THE BRITISH CONSTITUTION IN THE TWENTIETH CENTURY

THE
BRITISH
CONSTITUTION
IN THE TWENTIETH CENTURY

edited by
Vernon Bogdanor

Published for THE BRITISH ACADEMY
by OXFORD UNIVERSITY PRESS

Oxford University Press, Great Clarendon Street, Oxford OX2 6DP

Oxford New York
Auckland Bangkok Buenos Aires Cape Town Chennai
Dar es Salaam Delhi Hong Kong Istanbul Karachi Kolkata
Kuala Lumpur Madrid Melbourne Mexico City Mumbai Nairobi
São Paulo Shanghai Singapore Taipei Tokyo Toronto

Oxford is a registered trade mark of Oxford University Press
in the UK and certain other countries

Published in the United States by Oxford University Press Inc., New York

British Library Cataloguing in Publication Data
Data available

ISBN 0–19–726319–4

Phototypeset by Intype London Ltd
Printed in Great Britain
on acid-free paper by
Antony Rowe Limited
Chippenham, Wiltshire

The British Constitution has always been puzzling and always will be.

The Queen, cited in Peter Hennessy, *The Hidden Wiring*,
Gollancz, 1995, p. 33

Contents

List of Illustrations

List of Tables

Notes on Contributors

Vernon Bogdanor is Professor of Government at Oxford University. His books include *The People and the Party System: The Referendum and Electoral Reform in British Politics* (1981), *Multi-party Politics and the Constitution* (1983), *The Monarchy and the Constitution* (1995) and *Devolution in the United Kingdom* (1999). *The Governance of Britain* will be published in 2004.

Rodney Brazier is Professor of Constitutional Law at Manchester University. His books include *Constitutional Practice* (1988), *Constitutional Reform* (1991) and *Ministers of the Crown* (1997). He is editor of de Smith and Brazier's *Constitutional and Administrative Law*.

John Curtice is Professor of Politics and Director of the Social Statistics Laboratory at Strathclyde University. He is also Deputy Director of the Centre for Research into Elections and Social Trends and Head of Research, National Centre for Social Research, Scotland.

Clive Emsley is Professor of History at the Open University. His books include *Policing and its Context, 1750–1870* (1983), *Crime and Society in England, 1750–1900* (1987), *The English Police: A Political and Social History* (1991) and *Gendarmes and the State in Nineteenth-century Europe* (1999).

David Feldman is Professor of Law at Birmingham University. His books include *The Law Relating to Entry, Search and Seizure* (1986) and *Civil Liberties and Human Rights in England and Wales* (2nd edn, 2002). He is currently Legal Adviser to the Joint Select Committee on Human Rights.

Brigid Hadfield is Professor of Law at Essex University. Her books include *The Constitution of Northern Ireland* (1989), (ed.) *Northern Ireland: Politics and the Constitution* (1992) and (ed.) *Judicial Review: A Thematic Approach* (1995).

Robert Holland is Professor of Imperial and Commonwealth History at London University. His books include *Britain and the Commonwealth*

Alliance, 1918–1939 (1981), *European Decolonisation: An Introductory Survey* (1985) and *The Pursuit of Greatness: Britain and the World Role, 1900–1970* (1991).

Jeffrey Jowell is Professor of Public Law at University College, London. His books include *Law and Bureaucracy* (1975) and *De Smith, Woolf, and Jowell's Judicial Review of Administration Action* (1995) and he has edited, with Dawn Oliver, four editions of *The Changing Constitution* (1985–2000). He is a member of the Council of Europe's Commission for Democracy Through Law (the Venice Commission).

Martin Loughlin is Professor of Law at the London School of Economics. His books include *Local Government in the Modern State* (1986), *Public Law and Political Theory* (1992), *Legality and Locality: The Role of Law in Central–Local Government Relations* (1996) and *Sword and Scales: An Examination of the Relationship Between Law and Politics* (2000). He was co-editor of *Half A Century of Municipal Decline* (1985).

Ian Loveland is Professor of Law at the City University. His books include *By Due Process of Law: Racial Discrimination and the Right to Vote in South Africa, 1855–1960* (1999), *Importing the First Amendment: Freedom of Expression in America, English and European Law* (1998), *Constitutional Law* (2000) and *Political Libels: A Comparative Study* (2000).

Geoffrey Marshall is an Honorary Fellow of The Queen's College, Oxford, where he was Provost from 1993 to 1999. His books include *Parliamentary Sovereignty and the Commonwealth* (1957), *Police and Government* (1965), *Constitutional Theory* (1971) and *Constitutional Conventions* (1984).

Paul Seaward is Director of the History of Parliament; until 2001 he was Deputy Principal Clerk in the House of Commons. His publications include *The Cavalier Parliament and the Reconstruction of the Old Regime* (1989), and he is currently working on Hobbes' *Behemoth* for the Clarendon Hobbes edition.

Anthony Seldon is Headmaster of Brighton College. His books include *Churchill's Indian Summer: The Churchill Government 1951–55* (1981), *Major: A Political Life* (1997) and, with Dennis Kavanagh, *The Powers Behind the Prime Minister* (1999). He is currently working on a biography of Tony Blair.

Paul Silk was formerly a Clerk in the House of Commons, and is now Clerk of the National Assembly for Wales.

Robert Stevens is Senior Research Fellow at the Constitution Unit, University College London. He was formerly Professor of Law at Yale University, Chancellor of the University of California–Santa Cruz, and Master of Pembroke College, Oxford. His books include *Law and Politics: The House of Lords as a Judicial Body, 1800–1976* (1978) and *The Independence of the Judiciary* (1993).

Rhodri Walters is a Clerk of Committees and Clerk of the Overseas Office in the House of Lords.

Diana Woodhouse is Professor of Law and Politics at Oxford Brookes University. Her books include *Ministers and Parliament: Accountability in Theory and Practice* (1994), *In Pursuit of Good Administration* (1997) and *The Office of Lord Chancellor* (2001).

Preface

While there is a multitude of works on British political history in the twentieth century and on contemporary British government, there is, I believe, no single volume providing a coherent interpretation of that elusive animal, the British constitution, in the twentieth century. The contributors to this volume hope that, bringing together as it does historians, lawyers and political scientists, it will encourage further research in the fascinating if unfashionable discipline of constitutional history.

Most of the chapters in this volume were discussed at a three-day workshop held at the British Academy in November 2000. The contributors would like to thank the discussants at the workshop who included Lord Butler of Brockwell (the former Cabinet Secretary), Dr David Butler of Nuffield College, Oxford, Sir Christopher Foster, Mr Michael Steed of the University of Kent, Sir Michael Wheeler-Booth (formerly Clerk of the Parliaments and currently a Fellow of Magdalen College, Oxford) and Dr Noel Whiteside of Warwick University. Sir Christopher Foster was generous enough to circulate detailed notes on the various papers and the contributors are particularly grateful to him. The contributors are also grateful to Mr Nick Barber of Trinity College, Oxford, and to Mr Michael Brock, Mr Richard Thorpe and Mr Dan Turnbull, for their helpful comments.

In addition, the workshop had the benefit of comments and criticism from a number of serving civil servants, and the contributors are grateful to Lord Wilson of Dinton (the former Cabinet Secretary) for encouraging civil servants to attend and take part in the discussion. But of course none of those who have generously criticised earlier drafts of these chapters are responsible for the arguments and conclusions of the final version, which are those of the contributors alone.

I should like to thank the Fellows of Brasenose College, and, in particular, the former Principal, Lord Windlesham, for creating so intellectually stimulating an environment in which to work. I should also like to thank Professor Fergus Millar for inviting me to edit this volume;

and, from the British Academy, Rosemary Lambeth, for her help in organising the workshop, James Rivington for his patience in waiting for the final typescript, and Peter Brown for casting a benevolent and paternal eye over the entire proceedings.

Vernon Bogdanor
Brasenose College, Oxford

1.
Introduction
VERNON BOGDANOR

I

When Bagehot came to write the introduction to the second edition of *The English Constitution* in 1872, he had little doubt that the constitution which he was describing was a model and an exemplar for liberals everywhere. 'The practical choice of first-rate nations', he declared, 'is between the Presidential Government and the Parliamentary; no State can be first-rate which has not a Government by discussion, and those are the only two existing species of that Government. It is between them that a nation which has to choose its Government must choose.' A wise nation would undoubtedly choose the English constitution, because that constitution was 'framed on the principle of choosing a single sovereign authority, and making it good', while the American constitution, by contrast, was framed upon the principle 'of having many sovereign authorities, and hoping that their multitude may atone for their inferiority'. The English model was superior precisely because it brought 'singleness and unity' to bear. 'The excellence of the English Constitution is . . . that in it the sovereign power is single, possible, and good'.[1] Most educated Englishmen of his day would almost certainly have agreed with Bagehot. They saw their constitution developing in an evolutionary and peaceful way towards democracy. The electoral reforms of the late nineteenth century, and, in particular, the 1867 Reform Act and the further reforms of the years 1883–5, together with the creation of representative county councils in 1888 and of district and parish councils in 1894, were taken by a later generation as confirmation of this view; and it was shared by socialists, as well as by liberals and conservatives.

By the end of the nineteenth century, however, doubts were beginning

---

[1] *The Collected Works of Walter Bagehot*, ed. Norman St John-Stevas, The Economist, vol. 5 (London, 1974), p. 202.

to creep in as to whether the constitution was really quite so splendid as Bagehot had suggested. 'We cannot', Sidney Low wrote in 1904, 'take the speculations and inferences of the critics belonging to the great middle-class era of English constitutional history as if they were of pontifical authority for the present day.'[2] Henry Maine, whose empirical examination of *Popular Government* was first published in 1885, had accepted the Whig contention that Britain was proceeding in an evolutionary and fairly peaceful manner in the direction of democracy, but denied that democracy had 'an inherent superiority over every other form of government'.[3] Popular government in Maine's view was something to be endured rather than welcomed. If, moreover, it had to be endured, it was better endured in its American form, because the American constitution, with its checks and balances, had shown that expedients could be found to mitigate the 'difficulties' attending the democratic experiment, and even perhaps to 'overcome' them.[4] Maine's view was echoed by the historian W. E. H. Lecky, who, in *Democracy and Liberty* (first published in 1896), discerned a 'declining respect for parliamentary government' in Britain, due to 'the tendency of democracy to impair the stability of government and the working of parliamentary institutions'.[5] He too looked longingly towards the United States, which seemed to have discovered constitutional checks to limit the power of unbridled democracy.

These worries about democracy were shared by the eminent jurist A. V. Dicey, but Dicey felt, in contrast to Maine and Lecky, that salvation should be sought, not in an American type of constitution, but in the referendum, a democratic means of checking the excesses of democracy:

> 'I think', wrote Dicey in 1894, 'that I should have preferred real Parliamentary government as it existed up to 1868. But I have not the remotest doubt that under the present condition of things sham Parliamentary government means a very vicious form of government by party, and from this I believe the referendum may partially save us.'[6]

---

[2] Sidney Low, *The Governance of England* (T. Fisher Unwin, 1904), p. 14.

[3] Henry Maine, *Popular Government*, 1890 edn (John Murray), p. vii.

[4] Ibid., pp. xi–xii.

[5] W. E. H. Lecky, *Democracy and Liberty*, 1899 edn (Longmans Green), pp. v, xi.

[6] A. V. Dicey to Leo Maxse, 2 February 1894, cited in Richard A. Cosgrove, *The Rule of Law: Albert Venn Dicey, Victorian Jurist* (Macmillan 1980), p. 207. The early twentieth-century debate on the referendum can be followed in part 1 of Vernon Bogdanor, *The People and the Party System: The Referendum and Electoral Reform in British Politics* (Cambridge University Press, 1981).

In the early years of the twentieth century, the empirical work of embryonic political scientists such as Moisei Ostrogorski, and of social scientists, such as Roberto Michels and Max Weber, seemed to offer a scholarly foundation for the forebodings of conservative critics of democracy. For their findings seemed to demonstrate that representative government required, for its effective operation, the development of a complex structure of political organisation, which would inevitably be dominated by political parties. These parties would in turn come to be dominated by elites which rapidly became disconnected from those whom they claimed to represent. James Bryce told his friend Dicey in 1919:

> The tendency to groups is a deadly bacillus in modern legislatures. When one re-reads Mill's 'Representative Government', are you not struck by the fact that he did not anticipate the development things have taken and the discredit into which legislatures have fallen.[7]

Organisation seemed inevitably to mean oligarchy and the organisations so essential to the working of the democratic system, the party machine in particular, seemed to be undermining the autonomy of the individual which democracy, in theory, was meant to enhance. So it was that, as a distinguished external observer of the British constitution, A. L. Lowell, president of Harvard, noticed in his book, *The Government of England* (published in 1908), there was in Britain 'discontent with some of the results of democracy, a feeling which finds vent in widespread criticism of representative institutions'.[8]

This discontent was buttressed from a quite different quarter, by the worries of those who believed that democracy was proving inimical to the idea of 'national efficiency'. During the 1890s, it was becoming apparent that Britain was being overtaken economically by Germany and the United States, while the poor quality of many army recruits during the Boer War seemed to show that Britain was failing to secure the physical health of much of her population. The answer, so it was alleged by critics such as the former Liberal prime minister, Lord Rosebery, was to refashion government along business lines. 'After all', Rosebery suggested in 1900, 'a state is in essence a great joint stock company with unlimited liability on the part of its shareholders'.[9]

---

[7] Bryce to Dicey, 29 August 1919, Bryce papers, Bodleian Library, MS 3 fo. 83.
[8] A. L. Lowell, *The Government of England* (Macmillan, 1908), vol. 1, p. 195.
[9] Rosebery, *Miscellanies*, vol. 2 (1921), quoted in G. R. Searle, *The Quest for National Efficiency: A Study in British Politics and Political Thought, 1899–1914* (Blackwell, 1971), p. 87.

There was a need, declared the editor of the influential periodical *The Nineteenth Century* in 1900, 'for conducting the business of the country, as administered by all the various Departments of State, upon ordinary business principles and methods'.[10] This meant, presumably, limiting the power of the House of Commons to interfere with the day-to-day working of government departments. The Commons should confine its role to strategic oversight, the role essentially of shareholders in a public company. Thus, while conservative critics had called for the executive to be made more subject to checks and balances on the American model, the national efficiency movement sought a stronger executive free from the irritating constraints of everyday politics. Yet precisely because the precepts of 'national efficiency' seemed to entail an unacceptable limitation upon the power of the House of Commons, the movement was able to make little headway until Lloyd George entered 10 Downing Street in December 1916.

For, despite the attacks made upon it, the Whig/Liberal approach remained the dominant public philosophy in Britain at the turn of the century. Liberals believed that the cure for the ills of the political system lay not in confining or limiting democratic government, but in improving its quality. They were most immediately concerned with completing the progress towards universal male suffrage, and with giving women the vote—although by no means all Liberals supported this latter objective—and with removing various anomalies in the electoral system such as plural voting. They sought also to increase popular control over government by limiting the powers of the House of Lords which, in 1900, still enjoyed, in theory at least, an absolute veto over legislation, a power generally used to obstruct Liberal but not Conservative legislation, so that, as Lord Rosebery told Queen Victoria in 1894, the Lords 'controls a Liberal but not a Conservative Government', something which he believed to be 'obnoxious to the conscience of the country as well as to its best interests'.[11]

These fundamental Liberal aims—universal suffrage and the reform of the House of Lords—were to be achieved during the second decade of the twentieth century, through the Representation of the People Act of 1918, sometimes known as the fourth Reform Act, and the Parlia-

[10] Searle, *The Quest*, p. 88.
[11] Lord Rosebery to Queen Victoria, 1 November 1894, *Letters of Queen Victoria*, ed. G. E. Buckle, 3rd series (John Murray, 1930–32), vol. 2, p. 439.

ment Act of 1911, which gave statutory definition to the relationship between the two houses and indeed clarified the relationship between the sovereign and his ministers.[12] At the same time, the apparent resolution of the Irish question in the years 1921–2 decided, for good, so it then seemed, the final territorial structure of the United Kingdom. To many Liberals, and indeed to most of those in other parties, the movement for constitutional reform seemed at last to have reached a successful conclusion. The Liberal Party itself was beginning its long period of decline. Thus, questions of constitutional reform came to be removed from the agenda of British politics, and the British constitution ceased to be a matter of contention between the two major parties: the Conservatives and Labour. Thus, while the first twenty years of the twentieth century proved to be a period of considerable constitutional change, they were to be followed by a period of constitutional quiescence which lasted until the 1970s.

II

At the beginning of the twentieth century, despite the worries of conservative critics, most educated people probably had little doubt that Britain's unwritten—more properly, uncodified—constitution, had, through its flexibility, served it well. Few wished to see this constitution replaced by a codified document, until the House of Lords, by rejecting Lloyd George's 'People's Budget' in 1909, gave the Liberal government no alternative but to limit, by statute, powers which had hitherto been limited only by convention. During the 'truce of God', between June and November 1910, an inter-party constitutional conference met in an abortive attempt to seek an agreed settlement to the problem of the House of Lords. This conference proved wide-ranging in its approach. It seemed indeed to be attempting, in the words of Asquith's biographers, 'nothing less than to convert the immemorial unwritten into a written constitution', by attempting to distinguish between various categories of legislation, 'ordinary', 'financial', and 'constitutional', this last category to be made subject to special

---

[12] For the 1918 Representation of the People Act, see Martin Pugh, *Electoral Reform in War and Peace, 1906–1918* (Routledge & Kegan Paul, 1978), and for the 1911 Parliament Act, see Roy Jenkins, *Mr Balfour's Poodle* (Heinemann, 1954), and Neal Blewett, *The Peers, the Parties and the People: The General Elections of 1910* (Macmillan, 1972).

safeguards.[13] However, the failure of the conference and the method by which the 1911 Parliament Act resolved the House of Lords question seemed to confirm the value of traditional procedures, and the issue of whether Britain should follow almost every other democratic nation by providing itself with a codified constitution was to disappear from the political agenda for over sixty years.

The existence of an uncodified constitution meant that the precise role of the constitutional sovereign in an emerging democracy remained undefined. By the end of the nineteenth century, admittedly, it had been widely accepted, both by politicians and constitutional theorists, if not by the sovereign herself, that she should not intervene in party politics. George V was perhaps the first sovereign who set out to be politically neutral, as Bagehot had prescribed, and did not attempt to pursue policies of his own.[14]

But, even with a politically neutral sovereign, there was much scope for debate as to what the sovereign's proper function ought to be during times of crisis. In the late nineteenth century, it had been accepted that the sovereign could perform a valuable role as mediator, and Queen Victoria had not hesitated to exercise this role during the crisis over the disestablishment of the Irish Church in 1869, and during the discussions on the Third Reform bill and the Redistribution bill in 1884–5. On both occasions, the queen had used her influence with the Conservatives to assist the passage of Liberal reforms. Edward VII sought to perform the same role when, in 1906, the House of Lords rejected the Education bill, and again during the crisis caused by the Lords' rejection of the 'People's Budget' in 1909. In 1910, however, Asquith was unwilling to trust George V to overcome obstacles to House of Lords reform, believing the king to be a Conservative partisan, and with views no different from, as Asquith was later to put it, 'the average opinion of the man in the tube'.[15] Signifi-

---

[13] J. A. Spender and Cyril Asquith, *Life of Herbert Henry Asquith, Lord Oxford and Asquith* (Hutchinson, 1932), vol. 1, p. 291. Accounts of this conference can also be found in Lord Newton's biography of *Lord Lansdowne* (Macmillan, 1929), and in John D. Fair's valuable book, *British Interparty Conferences: A Study of the Procedure of Conciliation in British Politics, 1867–1921* (Oxford University Press, 1980). The minutes of the meetings of the conference have been preserved in the papers of Austen Chamberlain in Birmingham University.

[14] H. J. Hanham, *The Nineteenth Century Constitution* (Cambridge University Press, 1969), p. 25.

[15] Michael and Eleanor Brock (eds), *H. H. Asquith Letters to Venetia Stanley* (Oxford University Press, 1982), p. 487, 18 March 1915. This was partly the result of injudicious comments about Asquith and Lloyd George, which George V had made as Prince of Wales. See Vernon Bogdanor, *The Monarchy and the Constitution* (Oxford University Press, 1995), pp. 67–8.

cantly, therefore, during the crises over the House of Lords in 1910–11, and Irish home rule in 1913–14, George V's role was to be reduced to that of facilitator; and in 1910, Asquith bluntly told the king that 'it is not the function of a Constitutional Sovereign to act as arbiter or mediator between rival parties and policies; still less to take advice from the leaders on both sides, with the view to forming a conclusion of his own'.[16] George V, however, was to perform the role of facilitator many times—in 1914, on Irish home rule, in 1915, on conscription, and in 1916 and 1931, following the resignations of incumbent prime ministers. On each occasion, he sponsored an inter-party conference at Buckingham Palace in an attempt to resolve differences. By 1931, indeed, George V seems to have forgotten Asquith's advice, because he sought actively to promote the formation of a National Government, which he believed to be the only form of administration capable of dealing with the economic crisis.[17] The twentieth century, however, was to confirm Namier's dictum that the influence of the sovereign was in inverse relation to the growth of party, and that it would be at its greatest during periods of party confusion, such as 1916 and 1931.[18]

Asquith accepted in the memorandum which he wrote for the king in 1910 that it was still 'technically possible for the Sovereign to dismiss Ministers who render to him unpalatable advice', while emphasising that the last time this prerogative had been exercised was in 1834 when William IV had in effect dismissed Lord Melbourne. Nevertheless, constitutional theorists of the weight of Anson and Dicey remained insistent that the sovereign, although he did not retain the power to insist upon a dissolution, *did* retain the power to refuse royal assent to legislation, provided that he was prepared to face the consequences, which might well include the resignation of the government. In 1946, the first parliamentary counsel, Sir Granville Ram, writing to Sir Edward Bridges, the Cabinet secretary, reminded him of what Dicey had said in a letter to *The Times* in 1913 concerning the refusal of assent: 'Its repose may be the preservation of its existence, and its existence may be the means of saving the Constitution itself on an occasion worthy of bringing it forth.'[19] Dicey,

---

[16] Spender and Asquith, *Herbert Henry Asquith*, vol. 1, pp. 305–6.
[17] See Vernon Bogdanor, '1931 Revisited: The Constitutional Aspects', *Twentieth Century British History* (1991). See also, on inter-party conferences, Fair, *British Interparty Conferences*.
[18] See L. B. Namier, 'Monarchy and the Party System' in *Crossroads of Power* (Macmillan, 1960), p. 213.
[19] Ram to Bridges, 3 June 1946, PRO T 273/237, cited in Bogdanor, *The Monarchy and the Constitution*, p. 132, showing that George V had seriously contemplated using his veto on home

of course, had in mind the possibility that the king might refuse assent to the Irish Home Rule bill, and we now know that George V seriously contemplated this course.

Moreover, while the sovereign no longer enjoyed the power to *insist* on a dissolution, there could be little doubt that he retained the power to *refuse* one, a power which George V contemplated exercising in October 1924, following the defeat of the first Labour government in the House of Commons; and there could be no doubt that it was for the sovereign to appoint a prime minister. It was Queen Victoria, rather than the Liberal Party, who chose Rosebery instead of Harcourt as prime minister in 1894—and she did so without bothering to consult Gladstone, the outgoing prime minister: similarly, in 1923, George V, not the Conservative Party, chose Baldwin rather than Curzon; and George VI, not the Conservative Party, chose Churchill rather than Halifax in 1940, albeit on the recommendation of the outgoing prime minister, Neville Chamberlain. The choices of Harold Macmillan in 1957 and Lord Home in 1963, were, however, somewhat different in that they were based on the wishes of the Cabinet in 1957, and on what were believed to be the wishes of the Conservative Party in 1963, rather than on the inclinations of the sovereign. The sovereign was now appointing not the person whom she personally thought would be the best prime minister, but the person whom, she was told, the Cabinet or the party believed would be the best prime minister. By the middle of the twentieth century, therefore, the personal prerogative of the sovereign to choose the prime minister had come to be severely limited, and it was to be even more drastically curtailed when the Conservatives decided, in 1965, to adopt an electoral procedure to choose their leader so as to avoid any repetition of the embarrassments of 1963. It seems that the Palace was pleased rather than saddened by this seeming restriction of the royal prerogative, because the sovereign had no wish to be embroiled in the controversies which would result from a disputed choice.[20]

---

rule. The quotation from Dicey is from his letter to *The Times*, 15 September 1913, reprinted in Sir Ivor Jennings, *Cabinet Government*, 3rd edn (Cambridge University Press, 1959), p. 545.

[20] Indeed, as early as 1947, George VI's private secretary, Sir Alan Lascelles, had written to Sir Edward Bridges, the Cabinet secretary, to tell him that 'a clear advance indication by the members of the party' as to who they wanted as their leader would assist the sovereign even though it might seem to derogate from his power. Lascelles to Bridges, 11 September 1947, RA GVI 131/80, cited in Bogdanor, *The Monarchy and the Constitution*, p. 99.

III

The precise role of the Cabinet under a system with an uncodified constitution was also unclear. At the beginning of the twentieth century, it still had no regular time of assembly nor fixed place of meeting, the date of meeting being fixed, usually at short notice, by the prime minister. There were no rules of order, no quorum, no agenda and no record or minutes of what was decided; and it was considered contrary to etiquette to take notes at a Cabinet meeting. The Cabinet had 'no office, no staff, no secretary, no rules, no corporate funds, no permanent location. It could not receive a letter or answer it, except through the first lord of the Treasury or some other of its members, for it has no note-paper, and no seal, and no petty cash to buy stationery or pay messengers . . . When it assembles the Cabinet finds that it has no corporate character. It might be a fortuitous conference of heads of departments at one of the public offices, or a meeting of party leaders at the Carlton Club.' The Cabinet, indeed, seems not to have been mentioned in any official document until, in December 1900, an MP, a Mr Bartley, moved an amendment to the Address to the effect that 'We humbly express our regret at the advice given to your Majesty by the Prime Minister in recommending the appointment of so many of his own family to offices in the Cabinet.'[21]

The functions of the Cabinet had, however, been described in 1889 in John Morley's biography of Walpole, a *locus classicus*, said to have enjoyed the imprimatur of Gladstone. Morley laid down four principles of Cabinet government. They were, first, 'the doctrine of collective responsibility'; second, answerability 'immediately to the majority of the House of Commons, and ultimately to the electors whose will creates that majority'; third, that 'the Cabinet is, except under uncommon, peculiar, and transitory circumstances, selected exclusively from one party'; and fourth, that 'the Prime Minister is the keystone of the Cabinet arch', occupying 'a position which, so long as it lasts, is one of exceptional and peculiar authority'. Morley argued that one of the advantages of the Cabinet system, as of the constitution, was its 'flexibility', which 'allows the Prime Minister in an emergency to take upon himself a power not inferior to that of a dictator, provided always that the House of Commons will stand by him'.[22]

These four principles were as much in evidence at the end of the

---

[21] Low, *The Governance of England*, pp. 37, 38, 29fn.
[22] John Morley, *Walpole* (Macmillan, 1889), pp. 154–60.

twentieth century as they were at its beginning. Certainly, most Cabinets were drawn from members of one party; in peacetime, coalition governments were short-lived and transitory experiments, except in the case of the National Government which was to rule Britain between 1931 and 1940.

It was alleged, at various times during the twentieth century, that prime ministers—for example, A. J. Balfour in 1903, Lloyd George, Neville Chamberlain, Winston Churchill, Harold Macmillan in 1962, Harold Wilson, Edward Heath, Margaret Thatcher or Tony Blair—were taking upon themselves powers 'not inferior to that of a dictator'. Much of the debate, however, concerning prime ministerial power was ahistorical because the protagonists to the argument failed to appreciate the force of Morley's qualifying clause 'provided always that the House of Commons will stand by him'. When that condition was removed—as Lloyd George, Neville Chamberlain and Margaret Thatcher were to find to their cost—their supposedly dictatorial power disappeared. It is doubtful, therefore, whether the twentieth century showed any trend towards increasing prime ministerial power as opposed to an ebb and flow of power determined by political vicissitudes; or, as Sidney Low put it as early as 1904, 'The precise amount of authority exercised by the Prime Minister must depend upon circumstances and his own character. If he is a Pitt, a Peel, a Palmerston, a Disraeli or a Gladstone, he may come near to being a dictator.'[23]

At the beginning of the twentieth century, it seems to have been generally accepted that the convention of collective ministerial responsibility could be suspended when a government was faced with a contentious issue. This was done by labelling the issue an 'open question', on which ministers were allowed to express conflicting views in public, the government not yet having reached a settled conclusion as to its policy. Female suffrage was generally treated in this way by Liberal Cabinets before the First World War. It was, in any case, difficult to enforce collective responsibility before the establishment of the Cabinet Secretariat in 1916, because there was no effective record of proceedings, and it was sometimes not clear precisely what had been decided. In 1900, Salisbury wrote to his nephew Arthur Balfour to say:

I am beginning to think that the rule of which we are rather proud, that

---

[23] Low, *The Governance of England*, p. 158.

there shall be no record of a Cabinet's proceedings is a mistake. I had imagined that the Cabinet had unanimously, and rather energetically resolved that the dispatch of Roberts about Spion Kop was not to be published yet there it was in the papers yesterday morning. I have not yet heard any explanation but I have no doubt it will be that Lansdowne [secretary of state for war] did not understand the resolution of the Cabinet as we did.

Balfour replied:

I agree with you that a brief record of Cabinet discussion would be a convenience. My own memory in such matters is very untrustworthy and I sometimes find it difficult, after our confused discussions, to recollect even the instructions I have received on matters which I have myself brought before it.[24]

At times, this uncertainty as to what had been decided could have serious consequences, as when Joseph Chamberlain believed that he had obtained a commitment from his Cabinet colleagues to retain the duty on imported corn imposed in the Budget of 1902, only to find that at least one minister was quite unaware that such a commitment had in fact been given.[25] This misunderstanding was a prime cause of the Cabinet crisis of 1903 on tariff reform which led to the resignation of five senior ministers, including Chamberlain himself. It was perhaps this episode to which Chamberlain's son, Austen, was referring when he told the House of Commons in 1922 that, under the old system, 'I have known Cabinets break up under the impression that they had settled something, and every Minister going away asking his neighbour what was the decision to which they had come.'[26] By 1916, with the establishment of Lloyd George's small war cabinet, precise records had become essential since departmental ministers were not members of the war cabinet, and some means had to be found by which they could be apprised of cabinet decisions. Before 1916, however, the only official record of Cabinet proceedings had been the report which the prime minister wrote to the sovereign after the meeting of the Cabinet, and which was seen by no other member of the Cabinet. Some of these reports, such as those from A. J. Balfour and Sir Henry Campbell-Bannerman, were quite perfunctory, and indeed almost insulting in their brevity. In November 1906, for

[24] Cited in W. H. Greenleaf, *The British Political Tradition* (Methuen, 1987), vol. 3, part 1, p. 698.

[25] G. H. L. Le May, *The Victorian Constitution* (Duckworth, 1979), p. 114.

[26] House of Commons Debates, 5th series, vol. 155, col. 224, 13 June 1922.

example, Campbell-Bannerman confined himself to informing Edward VII that 'the Cabinet met today and was entirely engaged with arrangements of public business for the conclusion of the session'. A year later, Lord Knollys, the king's private secretary, wrote that these perfunctory reports were 'really making an absolute fool of the King'.[27]

The doctrine of the 'open question' could hardly survive the development of modern media relations, but the twentieth century was to see three instances of specific 'agreements to differ'—in 1932, under a coalition government, on the issue of the tariff; in 1975, on whether the government should recommend acceptance in a referendum of the renegotiated terms providing for Britain's continued membership of the European Community; and in 1977, on direct elections to the European Parliament. Nevertheless, the doctrine of the 'open question' has been replaced less by the 'agreement to differ', than by the informal leak and the confidential briefing. These allowed a minister to indicate reservations about a particular policy of the government in which he or she served, while continuing nevertheless to remain in it. The 'open question' or the 'agreement to differ', had, however, been formal procedures in relation to issues on which a government had been unable to come to a settled view. The leak or the confidential briefing, by contrast, was an informal procedure in relation to matters on which a government had at least purported to have come to a settled view.

But the main differences between an early and a mid-twentieth century Cabinet lie elsewhere. Cabinet meetings at the beginning of the twentieth century were, despite the Boer War, infrequent, and indeed in September and October 1901 the Cabinet did not meet at all. In a speech at Oldham in October 1901, the chancellor of the Exchequer, Sir Michael Hicks-Beach, apologised for this, but said that 'There are such things as interviews between ministers . . . there are official messengers who carry communications between different departments'. Sidney Low called this remark: 'a rather plain-spoken admission that the formal Council, the pledge of solidarity and collective responsibility has been virtually superseded by informal interviews and communications between certain selected members of the Cabinet'.[28] Even so, the Cabinet took many more formal decisions than it was to do at the end of the twentieth century, by which time it had been reduced to such a degree of informality that it

[27] Philip Magnus, *King Edward the Seventh* (John Murray, 1964), pp. 355, 282.
[28] Low, *The Governance of England*, p. 169fn.

seemed to be becoming, once again, a 'meeting of friends' as eighteenth-century Cabinets had been.

In 1900, there was just one Cabinet committee, on defence, established by Lord Salisbury in 1895. By 1903, it had become an advisory council and it was renamed the Committee of Imperial Defence, and chaired by the prime minister, with its own secretariat. Its secretary from 1912 was Sir Maurice Hankey, who was to become the first Cabinet secretary in December 1916, when Lloyd George established the Cabinet Office to take minutes of Cabinet proceedings and to co-ordinate the work of the departments.

By the time of the Attlee government after 1945, Cabinet committees had become both permanent and functionally orientated. Yet, by the end of the twentieth century, this institutionalisation itself seemed to be but a passing phase, for the committee system in turn appeared about to be superseded by various bilateral and informal procedures, which prime ministers such as Lord Rosebery or Lord Salisbury might have had little difficulty in recognising. Certainly the Cabinet system at the end of the twentieth century displayed as much 'flexibility' as Morley had found at the end of the nineteenth, and it seemed well able to accommodate the styles and vagaries of prime ministers with very different aims and predilections.

In no field of policy did the power of the prime minister seem more extensive at the beginning of the twentieth century than in foreign and imperial affairs. Under Conservative governments, it was customary at the turn of the century for only an inner ring of ministers, sometimes just the prime minister and the foreign secretary, to see the boxes of foreign despatches. Lord Rosebery, the Liberal imperialist, had adopted the same practice during his own short-lived government of 1894–5. Radicals regularly inveighed against the prerogative in foreign and imperial affairs and, in March 1886, Labouchere proposed in the Commons that no territories should be added to the Empire without parliamentary consent, a motion that was lost by just four votes. A. J. Balfour, as leader of the House of Commons in 1901, instructed the under-secretary for foreign affairs not to answer supplementary questions on foreign affairs in the House, since it was impossible to carry on negotiations if the Foreign Office was to be made subject to detailed questioning in Parliament.[29]

---

[29] A. P. Thornton, *The Imperial Idea and its Enemies: A Study in British Power* (Macmillan 1958), pp. 85–6.

Morley did not, in his account of Cabinet government, mention individual ministerial responsibility as a convention of the constitution. This principle seemed as much or as little in evidence at the end of the twentieth century as it was at its beginning. For, as S. E. Finer showed in a classic article published in 1956, two years after Crichel Down and the resignation of the minister for agriculture Sir Thomas Dugdale, the convention, or supposed convention, had been more disregarded than observed since the mid-nineteenth century, there having been but seven ministerial resignations between 1855 and 1914 which could be attributed to the doctrine; and it was 'very difficult to deduce from these incidents anything resembling a rule'.[30] A minister, according to Sidney Low, 'may have cost the country thousands of lives and millions of pounds, by launching an ill-arranged expedition into the heart of a distant continent, too late for it to be of any use; and his defeat may eventually be brought about because his colleagues have decided—perhaps in opposition to his own wishes—to put an unpopular tax on bread or beer'.[31] At the beginning of the twentieth century, it was 'commonly said that the ministers are severally responsible to Parliament for the conduct of their own departments, and jointly responsible for the general policy of the government'. But, 'Like many other maxims of the British constitution, this has the advantage of being sufficiently vague to be capable of different interpretations at different times. With the growth of the parliamentary system and the more clearly marked opposition between the parties, the joint responsibility has in fact become greater and the several responsibility less.'[32]

Nevertheless, the existence of this supposed convention helped to obscure the extent to which the influence of the bureaucracy was beginning to grow in the new century with the expansion of the state. 'How is it', the Liberal publicist Ramsay Muir argued, in 1910, 'that the Englishman is almost unconscious of the existence of so huge and efficient a power, controlling his life. The explanation is to be found in the fact that during the period in which this power has grown up, and thrown its tentacles round every part of the nation's activity, there has been an almost total silence about the men who have wielded it.' This was because the convention of individual ministerial responsibility provided

---

[30] S. E. Finer, 'The Individual Responsibility of Ministers', *Public Administration* (1956), 377–96. See, on Crichel Down, both I. F. Nicolson, *The Mystery of Crichel Down* (Clarendon Press, 1986), and J. A. G. Griffith in *Contemporary Record*, 1987.

[31] Low, *The Governance of England*, p. 148.

[32] Lowell, *The Government of England*, p. 71.

that the civil servant was 'never publicly, however he may be privately, blamed'.[33] An uneasy awareness was growing, however, that civil servants were not confining themselves to the role of passive advisers as the theory of ministerial responsibility would seem to require. The influence, for example, of Robert Morant, assistant private secretary to the Duke of Devonshire, Lord President of the Council, on the Education Act of 1902 was profound. Indeed, its passing, according to Sir Lewis Selby Bigge, writing in the *Dictionary of National Biography*, 'was largely due to his vision, courage and ingenuity ... his achievement ... is one of the romances of the civil service'. Morant, moreover, was 'assuredly far better known to the vast number of teachers and educational administrators now to be found in England than any of the quickly shifting ministers who come and go in the Education Office'.[34]

In 1905, a further example of civil service influence was revealed to the public when George Wyndham, Irish secretary in the Unionist government repudiated a scheme of devolution which his undersecretary, Sir Anthony MacDonnell, an Irish Catholic in sympathy with the nationalists, had helped to formulate, because it went further than Unionists were willing to countenance. MacDonnell was censured by the Cabinet, but Wyndham nevertheless was forced to resign. Three years later, in 1908, William Beveridge entered Whitehall as a non-established civil servant to help prepare legislation on labour exchanges and unemployment insurance. Civil servants were, so it seemed, coming to play a creative role in government which was not easy to reconcile with traditional constitutional nostrums.

IV

Parliament at the end of the nineteenth century displayed many of the features—subordination to the executive, overcrowding of the parliamentary timetable, excessive burden of legislation, control by the party whips, decline of the private member—often attributed by the unhistorically minded to the present day. In 1894, Sidney Low wrote an article entitled 'If the House of Commons were Abolished?', in which he insisted that abolition 'would not necessarily bring the Constitution to a standstill ... The main difference would be that we should then recognise

---

[33] Ramsay Muir, *Peers and Bureaucrats* (Constable, 1910), pp. 22, 23.
[34] Muir, *Peers and Bureaucrats*, p. 24.

the real character of our system of government, as it has developed itself in comparatively recent years . . .'. Not the House of Commons but the 'Cabinet and the Caucus' were 'the real, efficient working parts of the political machine. So far as law-making goes, there is no room for the House of Commons between those upper and nether millstones.'[35]

'Members of Parliament are slow to realise', Sir Almeric FitzRoy, clerk to the Privy Council, pointed out in 1901, in comments that could have been made at almost any time during the twentieth century, and certainly at its end, 'how rapidly the credit of the House of Commons as an institution is declining . . . The power of the Press, and the creation, partly thereby and partly by the operation of other agencies, of a public opinion independent of and indifferent to the claims of the popular Chamber, have relegated Parliament as a political mouthpiece, to a subordinate position, where, if it so wills, it can still play a useful though less authoritative part.'[36] Bagehot had declared in *The Economist* in 1874 that the literary, scientific and philosophical worlds were hardly comparable in dignity to the political. 'I wrote books . . . and I was nobody; I got into Parliament, and before I had taken my seat I had become somebody.' By 1904, however, Sidney Low felt that 'we have moved rapidly in the intervening space. No one, I suppose, would now contend that a famous author, a popular preacher, a distinguished man of science, or even a successful actor, is less in the public thoughts than any of the politicians, except some half-dozen leaders of the very first rank.' The House of Commons, Low declared, had become a mere electoral college, 'a kind of preparatory school for the polls'.[37]

This was partly, but by no means wholly, a consequence of procedural change. The reforms of the 1880s and afterwards, introducing the closure and the guillotine, a reaction to obstruction by the Irish nationalist members, had made it more difficult for backbenchers or minority parties to hold up government business, and they gave the government nearly complete control over the legislative timetable.[38] The permanent standing committees established in 1907, to which all legislation except financial

---

[35] Sidney Low, 'If the House of Commons were Abolished?', *The Nineteenth Century* (December 1894), 847, 850–1.

[36] Sir Almeric FitzRoy, *Memoirs* (Hutchinson, 1928), vol. 1, p. 49.

[37] *Collected Works*, vol. 6, p 55. Low, *The Governance of England*, pp. 97, 104.

[38] See, for a contemporary estimate, A. L. Lowell, 'The Influence of Party upon Legislation', *Annual Report*, The American Historical Association, 1901.

bills, bills of constitutional importance or bills confirming provisional orders, were to be sent, did little to counter this trend, because these committees turned out to be as adversarial in their nature and as much open to the dominance of the whips as the floor of the House. Moreover, the closure was applied to debates in standing committees as well as to debates on the floor of the House. At the same time, the growing strength of party organisation made it more difficult for an independent-minded backbencher to defy the whips. By 1896, Augustine Birrell was complaining that, while 'At one time the private Member had an opportunity of making some reputation by legislative effort, . . . now he had hardly any chance. His occupation was well nigh gone, and there was nothing for him to do but to stroll listlessly about the Lobbies, and to come in and out when a Division is threatened.'[39] Lowell's analysis of divisions in the House of Commons showed that party cohesion was almost as strong as the beginning of the twentieth century as it was to be at its end.[40] To one MP, indeed, it seemed that 'the actual Government of this country is properly, neither a Monarchy nor a Democracy, but mainly an alternation of two traditional Oligarchies . . . managing the members of its Parliamentary following through a dexterous blending of menace, cajolery and reward'.[41] In fact, however, party cohesion resulted less from oligarchic control than from a stronger identification of backbench MPs with the causes for which their party stood, and even perhaps from a greater willingness of party leaders to respond to the concerns of their followers.[42]

One of the two 'traditional Oligarchies', however, the Conservative, or Unionist Party, as the Conservative–Liberal Unionist coalition was known until 1921, had the advantage of a permanent majority in the upper House, the House of Lords. This majority had been considerably strengthened by the home rule split in 1886, for, while in the Commons only a minority of Liberal MPs became Liberal Unionists, in the Lords, a majority of Liberal peers were found to have broken with their party, and the Liberals found themselves severely under-represented in the Lords. Indeed, the seventy-five peers who in 1909 voted for Lloyd

---

[39] House of Commons Debates, 4th series, vol. 37, col. 1278, 27 February 1896.
[40] Lowell, 'The Influence of Party upon Legislation in England and America'. See also Samuel Beer, *Modern British Politics* (Faber, 1966), p. 257.
[41] Robert Wallace MP, *The Nineteenth Century* (1895), 192–3.
[42] Hugh Berrington, 'Partisanship and Dissidence in the Nineteenth-century House of Commons', *Parliamentary Affairs* (1967–8), 349.

George's 'People's Budget' 'constituted the largest pro-Liberal vote in the Lords on a major issue for 25 years'.[43]

Moreover, the Lords, according to Lord Salisbury, enjoyed the constitutional right, indeed the duty, of ensuring that 'fundamental' legislation enjoyed the support of the electorate before it was passed. This theory of the mandate meant that the Lords could justifiably reject 'fundamental' legislation, thereby forcing a dissolution so that voters could pronounce on its merits. In practice, however, the mandate argument was used less to check 'fundamental' legislation, than to destroy those parts of the Liberal programme which peers thought were unpopular in the country. Salisbury's theory would not only have placed the Commons in a position of constitutional inferiority to the Lords; it represented also, in the words of the Liberal MP Sir Charles Dilke, 'a claim for annual Parliaments when we are in office, and septennial Parliaments when they are in office'.[44] The power of the Lords had been most graphically displayed in 1893, when Gladstone's second Home Rule bill, having been passed by the Commons, was destroyed in the Lords by a vote of 419 to forty-one. The aged prime minister had sought to dissolve so as to rally the country in a campaign of 'peers versus people'; but his colleagues refused to countenance it, and the conflict was postponed for sixteen years, to 1909, when the Lords rejected Lloyd George's 'People's Budget', 'until', in the words of the motion of the Unionist leader in the Lords, Lord Lansdowne, echoing Salisbury's mandate doctrine, 'it has been submitted to the judgment of the country'. In rejecting the Budget, however, the Lords were testing this doctrine to destruction, and their powers were, for the first time, restricted by statute in the Parliament Act of 1911.

Defenders of the House of Lords appreciated that it was not in a particularly strong position to resist the depredations of left-wing governments because of its hereditary composition. During the early part of the century, therefore, Unionist peers, afforced by the ex-Liberal prime minister, Lord Rosebery, agreed to depart from the hereditary principle if that was necessary to strengthen the upper House. The Rosebery resolutions debated in the Lords in March 1910 had as one of their three principles 'acceptance of the principle that the possession of a peerage

[43] Andrew Adonis, *Making Aristocracy Work: The Peerage and the Political System in Britain, 1884–1914* (Clarendon Press, 1993), p. 21.
[44] S. Gwynn and G. Tuckwell, *Life of the Right Hon. Charles Dilke* (John Murray, 1917), vol. 1, p. 371. The House of Commons had a maximum term of seven years until the Parliament Act of 1911 reduced it to five. For the doctrine of the mandate, see Bogdanor, *The People and the Party System*, pp. 17–20.

should no longer of itself give the right to sit and vote in the House of Lords'. The Liberals, however, refused to consider the question of composition of the Lords until the issue of powers had been settled.[45] 'To set up an elective Second Chamber', Asquith believed, 'would be to destroy the unique character of the House of Commons, and to introduce a new dimension into the heart of the Constitution.'[46] Indeed, an elective second chamber might well have proved to be even more of a menace to a government of the Left than the hereditary chamber had been.

V

Westminster of course was not merely the Parliament of the United Kingdom. It was also the Imperial Parliament. As the Imperial Parliament, Westminster held sway over 410 million people, of whom just 41.5 million lived in Britain, while 294 million lived in the Indian Empire.[47] At the beginning of the twentieth century, Britain was fighting her last imperial war against the Boers, and the imperial issue lay at the heart of politics. There was, in particular a lively debate as to how Britain's relations with the self-governing colonies should be ordered. The idea of imperial federation was much in the air, and gave rise to the same concerns as the idea of European unity was to do at the end of the century. For both imperial federation and European unity threatened the fundamental constitutional tenet of parliamentary sovereignty. It was, therefore, unclear to what extent Westminster, despite the much-vaunted 'flexibility' of the British constitution, was able, even if it wished, to share power with other member states, joined together for a common purpose in the self-governing Empire. Tariff reform, moreover, which seemed to its proponents a practical attempt at realising the imperial idea, was to break up the Conservative Party in 1903, and condemn it to its longest period of opposition in the twentieth century; while Europe was to play a large part in splitting the Labour Party in the 1980s, and condemning Labour in turn to its longest period in opposition between 1979 and 1997; it was then to threaten, in turn, the unity of the Conservatives after the Maastricht Treaty of 1992. Throughout these party battles,

---

[45] Jenkins, *Mr Balfour's Poodle*, p. 50.
[46] Spender and Asquith, *Life of Herbert Henry Asquith*, vol. 2, p. 350.
[47] Ronald Hyam, 'The British Empire in the Edwardian Era', p. 48, in Judith M. Brown and William Roger Louis (eds), *The Oxford History of the British Empire*: vol. 4, *The Twentieth Century* (Oxford University Press, 1999).

at the beginning as at the end of the twentieth century, Britain strenuously resisted the federal principle, both in its relationships with outside powers, and as a means of resolving the problem of holding together the separate national components of a multinational state.

Nevertheless, the difficulties of governing a great empire from Westminster had led some observers at the beginning of the twentieth century to the view that Parliament was no longer an efficient instrument for the conduct of business. Britain's increasing imperial responsibilities together with the demands of social and economic legislation seemed to be imposing new strains which Westminster was ill-equipped to meet. 'The whole future of this Empire', Alfred Milner feared, 'may turn upon the whims of men who have been elected for their competence in dealing with Metropolitan tramways or country pubs.'[48] Adherents of national efficiency sought, as we have seen, to weaken parliamentary scrutiny, while imperialists dreamt of a federation of the Empire and a Parliament of the Empire which would be able, so they believed, to consider imperial affairs in greater depth than Westminster could do. At the same time, devolution was hailed as a remedy for the congestion of parliamentary business. Some Liberals sought to use the issue of Irish home rule as a lever to secure 'home rule all round' or federalism, an idea first proposed by the former Liberal prime minister, Earl Russell, in 1872. There was in addition some pressure in Scotland and Wales, though it was by no means as great as in Ireland, for home rule. England, admittedly, constituted a difficulty, since, as Winston Churchill declared in a Cabinet memorandum in 1911, 'It seems . . . absolutely impossible that an English Parliament, and still more an English Executive, could exist side by side with an Imperial Parliament and an Imperial Executive'.[49] He therefore proposed, as an alternative, regional devolution within England, as Gladstone had done during the Midlothian campaign, and as the Blair government was to do at the end of the twentieth century.

The original draft of the 1912 Home Rule bill was to provide for a scheme of Grand Committees for England, Scotland and Wales with wide legislative powers of a similar scope to those proposed for the Irish Parliament; and it was entitled 'Government of Ireland and House of Commons (Devolution of Business) bill'. Although the scheme for Grand Committees was dropped from the final draft of the bill, nevertheless

---

[48] Alfred Gollin, *Proconsul in Politics* (Macmillan, 1964), p. 314.
[49] Cabinet Papers, Cab. 37/105/16, and Cab. 37/105/18, cited in Hanham, *The Nineteenth Century Constitution*, p. 131.

Asquith, in recommending home rule to the Commons, declared that it was 'the first step and only the first step in a larger and more comprehensive policy'.[50] Such a 'larger and more comprehensive policy' was by no means anathema to all Unionists, since there were some, especially in the Round Table group, who believed that home rule all round would avoid the separatist taint of a concession confined just to Ireland. 'There was', declared the Unionist MP Halford Mackinder, in a Commons debate on devolution in 1919, 'safety in numbers. In the number of subordinate Parliaments there is safety, for the majority of subordinate Parliaments will be able to exercise restraint on the recalcitrant Parliament that would cut itself adrift or otherwise misbehave.'[51] Devolution need not, therefore, be a step towards separation. Indeed, Sir Edward Carson, the Irish Unionist leader, argued in 1919 that it could 'if properly carried out . . . lead to closer union'.[52]

The idea of home rule all round attracted considerable support immediately after the First World War, when many believed that a new constitutional structure would be needed to meet the problems of a new age. In 1919 a joint conference on devolution was established, containing members from both Commons and Lords, under the chair of the speaker, James Lowther, who had, in a previous conference in 1917, achieved agreement on the difficult issues of franchise reform and female suffrage. But, as Lowther was to report ruefully to the prime minister in 1920, the devolution conference had been 'more successful in bringing out into the open, than in solving, the doubts and difficulties that surround the task of recasting the British constitution with the aid of imperfect analogies supplied by other countries, which under totally dissimilar conditions have adopted federal principles of government for the purpose of uniting previously separate states'.[53] The conference failed to agree a solution, and such proposals as it made proved abortive. The issue no longer excited the public, even in Scotland and Wales. Indeed, with the departure of most of Ireland from the United Kingdom in 1921–2, the political dynamic which might have led to home rule all round disappeared for over fifty years.

---

[50] House of Commons Debates, 5th series, vol. 36, col. 1043, 11 April 1912. See also Patricia Jalland, 'United Kingdom Devolution 1910–14: Political Panacea or Tactical Diversion?', *English Historical Review* (1979), 765–7; and Vernon Bogdanor, *Devolution in the United Kingdom* (Oxford University Press, 1999), pp. 44–50.

[51] House of Commons Debates, 5th series, vol. 116, col. 1930, 3 June 1919.

[52] Ibid., col. 1898.

[53] Letter from Mr Speaker to the Prime Minister, Cmd 692, 1920, p. 38.

VI

Despite the frequent complaints that Parliament was overloaded, central government at the beginning of the twentieth century was responsible for far fewer functions than it was at its end. Partly of course this was because many public functions which are now taken for granted, for example, the provision of a health service and the regulation of the economy, were not thought to be the responsibility of the state at all. But many other important functions—such as transport and housing, as well as gas, water, electricity supply and other public utilities—remained with local authorities, which derived their powers from local acts. Indeed, before the National Insurance Act of 1911, it was customary to entrust new public functions to local authorities rather than to central government. Joseph Chamberlain, mayor of Birmingham from 1873 to 1876, and a pioneer in the development of local public services, so-called 'gas and water socialism', had declared in 1885:

> the most fruitful field before reformers at the present time is to be found in an extension of the functions and authority of local government. Local government is near the people. Local government will bring you into contact with the masses. By its means you will be able to increase their comfort, to secure their health, to multiply the luxuries which they may enjoy in common, to carry out a vast cooperative system for mutual aid and support, to lessen the inequalities of our social system, and to raise the standard of all classes in the community.[54]

Chamberlain's example was to be rapidly followed by the London County Council, established under the Local Government Act of 1888, and by other large urban authorities. In 1935, the editors of a book entitled *A Century of Municipal Progress, 1835–1935* could celebrate the centenary of the Municipal Corporations Act of 1835, by imagining 'a reformer who had grown grey in the struggles of the nineteenth century over local government' revisiting Britain. 'He would be chiefly struck by the scope and importance of the new tasks that now fall to local authorities . . . the result partly of the energetic teaching of thinkers; partly of the successful experiments of the early London County Council; partly of the democratic movement that started in 1906.'[55]

Continental observers also admired the development of local govern-

---

[54] Cited in Greenleaf, *The British Political Tradition*, vol. 3, part 1, p. 38.
[55] J. L. Hammond, 'The Social Background, 1835–1935', in H. J. Laski, W. Ivor Jennings and W. A. Robson (eds), *A Century of Municipal Progress, 1835–1935* (Allen & Unwin, 1935), p. 53.

ment in Britain. Indeed they saw it as reflecting a peculiarly British penchant for self-government, and as the expression of a strong sense of local patriotism, which seemed absent in much of the Continent. The strength of local self-government was for these observers the secret of the success of representative democracy in Britain. Shortly after the passage of the Local Government Act in 1894, which provided for the establishment of district councils and of elective parish councils for every village with a population of over 300, and for some which were even smaller, the great Austrian constitutional lawyer Josef Redlich declared that 'the whole field of internal administration, if one except the City of London, now lay under the control of popularly elected bodies'.[56] In consequence,

> The grand principle of representative democracy has now been fully applied to local government ... England has created for herself 'self government' in the true sense of the word. She has secured self government—that is to say, the right of her people to legislate, to deliberate and to administer through councils or parliaments elected on the basis of popular suffrage ... And this is the root of the incomparable strength of the English Body Politic.'[57]

VII

In 1900, moreover, despite what Redlich wrote, Britain was very far from being a 'representative democracy'. The franchise was restricted primarily to householders, while complicated registration requirements meant that, before 1918, only around 60 per cent of adult males had the vote.[58] Some males, moreover, enjoyed more than one vote if they owned property in more than one constituency or if they were university graduates. In the January 1910 general election, the number of plural voters was, apparently, greater than the majority of the winning party in no fewer than seventy-eight county constituencies. The vote, before 1918, was as much a reward for owning property or being a graduate of a university as a right of the citizen. Indeed, Britain by 1914 was 'the only major western democracy not to have achieved a practical universal male suffrage, and it was not until 1918 that the system of "democracy tem-

---

[56] Josef Redlich, *Local Government in England* (Macmillan, 1894), vol. 1, p. 213.
[57] Cited in Bryan Keith-Lucas, *Parish Councils: The Way Ahead*, The Fourth Mary Brockenhurst Lecture (Devon Association of Parish Councils, 1985), p. 1.
[58] Neal Blewett, 'The Franchise in the United Kingdom, 1885–1918', *Past and Present* (1965).

pered by registration" was abolished'.[59] Moreover, the failure to redistribute electoral constituencies in accordance with changing population movements meant that there remained gross discrepancies in constituency size, especially between the component parts of the United Kingdom. In England at the beginning of the twentieth century, there was on average one MP for every 66,971 people, in Ireland one MP for every 44,147 people.[60] A vote in Kilkenny, it was alleged in 1910, was worth twenty votes in Romford.[61] It was, however, difficult to transfer seats from Ireland to England, for fear of arousing the wrath of the Irish nationalists; and when the Unionists in 1905 mischievously proposed to do so, the Irish argued that this would violate the Act of Union which had allotted to Ireland one hundred MPs in the House of Commons![62]

The Reform and Redistribution Acts of 1884–5, however, had set in motion an important principle, namely that the House of Commons represented not communities but individuals. 'The ancient idea of the representation of communities', declared F. W. Maitland, the constitutional historian, 'or organised bodies of men, bodies which, whether called boroughs or counties, constantly act as wholes, and have common rights and duties, has thus given way to that of a representation of numbers of unorganised masses of men, or of men who are organised just for the one purpose of choosing members.'[63] The reforms of the 1880s established single-member constituencies as the norm, with only twenty-seven two-member constituencies being retained. Many of these single-member constituencies were, especially in the cities, artificial creations, and they tended to separate parliamentary representation from local representation, so eroding the idea of territorial representation and helping to weaken local and territorial loyalties. Indeed, the decline of local loyalties would prove to be one of the dominant themes of the twentieth century. In the words of one authority: 'For the first time it could clearly be seen that parliamentary constituencies were artificial creations formed to give a basis of legitimacy to the politicians at Westminster rather than local communities. Henceforth, national and

---

[59] J. G. Bulpitt, *Territory and Power in the United Kingdom* (Manchester University Press, 1984), p. 115.
[60] Lowell, *The Government of England*, p. 201.
[61] Muir, *Peers and Bureaucrats*, pp. 22–3.
[62] Lowell, *The Government of England*, p. 201.
[63] F. W. Maitland, *The Constitutional History of England* (Cambridge University Press, 1908), p. 363.

regional political issues were to be more important than local factors in deciding the results of elections.'[64]

Moreover, the single-member constituency would, so Ostrogorski feared, increase the power of the party machine, the caucus, and weaken minorities within parties. For the majority would enjoy 'a monopoly of the representation, and the Caucus has a monopoly of the majority'.[65] The new system had enabled Gladstone to hold together a naturally fissiparous Liberal Party, while, in the twentieth century, it helped the party leaders to overcome rebellion. It thus militated against the formation of strong and effective centre parties, whether an alliance of Liberal imperialists and Unionist free traders, at the beginning of the century, or the Social Democrat Party, the SDP, in the 1980s. 'Without Proportional Representation', Sir John Lubbock, a Liberal Unionist free trader, declared, 'a central party is, I believe, impossible. A system of election such as ours favours two extremes, and crushes out moderate men and independent thinkers.'[66] The settlement of 1884–5, although it was very far from yielding even universal male suffrage, nevertheless exerted a fundamental influence on twentieth-century politics by reinforcing the two-party system and preventing party fragmentation.

Even so, the early years of the twentieth century were marked by a lively argument on the merits of different electoral systems. Indeed, it was against the background of a likely further extension of the franchise, resolving the issues of both plural voting and female suffrage, that the Proportional Representation Society, first established in 1884, was refounded in 1905. The society argued for the single transferable vote, the only form of proportional representation seriously considered in Britain until the 1970s. This received some support from Conservative free traders, fearful of being extruded from the party through the operation of the Chamberlain machine, and also from minorities in the Liberal and Labour parties.

But the party leaders were on the whole unsympathetic to proportional representation. 'I am afraid', Sir Charles Dilke, one of the architects of the 1884–5 settlement, was to tell the Royal Commission on Electoral Systems in 1910, 'that the party leader now, as in former times,

---

[64] H. J. Hanham, *The Reformed Electoral System in Great Britain, 1832–1932* (Historical Association, 1968), p. 26.
[65] Moisei Ostrogorski, *Democracy and the Organisation of Political Parties* (Macmillan, 1902), vol. 2, p. 536.
[66] Horace G. Hutchinson, *Life of Sir John Lubbock, Lord Avebury* (Macmillan, 1914), vol. 2, p. 276.

takes the view that any resistance to that tendency, or that effect, of single-member constituencies or of majority representation is a device to preserve in a glass case or under a glass shade a specimen on which he desires to trample with a boot. That, I think, is the party leader's usual view.'[67] The Chamberlainites, who were becoming the majority faction amongst the Unionists, sought to destroy the free traders, not to conciliate them, while the Liberals and Labour believed that the electoral agreement signed by Herbert Gladstone, the Liberal chief whip, and Ramsay Mac-Donald, secretary of the Labour Party, in 1903, would allow them to build a progressive alliance under the existing electoral system. Ramsay MacDonald believed that Labour would eventually become the majority party and so benefit from the plurality electoral system; and he persuaded Labour to oppose any change in the electoral system. Thus Labour, almost alone among west European social democratic parties, came to reject proportional representation.

The Liberals, who had benefited from the plurality system in 1906, had no wish to replace it with a system which would make them once again dependent on the Irish nationalists for their parliamentary majority, as they had been between 1892 and 1895, and were to be again after 1910. J. Renwick Seager, secretary of the Registration Department of the Liberal Central Association, told the Royal Commission on Electoral Systems in 1910:

> Proportional representation is a matter scarcely ever talked about ... The Liberal agents as a whole, so far as I know, are none of them in favour of it; and as to the organisations, I do not know of one Liberal organisation that has ever passed a resolution in favour of it.'

Seager himself was opposed to proportional representation because 'the effect to my mind would be that the number of bores and cranks in the House would be largely increased, apart from the personal interests of trade or religion'.[68]

Some leading Liberals, however, were becoming fearful that Labour might succeed in breaking out of the constraints imposed upon it by the Gladstone–MacDonald pact. They therefore made sympathetic noises towards the alternative vote or two-ballot systems, which would prevent the left-wing vote being split; it was probably for this reason that Asquith had set up, in 1908, the only Royal Commission on Electoral Systems

[67] Cd 5352, minutes, para. 1496.
[68] Cd 5352, 1910, minutes, paras 981, 849, 940.

ever to have been established in Britain. This Commission reported in 1910 in favour of the alternative vote, with just one dissentient who favoured proportional representation. The Commission, however, gave a scathing verdict on the working of the plurality system in single-member constituencies as it had been established by the Third Reform Act of 1884:

> Whether the authors of the Bill of that year did or did not believe that the single-member constituency would secure a general correspondence between the support in votes and the representation of the two great parties, such a belief was no doubt widely held at the time. It has proved to be unfounded. Majorities in the House have shown a very great, and at the same time variable disproportion to majorities in votes, and there is nothing in the system to warrant the belief that such exaggerations will not recur.

Moreover, the plurality system 'misleads the nation as to the actual state of feeling in the country. In the House of Commons it encourages ambitious legislation for which there is no genuine demand.'[69]

Both Liberals and Labour toyed with the alternative vote rather than proportional representation at various times in the twentieth century, seeing it as an essential precondition of a realignment of the Left. In 1930, indeed, Ramsay MacDonald's second minority Labour government introduced an Electoral Reform bill, providing for the adoption of the alternative vote. The bill passed the Commons, but was subjected to wrecking amendments in the Lords, and the government fell before the provisions of the Parliament Act could be applied. Governments were, however, much more wary of proportional representation which did not appear in the manifesto of any political party until adopted by the independent (Asquithian) Liberals in their 1922 manifesto, but by that time proportional representation had come to be seen as a device to rescue the dying Liberal Party, rather than as a reform worthy of appraisal on its own merits.

VIII

Proportional representation, however, and even perhaps reform of the House of Lords, excited the political class more than it did the people; female suffrage was probably the only constitutional reform to ignite

---

[69] Cd 5163, 1910, Report, para. 90.

popular interest in the early part of the twentieth century. It is of course dangerous to make assumptions about popular opinion in the days before opinion polls, but it is doubtful whether large numbers of the voting public shared the criticisms of the British constitution put forward by the jurists or the social scientists. Indeed, the very high polls of 1910— 92 per cent of registered voters went to the polls in January 1910 and 89 per cent in December even though the Register was very old—suggest that this was so. While it is true that the British constitution, unlike its codified counterparts, did not provide for formal limits to the power of government, nevertheless, the British seemed to possess, more than their continental neighbours, a constitutional sense, a sense that power, even when sovereign, should be exercised with restraint and with due deference to the rights of minorities. Thus the twentieth century began with a sense of optimism, only partly tempered by warning voices and forebodings. To the majority, however, there must have seemed no reason why the Imperial Parliament should not continue to govern a United Kingdom, which included of course the whole of Ireland, in perpetuity, through the procedures which Bagehot had consecrated over thirty years earlier. 'The final test of a constitution', after all, so it has been said, 'is whether it works'.[70] At the beginning of the twentieth century, the British constitution seemed triumphantly to have passed that test.

[70] Le May, *The Victorian Constitution*, p. 188.

2.
The Constitution: Its Theory and Interpretation

GEOFFREY MARSHALL

'The theory of the constitution' is a phrase of considerable obscurity, since both 'theory' and 'constitution' are commonly used in a number of different ways. Before asking what theories about the constitution have been held in Britain during the twentieth century it may be prudent to consider briefly the general meaning or meanings of the term 'constitution' and how they may apply to the political arrangements of the United Kingdom. This itself is one form of constitutional theorising among many and almost everyone who writes about the British constitution engages in it.[1] Tocqueville's much quoted allegation that there is no English constitution carries an implicit theory about the general nature of constitutions. For our present purposes we had better assume that this theory—or at least its application—is false and that we can find a meaning for the term that permits theories to be held about the British constitution other than that it is non-existent.

Definitions of 'constitution'

The definition offered by the *Concise Oxford Dictionary* is—in the manner of dictionaries—not very precise. It tells us that a constitution is 'the body of fundamental principles or established precedents according to which a state or other organisation is acknowledged to be governed'. On the face of it this description does not exactly match the contents of many constitutions. Most contain numerous provisions that are not in

[1] See, for example, Eric Barendt, 'Is there a United Kingdom Constitution?', *Oxford Journal of Legal Studies* (1997), 137; Rodney Brazier, 'The Constitution of the United Kingdom', *Cambridge Law Journal* (1999), 96; Neil MacCormick, 'Does the United Kingdom have a Constitution?', *Modern Law Review* (1978), 1.

any obvious sense fundamental. The constitution of the United States, for example, contains the stipulation that Congress shall meet each year on the third day of January unless they appoint a different day. So some further elaboration is clearly needed.

Sir Kenneth Wheare in his *Modern Constitutions*[2] writes that the word constitution was commonly used in two senses, which for convenience we may call senses (a) and (b). In the first or wider sense it may be used to describe 'the whole system of government of a country, the collection of rules which establish or regulate or govern the government'. These rules are partly legal and partly non-legal—taking the form of 'usages, undertakings, customs or conventions which are not less effective in regulating the government'. By contrast the narrower sense (b) of constitution describes a selection of purely legal rules, which has usually been embodied in one document or in a few closely related documents. Usually, though perhaps not necessarily, the rules included in the constitutional document or documents require a more complex procedure for their repeal and amendment than other legislative enactments within the system.

This twofold classification suggests a number of reflections. One is that it is not a distinction simply between the legal and the non-legal rules that govern the government. For this reason we might posit a third sense of constitution—sense (c), which might describe a sense of constitution wider than (b) but narrower than (a)—namely not a mere historical selection but all the basic legal rules that define the structures and procedures of government and the relations between government and citizens. The constitution of the United States in this sense would not be found in the brief document that carries that title but would be contained also in numerous Acts of Congress (for example those delimiting the jurisdiction of the Supreme Court) and also in state constitutions and in the voluminous decisions of the Supreme and federal courts. Similarly, the constitution of Canada in sense (b) might be said to be contained in the historic Constitution Acts of 1867 and 1982, but in law the constitution of Canada (by the provisions of section 52 of the 1982 Constitution Act) includes a long list of other enactments including the Manitoba, Alberta and Saskatchewan Acts, a number of British North America Acts and the Statute of Westminister. This is not quite the constitution in sense (c) as we have defined it, since it does not include the legal rules stemming from the federal and provincial courts, or for

---

[2] *Modern Constitutions* (Oxford University Press, 1951), ch. 1.

that matter from the constitutions of the provinces. So Canada may be said to have a constitution in four senses.

Four distinguishable senses of 'constitution', therefore, would be:

(a) the combination of legal and non-legal (or conventional) rules that currently provide the framework of government and regulate the behaviour of the major political actors;

(b) a single instrument promulgated at a particular point in time and adopted by some generally agreed authorisation procedure under the title 'constitution' (or equivalent rubric such as 'basic law');

(c) the totality of legal rules, whether contained in statutes, secondary legislation, domestic judicial decisions or binding international instruments or judicial decisions, that affect the working of government;

(d) a list of statutes or instruments that have an entrenched status and can be amended or repealed only by a special procedure.

In which sense then does the United Kingdom have a constitution? Clearly it has a constitution—as does every state—in sense (a). It has never—apart from a brief period under the Protectorate—had a constitution in sense (b). It does—again in common with all other states— have a constitution in sense (c), though not in sense (d). It might well be argued that sense (b) is the least important of the three and that the United Kingdom's situation is less exceptional than is commonly imagined. References to the celebrated absence of the British constitution, or to its unwritten constitution, in fact generally signal only the absence of a constitution in sense (b), that is a document with historical significance and a specific title. But, in the more important senses (a) and (c), the United Kingdom is in the same position as every other state. Moreover, in every state there is a problem about characterising the non-legal rules of the constitution. Should they be spoken of as unwritten or informal? Neither term seems appropriate. Conventional or customary rules are to be found in written form: they are not passed from person to person by word of mouth. In some cases their form is as clear and ascertainable as many rules of law. In other cases their exact formulation or their interpretation is uncertain or controversial. But that is true also of the legal rules of the constitution. Since there is no single term that is obviously applicable they might just as well be called the non-legal or conventional rules of the constitution. Although it is often suggested that these rules play a larger role in the British constitution than elsewhere, it is not clear, when we are considering the constitution in its most important senses—(a) and (c)—that this is true. It would be difficult to produce any calculation about the proportion of legal to conventional rules because of a second difficulty of characterisation that affects all constitutions equally. We cannot state the number of constitutional laws because there is no clear boundary to be drawn between laws that are part of the constitution and laws that are not. The characterisation of laws as constitutional or criminal or administrative is over a large area conventional.[3] (Is the legislation about local government or criminal justice or race relations constitutional in character?) Talk of codifying the constitution in the United Kingdom implicitly refers to a document in sense (b).[4] But in the more important senses (a) and (c) no state— certainly not the United States—has a codified constitution or would think of producing one. Since the real constitution is indefinite as to its boundaries the task is beyond human capacity.

Constitutional theorising

If we know what our constitution is, what of its theory? The American constitutional historian Edward Corwin defined constitutional theory as 'the sum total of ideas of some historical standing as to what the constitution is or might be'. This tells us not a great deal, besides appearing to disqualify as theory novel ideas of no historical standing. An alternative suggestion might be that constitutional theory comprises any fairly general set of ideas about the legislative, executive or judicial branches of government. That formulation in turn seems incomplete, since it leaves out of account the fact that constitutional relationships do not obtain exclusively between branches of government but between government, or one of its elements on the one hand and citizens or groups of citizens on the other, perhaps also with other states and their citizens. There are also some general internal problems of governmental organisation that do not relate to functional relationships between branches of government but rather to the geographical distribution of power within the state. In addition, much theorising consists in the analysis of particular structural concepts of some traditional importance—for example sovereignty, the

---

[3] A point made persuasively in F. W. Maitland's *Constitutional History of England* (Cambridge University Press, 1908). See 'The Definition of Constitutional Law' at pp. 526–39: 'Our whole constitutional law seems at times to be but an appendix to the law of real property.'
[4] See the heroic (but hopeless) attempt to codify the constitution by the Institute for Public Policy Research, *The Constitution of the United Kingdom* (1991).

separation of powers, the rule of law, convention, federalism, devolution, judicial review, representation, the mandate, referenda and so on. Nor are we at the end, because there is also a universe of concepts that concern limitation on state powers and the general categories that figure in bills of rights—equality and equal protection, freedom of expression and movement, rights to property, due process and the like. All of these topics involve a mixture of legal and non-legal issues and the form of discourse may be descriptive, prescriptive or historical.

An interesting subcategory, mainly found among historians is that of analogical characterisation in which some simile or metaphor is invoked to describe the general nature of our constitutional arrangements. Those who wrote about the constitution in the nineteenth century and early twentieth century were endlessly fertile in their invention of literary images designed to convey one or other characteristic of the so-called unwritten constitution—its fluidity, adaptability, evolutionary character and so on. From writers such as Bagehot, Low, Lowell and Marriott we learn that the constitution is a growing edifice, that it resembles a human structure, that it is an ever changing suit of clothes or a 'goodly tree of freedom'. The last phrase is that of William Edward Hearn in *The Government of England, its Structure and its Development* (1867). Unlike 'the mechanical contrivances of political inventors' which have crumbled away in the hands of their projectors, the stately bulk of the British implant is 'deeply rooted in the habits and affections of the people' and 'like that typical mustard tree in whose overshadowing branches the fowls of the air find shelter it affords in the evil days to many a weary wing and many a scared and fluttering guest a secure asylum and an inviolable home'. This form of eulogy has been less commonly indulged in recent times, but the boundaries of constitutional theory are widely spread and most of its varieties can be found in the twentieth century.

Constitutional interpretation

One form or subcategory of constitutional theory is constitutional interpretation. But 'interpretation' is a vague term and it can have different applications when applied to the different senses of 'constitution'. The American example illustrates this well enough. In relation to sense (b) — the historic document—there is a familiar and much debated set of interpretive questions. Should the intentions of the constitution's framers be used as a guide to its current meaning? Should it be read historically, textually or morally? In an American context judicial interpretation also commonly concerns not merely the reading or interpretation of the constitution's terms, but the various questions that fall under the heading of judicial review. How should the power of invalidation of federal and state legislation be exercised? Should the power be used in an activist or in a minimal and restrained fashion? What standards of scrutiny—high, low, or intermediate—should be applied to legislation when reviewing it in the light of the restraints imposed in the constitution and the Bill of Rights? Should the judiciary treat economic legislation and that affecting civil and political rights in the same way? Problems of interpretation and application also arise within the boundaries of particular provisions in the constitution. What meaning is to be given to the term 'speech' in the First Amendment—or to 'state action' in the Fourteenth Amendment?

In relation to the constitution in sense (c)—the full range of legal rules outside the confines of the historic legal document that affect the basic structure of government—there will also be interpretive questions about the methodology of statutory interpretation and about the role of presumptions of constitutionality.

If we turn now to the constitution of the United States in its widest sense, sense (a)—the whole body of rules that regulate government — we can find 'interpretations' of the constitution in a different sense. They may represent competing views about the ways in which the branches of government, or the federal and state elements in the system do or should operate. They can be interpretations of a descriptive or historical or normative character. Works such as Woodrow Wilson's *Congressional Government* or Bryce's *American Commonwealth* paint differing pictures of the governmental machinery. Wilson may tell us that 'the predominant and controlling form, the centre and source of all regulative power is Congress'.[5] Later analysts may say that an executive presidency has evolved into a leadership presidency or has become an 'imperial presidency'.

Analogues to both kinds of interpretation can be seen in British constitutional writing. Our constitution in sense (c) raises problems of statutory interpretation and the elucidation of common law principles. With the addition of Community law obligations within the constitution and with the addition of human rights legislation interpretive problems of judicial review in the American sense have been added. Our constitution in sense (a) moreover is not lacking in interpretive analyses. A

---

[5] *Congressional Government* (Columbia University Press, 1913), p. 11.

number of them were described by Professor J. C. Rees in a lecture 'Interpreting the Constitution' in 1955.[6] One such interpretation or view-point, he said, was to be found in the writings of Sir Ivor Jennings, which could be summed up as the liberal toleration model embodying decision by majority vote in Parliament, free discussion and deference to the electorate. A second interpretation was to be found in the writings of Sir Ernest Barker, which by contrast with majority vote or government by number was concerned with the moral basis of democracy. A third view, seen in the work of L. S. Amery, portrays the constitution as a balance between two independent elements—the Crown and the People—the authority of the Crown being original. A fourth model was seen in the economic interpretation of the constitution propounded in various versions by Harold Laski, in which the machinery of government and its activities reflect and respond to the need of a particular social class. Much could no doubt be said about these models, particularly about their mutual consistency or exclusivity. Rees said, plausibly enough, that it is impossible to describe the constitution without interpreting it and in some sense or other this must be so. The character of description varies with its objects. Where the object is a process or a set of institutions their operation or evolution must involve causal explanations and, although causes and explanations may in principle involve matters of fact, where the matters of fact are complex rather than simple, matters of fact easily merge into matters of opinion and theory.

This point appears clearly enough if we think of more recent inter-pretive theses. One example might be the suggested transition of the British system of government from a Westminster to a Whitehall model—first propounded in the 1960s by Professor A. H. Birch (in his work on *Representative and Responsible Government*). Another might be Richard Crossman's thesis about the replacement of collective cabinet government by prime-ministerial or quasi-presidential government. But what—apart from the confused border line between describing and commending constitutional arrangements—these models show is that constitutional theorising is a somewhat disconnected heap of activities that embraces descriptive, historical and normative writings and includes the pro-pounding of general models, the elucidation of general principles or doctrines both legal and non-legal and the elucidation and application of particular rules, both of law and convention.

---

[6] Leicester University Press, 1955.

Constitutional documentation

Why, we might ask, is the twentieth-century constitutional history of England not written? Where are the volumes that continue the work of Hallam, Maitland, Dicey and Erskine May? Perhaps some mention might be made of the work of Arthur Berriedale Keith who, besides chronicling at length the development of the British dominions, published in 1940 two volumes on *The Constitution of England from Queen Victoria to George VI*. On a more restricted theme and in a more analytical vein there have been detailed studies of cabinet government by Sir Ivor Jennings and by John Mackintosh. But there are not many such.[7]

One difficulty has been the indefinite extent of the constitution (in the senses we have defined as (c) and (a)). Of course in this sense there has been no adequate history of the constitution of the United States or France. The entirety of the materials is unusable and the task of selection is unmanageable. The problem is an extending one. Compare the content of the volumes of constitutional documents and materials that were confidently compiled and issued even fifty years ago—often covering two or three centuries of constitutional development. They would typically contain extracts from a handful of statutes of obvious constitutional importance (the Bill of Rights, Act of Settlement, the Parliament Acts, Representation of the People Acts, Public Order Act), together with some extended quotations from Hansard and a selection of extracts from leading cases on matters such as the powers of the Crown, parliamentary privilege, martial law, public order and judicial remedies.

Consider now the plight of a would-be compiler of a similar volume for the second half of the twentieth century. A multitude of public documents, reports of commissions and parliamentary select committees exist, many of them multi-volumed or running to hundred of pages. The same is true of major statutes and law reports. Their content cannot be represented by a few selected pages and they cannot be included in full. The case-law particularly is hardly reducible to a few leading cases and now includes voluminous European materials. The relevant law may on its face be classified as criminal law, or education or immigration or social services law, or human rights law or devolution law. How in this situation is the development of something labelled 'the constitution' to be documented, described or interpreted? Only perhaps in the manner

---

[7] For a survey of writing on the constitution over the past forty years see Nevil Johnson, 'Then and Now: The British Constitution', *Political Studies* (2000), 118.

of Dicey by selecting (if it is still possible) what seem to be leading principles and attempting to relate the expanding mass of legal and political materials to them.

With some slight modification the themes of Dicey's *Law of the Constitution*[8] may still serve the purpose—though each could profitably have a substantial volume devoted to it. First, perhaps, the development of the conventional basis of the constitution and its relation to the legal components. Secondly, the legal foundations of the constitution and the character of parliamentary authority. Thirdly, the rule of law and the application of human rights as between government and citizen. Each of these has provided a focus for ample interpretive debate over the course of the century.

Interpreting 'convention'

Since the publication of Dicey's classic analysis of the conventions of the constitution discussion has focused on at least five separable issues: the scope and purpose of convention; the grounds and causes of obedience to convention; the mode of establishment of convention; the relation between convention and law; and the desirability of codifying conventions or (more radically) of embodying the conventions in a written constitution.

As to scope and purpose, Dicey saw conventions as being in the main 'rules intended to regulate the exercise of the whole of the remaining discretionary powers of the Crown'. Whilst this summation is true of the central convention that has effectively transferred prerogative powers into the hands of ministers, requiring the Crown to act on advice in almost all executive functions and in assenting to legislation, it does not accurately describe the role of all the major conventions: for example those that relate to the activities of the two Houses of Parliament internally and in relation to each other; or the mutual relationships of government and opposition; or of ministers and civil servants; or the external rules governing the relations of the United Kingdom and the members of the Commonwealth. Nor does it have any bearing on the most fundamental (though generally unstated) convention that requires the sovereign legislative powers of Parliament to be exercised in accord-

---

[8] *Introduction to the Study of the Law of the Constitution*, 10th edn, ed. E. C. S. Wade (Macmillan, 1959). For a recent assessment of Dicey's views see the articles on 'Dicey and the Constitution' in *Public Law* (1985), 583–744.

ance with various presumptions designed to restrain their theoretically unlimited scope.

Dicey's analysis remained more or less unchanged and unchallenged through the various editions of his book, of which the eighth edition appeared in 1915, and it was reprinted through the 1920s and in 1931. In 1933, however, Sir Ivor Jennings published *The Law and the Constitution* (which itself became a popular classic going through five editions until 1959). Jennings attacked Dicey on a number of fronts. As to convention he challenged Dicey's theses that conventions were obeyed because a breach of convention ultimately entailed a breach of law and that conventions were distinguishable from law on the ground that they were not recognised or enforced in the courts. On the first point Dicey can be defended on the ground that his example of the legal difficulties that would attend a government in attempting to raise taxes if it had lost the confidence of the House of Commons but refused to resign was not advanced as a general ground of obedience to convention, since he freely admitted other examples of breaches of convention (changing the basic legislative procedures of Parliament or suspending the Habeas Corpus Acts) which would produce no subsequent illegal consequences.

On the second point Jennings' attack on Dicey is unclearly expressed and to some degree inconsistent. In various editions of *The Law and the Constitution* he argued that there was 'no fundamental distinction between law and convention' or at least 'no distinction of substance'. On examination, however, Jennings appears to be saying merely that there are considerable similarities between law and convention. Both, he thought, had a political character and the enforcement of each rested on acceptability. That they share these characteristics does not, however, in itself show that there are not from other points of view important distinctions to be made between them. Jennings, in fact, conceded this in the third edition of *The Law and the Constitution*, saying that there was 'a formal distinction of the kind recognised by Dicey',[9] one feature of the difference being that it was not a court that decided when a convention had been broken. It does not seem therefore that Jennings and Dicey were as much at odds on this issue as is usually supposed.

In 1936 Jennings produced the first edition of *Cabinet Government*, the *locus classicus* of the inter-war conventions of the British parliamentary system. Perhaps the most frequently quoted passages in later years were, however, those that appeared in the first edition of *The Law and the*

---

[9] *The Law and the Constitution* (University of London Press, 1943), p. 113.

Constitution three years earlier and which related to the role of precedent in the establishment of conventions. 'We have', he writes, 'to ask ourselves three questions: first, what are the precedents? Secondly, did the actors in the precedents believe that they were bound by a rule? And thirdly, is there a good reason for the rule?'[10] It had sometimes been thought, he said, that the king's choice of Baldwin in 1923 instead of Lord Curzon created the convention that the prime minister must always be in the House of Commons. But it certainly did not if the king did not regard himself as bound by such a rule. Jennings did not, however, elaborate on these criteria or their potential inconsistency as much as might have been hoped. Suppose that King George V had regarded himself as bound by the rule but that there was no good reason for it. Suppose that he had not regarded himself as bound by the rule but that there was a good reason for it and perhaps a series of precedents. When the persons concerned did regard themselves as bound, Jennings concluded, the convention might still be broken with impunity. But, if the convention were supported by precedents and good reasons, presumably those who broke the convention would be breaking the convention mistakenly and unconstitutionally.

Jennings, in other words, did not allot any degrees of relative priority to his criteria. Implicitly, however, many modern textbook definitions of convention appear to allot a high, indeed crucial, importance to the beliefs of the actors concerned when they deem conventions to be rules of practice that are regarded as morally or politically binding by those who work the constitution. Whatever the stated criteria, however, politicians may be mistaking the precedents or failing to perceive the rationale of a conventional rule that they are failing to observe. Of course, if all politicians, or even a majority of them, fail in this way the conventional rules (like the rules of a language) will become whatever it is that anyone does. But at any one time the rules—as with linguistic usage—can be misinterpreted or misread.

This suggests that the effectiveness and binding character of conventions differs from that of law at least in the sense that there are no authoritative interpreters, or even in some cases agreed formulations, of important conventional rules. Thus the status of important individual conventions may be open to challenge on the basis of fresh arguments about the precedents that allegedly support them. It was possible, for

---

[10] *The Law and the Constitution* (University of London Press, 1933), p. 109.

example, for S. E. Finer, in a much quoted article in 1956,[11] to allege that there were insufficient uncontroversial precedents to support the existence of the generally accepted convention of individual ministerial responsibility. Moreover, if politicians misread or misconstrue or ignore the relevant precedents there is in the United Kingdom no appeal to any court, ombudsman or official interpreter of the constitution's basic rules.

That this might not be a necessary feature of a conventional consti-tution was demonstrated by Commonwealth experience in the 1980s. The crisis in Canada over the patriation of the constitution furnished an example of conventions being the subject of judicial arbitration. The Supreme Court of Canada was able, under the provisions of federal and provincial legislation providing for advisory opinions to be given on a variety of matters not confined to legal issues, to hand down an opinion which was essentially on the question whether, and in what form, the consent of the provinces was required by the conventions of the federal constitution for the action of the federal government in requesting British amendments to the existing legal framework.[12] The Supreme Court's reply to the question was: 'As a matter of constitutional convention — Yes. As a matter of law—No.' This event has provoked a continuing debate about the traditional separation between law and convention. The court itself signified its clear agreement with Dicey's view that conven-tions are not laws and are not enforcible in the courts. But a non-legal rule that is declared to exist by a court has a curious status. It brings out, perhaps, that there is an uncertainty in the notion of recognition or enforcibility by a judicial body. Conventional rules may be given some legal effect or status when courts use them to interpret unclear rules of strict law, or to extend existing rules of law. Distinctions can still be drawn, as they can when non-legal rules of other kinds figure in judicial proceedings—as the rules of trade unions or universities or political parties may do. When an appeal is made to a court about the breach of such rules it might be said that what is being judicially enforced is an independently existing legal obligetion to operate these bodies of rules correctly—an obligation which does not exist at present in relation to the conventional rules of political behaviour; though, no doubt, judicial creativity might in future create such an obligation. Until such time

---

[11] 'The Individual Responsibility of Ministers', *Public Administration* (1956), 377.
[12] *Reference Re Amendment of the Constitution of Canada* (1982) 125 DLR (3d) 1. For the background, see House of Commons, First Report from the Foreign Affairs Committee, HC 42(1) (1980–1) *British North America Acts: The Role of Parliament*; and Geoffrey Marshall, *Constitutional Conventions* (Clarendon Press, 1986), ch. 11.

Dicey's distinction between law and convention can still with some difficulty be maintained, but the lines between direct enforceability and various forms of indirect application or judicial consideration are not easy to draw. What is perhaps more interesting is that where for whatever reason courts pronounce on conventions their decisions are accorded some authority and cannot easily be ignored.

Can the same be said (we may wonder) of other forms of official certification that fall short of embodying conventions in legislation. A difficult exercise of this kind was attempted in Australia between 1982 and 1985, when a constitutional commission (or 'Convention') was set up to attempt a codification of the major conventions of the Australian parliamentary system.[13] In 1985 the commission set out a list of eighteen conventions governing the relationships of the prime minister, the governor-general and the House of Representatives. The report was prefaced by the statement that 'This Convention recognises and declares that the following principles and practices shall be observed as conventions in Australia.' This method of establishing the content and authority of constitutional conventions presents, it must be admitted, some difficulties. Unlike the courts, a convention or government-appointed committee has no special hold on the public imagination or claim to deference and it is unclear what the effect or significance of promulgating a declaration of this kind can be. Unless or until the committee's conclusions are embodied in legislation (when they would cease to be conventions) there seems no very good reason for anyone to defer to the views of such a body. The existing historical precedents and bases of the conventions cannot be changed by decree. Nor is it clear whether the publication of such a list of declared or supposedly certified conventions implies that no further change in them can take place except by a similar process. Happily, no analogous exercise has been attempted in the United Kingdom. Who would trust a committee to define the definitive rules of parliamentary government, or, if they attempted it, feel precluded from arguing that they had got them wrong?

In the 1990s academic debate on the character of convention continued. In 1991 a Canadian political scientist, Dr Andrew Heard, suggested a new classification of conventional rules based on their

---

[13] See C. Sampford and D. Wood, 'Codification of Constitutional Conventions in Australia', *Public Law* (1987), 237 and C. Sampford, 'Recognise and Declare: An Australian Experiment in Codifying Conventions', *Oxford Journal of Legal Studies* (1987), 369.

varying degrees of obligation and specificity.[14] He distinguished, first, fundamental conventions—rules basic to the constitution, fixed in form and supported by general agreement. Second were 'meso-conventions' whose details and application might change without any major change to the workings of the political system. Third there might be 'semi-conventions'—rules prescribing desirable patterns of behaviour that might on occasion be disregarded without damage to the system. Fourth came 'infra-conventions' comprising rules that support some constitutional principle but which are characterised by controversy either as to the principle concerned or as to the formulation of the terms in which it should be framed. Fifth, there could be said to be usages based on habit, or ceremonial symbolism but not stemming from or intended to support any constitutional principle.

The acknowledgement of a hierarchy of conventional rules with differing degrees of generality, importance, authority and specificity, together with some uncertainty as to which rules belong to which category, complicates codification exercises such as those attempted in Australia or in other Commonwealth countries. It complicates equally, or even more so, proposals to enact a written constitution for the United Kingdom that would incorporate both the existing legal and non-legal constitutional rules and principles in a single document. It is perhaps one of the major arguments against such a utopian (or Cromwellian) enterprise.

Interpreting parliamentary sovereignty

In 1900 Dicey's account of the doctrine of parliamentary sovereignty would have gained general assent. It was, from a legal point of view, he said, the dominant feature of our political institutions. It meant that Parliament (defined as the Queen, Lords and Commons acting together) had the right to make or unmake any law and that no person or body had a right to override or set aside its legislation. The unlimited power of Parliament did not extend (paradoxically) to all kinds of legislation, since it was incapable of enacting unchangeable laws. A limitation on future action—if it were such—could be imposed in only two ways. Parliament could extinguish or dissolve itself, leaving no means by which a

---

[14] Andrew Heard, *Canadian Constitutional Conventions: The Marriage of Law and Politics* (Oxford University Press, 1991), ch. 7.

subsequent Parliament could be summoned; or it could transfer the entirety of its sovereign authority to another person or body of persons (as did the former Parliaments of Scotland and England at the Union).

An inquiry into the way in which Dicey's doctrine has evolved in the twentieth century leads the inquirer along an uncertain trail. Perhaps one clue at the outset can be found in a footnote in Dicey's first chapter (at page 67 of the fifth edition) where he remarks that Henry Sidgwick's account of sovereignty, though differing from his own, was 'full of interest and instruction'. Sidgwick is possibly an underestimated figure in the history of sovereignty. In his *Elements of Politics* first published in 1891 he discussed Austin's thesis that sovereignty in its nature could not be limited. In any legal system there was usually, he said, a body or complex system of bodies that had no legal limits to its power to alter the law. But its structure had to be legally determined and there were in that sense legal limitations of great importance since it could be prevented from acting except under certain conditions by the legal rules determining its structure and procedure. This may be the first clear promulgation of the idea that there is a distinction between rules that restrict the area of sovereign power and rules that are constitutive of the sovereign body in question and define and delimit the manner and form in which its authority is exercised. Dicey himself had of course pointed out that the authority of Parliament could only be exercised by the Queen and both Houses. The rules that require this would be rules of common law, whilst the rules that prescribe the procedures of each House are determined by the law and practice of Parliament, and the royal assent to legislation is a prerogative act. But common law, the practice and privileges of each House and the royal prerogative are all subject to alteration by statute, and Dicey did not press the question how far any of these rules or procedures could be changed. The theoretical possibility of limiting future legislative activity by an alteration in the manner and form of law-making had, however, been hinted at during Dicey's lifetime by Sir John Salmond. In his *Jurisprudence*, first published in 1902, he asked why a statute providing that no future statute should be repealed except by an absolute majority of all the members in each House could not create good law.

Salmond's question went unanswered. But in 1911 in enacting the Parliament Act the then elements of the King in Parliament did effect a change in the procedure of enactment to provide that legislation rejected by the Lords and re-passed by the Commons could be enacted by two elements only, namely the King and the Commons. Whether the effect of the Parliament Act was to create a solemn form of delegated legislation by the Parliament of the United Kingdom to two of its elements rather than to create an alternative form of primary enactment has been the subject of controversy.[15] But the enacting formula of the 1911 Act ('Be it enacted . . .') and the passage by the King and Commons of the 1949 Parliament Act suggested that an alternative manner and form of primary legislation had been created. Two further questions remained unanswered however. Could the rules have been changed not simply for a defined class of legislation but for all legislation; and could the legislative process have been changed not to simplify it but to make it more complex—to provide, for example, that certain legislation should require passage by a special majority before receiving the royal assent; or that an additional procedure, such as approval by a referendum majority should be added to the legislative process? And does it matter whether such a procedure is required as a prerequisite to enactment or as a post-enactment condition of the legislation being brought into operation? (Sixty-seven years later, in 1978, the Scotland Act incorporated a referendum requirement as a condition of the Act's continuing operation, so that failure to achieve the special majority required repeal by resolution. But could the referendum vote have been made either a condition precedent to the enacted measure being brought into operation or a condition precedent to the royal assent?) These questions broach the thorny question of entrenchment of legislation and the possibility of its enactment by a sovereign legislature possessing the characteristics described by Dicey.

During the inter-war years we can trace the history of this argument and the manner in which it progressed under the stimulus of a number of developments in the Commonwealth and in the United Kingdom's relations with the then British dominions. An influential figure was the Australian scholar Richard Latham, whose brief monograph *The Law and the Commonwealth*, published in 1937, six years before his death on active service, adopted an original and unusual approach to the constitutions of the Commonwealth countries, drawing on the juristic theory of Hans Kelsen. Latham argued that the sovereign authority in a legal system could not be the ultimate source of law. His, or its, powers must be derived from the basic rule or grundnorm of the legal system. 'Where

---

[15] See H. W. R. Wade 'The Basis of Legal Sovereignty', *Cambridge Law Journal* (1955), 193–4; A. W. Bradley, 'The Sovereignty of Parliament—in Perpertuity?', in Jeffrey Jowell and Dawn Oliver, *The Changing Constitution*, 3rd edn (Clarendon Press, 1994).

the purported sovereign is anyone but a single actual person the desig-
nation of him must include the statement of rules for the ascertainment
of his will, and these rules, since their observance is a condition of the
validity of his legislation, are rules of law logically prior to him. Further,
the mere assertion of the omnipotence of a sovereign leaves completely
uncertain the fundamental question whether or not he can bind himself.'[16]
Latham referred at this point to the decisions in the High Court of
Australia and the Privy Council in *Attorney-General of New South Wales*
v. *Trethowan*.[17] In that case both courts upheld a New South Wales
entrenching statute requiring any future abolition or changes to the
constitution of the upper House to be approved by referendum before
being presented to the governor for the royal assent. The New South
Wales legislature, however, was expressly authorised under the terms of
the Colonial Laws Validity Act to make laws about its own powers and
procedures. Although there were dicta in the *Trethowan* case about the
possible application of the principle to the Parliament of the United
Kingdom, no clear constitutional grundnorm positively authorised the
British sovereign legislator to make laws about its own law-making
procedure. This proved to be something of a difficulty when the Imperial
Parliament attempted in 1931 to do what Dicey's theory asserted to be
impossible, namely to limit or abdicate its own powers over particular
geographical areas whilst itself remaining in existence. The object of the
Statute of Westminster was to concretise into law the conventional equality of the dominions with the United Kingdom by conferring sovereign
authority over their own constitutions on their Parliaments. In form,
however, the statute preserved or acknowledged the theoretical sovereign
authority of the United Kingdom Parliament by providing that no future
legislation should extend to a dominion as part of its law unless it was
expressly declared in the statute that the dominion in question had
requested and consented to the enactment.[18]

In 1933, in the first edition of *The Law and the Constitution*, Ivor
Jennings suggested that this requirement could be regarded as a manner
and form provision changing the permissible future shape of legislation
for the dominions. Citing the *Trethowan* case, Jennings propounded the

---

[16] R. T. E. Latham, *The Law and the Commonwealth* (Oxford University Press, 1949), p. 523.
Latham's essay was first published in 1937 in W. K. Hancock, *Survey of British Commonwealth
Affairs* (Oxford University Press), vol. 1.
[17] *Commonwealth Law Reports*, 394; [1932] AC 526
[18] See K. C. Wheare, *The Statute of Westminster and Dominion Status*, 5th edn (Oxford
University Press, 1953), ch. 6.

45

general view that the sovereignty of Parliament did not exclude the possibility that the sovereign legislature might impose legal restraints upon itself because its power to change the law extended to the power to change the law about the way in which law should be made. This is perhaps the first clear expression of what later came to be labelled the 'new view' of sovereignty. Its essence lies in the supposition that legal supremacy relates essentially to the possession of an unlimited area of power, but that rules that simply define the procedures through which legal changes are effected are not fetters or limits on power and do not constitute restrictions on sovereignty.

That general thesis received further support from litigation in South Africa after the Second World War, turning upon the continuing validity of the so-called entrenched clauses in the South African constitution which required certain legislation to be passed by a two-thirds majority in a joint session of both Houses of Parliament. Since these provisions were in the South Africa Act—a British Act of Parliament, which since the passage of the Statute of Westminster the South African Parliament was entitled to amend in the exercise of its newly acquired sovereignty— the nationalist government, lacking a two-thirds parliamentary majority, attempted to remove the entrenched clauses by a simple majority statute. In 1952 in *Harris* v. *Dönges*[19] the Appellate Division of the South African High Court declared this purported legislation to be ineffective. When properly assembled, it held, the sovereign Parliament of South Africa could legislate for any purpose. But a prior question to be answered was what constituted the Parliament of South Africa for the purpose in hand. There were in effect two Parliaments in South Africa— one capable of acting by simple majority, the other constituted by a two-thirds majority in a joint sitting. The simple majority of members who had purported to enact the challenged legislation were not authorised to enact anything and were not Parliament.

None of this provided conclusive evidence or judicial support for the supposition that the sovereign Parliament of the United Kingdom, which is not defined in any constitutional instrument, was capable in effect of redefining itself for particular purposes by imposing on itself binding rules defining what would constitute legislation for the legislative objects

[19] 1 TLR 1245. The decision in this case leaned heavily upon the argument developed by D. V. Cowen in his *Parliamentary Sovereignty and the Entrenched Sections of the South Africa Act* (Juta, 1951). On the subsequent litigation see Geoffrey Marshall, *Parliamentary Sovereignty and the Commonwealth* (Clarendon Press, 1957), ch. 11.

in question. Nevertheless, it provided material for a juristic remodelling of the general theory of legislative sovereignty.[20] The Commonwealth cases almost certainly provided some stimulus to the proposal made in Professor H. L. A. Hart's *Concept of Law*, which first appeared in 1961, that there might be two alternative models of sovereignty to which logic offered no relative priority. One form of sovereignty he dubbed 'continuous', the other 'self embracing'. The first is allotted power by the ultimate rule of recognition (or grundnorm) of the legal system to make laws of any kind in the same form and by the same process for all purposes, but is not permitted to make laws changing or affecting its own powers. The second has power to make laws that modify or even destroy its own law-making powers. Whether the British sovereign is of the first or second kind has importance for the jurisprudence of the Commonwealth, for relations with the law of the European Union and for the enactment of legislation with a fundamental or protected status— such as human rights legislation and devolution provisions. In 1978 the House of Lords Committee on the Bill of Rights[21] concluded that a Bill of Rights could not be entrenched, although no coherent argument for this conclusion was presented. It cannot be said that any clear judicial authority supports any version of the revised or self-embracing theory of sovereignty. Nevertheless, there are arguments of principle that weigh in its favour. The only way to make sense of the process by which autonomy has been conferred on Commonwealth countries is to suppose that (contra Dicey) Parliament is capable of restricting the future application of its powers by reference to particular areas. If Canada is to be an independent nation, the provision that no legislation subsequent to the passage of the 1982 Canada Act shall extend to Canada must be regarded as different from the provision in section 4 of the Statute of Westminster and be treated as unrepealable. Moreover, if Parliament were to be treated as continuously sovereign in its present form, then changes in that form which are generally assumed to be possible—such as abolition of the House of Lords or removal of the monarchy—would

---

[20] In the last thirty years there has been a considerable volume of writing on this theme. See, for example, R. F. V. Heuston, *Essays in Constitutional Law*, 2nd edn (Stevens, 1964) ch. 1; O. Hood Phillips, 'Parliament and Self-limitation', *Cambrian Law Review* (1973), 71; George Winterton, 'The British Grundnorm: Parliamentary Sovereignty Re-examined', *Law Quarterly Review* (1976), 591; and the literature cited in ch. 4 of S. de Smith and Rodney Brazier, *Constitutional and Administrative Law*, 8th edn (Penguin, 1998).
[21] HL 176 (1977–8).

have to be regarded as legally unachievable. Believers in the continuous sovereignty theory, therefore, have some hurdles to surmount.

Unfortunately, no issue has been before the British courts that would test judicial readiness to contemplate revision of the traditional sovereignty doctrine. Perhaps an exception was *MacCormick* v. *Lord Advocate*[22] in 1953 when it was said in the Court of Session that the powers of the United Kingdom Parliament might not extend to altering fundamental articles of the Act of Union. No court, however, has claimed jurisdiction to set justiciable limits to an Act of Parliament. In 1969, in *Madzimbamuto* v. *Lardner-Burke*, Lord Reid said emphatically that, although there were some things that might be regarded as unconstitutional in the sense of being morally or politically wrong, 'this does not mean that it is beyond the power of Parliament to do such things. If Parliament chose to do any of them the courts could not hold the Act of Parliament invalid.'[23] In the last two decades, however, a more radical scepticism about the sovereignty of Parliament has shown itself in both academic and judicial quarters. Lord Woolf (though extra-judicially) in 1994 expressed the view that 'there are limits to the sovereignty of Parliament which it is the courts' inalienable responsibility to identify and uphold'.[24] In a similar vein it has been suggested by Sir John Laws that in a free and rational society (presuming ours to be such) there are certain rights that cannot be supposed to be at the disposal of governments. There must, he argued, be a higher order law than the command of legislators which is not within their unlimited control.[25] A higher order law might of course simply be a superior positive norm as in Commonwealth constitutions. A perhaps surprising development in Australia has been the willingness of the Australian High Court in the 1990s to discover in the structure of the constitution rights limiting the powers of the federal legislature that are not explicitly enacted but held to be implied in the machinery of representative government.[26] In the United Kingdom by contrast the only available source of judicial authority to control the legislative authority of Parliament is the common law. Its role in the formation and perpetuation of the legislative sovereignty principle has in recent years become

---

[22] 1953 SC 396.
[23] [1969] 1 AC 645 at 723.
[24] See '*Droit Public*—English Style', *Public Law* (1995), 57, 69.
[25] 'Law and Democracy', *Public Law* (1995), 72.
[26] See H. P. Lee, 'The Australian High Court and Implied Constitutional Guarantees', *Public Law* (1993), 606.

the subject of renewed and vigorous debate, on both historical and juristic grounds.

Some judges and some jurists have been prepared to say that there are rights so fundamental to the common law that they are not to be supposed to be at the disposition of Parliament. In his book *Law, Liberty and Justice*,[27] for example, T. R. S. Allan argued for the presumptive limitation of legislative authority. Parliament, he suggested, is conceded its law-making supremacy, but within the overall restraints of the constitutional scheme as a whole. Statutes are entitled to general respect but not unlimited deference. Proponents of what might be called the 'still newer view' of sovereignty have in some cases found inspiration in the jurisprudential theories of Ronald Dworkin. In the (allegedly positivistic) universe of legal rules described in Hart's *Concept of Law* a legal system might, if its rule of recognition so provided, contain a legislature with limited or unlimited powers and in the second case with or without authority to impose limitations on its own powers. In Dworkin's imperial legal kingdom, however, the final criteria of valid law-making must be related to the overall purposes of the system and in liberal kingdoms must be related to its moral and political values. Alongside this jurisprudential doctrine there is also to be found a parallel historical thesis claiming to be in fact more traditional than the prevailing orthodoxy and alleging that parliamentary sovereignty in its present shape is a relatively modern doctrine invented by positivist followers of Hobbes and Austin, and superseding the older tradition in which parliamentary authority was held to be controllable by the common law.

More recently still, these arguments have been the subject of a counter-attack, both historical and juristic, by Professor Jeffrey Goldsworthy of Monash University in his work *The Sovereignty of Parliament: History and Philosophy*.[28] Professor Goldsworthy argues that, although there was an acceptance by theorists of natural law that human law was subordinate to divine law, that belief was consistent with the absence of any supposition that the King's laws made in Parliament could be rejected or overturned in a court of law. Parliamentary sovereignty originated in the powers of the King to make law. As the source of legal jurisdiction it was never supposed that he could be subject to the jurisdiction of his own courts. Breach of the natural laws which bound the sovereign was subject to control only by rebellion or resistance. On

---

[27] Clarendon Press, 1993.
[28] Clarendon Press, 1999.

the jurisprudential front, appeal is made to Hartian theory to argue that, although judges have the duty to decide how rules of law should be applied, the determination of what, in a given legal system, is to count as valid law is not within the sole power of the judiciary to decide but is a product of the understanding of officials in all three branches of government and of the legal community as a whole. This understanding does not, it is argued, support judicial limitation of Parliament's legislative powers in the United Kingdom.

These divergent views show the philosophical and historical uncertainty with which Dicey's doctrine has become enveloped at the turn of the century. Whatever conclusions may eventually be drawn, more practical concerns to do with European Union law have underlined the importance of the judiciary as potential remoulders of the sovereignty principle. Since the passage of the European Communities Act in 1972, which allotted, or purported to allot, a special status to community law within the United Kingdom, and more especially since the decision in the *Factortame* case, in which an Act of Parliament was for the first time 'disapplied' as being in conflict with Community law, some difference of opinion has existed as to whether the British judiciary has acquiesced in a legal revolution, abandoning a crucial element in the doctrine of parliamentary sovereignty.[29] From one view it can be argued that the European Communities Act has been interpreted in a way that effectively deprives subsequent Parliaments of their right to make their expressly framed legislation prevail. A less drastic view may, on the other hand, be taken. Although the courts appear to have treated the 1972 Act in a special and unprecedented way and to have abandoned the notion of implied repeal as an incident of the sovereignty principle, they have not yet expressly abandoned the view that the Queen in Parliament is capable both of repealing the 1972 Act in whole or part and of amending it in such a way as to confirm the power of Parliament to make an Act of Parliament prevail over inconsistent Community law in its application to the United Kingdom. If the courts were to decide at any point that Parliament has abdicated or abandoned its power to legislate in this way then a radical change would certainly have taken place in the doctrine of sovereignty. If Parliament did so abdicate its powers it must have

---

[29] See H. W. R. Wade, 'Sovereignty—Revolution or Evolution', *Law Quarterly Review*, 112 (1996), 568; and Paul Craig, 'Sovereignty of the United Kingdom Parliament after *Factortame*', *Year Book of European Law* (1991), 221; and Neil MacCormick, *Questioning Sovereignty: Law, State and Nation in the European Commonwealth* (Oxford University Press, 1999), ch. 6.

done so in 1972 under the law as it then was. It would be difficult to argue that the law at that time permitted such a conclusion to be drawn. If the judiciary were to rewrite the constitutional history of the past three decades so as to decide otherwise and that were to be accepted by the other branches of government and by the political community, then in truth a judicial revolution would have occurred.

Interpreting the rule of law

Dicey's much quoted description of the rule of law nominally contains four elements. First, the principle *nulla poene sine lege;* that no man can be punished except for a breach of law— a more or less tautological proposition. Secondly, the law should exclude the exercise of arbitrary, or even wide discretionary powers in the hands of government. Thirdly, there should be equality before the law, in the sense that all legal issues, whether involving citizens or government, should be dealt with in the same courts. Fourthly (and somewhat oddly), the rights of citizens are to be drawn—at least in the English model—not from any special consti-tutional code but from the provisions of ordinary legislation and the common law. It is worth noting that although these general principles are often rehearsed as if they exhaust Dicey's delineation of the rule of law, the contents of part II of *The Law of the Constitution* include a number of more substantive ingredients, such as freedom of discussion and public assembly and the subordination of the army to the rules of common law. Nevertheless, during the greater part of the first half of the twentieth century, debate on the rule of law as Dicey was understood to have expounded it, turned in large part on the executive discretion and pro-cedural equality before the law principles. In the early editions of *The Law of the Constitution* Dicey certainly illustrated his equality thesis by his assault on the system of *droit administratif,* which in its French manifes-tation allegedly threatened the supremacy of law by subjecting disputes involving government officials to a separate regime of tribunals. What everyone now knows is that Dicey came to acknowledge the growth of administrative law in England and to reassess his earlier condem-nation of the divided French jurisdiction. It is true is that Dicey adjusted his account of the French system in successive editions of his book.[30]

---

[30] See the analysis in F. H. Lawson's articles 'Dicey Re-visited', *Political Studies* (1959), 109 and 207.

Yet, despite its prominence, the French system was merely a striking but perhaps incidental example of the thesis from which he never resiled. The change in the character of legislation in the first years of the century was a process that he indeed recognised. In the second edition of *Law and Opinion in England*, published in 1914, he set out the accumulation of law that marked, in his eye, the growth of collectivism—in particular the pensions legislation of 1908, the National Insurance Act of 1911, the trade union legislation of 1906 and 1913 and the Finance Act of 1910. In 1915 he contributed to the *Law Quarterly Review* his article on 'The Development of Administrative Law in England', commenting on the decision of the House of Lords in *Local Government Board* v. *Arlidge*.[31] He recognised (whilst clearly regretting it) that the exercise by government departments of adjudicatory powers was 'in harmony with the legislative opinion dominant in 1915' which implied that in exercising such powers departmental officers should act not in accordance with the procedures of a court of law but according to the rules which govern the fair transaction of business in a public department. Nonetheless, he believed that the rule of law was preserved in the sense that the courts could still be counted on to ensure that departments conformed themselves strictly to their statutory powers and to dealing with any actual and provable breach of law. The ability of the courts to do this, however, might clearly be handicapped to the extent that the law applicable to departments might not require compliance with the common law rules of natural justice and might in various ways exclude the jurisdiction of the courts. This point was noted more explicitly in *Law and Opinion in England*, where, after conceding that administrative law 'has some distinct merits', Dicey remarked that it had also two defects which had until recent years prohibited its existence in England. First, administrative tribunals tended to be protected from judicial review by exclusionary rules and, secondly, they often had connections with the government of the day. It could be argued therefore that Dicey's objections to what he called 'administrative law' and to the damage by collectivist legislation to the rule of law were not so much to the substance of the social measures which he accepted as being in line with parliamentary and public opinion but to the acquisition under much of this legislation of unreviewable powers by departments of government in their exercise of judicial and quasi-judicial functions. In this he was putting forward views that were not markedly different from the concerns of later

---

[31] [1915] AC 120.

reformers of administrative law and that led in time to the appointment of the Committee on Ministers' Powers in 1929 and, in 1955, to the Franks Committee on Tribunals and Enquiries.

There is a passage also in Dicey's 1915 article that could have been penned by many later would-be reformers of Parliament of all political persuasions on the weakness of ministerial responsibility as a control of administrative action. In *Arlidge*, the Lord Chancellor had said (as did many other judges in the 1940s and 1950s when judicial control was generally conceded to be at its weakest) that Parliament, to which the minister in charge was responsible, could review what had been done. Dicey remarked that 'any man who will look plain facts in the face will see in a moment that ministerial liability to the censure, not in fact by Parliament, nor even by the House of Commons but by the party majority who keep the government in office is a very feeble guarantee indeed against the action which evades the authority of the law courts'.[32] Dicey's many critics, including Ivor (later Sir Ivor) Jennings were perhaps over-ready to treat his rule of law analysis as merely the expression of a Whig dislike for social regulation. That he certainly had, but there can be distinguished in the pages of *The Law of the Constitution* arguments about judicial and legislative control of administrative action that deserved and later got more objective consideration.

It might be argued that the beginning of this process was the publication in the 1920s of a series of works drawing attention to the increasing importance of executive rule-making. In 1921 Cecil Carr (later counsel to the speaker) published a short study of delegated legislation.[33] In the United States in 1927 John Dickinson published *Administrative Justice and the Supremacy of Law*. Perhaps most importantly in 1929 Lord Hewart of Bury, chief justice and former attorney-general, wrote *The New Despotism*. It is an indication of the ideological flavour taken by the debate on the control of administrative powers in the inter-war years that Hewart's book—which is more often referred to than read—has been consistently and unfairly traduced. Harold Laski, for example, in his post-war *Reflections on the Constitution*, described it as 'Lord Hewart's notorious pamphlet'. One might not guess from this description that it was a work of some 300 pages, containing an admittedly strongly expressed but

---

[32] See appendix 2 of the 10th edition of *The Law of the Constitution*, p. 498. Dicey's article is reprinted from *Law Quarterly Review* (1915), 31.

[33] *Delegated Legislation* (Oxford University Press, 1921). See also his later study *Concerning English Administrative Law* (Oxford University Press, 1941).

nonetheless substantial argument about the growth of administrative discretion. That it was a surprising publication by a serving member of the judiciary was true and it was also true that Hewart was a man of conservative Liberal sympathies. But those considerations should not have been thought by some academic critics to have relieved them of all responsibility for considering the merits of his arguments. The burden of his attack was not on the content of legislation, primary or secondary, but on the procurement by government of statutory provisions that had placed a large and increasing field of departmental activity beyond the reach of judicial control. It was, he said, 'a strong thing to place the decision of a minister in a matter affecting the rights of individuals beyond the possibility of review by the courts of law'. De Lolme, he added, had held that 'Parliament could do anything but make a man a woman or a woman a man.' But what would De Lolme have said to the suggestion that Parliament should enact that a particular individual should have power at his pleasure to override its enactment? Such an individual, he added, would not have found it difficult, if he could (a) get legislation passed in skeleton form; (b) fill up the gaps with his own rules, orders and regulations; (c) make it difficult for Parliament to check the said orders, rules and regulations; (d) secure for them the force of statutes; (e) make his own decisions final; (f) arrange that the fact of his decision should be conclusive proof of its legality; (g) take power to modify the provisions of statutes; and (h) prevent and avoid any sort of appeal to a court of law.[34] A similarly stringent view was to be found in the work of C. K. Allen, whose book *Law in the Making*[35] appeared in 1927. Allen—later professor of jurisprudence in the University of Oxford— was described by Laski as 'an academic lawyer whose hatred of change is even greater than his persuasive rhetoric'.[36] Nevertheless both Hewart and Allen were taken seriously by the Committee on Ministers' Powers, set up in 1929, and the committee's report in 1932[37] reflected many of their criticisms. 'Henry VIII clauses', conferring power on a minister to modify provisions of Acts of Parliament, should, the committee said, be banned in all but the most exceptional cases, as should the use of clauses designed to exclude the jurisdiction of the courts. A further recommenda-

---

[34] *The New Despotism* (Ernest Benn, 1929), p. 21.
[35] Clarendon Press, 1927. His other polemical attacks on administrative lawlessness were *Bureaucracy Triumphant* (Oxford University Press, 1931) and *Law and Orders*, 1st edn (Stevens, 1945).
[36] *Reflections on the Constitution* (Manchester University Press, 1951), p. 38.
[37] Cmd 4060 (1932).

tion of the committee was that each House of Parliament should set up a committee to scrutinise regulations made in the exercise of delegated powers. That proposal was not implemented until after the Second World War, shortly before another lacuna in the rule of law was filled by the passage of the Crown Proceedings Act in 1947, which removed the anomalous exemptions enjoyed by the Crown in civil litigation. That exemplification of the stately pace of constitutional reform in the United Kingdom had its origin, interestingly enough, in a committee on Crown proceedings under the chairmanship of Lord Hewart which in 1927 had drafted a Crown Proceedings bill essentially similar to that which found favour with the post-war Labour government twenty years later.

Some theory about theorists

The undoubtedly political character of the debate on the rule of law and its application in the United Kingdom has stimulated a certain amount of theorising about implied theories of the state allegedly supported by the disputants. One such categorisation divides them into 'red light' and 'green light' theorists.[38] Red light theorists, it has been suggested, see the aim of administrative law as that of curbing or controlling the state and its agents. Green light theorists are more sympathetic to the use of executive power to provide welfare or community services and are suspicious of judicial controls on state activity. Red light theorists have also been charged with holding a belief in legal positivism, together with a number of associated attitudes, such as a mechanical view of the judicial process, a superstitious attachment to the separation of powers and a belief that law can be detached from politics. A selection of putatively red and green light writers on administrative law looks oddly like an Oxbridge versus an LSE view of the constitution, typified on the one hand by Dicey, Hewart, Allen and Wade and on the other by Jennings, Robson, Laski and Griffith. But there are some oddities in this juristic team selection. The notion of a progressive or non-progressive attitude to the state is a vague one. If state action means executive action, sympathy with it is not a constant element in progressive political opinion at all times and places, especially when it involves the action of police, immigration officials, social security officers or right-wing home secretaries. Moreover, the association of red light theory with a supposedly

---

[38] On this distinction and its implications, see C. Harlow and R. Rawlings, *Law and Administration* (Weidenfeld & Nicolson, 1984).

conservative tradition of legal positivism is unfair both to positivists and green light theorists. Traditionalism (or for that matter legal conceptualism or mechanical jurisprudence) has no necessary connection with legal positivism. And legal positivists, though wishing to exclude consideration of justice or morality from the *definition* of law, have certainly not been reluctant to criticise particular laws or legal arrangements on moral grounds. Many green light theorists have been legal positivists or Benthamites without prejudice to their green light status. It would also be a mistake to associate red but not green light theorists with an attachment to the rule of law.

Multiple concepts of the rule of law

Opposition to legal positivism is not irrelevant to the sense which a legal theorist may attach to the idea of the rule of law since it will rule out certain kinds of legislative provisions as coming within the idea of law. This complicates in some degree the dispute that has occurred in recent years about the breadth and content of the rule of law doctrine and whether it should be given a formal or a substantive meaning. A purely formal theory which equates the rule of law merely with the existence of a system of laws passed in due form seems (given the context in which arguments about the rule of law occur) to be too thin and to provide no basis for criticism of unsatisfactory or tyrannical legal regimes provided that they observe minimal requirements of formality. On the other hand, too substantive an account that includes in the requirements for observing the rule of law compliance with a lengthy list of criteria based on rights or justice may fail to give it a useful or distinctive meaning. 'The adoption of a fully substantive conception of the rule of law', it has been argued, 'has the consequence of robbing the concept of any function which is independent of the theory of justice which imbues such an account of law.' We should conclude therefore that 'the rule of law is just one of the virtues by which a legal system may be judged . . . It is not to be confused with democracy, justice, equality (before the law or otherwise) human rights of any kind or respect for persons or for the dignity of man.'[39]

Unhappily, there does not seem to be any clear or simple dividing line between the formal and substantive rule of law concept. There seems to be a continuum, along which four stages might be distinguished, and

[39] Joseph Raz, 'The Rule of Law and its Virtue', *Law Quarterly Review* (1988), 195, 196.

it may not be clear in every case at which point along this continuum particular theorists should be located. In the first place we might posit a purely formal sense in which the laws of a system are duly enacted in accordance with established formal criteria. Several things might be said about the utility of this model or concept. One is that it is probably not a concept that anyone has ever adopted. Another is that a natural lawyer or non-positivist would not regard this variant as available since it could not be regarded as envisaging a possible model of a legal system.

In the second place we might wish to include as part of the rule of law compliance with what the American legal theorist Lon Fuller dubbed the 'internal morality' of law.[40] This is a set of procedural virtues such as generality, clarity, consistency, comprehensibility, prospective application and impartial adjudication. F. A. Hayek's discussion of the rule of law places considerable emphasis on generality in the sense of compelling legislators to operate through the medium of general rules. There are conceptual difficulties about this proposal since what is to count as a non-general rule is not easy to specify. (Does a rule fail in generality if it applies to particular persons or groups or classes of person or enterprise?) Moreover, mere generality does little to protect against illiberal laws since there is nothing impossible in the notion of wicked or tyrannical general rules. However, some of the requirements of internal morality in Fuller's sense go further than the mere legality that is implied in the most formal rule by-law concept.

A third and still less formal notion of the rule of law might incorporate a requirement that the law should respect constitutional values such as equality, non-discrimination (on enumerated or non-enumerated grounds) and rationality or proportionality and possibly some particular rights that are of special relevance to decision-making procedures in an equal and open society—for example free speech and guarantees of fair elections.

Fourthly and most substantive, the rule of law might be equated with a legal system that complies with all the major constitutional rights that are thought important in a developed liberal democratic society.

Which of these concepts can be attributed to Dicey has been the subject of some disagreement. It has been argued that the references to various rights in Dicey's description of the English legal system are not

[40] *The Morality of Law* (Yale University Press, 1969), ch. 2.

part of his account of the rule of law and that it is predominantly formal.[41] On the other hand, although Dicey's initial discussion of the rule of law refers to a number of formal or procedural matters, chapters 5 to 12 of *The Law of the Constitution*, which deal with the right to personal freedom, freedom of discussion, the right of public meeting, the rights of soldiers and civilians under martial law, taxation and the legal and political responsibilities of ministers, are all placed within part II of the book, which is entitled 'The Rule of Law'; the reader could be forgiven for thinking that Dicey intended them to form part of an account of what the rule of law meant for Englishmen. Moreover, although the absence of arbitrary discretion and equality before the law have procedural senses, equality is more than identical situation and requires criteria of relevance for identifying permissible grounds for discriminating between persons and groups. Such grounds cannot be purely formal.

Faced with this battery of possible uses for the rule of law concept, it is not easy to decide what usage should be preferred. One tactic for critics and public lawyers might simply be to decline to referee the situation and to urge those who make reference to the rule of law to specify if they are using a substantive version of the theory and if so what particular values or theory of justice provides the basis for their argument. Perhaps it might be noted that it need not be the case that the meaning attached to the rule of law will entirely depend upon what one understands by the term 'law'. Attachment to a theory of legal positivism, for example, need not rule out the use of a substantive concept of the rule of law. Positivists are not prevented from wishing to have laws that comply with moral criteria or from wishing positive constitutional law to make compliance with rights a condition of legal validity. Most theorists, however, clearly wish to commend a particular usage, and most recent commentators[42] appear to concur in the view that the rule of law should be understood as having a restricted application that is not coincident with constitutionalism in general or with all the legal requirements that might be made by a theory of justice. Joseph Raz, for example, has argued that if justice, equality or human rights of any kind are included in the rule of law the term would lack any useful function. Perhaps there are two possible reactions to this. One is that, particularly in the second

---

[41] See Paul Craig 'Formal and Substantive Conceptions of the Rule of Law', *Public Law* (1997), 467 at 470–4.

[42] For example T. R. S. Allan, *Constitutional Justice: A Liberal Theory of the Rule of Law* (Oxford University Press, 2001); and Jeffrey Jowell, 'The Rule of Law Today', in Jeffrey Jowell and Dawn Oliver (eds), *The Changing Constitution*, 4th edn (Clarendon Press, 2000).

half of the twentieth century, custom, both national and international, has clearly favoured a general usage for the term 'rule of law' that includes compliance with at least the major constitutional rights, and it may be too late to reverse this tendency even if this means that the term now shades imperceptibly into the more general idea of constitutionalism. The second possible reaction might be to wonder whether in the light of this we should simply draw the conclusion that the rule of law concept does indeed now lack any useful function. It is not a term that plays much part in constitutional debate in the United States, for example, since that tends to be focused on particular constitutional notions such as equal protection, due process of law or the separation of powers—all of which might be thought constituents of the rule of law in one of its substantive senses. If institutions are to be criticised as failing to meet standards of constitutional or procedural propriety the accusation that they are infringing the rule of law can perhaps more usefully be replaced by specifying the particular form of legal or constitutional impropriety that is in question. Since it lacks both precision and an agreed usage, the rule of law may not now be an essential item in the vocabulary of constitutional discourse.

Constitutitional limitations and human rights

A striking feature of the constitutional history of the United Kingdom in the second half of the twentieth century was the extension of control over the discretionary activities of government—a development to which both Dicey and the so-called red light theorists of the 1930s, 1940s and 1950s might have given their approval. A landmark was the appointment and implementation of the recommendations of the Franks Committee, whose report in 1957[43] concluded that tribunals (whose independent status Dicey had questioned) should be regarded as 'machinery provided by Parliament for adjudication, rather than as part of the machinery of administration', and that all administrative procedures should be characterised by 'openness, fairness and impartiality'. That was followed in 1967 by the creation of the parliamentary commissioner for administration, whose activities were intended by government to eschew the examination of the merits of departmental discretion and policy, but which by usage were extended to embrace in effect a control of official unfairness or irrationality. Along with these developments went the

---

[43] Cmnd 218 (1957).

much chronicled expansion in the scope of judicial control. By 1985 Lord Roskill could say that there had been 'as a result of judicial decisions since about 1950 . . . a radical change in the scope of judicial review . . . described, but by no means critically, as an upsurge of judicial activism'. The reasons for this may not have been fully explained but the results were clear. In decisions such as *Ridge* v. *Baldwin*,[44] *Anisminic* v. *Foreign Compensation Commission*,[45] *Council of Civil Service Unions* v. *Minister for the Civil Service*[46] and *M*. v. *Home Office*,[47] the courts significantly resisted unfettered discretion, narrowed official immunities and expanded the grounds of review. Whether this has been on the basis of a direct or indirect application of parliamentary intention authorising judicial application of the *ultra vires* rule or in the exercise of an inherent common law function to set the bounds of legality (subject to a potential override by Parliament) is a question that has divided academic theorists in recent years and seems unlikely to be definitively settled.[48]

A further extension in the judicial role was foreshadowed in the campaign to procure the enactment of a Bill of Rights that culminated in the passage of the 1998 Human Rights Act. The modelling of the legislation on the minimal New Zealand Bill of Rights, so as to preclude judicial invalidation of Acts of Parliament and confine the courts to an extended interpretative role in the application of European Convention rights to the United Kingdom produced both red and green light reactions—one school of thought stigmatising the Act as an enfeebled form of Human Rights legislation, the other praising it as an ingenious and democratic compromise between the rights principle and that of legislative supremacy. Whichever view is right, there are some radical rule of law questions to be answered by the British judiciary at the turn of the century under the now mandatory interpretive guidance of the European Court of Human Rights. One is what sort of separation of judicial power is required by the principle of impartial adjudication. In a Scottish case, *Starrs* v. *Ruxton*,[49] the arrangements for the appointment of temporarary sheriffs were held to be insufficient to guaranteee judicial independence,

---

[44] [1964] AC 40.
[45] [1969] 2 AC 147.
[46] [1985] AC 374.
[47] [1994] 1 AC 377.
[48] See Paul Craig, 'Competing Models of Judicial Review', *Public Law* (1999), 428; and C. Forsyth, 'The Ultra Vires Doctrine in a Constitutional Setting: Still the Central Principle of Administrative Law', *Cambridge Law Journal* (1999), 129.
[49] 2000 SLT 42 HJC.

and in *McGonnell* v. *United Kingdom*[50] the Strasbourg court held the mixture of legislative and judicial powers in the legal system of Guernsey to be a violation of Article 6 of the Convention. Are there, we may wonder, elements in the mixture of judicial and legislative offices in the British constitution that might come into question as adjudication of the Convention provisions progresses? It may be that the central provision of the Human Rights Act itself, that denies full justiciability to the Convention rights scheduled to the Act and which provides only an uncertain opportunity of a parliamentary remedy dependent on the decision of the ministers whose acts have been the subject of complaint, is vulnerable to attack under Article 13 of the European Convention which guarantees an effective remedy to everyone whose rights and freedoms have been violated. Article 13 was omitted from the Act, either from abundant caution or lack of scruple or for other reasons, but the question can still be tested in Strasbourg.[51]

The cryptic wording of the Human Rights Act creates a number of posers for the judiciary. One of them is the meaning and scope of the term 'public authority' on whom the obligation to act conformably with the Convention rights is placed. Another is the uncertain relationship between the giving of declarations of incompatibility and the manipulation of the terms of statutes to achieve conformity with Convention rights. That raises the issue whether the terms of the Human Rights Act can be taken to have changed the existing rules for the interpretation of statutes. Yet another issue is the extent to which the courts, as public authorities, will be bound to give effect to Convention rights in disputes arising between private litigants as well as in disputes between citizens and the state.

Certainly any future Dicey, recording the progress of the rule of law in twentieth-century Britain would be bound to conclude that the constitution underwent significant and accelerating change in the period from 1960 onwards. At the midway point British constitutional arrangements could still be described as embodying a bundle of traditional doctrines. They could be summed up as parliamentary sovereignty,

---

[50] European Court of Human Rights, 28488/95, *The Times*, 22 February 2000.

[51] The impending impact of the Human Rights Act that came into operation in England and Wales in October 2000 provoked a substantial amount of anticipatory debate. See (among many commentaries) Basil Markesinis (ed.), *The Impact of the Human Rights Bill on English Law* (Clarendon Press, 1998); S. Grosz, J. Beatson and P. Duffy, *Human Rights: The 1998 Act and the European Convention* (Sweet & Maxwell, 2000); and Richard Clayton and Hugh Tomlinson, *The Law of Human Rights* (Oxford University Press, 2000).

crown prerogative, legislative privilege and administrative discretion. At the close of the century all of these had been subjected to a prolonged process of questioning based on the principle that no power can be absolute or unreviewable or immune from challenge in the light of rights-based principles such as fairness, equality, rationality, proportionality and perhaps some form of the separation of powers. This tendency will no doubt be reinforced as the constitution of the United Kingdom becomes increasingly enmeshed with the constitution of Europe and its interpretation becomes increasingly European.

Queries and conclusions

Some commonly posed questions such as 'Can anything in the United Kingdom be clearly said to be unconstitutional?' and 'Who are the interpreters of our constitution?' require, as we have seen, fairly complicated answers, because there are as many varieties of interpretation and constitutionality as there are senses of 'constitution'. One obvious form of interpretation is judicial interpretation of the large and indeterminate number of statutes and secondary legislation that make up the legal elements in the constitution. In relation to the legislation providing for the exercise of devolved powers, the Judicial Committee of the Privy Council, in addition to the ordinary courts, has assumed an important interpretative role; and some of our principles of government are interpreted for us outside the United Kingdom in the judicial organs of the European Union. In relation to the conventional rules of the constitution, interpretation is a role shared by politicians and academic commentators but the difficult questions here do not have definitive answers.

In some respects, perhaps, the conventional rules that regulate certain areas of governmental behaviour have become more crystallised and less debatable in recent years with the promulgation and general acceptance of codes of practice (for civil servants, ministers and members of Parliament for example). Here the numerous ombudsmen and regulators have become important and semi-authoritative interpreters of our constitutional morality. Thus, old questions are sometimes resolved, though new ones may appear. At the present time two areas of conventional uncertainty are the activities of the upper House in relation to government policy and the constitutional role of the referendum. As to the latter, it seems likely that such changes as modification of the electoral system, the adoption of the single European currency and further legislative changes to the unitary structure of the United Kingdom will produce demands for referenda and that these demands will receive fairly broad political support. In terms of the Jennings criteria for the creation of conventions (precedents, supporting reasons and feelings of obligation among political actors) it might well be thought that sufficient grounds exist for the existence of a referendum convention. Certainly the argument that referenda are inconsistent with parliamentary government has lost the plausibility it might once have had.

As to the legal aspect of the constitution a question commonly raised—but to which no simple answer exists—is whether the sovereignty of Parliament remains a central feature of our constitution. This is sometimes related to the question whether the constitution has finally thrown off the legacy of Dicey. That, perhaps, is an easier query to answer if we relate it to the three parts of Dicey's classic text. What elements of Dicey's philosophy, we may wonder, have in recent times actually placed any serious restrictive rein on our thinking? Neither his political standpoint nor his particular application of the rule of law idea to administrative jurisdiction has played any influential role in our affairs for the past fifty years. In the matter of convention, on the other hand, Dicey's major insight as to its character, though modified by further reflection, has not been displaced, so has no need of repudiation. And, on the question of parliamentary sovereignty, the situation, whatever it is, has not been dictated or constrained by anything in Dicey's exposition of the law as it was in 1885. Dicey did not invent or establish the sovereignty of Parliament and we are not striking off any Dicey-ite fetters in modifying it.

Whether parliamentary sovereignty remains an essential feature of the constitution is a complex and somewhat unclear matter. It is palpably true that in a day-to-day (or year-to-year) sense we are no longer governed by the Queen in Parliament. Nor can we with any confidence any longer venture the aphorism that the British constitution can be summed up in the proposition that 'There shall be a Parliament and it shall do as it pleases.' Over a wide and extending field Parliament's enactments are subject to the need to comply with the superior authority of rules issuing from the European Union's legislative and judicial organs. Nevertheless, in the more fundamental juridical sense in which the problem translates into the question whether legislative authority in and over the United Kingdom has been abdicated by the Queen in Parliament, the answer appears to be that which Dicey would have given, namely that the only manner in which Parliament could abdicate its authority would be by abolishing itself, and it has not done so. The judiciary has treated the 1972 European Communities legislation as a declaration by Parliament that all future legislation should (at least until further notice) be interpreted so as to conform to Community legislation. But, however the courts manipulate post-1972 statutes, that presumption, however forceful, cannot, on our existing principles, operate either to disable future express amendments of the 1972 European Communities Act or to prevent legislation that might be expressed so as to have effect notwithstanding anything to the contrary in Community law.

The preservative impact on parliamentary sovereignty of the Human Rights Act is in principle even clearer. Of course, there would have been nothing inconsistent with parliamentary sovereignty in the passage of an unentrenched Bill of Rights that took precedence over existing inconsistent legislation. That would not have been a derogation from, but an assertion of legislative sovereignty (as, for example, was the passage of the Canadian Federal Bill of Rights of 1960). That such legislation permits the courts to invalidate or hold inoperative Acts of Parliament is merely a consequence of the rule that later statutes supersede earlier statutes with which they are inconsistent. The Human Rights Act of 1998, however, not only preserves the validity and operation of any incompatible primary legislation but, unlike the European Communities Act of 1972, contains no categorical presumption that all future legislation should conform to the rights set out in the Convention. The upshot of section 3 of the Act is that all future legislation should conform unless Parliament decides in clear terms and in the exercise of its sovereignty that it should not. The courts may issue a declaration of incompatibility, but it then remains for Parliament to decide whether its view should prevail.

Nonetheless, the human rights legislation has radically changed the way in which legislation is drafted and the conditions under which executive authority is exercised and it is no flight of fancy to say that it will transform a large part of the constitution. The need to comply with the impartial adjudication guarantees of Article 6 is likely to have far-reaching effects not only on the criminal law but on many fields of national and local policy-making that have adverse impacts on individual or corporate interests. It may be that the doctrine of ministerial responsibility will come to have an increasingly narrower application as fields of executive activity become subject to judicial supervision. The discretionary powers of the Crown and the royal prerogative may have to be exercised in a different manner. The traditional privileges of Parliament are to some degree protected, since Parliament and its constituent parts are not public authorities for purposes of the Human Rights Act. But that restriction itself, along with other features of the Act, may turn out to be inconsistent with the European Convention as interpreted in Strasbourg and may require future amendment. All of this leads to the conclusion that the pace and direction of constitutional change are no longer exclusively dictated by politicians and legislators. As Bishop Hoadly had it, those who have authority to interpret the law are the true law-givers. When their remit compels them to decide what governmental restraints on individual rights and liberties are necessary in a democratic society, it is plain in what forum the debate on the role of the state in twenty-first-century Britain will have to be conducted.

Bibliography

General works and commentary

W. R. Anson, *The Law and Custom of the Constitution*: vol. 1, *Parliament* (ed. M. L. Gwyer), 5th edn (1922); vol. 2, *The Crown* (ed. A. B. Keith), 4th edn (Clarendon Press, 1935).

A. B. Keith, *The Constitution of England from Queen Victoria to George VI*, 2 vols (Macmillan, 1940).

H. J. Laski, *Reflections on the Constitution* (Manchester University Press, 1951).

L. S. Amery, *Thoughts on the Constitution*, 2nd edn (Oxford University Press, 1953).

A. V. Dicey, *Introduction to the Study of the Law of the Constitution*, 10th edn, ed. E. C. S. Wade (Macmillan, 1959).

W. I. Jennings, *The Law and the Constitution*, 5th edn (London University Press, 1959).

R. F. V. Heuston, *Essays in Constitutional Law*, 2nd edn (Stevens, 1964).

Geoffrey Marshall, *Constitutional Theory* (Clarendon Press, 1971).

Institute for Public Policy Research, *The Constitution of the United Kingdom* (1991).

Ferdinand Mount, *The British Constitution Now: Recovery or Decline?* (Heinemann, 1992).

Vernon Bogdanor, *Politics and the Constitution: Essays on British Government* (Dartmouth, 1996).

Colin Munro, *Studies in Constitutional Law*, 2nd edn (Butterworths, 1999).

Jeffrey Jowell and Dawn Oliver (eds), *The Changing Constitution*, 4th edn (Clarendon Press, 2000).

F. H. Lawson, 'Dicey Re-visited', *Political Studies* (1959).

Neil MacCormick, 'Does the United Kingdom have a Constitution?', *Modern Law Review* (1978).

'Dicey and the Constitution', *Public Law* (1985).

Eric Barendt, 'Is there a United Kingdom Constitution?', *Oxford Journal of Legal Studies* (1997).

Rodney Brazier, 'The Constitution of the United Kingdom', *Cambridge Law Journal* (1999).

Nevil Johnson, 'Then and Now: The British Constitution', *Political Studies* (2000).

K. D. Ewing, 'The Politics of the British Constitution', *Public Law* (2000).

Neil Walker, 'Beyond the Unitary Concept of the British Constitution', *Public Law* (2000).

Constitutional practice and convention

W. I. Jennings, *Cabinet Government*, 3rd edn (Cambridge University Press, 1959), ch. 1.

K. C. Wheare, *The Statute of Westminster and Dominion Status*, 5th edn (Oxford University Press, 1959).

Geoffrey Marshall, *Constitutional Conventions: The Rules and Forms of Political Accountability* (Clarendon Press, 1986).

Andrew Heard, *Canadian Constitutional Conventions: The Marriage of Law and Politics* (Oxford University Press, 1991).

Rodney Brazier, *Constitutional Practice: The Foundations of British Government*, 3rd edn (Oxford University Press, 1999).

Colin Munro, 'Laws and Conventions Distinguished', *Law Quarterly Review* (1975).

Eugene Forsey, 'The Courts and the Conventions of the Constitution', *University of New Brunswick Law Journal* (1984).

Rodney Brazier, 'The Non-legal Constitution: Thoughts on Convention, Practice and Principle', *Northern Ireland Legal Quarterly* (1992).

J. Jaconelli, 'The Nature of Constitutional Convention', *Legal Studies* (1999).

The sovereignty of Parliament

R. T. E. Latham, *The Law and the Commonwealth* (Oxford University Press, 1949).

Geoffrey Marshall, *Parliamentary Sovereignty and the Commonwealth* (Clarendon Press, 1957).

W. I. Jennings, *The Law and the Constitution*, 5th edn (University of London Press, 1959), ch. 4.

Neil MacCormick, *Questioning Sovereignty: Law, State and Nation in the European Commonwealth* (Oxford University Press, 1999).

Jeffrey Goldsworthy, *The Sovereignty of Parliament: History and Philosophy* (Clarendon Press, 1999).

H. W. R. Wade, 'The Basis of Legal Sovereignty', *Cambridge Law Journal* (1955).

O. Hood Phillips, 'Parliament and Self-limitation', *Cambrian Law Review* (1973).

G. Winterton, 'The British Grundnorm: Parliamentary Sovereignty Re-examined', *Law Quarterly Review* (1976).

Paul Craig, 'Sovereignty of the United Kingdom Parliament after *Factortame*', *Year Book of European Law* (1991).

H. W. R. Wade, 'Sovereignty—Revolution or Evolution', *Law Quarterly Review* (1996).

T. R. S. Allan, 'Parliamentary Sovereignty, Law, Politics and Revolution', *Law Quarterly Review* (1997).

A. W. Bradley, 'The Sovereignty of Parliament in Perpetuity?', in Jeffrey Jowell and Dawn Oliver (eds), *The Changing Constitution*, 4th edn (Clarendon Press, 2000).

The rule of law and the separation of powers

R. A. Cosgrove, *The Rule of Law: Albert Venn Dicey, Victorian Jurist* (Macmillan, 1980).

J. A. G. Griffith, *The Politics of the Judiciary*, 4th edn (Fontana, 1991).

Lord Woolf and J. Jowell, *De Smith, Woolf and Jowell, Judicial Review of Administrative Action*, 5th edn (Sweet & Maxwell, 1995).

C. Forsyth, *Judicial Review and the Constitution* (Hart, 2000).

Robert Stevens, *The English Judges: Their Role in the Changing Constitution* (Hart, 2002).

J. G. Wilson, 'Altered States: A Comparison of Separation of Powers in the United States and in the United Kingdom', *Hastings Constitutional Law Quarterly* (1990).

Eric Barendt, 'Separation of Powers and Constitutional Government', *Public Law* (1995).

Paul Craig, 'Formal and Substantive Conceptions of the Rule of Law: An Analytical Framework', *Public Law* (1997).

Lord Woolf, 'Judicial Review: The Tensions between the Executive and the Judiciary', *Law Quarterly Review* (1998).

T. R. S. Allan, 'The Rule of Law as the Rule of Reason: Consent and Constitutionalism', *Law Quarterly Review* (1999).

Jeffrey Jowell, 'The Rule of Law Today', in Jeffrey Jowell and Dawn Oliver (eds), *The Changing Constitution*, 4th edn (Clarendon Press, 2000).

Sir David Williams, 'Bias, the Judges and the Separation of Powers', *Public Law* (2000).

The Rt Hon. Lord Steyn, 'The Case for a Supreme Court', *Law Quarterly Review* (2002).

Human rights and the constitution

University of Cambridge Centre for Public Law, *Constitutional Reform in the United Kingdom: Practice and Principles* (Hart, 1998).

University of Cambridge Centre for Public Law, *The Human Rights Act and the Criminal Justice and Regulatory Process* (Hart, 1999).

R. Clayton and H. Tomlinson, *The Law of Human Rights*, (Oxford University Press, 2000), vols 1 and 2.

J. Cooper and A. Marshall-Williams, *Legislating for Human Rights: The Parliamentary Debates on the Human Rights Bill* (Hart, 2000).

S. Grosz, J. Beatson and P. Duffy, *Human Rights: The 1998 Act and the European Convention* (Sweet & Maxwell, 2000).

Tom Campbell, K. D. Ewing and Adam Tomkins (eds), *Sceptical Essays on Human Rights* (Oxford University Press, 2001).

David Feldman, *Civil Liberties and Human Rights in England and Wales*, 2nd edn (Oxford University Press, 2002).

Lord Lester, 'Human Rights and the British Constitution', in Jeffrey Jowell and Dawn Oliver (eds), *The Changing Constitution*, 4th edn (Clarendon Press, 2000).

F. Klug and C. O'Brien, 'The First Two Years of the Human Rights Act', *Public Law* (2002).

3.
The Monarchy
RODNEY BRAZIER

I

Elizabeth II's Golden Jubilee was commemorated in 2002. Her fifty years as sovereign were remarkably free of the kinds of constitutional difficulties that had afflicted her great-grandfather, Edward VII, her grandfather, George V, her uncle, Edward VIII, and her father, George VI. During their reigns the British constitution had to cope, for example, with a clash of wills between the Commons and the Lords, demands for equal voting rights, the horrors of two world wars and a civil war in Ireland, an irreconcilable breach between a king and his government, several tricky successions to the premiership, and the appointment in peacetime of a ministry of all the talents as a response to fear of financial collapse. By contrast to strains such as these, the monarchy in the person of Elizabeth II has enjoyed fifty years of relative calm. That tranquillity has, admittedly, been disturbed by two political skirmishes in the Conservative Party over the choice of a new prime minister, in which the queen was unavoidably implicated, and latterly by demands that the institution, including the royal family, modernise itself. That the queen has been acknowledged so widely as an outstanding example of a constitutional monarch is not, however, entirely the result of her own personal qualities. Constitutional developments occurring before her father's death had reduced the need for royal intervention in political affairs. Thus, for instance, the cardinal convention of the British constitution that the sovereign must, in the end, act on ministerial advice (save in exceptional circumstances) had come to be fully accepted: as a result, the monarchy had already come to underpin parliamentary government rather than to rival it. Universal suffrage had been achieved long before 1952, and indeed the last inconclusive general election had occurred over twenty years before in 1929; politicians had accepted that elections were the most forceful expression of popular will, to which effect had to be given in government formation; the sovereign's involvement in the transfer of power between the political parties had become largely formal.[1] Although the queen played a personal role in 1957 and in 1963 during two prime ministerial succession crises, the need for her to do so disappeared after 1965 when the Conservatives fell into line with the other main parties by adopting a formal balloting system to elect their leader.[2] Nor was it at all likely that the queen would be called upon to resolve parliamentary deadlock by creating a mass of new peers, given the acceptance by both Houses of Parliament long before her accession of a statutory concordat which would govern legislative disputes between them.[3] Against that constitutional backdrop, however, the personal contribution of the queen to national affairs stood out. She conducted herself according to the highest standards set by her predecessors in the twentieth century, fortunately untroubled by constitutional alarums on the scale endured by them.

It would be impossible to consider in depth the whole twentieth-century history of the British monarchy within the confines of this chapter.[4] Some matters have to be ignored. In particular, it is not possible to do justice to the sovereign's role in relation to the Empire and the Commonwealth. This is regrettable, partly because the positions of head of the Commonwealth and head of state of Commonwealth realms have given the British monarchy an international dimension which other monarchies lack.[5] Nor does this chapter reflect at all adequately the symbolic and social functions of the sovereign. She is a symbol of the nation, a

---

[1] Only one general election was to be inconclusive during the last half of the twentieth century, that held in February 1974, and even then the queen was not required to resolve the deadlock.

[2] As a result the sovereign was likely to be called on only if agreement on a new prime minister could not be reached within the relevant political party, or if (following the election of a hung Parliament) politicians could not agree on the type of government to be formed.

[3] The Parliament Act 1911 was used five times before 2000, in order to secure enactment of the Government of Ireland Act 1914, the Welsh Church Act 1914, the Parliament Act 1949, the War Crimes Act 1991 and the European Parliamentary Elections Act 1999.

[4] There are several good works on the reigns of sovereigns since Victoria which throw light on the institution during the twentieth century. They are listed in the bibliography in Vernon Bogdanor, *The Monarchy and the Constitution* (Oxford University Press, 1995). Ben Pimlott, *The Queen: A Biography of Elizabeth II* (HarperCollins, 1996) is a significant subsequent publication; and Sarah Bradford, *Elizabeth: A Biography of Her Majesty the Queen* (Heinemann, 1996) is also useful.

[5] On the other hand, the constitutional crises which have beset Commonwealth states such as Grenada and Fiji have primarily involved the relevant governor-general rather than the sovereign personally. On governor-generals see David Butler and D. A. Lowe (eds), *Sovereigns and Surrogates: Constitutional Heads of State in the Commonwealth* (Macmillan, 1991).

focus for national loyalty transcending political partisan rivalries. As with her predecessors, the queen personifies the state and the nation, their history, stability, and continuity. The sovereign recognises success and achievement, especially through the honours system, and encourages citizens to do good by each other.[6] These are all important functions, but full credit cannot be afforded to them here. Rather, I intend to concentrate on three themes. I want to see how the constitutional power enjoyed by the sovereign as late as one hundred years ago was even then giving way to constitutional influence, a process which accelerated during the last century. Then I set out the changes which Parliament made to the law touching the Crown. Lastly, I try to assess, in the light of recent changes to the British constitution, the main roles of the monarchy in the decades ahead.

II

During the twentieth century, constitutional monarchy continued to adjust from a position of power to one of influence in constitutional and political affairs. The scope for the use of the sovereign's personal discretion, and therefore of his or her constitutional power, was reduced during that time in a number of areas which are of critical importance to the constitution.

In the whole range of conventions recognised by the British constitution, it is universally acknowledged that the most important by far is that which requires that, save in extraordinary cases, the sovereign should act on ministerial advice.[7] That principle had been embraced by ministers and accepted by sovereigns since Victoria's reign, but the extent of the convention remained a matter for debate between the main constitutional actors. So George V was clear that, if circumstances required it, he could use the sovereign's legal power to withhold royal assent to legislation, and could make his own choice of prime minister. Thus, during the crisis over the Home Rule bill in 1912–14 the king used the

---

[6] See Frank Prochaska, *Royal Bounty: The Making of the Welfare Monarchy* (Yale University Press, 1995).

[7] This is the opinion of all constitutional commentators (subject to verbal differences). Indeed, it was also the considered opinion of the queen's private secretary expressed in a letter to *The Times*, 29 July 1986. Sir William Heseltine wrote: 'Whatever personal opinions the sovereign may hold or may have expressed to her Government, she is bound to accept and act on the advice of her Ministers.' He did not allude to those exceptional circumstances in which advice might be rejected (a possibility which will be considered below).

implied threat of veto in an effort to persuade ministers to reach a consensual settlement;[8] his choice of Stanley Baldwin as prime minister in 1923 was a personal and reasoned choice made between Baldwin and Lord Curzon. Now it cannot be argued at all convincingly that the sovereign is bound in every circumstance to do the bidding of ministers, for that would reduce the head of state to a mere automaton. Nor could any such argument take account of situations in which there were no ministers who could offer advice (because the prime minister or the government or both together had resigned), or where advice offered was unacceptable (such as Stanley Baldwin's view expressed to Edward VIII that he would marry Mrs Simpson as king contrary to the wishes of the Cabinet).[9] But the reasons underlying the convention, and the understanding that it should operate liberally in favour of ministers, became clearer and stronger in the first part of the century.

As late as 1903 the sovereign was able to undertake a visit to another European capital, Paris, without obtaining ministerial approval for the trip—and, indeed, without even telling his government that he intended to go.[10] Edward VII's initiative gave a powerful personal boost to what became the Anglo-French Agreement of 1904 inaugurating the *Entente Cordiale*, but in terms of constitutional history that is of less significance than that it marked one of the last actual assertions of constitutional independence by a sovereign.[11] When the nature of the convention concerning ministerial advice became crucial a few years later, during the crisis over the passage of the Parliament bill, H. H. Asquith was to set out his understanding of the king's constitutional position in trenchant terms. It came in a minute sent to George V in December 1910:

> The part to be played by the Crown . . . has happily been settled by the accumulated traditions and the unbroken practice of more than seventy years. It is to act upon the advice of Ministers who for the time being possess the confidence of the House of Commons, whether

---

[8] See, for example, Sir Harold Nicolson, *King George V: His Life and Reign* (Constable, 1952), p. 233; Bogdanor, *The Monarchy and the Constitution*, pp. 122–35.

[9] Edward VIII only sought formal advice from the prime minister on the possibility of a morganatic marriage, and on whether and if so when he should broadcast to the nation and the Empire: see Bogdanor, *The Monarchy and the Constitution*, pp. 136, 141. But Baldwin's view on the substantive matter was clearly communicated to the king, albeit not technically as formal ministerial advice: it came to the same thing.

[10] Sir Frederick Ponsonby, *Recollections of Three Reigns* (Eyre & Spottiswoode 1951), pp. 59–60: 'Whether he anticipated opposition on the part of the Government . . . I never knew . . .'.

[11] On Edward VII generally, see Sir Philip Magnus, *King Edward the Seventh* (John Murray, 1964).

that advice does or does not conform to the private and personal judgement of the sovereign. Ministers will always pay the utmost deference, and give the most serious consideration, to any criticism or objection that the Monarch may offer to their policy; but the ultimate decision rests with them; for they, and not the Crown, are responsible to Parliament.[12]

Asquith's formulation encapsulated the constitutional position that was to obtain in the British system of government during the twentieth century. Its acceptance by successive sovereigns was an acknowledge-ment that parliamentary democracy, rather than the power of the sovereign, had become the prime engine of government. Even after the passage of the Representation of the People Act 1884 only some 60 per cent of the adult male population (or about 28 per cent of the population as a whole) had the vote.[13] All adult men, and women over 30, had to wait until 1918 for the franchise; not until 1928 were women made equal with men by being allowed to vote at 21. By 1928, therefore, the outcome of a general election had to be accepted as a reasonably accurate expression of the people's will, and one to which politicians and the sovereign had to attach decisive weight. Accordingly, the number of seats obtained in the House of Commons was to be *the* determining factor in the appointment of prime ministers and governments, and this development gave rise to what was to become the constitutional convention that the prime minister must sit in the representative House.[14] Parliamentary democracy, in this instance as expressed through the ballot box, was to become the undisputed chooser of prime ministers, save for cases in which the people spoke with an uncertain voice and returned a hung Parliament. That fact gave to ministers undisputed political authority: they represented the political will of the masses; the sovereign could make no such claim. The rebalancing of power was to be confirmed and set for ever by the abdication crisis: for that momentous event made clear beyond doubt that in any irreconcilable clash of will between sovereign and ministers the prime minister's will in general prevails, at least in cases where no alternative government can be found.[15] Indeed,

---

[12] R.A. GV 0 2570/11.

[13] Colin Turpin, *British Government and the Constitution: Text, Cases and Materials*, 4th edn (Butterworth, 1999), p. 19.

[14] George V's choice of Baldwin over Curzon was made, in part, because the Labour Party, with 142 MPs, had no representation in the House of Lords.

[15] The sovereign has reserve powers, which are considered later.

another enduring legacy of the abdication was to be the tenacity with which the queen has held to the view that the duty to wear the Crown endures for life.[16]

Universal franchise also meant that politicians had greater authority to undertake government-making themselves rather than having to rely on a royal intervention. Thus, for example, while in 1923 the king's private secretary,[17] Lord Stamfordham, conducted informal and confidential talks which helped to install Ramsay MacDonald's first government in office (Stanley Baldwin having first met, and been defeated in, Parliament), by complete contrast in 1929, Baldwin having lost his majority at the general election, declined to repeat the 1923 process but resigned straight away. The people, for better or worse, had spoken at that election; they did not accord victory to the Conservative government; if (as it turned out) Labour could govern with the tacit support of the Liberals, so be it. It so happened that the voting system was only to fail to give one party a majority of Commons seats on one further occasion during the twentieth century. So fully accepted had the notion become that political decisions about government formation should be left (at least in the first instance) to politicians that the queen was not called upon to perform an active role when the hung Parliament of February 1974 was returned.[18] Moreover, even when a prime minister was to resign between general elections, leaving a royal decision to be made about the succession, the scope for intervention was removed in 1965 when the Conservatives adopted leadership election rules.[19] Since then, all the main political parties have had a clear method of replacing a leader, and if he or she were also prime minister there was no reason why the sovereign should wish to pre-empt a party's choice, or to rely on informal soundings which, as in 1957 and 1963, were to lead to

---

[16] The queen declared as much publicly in, for example, her first Christmas Day broadcast as sovereign, in which she asked for prayers that she might be able to serve God 'and you all the days of my life': quoted in Pimlott, *The Queen*, p. 190.

[17] The office of private secretary to the sovereign is of central importance in the working of the constitution. Because of the exceptional discretion required of its holders relatively little information is available about the influence of successive private secretaries. The best factual account remains Sir John Wheeler-Bennett, *King George V: His Life and Reign* (Macmillan, 1958), appendix B.

[18] See generally Rodney Brazier, *Constitutional Practice*, 3rd edn (Oxford University Press, 1999), ch. 3.

[19] The rules were put in place to avoid any recurrence of the embarrassing events surrounding Harold Macmillan's resignation and the choice of his successor by, in Iain Macleod's famous and damning phrase, 'the magic circle'.

subsequent disputes about whether the results were reliable.[20] So, in particular, the choices of James Callaghan to replace Harold Wilson in 1976 and of John Major to replace Margaret Thatcher in 1990 were made by their respective parties without any assistance from Buckingham Palace. While the succession to the premiership had been far from automatic on nine occasions in the period from 1902 to February 1974,[21] there was to be little difficulty in choosing a prime minister during the final quarter of the twentieth century (which witnessed six general elections and four changes of occupant at 10 Downing Street). It is impossible to argue with the results of secret ballots.

While the cardinal convention that ministerial advice must be accepted in most cases was becoming fully accepted, one area in which advice was unlikely to be offered at all was in the matter of controlling the House of Lords. The passage of the Parliament Act 1911 established statutory rules to govern legislative disputes between the two Houses, and as a result it was most unlikely that any sovereign after 1911 would be advised to create masses of new peers in order to mould the House of Lords to the wishes of the House of Commons. Edward VII and George V had had to consider whether to guarantee such creations, and if so on what conditions,[22] but after the passage of the Parliament Act, governments knew that at worst the Lords could hold up legislation approved by the Commons by two years (and, after the 1949 Parliament Act, by one year).

The full acceptance of this cardinal convention, however, confirmed a much greater shift in real power than might be assumed at first sight. For it had a radical and pervasive effect on the law of the royal prerogative. Once the notion that the sovereign should do that which ministers advised had taken hold, the sovereign became obliged, in the main, to use prerogative powers as advised by ministers. These powers remain vast even now: they encompass matters as diverse as the disposition of the armed forces (and, indeed, the declaration of war), the making of treaties, the conduct of foreign and Commonwealth relations, the regulation of the civil service, the exercise of patronage in the Church of England and in relation to many public bodies, and much more. The

---

[20] The notion that the sovereign, where possible, should wait for the relevant political party to elect a replacement for a leader and prime minister who had resigned, and then appoint the replacement as prime minister, had been mooted as early as 1947 by the king's private secretary, Sir Alan Lascelles: R.A. P.S. GVI C131/80.

[21] In 1916, 1923, 1923–4, 1929, 1931, 1940, 1957, 1963, and February 1974.

[22] Nicolson, *King George V*, chs 9 and 10.

exercise of some of these powers requires the sovereign to give assent to prerogative Orders in Council; subordinate law-making of that kind gives to ministers vast law-making authority which they would otherwise have to take through primary legislation. Other prerogative powers are used even more easily than that, requiring no legislative action of any kind. The further development of constitutional monarchy in the twentieth century had, in effect, transformed many aspects of the royal prerogative into ministers' executive powers.[23]

And so the supremacy of parliamentary democracy over royal power means that the sovereign must appoint to ministerial office those recommended by the prime minister; dissolutions of Parliament normally take place on request; royal assent to legislation must be granted when ministers so advise; ministers have executive powers thanks to so much of the royal prerogative in practice being at their disposal; and so on. That supremacy also means that it is settled that the sovereign does not have a free hand in the appointment of a prime minister, but must appoint that member of the House of Commons who has or could obtain its confidence. But all this does not mean that the twentieth century saw the sovereign become a mere adornment for the political doings of ministers. For in 2000 the sovereign retained that constitutional influence which has been substituted for power; and the sovereign also remains the repository of reserve powers to be used in any constitutional emergency. I explore these matters in turn.

Throughout the twentieth century the sovereign continued to personify the nation and remained a focal point for national unity.[24] Such a symbol must transcend partisan politics. Certainly, if a sovereign is to exercise influence over ministers it will be of critical importance that the head of state is perceived to be politically neutral. Any hint of partisanship would destroy the prospect of any weight being attached to a sovereign's views by a government whose politics were seen to be out of accord with those of the head of state. A potentially dangerous hour struck for constitutional monarchy in 1924 when the first-ever Labour government assumed office. While deeply conservative in his personal habits, and of a Conservative persuasion in politics, George V was at the

---

[23] I have explored this development more fully in 'Constitutional Reform and the Crown', in Maurice Sunkin and Sebastian Payne (eds), *The Nature of the Crown: A Legal and Political Analysis* (Oxford University Press, 1999), ch. 13.

[24] In Great Britain at least. The Crown was a divisive factor in Ireland before the independence of the Irish Free State in 1922.

same time a conciliator.[25] One false step towards the Labour Party, one partisan word or deed, would have damaged the monarchy. But the king behaved impeccably. He received MacDonald in a friendly way, and subsequently set out some basic constitutional points in a memorandum[26] for a politician who had never held ministerial office, and whose party had never governed alone before. George V was to take every opportunity publicly and privately to show his trust in the new order.[27] Indeed, 'when old friends presumed on their intimacy to commiserate with him on the affliction of a socialist Government they were sharply rebuked for their pains'.[28] He would criticise the new ministers in private and to their faces, certainly; but the king's wise decision to deal with Labour ministers as he had their Liberal and Conservative predecessors set a standard which has been followed by his successors. This was a remarkable political and constitutional achievement. From that time the sovereign has fulfilled the constitutional functions of that office with scrupulous impartiality in relation to governments of different party colours.[29] It is only on that basis that the sovereign could continue to enjoy rights which, being based in constitutional convention, are as ultimately insubstantial as any other matter rooted only in non-legal rules. Of equal importance, the stance of political neutrality struck in private must be carried over into the public domain: the political predilections of the sovereign during his or her lifetime must remain unknown to the public. It would be damaging to the relationship between sovereign and ministers if it were known that the sovereign preferred one party over another. Clearly, every sovereign will have views about some issues which may not always coincide with those of the government. Indeed, the sovereign's opinions could not always be the same as those of every

---

[25] As Sir Robert Rhodes James has aptly put it, '[T]he most important political theme of his approach to the role of the monarch was to encourage settlements, sincerely believing that sensible solutions to complex matters could be arrived at if sensible men met in private to resolve their difficulties': *A Spirit Undaunted: The Political Role of George VI* (Little, Brown, 1998), p. 42.

[26] R.A. K. 1917.

[27] Kenneth Rose, *King George V* (Macmillan, 1983), p. 329; Nicolson, *King George V*, p. 502.

[28] Rose, *King George V*, p. 328.

[29] George V has been criticised for being politically biased in the formation of the National Government in 1931. On the other hand, he acted for the most part on the advice of his prime minister, MacDonald; and when he went further in persuading MacDonald to remain in office and the other party leaders to join a National Government, he acted swiftly as a constitutional facilitator in a way that the economic emergency seemed to require. For a balanced account which includes references to those who have criticised the king's conduct, see Rose, *King George V*, pp. 373–9.

set of ministers. But the trick, first worked by George V and continued throughout the last century, is to keep personal political attitudes hidden from public gaze. It follows that the principle of confidentiality between the Crown and ministers is always maintained.[30]

A sovereign exercises influence in governmental matters by using conventional attributes famously summarised by Bagehot as the rights to be consulted, to encourage and to warn ministers. That formulation has occasionally been rendered as the rights to *advise*, to encourage and to warn, but a sovereign cannot offer advice nor support action, nor counsel against proposed action without knowing what ministers are doing. Perhaps, therefore, it is more accurate, albeit more prolix, to say that the sovereign has five conventional rights rather than three—to be informed, to be consulted, to advise, to encourage and to warn. A right of information would embrace even those cases where the sovereign is not expected to take any action, but is merely being made aware of what is happening.[31] A right to be consulted, however, necessarily involves the notion that the sovereign may wish to express a view about the subject-matter, or indeed may have to exercise a prerogative power in order to give legal effect to it. Personalities and relationships have affected the giving of information and of consultation to a significant degree. At one extreme, Lloyd George's treatment of George V bordered on the contemptuous,[32] while at the other Ramsay MacDonald kept him better informed than any of his predecessors had done.[33] During the twentieth century Harold Macmillan was probably the last prime minister to devote significant amounts of time to informing the queen in writing about governmental matters.[34] While much information can be

---

[30] As George V assured MacDonald at his first audience in 1924, the sovereign does not discuss government business with anyone other than his private secretary and assistant secretaries: Lord Stamfordham's note, R.A. K. 1918 164. Indeed, as the private secretary to the queen put in his letter to *The Times*, 29 July 1986 (see note 7 above), 'The sovereign is obliged to treat her communications with the Prime Minister as entirely confidential between the two of them.' The Freedom of Information Act 2000, s. 37, rightly exempts from disclosure communications with the queen, the royal household, or the royal family, and communications about the conferring of honours.

[31] The sovereign receives much information, of course, from the private secretary.

[32] 'What made matters worse was that the King often did not receive the Cabinet minutes and his letters went unanswered': Rhodes James, *A Spirit Undaunted*, p. 60.

[33] Ibid., p. 78.

[34] His autobiography is replete with references to those long letters and reports: see Harold Macmillan, *Riding the Storm* (Macmillan, 1971), *Pointing the Way* (Macmillan, 1972), *At the End of the Day* (Macmillan, 1973), passim.

conveyed in this way,[35] only by meeting one another can sovereign and prime minister exchange views fully. At such audiences only the two principal constitutional actors are present, and afterwards no formal minutes are routinely written, although the sovereign's private secretary may make a note of anything which the sovereign mentions to him after an audience. Such audiences are a way for the sovereign to probe actual or proposed policy. Before the Second World War the number of audiences given to prime ministers by the sovereign varied, depending on political circumstances as well as the inclination of prime ministers to seek them. For example, Edward VIII accorded Baldwin only nine in his year-long reign despite the personal constitutional crisis which developed around the king.[36] By 1940, audiences had become weekly lunches each Tuesday,[37] enabling George VI and Winston Churchill to form one of the closest-ever partnerships between sovereign and prime minister.[38] That weekly pattern persisted after the war. The queen has given an audience to the prime minister each week when Parliament was sitting and both were in London, normally on Tuesdays in the early evening. All of the queen's former prime ministers have testified to the usefulness to them of these meetings.[39] It is against that background of being informed and consulted that a sovereign, where appropriate, can offer advice, encouragement, and warnings.

The giving of counsel by a sovereign in a sensitive manner, and the due consideration of it by a prime minister, illustrate the symbiotic relationship between the head of state and the head of government which became established during the twentieth century. The sovereign has been able to draw on his or her experience of public affairs and to offer an opinion based on what has gone before—perhaps even long before the prime minister entered public life; the prime minister, while not obliged to accept the sovereign's view, will usually see the value of what has been said and at least take it into account before proceeding.[40] It is unnecessary to compile here an exhaustive catalogue of such instances,

---

[35] The queen spends between two and three hours a day reading official papers: *Report of the Select Committee on the Civil List*, HC 29 (1971–1972), Minutes of Evidence, Appendix 13, para. 3 (Memorandum of the Queen's Private Secretary).

[36] Rhodes James, *A Spirit Undaunted*, p. 206.

[37] Wheeler-Bennett, *King George VI*, p. 446.

[38] Ibid., ch. 9.

[39] Brazier, *Constitutional Practice*, p. 33, note 48, and see below note 42.

[40] For the principal instances of this process, and the sources for them, see Brazier, *Constitutional Practice*, pp. 184–9.

especially since most are well known. But some examples of that process during the last century can be recalled briefly to show it at work. Thus, for instance, George V told MacDonald at his first audience, among other things, that it was too much for a prime minister to be his own foreign secretary (although MacDonald retained the Foreign Office during his first, brief premiership). His successor was told to get to grips with such questions as housing, unemployment, the cost of food, and education, and Baldwin was also warned later against the government being too provocative during the General Strike. George VI supported Neville Chamberlain in the policy of appeasement, and gave at least equal succour to Chamberlain's successor in the prosecution of the very opposite of that policy; the king counselled Winston Churchill not to set to sea with the Allied forces on D-Day (a warning that was accepted, just in time). George VI counselled two prime ministers about proposed ministerial appointments (Churchill against his wish to bring in Lord Beaverbrook in 1940—a warning not accepted; and Clement Attlee that Hugh Dalton should not become foreign secretary—a warning heeded, probably). The lack of official published information from the queen's reign means that it is impossible to assess fully her influence on ministers. It is known that most of her predecessors in the twentieth century had more influence on public affairs than was publicly appreciated during their reigns, and the queen may well have influenced affairs more than we know now. There is speculation about the queen's role, but it is known, for example, that she encouraged the government in the person of James Callaghan as foreign secretary in 1976 to go ahead with a planned initiative towards the illegal regime in Rhodesia (gratefully accepted, although like so many others the initiative failed).[41] It is certainly clear that the queen has been able to exercise influence by putting her views to ministers based on her broad and deep knowledge of public affairs, because her former prime ministers have said as much.[42] The stating of a royal view, leading sometimes to a change of mind, is a permanent aspect of the constitution which permits a benign influence on, or in more prosaic terms provides a further source of policy advice for, any government.

[41] James Callaghan, *Time and Chance* (Collins, 1987), pp. 378–82.
[42] See, for example, Edward Heath, *The Course of My Life* (Hodder & Stoughton 1998), pp. 317–19; Margaret Thatcher, *The Downing Street Years* (HarperCollins, 1993), p. 18 ('Her Majesty brings to bear a formidable grasp of current issues and breadth of experience'); John Major, *John Major: The Autobiography* (HarperCollins, 1999), p. 508 ('I hope Tony Blair seeks her advice and heeds her response. I found them invaluable on many occasions').

As a matter of law the Crown enjoys a large number of powers which are enshrined in that part of the common law known as the royal prerogative.[43] The sovereign's active participation in the use of many of these powers is necessary for them to be exercised effectively in law. While most prerogative powers fall to be used by the sovereign on ministerial advice, it is from the same legal source—the royal prerogative—that sovereigns have enjoyed powers which would only be considered for use in a constitutional emergency in which the sovereign could not accept ministerial advice. These reserve powers[44] embrace the sovereign's power to insist on, or to refuse, a recommended dissolution of Parliament, to refuse royal assent, and to dismiss ministers. But the setting out of that list immediately prompts the question whether it can be said that, in the light of twentieth-century constitutional history, such emergency, reserve powers still exist. For they seem redolent of a form of monarchy that passed away in 1688 or (according to taste) by the time that representative government had become fully established in the United Kingdom. The question posed, however, is not precise enough. The *powers* still exist, because they are part of the royal prerogative which is itself part of the common law. Rules and powers which are part of the common law do not become extinct merely through lack of use.[45] Common-law attributes can be amended or abrogated by an exercise of parliamentary sovereignty, and there are several examples from the last hundred years of Acts that were passed to do just that in relation to the prerogative.[46] But no legislation has been enacted in order to limit, let alone abolish, the Crown's constitutional prerogatives, whether of the routine or the reserve varieties. In law all those powers remain. Because in ordinary circumstances the prerogative powers are, by constitutional convention, exercised on ministerial advice they form part of the government for which ministers are accountable to Parliament and through it to the people. Granted, though, that the reserve powers exist in law as much in 2000 as they did in 1900, are they perhaps properly considered as existing in a lumber-room to which are quietly consigned bits of

---

[43] For an excellent survey of the history of the prerogative see D. L. Keir and F. H. Lawson, *Cases in Constitutional Law*, 6th edn (Clarendon Press, 1979), ch. 2.

[44] Sir Ivor Jennings described these powers as 'personal prerogatives': *Cabinet Government*, 3rd edn (Cambridge University Press, 1959), ch. 13; see also Geoffrey Marshall, *Constitutional Conventions* (Clarendon Press, 1984), ch. 2.

[45] See, for example, *McKendrick v. Sinclair* (1972) SLT 110 at 116.

[46] Notably through the Crown Proceedings Act 1947.

the British constitution for which no practical use remains? That is a superficially attractive way of looking at the matter. After all, parliamentary government has flourished in the twentieth century. Sovereigns have understood the need to act with restraint, rarely even considering the use of reserve powers; ministers have accepted the obligations of constitutional rules, and have tried to act 'constitutionally'. Thus sovereigns have not regularly insisted on dissolving Parliament or refusing royal assent, just as ministers have not demanded dissolutions in circumstances in which the sovereign would feel constrained to refuse, and have not declined to resign having lost a general election. But it would be misleading and unwise to open the lumber-room door in order to toss in the reserve powers only on the basis that for a century and more they have not been needed.

It would be a very strange state whose constitutional law recognised that the head of that state possessed legal rights for use as the final arbiter of constitutionalism, but which allowed no indication of the circumstances in which they might have to be used. Indeed, on a small number of occasions in the last century two sovereigns were clear that they might have to use their reserve powers against the wishes of ministers. Both Edward VII and George V were of the view that the king had the right to insist on a general election before agreeing to a mass creation of peers in order to coerce the House of Lords.[47] In the same constitutional crisis George V initially decided to refuse a dissolution in November 1910, although he changed his mind after discussing the matter with senior ministers;[48] but clearly he was of the opinion that a refusal could be persisted in if the circumstances justified it. Although no bill passed by Parliament since 1708 has been vetoed by the sovereign, as late as 1914 George V thought that the power to veto was extant and he considered using it in relation to the Government of Ireland bill, although in the end he reluctantly assented to it.[49] There has been no suggestion from royal advisers at any time during the last century that such prerogatives have been taken to have disappeared, and indeed constitutional commentators have spent much time covering paper with analyses of the circumstances in which the reserve powers properly might be used.

[47] Jennings, *Cabinet Government*, pp. 428–48; J. A. Spender and Cyril Asquith, *Life of Herbert Henry Asquith, Lord Oxford and Asquith* (Hutchinson, 1932), vol. 1, pp. 261, 398.
[48] Jennings, *Cabinet Government*, p. 424; but see Nicolson, *King George V*, pp. 125–39, Rose, *King George V*, pp. 115–25.
[49] See note 8 above.

They would not have so directed their energies unless they believed that such situations existed.[50]

The United Kingdom has no supreme court which could ensure that in the last resort the political actors behave in conformity with the norms of the constitution; Parliament is dominated by the government; voters cannot precipitate a general election; the only insurance of constitutional propriety in a dire emergency is the sovereign. Representative parliamentary government has, however, ensured that governments are fully subject, in time, to the electorate: they know that they risk dismissal by an informed electorate if they were to do grave constitutional wrong. Because of that, the use of the sovereign's reserve powers has ceased to be a weapon of first resort against politicians who might be tempted to depart from the constitutional straight and narrow. Equally, the cardinal convention that sovereigns act on ministerial advice, accepted fully in ordinary circumstances, reassures ministers that the sovereign would not dream of acting on his or her personal discretion in such circumstances. There was, therefore, no suggestion that the queen would do other than assent to the legislation to devolve powers to Scotland, Wales, and Northern Ireland, even if she had had private reservations about the consequent loosening of the bonds which bind together the constituent parts of the United Kingdom. How much has changed can be seen by remembering how close her grandfather came to trying to block home rule for Ireland.

III

Constitutional lawyers can be criticised for failing to give clear answers to constitutional questions that crop up from time to time. Often a reasonable defence is that the rules that govern many such issues are conventional in character, and as such lack the precision of the law. But the twentieth century saw the enactment of new rules about several aspects of the Crown,[51] so that today there is a significant corpus of Crown statute law.

---

[50] See, for example, Brazier, *Constitutional Practice* pp. 189–97; A. W. Bradley and Keith Ewing, *Constitutional and Administrative Law*, 12th edn (Longman, 1997), pp. 262–8; S. A. de Smith and R. Brazier, *Constitutional and Administrative Law*, 8th edn (Penguin, 1998), pp. 122–8; Jennings, *Cabinet Government*, ch. 13; Marshall, *Constitutional Conventions*, chs 2, 3. Those analyses will not be pursued here.

[51] For discussion of the Crown (as distinct from constitutional monarchy) see Sunkin and

In several respects the law concerning the monarchy was unsatisfactory at the beginning of the twentieth century. A new sovereign was still obliged by the Bill of Rights 1689 and the Act of Settlement 1701 to utter oaths which, while designed to ensure that the sovereign was in communion with the Church of England, were uniquely offensive to his or her Roman Catholic subjects. Again, had a sovereign succumbed to an illness of such a severity that a regency was required, no legal framework existed in 1900 under which a regent could take office. Were a sovereign to decide to abdicate, then (perhaps not surprisingly) no law prescribed the events which would give effect to it. More importantly from a practical point of view, at the dawn of the twentieth century the king in law could still do no wrong, and he and his ministers were legally immune from actions in the courts for wrongdoing committed against the king's subjects.[52] Indeed, Parliament's will, as expressed in statute, did not bind the Crown at all unless a given statute said so expressly or by necessary implication: the king's ministers and his other servants were helped by that rule to escape liability for what, for subjects, would be breaches of that statute's terms.[53] In particular, the Crown was immune under that doctrine from liability to pay taxes imposed by statute. Many of these undesirable legal rules were to be changed—some drastically—in the years after Edward VII's succession.

The first statutory intervention was made in time for George V's coronation. Victoria and her predecessors had been required by legislation passed in the aftermath of the Glorious Revolution to swear oaths in terms obnoxious to Catholics. The Accession Declaration Act 1910 removed the worst excesses of the seventeenth-century statutory diatribe against Catholicism,[54] and in its place were substituted rules requiring a new sovereign to declare (at the first meeting of Parliament after the accession or at the coronation) that he or she was a faithful Protestant, and (at the coronation) to take an oath to govern in specified ways, including a duty to maintain the Protestant reformed religion.[55] The 1910

Payne, *The Nature of the Crown*, especially the excellent ch. 3 by Martin Loughlin, 'The State, the Crown and the Law'.

[52] Unsatisfactory remedies existed, such as the petition of right: they were much too favourable to the Crown.

[53] This remains the case: *Lord Advocate* v. *Dumbarton District Council* [1990] 2 AC 580.

[54] Thus the Act removed from the oath all references to 'papist', 'popish princes', and the 'popish religion'.

[55] See Brazier, 'The Constitutional Position of the Prince of Wales', *Public Law* (1995), 401 at 411–12. In fact the terms of the coronation oath as actually taken were to be modified subsequently without statutory authority.

Act did nothing to affect the legal rule that the sovereign must be in communion with the Church of England,[56] and although the offensive terms of the seventeenth-century settlement were deleted,[57] the bar against any non-Anglican ascending the throne remained: only a person in communion with the Church of England could ascend or remain on the throne.[58]

The second change to the legal regime for the monarchy was to come twenty years after that. The monarchy had helped to unify the British Empire. But the Empire was already evolving into a Commonwealth, in that the old dominions were in practice self-governing and in effect largely independent. As part of that evolution it was agreed at the imperial conference in 1930 that any change in the law touching the succession to the throne or the royal style and titles would require the assent of the Parliaments of the dominions as well as of the Parliament of the United Kingdom, a new convention which was to be recited in the preamble to the Statute of Westminster 1931.[59] The purpose of this recital was to ensure that wherever the sovereign was head of state the same rules of succession would apply. That precept was to maintain its force even as independence seeped through the Empire, for by 2000 fifteen Commonwealth states still acknowledged the queen of the United Kingdom as their queen. Although the preamble does not constitute a rule of statute law,[60] its terms were to be followed as if they were law on three occasions in the twentieth century. Two of them involved changes to the royal titles—on the laying to rest of the title of Emperor of India in 1948 following India's transition to republican status, and on the adoption by Elizabeth II of separate titles for her several realms in 1953. On both occasions the dominions gave their assents.[61]

But it was the third instance that was to have the most dramatic consequences for the monarchy, when Baldwin consulted the dominion prime ministers in 1936 to ascertain whether the dominions would

---

[56] Act of Settlement 1701, s. 3.

[57] But not the bar against the sovereign marrying a Catholic, which Catholics consider offensive to them: a sovereign could marry any non-Catholic and remain on the throne.

[58] See note 56.

[59] See Chapter 16.

[60] It is merely an aid to the interpretation of the statutory rules in the body of Acts of Parliament.

[61] It was to become accepted in the laws of the Commonwealth that the Crown was divisible: thus the Crown of Canada is separate from the Crown of the United Kingdom, although worn by the same person: see *R. v. Secretary of State for Foreign and Commonwealth Affairs, ex p. Indian Association of Alberta* [1982] 1 QB 892.

approve of Edward VIII's proposed morganatic marriage. That crisis brought the Statute of Westminster into stark constitutional relief. The prevailing opposition in the dominions matched that of all the party leaders in the United Kingdom, with conclusive results for the king's future. His Majesty's Declaration of Abdication Act 1936 confirmed the lesson from 1689 that the monarch reigns at the sufferance of Parliament. While no one in (say) 1900 would have needed for a moment to discover the constitutional mechanics needed to effect an abdication (if, indeed, there were any), the Statute of Westminster 1931 was unwittingly to provide the model for part of the necessary machinery, and the events of 1936 were to put in place the final piece of the template for the general doctrine that a sovereign must either accept ministerial advice, or in an irresolvable clash of wills must find another government, or abdicate.

It was the family circumstances of the departed king's successor that caused a further change in Crown law. At the beginning of George VI's reign his two daughters were aged ten and six respectively. If there had been a demise of the Crown before Princess Elizabeth had reached the age of eighteen a regency would have been required, but there was no standing legal arrangement for that contingency. With the ready agreement of his government what became the Regency Act 1937 was enacted, which (taken together with the Regency Acts of 1943 and 1953) provides a code governing the appointment and powers of a regent if a sovereign were to succeed while under the age of eighteen, or if the sovereign were to become incapacitated. The Act as amended also provides for the appointment of counsellors of state when a sovereign is ill (though not so incapacitated as to require a regency) or is absent from the United Kingdom. No regency was required during the twentieth century, although counsellors of state were appointed under these Acts during George VI's illnesses and many times during the queen's overseas tours.[62]

The last hundred years witnessed several statutory changes to the royal prerogative. True, a host of miscellaneous and relatively minor prerogatives—themselves feudal remnants—remained much the same in 2000 as they had been in 1900,[63] altered here and there by statute.[64]

---

[62] Counsellors of state were appointed by George V on his illness in 1928 and in 1936. This was done under the royal prerogative, with privy counsellors present, and attested to by warrant signed by the king.

[63] For a list, see Brazier, 'Constitutional Reform and the Crown', in Sunkin and Payne, *The Nature of the Crown* pp. 244–5.

[64] For example, the prerogative right to mint coinage is now exercised mainly on the basis of statute.

That the Crown has (for instance) the right to sturgeon, certain swans, and whales, does not matter very much. But other legal prerogatives have great practical significance for citizens, and Parliament has legislated in recent decades so as, for instance, to regularise the preference given to the Crown on a debtor's bankruptcy, to reduce dramatically the Crown's advantage in the rule that time does not run against the Crown in legal proceedings, to cut back the effect of the maxim that the Crown can do no wrong, and to state in particular situations that a given statute does, indeed, bind the Crown and its servants (so that, for example, the immunity that had exempted NHS bodies from environmental health legislation has been abolished). Of the statutory reforms, those that have chipped away at the prerogative of perfection are the most important.[65] While the queen can no more be prosecuted or sued for an alleged wrong committed by her personally than could her predecessors, the logical extension of the principle that, in law, the Crown can do no wrong produced a stain on the fabric of the constitution. The principle had been extended as a legal defence to deny remedies to citizens for wrongs committed by emanations of the Crown (or the state), whether they were breaches of contract, or tort, or ministers' misdeeds. Parliament and the courts have been removing that stain since the late 1940s,[66] but it has been a slow process, and even at the turn of the millennium it was far from complete. Now it may be objected that this 'lawyers' law' has little to do with constitutional monarchy: but it has. Critics of a monarchical system can point to these discriminatory legal rules as part of a case that monarchy itself is outmoded. Governments and Parliament (and, indeed, the courts) have recognised from time to time that particular legal effects of the prerogative are impossible to defend, and have taken action to change them. This is the contribution of lawyers and parliamentarians, made during the twentieth century, to the modernisation of the monarchy, a process which was started long before the phrase entered public debate.

Most of the constitutional elements which contribute to the financing of the monarchy were in place by the middle of the nineteenth century, and so do not form a central part of the history of the last century.[67] Changes during the last hundred years—such as the decision in 1972 to

---

[65] See Brazier, 'Constitutional Reform and the Crown', pp. 345–6.
[66] The main statutory changes were contained in the Crown Proceedings Act 1947.
[67] See Philip Hall, *Royal Fortune: Tax, Money and the Monarchy* (Bloomsbury, 1992), ch. 2; Adam Tomkins, 'Crown Privileges', in Sunkin and Payne, *The Nature of the Crown*, ch. 7.

fix civil list payments for ten-year periods at a time—were adjustments which involved no great issue of constitutional principle. But one reform had its origins in the history of the law of the royal prerogative. For, if the questions are posed 'Why is the monarch not obliged under the law to pay income tax like anyone else?' or 'Why was Victoria's agreement in 1842 to pay the newly reintroduced income tax merely voluntary?', the answers can be found only in the legal principle that the Crown is immune from the provisions of statute unless the Act provides to the contrary. Taxes can be raised only under statutory authority: none of the tax statutes provides that the Crown shall pay tax. If any sovereign were to pay taxes on his or her personal income or wealth, this would be because he or she had volunteered to do so. The queen's decision in 1992 to pay income, capital gains, and inheritance taxes on her personal income and wealth[68] was taken as a voluntary acceptance that her *private* wealth should not be immune from taxation.[69]

IV

During the final decade of the last century there was much talk of the need for the monarchy to modernise itself.[70] Certain actions by the queen appeared to be based on an acceptance that change was, indeed, necessary. For instance, the queen and the Prince of Wales decided to pay certain taxes;[71] the queen fully accepted that the decision whether to commission a replacement for the royal yacht was one for ministers (who decided against a replacement for *Britannia*); the ceremonial at the state opening of Parliament was simplified slightly (although it took a seasoned eye to spot the differences); the queen's public engagements were extended so that she could meet more 'ordinary' people; whole days were devoted to visits by her of particular groups (such as the voluntary services); and so on. Some of these changes were introduced to offset

---

[68] There will, however, be no inheritance tax in relation to bequests to the sovereign's successor. The queen also agreed to reimburse civil list payments made to her for all members of the royal family other than herself, the queen mother, and the Duke of Edinburgh.

[69] For the detailed arrangements see the prime minister's statement at HC Deb., vol. 218, col. 1111, 11 February 1993.

[70] See, for example, Robert Blackburn and Raymond Plant, 'Monarchy and the Royal Prerogative', in Blackburn and Plant (eds), *Constitutional Reform: The Labour Government's Constitutional Reform Agenda* (Longman, 1999), ch. 6.

[71] For the details see *Royal Finance*, 2nd edn (Her Majesty the Queen, 1995).

criticism of the royal family's immediate actions following the death of Diana, Princess of Wales, conduct which led to accusations that the queen and others were out of touch with and indeed remote from the feelings of most people.[72] For all the media and political talk of modernisation, however, it cannot be said that (apart perhaps from the decision to pay certain taxes) these changes amounted to very much in purely constitutional terms, although the symbolism involved was significant. Nor did the monarchy start to reform itself for the first time in the 1990s. Rather, such alterations as there were during that time are best viewed as part of the continual process of adaptation which has taken place in the monarchy since the reign of Victoria: monarchy has had to 'accommodate itself' to a constantly changing society.[73] But a very different and much more significant engine for change in the responsibilities of the institution arrived in 1997 with the advent of the Labour government under Tony Blair. For the new government had a mandate for the most ambitious programme of constitutional reform ever sought from and granted by the British electorate, a programme which in several respects was to affect the monarchy.

Moves towards self-government within a unitary state carry a risk that the glue which binds that state together may lose its potency. Partly to reduce that risk the sovereign's role in the United Kingdom was stressed in the Labour government's devolution plans for Scotland and Wales. Ministers spoke of Scotland 'of course' remaining an integral part of the United Kingdom, with the queen as head of state in it,[74] and of the National Assembly for Wales being a Crown body, with the queen fulfilling specific functions in relation to it.[75] The symbolism of the queen formally opening the new Scottish Parliament and the Welsh National Assembly was clear: while legislative power was being passed to Edinburgh and power to pass secondary legislation to Cardiff, this was under the continuing ultimate legislative sovereignty of the Queen in Parliament at Westminster. This legal fact was to be underlined by the requirement that all members of the Scottish Parliament and National Assembly members take the oath of allegiance to the queen, as prescribed

---

[72] Certainly, the queen's decision to make a live television broadcast in the wake of the death, and the decision to fly the union flag over Buckingham Palace in the queen's absence, so that it might be lowered to half mast as a mark of mourning, were two responses to that criticism.

[73] Bogdanor, *The Monarchy and the Constitution*, p. 303.

[74] *Scotland's Parliament*, Cm 3658 (1997), para. 4.2.

[75] *A Voice for Wales*, Cm 3718 (1997), paras 1.20–1.21.

by the new constitutional statutes. In Scotland, too, bills passed by the Parliament would require royal assent before they could become law; the Scottish first minister—although elected by the Parliament and proposed for office by the presiding officer—was to be appointed to office formally by the queen, who would give him or her a warrant of appointment and custody of the Scottish seal.[76] The first minister was to have direct access to the queen—including occasional private audiences—similar to that enjoyed by the British prime minister. Moreover, in the constitutional emergency which might arise from the Scottish Parliament at any time being unable to nominate a first minister, or itself voting for a dissolution, the queen was given a statutory discretion whether to bring about a dissolution.[77] Northern Ireland—as many people in Great Britain tend to put it in a rather mealy-mouthed way—is different: and this was to be reflected in the devolution settlement based on the Good Friday Agreement and the Northern Ireland Act 1998. For obvious reasons the queen's constitutional role in Northern Ireland has to be a balanced one. She was not asked to open the Northern Ireland Assembly; she was given no responsibilities, not even formal ones, in government-making there; but royal assent was to be required for bills. In all three of the devolution settlements it was to be the queen's Privy Council—or rather its Judicial Committee—which was to be the final arbiter of the constitutionality of laws passed (or to be passed) by the Parliament and the Assemblies. Thus the sovereign was accorded new constitutional roles, duties, and powers the like of which had only been seen in the United Kingdom once before in the twentieth century, in relation to the Parliament of Northern Ireland from 1921 to 1972. Symbolically, legally, and constitutionally, the queen has new functions today in relation to legislatures and executives which were at best pipe-dreams in 1900. While the practical significance for the monarchy of those institutions cannot yet be assessed, these developments will ask more from it. Far from having less to do than in the late twentieth century, the

---

[76] The seal is the first minister's as keeper of the Scottish seal: Scotland Act 1998, s. 45(7). That method of appointment implements a model which has been proposed by some (including the Liberal Democrats) for Westminster, under which the British prime minister would be nominated by the speaker following a vote in the House of Commons. It is, however, highly unlikely that the main political parties would surrender their ability to manoeuvre in a hung Parliament by ceding their decision-making to the House of Commons itself.

[77] Scotland Act 1998, s. 3. The dissolution would be proposed by the presiding officer, but the queen then 'may take steps to effect it', ibid., s. 3(2). The queen would be likely to act on the presiding officer's proposal, save in exceptional circumstances.

sovereign is busier now, performing duties in relation to the new assemblies and executives, being seen more in Scotland and in Wales, acting as a unifying symbol of the whole kingdom which has a constitutionally weaker central government and legislature.

If the Labour Party's 1997 general election manifesto commitment to a formal reconsideration of the voting system for the House of Commons were to produce a more proportional electoral system,[78] it would in theory be possible that the sovereign might once again become involved in government-making. The trend during the twentieth century was in the opposite direction—to reduce the need for royal intervention in that process. That trend took place against the background of the political parties themselves resolving questions which had earlier exercised sovereigns, and of general elections which normally resulted in one party obtaining a majority. There is a general assumption that any change in the voting system which produced more hung Parliaments would necessarily involve the queen more in government-making.[79] It is unclear to what extent the Jenkins Commission's alternative vote-top-up system would produce more hung Parliaments;[80] it is also unclear when— indeed, whether—there will be a referendum on it.[81] But in the light of twentieth-century experience it is possible to be sanguine. If there were to be more inconclusive general elections, it is probable that the queen would follow the February 1974 precedent and allow the politicians to resolve the problem for themselves. The sovereign's intervention could prove little more than a formality, unless, of course, politicians were to fail to agree. Indeed, the new and hung Scottish Parliament in 1999 itself easily produced a coalition;[82] the reserve powers set out in the Scotland

---

[78] As proposed by the *Report of the Independent Commission on the Voting System*, Cm 4090 (1998).

[79] Any lessons which may be drawn from New Zealand's recent switch from first past the post to proportional representation will no doubt be considered at Buckingham Palace.

[80] The Jenkins Commission claimed that, since 1979, only the 1992 general election would have resulted in a hung Parliament. Some commentators have said, however, that if elections from 1945 to 1974 were taken into account several more instances of inconclusive results would have occurred.

[81] The Labour Party seems to have watered down its original commitment to place the recommended alternative system before the electorate, and instead may offer a choice between the status quo and the alternative vote system.

[82] The Northern Ireland Assembly also produced a coalition Executive, but it is governed by detailed statutory rules in the Northern Ireland Act 1998 which are designed to create a coalition reflecting the membership of the Assembly. (The Welsh National Assembly initially supported a minority Executive, then a coalition, but there is no royal role in the formation of the Executive.)

Act which provide for royal decision-making in a Parliament that could not agree on a first minister were not needed and will perhaps remain unused. Labour's 1997 manifesto also doomed hereditary peers, and out they—or all except 92 of them—duly went in 1999. It was remarkable that in all the attacks which were mounted against the hereditary principle before and during the passage of the House of Lords Act of that year, few sought to put the hereditary monarchy in the same sights as the hereditary peers.[83] Indeed, what might have been a weakening moment for the monarchy passed with seemingly little effect on it: perhaps the argument was accepted, however reluctantly in some quarters, that, while a hereditary legislative chamber is hard to justify, a hereditary constitutional monarch can be justified convincingly—as, indeed, it has been in seven other European Union and fifteen other Commonwealth states. Moreover, a concerted republican effort was repelled in Australia in the same month as the hereditaries were expelled from the Westminster Parliament.[84] Australian republicans vowed, it is true, to force the issue again; and it is likely that New Zealand will make a test of opinion on republicanism there one day. It is possible that the number of realms recognising the British sovereign as head of state may be reduced in the next few years, but there is no irresistible tide of republicanism washing around the Commonwealth.[85] Given the personal popularity of the queen in the United Kingdom it seems unlikely that republicanism will gain much ground there while she is on the throne, where she may remain for another twenty years or more. Indeed republican sentiment has remained weak in the United Kingdom throughout the twentieth century.[86] The political parties took account of that: none engaged, or wished to be associated with, the principle of republicanism.[87]

Having been in place and undisturbed for hundreds of years, the rules concerning the succession to the throne came under consideration in Parliament in the last years of the twentieth century, and the rule that

[83] Indeed, only a handful of parliamentarians made any connection between that legislation and hereditary monarchy.

[84] In November 1999 Australia voted 55 per cent to 45 per cent against a proposed republican model.

[85] Outside the antipodes republicanism may be strongest at present in Jamaica, Barbados, and Antigua and Barbuda: see Colin Munro, 'More Daylight, Less Magic: The Australian Referendum on the Monarchy', *Public Law* (2000), 5.

[86] Frank Prochaska, *The Republic of Britain* (Allen Lane, 2000).

[87] For a republican case made at the end of the twentieth century see Jonathan Freedland, *Bring Home the Revolution: The Case for a British Republic* (Fourth Estate, 1998).

males take precedence in the line of succession appeared set to be reformed. In response to a private peer's bill introduced in the 1997–8 session, the government announced that it was considering how to take change forward.[88] Ministers had consulted the queen, who had no objection to the government's view that daughters and sons should be treated in the same way in determining the line of succession to the throne. At the time of writing, though, no legislation has been proposed. Again, both in the Westminster and Edinburgh Parliaments formal moves were taken to remove the discriminatory statutory rules which prevent adherents of the Roman Catholic faith, and those who marry Catholics, from acceding to or remaining on the throne. But the government set its face against such a change, the prime minister explaining that the government's heavy legislative programme, the complexity of the issue (which included the amendment or repeal of a number of items of legislation), the requirement of Commonwealth consents, and the other major constitutional issues raised by the proposed change, meant that it would take the matter no further.[89] Behind any such move might lie the wider question of disestablishment of the Church of England, a possibility that the political parties seem content to leave to the Church itself. Thus, while progress on that aspect of the statutory qualities required of a sovereign in the twentieth century appears to be stalled, it may be that by the time Prince William comes to the throne his descendants might enjoy sex equality as far as the succession to him was concerned (although any practical effect of a legal change would be apparent only if his first-born were to be female).

For most of the twentieth century sovereigns and their closest advisers recognised the continuing need to adapt the institution of monarchy so as to reflect changes in British society. That involved further erosions in the sovereign's power. In return, the ability of sovereigns to continue to use their conventional rights of influence was accepted and indeed welcomed by prime ministers, at least during and after the Second World War. Improvements were made to the law touching the Crown. In recent years the sovereign's responsibilities have been expanded within the reshaped United Kingdom constitution. The contemporary monarchy is obviously different from that which existed in 1900, but continues to perform very useful, albeit limited, functions in the modern British state.

---

[88] Lord Williams of Mostyn, Minister of State, Home Office, HL Deb., vol. 586, cols 914–17, 27 February 1998.
[89] Tony Blair at HC Deb., vol. 341, col. 57, written answers 13 December 1999.

Bibliography

Primary sources

Statutes

Accession Declaration Act 1910
Act of Settlement 1701
Bill of Rights 1689
Crown Proceedings Act 1947
Government of Wales Act 1998
His Majesty's Declaration of Abdication Act 1936
House of Lords Act 1999
Northern Ireland Act 1998
Parliament Act 1911
Parliament Act 1949
Regency Acts 1937–53
Representation of the People Act 1884
Scotland Act 1998
Statute of Westminster 1931

Cases

Lord Advocate v. *Dumbarton District Council* [1990] 2 AC 580.
McKendrick v. *Sinclair* (1972) SLT 110.
R. v. *Secretary of State for Foreign and Commonwealth Affairs, ex p. Indian Association of Alberta* [1982] 1 QB 892.

Royal archives

R.A. K. 1917.
R.A. K. 1918 164.
R.A. GV 0 2570/11.
R.A. P.S. GVI C131/80.

Official papers

Report of the Independent Commission on the Voting System, Cm 4090 (1998).
Report of the Select Committee on the Civil List (1971–1972), HC 29.
Scotland's Parliament, Cm 3658 (1997).
A Voice for Wales, Cm 3718 (1997).

Secondary sources

Books

Bogdanor, Vernon, *Multi-party Politics and the Constitution* (Cambridge University Press, 1983).
Bogdanor, Vernon, *The Monarchy and the Constitution* (Clarendon Press, 1995).

Bradford, Sarah, *Elizabeth: A Biography of Her Majesty the Queen* (Heinemann, 1996).

Bradford, Sarah, *King George VI* (Weidenfeld & Nicolson, 1989).

Brazier, Rodney, *Constitutional Practice*, 3rd edn (Oxford University Press, 1999).

Butler, David, *Governing without a Majority*, 2nd edn (Macmillan 1987).

Butler, David and Lowe, D. A. (eds), *Constitutional Heads of State in the Commonwealth* (Macmillan, 1991).

Dale, Sir William, *The Constitutional Structure of the Commonwealth* (Oxford University Press, 1960).

Dimbleby, Jonathan, *The Prince of Wales* (Little, Brown, 1994).

Donaldson, Frances, *Edward VIII* (Weidenfeld & Nicolson, 1974).

Freedland, Jonathan, *Bring Home the Revolution: The Case for a British Republic* (Fourth Estate, 1999).

Hall, Philip, *Royal Fortune: Tax, Money and the Monarchy* (Bloomsbury, 1992).

Haseler, Stephen, *The End of the House of Windsor: Birth of a British Republic* (I. B. Tauris, 1993).

Jennings, Sir Ivor, *Cabinet Government*, 3rd edn (Cambridge University Press, 1959).

Magnus, Sir Philip, *King Edward the Seventh* (John Murray, 1964).

Marshall, Geoffrey, *Constitutional Conventions* (Clarendon Press, 1984).

Nairn, Tom, *The Enchanted Glass: Britain and its Monarchy* (Radius, 1988).

Nicolson, Sir Harold, *King George V: His Life and Reign* (Constable, 1952).

Pimlott, Ben, *The Queen: A Biography of Elizabeth II* (HarperCollins, 1996).

Ponsonby, Sir Frederick, *Recollections of Three Reigns* (Eyre & Spottiswoode, 1951).

Prochaska, Frank, *Royal Bounty: The Making of the Welfare Monarchy* (Yale University Press, 1995).

Prochaska, Frank, *The Republic of Britain* (Penguin, 2000).

Rhodes James, Sir Robert, *A Spirit Undaunted: The Political Role of George VI* (Little, Brown, 1998).

Robilliard, St John A., *Religion and the Law: Religious Liberty in Modern English Law* (Manchester University Press, 1984).

Rose, Kenneth, *King George V* (Macmillan, 1983).

Wheare, K. C., *The Statute of Westminster and Dominion Status*, 5th edn (Oxford University Press, 1953).

Wheeler-Bennett, Sir John, *King George VI: His Life and Reign* (Macmillan, 1958).

Ziegler, Philip, *King Edward VIII* (Collins, 1990).

4.
The Cabinet System

ANTHONY SELDON

This chapter explores how the Cabinet system changed between 1900 and 2000. The first section looks at how the Cabinet system operated and what it meant in 1900; we then examine the Cabinet system at twenty-year intervals from 1920 and 2000. Every individual year in the century was unique, with particular concerns and conditions which affected the operation of the Cabinet system; twenty-year intervals nevertheless permit us to see the system evolving over the course of the century. Ten-year intervals would have revealed shorter term fluctuations[1] but would not have altered the broad conclusions about change over the twentieth century, which show a steady transition through a number of distinct stages from Cabinet in 1900 being *the* decision-making body to a highly personalised and fluid system in 2000. Cabinet thus reverted to what it was in the eighteenth century: a regular discussion among political friends.[2]

Only one departure from the twenty-year rhythm occurs: 1940 was the first full year of war, and hence was excessively atypical, so 1939 is examined in its place. The second section explores the changes that occurred in the Cabinet system over the hundred years, and the third and final section explores why the changes have taken place.

Describing how the Cabinet system changed over the last century has two main difficulties. There was no agreed 'rule book' on how British government was to be organised and run, and how and where decisions

---

[1] One can point to clear examples of prime ministerial power and Cabinet subservience at the beginning of the period, including Gladstone's preparing the Government of Ireland bill in 1886 without reference to Cabinet, or Balfour dismissing his free trade ministers in 1903. One can also point to examples of Cabinet being the key decision-taking body at the end of our period, as over the Maastricht debates in 1993. But short-term fluctuations do not upset the broad view of change over the century. Cabinet by 2000 was a very different body to Cabinet in 1900.

[2] Lord Butler of Brockwell, 'Cabinet Government', Attlee Foundation Lecture, Mansion House, London, 18 March 1999; and Peter Riddell, 'Blair as Prime Minister', in Anthony Seldon (ed.), *The Blair Effect* (Little, Brown, 2001), p. 32.

were to be taken. There are thus problems understanding how decisions were taken in practice compared to how they were to be taken in theory, or how they were supposed to be taken based on limited organisation charts, or according to convention. 'It is an illusion to suppose that, whatever arrangements are made, it will ever be possible to arrange the business of the Cabinet and its committees on the ideally tidy and orderly basis which the critics seem to have in mind,' complained a Cabinet official in 1964.[3]

A second difficulty stems from the uneven nature of the evidence. Three principal sources can be consulted. Cabinet minutes at the Public Record Office (PRO) are in existence only from the time the Cabinet Secretariat was created in 1916, and they are unavailable after 1972 because of the thirty-year rule. Only three of the six cross-sections, 1920, 1939 and 1960, could thus make use of this source.[4] Cabinet and Cabinet committee minutes can give a misleading impression of the discussions they are purporting to describe. They are written, not for historical accuracy, but to facilitate administrative efficiency.

The second source is created by those with first-hand experience of the Cabinet system, and includes oral interviews, private papers, diaries and published memoirs. But personal testimony is often a flawed source. Ministers' accounts are especially unreliable, in part because ministers are rarely dispassionate observers, and because they lack perspective. Few ministers had more than ten years' experience of the Cabinet system, and they could rarely comment reliably on how the system changed over time. If they returned to government after a period in opposition, they were usually returning to a higher position in government and this created a different point of observation. Senior officials are more objective, but they are usually seconded to the Cabinet Secretariat office for fixed periods, so they generally lack a long-term perspective. Until recently, officials have been reluctant to speak to researchers and, while they can to some extent fill the gap in the public record over the last thirty years, they are more circumspect the closer they come to the present day. Even the most senior Cabinet Office officials are not without their own distortions in perspective. The most useful published sources

---

[3] P. Catterall and C. Brady, 'Cabinet Committees in British Governance', *Public Policy and Administration* (1998), 81.

[4] The Cabinet Office, which was well-disposed to this chapter in general, refused to disclose information for 1980 and 2000 including the frequency of Cabinet committee meetings, or the number of papers put up to Cabinet. It justified its inability to help by referring to *Open Government: Codes of Practice on Access to Government Information*, 2nd edn (1997).

are the diaries and letters of inter-war assistant Cabinet secretary, Tom Jones (1969–71),[5] and Stephen Roskill's three volumes on the first Cabinet secretary, Sir Maurice Hankey (1970–4).[6] The gap in diaries or memoirs by, or detailed biographies about, all Cabinet secretaries since Hankey further impedes understanding, because these powerful individuals possess an unrivalled understanding of how the Cabinet system operated in practice.

Third are written accounts by commentators and academics, the least satisfactory source of the three. Important information, however, is found in Jennings (1959),[7] Mackintosh (1977),[8] Gordon Walker (1972),[9] Hennessy (1986),[10] Burch and Halliday (1996),[11] James (1999)[12] and Hennessy (2000).[13] But all are handicapped by the problems with, and the unevenness of, the first two types of primary source. Much has been written about whether Britain has developed a presidential rather than Cabinet government, about the 'core executive' and the Cabinet's place as just one among several bodies co-ordinating a complex governmental process. The decision has been consciously taken in this chapter, on grounds of space and personal taste, to focus on primary sources rather than to discuss the academic debates in the secondary literature. The best means for following these debates—which can be arid, or circular, or both—are two recent and lucid books, James (1999)[14] and Hennessy (2000).[15] The aim here has been to engage with the primary evidence, and to attempt a piece of historical analysis rather than political science.

Six cross-sections

Cabinet in 1900

1900 was the first full year of the Boer War. Lord Salisbury was in his twelfth year as prime minister and nearing the end of his tenure (he

---

[5] Thomas Jones, *Whitehall Diary*, ed. Keith Middlemas (Oxford University Press, 1969–71).

[6] Stephen Roskill, *Hankey: Man of Secrets*, 3 vols (Collins, 1970–4).

[7] Sir I. Jennings (ed.), *Cabinet Government*, 3rd edn (Cambridge University Press, 1959).

[8] J. Mackintosh, *The British Cabinet*, 3rd edn (Stevens, 1977).

[9] P. Gordon Walker, *The Cabinet*, revised edn (Heinemann Educational, 1972).

[10] P. Hennessy, *Cabinet* (Blackwell, 1986).

[11] M. Burch and I. Halliday, *The British Cabinet System* (Harvester Wheatsheaf, 1996).

[12] Simon James, *British Cabinet Government*, 2nd edn (Routledge, 1999).

[13] P. Hennessy, *The Prime Minister: The Office and its Holders since 1945* (Allen Lane, 2000).

[14] James, *British Cabinet Government*.

[15] Hennessy, *The Prime Minister*.

retired in 1902). The precise function and remit of Cabinet meetings in 1900 and the extent of any committees is hard to judge,[16] in large part because there was no Cabinet Secretariat until 1916, and there are no consecutive records of meetings other than the Committee of Imperial Defence. The principal source of information on what happens in Cabinet are the letters the prime minister of the day sends to the monarch. In 1900, Salisbury wrote twenty-six letters (all but four written on paper from the Foreign Office, where he preferred to work and hold Cabinet meetings rather than at Number 10), all of which are on file at the PRO. Even this number is not a completely reliable indicator of the number of Cabinet meetings, because some of these letters are also responses to questions raised by Queen Victoria, rather than purely minutes/notes of actual Cabinet meetings.[17]

The format Salisbury uses to begin his letters is: 'Lord Salisbury with his humble duty to Your Majesty respectfully submits that a Cabinet Council was held today.'[18] The letters use 'Cabinet Council' and 'Cabinet' interchangeably. Although in his letter dated 23 February, he says the 'weekly' Cabinet was held today,[19] the meetings were not, in fact, held weekly. Cabinet met six times in February, but only four times in March and April combined (on the evidence of Salisbury's letters). There were no Cabinet meetings between 3 August and 17 November. In his letter of 4 August, Salisbury says 'it was the last Cabinet to be held before the recess'.[20]

What of Cabinet committees? Their origins have been traced back to 1716, and sub-Cabinet ministerial meetings on defence issues in particular were not uncommon in the eighteenth and nineteenth centuries.[21] When the Conservatives were returned to office in 1895, Salisbury constituted a Defence Committee under the lord president, the Duke of Devonshire, a move prompted by the 1890 Hartington Commission which examined the need for better co-ordination between the two defence departments, the War Office and the Admiralty. A letter of 8 December shows that proposals to entrench this existing Defence Com-

---

[16] Mackintosh, *The British Cabinet* reports twenty-six references to Cabinet committees before 1900. With the exception of an *ad hoc* Defence Committee spasmodically in the 1850s, the committees were concerned with the drafting of legislation.

[17] Document from the Public Records Office (PRO) in Kew, CAB 41/25/01.

[18] (PRO) CAB 41/25/29.

[19] (PRO) CAB 41/25/33.

[20] (PRO) CAB 41/25/48.

[21] Catterall and Brady, 'Cabinet Committees', 70.

mittee were a subject of some controversy. The principal catalyst for the move was the peculiar demands of the Boer War: the previous major war, the Crimean, had prompted the establishment of a War Committee in August 1855, so a precedent existed. In June, Salisbury complained that the 'discussion . . . took some time and to no distinct result. It concerned the constitution of the Defence Committee . . . the subject will be reviewed week to week.'[22]

The future role and importance of Cabinet committees more generally were the cause of some debate and difference between senior members of the 1900 Cabinet. Although this discussion had general implications, it was particularly focused on the Defence Committee. A memo by Devonshire dated 2 November states that 'The [Defence] Committee has not been . . . more than an informal Committee of the Cabinet . . . The Committee has met rarely, and generally without any definite agenda . . . No minutes have been kept . . . [it] has perhaps relieved the Cabinet from some professional discussion'. He then goes on to propose certain changes; the committee should 'meet at certain definite intervals, that it should have a Secretary or Joint Secretaries, and that agenda for its meetings should be prepared . . . Minutes kept'.[23]

A memo by George Goschen, the first lord of the Admiralty, dated 22 November 1895, had argued, however, that Cabinet committees should be kept limited, because otherwise members would not be able to do all their work efficiently.[24] Lord Lansdowne, secretary of state for war, argued for the merits of informal committees that would meet during the parliamentary recess.[25] Goschen, however, with remarkable prescience, cautioned that 'it would be a strong thing for a Committee to have the right to decide a matter without appeal. The Cabinet must surely have the power of ultimate review.'[26] Goschen was anxious for the Defence Committee to have strictly limited jurisdiction, only over those areas not the sole responsibility of the War Office or the Admiralty.[27]

On 20 January, the Defence Committee met, and the records describe the outcome as follows: 'Paragraph 5: The War Office was authorized to take action in accordance with the Secretary of State's recommendation.'[28]

---

[22] (PRO) CAB 41/25/51.
[23] (PRO) CAB 37/53/71.
[24] (PRO) CAB 37/53/71.
[25] (PRO) CAB 37/53/71.
[26] (PRO) CAB 37/53/71.
[27] Mackintosh, *The British Cabinet*, p. 277.
[28] (PRO) CAB 37/52/05.

In paragraph 7, it was decided to raise twelve new battalions—the inducement for men to join being a 'bounty' to be fixed 'in consultation with the Treasury'.[29] This record certainly shows that the Defence Committee possessed the power to make important decisions on its own, and indeed that efficient records were being made, despite what Devonshire thought.

Records of the Defence Committee (dated 22 January) do not always allow one to reach firm conclusions about the committee's jurisdiction. Garnet Wolseley (commander-in-chief of Britain's armed forces, 1895–1900) had written a letter to the secretary of state for war urging an increase in the number of army battalions. This letter was presented to the Defence Committee. In Lansdowne's minutes, which are the only surviving record of this meeting in the PRO, he completely dismisses Wolseley's plea. It is hard to tell—impossible going solely by the public records—whether this dismissal reflects the discussion of the committee or Lansdowne's personal views.[30]

The records of Defence Committee meetings in general, however, appear to show that, once agreement had been reached on an issue, the departments concerned went away and implemented it. Cabinet did not have to review everything the committee did. It is important, however, not to exaggerate the importance of the embryonic committee system in 1900, nor indeed the Defence Committee, which had only a limited role in the conduct of the war. After the Boer War was over, the Defence Committee was reconstituted in December 1902 with the task to think and plan strategically. In February 1903 it was re-titled the Committee of Imperial Defence (CID). This was the first major reform to the Cabinet system in the twentieth century, even if the CID lost some of its unifying influence as the War Office and Admiralty began to go their own ways—until the First World War prompted the need again for close co-ordination. Apart from the Defence Committee, no Cabinet committee appears to have met in 1900. The 'Cabinet system' was thus very simple: full Cabinet, and the one subordinate committee.

The precise content of Cabinet meetings in 1900 is difficult to ascertain, because there were no agenda nor minutes. Nevertheless, the Cabinet papers of the year do provide a clear indication of the preoccupations of the day. Unsurprisingly, the papers are dominated by the Boer War and the Empire. Most Cabinet papers of this period are of four kinds:

---

[29] (PRO) CAB 37/52/05.
[30] (PRO) CAB 37/52/05.

copies of correspondence; memoranda on issues, laying out options and generally making a recommendation; purely factual papers – detail which Cabinet needed to make a decision; and draft bills with explanations/critiques/arguments. Table 4.1 analyses the frequency with which key topics are mentioned in the Cabinet papers.

Table 4.1 Key issues in Cabinet, 1900

Issues	Number of papers in which mentioned
Boer War and South Africa	31
Defence	24
Foreign affairs and Empire	24
Economic affairs	5
Miscellaneous	8

An insight into the system in operation for co-ordinating government at the centre came in February 1900, when the Eastern Extension Telegraph Company sought to secure and extend its cable monopoly (along with other business partners) in China. The whole debate on the extension of the monopoly with and within government seems to have been carried out solely through correspondence (excepting, of course, informal discussion, of which there are few records). The Foreign Office sent out letters about the proposals to the India Office, the Colonial Office and the Treasury. These departments replied with their views. The Treasury responded with a letter about (a) the wording of the contract; and (b) the desirability of monopoly. This was addressed to the Foreign Office (FO). The FO forwarded the letter to the General Post Office (GPO), asking for comments and views. The GPO responded to the Treasury letter, and letters from the Colonial Office and the India Office after two months. These letters were addressed to the FO which forwarded it to the Treasury which responded to the FO. The system appears to have been overly drawn-out, and itself suggests the benefit, with government's work increasing in size and complexity, of having an extended system of Cabinet committees to co-ordinate government thinking.

Collective Cabinet responsibility for decisions was feeling the strain in 1900, even with a Cabinet system far simpler than anything that was to follow. In a letter dated 24 April—which was printed for and circulated to Cabinet—Lansdowne said, regarding the publication of the Spion Kop despatches during the Boer War: 'Our [the Cabinet] decisions are not always very distinctly intimated to the Ministers who have to carry them out, but in this case I can recall nothing which, in my understanding, bore any resemblance to such a decision as was, I am now told, arrived at.'[31] Lansdowne claimed that, as he had nothing to do with the decision, he felt estranged from it—laments which many a modern Cabinet minister would share. Lansdowne's biographer records Salisbury wondering whether 'our traditional practice of not recording Cabinet decisions is a wise one!'[32]

A. J. Balfour, the first lord of the Treasury, and Salisbury's successor in 1902, had his own criticisms of the quality of Cabinet discussion:[33] ' . . . our discussions are not so profitable as they might be', he said, because ' . . . as soon as we meet we seem to get immersed in some question of detail, and never come to a decision upon the broader lines of policy, in harmony with which all questions of detail should be settled'.[34] Lord George Hamilton (secretary of state for India) shared Balfour's view, denouncing Cabinet in a letter to Lord Curzon in September 1900 as 'a most effete organisation. This is mainly the Chief's fault. He won't press for a decision, he does not keep people to the point, and all sorts of irrelevant trivialities are discussed *ad nauseum* to the exclusion of affairs of real importance.'[35]

The powerful and ubiquitous hand of the Treasury can be seen in the records, although control was not as pervasive as it came to be after the First World War. In May 1900, on the subject of increasing reserves of armaments and military stores, Lansdowne said: 'There has been a considerable amount of official and unofficial discussion between the Treasury and the War Office.'[36] As a result of the discussion, the Treasury offered a compromise. If the War Office accepted this position, then the Treasury would accept the 'remainder of the proposals with a few reservations on minor points. If the War Office declines, the Treasury withdraws its concession.'[37] This horse-trading seems typical, and Lansdowne took the matter to Cabinet only because he found the Treasury's terms unacceptable.

---

[31] (PRO) CAB 37/52/43.

[32] Thomas Wodenhouse Legh, Baron Newton, *Lansdowne: A Biography* (Macmillan, 1929), p. 184.

[33] Though his leadership saw Cabinet become 'notoriously informal', where 'senior civil servants were shocked to hear ministers addressing each other in Cabinet by their Christian names'. From Jane Ridley and Clayre Percy (eds), *The Letters of Arthur Balfour and Lady Elcho 1885–1917* (Hamish Hamilton, 1992), p. 197.

[34] (PRO) CAB 37/52/27.

[35] Andrew Roberts *Salisbury: Victorian Titan* (Weidenfeld & Nicolson, 1999), p. 605.

[36] (PRO) CAB 37/53/51.

[37] (PRO) CAB 37/53/51.

So what precise role did Cabinet play in 1900? It was clearly the core decision-making body. The Defence Committee was the only sub-group in existence, and it was demonstrably subordinate to full Cabinet. Secondary decisions could be taken interdepartmentally. No rule book existed dictating which decision should be taken at Cabinet, and which could be taken below. But the convention of Cabinet supremacy on all decisions judged to be primary can be clearly seen. Great stress was put on keeping Cabinet informed of all important matters. During the winter months of the Boer War in 1900–1, for example, the commanders in South Africa telegraphed the secretary of state for war with the latest news. Copies of these telegrams were released to Cabinet either on the same day or the next. The official documents also suggest a sense of collective decision-making, with phrases like 'we ought to' or 'we should consider' cropping up frequently. Cabinet, and not Salisbury, nor a departmental head, is referred to as the ultimate authority and had the 'power of ultimate review'. There are references to schemes being sanctioned by Cabinet, and there is a sense of Cabinet being powerful and sovereign, even if the mechanics of government and the volume of business meant it was regularly bypassed on secondary matters.

There is no doubt that Cabinet in 1900 was *the* prime decision-making body.

Cabinet in 1920

In January 1920, the First World War had been over for just more than a year, and the forceful David Lloyd George had just begun his fourth year as prime minister. The coalition government created in December 1916 had been continued into peacetime and through the general election of December 1918. Throughout much of 1919, the unusual arrangement had existed of the War Cabinet continuing in existence alongside the reconstituted yet subordinate full Cabinet, which focused on domestic issues. The bodies were 'merged' in October 1919.[38]

Eighty-two Cabinet meetings were held in 1920 (see Table 4.2) compared to a probable only 26 in 1900. Meetings were mostly held in 10 Downing Street though some were held in Andrew Bonar Law's room

---

[38] John Turner, 'Cabinets, Committees and Secretariats: The Higher Direction of War', in Kathleen Burk (ed.), *War and the State: The Transformation of British Government 1914–1919* (George Allen & Unwin, 1982), p. 76.

in the House of Commons (Bonar Law was Conservative Party leader and lord privy seal).[39]

Most meetings were chaired by Lloyd George; but Bonar Law chaired every meeting from 12 April to 19 May, when the prime minister was away from London. Cabinet secretary, Sir Maurice Hankey, complained in his diary: 'This week (8 May) I have had to shove along the Cabinet under Bonar Law.'[40] Most meetings began around 11.30am or 12 noon. A few, however, were held in the evening—the latest starting time was 7pm, on 9 August. There were two meetings in a day on five occasions— 29 January, 13 December, 17 December, 29 December and 30 December. No meetings were held from 17 August to 14 September—almost a month, compared to more than three months without a meeting in the late summer and autumn of 1900.

Table 4.2 Cabinet meetings held in each year, 1920–30

Year	Number of Cabinet meetings
1920	82
1921	93
1922	72
1923	59
1924	67
1925	61
1926	67
1927	64
1928	58
1929	55
1930	73

Dramatic differences can be seen in the records of Cabinet meetings for 1900 and 1920. In 1920, every Cabinet meeting had at least one official, if not two, from the new Cabinet Secretariat, recording minutes.[41] In 1920 the two officials most often present were Sir Maurice Hankey, the long-serving Cabinet secretary (1916–38) and his assistant Thomas Jones, or both. These officials were completely trusted by ministers, despite the comparative novelty of their positions—Hankey, for example, was sent a copy of 'a very secret memorandum' from R. P. M. Gower, on behalf

---

[39] On 12 April 1920, a message was circulated at 11am that Bonar Law wanted a Cabinet called at 12 o'clock, which met at the appointed hour 'in the dining-room at No. 10 as advantage was being taken of the absence of the P.M. to clean the Cabinet room': Jones, *Whitehall Diary*, vol. 1, p. 111.

[40] Stephen Roskill, *Hankey, Man of Secrets*: vol. 2, *1919–31* (Collins, 1972), p. 164.

[41] John Turner, *Lloyd George's Secretariat* (Cambridge University Press, 1980) pp. 19–21.

of the chancellor, and asked to 'arrange for the papers to be discussed at Cabinet in about a week or ten days time'.[42]

The minutes are detailed and tell us who attended Cabinet, who was in the chair, where the meetings were held, and at what time. Agendas were issued in advance of meetings and constituted the summons to the meetings. In theory, the agenda was settled by the prime minister. In practice, Hankey finalised it. The first item was usually foreign affairs, followed by domestic topics. The minutes are laid out in strict bureaucratic fashion with numbers for issues discussed.

The minutes faithfully record every discussion and conclusion of Cabinet, including parliamentary business, an area not recorded in Salisbury's letters of 1900 to Queen Victoria, but one which was to play such an important standing part in Cabinet agendas as the century evolved. Attached to minutes of most Cabinet meetings are several appendices, which are the papers Cabinet had before them at the time. Contrast this with 1900, when, as Andrew Roberts said, it was considered 'bad form' for ministers to record any notes of Cabinet meetings; and it was common practice for papers to be dropped in the coal fire after the meeting had been concluded.[43]

Despite the zealous professionalism in 1920, the system was not foolproof. In a Cabinet meeting on 11 February, the accuracy of the draft conclusions of the new Finance Committee was disputed: 'It was suggested that the above record did not correctly interpret the intentions of the Finance Committee.'[44] The minutes record the decision in favour of the immediate and entire withdrawal of an army division from India. The Cabinet records say that some ministers queried whether the government of India should have been consulted before the force was withdrawn. Lloyd George, however, said that, according to his recollection, the Finance Committee record was accurate.

The Cabinet system had developed greatly since 1900.[45] During the war a number of committees were established to oversee detailed business and to co-ordinate Whitehall departments and the vastly expanded Prime Minister's Office at Number 10. Many committees were transitory or *ad hoc*. But in June 1918, as the focus was switching to the post-war world, two standing committees—Home Affairs and Economic Defence

[42] (PRO) CAB 23/20/272.
[43] Author's interview with Andrew Roberts, 04.04.1999.
[44] (PRO) CAB 23/20/127.
[45] Turner, 'Cabinets, Committees and Secretariats', p. 64.

and Development—were established by Lloyd George, and both took decisions on minor or uncontroversial topics without reference to full Cabinet. There are numerous references in the 1920 records to Cabinet agreeing to refer a question to a committee, which could have the authority to settle it *on behalf of* Cabinet. On 7 January Cabinet debated the post-war future of the territorial force and decided that the 'subject be submitted to a Cabinet Committee . . . for consideration and report'.[46] But, later on in the same meeting, Cabinet decided to delegate decision-making completely: 'to refer the question of de-control without compensation to the Home Affairs Committee, with instructions to settle the matter on behalf of the Cabinet'.[47]

Committees were either standing, such as the Home Affairs Committee, or *ad hoc*, such as the committee set up to hammer out government policy for the future of Ireland. Several of these *ad hoc* committees, as records for the 1920s as a whole reveal, continued over long periods. The exact constitutional position of Cabinet and Cabinet committees was imprecise, and remained the subject of concern for some politicians. Austen Chamberlain, the chancellor of the Exchequer, described the Home Affairs Committee as 'almost a Cabinet within a cabinet!'[48] Again and again, one sees British government being run by convention, rather than by a rule book decreeing exactly which decisions should be taken at which level, and by which body.

Cabinet seemed at times almost carried away with the powerful new committee instrument it had at its disposal. A snapshot of a spawning Cabinet committee system can be seen in the Cabinet's setting up of a Pensions Committee on 11 March.[49] The committee duly reported: 'The Committee recommends that an Inter-Departmental Committee should be appointed to consider the best machinery for giving effect to the above recommendations.'[50]

Despite the occasional worries expressed by ministers in the official papers that Cabinet was setting up too many committees, there is no doubt that most ministers accepted that they were being set up as a response to a real need. The scope of government had grown considerably in the twenty years up to 1920—as the trebling in the number of Cabinet meetings from 1900 to 1920 itself indicates—and it was found

[46] (PRO) CAB 23/20/35.
[47] (PRO) CAB 23/20/38.
[48] Sir Charles Petrie, *The Life and Work of the Rt Hon. Sir Austen Chamberlain* (Cassell, 1940), vol. 2, pp. 138–43.
[49] (PRO) CAB 23/20/237–40.   [50] (PRO) CAB 23/21/97.

to be increasingly difficult for Cabinet to make every important decision in the post-war world, with government adopting new economic and social commitments, and enhanced overseas work in the new era of the League of Nations and multilateral diplomacy (Lloyd George himself attended nine international conferences in 1920 alone), and with problems in Ireland remaining a major concern as they had been just before and during the First World War.

Despite the growing use of committees, Cabinet still remained the hub of the political system. In the meeting on 4 February, Cabinet granted a three-man committee 'full Cabinet powers' to complete the king's speech, but added the crucial caveat that the speech should be completed according to certain principles, which the *full* Cabinet proceeded to discuss and state.[51] Also, as Lord Curzon, the foreign secretary, angrily wrote, Cabinet was important enough to go against the advice of the prime minister and 'two successive foreign secretaries'[52] on an important foreign policy issue (the question of the Turks in Constantinople, on which more below).

A new body had made an appearance in late 1919. This is the 'Conference of Ministers', an *ad hoc* group of ministers and others who met to discuss certain specific problems and issues. These conferences varied in size from three to ten ministers. Also present were senior officials from the Treasury and other key departments. 'Conferences' could have Cabinet powers—for example, a conference that met on 4 May 1920 at Downing Street considered a memorandum by the Ministry of Transport concerning a draft bill. Crucially, conferences were often initiated by Cabinet committees to discuss a problem and report to *Cabinet*. The conference fell short of being an inner Cabinet because the prime minister was not always present, the membership varied and because officials and even non-governmental figures were in attendance. The name 'conference' derived from the fact that, as non-ministers could be present, it would be inappropriate to call them 'Cabinet' committees. Conferences disappeared with Lloyd George's departure in 1922, when incoming Prime Minister Bonar Law axed them, replacing them wholly by Cabinet committees: 159 conferences met between October 1919 and September 1922.

The official records reveal quite how central to government the economy and social welfare had become. The unparalleled devastation

---

[51] (PRO) CAB 23/20/77.
[52] (PRO) CAB 23/20/30.

and disruption caused by the war meant reconstruction had to have the highest priority—'The war fundamentally altered the shape and size of British government.'[53] Cabinet discussed at length the state of the economy, unemployment and the level of government spending and, more fundamentally, how the state of the economy affected the British people. The key areas of discussion in Cabinet meetings were therefore defence, foreign policy, Empire, economic affairs and social welfare. With the expanding size of government, especially over domestic policy, the Treasury had acquired a tighter grip on Cabinet by 1919–20. During the war, the Treasury had, to some extent, lost control of spending, in part because of Lloyd George, the expense of the war itself, and the actions of the business people running the production departments, especially the Ministry of Munitions. The Treasury powerfully reasserted its position after the war. As a result, every Cabinet spending decision had to be agreed with the Treasury.[54]

There is one outstanding example of Cabinet independence and importance in the year. In January, Cabinet was much occupied with the question of the Turks in Constantinople. Were they to be able to remain in control in Constantinople under British and international supervision, or were they to be turned out? This subject excited much debate, with a 'conference' discussing it in addition to lengthy and protracted argument in Cabinet. Curzon wanted the Turks out so that the British would control the Straits. In the end, Cabinet decided against Curzon, and Turkish possession was included in the Treaty of Sèvres. The records recall Curzon's response: 'I ask to place on record my earnest and emphatic dissent from the decision arrived at by the majority of the Cabinet yesterday—in opposition to the advice of the prime minister and two successive foreign secretaries—to retain the Turk in Constantinople.'[55] This clearly shows that Cabinet was prepared to be independent and take decisions contrary to the wills of the prime minister and foreign secretary.

The unusual conditions of Lloyd George needing to maintain the Coalition gave Cabinet as a whole in 1920, as it did individual ministers, a peculiar authority, which offset the powerful position Lloyd George had acquired personally, particularly on the world stage. Cabinet's insist-

---

[53] Eunan O'Halpin, *Head of the Civil Service: A Study of Sir Warren Fisher* (Routledge, 1989), p. 29.
[54] Ibid., pp. 29–31.
[55] (PRO) CAB 23/20/30.

ence that Soviet Russia not be accorded recognition was another occasion when he was overruled by Cabinet. By 1920 Cabinet had become the principal decision-taking body in government. Although Cabinet could assert itself when it wished, no longer just secondary but also primary issues were being settled at Cabinet committee level. Cabinet committees thus took decisions as representatives of the full Cabinet.

Cabinet in 1939

In January 1939, Neville Chamberlain was in his second year as prime minister at the head of the National Government. In contrast to his predecessor Stanley Baldwin, he was a crisp chair of Cabinet and its committees. Forty-nine meetings of Cabinet were held until 2 September 1939, the day before Britain declared war on Germany. The War Cabinet then met 123 times until the end of the year. Meetings of the peacetime Cabinet were mostly held at 10 Downing Street on Wednesdays at 11am, which seemed to have become an accepted time. In the meeting on 24 April 1939, for example, the prime minister specifically sought to reschedule the time of the next regular Wednesday meeting: 'The Prime Minister asked his colleagues to take note that it would be necessary for the Meeting on the 26 April to be at 10.0 a.m. in order that he might . . . see the . . . Leaders of the opposition before lunch time on that day.'[56]

The War Cabinet necessarily had quite a different rhythm. At its first meeting, it was decided that meetings should be held daily, at 11.30am at 10 Downing Street.[57] Meetings could be held at irregular times in emergencies, as foreshadowed by the meeting on 2 September 1939 at 11.30pm when Cabinet debated what action to take about Hitler and Poland. The minutes record: 'The Cabinet was called together at very short notice and a number of Ministers did not arrive until a considerable time after the proceedings had started.'[58] The meeting terminated at around 12.15am on 3 September.

The size of the Cabinet in 1939 (until 2 September) was between twenty and twenty-three, a relatively fixed number compared to twenty in 1920 and twenty to twenty-two in 1960. The composition of these Cabinets changed, however, especially between 1939 and 1960. The compositions of the peace and War Cabinets are listed in Table 4.3.

[56] (PRO) CAB 23/99/23.
[57] (PRO) CAB 65/01/16.
[58] (PRO) CAB 23/100/474.

Table 4.3 Cabinet in 1939

Chamberlain's peacetime Cabinet	
1	Prime minister
2	Chancellor of the Exchequer
3	Home secretary
4	Foreign secretary
5	Secretary for dominion affairs
6	Secretary for colonies
7	Lord privy seal
8	Secretary of state for India
9	Secretary of state for air
10	First Lord of Admiralty
11	President of the Board of Trade
12	Minister of labour
13	President of the Board of Education
14	Lord president of Council
15	Minister for co-ordination of defence
16	Secretary of state for war
17	Secretary of state for Scotland
18	Minister of agriculture and fisheries
19	Minister of health
20	Minister of transport
21	Chancellor of duchy of Lancaster
22	Lord Chancellor
23	Minister without portfolio
War Cabinet posts after 3 September	
1	Prime minister (Chamberlain)
2	Chancellor of the Exchequer (Simon)
3	Foreign secretary (Halifax)
4	Minister for co-ordination of defence (Chatfield)
5	Lord privy seal (Hoare)
6	Secretary of state for war (Hore-Belisha)
7	First Lord of Admiralty (Churchill)
8	Secretary of state for air (Wood)
9	Minister without portfolio (Hankey)
10	Minister of supply (Burgin)

On the declaration of war with Germany, all members of Cabinet voluntarily surrendered their portfolios to Neville Chamberlain: on the evening of 3 September 1939 he announced the formation of the War Cabinet, with just nine members. The Committee for Imperial Defence, whose work it subsumed, was immediately disbanded. The form of the Cabinet records, however, remained largely the same as in 1920, with the same professionalism and format evident. Edward Bridges (1938–47) had now replaced Hankey as Cabinet secretary after his twenty-two year stint. Hankey had forged and shaped the Cabinet Office: Bridges continued Hankey's traditions, especially in his first years.

One difference—superficial as it may seem—but indicative of a greater degree of bureaucratisation, is that agendas in 1939 were attached to the rest of the minutes for Cabinet meetings. Agendas were typed and circulated prior to the meeting; the agenda for the Cabinet meeting on 2 March is dated 24 February 1939. Meetings that did not have agendas were those called at short notice—such as meetings on 18 March and 20 March 1939. Agendas in 1939 were beginning to take on a more standardised form. The issue of 'Palestine', for example, was almost always present, with an 'if required' in brackets after it, but agendas had not yet acquired the parliamentary, home affairs, overseas affairs sequence of latter years.

The records for the meeting on 7 June are unusual, because there are handwritten corrections to the records: ' . . . it was clear that Italy would respond very favourably to any overtures from France' was the typed minute; 'was clear' was scratched out and 'might be hoped' was handwritten above it while 'very' was scratched out altogether. The modified record reads: 'it might be hoped that Italy would respond favourably to any overtures from France'.[59] This type of handwritten correction is very rare in 1939.

A continuing feature is that the records omit to mention any details of the Budget. This was done deliberately: as the records state, 'In view of the great importance of secrecy, the details, in accordance with precedent, are not recorded in the Cabinet minutes.'[60]

Bilateral and trilateral decision-taking meetings with the prime minister that became prevalent in the last third of the century were already in evidence in 1939. On 18 January, for example, the issue of currency legislation was raised, and the minute reads: 'What the Chancellor asked, if his colleagues agreed, was that he should settle the terms of the legislation as soon as he could with the Prime Minister, and that he should be authorised to bring the Bill before the Committee of Home Affairs in time for its presentation to the House.'[61] His colleagues posed no objection.

Prior to his asking the Cabinet for permission to settle it with the prime minister, Sir John Simon, the chancellor, had made a statement on currency legislation to Cabinet. His statement is almost exactly the same, with only a few changes in words, as his briefing from his officials, or,

[59] (PRO) CAB 23/99/305.
[60] (PRO) CAB 23/99/305.
[61] (PRO) CAB 23/97/41.

as one put it, 'the stuff which we have suggested to the Chancellor that he should say at the Cabinet tomorrow'.[62] These words appear in a letter written to Sir Edward Bridges by Sir Richard Hopkins (later permanent secretary at the Treasury, 1942–5). At the time, Hopkins was second secretary to the Treasury, and the 'we' refers to the Treasury civil servants. Cabinet ministers since the emergence of the 'modern' civil service in the mid-nineteenth century had often reflected what their departmental briefing advised them, but the records do not always allow one to see it so blatantly.

During 1938, Chamberlain had become used to taking key decisions with his three most senior and trusted Cabinet colleagues, Simon (chancellor), Sir Samuel Hoare (home secretary) and Lord Halifax (foreign secretary from February). During the Munich crisis that autumn, these four met and settled policy before telling Cabinet. Here one sees clear evidence of an 'inner Cabinet' in operation, something which occurred periodically throughout the century, depending on the prime minister's taste, and the political position. Chamberlain's grouping contained the few posts considered the most senior in Cabinet: at other times, the prime minister might form an inner Cabinet containing trusted favourites who might not always hold the most senior posts.

What also becomes clear is that, during 1939, Cabinet committees were taking an even bigger role than in 1920. The 1920s and 1930s saw Cabinet committees spawn to become an accepted and essential feature of the Cabinet system. The Committee of Imperial Defence was used to taking decisions independently of Cabinet. The Home Affairs Committee oversaw domestic policy and, critically, also legislation, which gave it a role of pivotal importance. The Foreign Policy Committee, created by Neville Chamberlain, had become another important new committee: Hoare conceded that its meetings 'tended to short-circuit the full Cabinet' but qualified it by saying that its decisions were always reported to the Cabinet and its approval obtained.[63] The records, however, do not always bear out Hoare's assertion. In October 1939, a powerful Military Co-ordination Committee was constituted, which took over some of the implementation tasks and authority of the disbanded Committee of Imperial Defence.

The purpose of the War Cabinet was very different from that of

---

[62] PRO CAB 23/97.

[63] Viscount Templewood (Sir Samuel Hoare), *Nine Troubled Years*, 1st edn 1954 (Greenwood Press, 1976), p. 290.

Chamberlain's peacetime Cabinet. The daily round of meetings provided a forum where members could compare notes, and where they were told what was going on elsewhere to co-ordinate the war effort. Because of the pressure of time, ministers often had to take decisions individually or bilaterally away from Cabinet, and so frequent meetings were essential if cohesion and understanding was to be retained.

Deliberation did occur in War Cabinets, but it was limited. On 5 September 1939, for example, a 'discussion took place on methods of expediting the France-Anglo-Turkish Treaty negotiations'.[64] After a brief exchange, the War Cabinet unanimously agreed that the United Kingdom wanted to have Turkey on its side; the sticking point was a gold bullion loan to Turkey. But, 'the discussion was not carried further in view of the fact that the Chancellor of the Exchequer and the Secretary of State for Foreign Affairs had arranged to meet later in the day to discuss the matter'.[65]

It was not necessary for the prime minister/chancellor/foreign secretary always to be present at the War Cabinet meetings. On 10 September, the War Cabinet meeting consisted of only three—lord privy seal, secretary of state for war and Lord Hankey—as well as the chiefs of staff, but they still made decisions on censorship, the response to Poland, and so on.[66]

The 1939 peacetime Cabinet was a transitional body. It was a blend of the principal decision-taking body of the inter-war years, and the principal ratifying body of the early post-war years. The growth of business, and a settled and increasingly sophisticated network of Cabinet committees meant, even in the absence of any blueprint of how the Cabinet system should be operating, that increasingly decisions were taken not only in committees, but were also merely being referred up to Cabinet for ratification on the nod. Cabinet committees were assumed to be representative of Cabinet at large, and contained not just the departmental specialists but also the political heavyweights who could have their legitimate say at that level.

Cabinet in 1960

In 1960, Harold Macmillan was in his fourth year as Conservative prime minister, and the party had just won its third general election in suc-

[64] (PRO) CAB 65/01/26.
[65] (PRO) CAB 65/01/27.
[66] (PRO) CAB 65/01/39.

cession, in October 1959. With Macmillan in Africa on his 'winds of change' tour from the beginning of the year until mid-February, Cabinet was chaired by Rab Butler, home secretary. Sixty-five meetings were held in 1960, but there does not seem to have been a regular rhythm to meetings, as there had been in 1939 and 1920. There was a bias to Tuesday mornings in 10 Downing Street starting at 10.30/11am, but several meetings were held on other days, particularly Thursdays, at different times and in different places (especially the prime minister's room in the House of Commons and from mid-year in Admiralty House, where Number 10 moved in July 1960 while 10 Downing Street was being rebuilt). There were no meetings held between 8 August and 15 September.

The composition of the Cabinet was now very different to pre-war days. The emergence of the secretary of state for defence as the key figure after the 1958 white paper meant that the three separate service ministers were no longer members of Cabinet. The post of secretary of state for India had ceased to exist on Indian independence in 1947. The minister of health was also out of Cabinet (albeit briefly, from 1952 to 1962). New positions—minister of housing and local government, minister of aviation and postmaster-general—reflected new governmental concerns and priorities. Table 4.4 shows a comparison of the composition of the Cabinets of 1920, 1939 (peacetime) and 1960.

The Cabinet system had burgeoned and consolidated since 1939. At the apex of the system were the standing committees. The Defence Committee ('Imperial' had been dropped from its title after 1939) was the longest standing committee, tracing its origins back to 1903 and before. In 1963, it merged with the Foreign Affairs Committee (which had enjoyed an irregular existence over the previous thirty-five years) to be called the Defence and Overseas Policy Committee. The Home Affairs Committee, created in 1917, was the second longest-serving committee, and considered and co-ordinated all domestic legislation and issues. It had periodically been known by the title the 'Lord President's Committee', and it had spawned three further standing committees: the Legislation Committee, created in 1940, which ensured that all bills accorded with decisions of the Cabinet; the Future Legislation Committee in 1945, which prepared the programme for the next parliamentary session; and the Economic Policy Committee, whose field was economic management and finance. A sixth standing committee in 1960 was the Atomic Energy Committee, although it ceased to exist as a separate entity in the early 1960s.

The standing committees all had a variety of subcommittees, which

Table 4.4 Cabinet posts in 1920, 1939 and 1960

	1920	1939	1960
1 Prime minister	•	•	•
2 Chancellor of the Exchequer	•	•	•
3 Home secretary	•	•	•
4 Foreign secretary	•	•	•
5 Secretary for dominion affairs		•	
6 Secretary for colonies		•	•
7 Lord privy seal*	•	•	•
8 Secretary of state for India	•	•	
9 Secretary of state for air		•	
10 First Lord of Admiralty	•	•	
11 President of the Board of Trade	•	•	•
12 Minister of labour	•	•	•
13 President of the Board of Education**	•	•	•
14 Lord president of Council***	•	•	•
15 Minister for co-ordination of defence		•	•
16 Secretary of state for war****	•	•	
17 Secretary of state for Scotland	•	•	•
18 Minister of agriculture and fisheries	•	•	•
19 Minister of health	•	•	
20 Minister of transport	•	•	•
21 Chancellor of duchy of Lancaster		•	•
22 Lord Chancellor	•	•	•
23 Minister of supply		•	
24 Chief secretary for Ireland	•		
25 Minister without portfolio	•	•	
26 Minister of housing and local government and Welsh affairs			•
27 Paymaster general			•
28 Minister of aviation			•

* Also minister for science in 1960.
** Also minister of education in 1960.
*** Also secretary of state for Commonwealth relations in 1960.
**** Also secretary of state for war and air in 1920.

had also grown in number and regularity since 1939, as had the number of *ad hoc* committees. (In 1960 these were called 'miscellaneous committees', and bore the name 'MISC' and then a number. 'MISC' alternated at change of governments with 'GEN', an abbreviation of 'general committees'. This alternation of name still exists today.) One such miscellaneous committee in 1960 was set up soon after the 1959 general election with the brief to consider student numbers in higher education. This body's work fed into the Committee on Higher Education under Lord Robbins which was set up in February 1961. Other miscellaneous committees were reconstituted at set times annually, such as the agriculture committee for the annual review of prices for farming produce.

These *ad hoc* committees were growing in number. On 19 July 1960, the prime minister set up a Cabinet committee to consider the question of assistance to Muscat and Oman. 'For this purpose he would invite the Paymaster General [Lord Mills] to act as Chairman of a small Committee of Ministers from the Foreign Office, the Treasury, the Colonial Office and the War Office.'[67] Some *ad hoc* committees could lie dormant. While discussing the immigration of coloured people on 26 July, for example, the home secretary said: 'It would . . . be useful if the Cabinet Committee which had previously examined this problem could be reconstituted in the autumn to keep it under review.'[68]

The records frequently show Cabinet as the body which legitimised decisions taken by individual ministers whose departments were in charge of that decision. The records show that Cabinet generally approved the minister's proposal: the raising of fundamental objections, and the overturning of decisions were rare.

Economic concerns dominated Cabinet discussions. The Budget was discussed in Cabinet on 2 April, but, as usual, no record was kept. Chancellor Derrick Heathcoat Amory sought in February to raise revenue by increasing NHS contributions by 1 shilling (5p): several policy ministers objected and the matter was passed on for resolution by the Economic Policy Committee.[69] In June, Heathcoat Amory was bewailing: 'Many firms were still not sufficiently export-minded: unlike their European competitors, they tended to concentrate too much on the easier home market.'[70] His caution convinced Cabinet to delay increasing old age pensions until at least April 1961 'when it could appropriately be financed by increased contributions'.[71] In these examples, one sees decisions being deferred to a standing committee, one sees Cabinet being used by the chancellor as a soundingboard to voice his concerns, and one sees it also being used as a decision-making forum.

In external affairs, it was colonial matters which dominated the first half of the year. By 1960, the government had decided that South Africa would gain independence on the basis of majority rule: the main questions were exactly how, the character of the future regime and its relationship with Britain. Deliberations in full Cabinet saw a mixture of genuine decision-taking and mere information giving. On 22 February,

[67] (PRO) CAB 128/34/192.
[68] (PRO) CAB 128/34/203.
[69] (PRO) CAB 128/34/38–40.
[70] (PRO) CAB 128/34/160.
[71] (PRO) CAB 128/34/136.

for example, Iain Macleod, colonial secretary, told Cabinet that Britain would assume financial responsibility for the East African Land Forces.[72] Lord Home, Commonwealth secretary, meanwhile went on his tour to southern Africa in mid-February with precise instructions from Cabinet about what he could say, including the offer of withdrawal of British 'reserved powers'[73] in Southern Rhodesia. Genuine debates took place in Cabinet in May and June on the issue of whether it was desirable for South Africa to remain as a republic within the Commonwealth, especially following the outcry at the Sharpeville killings in March.

In relations with the superpowers, one again finds conflicting views from the records of Cabinet's precise jurisdiction. On some occasions Macmillan and his subservient foreign secretary Selwyn Lloyd seem to be merely keeping Cabinet informed. On other occasions Cabinet is deciding and even checking the prime minister. Macmillan seems to have had a largely free hand in preparing for the summit meeting planned for July in Paris, but cancelled following the shooting down of the American U-2 spy plane over the Soviet Union on 1 May. Macmillan told Cabinet it was 'too early to decide whether the Soviet Government had deliberately decided to pursue a more aggressive policy'.[74] But it was Cabinet which debated whether Macmillan should attend the UN General Assembly in late September: at its meeting on 22 September, Cabinet decided Macmillan should attend so that 'the case for the West was fully presented'.[75] Cabinet also played a key role in 1960 in deciding whether Britain should apply to join the EEC. A prolonged debate took place on 13 July, with firm opinions on either side: Macmillan concluded the discussion saying he would tell the House that the government saw 'insuperable difficulties in the way of our accepting membership of the Community'.[76]

Cabinet was clearly dominant in discussions over Britain's strategic defence, albeit influenced heavily by the opinions of the Defence Committee. On 13 April, Cabinet accepted the Defence Committee's recommendation to scrap Britain's independent ballistic nuclear missile capacity, Blue Streak.[77] Macmillan had discussed with the Americans in Washington in March the possibility of their stationing US Polaris missile

[72] (PRO) CAB 128/34/62.
[73] (PRO) CAB 128/34/58.
[74] (PRO) CAB 128/34/144.
[75] (PRO) CAB 128/34/224.
[76] (PRO) CAB 128/34/182.
[77] (PRO) CAB 128/34/119.

submarines in Scotland. Cabinet recommended that Loch Linnhe be offered to the USA, but Macmillan told Cabinet on 28 July that President Eisenhower regarded it as unsuitable, and he wanted a base on the Clyde.[78] Cabinet accordingly decided 'in view of the importance of preserving the special relations between the two countries'[79] to offer the Americans the facilities they sought, despite the likely local objections.

When Cabinet criticised or made suggestions, it was usually on political rather than expert grounds. On 27 October, for example, the timing of the introduction of legislation for increasing the NHS contribution was being debated. The Treasury view was that 'the decision should be announced after . . . the coming into operation of the new graduated pensions scheme in the following April'[80] since that would reduce the inconvenience and disruption to employers and businesses. That is sound economic sense, but Cabinet pointed out 'that the increase in the Health Service contribution would be more easily justified if it were presented in the context of the substantial increase in Government expenditure . . . revealed by the Estimates for the following financial year'.[81] Later on in the same minute, the Cabinet agreed 'that the necessary legislation should be introduced at the time the Estimates for the financial year 1961–62 were published'.[82]

The Cabinet did take important decisions while Macmillan was away on his long tour in Africa. On 26 January, for example, Cabinet discussed wage increases for railway workers and the possibility of industrial action by the railway unions. The Cabinet then said: 'the Minister of Transport should authorise the Chairman of the British Transport Commission to offer the railway unions an interim wage increase of not more than 4 per cent'.[83] Minister of labour Edward Heath reported that the unions rejected the offer. Cabinet agreed, albeit reluctantly, that this offer should be increased to 5 per cent,[84] which the unions accepted.

There is a counter-example where Cabinet deferred to Macmillan. On 3 February, Cabinet—still bereft of the prime minister—discussed a German request to build warships of 6,000 tons displacement and to manufacture influence mines. These were not allowed under the Brussels

---

[78] (PRO) CAB 128/34/212.
[79] (PRO) CAB 128/34/212.
[80] (PRO) CAB 128/34/243.
[81] (PRO) CAB 128/34/243.
[82] (PRO) CAB 128/34/244.
[83] (PRO) CAB 128/34/32.
[84] (PRO) CAB 128/34/52.

Treaty. The foreign secretary Selwyn Lloyd proposed that the Germans should be allowed the warships but not the mines. Cabinet agreed, but only 'Subject to the Prime Minister's comments'.[85]

In general, the 1960 records point to a Cabinet that was still the prime arbiter of the main political and economic decisions of the day. Recommendations from Cabinet committees, especially the principal standing committee, or directly from Cabinet ministers, clearly influenced Cabinet enormously. Subsidiary decisions were often decided below Cabinet, in committees, in *ad hoc* meetings and in departments, as Cabinet secretary Sir Norman Brook noted in 1961: 'we are doing rather less of our collective business at formal meetings of the Cabinet'. Macmillan, however, felt that, despite this, 'on the whole I think Ministers feel reasonably in the picture',[86] Cabinet indeed could and did overrule committees, as well as overrule the prime minister and other key ministers. In 1960, Cabinet was still the supreme body dominating the British body politic.

Cabinet in 1980

In 1980, Margaret Thatcher was entering her second year as prime minister and the Conservatives had been in office since May 1979. Outside the holiday periods, Cabinet met weekly at Number 10 on Thursdays, usually at 11am, and would run on until about 1pm. Mrs Thatcher was wary of letting meetings last longer because the press would think a crisis was looming: equally, she could spin out meetings on occasion— if she believed ending a meeting early would give the public a bad impression. In 1980, there were 45 meetings, the second highest number in any one year of her premiership. (1982, the year of the Falklands campaign, saw the most Cabinet meetings.) The major change in frequency had come in 1977, when Cabinet began to meet just once weekly, the average number of meetings falling from 60 to 40 a year.

Agendas in 1980 followed a common pattern. The business was of two kinds: with and without papers. Meetings opened with two standing items, for which papers were not circulated. Parliamentary affairs for the following week came first. Before the Cabinet, Mrs Thatcher chaired a half-hour meeting with the business managers of both Houses (i.e. the leaders of the Commons and Lords and the chief whips in both houses)

---

[85] (PRO) CAB 128/34/37.
[86] Catterall and Brady, 'Cabinet Committees', 67.

as well as the chief press secretary, so that she could be well briefed for the Cabinet. At Cabinet, the leader of the House opened the first item by giving a report on forthcoming business in the House of Commons. If there were no remarkable items, Mrs Thatcher would keep discussion of this first item to below thirty minutes. She would sometimes seek advice on how to handle the twice-weekly prime minister's questions; the second of the week took place in the House of Commons that afternoon. Ministers would raise concerns about the passage of their departmental business. A briefer discussion about business in the House of Lords took place. By the mid-1980s, a new standing item began to appear on the agenda, which was home affairs (hitherto incorporated in the parliamentary item on the agenda). After home affairs began to appear as a discrete item, ministers in charge of domestic departments had extra opportunities to raise current issues and problems.

Second came foreign affairs. Mrs Thatcher invited the foreign secretary, in 1980, Lord Carrington, to report to ministers on developments in the world of interest to Britain. These reports were found to be entertaining in both delivery and content, and it was rare for ministers to check the foreign secretary. When he had finished speaking, however, they did have the opportunity to ask questions, although the Overseas (hitherto Oversea) and Defence Committee had become the undisputed forum where primary and controversial issues were decided, while the routine and non-controversial decisions were taken interdepartmentally, or at bilateral and trilateral meetings. European Community affairs were discussed at the end of the second item.

The second part of the meeting was devoted to *ad hoc* subjects for which papers had usually been circulated in advance. If there were financial implications, the figures had to be agreed beforehand with the Treasury, which also possessed the right to demand that a matter be raised in full Cabinet. In 1980, there would typically be between one and four items raised under this heading. In July, Cabinet determined the overall level of public expenditure for the following three financial years, though in general Mrs Thatcher disliked discussing detailed public expenditure items in Cabinet. This July Cabinet, one of the most important of the year, had first begun to meet to decide public expenditure questions in the 1960s. Difficult spending decisions were taken over the summer and early autumn in an *ad hoc* committee, given the name MISC 62 (which meant it was the sixty-second such *ad hoc* committee to be set up under Mrs Thatcher's premiership). It was colloquially called the 'Star Chamber'.

Cabinet by 1980 was clearly ceasing to be the core body in British government. Decision-taking had passed squarely to the four principal standing committees: Home and Social Affairs (H) (an amalgam of the Home Affairs and Social Services Committees of 1960), Economic Affairs (EA), Overseas and Defence (OD) and Legislation (L) (which incorporated future legislation). The first three of these committees had a complex system of subcommittees in 1980. Important decisions on individual subjects were also debated and decided in the *ad hoc* committees (called MISC until the 1964 general election, GEN until 1970, MISC until 1974, GEN until 1979, and MISC again under the Conservatives). Compared to 1960 and earlier, standing Cabinet committees had become the key committees where decisions were taken and on which ministers wanted to serve. Chairing of standing committees was largely preordained, but Mrs Thatcher exercised more influence than her predecessors in appointing chairs of committees where she had discretion. She was content for committees to take decisions on unimportant issues, on important issues in which she was not interested, on important issues where she would have expected the committee to have reached the same decisions that she would have done and on important issues where she knew she would dislike the outcome but could do nothing about it.[87]

Mrs Thatcher thought the Cabinet system she inherited in 1979 was overblown and excessively bureaucratic: she thought that too much went to Cabinet and indeed to Cabinet committees. Increasingly from 1979/80, decisions were taken by her in small groups of ministers on either a bilateral or a multilateral basis. These were not Cabinet committees and were not serviced by the Cabinet Office. She found this a convenient way of conducting business and she found such caucus meetings much easier to control, not least because she found herself outnumbered in 1980 by the 'wets', who were ideologically opposed to her new style of free market Conservatism.

Mrs Thatcher's bypassing of the Cabinet system was increasingly resented by those ministers who felt uninvolved in decisions while still bound by collective responsibility. Two senior ministers—Francis Pym, defence secretary, and Jim Prior, employment secretary—complained to William Whitelaw, *de facto* deputy prime minister, and to Sir Robert Armstrong (Cabinet secretary 1979–87) about her taking decisions with

---

[87] From a letter from Sir Christopher Foster to Anthony Seldon, 20.10.00, and Sir Christopher Foster, *The End of Cabinet Government?* (Public Management & Policy Association, 1999), p. 6.

groups outside the Cabinet system.[88] This style was a principal reason why she was felt to be replacing 'Cabinet government' by 'prime ministerial government'. Although she was to bypass the Cabinet committee structure much more after her victory in the 1983 general election, this style of government was already clearly in evidence in 1980. Another reason why she was felt to be bypassing Cabinet government was that she liked to announce what she wanted at the start of a meeting, and she would then defy her ministers to disagree with her.

The Treasury, the undisputed dominant department in Whitehall, was still growing in importance, although it had ceded in the 1960s to the Cabinet Office the chairing of all official committees. (These were committees composed entirely of civil servants, which emerged before the Second World War[89] to shadow ministerial committees, but which tended to work by correspondence rather than by meetings. By the 1970s, official committees were on the wane and by 1980 rarely met.)[90] Already in 1980 the Treasury was deciding key economic issues with Number 10 outside the Cabinet system, and this trend was to continue throughout the 1980s and 1990s. The close ideological identity in 1980 between Mrs Thatcher and her chancellor Sir Geoffrey Howe helped enhance the Treasury's position.

What function then did Cabinet have in 1980? Committee chairs occasionally sought ratification of decisions already taken but such ratifications were the exception, occurring only when decisions taken at committee level were considered of peculiar economic, social or external importance or when the matter was highly sensitive or where it was exceptionally politically controversial. In general, Cabinet ministers in 1980 only heard about committee decisions through reading the committee's minutes. Few decisions were taken in Cabinet in 1980. Southern Rhodesia, in the process of becoming the independent Zimbabwe under Robert Mugabe, was debated at length and important decisions on its future were taken in Cabinet.

But, if decisions in general were no longer being taken in Cabinet, why was it necessary for ministers to meet together at all in 1980? Discussion under the parliamentary business agenda item afforded an opportunity for the business managers to communicate, tactics to be debated and ministers to air their concerns and receive advice on how to handle their

---

[88] Private information.
[89] S. S. Wilson, *The Cabinet Office to 1945* (HMSO, 1975), p. 56.
[90] From a letter from Sir Christopher Foster to Anthony Seldon, 20.10.00.

departments' business in both Houses. The foreign affairs discussion provided a useful briefing and an opportunity to share points of view—this was before the European Community became such a contentious subject between ministers in the mid–late 1980s. The second part of the agenda gave ministers the chance to raise subjects with background papers circulated beforehand. In general, the function of Cabinet was to allow ministers to feel part of the same team, to benefit from advice and camaraderie and to feel a sense of ownership which was essential if ministers were to continue to be collectively responsible in an increasingly splintered and complex governmental process. The classic Cabinet system, with a complex pattern of standing and *ad hoc* committees beneath it, was beginning to break down, under political and administrative pressures. But Cabinet itself was still the supreme discussion body of British government, even if decision-taking had passed elsewhere.

Cabinet in 2000

In 2000, Tony Blair was in his fourth year as prime minister. The outward pattern had changed little. Cabinet was still meeting weekly outside holiday periods, at 10.30am at Number 10 on Thursdays. But meetings lasted little more than an hour, compared to the two hours in 1980 and in earlier years.[91] The frequency declined marginally under Blair: the average number of meetings annually in 1980–90 was 42, but it met on 36 occasions in 1997; 37 in 1998; 35 in 1999; and 36 in 2000. Table 4.5 lists the number of meetings from 1969 to 2000.

All the big political issues of 2000 were mentioned in Cabinet, but this was mainly to air the presentational issues surrounding them. So where were decisions being taken, and where were the debates occurring in 2000? First, formal decisions on major issues of government policy involving a number of different departments would be made by Cabinet committees; external decisions, as with Kosovo, or domestic decisions, such as government policy on genetically modified food, were taken in this forum. Second, decisions were taken in *ad hoc* groups, usually but not necessarily with the prime minister present, as over the slaughter of pigs in the swine fever outbreak in August 2000. Third, decisions were taken in bilaterals between the prime minister and one other minister, especially where the decision affected that one ministerial department

---

[91] Peter Riddell argues that Cabinet often lasted 'much less' than an hour; 'Blair as Prime Minister', p. 32.

Table 4.5 Cabinet meetings held in each year, 1969–2000

Year	Number of Cabinet meetings
1969	61
1970	72
1971	63
1972	59
1973	63
1974	63
1975	56
1976	57
1977	41
1978	44
1979	40
1980	45
1981	41
1982	53
1983	38
1984	41
1985	37
1986	42
1987	37
1988	40
1989	39
1990	40
1991	38
1992	40
1993	40
1994	40
1995	40
1996	41
1997	36
1998	37
1999	35
2000	36

principally, or where speed was essential. Fourth, decisions were taken in bilaterals between just two ministers, and even major decisions would be reached by correspondence rather than by convening committees, Cabinet or otherwise. Finally, major decisions were taken by Blair, Gordon Brown and John Prescott. The Blair–Brown nexus was particularly important, confirming the enduring importance of the Treasury, and Brown in particular, who dominated the Public Spending Committee (PSX) and the Cabinet's Economic Committee (EA), which rarely met in 2000.[92] Brown expanded the number of his own policy advisers in the

---

[92] Hennessy, *The Prime Minister*, p. 513.

Treasury; acting on his own, or by convening his own bilaterals, he would regularly bypass not just Cabinet but the whole Cabinet committee system.

Blair's expanded Number 10 was also the focus of many decisions which were then communicated to the Cabinet. As a senior Cabinet Office official put it, 'the Cabinet system is all much more flexible now than it was. The system works as long as Number 10 and the Cabinet Office are told what is going on. Nothing today is black and white. Reality is very different to how it is described in books and articles.'[93] As Peter Riddell wrote in 2000, on a wide range of issues 'Blair has not used Cabinet committees and has either worked through *ad hoc* groups . . . or bilaterally with relevant departmental ministers'.[94]

If decisions were all taken below Cabinet, and if the system was as flexible as the source suggests, why did Cabinet not disappear and cease to exist? Why in 2000 were twenty-two busy men and women prepared to lose part of a morning each week to attend Cabinet meetings, as well as time beforehand reading and occasionally preparing Cabinet papers? It is clear that Cabinet's main function and justification in 2000 was that of the one and only forum where the government's most senior ministers and heads of departments met, where issues could be aired, and where disagreements not settled outside could be vented. By meeting together, a sense of teamwork was engendered, ownership offered, and the lingering yet still vital doctrine of collective responsibility could be given expression. Ministers were brought up to speed on developments in the European Union and abroad, in the Scottish and Welsh Assemblies, and the crucial issue (to this government) of media management could be considered.

The agenda in 2000 was composed of three standing items, which were then followed by a discussion of Cabinet papers, if any, by now uncommon.[95] The first item was parliamentary business, generally the shortest. It was all very orderly: business in the House of Commons, whipping issues, then House of Lords business followed by a general discussion of pressing parliamentary issues. Any minister could raise

---

[93] Private information.

[94] Riddell, 'Blair as Prime Minister', p. 33.

[95] 'In contrast to what I remembered of the 1960s and 1970s, I cannot overstate my astonishment at finding, with rare exceptions, that in the 1990s Cabinet papers are no longer circulated.' Foster, *The End of Cabinet Government*, p. 20. The Cabinet Office refused to provide information on the number of Cabinet papers.

topics, and declare what parliamentary problems were foreseen in their areas, so that ministers could be forewarned.

The second item covered domestic business. The Cabinet Office would give Blair a brief of what he wanted to raise or what ministers had told the Cabinet Office they wanted to raise: 'This item writes itself', said an official, 'you can judge what issues will come up by following the correspondence between ministers.' There was also a systematic look at announcements over the coming week, which one Number 10 aide described as 'a warning and information system'.[96] The Strategic Communications Unit, a Blair innovation, made its impact in this section of the agenda, and ministers were given briefings on how they should respond to different questions that might crop up. 'It is very useful as the expectation today is that Cabinet Ministers know everything that is going on,' opined one.[97] During this second agenda item Blair might invite a minister, such as Gordon Brown, to talk on the economy, or John Prescott, on transport.

Overseas business came third. Blair invited Robin Cook, foreign secretary, to speak; he would use the opportunity to address ministers on the pressing issues as he saw them. This was the slot when the defence secretary and overseas development secretary might also speak. Said one observer, 'it is their chance to inform, to brief everyone on the arguments and to check everyone is happy'.[98] And if they are not? Generally, lone discordant voices were not raised. The dissenting minister might have raised the objections at the Overseas and Defence Policy Committee. If he or she was not a member, or the meeting has passed, they must hold their counsel.

The formal Cabinet system, with four main standing committees, subcommittees and *ad hoc* Cabinet committees, was much as it was in 1980, but the practice, which was beginning to loosen up in 1980, had become much looser still. The volume of decisions going through committees had declined enormously. Decisions were much more likely to go down the Cabinet committee route if Blair had no particular interest in a topic—which included great swathes of lower profile government work. Lord Irvine, the Lord Chancellor, was a key chair and he liked utilising the Cabinet committee system. On occasions in 2000 he briefed

---

[96] Private information. See chapter on Blair in Dennis Kavanagh and Anthony Seldon, *The Powers Behind the Prime Minister: The Hidden Influence of Number Ten*, 2nd edn (HarperCollins, 2000), pp. 251–96.
[97] Private information.
[98] Private information.

Cabinet on where the debate was within a committee, to test the water. But everyone knew that, when decisions went down that path, the Cabinet committee would be the final arbiter. No decisions were taken in Cabinet in 2000. One of the handful to be taken in Cabinet under Blair since 1997 was the decision to proceed with building the Millennium Dome. It went to Cabinet twice, with Mandleson arguing strongly for it. The sense of both meetings was against. On the second occasion it was raised, Blair had to leave the Cabinet before the discussion. Prescott chaired the meeting, which was broadly against the Dome again; Blair was told about the discussion, then reversed the 'decision'.[99]

The Cabinet system in 2000 had changed utterly when compared with its position in 1900. The system in 2000 was the most informal of the six studied. Cabinet Office officials admitted that it would be very difficult to write an organisation chart on how the Cabinet system was operating, or even how it should have been operating, in 2000.[100] Blair referred to ministers not by their titles, as had been standard before 1997, but by their first names. First names were also used in the correspondence. It is an indicative change from the formality that existed even in 1980.

How has the Cabinet system changed?

The Cabinet system has moved through five phases from 1900 to 2000:

1. *Cabinet as the sole decision-making body.* This was the case from 1900 until the First World War, with the qualification that Cabinet 'committees', which had existed *ad hoc* since the eighteenth century, and the Committee of Imperial Defence, set up in 1903, could be the forums where decisions were effectively taken (though the CID lost much of its authority after 1905). Cabinets had the right to challenge and indeed overturn these decisions. Individual decisions could also be taken by the prime minister alone, or in consultation with two or three others.

2. *Cabinet as the principal decision-taking body.* This description holds true from the First to the Second World War. Decisions were increasingly taken in Cabinet committees, which expanded greatly in number during and after the First World War. Although Tom Jones complained that Cabinet was weak in allowing too many decisions to

---

[99] Private information.
[100] Private information.

be taken by committees, it was inevitable that this should be so, given the volume of business. Decisions were, however, always reported to Cabinet for acceptance, or not. The principal qualification is that a determined prime minister could take decisions on his own, or with a few close Cabinet colleagues, as Neville Chamberlain did in the autumn of 1938. Sir Maurice Hankey (1916–38) and Sir Edward Bridges (1938–46) were the Cabinet secretaries who presided over this phase in the Cabinet system's evolution.

3.   *Cabinet as the principal decision-ratifying body.*   This was the case from the Second World War until the late 1970s. After the Second World War, the Cabinet committee system came of age and reached a high point under the Cabinet secretaryships of Sir Norman Brook (1947–62) and Sir Burke Trend (1963–73), two consummate Whitehall mandarins and sticklers for correct form. Decisions were taken mainly in Cabinet committees, but important decisions would always be presented for ratification (if not always discussion) by ministers to full Cabinet, which could very occasionally reverse those decisions.

4.   *Cabinet as the supreme discussion and information-giving body.* This was the case through different guises from the late 1970s until 1997. The reduction in the number of meetings to once a week in 1977 was significant, as was Mrs Thatcher's spurning of the Cabinet/Cabinet committee system from 1979/80 and even more from 1983. Ministers would now learn about Cabinet committee decisions purely from Cabinet minutes sent to their private offices. Under John Major, especially from 1990–2, Cabinet returned to how it had operated in phase 3, and even phase 2: but an increasingly hostile atmosphere, and divisions within his Cabinet, meant he came to trust Cabinet and even Cabinet committees less and less.

5.   *A personal system.*   Under Tony Blair since 1997, and under Sir Richard Wilson as Cabinet secretary (1998–2002), an even more informal system of conducting business at the heart of government had emerged. There was more fluidity, and less of a reliance on set procedures, than at any point in the century. Cabinet had become, in the words of one senior Cabinet Office figure, the occasion where political colleagues met together for team-building and a weekly exchange of views. The imperatives of co-ordinating thinking in the light of the European Union, devolution, with the need to monitor developments in the Scottish Parliament and Welsh National Assembly and the need to manage the media all helped ensure that the weekly meetings had purpose and value. Whether this post-modern Cabinet system survives Blair's departure, or

a more hostile environment such as Major faced after 1992, has yet to be seen.

Why has the Cabinet system changed?

There are eleven reasons which explain the evolution through the five phases of the Cabinet system in the last century. These are listed in roughly chronological order:

1. *The need to involve expert opinion from outside the body of Cabinet ministers.* This decision helps explain the formation of the Defence Committee/Committee of Imperial Defence on which sat the chiefs of staff.

2. *Drafting legislation to be put to Parliament.* Cabinet committees in the nineteenth century were almost exclusively concerned with drafting legislation. The legislation role later became a key function of the Cabinet system as it usurped some of the role of the legislature in the twentieth century.

3. *The end of Britain's isolation and its entry into an interdependent world of international diplomacy in the twentieth century.* This factor helps explain the formation of the Committee of Imperial Defence and later the Foreign Affairs Committee.

4. *Increasing involvement of government in social and economic questions from the early twentieth century.* The Liberal governments from 1905, notably with the Old Age Pensions Act of 1908 and the National Insurance Act of 1911, laid the foundations of the welfare state. The enduring impact of the First World War,[101] legislation in the 1920s and 1930s, and changes in economic thinking in the 1940s were also responsible for governments playing a greater part in the economic and social policy of the nation. Domestic committees, beginning with the Home Affairs Committee, were needed to oversee and co-ordinate this governmental activity. The creation of the Cabinet Office/Secretariat in 1916 provided the organisation which could service a complex bureaucracy. It not only permitted but also encouraged the expansion of Cabinet committees.

5. *The emergence of the Treasury in the 1910s as the dominant Whitehall department.* This is significant, because the Treasury rapidly discovered

---

[101] Turner, 'Cabinets, Committees and Secretariats', p. 78.

it could control and contain decision-making within the Cabinet committee system as it emerged early in the century.

6. *Personalities.* Some prime ministers—for example, Clement Attlee as deputy prime minister (1940–5) and then prime minister (1945–51)—welcomed the growth of committees. Other prime ministers—for example, Mrs Thatcher (1979–90) and Tony Blair (1997–)—have tried to bypass Cabinet and Cabinet committees. Cabinet secretaries have always had immense influence over the conduct of policy-making. Hankey (1916–38) and Brook (1947–63) were particularly influential in shaping the system. Others like Sir Robert Armstrong (1979–87) and Sir Robin Butler (1987–97) sought to resist Mrs Thatcher's attempts to short-circuit the Cabinet system, but to little effect. Sir Richard Wilson (1998–2002) co-operated, apparently happily, with Blair's marginalising of the Cabinet committee system as it emerged at the end of the last century.

7. *Pressure of time.* Whereas the number in Cabinet remained largely static over the twentieth century at about twenty and the number of Cabinet meetings a year fell by about half, the pressure of business increased out of all proportion. It became clear as early as the 1910s and 1920s that Cabinet could not possibly debate all issues, and decision-taking would have to be delegated to subordinate committees which would nevertheless be representative of Cabinet as a whole and which would contain those ministers with most direct interest in matters being discussed.

8. *The media.* The growth of political television in the 1960s and the electronic media in the 1970s and 1980s meant that instant responses were being demanded from Number 10, not just from within Britain but worldwide. Decisions could not always wait until the next Cabinet or Cabinet committee meeting.

9. *Leaking by Cabinet ministers and their aides.* The growth of leaking from the Wilson government of 1964–70, vividly recounted in the Crossman diaries, and redressed only temporarily by the Heath Cabinet of 1970–4, meant that prime ministers and others were increasingly reluctant to air their true thoughts in Cabinet. This meant that with particularly leaky Cabinets, for example John Major's of 1992–7, discussions could be very anodyne: sensitive and controversial issues were kept away from the whole Cabinet committee system.

10. *Increasing departmental interdependence.* Although interdependence grew from early last century, entry into the European Economic Community in January 1973 increased it enormously. Every Whitehall

department has a European Union section, and the European Secretariat of the Cabinet Office plays a commanding role co-ordinating British European policy and administration. Membership of the EU also means that ministers attend European Councils and take decisions without ratification by Cabinet/Cabinet committee.

11. *Changes to the doctrine of collective Cabinet responsibility.* The doctrine for much of the last century meant that ministers were collectively involved in government decisions, and were bound to remain loyal to the decisions in public even when they disagreed. By 2000, it was common for ministers to leak, or announce, decisions to the media, or to Parliament, and even Cabinet ministers will have played no personal or representative part in those decisions. Only if they protest in public will collective responsibility be engaged; they usually remain quiet, either because they fear dissent will jeopardise their position, or because they appreciate that they know insufficient detail to dispute the decision. But over the Millennium Dome, because Cabinet ministers felt they had been overruled by Blair in the summer of 1997, they did not feel bound by collective responsibility and openly criticised the building when it ran into trouble.

The Cabinet system changed greatly in the twentieth century: from one in 1900 with a crucial apex but little substructure, to a system for much of the century with Cabinet remaining at the apex but with decision-taking moving down to a sophisticated and highly bureaucratic substructure, to one where, by 2000, both apex and superstructure had become fluid and where the whole system could be bypassed by other organisations, notably Number 10 and the Treasury and by powerful individuals, above all Blair and Brown. But this does not preclude a return in the future to a more formalised Cabinet system in the twenty-first century.

Only time will tell whether the new century will see a further restoration of Cabinet government or a further withering away of its institutional foundations.

Note. The author would like to thank Pranay Sanklecha and Teresa Goudie for their research, and John Barnes, Vernon Bogdanor, Christopher Foster, Peter Snowdon and Dennis Kavanagh for reading an earlier draft.

Bibliography

Primary sources

Public Record Office

Documents from the Public Records Office (PRO) in Kew.
(PRO) CAB 23/20/30, 35, 38, 77, 127, 237–40, 272.
(PRO) CAB 23/21/97.
(PRO) CAB 23/97/01, 41.
(PRO) CAB 23/99/23, 305.
(PRO) CAB 23/100/474.
(PRO) CAB 37/52/05, 27, 43.
(PRO) CAB 37/53/51, 71.
(PRO) CAB 41/25/01, 29, 33, 48, 51.
(PRO) CAB 65/01/16, 26, 27, 39.
(PRO) CAB 128/34/32, 37–40, 52, 58, 62, 119, 136, 144, 160, 182, 192, 203, 212, 224, 243, 244.

Interviews

Various interviews were conducted for this chapter: nearly all were 'off the record'.

Memoirs and diaries

Benn, A., *Against the Tide: Diaries 1973–76* (Hutchinson, 1989).
Butler, Lord, *The Art of the Possible: The Memoirs of Lord Butler* (Hamish Hamilton, 1971).
Cabinet Office, 'Cabinet Committee Business: A Guide for Departments' (1995).
Cabinet Office, 'Cabinet Committee Business: A Guide for Departments, Revised Version' (1997).
Castle, B., *The Castle Diaries: 1974–76* (Weidenfeld & Nicolson, 1980).
Castle, B., *The Castle Diaries: 1964–70* (Weidenfeld & Nicolson, 1984).
Crossman, R., *The Diaries of a Cabinet Minister*: vol. 1, *Minister of Housing 1964–66* (Hamish Hamilton, 1975).
Crossman, R., *The Diaries of a Cabinet Minister*: vol. 2, *Lord President of the Council and Leader of the House of Commons 1966–68* (Hamish Hamilton, 1976).
Crossman, R., *The Diaries of a Cabinet Minister*: vol. 3, *Secretary of State for Social Services 1968–70* (Hamish Hamilton 1977).
Fyfe, David Maxwell, *Political Adventure: The Memoirs of the Earl of Kilmuir* (Weidenfeld & Nicolson, 1964).
Jones, Thomas, *Whitehall Diary*, ed. Keith Middlemas (Oxford University Press, 1969–71).
Lawson, N., *The View from No. 10: Memoirs of a Tory Radical* (Bantam, 1992).
Macmillan, Harold, *At the End of the Day 1961–1963* (Macmillan, 1973).
Mallaby, G., *From My Level: Unwritten Minutes* (Hutchinson, 1965).

Ridley, Jane and Percy, Clayre (eds), *The Letters of Arthur Balfour and Lady Elcho 1885–1917* (Hamish Hamilton, 1992).

Roskill, Stephen, *Hankey, Man of Secrets*: vol. 1, *1877–1918* (Collins, 1970).

Roskill, Stephen, *Hankey, Man of Secrets*: vol. 2, *1919–31* (Collins, 1972).

Roskill, Stephen *Hankey, Man of Secrets*: vol. 3, *1931–63* (Collins, 1974).

Templewood, Viscount (Sir Samuel Hoare), *Nine Troubled Years*, 1st edn 1954 (Greenwood Press, 1976).

Secondary published sources

Books

Aldous, Richard and Lee, Sabine (eds), *Harold Macmillan: Aspects of a Political Life* (Macmillan, 1999).

Amery, L. S., *Thoughts on the Constitution* (Oxford University Press, 1947).

Bagehot, Walter, *The English Constitution*, 1st edn 1867 (Collins, 1963).

Barnes, J., 'The Prime Minister's Role in Foreign Affairs and Economic Policy: Creeping Bilateralism in Action?', in James, S. and Preston, V., *New Politics, Old Politics: Essays in Political History since 1945* (André Deutsch, 1999) .

Berrill, K., 'Strength at the Centre: The Case for a Prime Minister's Department', in King, Anthony, *The British Prime Minister*, 2nd edn (Duke University Press, 1985).

Burch, M. and Halliday, I., *The British Cabinet System* (Harvester Wheatsheaf, 1996).

Burk, Kathleen (ed.), *War and the State: The Transformation of British Government 1914–1919* (George Allen & Unwin, 1982).

Cross, J. A., *Sir Samuel Hoare: A Political Biography* (Jonathan Cape, 1977).

Daalder, Hans, *Cabinet Reform in Britain 1914–63* (Oxford University Press, 1964).

Davies, Sir Alfred, *The Lloyd George I Knew* (Henry E. Walter, 1948).

Dunleavy, P., 'Estimating the Distribution of Positional Influence in Cabinet Committees under Major', in Rhodes, R. and Dunleavy, P. (eds), *Prime Minister, Cabinet and Core Executive* (Macmillan, 1995).

Dutton, David, *Simon: A Political Biography of Sir John Simon* (Aurum Press, 1992).

Foster, Sir Christopher, *The End of Cabinet Government?* (Public Management & Policy Association, 1999).

Hennessy, P., *Cabinet* (Blackwell, 1986).

Hennessy, P., *Whitehall* (Secker & Warburg, 1989).

Hennessy, P., *The Hidden Wiring: Unearthing the British Constitution*, revised edn (Indigo, 1996).

Hennessy, P., *The Prime Minister: The Office and its Holders since 1945* (Allen Lane, 2000).

James, Simon, *British Cabinet Government*, 2nd edn (Routledge, 1999).

Jennings, Sir I. (ed.), *Cabinet Government*, 3rd edn (Cambridge University Press, 1959).

Jones, G., 'Development of the Cabinet', in Thornhill, W. (ed.), *The Modernisation of British Government* (Pitman, 1975).

Judd, Denis, *Radical Joe: A Life of Joseph Chamberlain* (Hamish Hamilton, 1977).

Kavanagh, Dennis and Seldon, Anthony, *The Powers Behind the Prime Minister: The Hidden Influence of Number Ten*, 2nd edn (HarperCollins, 2000).

Legh, Thomas Wodehouse, Baron Newton, *Lord Lansdowne: A Biography* (Macmillan, 1929).

Mackie, T. and Hogwood, B., *Unlocking the Cabinet: Cabinet Structures in Perspective* (Sage, 1985).

Mackintosh, J., *The British Cabinet*, 3rd edn (Stevens, 1977).

O'Halpin, Eunan, *Head of the Civil Service: A Study of Sir Warren Fisher* (Routledge, 1989).

Rhodes, R. and Dunleavy, P. (eds), *Prime Minister, Cabinet and Core Executive* (Macmillan, 1995).

Riddell, Peter, 'Blair as Prime Minister', in Seldon, Anthony (ed.), *The Blair Effect* (Little, Brown, 2001).

Roberts, Andrew, *Salisbury: Victorian Titan* (Weidenfeld & Nicolson, 1999).

Seldon, Anthony (ed.), *The Blair Effect* (Little, Brown, 2001).

Skidelsky, Robert, *John Maynard Keynes: Fighting for Britain 1937–1946* (Macmillan, 2000).

Thomas, G., *Prime Minister and Cabinet Today* (Manchester University Press, 1998).

Trend, Lord (Burke), 'Norman Brook', in Williams, E. and Nicholls, C. (eds), *Dictionary of National Biography 1961–70* (Oxford University Press, 1981).

Turner, John, *Lloyd George's Secretariat* (Cambridge University Press, 1980).

Turner, John, 'Cabinets, Committees and Secretariats: The Higher Direction of War', in Burk, Kathleen (ed.), *War and the State: The Transformation of British Government 1914–1919* (George Allen & Unwin, 1982).

Walker, Patrick Gordon, *The Cabinet*, revised edn (Heinemann Educational, 1972).

Wilson, S. S., *The Cabinet Office to 1945* (HMSO, 1975).

Articles

Armstrong of Ilminster, Lord, 'Cabinet Government in the Thatcher Years', *Contemporary Record* (1994).

Brady, C., 'Collective Responsibility of the Cabinet: An Ethical, Constitutional or Managerial Tool?', *Parliamentary Affairs* (1998).

Catterall, P. and Brady, C., 'Managing the Core Executive', *Public Policy and Administration* (1997).

Catterall, P. and Brady, C., 'Cabinet Committees in British Governance', *Public Policy and Administration* (1998).

Hunt of Tamworth, Lord, 'The Failings of Cabinet Government in Mid to Late 1970s', *Contemporary Record* (1994).

Seldon, Anthony, 'The Cabinet Office and Coordination 1979–87', *Public Administration* (1990).

Weller, P., 'Do Prime Ministers' Departments Really Cause Problems?', *Public Administration* (1983).

Lectures

Butler, R., 'The Changing Civil Service', Address to ESRC Whitehall Programme conference and author's note of questions and answers, 24 September 1997.

Butler of Brockwell, R., 'Cabinet Government', Attlee Foundation Lecture, Mansion House, London, 18 March 1999.

Hunt of Tamworth, Lord, 'Cabinet Strategy and Management', Lecture to the RIPA/CIPFA Conference, Brighton, 6 June 1983.

5.
The House of Commons[1]

PAUL SEAWARD AND PAUL SILK

The nineteenth-century legacy

'For a quarter of a century', wrote one critic in 1858, 'Parliamentary Government has been established in this country with greater purity and efficiency than it ever possessed before ... innumerable measures of unequalled public importance have been adopted in rapid succession by the legislature; and while discord has shaken, and despotism subdued, almost every other great nation in Europe, the people of England have never been more heartily attached to their institutions, or more happily at peace among themselves'.[2] With a constitution reinvigorated and purged of the pernicious effects of executive dominance and housed in a splendid new building, the Victorian legislature basked in an unprecedented prestige and self-confidence. Although party was the essential principle on which Parliament's ability to function was based, it was party with much of its potency removed. Members were, wrote Walter Bagehot in 1865, 'Whigs, or Radicals, or Tories, but they are much else too. They are common Englishmen, and ... "hard to be worked up to the dogmatic level". They are not eager to press the tenets of their party to impossible conclusions.'[3] Parliament had its detractors, who could point to its many imperfections as an efficient legislature: Lord Salisbury in 1864 commented that the proceedings of the House of Commons were 'uncouth, complicated, often unmeaning, founded upon circumstances which have ceased to exist, often defensible by no reasons applicable to the present state of things, and liable at any time to misuse, which

[1] For a survey of the House of Commons in the first half of the century, see Stuart Ball, 'Parliament and Politics in Britain, 1900–1951', *Parliamentary History* (1991).
[2] *Edinburgh Review*, 219 (July 1858), quoted in A. Hawkins, 'Parliamentary Government and Victorian Political Parties', *English Historical Review* (1989).
[3] Walter Bagehot, *The English Constitution*, ed. R. H. S. Crossman (Fontana, 1963), p. 159.

would bring the whole business of the country to a standstill'.[4] But the inefficiency with which it conducted its business did not affect Parliament's place at the centre of politics and the constitution, nor of the British sense of self-identity.

The confidence of the Victorian Parliament was tempered, though, by an uncomfortable sense of the contingency of Parliament's status and prominence and the dependence of the fundamental consensus about its role on the narrowness of its recruiting grounds. And certainly, although there was no immediate and dramatic change, the passage of the 1867 and 1884 Reform Acts did bring about a much more radical transformation in the tempo and the atmosphere of the Victorian Parliament than the 1832 Act had done. Members became more assiduous, more talkative, more party political. The effect of the democratic electorate was seen, especially by foreign observers, in the increasing dominance of parties over members. Ostrogorski bemoaned the way that the caucus had greatly enhanced the power of party leadership and eroded the independence of the individual member: 'The right and the power of the Members to revolt at any moment against those who lead them, and the authority with which tradition and the essence of the party system has clothed the latter, maintained between both the equilibrium which ensured the working of the government and preserved the freedom of the assembly. This equilibrium is now destroyed in favour of the leaders.'[5] The growing influence of external party organisations threatened to reduce members to no more than mandated delegates. Dicey warned that 'the reason for alarm is not that the English executive is too strong, for weak government generally means bad administration, but that our English executive is, as a general rule, becoming more and more the representative of a party rather than the guide of a country'.[6]

It was not only in Britain that people complained about the decline of representative institutions. James Bryce wrote in 1921 that 'every traveller who, curious in political affairs, enquires in the countries which he visits how their legislative bodies are working, receives from the elder men the same discouraging answer. They tell him, in terms much the same everywhere, there is less brilliant speaking than in the days of their own youth, that the tone of manners has declined, that the best citizens

[4] *Lord Salisbury on Politics*, ed. Paul Smith (Cambridge University Press, 1972), p. 43.
[5] M. Ostrogorski, *Democracy and the Organisation of Political Parties* (Macmillan, 1902), pp. 1, 606.
[6] A. V. Dicey, *Introduction to the Study of the Law of the Constitution*, 8th edn (Macmillan, 1915), p. lvi.

are less disposed to enter the Chamber, that its proceedings are less fully reported and excite less interest, that a seat in it confers less social status, and that, for one reason or another, the respect felt for it has waned.'[7] Parliament in Britain may have been less prone than elsewhere to succumb to (as Winston Churchill put it in 1930) 'party organisations, to leagues and societies, to military chiefs or to dictatorships in various forms'.[8] In Britain, though, the perception of decline was made more acute by the keenly held belief in a mid-Victorian parliamentary golden age, which had set a standard for the independent-minded and sceptical examination of government. That standard would inevitably be in conflict with the increasing pressure to enact laws that derived from the widening scope of governmental activity, the development of the party programme and the growth of a democratic electorate.[9] Caught between widely different expectations of its role, Parliament often disappointed in both, provoking complaints both about its declining power and independence, and about its ineffectiveness as a means of legislating radical programmes of social, economic and constitutional change.

Members of Parliament

Full-time or part-time

Those out of sympathy with the advent of democracy regarded the early twentieth-century House of Commons as a chamber of party pygmies compared with their independent-minded Victorian predecessors. During 'the Palmerstonian era', Dicey commented in the eighth edition of the *Introduction to the Study of the Law of the Constitution*, a few members 'each possessed an authority inside and outside the House which is hardly claimed by any Member nowadays who neither has nor is expected to obtain a seat in any cabinet'.[10] The mass-member party may have discouraged some outstanding individuals from entering politics: but the trend was rather towards the professionalisation of politics and politicians. The mid-Victorian House was already dominated by a cadre

---

[7] James Bryce, *Modern Democracies* (Macmillan, 1921), vol. 2, p. 367.

[8] Winston Churchill, *Parliamentary Government and the Economic Problem* (Oxford University Press, 1930); see also Ronald Butt, *The Power of Parliament* (Constable, 1967), pp. 116–24.

[9] For an account of the impact of a reforming government on the legislative programme, see Agatha Ramm, 'The Parliamentary Context of Cabinet Government, 1868–74', *English Historical Review* (1984).

[10] Dicey, *Introduction to the Study of the Law of the Constitution*, p. lvi.

of gentleman-professionals; the fall in the number of members from a limited pool of landed families became precipitous after the 1880s.[11] From 1900 the election of Labour members from among the skilled or semi-skilled working class had a considerable impact in changing the atmosphere of the House; but after 1922 the proportion of professionals in the Parliamentary Labour Party rose steeply, and on both left and right the gap left by the country gentry was filled from the ranks of the professional middle class.[12] Women were first elected in 1918; but not until the last three elections of the century (1987, 1992 and 1997) did they become a significant presence in the Commons—and even at its end they counted for only a little more than one sixth of the membership.[13]

With members being drawn from a wider variety of social backgrounds the development of a system of payment for members was natural and essential; but for some it implied not only an undesirable professionalisation of their role but also an extension of the control of the party. Enoch Powell, during a debate on the introduction of a specific system of allowances in 1971, told the House that 'the change which will come about as a result of this alteration in our status—because of our becoming increasingly assimilated to full-time, pensioned employees— is that those who have the voice to say whether we shall or shall not be candidates of our party at a General Election gain a great accession of power over the individual and, thereby, indirectly, over the House'.[14] The rise in working-class representation had originally been dependent on the financial backing provided usually through trade union sponsorship; a House of Lords judgement of 1909 against the compulsory levy of trade union members for the purpose of supporting members of Parliament forced the Liberal government of 1910 to honour the party's twenty-year-old commitment and introduce a salary for members in August 1911, set at £400, part of which was regarded as an allowance for parliamentary duties. Governments found it difficult, though, to maintain its value, especially close to a general election, or in times of economic hardship. The eventual (though not entirely successful) solution was to try to

---

[11] Ellis Archer Wasson, 'The House of Commons 1660–1945: Parliamentary Families and the Political Elite', *English Historical Review* (1991); Michael Rush, 'The Members of Parliament', in S. A. Walkland (ed.), *The House of Commons in the Twentieth Century* (Oxford University Press, 1979), p. 97.

[12] Rush, 'The Members of Parliament', pp. 114–15.

[13] 41 women in 1987, 60 in 1992 and 120 in 1997: the previous highest figure was 29, in 1964. The numbers are given in David and Gareth Butler, *British Political Facts, 1900–2000* (Macmillan, 2000), p. 261.

[14] HC Deb., 5th series, vol. 828, cols 1155–6, 20 December 1971.

remove it from the political arena by making members' salaries subject to periodic review, preferably by an outside body. In 1963 the Lawrence Committee (the Committee on the Remuneration of Ministers and Members of Parliament) rejected the notion of an automatic link between members' pay and civil service pay,[15] but eight years later parliamentary pay became one of the responsibilities of the Top Salaries Review Body, which has made recommendations for increases in members' pay at regular intervals thereafter, and in 1983 the House decided to link members' pay to that of a senior civil servant.[16] Members also received separate allowances from 1969.[17]

If the development of a system of proper remuneration for members enabled them to become full-time parliamentarians, the development of a system designed to deal with conflicts of interest acted (some alleged) to prevent them from being anything else. The requirement that a member does not vote on a question in which he or she has a direct personal pecuniary interest is an ancient one;[18] but dissatisfaction with the essentially voluntary practice of declaration was expressed on a number of occasions after 1945, and a 1969 scandal prompted the establishment of a select committee (the Strauss Committee) to consider the rules and practice of the House on the declaration of members' interests. It proposed a code of conduct, but rejected the idea of a register. The government, though, preferred to rely solely on 'the general good sense of Members'. The Poulson case, however, revived the issue, and in May 1974 the Labour government proposed a resolution, accepted by the House, for a compulsory register, to be overseen by a select committee. From 1974 until the early 1990s the Committee on Members' Interests reviewed complaints that members had failed properly to declare their interests. But in the 1990s the system was placed under increased strain from the growth of professional parliamentary lobbying,[19] and a handful of notorious cases (including the so-called 'cash for questions affair' in 1994)[20] prompted the government to appoint a non-parliamentary

---

[15] Michael Rush and Malcolm Shaw (eds), *The House of Commons: Services and Facilities* (Allen & Unwin, 1974), p. 191.

[16] The link was temporarily suspended between 1992 and 1993.

[17] Rush, *The House of Commons: Services and Facilities*, ch. 6.

[18] See Erskine May's *Treatise on the Law, Privileges, Proceedings and Usage of Parliament* 18th edn (Butterworths, 1971), pp. 398–403.

[19] For the growth in lobbying companies, see Philip Norton, 'The United Kingdom Parliament under Pressure', in *Parliaments and Pressure Groups in Western Europe*, ed. Philip Norton (Frank Cass, 1999), p. 23.

[20] See First Report of the Committee for Privileges, Session 1994–5, HC 351.

committee, the Committee on Standards in Public Life (the Nolan Committee) to review its operation. The committee recommended the replacement of the existing system with a more elaborate mechanism allowing more sophisticated investigation of complaints against members. It was accepted by the House in 1995, but it was to remain subject to the oversight of a Commons committee, which would determine any penalties to be imposed, retaining the House's control over the regulation of the conduct of its own membership.[21] These pressures confirmed and intensified the tendency of members of Parliament to become 'career politicians',[22] and, despite resistance, by the end of the twentieth century the transition to a conception of membership of the House of Commons as full-time, salaried employment was virtually complete. With it went a redefinition and expansion of the role.

Members and constituencies

The greatest change came in the relationship between the member and the constituency. In the early part of the century, as for previous centuries, members recognised the need to nurture the loyalty of their constituencies with at least occasional appearances, judicious benefactions or public works. Over the course of the century, however, the relationship between members and their constituencies changed significantly: members found themselves increasingly preoccupied with the personal difficulties of their constituents and drawn in to helping them to resolve them on an individual basis. It was common to date the change to the period immediately after 1945, when Parliament was preoccupied with the establishment of the welfare state: Sir Charles Ponsonby wrote in the 1960s that 'before 1939, unless there was some controversy afoot, I rarely received more than ten or twenty letters a week . . . But after the election of 1945, everything was changed . . . suddenly the MP ceased to be a politician and potential statesman and became an official of the welfare state. Thousands wanted houses; old people wanted pensions; ex-service men wanted jobs; everybody wanted something, and "write to your MP" became a cliché . . . the wretched MP was snowed under'.[23] The new

---

[21] First Report of the Committee on Standards in Public Life, Cm 2850-I, pp. 22–3.

[22] See Anthony King, 'Rise of the Career Politician', *British Journal of Political Science* (1981), 249–85; and see Peter Riddell, *Honest Opportunism* (Hamish Hamilton, 1993).

[23] Sir Charles Ponsonby, *Ponsonby Remembers* (Alden, 1965), p. 11, quoted in Donald D. Searing, *Westminster's World: Understanding Political Roles* (Harvard University Press, 1994), p. 443; The *Oxford English Dictionary*'s earliest example of the word 'surgery' used for the regular open sessions held by members in their constituencies dates from 1951.

involvement and concern with the points where the individual met the state was one of the motives for the establishment of an ombudsman (the parliamentary commissioner for administration) in 1967, access to whom was to be mediated by the MP. Older assumptions about the proper activity of a member of Parliament, though, remained firmly embedded until at least the 1960s,[24] and even in the early 1970s one knight of the shire could sketch his parliamentary activities thus: 'I hunt three days a week, always. Probably hunt four days a week. I don't get any letters anyhow. I only have a secretary part-time. I have one woman, at home, who deals with Parliamentary letters on a Monday and that's it.'[25]

Members and parties

Despite the growing preoccupation of members with their constituencies, constituency parties never turned into caucuses, determined to treat the member as their delegate. With some exceptions (Suez and, more recently, Europe, on the Conservative side; the arguments in the 1980s, especially prompted by the activities of the Campaign for Labour Democracy, on the Labour side), they accepted the conventional Burkean view on the relationship of electors and representatives. Party influence, over both constituencies and members, largely came from the centre. What was true was that the cohesion of the parties and the influence of their leaders within Parliament had by the beginning of the century already become more strongly established than for almost all of the previous one and never significantly retreated.[26] For most of the century it was conventional to lament the disappearance of members' independence; but party discipline became particularly tight after 1945. During the four post-Second World War Parliaments the proportion of divisions involving even one dissenting member did not rise above 7 per cent. Richard Crossman wrote in the early 1960s that 'the point of decision has now been removed from the division lobby to the party meeting upstairs. The debate on the floor of the House becomes a formality, and the division which follows

---

[24] Philip Norton and David M. Wood, *Back from Westminster: British Members of Parliament and their Constituents* (University Press of Kentucky, 1993).

[25] Searing, *Westminster's World*, p. 181.

[26] For voting cohesion in the nineteenth century, see Hugh Berrington, 'Partisanship and Dissidence in the Nineteenth Century House of Commons', *Parliamentary Affairs* (1967–8) and John D. Fair, 'Party Voting Behaviour in the British House of Commons 1886–1918', *Parliamentary History* (1986), 65–82.

it a foregone conclusion.'[27] Defenders of the system argued that governments would temper their public policy in order to avoid losing
supporters from their own side. But, though demonstrating that independent minds continued to exist in Parliament, the argument could not
contradict the claim that Parliament was no longer itself the forum in
which they could exercise their influence to any effect. Yet party control
has not been consistently maintained so strongly, and at some periods has
weakened markedly. In the 1970s the number of divisions involving
dissenting votes grew, to an average of 20 per cent in the 1970–4 Parliament and to 28 per cent in the 1974–9 Parliament.[28]

The system for the enforcement of party discipline was already well-
developed by 1900. The government whips (the chief whip and three
others) acted as 'the aides de camp, and intelligence department, of the
Leader of the House. In the former capacity they arrange for him with
the whips on the other side those matters in which it is a convenience
to have an understanding.' They decided who would go on select committees, and arranged the time at which 'some test vote on some great
measure will take place'. Each party's whips would take it as their
business to know the temper of the party, and to spot the least sign of
disaffection or discontent. Members who intended to vote against the
party were expected to notify the whip. The pressure which whips were
supposed to bring to bear on recalcitrant and independent-minded
members gave their work a sulphurous reputation, characterised by the
legendary 'dirt book' which Edward Short claimed to have discontinued
when he became Labour chief whip in 1964.[29] Lowell in 1908, though,
noticed the limitations on the whips' power: 'any direct attempt by the
whips to bring pressure upon a Member through his constituents would
be likely to irritate, and do more harm than good. But it is easy enough,
in various ways, to let the constituents know that the Member is not
thoroughly supporting his party; and unless his vote against the government is cast in the interest of the constituents themselves, they are not
likely to have much sympathy with his independence.'[30] For most of the

---

[27] R. H. S. Crossman, 'Introduction', in Walter Bagehot, *The English Constitution* (1963; Fontana paperback edn 1981), p. 43.
[28] Philip Norton, *Dissension in the House of Commons, 1945–74* (Macmillan, 1975), p. 609; *Dissension in the House of Commons, 1974–79* (Clarendon Press, 1980), p. 425; see also Philip Norton, 'Behavioural Changes: Backbench Independence in the 1980s', in Norton, *Parliament in the 1980s* (Blackwell, 1985), p. 36.
[29] Edward Short, *Whip to Wilson* (Macdonald, 1989), p. 61.
[30] A. L. Lowell, *The Government of England* (Macmillan 1908), vol 1., ch. 25, quotation from p. 453.

time negotiators and fixers, rather than arm-twisters, the paths of the government whips were oiled by the support they enjoyed in the persons of the private secretaries to the government chief whip, a post held by only three people between 1919 and 2000, and to which has been attributed an extraordinary degree of influence in British politics.[31]

Parties, though, were held together only partly by the threat of discipline or the loss of the whip (a rare event),[32] and rather more by the increased *esprit de corps* of the parliamentary parties, reflected in the development of organisations representing the parliamentary membership of the major parties in the first quarter of the century. The Parliamentary Labour Party (PLP) had its origins in the party's need to maintain a separate identity during its co-operation with the Liberals from 1900. The PLP was formed in 1906, and from the start was a relatively formal body. The Conservative 1922 Committee was set up on a much more informal basis by new Conservative members elected in 1922; under the patronage of the chief whip, it acquired a minor role in the organisation of the party in Parliament. The party leadership were reluctant to go beyond that, though, having set up a separate system of backbench committees in 1924; but throughout the 1920s it established itself as a significant part of the party's internal arrangements, before a period of eclipse in the 1930s. Only after the Second World War did it establish itself more permanently.[33] The Liberals, too, were having regular party meetings from the 1920s. The influence of these organisations over their party leaderships was limited, especially when the party was in government: but they formed an essential channel of communication between members and a sometimes isolated leadership. Each of them succeeded in establishing control over the party's choice of leader, rather later for the Conservatives, for whom an electoral system was adopted only in 1965: but in 1976 members of the Liberal Party, and in the 1990s members of the Labour and Conservative parties in Parliament, lost complete control of the choice of leader, which was diffused more widely in their respective parties.

---

[31] See, for example, R. H. S. Crossman, *The Diaries of a Cabinet Minister* (Hamish Hamilton, 1976), vol. 2, p. 625. The three holders of the post were Sir Charles Harris (1919–61), Sir Freddie Warren (1961–78) and Sir Murdo Maclean (1978–2000).

[32] See D. and G. Butler, *British Political Facts, 1900–2000*, pp. 244–9, for a list of changes of allegiance, and losses of the whip.

[33] Stuart Ball, 'The 1922 Committee: The Formative Years 1922–45', *Parliamentary History* (1990).

The organisation of business

Even if the essential decisions were now taken elsewhere, the House at the end of the century still took as long as it did at its beginning to agree to them formally—with the result that the House of Commons continued to sit for notoriously long hours. 'For my own part', Balfour told the House in 1902, 'I have never been able to understand why of all his Majesty's subjects a Member of Parliament should be the one who never knows when he is to dine or when he is to sleep.'[34] The complaint was never overcome for the remainder of the century, despite an apparently irreversible trend towards the planning of the business of the House. Ramsay MacDonald told a Procedure Committee in 1931 that 'the length of our sittings is getting absolutely intolerable . . . unless we can manage to shorten the sittings of the House of Commons, without materially diminishing its output, the machine is going to break down on account of the weight that is upon it'.[35] Successive governments struggled with the attempt to reduce sitting hours and days, without reducing the amount of business dealt with, nor the amount of detailed consideration given to it.

At the beginning of the century it had been only relatively recently that the House had established a routine pattern of sittings: 'its freedom as regards the hour and time for sitting, working and rising', noted the 1893 edition of Erskine May, 'was almost wholly uncontrolled prior to the year 1888'. In 1888 the House set a regular time for the beginning of its sitting (3pm every day except Wednesday, when it was 12 noon) and for rising (the moment of interruption, fixed at midnight, was intended ordinarily to be the end of significant business). As part of the changes made by Balfour in 1902 the opening of a sitting was brought forward to 2pm; the short day on Wednesday was swapped for a short day on Friday; and provision was made for a break for dinner between about 7.30 and 9pm. These arrangements were further altered in 1906: the dinner break was dropped; the normal opening of a sitting was put back, in partial compensation, to 2.45pm, and the moment of interruption brought forward to 11pm; they remained essentially the same for the rest of the century.[36]

[34] HC Deb., 4th series, vol. 101, col. 1363, 30 January 1902.
[35] HC (1930–1), 161, Q. 175.
[36] Apart from during the Second World War. The time of sitting on Friday was altered on 21 December 1927 to 11am, with a moment of interruption at 4.00pm; these became the

The House's annual calendar and sitting hours have rarely been deemed satisfactory: their main virtue has generally been seen as allowing members to pursue other professional activities during much of the day, or else to free much of the ordinary office hours for ministers.[37] The movement to later sittings during the nineteenth century perhaps had much to do with the growing tendency to combine membership of the House of Commons with a profession. But, however convenient for those with careers to pursue in the courts or elsewhere, the House's annual and daily schedule have long been held a considerable nuisance for others. One member told the House in 1902 that 'as one who had had experience of public business on the London County Council, he thought that an immense amount of time was wasted at present. The other evening he had seen a Member whose time was so unoccupied that he was knitting a pair of stockings in the smoking-room. He thought that was a curious occupation for a Member of that House.'[38] Procedure Committees reviewed the issue in 1967–8, 1977–8 and 1986–7, and a separate committee, the 'Jopling Committee', did so again in 1991. An experiment in 1967 with morning sittings for finishing business left over at 10pm the night before was judged unsuccessful 'partly because many Members found the procedure inconvenient and partly because the government had difficulty in finding suitable business to take in the morning when many Members and Ministers were engaged in Committees or elsewhere'.[39] The experiment had no appreciable effect on the number of late sittings.[40] The awkwardness of the issue of late sittings was laid out by the 1986–7 committee: 'without a radical shift in the

---

basic sitting hours for all days of the week in wartime by a series of sessional orders, beginning in September 1940. In 1945 the old pattern of sitting was restored: on Mondays to Thursdays the House was to sit at 2.15pm, with a moment of interruption at 9.15pm; on Fridays the House would sit from 11am to 4.30pm. On 12 April 1946 a sessional order introduced the hours which obtained for the rest of the century: 2.30pm to 10.30pm with a moment of interruption at 10pm. These arrangements were embodied in a standing order on 4 November 1947. In January 1980 the hours for Friday sittings were changed to 9.30am to 3pm. In the 1966–7 session an experiment was conducted with morning sittings on Mondays and Wednesdays. It was not continued after the end of the session; but in 1994 morning sittings on Wednesdays were reintroduced as one of the 'Jopling' reforms. They were dropped, though, in 1999 as a result of the creation of the separate 'Chamber' in Westminster Hall. At the same time, an experiment was begun with an earlier beginning and ending for sittings on Thursdays.

[37] See Earl Winterton, HC (1930–1), 161, p. 330.

[38] HC Deb., 4th series, vol. 103, cols 662–3, 20 February 1902.

[39] HC (1977–8), 558, para. 9.8.

[40] Walkland, *The House of Commons in the Twentieth Century* (Clarendon Press, 1979), p. 510.

parliamentary day, or without reference of much more business to committees off the floor, little can be done unless the volume of business decreases considerably'.[41] The most thorough review of the issue, by the Jopling Committee, could recommend only cautious moves to morning sittings on Wednesdays, an earlier time of sitting on Thursdays, and a small increase in the use of committees for delegated legislation.[42] But by the 1997 Parliament the House was again sitting as long as ever. As Figure 5.1 shows, no attempt to reform sitting hours has, in fact, had more than a marginal effect: only war has had a serious impact on the average number of hours the House sits each day, and the trend has otherwise been steadily, though not dramatically, upwards. Figure 5.2 shows—less strikingly—the pattern of annual sessions.

The dominance of the executive

The principle of the government's control over a sizeable slice of the time of the House was relatively well established by the beginning of the century. Days were either order days (days when business already established had precedence over new business); or notice days (days for introducing new business). Mondays, Wednesdays, Thursdays and Fridays were order days; Tuesday was the notice day. The government could place its own business at the head of the order paper on Monday, Thursday and Friday. The operation of this already confusing system in practice was, however, haphazard. Even though it was earmarked for the government, Friday was by custom normally occupied by debates on going into Committee of Supply, which were, in effect, an opportunity for almost unrestricted debate for private members. As the remaining two days were inadequate for government business, the government increasingly colonised much of the rest of the time. Balfour sketched out the problem in introducing his package of standing order reforms of 1902: 'At present', he argued, 'by our standing orders, the Government have Mondays and Thursdays, and nothing else. No Government can, or for years has, conducted the public business entrusted to it on that very limited asset. It must come for more time; and the result is that the arrangements of private Members as regards their Motions and Bills are thoroughly upset.'[43] Balfour's proposals set out precisely at which sittings government business should have precedence, and had an immediate

---

[41] HC (1986–7), 350, para. 40.
[42] HC (1991–2), 20-I, para. 4.
[43] HC Deb., 4th series, vol. 101, col. 1363.

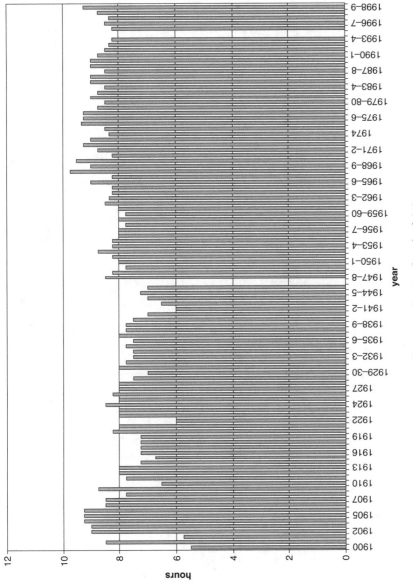

Figure 5.1. Average length of sitting

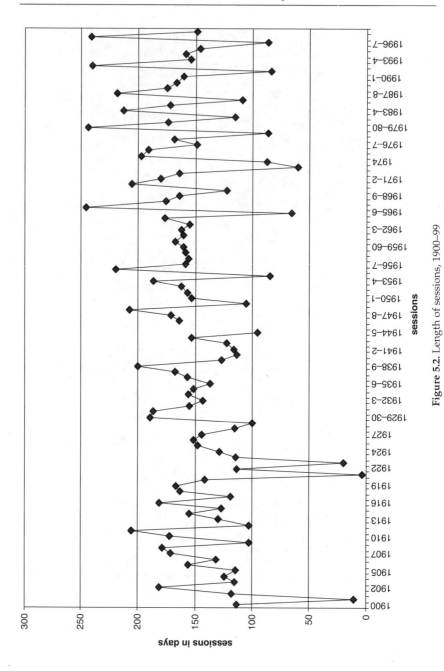

Figure 5.2. Length of sessions, 1900–99

impact in reducing the amount of time claimed from other business by the government. But, despite the vehement opposition they raised, the reforms did not in fact have a huge impact on the actual time left to private members. Lowell commented that before 1902 'in a normal year about thirty parts of the session out of a couple of hundred were given to private Members' (in other words government business took up about 85 per cent of the time); and though he accepted 'that the share of time reserved for private Members is small', he went on to say:

> although their lamentations over confiscation of their sittings by the government have been constant, the actual time at their disposal has not, in fact, been seriously diminished of late years. An examination of the parliamentary papers shows that in the ten years from 1878 to 1887 government business actually had precedence on the average in eighty-three per cent of the sittings, and during the following decade in about eighty-four and a half per cent. This is very little less than the proportion that now prevails. The recent rules have merely sanctioned by permanent standing order a practice that had long been followed in an irregular way by special resolutions adopted during the course of the session.[44]

Yet, even as reorganised by Balfour, private members' time was frequently poached by government, particularly when there was a heavy legislative programme to get through. In 1928–9, 1931–2, 1934–5 and for the whole of the Second World War and some time after it, almost all of private members' time was appropriated. Eventually in 1951 standing orders set aside a specified number of days for private members' bills and ballotted motions, a small fenced reservation in a territory now indisputably commanded by the government. This, too, was subject to encroachment, and the ballotted motions were ultimately removed in exchange for an increase in bill time. The motions were little lamented, for, as Ivor Jennings had said, they were 'usually completely useless' when they came from the government side, or 'usually in substance Opposition motions' when they came from the opposition side. Even in 1931 it was commented that the motions were usually provided by the whips.[45]

It is possible to exaggerate the degree to which private members' opportunities have been chipped away this century, for the process had been going on well before 1900. Laski, in his little book on the constitution in 1951, dismissed the notion, recalling a dinner to which he had been

---

[44] *The Government of England*, vol. 1, p. 312.
[45] I. Jennings, *Parliament*, 2nd edn (Cambridge University Press, 1957), pp. 362–3.

invited in about 1923, at which 'the host complained that the private Member, in the post-1918 period, was reduced to a shadow of what he had been in the days of Mr Gladstone, and how he was answered by Mr Birrell who reminded him of a dinner, at which they had both been present, with Mr Gladstone in the later eighties when the great man, who had then been for nearly sixty years in the House of Commons, told his two younger colleagues that the private Member of this generation was but a shadow of what the private Member had been in what he evidently regarded as the golden age—the period between the Reform Act of 1832 and the disruption of the Conservative Party by Sir Robert Peel'.[46] But that private members' opportunities have been progressively reduced is undeniable, and they exist now scarcely more than vestigially: in bills which require the at least tacit consent of government and opposition to proceed, or in adjournment motions devoted to constituency matters. Figure 5.3 shows for part of the century the fluctuating amount of time available to private members. The 1951 standing order introduced a period of much greater stability.

Making the law

The increase in the volume of (especially) government legislation during the nineteenth century had strained the capacity of the House to deal with it, and had been one of the engines of Victorian procedural reform. Despite the precedence now given to its business, the government remained dogged by the difficulty of processing its legislation. Lowell in 1908 was already remarking on the incapacity of Parliament to deal with any more bills: 'the legislative capacity of the House of Commons has nearly reached its limit. What is more, it is small, and markedly smaller than in the past. In the decade beginning with 1868, ninety-four government bills on the average became law each year, but of late the number has not been half so large, and private members' bills have fallen off in the same proportion. The fact is that a growth in the number of members who want to take part in debate, a more minute criticism, and a more systematic opposition, have made the process of passing a bill through the House increasingly difficult.'[47]

To governments which had come to power believing that they had a

---

[46] H. J. Laski, *Reflections on the Constitution* (Manchester University Press, 1951), p. 29.
[47] Lowell, *The Government of England*, vol. 1, p. 356.

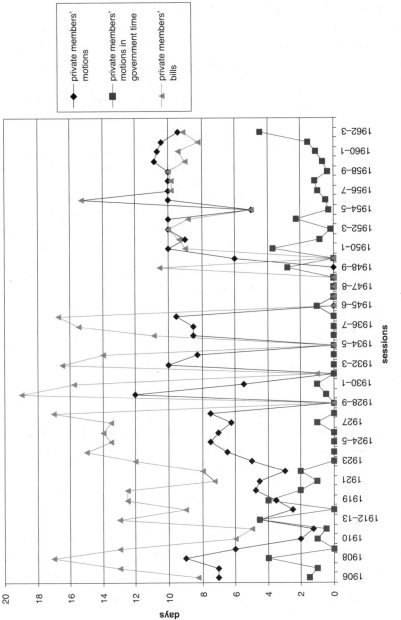

Figure 5.3. Private members' business

strong mandate for social, economic or constitutional change the problem was increasingly frustrating. If an electorate had given specific approval to a party programme, it seemed less reasonable, less legitimate, to attempt to prevent its passage. Their opponents, appealing to the distaste for the idea that the Commons might be a 'legislative machine', would insist that what was wanted was not more legislation, but rather 'more legislation but of a better sort'.[48] W. H. Greenleaf described the battlelines:

> The libertarian, wishing, as he does, to restrict the field of government action, will necessarily stress the need to revivify Parliamentary powers of inquisition and control and to limit the flow of statute-making. On the other hand the collectivist will tend to see Parliament as a legislative machine, a means of processing and legitimizing the evermore numerous proposals of the executive for the achievement of the general good; and in the last resort he will allow no procedural device or scrutiny to stand in the way. In an extreme case this attitude reveals a potential almost Cromwellian in its nature as with the idea that it might be necessary to supersede Parliament in favour of the more efficient process of government by decree. Procedural reform may thus be opposed precisely because it can make government weak.[49]

Drastic, executive-minded solutions to the problem were rather gingerly touted in Labour Party circles during the 1920s and 1930s, as they became aware that the difficulty of legislating would block its programme of reform. One delegate at the Labour Party conference in 1933, discussing a motion put forward by Stafford Cripps, argued that 'Parliamentary procedure, apart from the House of Lords, was devised to protect property from the King. It is being used now to protect property from the people, and Socialism involves the transference of property and the abolition of the powers of property. We have got, therefore, to be prepared to recast the whole form of procedure by democratic government in order to carry through our programme.'[50] In government, though, party leaderships took a more cautious and pragmatic line, and searched for some device which would protect the ability of the opposition and indi-

---

[48] Lt-Col. Lockwood in 1907, quoted by Walkland, *The House of Commons in the Twentieth Century*, pp. 253–4.

[49] W. H. Greenleaf, *The British Political Tradition* (Methuen, 1987), vol. 3, part 2, pp. 763–4. See also Geoffrey Marshall, 'The Analysis of British Political Institutions', in *The British Study of Politics in the Twentieth Century*, ed. J. Hayward, B. Barry and A. Brown (Clarendon Press, 1999), p. 260; Miles Taylor, 'Labour and the Constitution', in *Labour's First Century*, ed. Duncan Tanner, Pat Thane and Nick Tiratsoo (Cambridge University Press, 2000).

[50] E. F. Wise, quoted by A. H. Hanson, 'The Labour Party and House of Commons Reform — II', *Parliamentary Affairs* (1957–8), 46.

vidual members to scrutinise legislation effectively while permitting the government certainty that it could get its legislation through the House. The tendency throughout the century, though, was nevertheless for legislative power to accrue to the executive, with the more determined attempts to extend it coming under progressive administrations with large reform programmes: the 1905 Liberal government, and the 1945 and 1997 Labour governments.

Standing committees

Standing committees had come to be seen in the nineteenth century as the principal solution to the logjam of government legislation. Proposed by Sir Thomas Erskine May and others on a number of occasions between 1854 and 1878, they were only adopted as part of Gladstone's package of measures to overcome the obstruction of Irish members. The obstruction of Irish bills in 1881 and the first session of 1882 had brought matters to a head. In the autumn session of 1882, Gladstone secured the House's approval for the establishment of two committees, one to deal with bills on the law, courts of justice and legal procedure, and the other for bills concerned with trade, shipping and manufactures. The committees were to have a permanent membership of between sixty and eighty with additional members nominated for any particular bill.[51] By 1900 the existence of standing committees was generally accepted. But the powerful idea that significant business must be dealt with on the floor of the House was reflected in a widely held view that committees should not be used for the consideration of controversial bills. The Chairmen's Panel in 1905 claimed that standing committees were originally intended 'to deal mainly with such classes of legislation as the consolidation and improvement of various branches of the law and other kindred matters'; 'it is not desirable to refer to standing committees bills which (1) arouse strong party or political controversy or excite religious susceptibilities, or (2) which are not referred to them by a substantial majority of the House'.[52] Nor did the powers available to the speaker to curtail debate apply to standing committees. Standing committees could do little, therefore, to help a government with a controversial legislative programme. The Liberal government of 1905, with its major reform mandate, sought

[51] G. M. Higgins, 'The Origin and Development of the Standing Committees of the House of Commons, with Special Reference to their Procedure, 1886–1951', D.Phil thesis (Oxford University, 1954).
[52] HC (1905), 261.

to make the committee system more useful. A major revision in 1907 meant that bills would routinely be referred to standing committees; that there would be four committees, rather than two, in three of which government bills were to have precedence; the committees were no longer limited by subject; and their chairmen were given powers to curtail debate. The government continued, though, to promise that the major controversial bills would be considered in committee of the whole House. The system was further expanded at the end of the First World War: the number of committees was increased to six in 1919 (although one was intended to deal with estimates, a role it soon abandoned).

Standing committees still suffered from a lack of effective whipping. Whips were not normally appointed to standing committees, and such whipping as was necessary was done by the minister's parliamentary private secretary, 'though not always efficiently'.[53] Standing committees were regarded as a place where there was much livelier, more interesting and freer debate: 'There is a different spirit from that which exists in the House itself. There is more freedom. There is a genuine feeling on the Grand Committee quite apart from the membership of political parties . . . You do not divide yourselves into flocks under the close supervision of the shepherds when you come to divide. There is something in the physical question of voting where you sit instead of having to pass the cold eye of the whip.'[54]

Standing committees lapsed during the Second World War. But, in anticipation of pressure for legislation after the war, the coalition government had begun consideration of means of accelerating the House's consideration of public bills,[55] and in 1945 the Labour government established a new Procedure Committee, with an instruction to 'report as soon as possible upon any scheme for the acceleration of proceedings on Public Bills which may be submitted to them on behalf of His Majesty's Government'.[56] The government's proposals pointed to a considerable increase in the legislative capacity of the standing committee system. The assumption would be that all bills would be referred to standing committee, the only exceptions being very minor bills expected to be passed quickly, and bills of 'first class constitutional importance'; the number of standing committees would be increased; committees would

---

[53] Jennings, *Parliament*, p. 276.
[54] Lord Robert Cecil in HC Deb., 5th series, 600–1, quoted in Jennings, *Parliament*, p. 227–8.
[55] Herbert Morrison, *Government and Parliament*, 3rd edn (Oxford University Press, 1964), p. 219.
[56] 24 August 1945.

sit for longer; and guillotines would be made applicable to bills in standing committee. There would be no limit on the number of committees established and, correspondingly, their size was reduced. The Procedure Committee endorsed most of the government's recommendations, and the requisite sessional orders were made in November 1945. Conservative objections that it was impossible to define bills of 'first class constitutional importance' were dismissed by Herbert Morrison, who characterised their position as 'that anything which in any way impaired the free working of the capitalist system of production and distribution involved revolutionary constitutional doctrine'.[57] From 1947 onwards, whips were regularly appointed to standing committees.[58] The 1945 changes effectively established the system of standing committees for the remainder of the century. But they had also spelt the end of the relative independence of standing committee proceedings from the party battle in the House, and, for those who lamented Parliament's role as legislative factory, the debates in standing committee came to be numbered among its least satisfactory features. Government backbenchers were made dumb by the presence of whips; ministers and opposition spokespersons would debate a bill with only a second-hand knowledge of what it meant; members with specialist knowledge of the subject of the bill were deliberately excluded from participation on the committee. 'The many hours spent on a Committee stage are usually frustrating and unproductive for most of the participants', wrote one of them in 1992.[59]

Restriction of debate: the closure and the guillotine

The other device fixed on in the 1880s for overcoming campaigns of obstruction aimed at government legislation were the closure (a motion, voted on as soon as made, to end further debate on the specific motion before the House) and the guillotine (a timetable, agreed to by the House in advance, which sets a limit to debate on a set of proceedings, normally on a bill). The closure was borrowed from continental practice in 1881 and enshrined in a standing order in 1882. It has been used ever since, without too much opposition. The power given to the chair to

[57] Morrison, *Government and Parliament*, p. 222. A later Conservative government, however, dismissed the then Labour opposition's claim that the bill to abolish the Greater London Council (the London Government Act 1985) was a bill of first-class constitutional importance.

[58] S. A. Walkland 'Government Legislation in the House of Commons', in *The House of Commons in the Twentieth Century*, pp. 272–3.

[59] John Garrett, *Westminster: Does Parliament Work?* (Gollancz, 1992), p. 51.

select amendments (sometimes referred to as the 'kangaroo closure') from 1919 (and extended to committees in 1932) was likewise relatively easily accepted. The guillotine, though, introduced in 1881 in the same context as the closure, has had a rougher ride. Unlike the closure, the imposition of the guillotine may mean that certain aspects of a bill are not scrutinised at all, and its use—particularly after its extension to standing committees in 1945—firmly tipped the balance of legislative power in favour of the government. As with the introduction of whips into standing committee, the effect was to provide more and more convincing ammunition for those who argued that the need was not for more but for better legislation.

Governments acknowledged the problem with the guillotine by, on the whole, using it sparingly, or else by seeking to use it through agreement with the opposition parties. Ramsay MacDonald suggested this sort of domestication of the guillotine to the Procedure Committee in 1931; the practice was in effect used on the Government of India bill in 1935; and the invention in 1946 of a business subcommittee to allot time to stages of a bill in standing committee was intended to achieve the same effect. The proposal that all legislation should be routinely 'programmed' from the start was put forward frequently, at least from the 1930s (and like most reform proposals, it has a long Victorian ancestry), by members of both main parties and individuals independent of either. Its backing by a Hansard Society Commission in 1992 influenced the further consideration of the issue by the Select Committee on the Modernisation of the House of Commons which was set up by the Labour government in 1997 partly out of a concern that it would be unable to achieve its ambitious programme of constitutional reform without further changes to parliamentary procedure. By reaching cross-party agreement on 'programmes' for these bills in the 1997–8 session, a breach of the convention that 'first-class constitutional bills' should not be sent to standing committees was avoided. The government's attempt to encapsulate this apparent acceptance of 'programming' in a more permanent arrangement in 2000, however, split the committee, and the House.

As a consequence of the devices now available to the government the legislative capacity of the Commons grew a little over the century. Not hugely, however: in 1908, the year Lowell made his remarks on the subject, sixty-nine Acts were passed. The same number were passed in 1997 (though this was a general election year). Figure 5.4 shows this basic stability in numbers. Yet, as significant as the actual number of bills passed has been the length and complexity of the bills concerned.

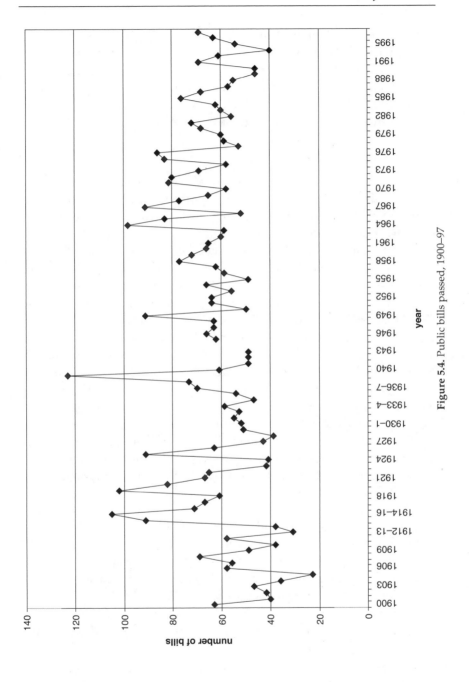

Figure 5.4. Public bills passed, 1900–97

Lowell's sixty-nine of 1908 took up 736 small pages; the sixty-nine of 1997 took up 3,073 large ones. Figure 5.5 shows the much more impressive growth in the paper consumed by government legislation. The amount of time occupied by the legislation has not grown greatly: as Figure 5.6 shows, up until the 1950s, at least, government bills were not occupying an increasing share of the House's time.

Delegated legislation

Opponents of the increasing tendency of governments to legislate had another target with the increasing conferment on ministers (and civil servants) of delegated powers. Delegated legislation had already been the subject of criticism before 1914: but it more than doubled in volume during the First World War, producing a strong reaction in the 1920s both within Parliament and outside it, particularly from those whose libertarian instincts were deeply touched by any extension to bureaucratic discretion. The arguments were put, most notoriously, by Lord Chief Justice Hewart in *The New Despotism* in 1929. Hewart accepted (grudgingly) that 'it may well be that departmental orders and regulations are, to some extent, unavoidable. But why should they be made behind the back of Parliament? . . . there is no good reason, why departmental officials should have, or seem to have, the power of legislating without Parliamentary authority'.[60] The government responded by setting up the Donoughmore Committee to review the issue. Reporting in 1932, the committee reaffirmed the need for delegated legislation, but accepted the case for increased safeguards, proposing a standard procedure for laying subordinate legislation before Parliament and a committee in each House to scrutinise all bills which would grant delegated powers and all statutory instruments laid.[61] No action was taken on the report, however, and the Second World War saw a further massive increase in law-making by ministerial rules and orders. Ultimately, the coalition government agreed in 1944 to set up a Commons Committee on Statutory Instruments on the grounds that 'without some concession to Parliament the Government is likely to have difficulty in securing their assent to legislation which contains regulation-making powers of a wider kind than would normally be thought possible'.[62] The Statutory

---

[60] Hewart, *The New Despotism* (Ernest Benn, 1929), p. 149.
[61] Report of the Committee on Ministers' Powers, Cmd 4060, summarised in Greenleaf, *British Political Tradition*, pp. 560–2.
[62] Quoted in Greenleaf, *British Political Tradition*, p. 571.

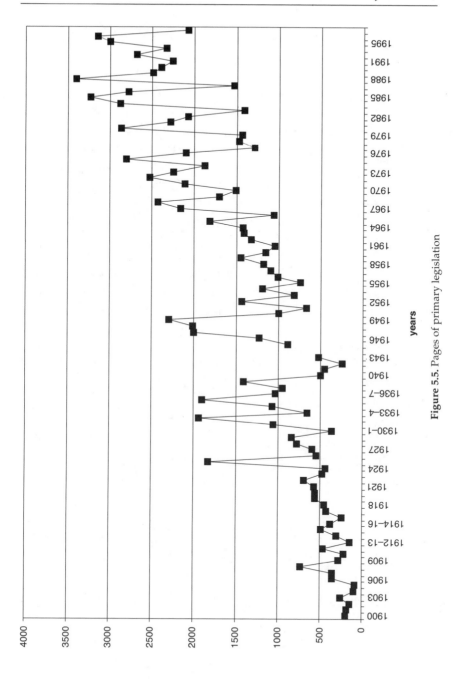

Figure 5.5. Pages of primary legislation

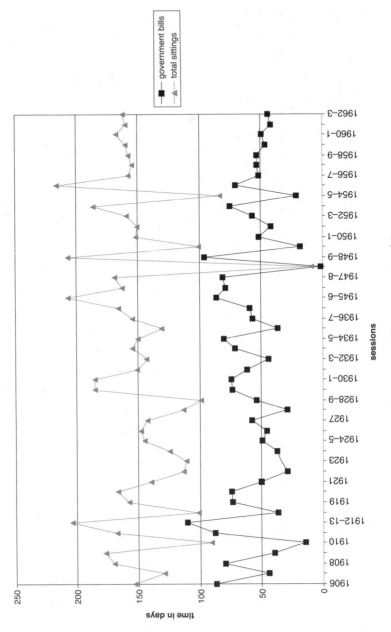

Figure 5.6. Government bills as proportion of time

Instruments Act 1946 also introduced the more systematic arrangements for delegated legislation suggested by the Donoughmore Committee. Yet it only affected a small category of all delegated legislation. Towards the end of the century, new variant forms of delegated legislation emerged— deregulation orders under the Deregulation Act 1994 and (although none were laid by the end of 2000) orders made under the Human Rights Act—and these were provided with special, extra levels of scrutiny, with committees of their own. But unhappiness about ordinary delegated legislation persisted because very few of the large number of instruments laid received significant parliamentary attention. Despite successive Procedure Committee reports with proposals for the more effective scrutiny of delegated legislation, few significant alterations were made to the post-war system.

Scrutiny of government

Financial scrutiny: the approval of the estimates

In 1900 the process of agreeing the estimates and the government's tax proposals—although considerably simplified following a set of reforms in 1896—would normally take up about a third of a session and would be the government's main objective. After the debate on the queen's speech the House would set up the Committee of Supply (to consider and authorise the government's estimates) and the Committee of Ways and Means (to consider and authorise the government's proposals for raising revenue). The debates in Committee of Supply proceeded through the government's individual estimates; the potential for wasting time on the general motion that the House resolve itself into Committee of Supply had been restricted in 1882 and the practice was limited to providing a series of routine, general debates on the army, the navy and the civil service. The order in which the various votes were considered was determined by the government, though normally after consultation with the opposition. Once the debates in supply were completed, the committee's resolutions would be reported to the House; then the Committee of Ways and Means would agree in turn to proposals made by the government, which would be reported to the House, and embodied in the Consolidated Fund bills.

The process was a long and sometimes agonising one. Even so, the belief that the House of Commons could effectively review the government's estimates, spotting inefficiency or unnecessary expenditure, was already generally recognised to be utopian. In practice, in fact, the supply debates were already seen mainly as the principal forum for general debate, and party-political debate in particular. Redlich described the process in 1908:

> Discussion of supply, in the first place, focusses the scrutiny of Parliament into the administration of the Empire: opportunities are afforded to private Members for remarks and comments upon the manner in which the services whose estimates are before the House discharged their public functions. Debate upon the estimates is therefore the appropriate occasion on which to advocate local claims or particular efforts for legislation and state action in a wide sense of the term. Reforms affecting any branch of the public service may thus annually be advocated. The estimates, again, furnish yearly recurring occasions for entering upon such subjects as general foreign policy, military and naval plans, or the world-embracing British trade and colonial policy. Secondly, with the central place in national affairs occupied by the state housekeeping, the topics introduced in its discussion give many opportunities for applying the great political principles which divide or unite the Government and the Opposition; the estimates are the battlefield where the great parties champion their respective causes, not only with reference to economic considerations, but also on grounds affecting national policy as a whole. And lastly, they furnish the traditional and appropriate occasions for challenging or calling for an expression of the confidence of the majority of the House in the Ministry and thus testing the political basis of their authority.[63]

Balfour's reforms of 1896, extended in 1902, were a first step in the process of abandoning the connection between the debates and financial scrutiny and converting the painful business of getting the estimates approved into a routine and certain—and, ultimately, almost purely formal—process. The reforms had provided for the main estimates to be voted on (whether or not debate had been exhausted) after an allotted period of nineteen days, and the resolutions of the Committee of Supply to be voted on by the House after a further day. The total of twenty days could be extended to twenty-three by the House if wished. The 'supply guillotine' did not, however, apply to supplementary estimates, excess votes and votes on credit.[64] The existence of a guillotine increased the significance of the order in which the votes were set down for approval, and Balfour offered the opposition effective control over it. The oppo-

---

[63] J. Redlich, *The Procedure of the House of Commons: A Study of its History and Present Form* (Constable, 1908), part 3, p. 136.

[64] M. Ryle, 'Supply and Other Financial Procedures', in Walkland, *The House of Commons in the Twentieth Century*, pp. 347–52.

sition was slow to pick up the offer but, over the next twenty or so years, it became normal practice for the votes to be debated to be chosen by the opposition, leaving private members with much reduced opportunities to initiate debate.[65] As a result, the debates tended to become even more than before set pieces, with the advantages of committee procedure, including detailed consideration and members speaking more than once, largely abandoned. As Michael Ryle wrote in the late 1970s, 'by the 1930s Supply days were being used as they are today, namely as the occasion for arranged and formal debates on policies and areas of administration chosen by the official Opposition of the day. They were thus essentially concerned with indirect rather than direct control of expenditure.'[66] Sometimes the votes on the estimates were taken purely formally and debate took place instead on a motion expressing an opinion on government policy. After the Second World War the shift to the more general debates on government policy and administration was recognised in a series of procedural changes, culminating in the formal abolition of the committees of Supply and Ways and Means in 1966–7 and the making of much of the supply procedure effectively formal and non-debated business. Any formal connection of the debates initiated by the opposition with the business of supply was jettisoned in 1982 on the recommendation of a Procedure Committee, since when the link between opposition debates and supply has been little more than a memory.[67]

The long gestation of the committee system

The decline of the Committee of Supply as a means of providing effective scrutiny of government expenditure was perhaps a token of diminishing interest in Victorian principles of economy, but the lack of detailed examination of the estimates was widely regarded as unsatisfactory. The obvious solution, proposed by a committee appointed in 1902 to look at ways of addressing the problem, was for a system of select committees to perform the function.

The proposal was strenuously resisted by governments reluctant to create any committee which might have the temerity to review, and even disagree with, government decisions, and might, they suspected, act as an upward, rather than a downward, pressure on expenditure. Not until 1912 were some of the committee's recommendations adopted, after

[65] Ryle, 'Supply and Other Financial Procedures', pp. 400–1.
[66] Ibid., p. 400.
[67] HC (1980–1), 118–1, paras 96–9.

pressure from backbenchers. The new Estimates Committee was barred from reviewing the policy behind the estimates. Lloyd George firmly told the House on introducing it that 'there must be no Committee which is to be a substitute for House of Commons responsibility; ... there must be no Committee that will accept responsibility for the policy it is examining'. Austen Chamberlain, for the opposition, was even more dubious: 'I am wholly opposed to the establishment of this Committee, which, in my opinion, will either be useless or will be in the highest degree mischievous.'[68] With support like this, the committee could hardly be expected to thrive, and it did not: 'Without previous preparation, without experience or aid, Members attempted to criticise the complicated plans which a department and the Treasury had taken more than one year to hammer out as the minimum requirements of the service, and to which they were committed.'[69] The committee was abandoned at the outset of the First World War. A much more effective Committee on National Expenditure was appointed in 1917 to appease cross-party backbench discontent, and it worked through departmentally related subcommittees. Before it succumbed to a revival of party-politics in 1921, the committee recommended the establishment of a permanent system of estimates committees, which could look in detail at the estimates, and whose reports would inform the debates in Committee of Supply. An Estimates Committee replaced it, despite the opposition of Austen Chamberlain, now chancellor of the Exchequer. Although regarded as toothless compared to its predecessor, it began to emulate the 1917 committee by working through subcommittees, and during the 1930s it abandoned the attempt to review the estimates in detail and began to conduct more general reviews of administrative activities.

During the Second World War the Estimates Committee lapsed and was replaced by a National Expenditure Committee, which operated in a more wide-ranging and comprehensive way than any of its predecessors. The suggestion after the end of the war by the clerk of the House, Sir Gilbert Campion, that a new committee be established, combining the functions of the Public Accounts Committee and the Estimates Committee, provoked a strong reaction among government ministers, who regarded the National Expenditure Committee as having taken a step too far in encroaching 'into the field of executive administration': 'the

---

[68] HC Deb., vol. 37, cols 367, 374.
[69] Basil Chubb, *The Control of Public Expenditure: Financial Committees of the House of Commons* (Clarendon Press, 1952), p. 91.

Committee got asking questions which, in the judgment of some of the Ministers at that time, were, so to speak, running rival with the executive responsibility of the Minister himself'. Herbert Morrison, giving evidence to the 1945–6 Procedure Committee, accepted that the committee's actions might have been reasonable during wartime, because the normal checks on government were much reduced, 'but the Government does not quite like the idea of going back to that system in conditions of peace'.[70] Instead of adopting Campion's proposal, the old Estimates Committee was revived. It was, however, expanded and given the power to appoint six subcommittees, and showed, in its inquiries, that it had learned much from the wartime committee. In particular, it did not limit itself (as suggested by its order of reference) to examination of the estimates, although its inquiries at least began by being firmly linked to financial scrutiny.[71] Commentators outside Parliament regarded it as constructive, particularly as it had accustomed departments 'to the dissemination of a great deal of information about their activities and organization, and . . . to listen sympathetically to parliamentary criticism'.[72]

Perhaps because of the committee's own tendency to push at the edge of its existing terms of reference, frequently making recommendations which were very close to, if not actually, about policy, perhaps because of the successful operation of a select committee covering the nationalised industries (on a temporary basis at first from 1951), during the 1960s the discussion about the Estimates Committee changed into advocacy of a much broader role of scrutiny than was permitted by the consideration of financial matters alone and was informed by a belief that Parliament had lost in a struggle for power with the executive and that a more systematic set of select committees might help it to win back the initiative.[73] The Procedure Committee in 1964–5 proposed extending the terms of reference of the Estimates Committee into 'how the departments of state carry out their responsibilities and to consider their Estimates of Expenditure and Reports'. Although the Labour government committed itself to an extension of the system of parliamentary committees in 1966, the changes introduced that year by the then leader of the House, Richard Crossman, disappointed many reformers.

[70] HC (1945–6), 189-I, Q. 3229.
[71] Chubb, *Control of Public Expenditure*, pp. 161–8.
[72] Nevil Johnson, 'Select Committees and Administration', in Walkland, *The House of Commons in the Twentieth Century*, p. 452.
[73] See, for example, Bernard Crick, *The Reform of Parliament* (Weidenfeld & Nicolson, 1964).

A Committee on Science and Technology was set up in 1966, followed by four 'departmental' committees—on Agriculture, Education and Science, Scottish Affairs, and Overseas Aid—and a Race Relations and Immigration Committee in 1968. This half-way house was commonly felt to be unsatisfactory, and a more coherent structure was established under the Conservative government in 1971, based on a Procedure Committee report of 1968–9. Under these arrangements, the Estimates Committee was replaced by an Expenditure Committee with six subcommittees, with terms of reference permitting examination of matters of policy as well as efficiency and economy in administration. Even so, the scrutiny it provided was widely regarded as unsystematic and uneven. A Procedure Committee report of 1978 argued for a single system of twelve committees, based on the main government departments. The Labour government—taken aback by the support the proposal had gained in the House—had to rethink its initial rejection of the idea;[74] but the system, a manifesto commitment of the Conservative Party, was eventually implemented by the new government in June 1979.

The 'new' select committee system did, as its proponents said it would, constitute a significant enhancement of the capacity for scrutiny of government activity by the House of Commons, and delivered the oversight of government, department by department, which reformers had demanded. But it was not quite the system the committee had proposed: the new committees were not given effective powers to send for ministers or to order the production of their papers and records; the opportunities for debates in the House on committee reports remained few. The weaknesses of the system were exposed in a series of *causes célèbres*, and were the subject of a steady stream of critical reports on their performance, highlighting too much control by whips; not enough opportunities for calling attention to their reports in the House; not enough research capacity; inadequate powers to insist on ministers giving evidence; lack of commitment and effort by members. Yet the select committee 'system' had finally become established as a permanent feature of the House of Commons; and it added a large new dimension to the scrutiny activity of Parliament.

Its creation, though, had been in spite of a constant sense that departmental select committees fly in the face of fundamental principles of British constitutional practice—in particular, the individual responsibility of ministers for policy and their accountability to Parliament as a

---

[74] See HC Deb., 5th series, vol. 963, cols 285–99, 383–5.

whole. Nowhere is the schizophrenic nature of the British Parliament in the twentieth century more apparent than in the debate over select committees; for the demands for a strengthened committee system which would clip the wings of an over-powerful executive did not go together with a challenge to those underlying principles of the constitution which barred them from becoming too effective. The only significant challenge to those principles during the century was the sustained campaign waged by the Labour MP, Fred Jowett, from 1913 to the 1930s for the abolition of the control of public departments by individual ministers and of the collective responsibility of the Cabinet, and their replacement—on the model of British local government—by a series of departmental committees composed of members of Parliament which would take administrative responsibility and initiate legislation. The scheme, proposed in an ILP report in 1924, was firmly rejected by Harold Laski, the mind behind an alternative report, which claimed that 'no committee can effectively direct administration for the essential reason that individual responsibility is the real root of all creative work in administration'; but also argued that such a committee system, with an innate tendency to compromise, would handicap a socialist majority from driving 'a great programme through the statute book'.[75]

For the most part the establishment and elaboration of the select committee system came about on the basis of a consensus that the committees' role was one simply of scrutiny and advice, and that this had no necessary effect on the constitutional balance. But some external observers cast a more jaundiced eye on the claim that select committees could be both effective and operate within the existing parameters of the British constitution, and were sceptical that the balance could be shifted without a significant recasting of some central parts of the British constitution. Nevil Johnson, for example, argued that it was unrealistic to believe (at least in the 1960s) that select committees could hold the key to a change in the relationship between government and Parliament. 'Such efforts cannot be expected of bodies which have no powers of decision and are under no obligation to vote, to say nothing of the party political neutralisation which remains an important condition of their ability to produce results and to secure attention.' He queried whether the belief that Parliament had declined seriously in relation to the executive and that 'something should be done to strengthen it as a representative institution capable of controlling the Executive' was com-

[75] Hanson, 'The Labour Party and House of Commons Reform—II', 39–42.

patible with a failure to question the doctrine of competitive two-party politics and ministerial responsibility.[76] The belief that significant increases in the effectiveness of select committees and the scrutiny function of Parliament more generally cannot really be conceded without upsetting the constitutional framework seems to have been shared by successive governments. A picture of the disposition of forces at the end of the century is provided by the exchange in 1999–2000 between the Liaison Committee and the government over its report on 'shifting the balance' between Parliament and the executive. The committee's advocacy of the popular idea of confirmation hearings by select committees of ministerial appointees met with the government's opposition to permitting committees to encroach upon its own territory: 'any indication that a ministerial appointment relied upon the approval of a Select Committee or was open to a Select Committee veto would break the clear lines of accountability by which Ministers are answerable to Committees for the actions of the executive'—'The role of the Select Committee has always been to scrutinise the actions and decisions of departments—not to take part in the decision making.'[77]

Questions

The development of the committee structure means that it is now the most effective system of scrutiny. But other forms—most obviously written and oral parliamentary questions—continue to provide opportunities to draw information out of the government and into the public domain. Parliamentary questions were already a regular, and growing, feature of the day in the House of Commons in 1900, taking place before the beginning of public business. The growth in the number of questions asked in the second half of the nineteenth century had been one element in the increasing stress under which the House was placed. It was already normal to give notice of questions and to ask supplementaries. Balfour in 1901 complained how questions 'take up the best hour in the day; they refer, for the most part, to very trifling subjects; they give rise to constant friction between the Chair and the Irish Members—very obstructive to the dignity of Parliament; and in the shape of supplementary questions asked without notice, they are constantly made the vehicle

---

[76] Nevil Johnson, in Walkland, *The House of Commons in the Twentieth Century,* pp. 462–3.
[77] The government's response to the First Report from the Liaison Committee on *Shifting the Balance: Select Committees and the Executive,* Session 1999–2000, Cm 4737, para. 17; see also HC Deb., vol. 363, col. 86.

for calumnious attacks on individuals'.[78] Balfour's package of reforms included setting a limit to questions (originally forty minutes, but subsequently growing to about an hour) at the beginning of each sitting; the introduction of a system for grouping questions to each minister, which progressively evolved into the current rota system; and the creation of a new procedure for answers to be given in writing, rather than orally. In 1909 a limit was introduced on the number of questions that any individual member could ask. 'Question time' maintained its status as a party-political slanging match, particularly after the introduction by Macmillan in 1961 of a fixed twice-weekly slot for questions to the prime minister, replacing the practice of prime minister's questions being taken each day after a certain number of questions to departmental ministers had been disposed of. The highly party-political nature of question time—and especially prime minister's questions—has been deprecated by virtually every parliamentary reformer ever since.

The introduction of written questions has been productive of a greater degree of light, and has become a major, though largely unsung, element in the process of parliamentary accountability. But written questions were slow to develop in this way until the 1960s, when they suddenly took off in popularity. The government, however, was able to limit the effectiveness of the scrutiny. It was said of Lloyd George that when, on a motoring holiday, he asked of a passer-by where he was and received the answer that he was in a car, he commented that it was the perfect answer to a parliamentary question, because 'it was true, it was brief, and it told him absolutely nothing he did not know before';[79] it was claimed that there was some evidence—especially in the exhaustive examination by Sir Richard Scott's inquiry into the extent to which information was provided to Parliament or concealed from it in response to parliamentary questions—that this was generally the spirit in which governments approached answering parliamentary questions. Although suggestions that the honesty with which governments gave answers should be policed by an external commissioner were not taken up, the introduction of a Freedom of Information Act right at the end of the century looked likely to produce the same effect.

---

[78] Quoted in D. N. Chester and N. Bowring, *Questions in Parliament* (Clarendon Press, 1962), p. 56.

[79] Philip Laundy, *Parliaments in the Modern World* (Dartmouth, 1989), p. 96, note 6.

Parliament, the United Kingdom and Europe

Sovereignty, the Union and the Empire

In 1900 the Westminster Parliament provided the focus of accountability and the centre of political authority for not only a Union of four countries, but also an Empire of 410 million people. The Colonial Laws Validity Act 1865 had specifically asserted Westminster's continuing power to legislate even for dominions such as the Australian states which had their own legislatures, although in 1915 Dicey wrote that 'the omnipotence . . . of Parliament, though theoretically admitted, has been applied in its full effect only to the United Kingdom'.[80] Benignly replicating itself across the globe, the Westminster Parliament was happy to shed over the course of the century most of its responsibilities for the dominions; but the rise of democracy and nationalist movements within the United Kingdom created periodic demands for the relaxation of Westminster's grip which became much more difficult to reconcile with the idea of Britishness and the identity of the Union—and also difficult to fit in within the assumption of a unitary Parliament. Federal solutions to devolution could not be comfortably fitted into a state one of whose parts was overwhelmingly larger than the three others; but asymmetrical devolution laid bare the differential balance of political power in separate parts of the United Kingdom and posed the 'West Lothian question'—why should the representatives of countries with devolved responsibilities continue to be allowed to vote on matters on which they had no electoral mandate? While recognising the demand for devolution, fear of the consequences for the existence of the Union and the awkward questions devolution posed for Parliament led governments to drag their heels on the subject until the political will for devolution became electorally impossible to ignore.

Ireland

Some form of home rule for Ireland, almost accomplished in 1914 following the neutering of resistance in the House of Lords by the passage of the Parliament Act in 1911, was guaranteed by the sweeping victory of Sinn Fein in the 1918 general election.[81] Lloyd George's Government

---

[80] A. V. Dicey, *Introduction to the Study of the Law of the Constitution*, 10th edn (Macmillan, 1959) p. xxvii.
[81] Seventy-three Sinn Fein members were elected, winning all but four seats outside Ulster.

of Ireland Act 1920, accurately described by A. J. P. Taylor as 'an arrangement of fantastic complexity',[82] brought into existence the Irish state and
removed Ireland as a significant issue of debate at Westminster for almost
fifty years. The separation of responsibilities between the new Northern
Ireland Parliament at Stormont and Westminster was rigorously enforced:
Speaker Whitley had ruled in 1923 that parliamentary questions on
devolved matters were outside the responsibility of British ministers and
could not therefore be asked.[83] That rule proved unsustainable as the
events of the late 1960s unfolded in Northern Ireland, despite efforts by
the Unionists to hold to the Whitley line when, for example, Gerry Fitt
attempted to secure an emergency debate on 2 December 1968 after riots
in Armagh.[84] After the suspension of Stormont, Northern Ireland affairs
occupied a great deal of parliamentary time for the last third of the
century, with the various schemes for constitutional change from the Sunningdale Agreement of 1973 to the Good Friday Agreement of 1999
coming under extensive scrutiny, and emergency legislation affecting
Northern Ireland alone (the Northern Ireland (Emergency Provisions)
Acts) and the United Kingdom as a whole (the Prevention of Terrorism
Acts) being introduced, renewed and frequently amended as the perception of security needs altered.

The sensitivity of Northern Ireland's politics made its reintegration
into the Westminster system especially difficult, and successive governments avoided getting to grips with the position of Northern Ireland
within Parliament. From having their own Parliament where domestic
legislation could be debated in detail and amended, Northern Ireland
members found themselves with fewer opportunities to influence legislation affecting the province than members for the remainder of the
United Kingdom had in respect of legislation affecting them. Stormont
primary legislation was replaced by Westminster secondary legislation,
subject to all intents and purposes to the same unsatisfactory and truncated parliamentary consideration as other delegated powers. The fiction
that Orders in Council under the Northern Ireland Act 1974 were primary
legislation was subjected periodically to the withering sarcasm of Enoch
Powell. Some procedural concessions were made to Northern Irish
interests, with a Northern Ireland Committee first established in 1974 as

[82] A. J. P. Taylor, *English History 1914–1945* (Clarendon Press, 1976), p.156.
[83] HC Deb., vol. 163, cols 1624–5.
[84] HC Deb., vol. 30, col. 1038ff.

a paler reflection of its Scottish and Welsh Grand counterparts.[85] As far as select committee scrutiny was concerned, the original position after the 1979 reforms was that each new departmental committee took responsibility for Northern Irish matters which fell within its subject area. This meant that there was little interest by predominantly Great Britain members in matters of specific Northern Ireland concern.

The quickening pace of constitutional negotiations in the last decade of the century reversed the tendency to delicate avoidance of the Irish question. A British–Irish Inter-Parliamentary Body was set up in early 1990 as a confidence-building body intended to complement other developments in British–Irish relations, but was boycotted by Unionists. On the other side, Unionists were supposed to be assured of Westminster's continuing involvement in Northern Ireland by a series of procedural concessions. A Select Committee on Northern Ireland Affairs was finally established in 1994, and at the same time the Northern Ireland Committee was given additional powers similar to those of the Scottish and Welsh equivalents. Although the Northern Ireland Select Committee and the Northern Ireland Grand Committee survived to the end of the century, by the late 1990s attention had shifted to the restoration of devolved powers back to Belfast, with the opening of the Northern Ireland Assembly in 1999.

Scotland

On 19 January 1988, at the first sitting of the First Scottish Standing Committee on the Housing (Scotland) Bill, Dennis Canavan, the MP for Falkirk West, decided to sit on the benches reserved for nominated members, though he was not a member of the committee. When he refused to withdraw, the sitting was suspended, but not before George Galloway had complained that Canavan might not be a member, although he was not showing the contempt of the committee that James Arbuthnot, a London Conservative MP and a whip, was by 'sitting stuffing envelopes in a committee on a Scottish Bill'. As John Home Robertson put it when the committee reassembled, 60 per cent of the seats on the committee were given to a party which had only 14 per cent of the Scottish vote.

Resentment at the participation of members from England in the discussion of exclusively Scottish matters was a feature of Scottish busi-

---

[85] See below for fuller description of these. The title of the Northern Ireland Committee was changed to the Northern Ireland Grand Committee on 9 March 1994.

ness at Westminster for much of the century; but, at its beginning, home rule for Scotland had largely been a Liberal cause. A Speaker's Conference was appointed in 1919 to consider the devolution of power from Westminster to subordinate legislatures; but its eventual report[86] was less than satisfactory, and was never debated. Impetus for a measure of home rule for the other Celtic nations waned after the establishment of the Irish Free State: the end of Irish pressure for home rule had collateral effects in Wales and Scotland, where those who supported devolution had been given something of a free ride by Irish home rulers. Another factor was the growth in Scotland and Wales, generally at the expense of pro-devolution Liberals, of a Labour Party which was essentially centralist and concerned with other issues. In 1932 during a debate on home rule, George Buchanan, Labour MP for the Gorbals, set out the party's views on the matter, arguing that 'no Parliament and no Government, local or national, will last or will have meaning for a people which does not wipe out needless poverty in the country which it governs'. The government offered remaining home rule opinion an abbreviated procedure for Scottish private bills, taken by one Scottish Conservative as 'proof that Scotland, if it requires development, will get it at the hands of the British Parliament'.

In any case, Scotland already possessed a measure of special treatment at Whitehall and Westminster. The Scottish Office had been created in 1885, along with a secretary of state open to questioning on the floor of the House. From 1907 there was a permanent standing committee on Scottish bills, generally known as the Scottish Grand Committee, though it formally received this title only in 1957. This committee's original sole purpose was to take the committee stage of Scottish bills not considered in committee of the whole House. There were several proposals through the first half of the century for the enhancement of its role, including those of the then clerk of the House, Sir Gilbert Campion, to the 1945–6 Procedure Committee, and in 1948 the committee was given extra powers to consider the second readings of Scottish bills and the Scottish estimates. The change was optimistically described by Kenneth Wheare as 'an attempt to make a kind of little Scottish House of Commons inside the House of Commons of the United Kingdom'.[87] It was certainly a

---

[86] Cmd 692.

[87] K. C. Wheare, *Government by Committee: An Essay on the British Constitution* (Clarendon Press, 1955), p. 161. See J. H. Burns, 'The Scottish Committees of the House of Commons, 1948–59', *Political Studies* (1960), and G. E. Edwards, 'The Scottish Grand Committee, 1958 to 1970', *Parliamentary Affairs* (1971).

reaction to burgeoning desire for parliamentary recognition of Scottish otherness, though criticised by many for its limited extent.[88] In 1957, a separate Scottish Standing Committee was established to consider the committee stage of Scottish bills.[89] This committee consisted of thirty Scottish members with not more than twenty other added members. A separate Scottish Grand Committee was simultaneously created to consider Scottish bills in principle (in effect, their second reading), and to hold six days on Scottish estimates and two days on which Scottish 'matters' might be debated on substantive motions. In essence, the new standing committee was intended to be more manageable, though the first bill it considered needed to be guillotined.[90] The one devolutionary concession was the limited introduction of 'matters' debates.

The growth in support for the Scottish National Party in the 1960s resulted in much greater pressure for Westminster change. A Select Committee on Scottish Affairs was established in February 1969, and chose first to examine the issue which was at the heart of Scottish public controversy—public funding in Scotland. Far more radically, a Conservative working group chaired by Sir Alec Douglas-Home reported in March 1970 to the party leader in favour of a Scottish Convention, sitting in Edinburgh as a third chamber of the United Kingdom Parliament. This did not find favour with the party leadership, and indeed the Scottish Select Committee was wound up in 1972, despite opposition complaints.

The Labour government of 1974 to 1979 proposed a more radical form of devolution, and debate on the Scotland and Wales bill in session 1976–7 and on the subsequent session's Scotland bill took up enormous swathes of time in both Houses. When the March 1979 referendum failed to be endorsed by 40 per cent of the Scottish electorate under a provision inserted into the Scotland Act by a backbench amendment made in the Commons against government opposition, and a Conservative government was subsequently elected, the pressure for devolution appeared to have receded. The Conservative government attempted to satisfy devolutionist sentiment with changes to the Scottish Grand Committee (which from 1981 was shorn of its non-Scottish members, permitted to meet in Edinburgh and allowed more days' debate on 'matters'), and to parallel the establishment of the departmentally related select committees by a

---

[88] HC Deb., 28 April 1948.

[89] A second Scottish Standing Committee was established in 1962–3.

[90] The controversial Miscellaneous Financial Procedures (Scotland) bill 1958 which introduced the 'block grant' system to Scotland.

Select Committee on Scottish Affairs.[91] But, despite the 1979 failure, pressure for change continued to grow during the Conservative administration, especially as a result of measures such as the early introduction of the ill-fated poll tax in Scotland. The decline in Conservative support north of the border posed increasing problems in dealing with Scotland at Westminster. The Scottish Affairs Committee was never even appointed during the 1987 to 1992 Parliament because of the difficulty in nominating it at a time when there were only ten Scottish Conservative MPs, most of them ministers. The final response of the Conservative period could be seen as an attempt to return in a watered-down form to the ideas of Sir Alec Douglas-Home. In July 1994, the Scottish Grand Committee was given power to hold question times, hear ministerial statements, consider secondary legislation and to meet anywhere in Scotland. Ministers from any department could participate in meetings. From July 1994 until the election of May 1997, the committee met on twenty-two occasions in Scotland and nine times at Westminster. Locations all over Scotland were chosen, and on one occasion the prime minister attended.[92] This was the embryonic Scottish Parliament identified by Wheare fifty years previously but, as an attempt to forestall devolution, the 1994 reforms were too little and too late, and failed to prevent the election nationally and in Scotland of a government committed to full-scale devolution. The Scotland Act was passed in the first months of the 1997 Labour government, and the Scottish Parliament first sat in May 1999.

Wales

The representation of Wales in the House of Commons throughout the twentieth century has reflected a far more radical electorate than that in England. For example, in the 1906 election, thirty-three of the thirty-four Welsh seats were won by Liberals, with the remaining seat going to Keir Hardie; in 1945, twenty-five of the thirty-six seats were won by Labour, seven by the Liberals and four by Conservatives or National Liberals. Yet specifically Welsh concerns were rarely heard at Westminster. A Welsh Parliamentary Party had been formed in 1888 to articulate Welsh aspirations in areas such as education, church disestablishment and land tenure. This had followed the first specifically Welsh Act—the Welsh

---

[91] Because of impending devolution, no proposals had been made by the 1977–8 Procedure Committee for the establishment of select committees to monitor the work of the Scottish or Welsh Offices.

[92] July 1996 in Dumfries.

Sunday Closing Act 1881. Disestablishment bills had, however, been unsuccessful in 1894 and 1895, and, in the judgement of K. O. Morgan, 'by the First World War, the Welsh Party was a familiar target for ironic scorn as its repeated, and always ineffectual, threats of revolt against the party leadership carried no conviction'.[93] The high point was the passage of the Welsh Church Act 1914 under the patronage of Lloyd George and the provisions of the Parliament Act 1911 without the assent of the Lords. Welsh MPs were reported as singing *Hen Wlad Fy Nhadau* in the Lobby. But in the inter-war period there was little consideration of specifically Welsh issues by the Commons, and no recognition that means should be found for allotting time to specifically Welsh business. Indeed, the word 'Wales' appears only once in the index to the Commons journals from 1930 to 1950. Efforts to push for Welsh administrative and legislative reform, such as the Wrexham Liberal MP Sir Robert Thomas's Government of Wales bill of 1922, were completely unsuccessful.[94]

Some concessions were forthcoming during the war: an Act on the Welsh language in 1942, and (although the demand for a separate secretary of state was rebuffed) the inception of a Welsh Day debate on 17 October 1944—the first of what later became annual debates held around St David's Day. The 1944 debate was famous for the speech of Aneurin Bevan criticising the idea that Welsh concerns were distinguishable from English concerns. In that view he represented a commonplace feeling in anglicised south-east Wales, but a different view from the majority of other Labour MPs who spoke. In the 1950s and 1960s, however, increased administrative devolution brought with it some parliamentary change. The home secretary was given the additional title of minister of Welsh affairs in 1951, and a minister of state was appointed (albeit sitting in the Lords) in 1957. Welsh MPs had shown that national concerns could influence their parliamentary behaviour when they voted, regardless of party, against the eventually successful Liverpool Corporation bill in the 1956–7 session—the bill which was so emotive in Wales because it provided for the flooding of the remote Welsh-speaking Tryweryn valley to provide water to Liverpool. A secretary of state was finally appointed in October 1964 by the new Labour administration. Giving ministers

[93] K. O. Morgan, *Rebirth of a Nation: Wales 1880–1980* (Clarendon Press, 1981), p. 32.

[94] The bill was introduced on 28 April 1922, and talked out on first reading. A deputation of Welsh MPs led by James Griffiths, the Labour MP (and eventual first secretary of state for Wales), went to see Chamberlain on 30 June 1938 to press the case for a secretary of state for Wales. They were rebuffed by the argument that Wales was not a parallel case to Scotland since it had no separate system of law and public administration.

specifically Welsh responsibilities meant Welsh parliamentary questions and adjournment debates, and, in session 1959–60, the appointment of a Welsh Grand Committee by sessional order. The sessional order was renewed each year until 1968–9, when a standing order was made. The Welsh Grand was at first a pale reflection of its Scottish counterpart, initially having power to consider only 'matters' referred to it by the House; but in 1974, the committee was given powers to consider the very few bills relating specifically to Wales. The Callaghan government adopted devolution for Wales; but as in Scotland (though more decisively) the proposals failed to attract the support of the required proportion of the electorate, and the succeeding Conservative governments were thrown back—as in Scotland—on means of satisfying the political interest in devolution through Westminster mechanisms. The task was made more difficult by the low level of Conservative parliamentary support in Wales. Three of the four secretaries of state for Wales from 1979 to 1997 represented English constituencies. When the Local Government (Wales) bill 1994 relating exclusively to Wales was introduced, the standing order providing that it should be committed to a standing committee 'so constituted so as to include all Members sitting for constituencies in Wales' had to be disapplied by a House whose party political make-up was wholly different from that of the MPs representing Welsh constituencies.

As in Scotland, the debate over devolution which developed in the final days of the Conservative administration from 1996 to 1997 saw the Tories making concessions on the role of the Welsh Grand Committee, in an unsuccessful attempt to satisfy the demand with something less. The establishment of the National Assembly for Wales by the Labour government in 1999, though, reflected the smaller support for devolution in Wales, because it was given only secondary legislative powers and no right to raise revenue. As in the case of Scotland, the competition for democratic supremacy between the Westminster Parliament and the devolved body in Cardiff is likely to become an important element of the constitutional history of the next century. But that question is likely to be exacerbated in the case of Wales where the model of secondary legislative power resting in Cardiff and primary legislative power in London is only sustainable on the basis of good will between the two administrations. As in the case of Scotland, Welsh MPs have also needed to adjust to the existence of a body which has taken over responsibility for areas of domestic policy which was previously theirs.

Europe

The impact on parliamentary institutions of Britain's entry into the European Economic Community has been as much a part of the debate on 'Europe' as the 'West Lothian question' has been part of the debate on devolution. From, and indeed before, the fraught passage of the European Communities Act 1972, the discussion of the impact of the EC on Westminster has been characterised by fears about the loss of control over legislation. The case of *Factortame* v. *Secretary of State for Transport*[95] which established almost twenty years after British accession that Community law had primacy over the statutes passed by Parliament, and which some held to have effectively extinguished the idea of parliamentary sovereignty, was widely regarded as confirming these fears, which grew with every broadening of the scope of the Community, in the Single European Act (1986), the Maastricht Treaty (1992) and the Amsterdam Treaty (1997). British participation in the European Parliament seemed no substitute for genuine national control over legislation: the Brussels and Strasbourg institution was regarded by many Westminster members with distaste, and its lack of an effective role, combined with the failure of credible pan-European political parties to be established left general objections to a 'democratic deficit' within the European institutions. Added to this, the mutual incomprehension of two Parliaments which worked in very different ways did nothing to remove the belief held in some quarters that the European Parliament could only survive by removing power from Westminster. Despite proposals for more imaginative linkages between Westminster and Europe, the effect of Europe on the House of Commons has been, formally at least, quite small and incremental: as the then leader of the House, John Biffen, commented in 1989, 'It is quite remarkable the extent to which we have not undertaken any fundamental alteration in our procedures to take account of what I think to be something almost without precedent in significance over the last generation or so.'[96]

Central to the concerns of many of the opponents of British entry into the EC was the loss of parliamentary influence on the making of regulations which—under the treaties—would eventually make their way into UK law with little scope for national customisation. A special select committee to consider the issue (generally known as the Foster

[95] [1990] 2 AC 85; *Factortame* v. *Secretary of State for Transport (No. 2)* [1991] 1 AC 603.
[96] Quoted by Vernon Bogdanor, 'Britain', in *Parliaments and Parties* ed. Roger Morgan and Clare Tame (Macmillan, 1996), p. 232.

Committee after its Conservative chair, Sir John Foster) was established in December 1972 and reported in February and again in October the following year.[97] The committee, whose members included anti-marketeers Michael Foot and Peter Shore, attempted in its reports to wrest back a measure of control to the House. Its recommendations were largely adopted by the Labour government of 1974. Among them was the establishment of a Select Committee on European Secondary Legislation (later, the European Scrutiny Committee) with power to consider draft proposals for legislation from the EEC Commission (together with other documents published by the commission for submission to the Council of Ministers); to report on whether these raised questions of legal or political importance, and to make recommendations, including recommendations for further scrutiny by the House. Assisted by a much larger and more expert staff than select committees had traditionally had, its job was to alert the House to any proposals of political significance. Over the period after 1974, it became central to the Commons scrutiny of European affairs. Other elements of the Foster package proved less long lasting with the sheer volume of European legislation emerging from Brussels. The Foster Committee had predicted a total of 300 European documents a year. By 1999, the figure had grown to almost 1,200 as the competencies of the EU increased. A special question time for EEC matters was abolished in 1986; it soon proved impractical to have a ministerial statement after each European Council meeting; and it became impossible to give up time on the floor of the House for the number of documents recommended for debate. From 1990 special committees were set up which combined the practice in ordinary standing committees with a session more akin to a statement in the House. Growing fears about the pressure and routinisation of the European legislation process forced the government to concede a convention—the so-called scrutiny reserve—preventing ministers from normally giving agreement in the Council of Ministers to any proposal for European legislation which had not completed the scrutiny process in both Houses.

---

[97] For a full discussion of the evolution of the scrutiny system in the House of Commons, see Priscilla Baines in *Westminster and Europe*, ed. Philip Giddings and Gavin Drewry (Macmillan, 1996).

The twentieth-century legacy

The decline of Parliament?

By the end of the twentieth century, the prestige and pre-eminence which Parliament possessed at its beginning was clearly no more. The passage of the European Communities Act and the *Factortame* case were, it was claimed, the first signs of a retreat from the principle of parliamentary sovereignty; Parliament's role in debating the issues of the day had been superseded by ubiquitous media discussion; its role in representing the people seemed threatened by the possibilities of direct democracy; and, dominated by the government, it seemed incapable of effectively fulfilling its job as principal scrutineer of the executive. From the Second World War onwards, the appearance of books with titles such as 'Can Parliament survive?', 'The Passing of Parliament' or 'Parliament under Pressure', testified to different shades of a received opinion.

Yet Parliament did survive, and even, in a modest way, thrived. Parliamentary sovereignty was, for sure, not an uncontested doctrine. Even at the beginning of the century, the certainty and clarity of Dicey's doctrine of parliamentary sovereignty was being contested with the perception that societies had made their own laws prior to the creation of Parliaments—and might do so again,[98] and the passage of the Parliament Act 1911 led even Dicey to consider in 1915 whether parliamentary sovereignty was still a valid doctrine. More serious challenges came in the last few years of the century from judges and academic lawyers, essentially on the same grounds as before, though now bolstered by the experience of considering rights derived from authorities other than Parliament: European Community law and the European Convention of Human Rights.[99] Yet these challenges were largely academic ones, with little clear effect on actual judgements; the incorporation into United Kingdom law of the Convention carefully preserved the sovereignty of Parliament against any claim that judges might hold an infringement of the Convention to invalidate United Kingdom statute; and, as the commitment to European law was itself defined by statute, repeal remained (theoretically) possible. The constraints on Parliament's right to legislate within its jurisdiction were moral and political, rather than

[98] D. G. Ritchie, *The Principles of State Interference*, 1891, quoted in M. Bentley, 'British Parliamentary Institutions and Political Thought, 1865–1914', *Parliaments, Estates and Representation* (1983), 43.

[99] Jeffrey Goldsworthy, *The Sovereignty of Parliament* (Clarendon Press, 1999), pp. 1–5.

legal. The political constraints grew, with devolution, as well as human rights and Europe; but parliamentary sovereignty was as applicable a doctrine in 2000 as it was in 1900.

Parliament's centrality to the political process had, however, become more doubtful. From time to time Parliament, or more particularly, the House of Commons, became squeezed in the dialogue between the electors and the executive: so squeezed, that occasionally commentators predicted that it would be squeezed out altogether. Even in 1893 Horace Seal envisaged that the 'units' of the 'Social Organism' would, 'themselves legislating from their own homes, in their own armchairs, at their own breakfast tables, . . . vote upon all important questions with as much ease as if they were filling up a census paper'.[100] Though this level of popular participation was scarcely realistic, the referendum was advanced now and then, although in a fairly limited role as a system for protecting the constitution from ill-considered or partisan alteration by a determined government with a secure majority. Although discussed during the constitutional crisis of 1909–11, the referendum never attracted significant support until the 1970s, and the arrival of a set of issues—European integration and UK devolution—which caused divisions within the parties as much as between them. More sustained systems of involving the people in legislative decision-making remain almost at the same visionary level as those advanced by Seal in 1893: but methodological and technological advance—the scientific opinion poll before the internet— has made the idea of voting at the breakfast table less absurd than a hundred years ago. Perhaps more significant than technological change has been the cultural change that it has encouraged: a decline of deference and of an assumption that members of Parliament could effectively represent the opinions of their electors. In some circles the idea achieved currency that modern media had made old-style representative democracy obsolete, that 'politics has now moved on from representational democracy to direct democracy, in which there is a need to win a daily mandate, in which strength comes from popularity and in which the public is much more fickle and discerning and the media far more hostile'.[101]

These challenges to Parliament were essentially, however, theoretical and speculative ones. The general view that the influence of government within Parliament had grown and was growing was considerably more

---

[100] Horace Seal, *The Nature of State Interference*, 1893, quoted in Bentley, 'British Parliamentary Institutions and Political Thought', 43.
[101] Philip Gould, quoted in *The Guardian*, 20 July 2000, p. 5, col. 2.

damaging to its prestige and authority. The arguments which led to the passage of the Parliament Act in 1911 and the special circumstances of the First World War, which provided a huge spur to the growth of executive dominance, seem to have been when the view first gained common currency. By 1917 the Liberal MP, Sir Charles Henry, could claim: 'For some time it has become apparent that the control of Parliament is being undermined, that the Executive and the permanent officials have assumed the power which, if not checked, threatens to become a menace to our Parliamentary life . . . Members of Parliament are no longer able to exercise the function which the electorate rely upon them to do.'[102] The Second World War gave this view further impetus. In 1963 Richard Crossman wrote in his influential introduction to Bagehot that 'it has often been observed that when they were plunged into total war in 1940, the British readily put their democratic constitution into cold storage, and fought under a system of centralised autocracy . . . what is not so often noticed is the extent to which the institutions and the behaviour of voluntary totalitarianism have been retained since 1945'.[103]

It was undoubtedly easier for a government to legislate and to obtain supply in 2000 than it was in 1900. Yet it is easy to overstress the growth in executive powers, and just as striking, over the course of the century, has been the survival of a belief in the importance of scrutiny and accountability, and the development of devices to assist that process— above all, of course, the creation of a select committee system, whose achievements in changing governments' minds may have been modest, but whose existence was the principal factor in ensuring the exposure to parliamentary and public criticism of vastly more information about government policy and administration than was available in 1900. And, despite the lament about the lack of media attention, the broadcasting of parliamentary proceedings by radio and television has provided much greater exposure of the reality of Parliament than before. Though it still failed to live up to the independence of spirit of the Victorian Parliament, Michael Ryle's judgement of 1995 was not unjust: 'the House of Commons is a much more lively and politically significant body than it was fifty years ago and, in particular, is far more effective today as a critical body than it has been for a very long time'.[104]

---

[102] HC Deb., 5th series, vol. 92, col. 1363, quoted in John Turner, 'The House of Commons and the Executive in the First World War', *Parliamentary History* (1991), 307.

[103] Crossman 'Introduction', in Walter Bagehot, *The English Constitution*, p. 56.

[104] 'The Changing Commons', in F. L. Ridley and M. Rush (eds), *British Government and Politics since 1945* (Oxford University Press, 1998), p. 149.

Note. Paul Seaward is grateful to G. W. Jones, Oonagh Gay, Jonathan Parry and Barry Winetrobe for reading and commenting on an earlier version of part of this chapter.

Bibliography

Official publications

Select Committee on Procedure, Report (1931–2), HC 129.
Select Committee on Procedure, First Report, *Procedure in the Public Business of this House* (1945–6), HC 9.
Select Committee on Procedure, First Report, *Procedure and Practice of the House; Public Bill Procedure; Committee system; Hours of sitting etc* (1977–8), HC 588.
Select Committee on Modernisation of the House of Commons, First Report, *The Legislative Process* (1997–8), HC 190.

Secondary sources

Ball, Stuart, 'Parliament and Politics in England, 1900–1951', *Parliamentary History* (1991).
Bentley, Michael, 'British Parliamentary Institutions and Political Thought 1865–1914', *Parliaments, Estates and Representation* (1983).
Berrington, Hugh, *Backbench Opinion in the House of Commons 1945–55* (Pergamon, 1973).
Bromhead, P. A., *Private Members' Bills in the British Parliament* (Routledge & Kegan Paul, 1956).
Butt, Ronald, *The Power of Parliament* (Constable, 1967).
Chester, D. N. and Bowring, N., *Questions in Parliament* (Clarendon Press, 1962).
Chubb, Basil, *The Control of Public Expenditure: Financial Committees of the House of Commons* (Clarendon Press, 1952).
Crick, Bernard, *The Reform of Parliament* (Weidenfeld & Nicolson, 1964).
Cromwell, Valerie, 'The Losing of the Initiative by the House of Commons, 1780–1914', *Transactions of the Royal Historical Society*, 5th series (1968).
Dicey, A. V., *Introduction to the Study of the Law of the Constitution*, 8th edn (Macmillan, 1915).
Higgins, G. M., 'The Origin and Development of the Standing Committees of the House of Commons, with Special Reference to their Procedure, 1886–1951', D.Phil thesis Oxford University (1954).
Garrett, John, *Westminster: Does Parliament Work?* (Gollancz, 1992).
Giddings, Philip (ed.), *Parliamentary Accountability* (Macmillan, 1995).
Goldsworthy, Jeffrey, *The Sovereignty of Parliament* (Clarendon Press, 1999).
Greenleaf, W. H., *The British Political Tradition* (Methuen, 1987).
Hewart, Gordon (Lord Hewart), *The New Despotism* (Ernest Benn, 1929).
Jennings, I., *Parliament*, 2nd edn (Cambridge University Press, 1957).

Laski, H. J., *Reflections on the Constitution* (Manchester University Press, 1951).

Lowell, A. L., *The Government of England* (Macmillan 1908).

Morrison, Herbert, *Government and Parliament*, 3rd edn (Oxford University Press, 1964).

Norton, Philip, *Dissension in the House of Commons, 1945–74* (Macmillan, 1975).

Norton, Philip, *Dissension in the House of Commons, 1974–79* (Clarendon Press, 1980).

Norton, Philip (ed.), *Parliament in the 1980s* (Blackwell, 1980).

Norton, Philip (ed.), *Parliaments and Pressure Groups in Western Europe* (Frank Cass, 1999).

Norton, Philip and Wood, D. M., *Back from Westminster: British Members of Parliament and their Constituencies* (University Press of Kentucky, 1993).

Ostrogorski, M., *Democracy and the Organisation of Political Parties* (Macmillan, 1902).

Redlich, J., *The Procedure of the House of Commons: A Study of its History and Present Form* (Constable, 1908).

Riddell, Peter, *Honest Opportunism* (Hamish Hamilton, 1993).

Ridley, F. F. and Rush, M. (eds), *British Government and Politics since 1945* (Oxford University Press, 1995).

Rush, M. and Shaw, M. (eds), *The House of Commons: Services and Facilities* (Allen & Unwin, 1974).

Searing, Donald M., *Westminster's World: Understanding Political Roles* (Harvard University Press, 1994).

Taylor, M., 'Labour and the Constitution', in *Labour's First Century*, ed. Duncan Tanner, Pat Thane and Nick Tiratsoo (Cambridge University Press, 2000).

Walkland, S. A. (ed.), *The House of Commons in the Twentieth Century* (Oxford University Press, 1979).

Wasson, E. A., 'The House of Commons 1660–1945: Parliamentary Families and the Political Elite', *English Historical Review* (1991).

Wheare, K. C., *Government by Committee: An Essay on the British Constitution* (Clarendon Press, 1955).

6.
The House of Lords

RHODRI WALTERS

'There are two things', observed Sir William Harcourt in 1895, 'that you can neither mend nor end: the House of Lords is one, the other is the Pope of Rome'.[1] These words were to prove, at least so far as they relate to the House of Lords, remarkably prophetic. The House of Lords was certainly not to be 'ended', although abolition was official Labour Party policy from 1977 to 1989. It was of course to be mended. Powers of veto were curtailed in 1911 and 1949; life peers were admitted in 1958; and all but ninety-two hereditary peers excluded in 1999. But the more comprehensive reforms promised in 1911 and attempted and then abandoned in 1968–9 never happened. The major political parties were, at critical moments of the century, content to leave the House of Lords with some of its legislative powers curtailed but otherwise largely unchanged. As the year 2000 drew to a close, the recommendations of the Royal Commission on the Reform of the House of Lords were still being discussed. Lords reform was undoubtedly one of the major political issues of the twentieth century, but it would do the House less than justice to view its constitutional role over that period solely in the context of the failed attempts at effecting wider change. What follows here is an outline account of what the House actually was; what it did; and when it started doing it.

Functions

In the twentieth century, the House of Lords, not being representative, could no longer vie with the House of Commons to be the 'forum of the nation'. But it remained, nonetheless, a chamber of the legislature, a forum of debate, a forum of scrutiny of the executive, and a court of

---

[1] Quoted in E. A. Smith, *The House of Lords in British Politics and Society 1815–1911* (Longman, 1992), p. 171.

final appeal for the United Kingdom. This chapter is not, however, concerned with the House's judicial function, which, although the scope of its jurisdiction was modified, in essence changed little.

The House's functions in the early part of the century were classically stated by the Bryce Conference on Reform of the Second Chamber in 1918.[2] The conference of thirty—set up in 1917 by the prime minister and drawn from the two Houses—had failed to agree across party lines on how to replace the almost exclusively hereditary membership, but it did agree on what the second chamber should do, namely to:

- cause sufficient delay to enable the government or the public, or both, to reconsider legislation passed by the House of Commons, in particular bills affecting the constitution or introducing new principles of legislation (before the passing of the Parliament Act 1911 the powers of delay were, ultimately, those of absolute veto: by the time of the conference the powers of delay were those of the suspensory veto over three sessions);
- examine and revise bills passed by the House of Commons;
- initiate bills on non-controversial issues with a view to facilitating their passage through the Commons; and
- hold 'full and free discussion of large and important questions' (debates) on matters on which legislation was not proposed.

For the sake of completeness, the following activities should also be added, namely to:

- examine private legislation (seemingly overlooked by Bryce);
- consider delegated legislation (much developed after 1917) and, after 1974, draft instruments of the European Union;
- scrutinise the activities of the executive by questions and in committee (to the extent that this may be deemed different from debate on 'large and important questions'); and
- safeguard the maximum duration of a Parliament at five years (to the extent that this is not foreseen in Bryce's provisions on delay).

The Bryce functions, *mutatis mutandis*, held good throughout the century[3]

---

[2] *Conference on the Reform of the Second Chamber*, Cd 9038 (1918).

[3] They were recognised explicitly in the Labour government's 1968 white paper, *House of Lords Reform*, Cmnd 3799, and the *Report of the Conservative Review Committee on the House of Lords* (1978, Home Report); and implicitly in the *Report of the Conservative Party's Constitutional Commission on Options for a New Second Chamber* (1999), and the *Report of the Royal Commission on the Reform of the House of Lords*, Cm 4534 (2000).

and were generally accepted across the political spectrum, though the manner in which the House discharged these functions varied greatly over the years as we shall see.

Powers

The powers available to the House of Lords in the discharge of its functions remained remarkably robust, notwithstanding the major modification of its legislative powers early in the century.

The House of Lords had entered upon the twentieth century with its powers intact, if somewhat undefined. There were certainly no statutory rules governing relations between the Lords and Commons in respect of public legislation. All bills required agreement of both Houses before they might be presented for royal assent; and the Lords initiated bills and amended or on occasion rejected outright bills brought up from the Commons. The Lords' powers over public legislation, other than bills of supply, were unfettered. If the Lords disliked any provisions in a bill they could amend them; if they disliked a bill in its entirety, they could reject it outright. Furthermore, in spite of the widening of the franchise and the growth of the House of Commons as a representative body, the Lords—or more particularly the Conservative members—took refuge in Lord Salisbury's 'doctrine of the mandate' to justify their use of these powers.[4]

It was this power of outright rejection, or veto, invariably used to frustrate measures laid before it by Liberal administrations—like Irish home rule and employers' liability in 1893—which conditioned the terms of the debate on reform as the nineteenth century ended. It is hardly surprising that, following the Lords' rejection of the 1909 Finance bill, the resolutions for Lords reform put forward by the Liberal government the following year and later enacted in the Parliament Act 1911 should have sought to curb the powers of veto. Under the terms of that Act the powers of the Lords to reject a bill outright were replaced by the so-called 'suspensory veto'. Any Commons public bill (except a bill to extend the life of a Parliament or a 'money' bill (see below)) which passed the Commons in three successive sessions, whether or not a

---

[4] The 3rd Marquis of Salisbury's 'doctrine', first elaborated in 1868, was that the will of the people and the views of the House of Commons did not necessarily coincide and that the Lords had a duty to reject—and hence refer back to the electorate—contentious bills, particularly those with constitutional implications.

general election were to intervene, could be presented for royal assent without the agreement of the Lords provided that (a) there had been a minimum period of two years between the Commons giving it a second reading in the first session and a third reading in the third session, and (b) that the Lords had received the bill at least one month before the end of each of the three sessions. A bill, under the Act, is deemed to be rejected by the Lords if it is not passed by the Lords without amendment or with such amendments only as may be agreed with the Commons. These provisions were further modified by the Parliament Act 1949 which reduced the three sessions to two and the minimum period between second reading in the first session and third reading in the second to one year. The effect of the Parliament Acts is to provide that, in respect of any bill to which the Acts might be applied, a period of thirteen months must elapse between second reading in the Commons and royal assent (between 1911 and 1949, twenty-five months). But the period of delay for which the House of Lords is responsible depends on a number of variables, the most important of which is the time taken to pass the bill in the Commons; the behaviour of the Lords in respect of the bill in the second session could also be significant if the Lords chose to protract proceedings rather than reject the bill outright; and the timing of the end of the second session would also be a determinant.

The effect of the Parliament Act 1911 on the House of Lords was profound. The replacement of its powers of veto with the suspensory veto was more than a technical adjustment. It was an assertion of the primacy of the Commons in legislative matters and a source of very great demoralisation of the upper House. A chamber of veto was forced to reinvent itself as a chamber of scrutiny and, as we shall see, it took a long time to make that adjustment.

In one area, that of 'supply', the Lords were already a less than equal partner to the Commons as the new century dawned. By ancient practice, reinforced by Commons resolutions of 1671 and 1678, the Lords did not initiate, change or alter bills 'of aids and supplies',[5] that is to say in modern parlance bills dealing with the imposition or repeal of taxes, or payments from the Consolidated Fund. Although in theory the Lords might reject outright such a bill (in 1860 they had rejected the Paper Duty Repeal bill), their long acquiescence in the Commons resolutions had virtually made it a rule that supply bills would not be interfered

---

[5] Erskine May, *Treatise on The Law, Privileges, Proceedings and Usage of Parliament*, 22nd edn (Butterworths, 1997), p. 797.

with. Indeed, there is evidence that the Lords were nervous of standing in the way of any bill with 'money' connotations—like the Old Age Pensions bill in 1908—whether supply or no.

The events leading to the passage of the Parliament Act 1911 had centred on the Lords' rejection of the Liberal government's Finance bill in 1909. Thus, in seeking to curtail the Lords' powers of veto over legislation, the 1911 Act made special provision for 'money' bills. Such bills must deal exclusively with such matters as taxation, public money and loans. Any bill, having been certified by the speaker of the Commons as a money bill and sent up to the Lords at least one month before the end of a session, may, if the Lords have not passed it without amendment within one month, be presented for royal assent without the Lords' agreement.

In practical terms, however, the money bill provision of the Parliament Act 1911 merely clarified a convention which had—save for rare lapses—been observed by the Lords for centuries and the provision has never been used to present a bill for royal assent. Ironically, the Finance bill of 1909, and indeed many finance bills since, would not have met the strict criteria for classification as a money bill. And the provisions of the 1911 Act did not prevent amendments being made to money bills. Indeed, at the behest of the executive, and with the agreement of the Commons, such amendments were in fact made on occasion. The fact nevertheless remains that all proceedings on supply bills or money bills were, save for a wide ranging debate on second reading of the Finance bill, taken merely formally in the Lords for most of the century. While the House might express its opinion upon public expenditure and taxation in debate and in select committees, it could only concur in matters of legislation.

But this reaffirming of Commons financial privilege enabled that House to rely on it for much of the century with total confidence as a reason for rejecting Lords amendments to other public bills. Such is the power of a 'privilege reason' that since 1931 the House of Lords has not insisted on any of its amendments rejected by the Commons on grounds of financial privilege.

The powers remaining to the Lords over general legislation were still very extensive, notwithstanding the provisions of the Parliament Acts. Their use was tempered in the latter part of the century by the convention that both Conservative and Labour oppositions refrained from voting against the second reading of any government bills which had featured in that party's election manifesto. This convention was established by the then Viscount Cranborne (later 5th Marquis of Salisbury) as leader of the Conservative opposition in the Lords from 1945 to 1951 and may be viewed as a *post facto* reworking of the old doctrine of the mandate. Having originated as no more than a code of conduct for an overwhelmingly large Conservative Party, it never enjoyed the status of a standing order of the House. Nonetheless, it was generally adhered to notwithstanding the changed circumstances brought about by the Parliament Act 1949 and by the erosion in the latter part of the century of the dominance of the Conservative Party.[6] But of course the restraint which it represented did not extend to amendments other than wrecking amendments, nor to non-manifesto bills.

The powers of the Lords over private legislation—that is to say legislation affecting private and particular interests and founded upon a petition by the body or person promoting it—remained co-equal to those of the Commons throughout the century. In adjudicating upon such bills, the two Houses still exercise both a legislative and judicial role and this is reflected in the quasi-judicial proceedings of any select committee on an opposed bill. While the House's powers remained intact, the scope for exercising them gradually shrank as other means of obtaining special powers evolved which avoided recourse to Parliament. An increasing number of functions came to be governed by public and general Acts—like naturalisation, divorce, municipal corporations and local government, water, and planning. Finally, under the terms of the Transport and Works Act 1992 (itself based on recommendations of a joint committee of both Houses) the remaining works bills—for railways and so on—were replaced by ministerial orders following public local inquiries.

Indeed, against this background of a decline in the significance of private legislation for both Houses, the House of Lords came to hold a certain pre-eminence over the Commons in the field of private local Acts. The local authority bills which were introduced following the repeal of all private local Acts by the Local Government Act 1972 were all started in the Lords and at the close of the century it was the practice for all private local bills to start in the upper House.

Delegated legislation under statutory procedures was not included

---

[6] J. A. G. Griffith and Michael Ryle (with M. A. J. Wheeler-Booth), *Parliament, Functions, Practice and Procedures* (Sweet & Maxwell, 1989), p. 505 lists some exceptions. Some commentators have raised the ambiguity of the convention so far as it concerns wrecking amendments, but in practice the convention was remarkably resilient. Any ambiguity lay more in the definition of what constituted a wrecking amendment.

in the Parliament Acts. Thus the House of Lords, in theory at least, had complete discretion over orders laid before Parliament—in the early years of the century under the Rules Publication Act 1893 and latterly under the Statutory Instruments Act 1946. Indeed, in October 1994 the House affirmed 'its unfettered freedom to vote on any subordinate legislation submitted for its consideration'.[7] In practice, however, because such orders cannot be amended but can only be approved or disapproved, the House fought shy of making full use its powers in this area.

In scrutinising the activities of the executive, the House has always been able to pose questions to ministers and receive ministerial responses to its debates because ministers have sat in the chamber. About half Salisbury's and Balfour's Cabinets were in the Lords, and about a third of Rosebery's and Campbell-Bannerman's. But already there were complaints from Liberal MPs that these were too many.[8] And just as the Marquis of Salisbury, at the dawn of the century, was the last prime minister to sit in the Lords (with the brief exception of the Earl of Home in 1963), so the role of the Lords in post-First World War Cabinets declined also. After 1945 it was unusual for members of Cabinet other than the leader of the House and Lord Chancellor to sit in the Lords although Churchill bucked the trend with seven lords in 1952. Mrs Thatcher's administrations of 1979 and 1983 had three, briefly four, in each; and Mr Blair's administration of 1997, while reverting to two, had a further two lords ministers attending (the chief whip and the minister of transport). But throughout the century junior ministers not in the Cabinet sat in the Lords, though not all ministries were always necessarily represented.[9] By the 1950s the number of ministers, including government whips who also acted as government spokespersons in the Lords, had settled at about fifteen. By the end of the century it had risen to twenty-one.

The Lords' powers of scrutiny and investigation also extended beyond the government. All Lords select committees had and still have an inherent power to send for persons and papers, just as the House itself— in theory at least—has the ultimate sanction of summoning a person to

[7] HL Deb., col. 956, 6 June 1994.

[8] Smith, *The House of Lords in British Politics and Society*, pp. 161–2.

[9] In early 1936 neither the Department of Agriculture nor the Foreign Office had ministerial representation in the Lords. See P. A. Bromhead, *The House of Lords and Contemporary Politics 1911–1957* (Routledge & Kegan Paul, 1958), p. 102.

the bar of the House.[10] While the House no longer does the latter, persons and papers are being sought almost every day by its committees.

Procedures

Compared with the twentieth-century House of Commons, the Lords continued to enjoy very considerable procedural freedoms both vis-à-vis the executive and internally. The disruption of Commons business by Parnell and his Irish supporters after 1875 had resulted in 1881 in the adoption in that House of closure motions, enabling the halting of debate by the executive; and of allocation of time orders (guillotine motions) restricting the time available for discussion of bills, or parts of bills, in committee and remaining stages. In 1907 standing committees were set up for taking the committee stage of most bills and closure motions extended to them; and in 1909 the power of selection of amendments for discussion was granted to the speaker.[11]

Thus, by the early years of this century it was already possible for the Lords to complain that Commons scrutiny of legislation was less than complete,[12] a refrain often repeated throughout the century. But more significantly these developments represented a considerable loss of power from Parliament to the executive. Thus Lowe, writing in 1904, described the Commons as 'a machine for discussing the legislative projects of ministers'; and Marriott, writing about the Lords in 1910, thought that the Lords had lost power not to the Commons as such but to the Cabinet, in relation to which the Commons had suffered a 'great decline'.[13] The terms of the Parliament Acts, it is true, gave the executive ultimate authority over the Lords but it never gained ascendancy by procedural devices over day-to-day business. Thus, in the Lords throughout the century all but the most minor bills continued to be taken on the floor of the House, with no means of curtailing debate, and no selection of amendments. Moreover, the government had no automatic control of the order paper and was obliged to proceed by negotiation to secure time for its own business and—by extension—to regulate the time available to private members and opposition parties. The century ended with a battle over procedures yet to be played out.

---

[10] May, *Treatise on The Law*, p. 616.

[11] W. H. Greenleaf, *The British Political Tradition* (Methuen, 1987), vol. 3, pp. 778–82.

[12] Andrew Adonis, *Making Aristocracy Work* (Clarendon Press, 1993), pp. 60–1.

[13] Bromhead, *The House of Lords and Contemporary Politics*, p. 141.

That is not to say that the century did not see some tightening of procedural freedoms, leading to restrictions on the number of questions, both oral and written, which might be asked; time limits on statements, unstarred questions and, if desired, debates; and limitations on third reading amendments. A Companion to Standing Orders of thirty pages in 1955 had grown to 247 pages by 2000 as the practices of the House increasingly came to be codified. For the most part, however, these changes were wrought not to give advantage to the executive over the Lords but to facilitate business as the House became more and more active in the last forty years of the century. They protected Lords from one another, so far as a self-regulatory environment would allow.

Composition of the House

The House of Lords began the century as a hereditary and aristocratic institution and ended it as a predominantly nominated assembly. Although the preamble to the Parliament Act 1911 had expressed the Liberal government's intention 'to substitute for the House of Lords as it at present exists a Second Chamber constituted on a popular instead of hereditary basis',[14] progress on changing the basis of membership was slow.

The Edwardian House of Lords consisted predominantly of the 600 or so hereditary peers of the English, Great Britain or United Kingdom peerages; twenty-eight Irish representative peers elected from among their number for life (no election took place after 1922 and they died out); sixteen Scottish representative peers elected from among their number at each general election (the practice ceased in 1963 when all Scottish hereditary peers were allowed to take seats); the two archbishops and twenty-four senior bishops of the Church of England (including Welsh bishops until 1920); and the current and retired lords of appeal in ordinary. The lords of appeal in ordinary, appointed under the Appellate Jurisdiction Act 1876, were life peers but the rest of the House other than the bishops were hereditary. They were also all men. Although some peerages could be held by women, they were not allowed to sit in the Lords.[15]

The idea of broadening the base of membership by introducing life

---

[14] 1 and 2 Geo. V, c. 13.
[15] Viscountess Rhondda tried to take her seat in 1922, but the Committee for Privileges found against her.

peers had been mooted as early as the 1880s by leading figures in the Lords like Rosebery, Salisbury and Dunraven[16] and, along with schemes for direct or indirect election, was to feature in most discussions of reform thereafter. But not until the passing of the Life Peerages Act 1958 was the hereditary mould finally broken. (This act also allowed women to be made life peers.) Further adjustments came in the Peerage Act 1963 which allowed female hereditary peers and all Scottish peers to sit in the Lords. (The chief purpose of this Act was to allow a hereditary peer to disclaim his peerage for his lifetime.) The hereditary element of the House thus remained intact, although very few new hereditary peerages were to be created after 1964, until the passing of the House of Lords Act 1999. Under the terms of that Act hereditary peers no longer sat in the Lords, save for seventy-five 'excepted' by election from their own party or group, fifteen elected by the whole House to serve as deputy speakers and committee chairs, and two (the Earl Marshal and Lord Great Chamberlain) *ex officio*.[17]

While it is possible to be fairly precise about the numbers of peers in the various categories over the course of the century, the effective House is a much more elusive concept. Not all peers were in receipt of writs of summons because, if hereditary, they may have been under 21 or, after 1963, have disclaimed for life. After 1958 any peer in receipt of a writ might apply for leave of absence. Of those who remained, many might attend only rarely or never.

Thus, throughout the century, the difference between average daily attendance and total potential membership—that is to say those peers in receipt of writs of summons—was enormous (see Table 6.1). Before the First World War the level of attendance at the House varied according to whether a Conservative or Liberal government was in power.[18] Although on occasion remarkably large numbers might turn out to vote—460 voted on the Irish Home Rule bill in 1893, 425 on the Finance bill in 1909—the general picture was very different and the attendance low. Notwithstanding a revival during the period of Liberal government

---

[16] Smith, *The House of Lords in British Politics and Society*, p. 141; Adonis, *Making Aristocracy Work*, p. 62.

[17] Under standing orders, after the end of the first session of the next Parliament following the passing of the Act any vacancy arising on the death of an 'excepted' peer will be filled by by-election in which only the other 'excepted' peers of the relevant group may vote.

[18] Adonis, *Making Aristocracy Work*, pp. 52–3. These figures tend to confirm Rosebery's view that 'When the Conservative Party is in power there is practically no House of Lords'; see Roy Jenkins, *Mr Balfour's Poodle* (Heinemann, 1954), p. 49.

Table 6.1 Composition of the House of Lords, sittings and attendance, 1900–2000

Session	Composition	Hereditary	Other	Life	Writs	Sitting days	Average sitting	Average attendance	Divisions	Average voting	Sittings after 10pm
1900					593	88	1h 53m	71	17	77	
1906					613	108	3h 02m	133	42	167	
1912					642	101	2h 07m	69	14	120	
1945–6						157	2h 52m		10		
1946–7						126	3h 50m	115	29		
1951–2	858	820	38	–	585	101	3h 35m	103	12		
1956–7	871	833	38	–	c.586	103	3h 54m	112	32		
1960–1	918	840	43	35	651	125	4h 48m	142	48		
1967–8	1,061	864	44	153	778	139	5h 47m	225	72		32
1972–3	1,080	838	41	201	806	128	5h 38m	240	73		15
1975–6	1,139	818	43	278	901	155	6h 15m	275	146		39
1980–1	1,178	803	45	330	936	143	6h 26m	296	184		53
1985–6	1,172	791	47	334	947	165	7h 21m	317	250		93
1990–1	1,194	779	44	371	980	137	6h 28m	324	104		42
1995–6	1,207	766	50	391	1,067	136	6h 53m	372	110		60
1998–9	1,325	758	53	514	1,210	154	7h 36m	446	99		89
1999–2000	693	92	54	547	690	177	7h 29m	347	192		91

Sources: 1900–12, in Adonis, *Making Aristocracy Work*, pp. 52–5, 60; thereafter House of Lords Information Office.

after 1906—there were often over 200 voting on that year's Education bill—there was a considerable falling off again after the passing of the Parliament Act 1911. As Lord Selborne wrote in 1932, 'From that moment attendance fell to smaller figures than ever known before, and has never recovered'.[19] Between the wars divisions of over 200 were rare and between 1919 and 1957 the average number of peers voting in divisions was eighty—far fewer than during the years immediately before the First World War.

Although the morale of the House seems to have recovered after 1945, patterns of attendance did not. The infusion of new blood after 1958, combined perhaps with the payment of subsistence allowances for attendance in 1957,[20] turned the tide and the years that followed saw a steady increase in attendance by the hereditary as well as the life members. Indeed, not until the mid-1980s did attendance by life peers begin to overtake that of hereditary peers. The effect of the House of Lords Act 1999 was to shift the balance for good, although seventeen hereditary peers other than those 'excepted' under the Act were subsequently awarded life peerages.[21]

In party terms, the political complexion of the House is set out in Table 6.2. As we can see it was overwhelmingly Conservative throughout the century. The defection of the Liberal Unionists after the home rule debates of 1886 and 1893 had left the Conservative Party with an untouchable numerical superiority which it was never to lose. The national collapse of the Liberal Party between the wars and the reluctance of the Labour Party—briefly overcome during the Attlee premiership 1945–51—to create hereditary Labour peers helped to delay numerical 'rebalancing' of party in the Lords. Indeed, this task almost defied the conventions governing the appointment of new peers and the House of Lords Act 1999 can be viewed as a radical prerequisite of a more even party distribution.[22]

The absolute majority enjoyed by the Conservative Party continued into the post-war years. But this control, evident into the 1960s, seems to have been eroded by the end of that decade with the creation of more Labour peers and the emergence of the crossbench peers as a group.

---

[19] Adonis, *Making Aristocracy Work*, p. 272.
[20] Travel expenses had been allowed since 1946.
[21] Ten former leaders of the House and peers of first creation, and seven on subsequent party lists.
[22] Ivor Richard and Damien Welfare, *Unfinished Business, Reforming the House of Lords* (Vintage, 1999), ch. 2, particularly pp. 51–2.

Table 6.2 Composition of the House of Lords by party (peers with writs and not on leave of absence)

	1906	1914	1952	1963	1968	1974	1986	1991	1999	2000
Conservative	461*	470	490	325	351	370	416	454	484	233
Liberal/Democrat	98	112	44	42	41	37	86**	70	72	63
Labour	–	–	63	63	116	134	119	116	193	201
Crossbench	–	–	–	–	–	–	244	255	355	163
Bishops	26	26	26	26	26	26	26	26	26	26
Independent/Other	44	59	203***	229	255	265	56	135	80	8
Total with writs etc.	613	642	826	685	789	832	947	1,056	1,210	694

* Includes Liberal Unionists.

** Includes Social Democrats.

*** Until the emergence of the crossbench peers as a group in 1965, this category is more of a catch-all balancing item than a group.

Sources: Adonis, *Making Aristocracy Work*, p. 20 for 1906 and 1914. The totals for 1906 and 1914 are those on the Roll of the Lords, roughly equal to peers in receipt of writs. Griffith and Ryle, *Parliament, Functions, Practice and Procedures*, p. 465 for 1952, 1963 and 1974; Cmnd 3799 for 1968; Silk and Walters, *How Parliament Works*, p. 144 for 1986; thereafter, House of Lords Information Office. (Before 1968, figures are based on information in *Vacher's Parliamentary Companion*: thereafter, figures are based on declarations by the parties themselves. Until 1986, these declarations include some peers who are on leave of absence and not in receipt of a writ. In 1968, the statistical effect of this was to overestimate Conservative and Liberal strength by around 10 per cent.)

These figures tell us little about the political allegiance of regular attenders. In the immediate post-war period, an interesting analysis of the voting habits of the first two sessions of the 1951 Parliament confirms Conservative superiority in absolute terms. Thus, of the 296 peers voting at least once, fifty-one were Labour, eight independent, fourteen Liberal, and 218 Conservatives. Of the sixty-five voting in at least half the divisions, forty-three were Conservative and twenty-two Labour.[23] This analysis also illustrates the much reduced fortunes of the Liberal Party and the fact that the independent crossbench peers had yet to emerge as a force in the House.

After 1967, the House occasionally compiled figures of regular attenders, who attended more than a third of the sittings in a session. This became the standard definition of the 'working' House and, as the figures set out in Table 6.3 show, while the Conservatives continued to have the largest representation, they consistently lacked an absolute majority from the late 1960s among regular attenders too.

In Table 6.4, a more sophisticated analysis by party affiliation of members attending on an 'average day' (in fact the total attendances by party divided by the sitting days) underscores the extent of the erosion of the Conservatives' position in the House in the late 1950s and 1960s. But equally it illustrates just how tenaciously the Conservative peers then held their position for the next twenty to thirty years. Following the 1997 election, Mr Blair's creation of new Labour life peers—regular in their attendance—had a marked effect on the relative strengths of the parties in the 1998–9 session, even before the House of Lords Act was passed. The figures for 1999–2000 show that the passing of the Act made that rebalancing more permanent.

By the last quarter of the century, then, Conservative Party dominance of the 'working' House was relative rather than absolute. Conservative administrations after 1970 were able to get their business through only with the support of others in the House—a highly significant development in the evolution of the Lords as a revising chamber. Although it remained in theory possible for the Conservative Party to win important divisions by strong whipping, analysis of session 1988–9 has shown that only rarely did the voting House differ from the working House. The appearance of the 'backwoodsmen', members attending fewer than 5 per cent of sittings, was rare. In no case did they sway the outcome of any

---

[23] Bromhead, *The House of Lords and Contemporary Politics*, p. 33, quoting Sydney Bailey's article in *The Spectator*, 20 November 1953.

Table 6.3 Working composition of the House of Lords by party (%)

	1967–8	1975–6	1983–4	1987–8	1998–9	1999–2000
Conservative	125 (43)	141 (43)	167 (43)	184 (46)	250 (45)	158 (35)
Labour	95 (33)	104 (32)	98 (25)	91 (23)	144 (26)	163 (36)
Liberal/SDP	19 (6)	24 (7)	46 (12)	51 (13)	55 (10)	57 (13)
Independent	52 (18)	60 (18)	76 (20)	73 (18)	110 (20)	72 (16)
Total	291 (100)	329 (100)	387 (100)	399 (100)	559 (100)	480 (100)

Sources: 1967–8 (October to August) in Cmnd 3799; thereafter derived from sessional information provided by the House of Lords Information Office.

Table 6.4 Average daily attendance (%) by party

	Conservative	Labour	Liberal/Liberal Democrat	Crossbench	Bishops, lords of appeal and others
1957–8	60.0	20.3	7.5	–	12.2
1970–1	45.3	27.5	5.5	10.3	11.4
1988–9	46.6	22.1	11.7	18.0	1.7
1998–9	37.0	34.4	10.6	15.9	2.0
1999–2000	35.3	36.0	11.4	15.4	1.9

Sources: 1970–1 in Baldwin, 'The House of Lords: Its Constitution and Functions', p. 11; 1988–9 in Shell and Beamish, *The House of Lords at Work*, p. 55; other years, based on data provided by the House of Lords Information Office and in Dod's and Vacher's *Parliamentary Companion*.

division. Indeed, only six divisions would have had a different outcome if the votes of members attending a third of sittings or fewer had been discounted.[24]

Both the 1968 white paper on Lords reform and the report of the Royal Commission in 2000 set great store by the role of the independent or crossbench peers and both, in their proposals for reform, sought to ensure their continuance. The Royal Commission proposed that its intended Appointments Commission should ensure that at least 20 per cent of members should be unaffiliated to any of the major parties. It is all the more interesting to reflect, therefore, that the significance of the crossbench peers is, in relative terms, of no great antiquity and largely post-dates the passing of the Life Peerages Act 1958 and the broadening of membership that followed.[25] Anecdotal evidence suggests that, thereafter, some hereditary peers who in a previous era would have taken a party whip now gravitated towards the crossbenches too.

Where did the members of the House of Lords come from? By the twentieth century, peerages were being granted by the Crown on the advice of the prime minister. New peerages would typically be granted as part of the birthday or new year honours lists (before the First World War this practice was variable), at the resignation of a prime minister, or at the dissolution of a Parliament. After 1958, and with greater regularity in the 1990s, miscellaneous lists—the so-called 'working peers' lists— supplemented these traditional lists. The granting of peerages was always an important aspect of the patronage exercised by the prime minister of the day, either on his or her own behalf or on behalf of the other political parties. Table 6.5, by showing the number of peers created by each administration between 1902 and the end of 2000, illustrates the use that successive prime ministers made of this patronage. It also shows how the passing of the Life Peerages Act allowed peerages to be even more freely bestowed than before.

At the end of the nineteenth century the House was still predominantly a landowning and aristocratic assembly which, if it did nothing else, gave aristocracy a continuing political role, still strongly placed in government.[26] After 1880 the rate of creations of new peerages had greatly increased. Between 1882 and 1911, 200 new peerages had been created

[24] N. D. J. Baldwin, in Donald Shell and David Beamish (eds), *The House of Lords at Work* (Clarendon Press, 1993), pp. 46–7.

[25] See also Lord Garner GCMG, 'Cross-bench Peers', in *The Parliamentarian* (1983). Their co-ordination as a group does not pre-date 1965.

[26] Adonis, *Making Aristocracy Work*, pp. 275–6.

Table 6.5 Peerage creations (excluding promotions) by administration, 1902–2000

Prime Minister	From	To	Creations	Annual average
Balfour	12.07.1902	05.12.1905	8	2.4
Campbell-Bannerman	05.12.1905	08.04.1908	31	13.2
Asquith	08.04.1908	07.12.1916	86	9.9
Lloyd George	07.12.1916	23.10.1922	92	15.7
Bonar Law	23.10.1922	22.05.1923	7	12.1
Baldwin	22.05.1923	22.01.1924	7	10.4
MacDonald	22.01.1924	04.11.1924	5	6.4
Baldwin	04.11.1924	08.06.1929	37	8.1
MacDonald	08.06.1929	07.06.1935	72	12.0
MacDonald (both periods)			*77*	*11.4*
Baldwin	07.06.1935	28.05.1937	29	14.7
Baldwin (all three periods)			*73*	*10.1*
Chamberlain	28.05.1937	11.05.1940	23	7.8
Churchill	11.05.1940	26.07.1945	60	11.5
Attlee	26.07.1945	26.10.1951	94	15.0
Churchill	26.10.1951	06.04.1955	37	10.7
Churchill (both periods)			*97*	*11.2*
Eden	06.04.1955	13.01.1957	18	10.1
Macmillan	13.01.1957	19.10.1963	100	14.8
Douglas-Home	19.10.1963	16.10.1964	31	31.2
Wilson	16.10.1964	19.06.1970	142	25.0
Heath	19.06.1970	04.03.1974	49	13.2
Wilson	04.03.1974	05.04.1976	83	39.7
Wilson (both periods)			*225*	*29.0*
Callaghan	05.04.1976	04.05.1979	60	19.5
Thatcher	04.05.1979	28.11.1990	216	18.7
Major	28.11.1990	01.05.1997	171	26.6
Blair (to end 2000)	01.05.1997	31.12.2000	205	55.9
Total			1,663	16.9

Source: Compiled by D. R. Beamish, House of Lords.

to bring the size of the House to 630. Of these, 33 per cent came from the public services and professions, 25 per cent from old landed families and 39 per cent from industry, commerce and finance. But a survey of one hundred of these new members indicates that fewer than half lacked an estate: and two-thirds of those enobled between 1885 and 1914 had also been members of Parliament. The broadening of the House's social base was, perhaps, less than deliberate before the First World War.

Professional backgrounds of peers created between 1916 and 1998 are summarised in Table 6.6. These summaries are very revealing. Landowners no longer feature, in confirmation of the accelerated decline of the landed aristocracy after the First World War.[27] Throughout the century

[27] David Cannadine, *The Decline and Fall of the British Aristocracy* (Yale University Press, 1990), in particular ch. 3, comprehensively charts the erosion of the economic and social standing of aristocracy—a process that began before the First World War.

MPs and former MPs continued to contribute the largest single group of new peers; and, if those with other political, trade union or local government backgrounds are added, it becomes clear that active politicians continued to provide nearly half the new creations even after the passage of the Life Peerages Act. Clearly, the House of Lords was always a highly political place, even if its politics may on occasion have been those of a slightly earlier political generation. But Table 6.6 also shows—at last—a greater diversity in background. Hidden among the MPs and politicians of the earlier period are, for the first time, members of the Labour Party, particularly after 1945. And, following the passing of the Life Peerages Act, new peers with backgrounds in academe, science and medicine, the voluntary sector, the arts and media, and local government become statistically significant for the first time. The House began to acquire a reputation as a chamber of experts who were eventually to play a prominent part not only in scrutiny of legislation but in establishing a new form of select committee activity. Many, of course, espoused traditional party allegiances but others did not and the crossbench 'tradition' as we now know it was born.

An analysis of the occupational background of members of the House in the early 1980s confirms the cumulative effect of these new creations. Only 44 per cent were landowners or farmers, compared with 33 per cent with a background in industry and commerce, 34 per cent in the professions, 15 per cent in the armed services, 10 per cent in the civil and diplomatic service and 44 per cent in public and political service. Of equal interest is the fact that only 6 per cent were former workers or trade unionists.[28] These figures well illustrate, with the reduced clout of the landowners and an increased diversity of occupational background, what a potpourri of expertise and special interests the House of Lords had become: but it had attained this state in a totally haphazard and unrepresentative way.

Finally, it should perhaps be observed that even on the eve of the 1999 reform the House of Lords was by no means the chamber of antiquity of popular imagination. Half the hereditary peerage held titles that post-dated 1880; and of course all the life peerages post-dated 1958.

---

[28] Baldwin in Shell and Beamish, *The House of Lords at Work*, p. 37. Baldwin's statistics are not mutually exclusive and are not intended to be a precise breakdown of the House's membership.

Table 6.6 Professional background of new peers created 1916–98 (%)

	MPs	Other political/ trade union	Commerce and industry	Military	Other public service	Law	Other	Academic and medical	Voluntary	Local government	Other	Total
1916–56	193 (51)	16 (4)	70 (18)	34 (9)	21 (6)	15 (4)	31 (8)					380
1958–98	354 (39)	49 (5)	127 (14)	13 (1)	55 (6)	47 (5)		99 (11)	21 (2)	40 (4)	95 (11)	900

Sources: Bromhead, *The House of Lords and Contemporary Politics*, p. 26; Peerage creations 1958–98, Lords Library Note 98/005. (Bishops and lords of appeal in ordinary are excluded.)

Sittings and business of the House

The Edwardian House was a very different place from its later twentieth-century counterpart in the way it conducted its business. The House sat at 4.00pm for public business, after the conclusion of judicial sittings. This lasted until the establishment of the Appellate Committee in 1948, which enabled the House to sit at 2.30pm (3.00pm on Thursdays). Until 1906 the House sat on every day of the week except Wednesday. Thereafter Wednesday replaced Friday as a sitting day. And it did not sit for long. In 1900 the average length of sitting was seventy-three minutes. After the Liberal victory of 1906, business picked up somewhat to between two and three hours a day.[29] But even this gives a misleading impression of industry. For all but the last eight weeks or so of a session, when government bills arrived from the Commons, the House rarely sat longer than twenty minutes. The sessions too were much shorter, beginning usually in February and finishing in August, with the Glorious Twelfth as an incentive to deliver the bills. Not until 1928 did sessions regularly begin in November.

After 1945, the years of the first Attlee administration saw an increase in both hours of sitting and the number of sitting days. Although the length of the parliamentary day remained at three and a half to four hours under the Conservatives, the number of sitting days fell back so that in its sitting arrangements at least the House of Lords of the early 1950s still had much in common with the early years of the century. After about 1960, as Table 6.1 shows, the inexorable rise of all indicators of business activity begins. By the extension of the sitting year, increased use of spillover periods after the summer adjournment and before the state opening, and increased resort to Friday sittings, the number of sitting days was increased by up to 50 per cent by the 1980s. In the last twenty years of the century, the average length of a sitting day in the Lords ranged between about six and a half and seven and a half hours. By the end of the century the House of Lords sat longer than any other parliamentary chamber in the world, other than the British House of Commons. And in the 1998–9 and 1999–2000 sessions, the House of Lords for the first time sat on more days than the Commons.

The organisation of business, by contrast, retained many of the characteristics of informality of the turn of the century. Then, as later, the

[29] See Adonis, *Making Aristocracy Work*, pp. 59–60; Smith, *The House of Lords in British Politics and Society*, p. 160.

government had no priority for its business and proceeded by negotiation with the official opposition. Under standing orders, bills had priority over other business on every day except Wednesday and, as the principal legislators, this gave successive governments some *de facto* advantage. In the early part of the century, business was arranged on a rather *ad hoc* basis between leaders and whips. By 1945 little had changed.[30] A week's business, perhaps a little more, would be tabled in the minutes of the House by the preceding Thursday. Subsequently, a notice of forthcoming business of up to two or three weeks ahead was also circulated by the Government Whips' Office, in lieu of a formal business statement which never caught on in the Lords.

The usual channels in the Lords also remained remarkably informal. The leader of the House and Government Chief Whips' Office acquired a continuing secretariat from 1935, in the person of Sir Charles Hendriks. After 1960 this service was provided by a clerk on secondment to the civil service as private secretary, supported by a small team of civil servants. Opposition parties had limited secretarial support, principally for the circulation of their notices. Following the introduction of financial assistance to opposition parties in 1975 secretarial and some research assistance became more feasible, particularly after separate provision was made for parties in the Lords in 1996. But the arrangement of business remained to the end highly personal to the government and opposition chief whips, facilitated by the private secretary.

Discharging the legislative function

Legislative veto

The House of Lords began the twentieth century more as a chamber of veto than a revising chamber and, because of its overwhelmingly Conservative complexion, its opposition was reserved for Liberal measures. The election of a Liberal government in 1906 led to some major disagreements but it was the Lords' rejection of the Finance bill in 1909 which eventually led, in 1911 and two general elections later, to the passing of the Parliament Act. This, as we have seen, limited the Lords' powers of veto to the 'suspensory' veto, a model first elaborated by John Bright as early as 1883.

Immediately after this modification of their powers, the Lords rejected

[30] See Bromhead, *The House of Lords and Contemporary Politics*, pp. 89–92.

the Government of Ireland bill and Established Church (Wales) bill in 1912 and 1913. Both bills were enacted in 1914 but their operation was suspended until after the war ended. The Temperance (Scotland) bill was fatally amended by the Lords in 1913 and passed, following a compromise, in 1914. Thus, for a while the Lords still behaved as they had in the years before 1911, admittedly on issues—Irish home rule and disestablishment—which historically had always aroused their ire.

The Lords rejected at second reading the Labour government's Education (School Attendance) bill in 1931 but the government fell and the bill was not proceeded with. Thus, for many years the only other bill to have been rejected outright and to be presented for royal assent under the 1911 Act was the Parliament Act 1949, reducing the suspensory veto to two sessions. There are a number of reasons why the 1911 Act was not used after 1914. First, except for two relatively short periods in 1924 and between 1929 and 1931, the Conservatives were dominant in peacetime government. Second, a considerable sense of demoralisation seems to have hit the House after the reality of the events of 1911 had sunk home. Third, by the time disagreements of principle became likely once again with the reformist agenda of the 1945 Labour government, the Salisbury convention had taken the sting out of outright Lords opposition to bills.

After 1949, the Parliament Acts were seldom resorted to, partly because of an increased reluctance on the part of the Lords to reject any government bill outright, whether a manifesto commitment or not, and partly because of the gradual evolution of the House from a chamber of veto to a chamber of scrutiny and amendment.

Notwithstanding these developments there comes a point in the exchanges between the Houses—normally when both Houses have taken up their position of disagreement on an amendment or amendments and insisted upon the disagreement—when a bill is deemed lost for the session. This resulted in the loss of the House of Commons Redistribution of Seats (No. 2) bill in 1969; of the Trade Union and Labour Relations bill in 1976, subsequently enacted without recourse to a final certificate under the Parliament Acts after the Lords withdrew their opposition in 1977; and of the Aircraft and Shipbuilding Industries bill in 1977, again enacted in the conventional manner in 1978 after the government removed part of the bill that had been found to be hybrid.

Indeed the House did not exercise its power of outright veto again until 1990 and 1991 when, following rejection at second reading in two successive sessions, the War Crimes Act received royal assent without agreement of the Lords—ironically, under a Conservative administration. In 1998 the European Parliamentary Elections bill was lost following disagreement over the electoral system proposed. The Lords rejected the reintroduced bill at second reading in the 1998–9 session thus enabling royal assent to take place under the Acts in time for the elections to proceed notwithstanding. Royal assent was also given under the Parliament Acts to the Sexual Offences (Amendment) bill, which lowered the age of consent for homosexual activity and buggery to 16, in the 1999–2000 session. And, as is considered more fully below, the Criminal Justice (Mode of Trial) (No. 2) bill was rejected at second reading and not further proceeded with.

Thus, the remaining powers of veto over legislation sanctioned by the Parliament Acts were seldom used. Like a nuclear deterrent, they proved cumbersome to operate and of indiscriminate effect. Instead, the House was to develop a more conventional armoury—that of constructive scrutiny and amendment.

Legislative scrutiny

Two functions recognised by Bryce as being appropriate for the second chamber—examining and revising bills passed by the Commons and initiating bills with a view to facilitating their passage through the Commons—together came to constitute by far the more important aspect of the House's work as a chamber of the legislature in the twentieth century, namely legislative scrutiny as opposed to legislative veto or delay. Indeed, so entrenched has the concept of the Lords as a 'revising chamber' become that it is widely assumed that the House always did it. But nothing could be further from the truth: in the early part of the century the House of Lords was 'a revising chamber notable for undertaking almost no revision'.[31]

In late Victorian and Edwardian Parliaments all important government bills were introduced in the Commons and they all arrived in the Lords during the last two months of the session. The result was chaos. As Lord Selborne, a minister in Salisbury's third ministry wrote, 'the proceedings are undignified and the work is badly done. It is not an abuse of language to apply the words "farce" and "scandal" to what takes place.'[32] Controversial bills tended to be opposed at second reading.

---

[31] Adonis, *Making Aristocracy Work*, p. 66.
[32] Ibid.

Others were rushed through after the most cursory consideration. On the rare occasions when detailed scrutiny was attempted—in 1906 the Lords spent sixteen sittings in committee of the whole House on the Education bill—the result was a mess. In the event, the Education bill was lost when the Lords insisted on their amendments.

Furthermore, after the Lords' powers of veto were modified in 1911, the House took a while to be weaned from its old habits, as we have seen. Between 1919 and 1945, no bills were rejected outright, and no bills were mutilated—even during the two periods of Labour government.[33] But it is not really possible to detect in the Lords' treatment of bills and in the character of the amendments they moved the emergence of a new consciousness as a revising chamber. On occasion the House was far from supine and Conservative peers were perfectly capable of creating difficulties for Conservative-dominated administrations. But the House was clearly driven by sectional interest and its chief concerns were reserved for bills on land, agriculture, coal mining, royalties and the like. Thus, amendments were insisted on for the Labour government's Coal Mines bill in 1930 and, in 1938, 117 amendments were made over eight days to the Conservative government's Coal Industry bill. Bromhead wrote in 1958 of this period, 'on uncontroversial matters the Lords made some contribution in the way of improvements to bills, and obliged the Government to explain its purposes or to accept modifications, but the positive contribution was less than in more recent years'.[34]

It is safe to say that not until after 1945 did the House acquire, and was seen to have acquired, the characteristics of a revising chamber. Constrained by its leader, Lord Salisbury, the Conservative Party's opposition to the Labour government's programme of nationalisation bills was muted. Thus, the eight nationalisation bills were subject to only forty-three divisions between 1945 and 1949, and over half of those were on the more keenly fought Iron and Steel and Transport bills. Moreover, an analysis of the 240 or so amendments made by the House to the Transport bill showed that while 200 were made for reasons of drafting or by way of fulfilment of undertakings, the forty-two made by the House against the wishes of the government were all reversed by

[33] The Education (School Attendance) bill was not proceeded with; the Unemployment Insurance bill, by contrast, was amended in 1930 whereas it would almost certainly have been rejected before 1914; and the Representation of the People bill, amended by the Lords, fell in 1931 because of the formation of the coalition government before Commons consideration.

[34] Bromhead, *The House of Lords and Contemporary Politics*, pp. 147–50.

the Commons. A similar fate befell Lords' amendments to the Iron and Steel bill, save for one which deferred the vesting day.

Nevertheless, Bromhead's description of the House's contribution to bills of this period is a classic statement of what a revising chamber might be:

> To the Government itself, the committee stages were often of great value, in providing opportunities for dealing with amendments not finally decided in the Commons, and for bringing forward new amendments in fulfilment of agreements reached with outside bodies. Similarly, many government amendments were made in order to improve drafting, to remove possible obscurities or inconsistencies in the texts. With most of these amendments it would not really be fair to give credit to the House of Lords as such; the Government and its draftsmen had had to work in a great hurry, and they merely used the committee and report stages in the Lords for introducing improvements or changes which they had not had time to prepare earlier. But in addition the Government was forced to deal with great numbers of amendments proposed by peers, mostly of the opposition. Some of these followed up the Commons proceedings, and some again were brought forward at the suggestion of outside bodies. Others were brought forward to deal with points which had passed unnoticed during the proceedings in the Commons. Several important bills had been hustled through the Commons under the guillotine, and some clauses were considered in detail for the first time in the Lords.[35]

The House of Lords came of age as a chamber of legislature at this time in one other respect. The number of bills introduced into the Lords as a legislative chamber of first instance greatly increased over pre-war levels—as many as twenty-two in 1947–8—because of pressure of business. Indeed, the Companies bill, a bill introduced into the Lords in 1947–8, was virtually rewritten in that House following extensive behind-the-scenes negotiations between the frontbenches and their advisers.

Although under the Conservatives after 1951 legislation was less controversial, the House continued to fulfil a revising role, mainly driven by the Labour frontbench; and it continued as a legislative chamber of first instance. In other words, it never looked back. It is interesting to speculate why the House had taken so long to establish for itself a reputation for legislative scrutiny. Clearly, it was a prerequisite that the House should no longer regard itself primarily as a chamber of veto and this view seems to have gained currency by the late 1920s. Second, its members had to be willing to devote both time to, and express an

---

[35] Bromhead, *The House of Lords and Contemporary Politics*, p. 158.

inclination for, an intellectual engagement in the subject matter of legislation in general rather than of that which appealed only to sectional
interest. The era of post-war reconstruction may have encouraged such
an approach. Finally—and perhaps most convincingly—the House had
to have an effective opposition, whatever the complexion of the government of the day, and not until the 1950s, following the creation of more
Labour peerages by Mr Attlee, did this begin to come about. The passing
of the Life Peerages Act 1958 further confirmed and strengthened the
second and third of these prerequisites, as the vigorous and protracted
opposition of certain Labour life peers to the London Government bill
in 1963 was to bear testimony.

Table 6.7 shows a broad picture of Lords' scrutiny of bills since 1946,
based on three complete sessions of a number of post-war Parliaments.
The number of bills amended by the House varied from Parliament to
Parliament. But this has to be seen in the context of an expanding statute
book—4,972 pages of legislation in the years 1948–50, rising to 5,641 in
1966–8, and 7,429 (larger A4 format) in 1987–9. As with so many other
indicators of House business, from the late 1960s the number of bills
amended, the number of amendments made and the number of divisions
(votes) on amendments all rose steeply, particularly in the 1980s. After
1974 it is possible to show that the House spent between 50 and 60 per
cent of its time in the scrutiny of government bills. Bearing in mind that
hours of sitting increased by between one and a half and two hours a
day over the same period (see Table 6.1), it is clear that by the last quarter
of the century the business of the House was increasingly being driven
by the consideration of legislation.

But bald statistics, as many other commentators have found, reveal
nothing about the importance of the amendments made—whether drafting, technical, substantive, or simply consequential upon other
amendments. Nor do they indicate their source. For the most part, opposition and backbench amendments were proposed with a view to
effecting a substantive modification of the policy of the bill in its application. In many cases, particularly from about 1980, these amendments
were furnished by outside bodies in addition to those proposed by
the political parties themselves, which often repeated amendments first
proposed by them in the Commons. Government amendments had a
more complicated provenance. Substantive amendments might be proposed to fulfil pledges made by ministers during Commons proceedings;
to introduce changes or new matter—sometimes very extensive —
generated by the sponsoring department; to respond to pressure brought

Table 6.7 The House of Lords and government legislation

Period	Total bills	Bills amended	Total amendments	Average per bill	Divisions	Government defeats	% sitting time on legislation
1946/7, 1948/9	126	62	2,626	42	64	53	–
1966–9	163	92	2,943	32	173	88	–
1970–3	118	60	2,854	48	440	22	–
1974–7	126	87	3,453	40	310	248	50
1979–82	115	59	3,835	65	634	40	52
1983–6	111	71	5,510	78	621	59	54
1987–1990	90	56	7,868	141	654	49	60
1992–5	93	47	5,476	117	407	42	51
1997–2000	103	79	10,396	132	450	95	57

Sources: Rush, 'The House of Lords: The Political Context', in Carmichael and Dickson, *The House of Lords, Its Parliamentary and Judicial Roles*, p. 17; *Report of the Conservative Review Committee* (1978), pp. 44–51; House of Lords Information Office; House of Lords Public Bill Office. (Consolidation bills, order confirmation bills, money and supply bills, and of course private members' bills are excluded.)

to bear during proceedings in Parliament (and more particularly the House of Lords itself); or in response to pressure from external sources as a result of direct discussion with the department or as a result of the involvement of members of the House during proceedings on the floor.[36]

Nor do statistics point up the fact that some bills attracted far more amendment than others. While it was very unusual for one of the government's 'programme' bills to go wholly unamended, the distribution of amendments could be very uneven. In the 1988–9 session, for example, five out of the seventeen bills amended by the Lords accounted for 82 per cent of all the amendments made, with as many as 702 being made to the Local Government and Housing bill and 488 to the Companies bill alone.[37] In 1998–9, seven of the thirty bills amended accounted for 82 per cent of all the amendments made.[38]

Successive governments were not slow to amend their own bills. Between 1970 and 1983, a half of all amendments moved were moved by the government. Of these just over a quarter were in response to undertakings given at earlier stages or to pressure groups and the remainder were initiated by the government.[39] The great majority of amendments actually made were government amendments.

The fate of Lords' amendments is of course another story. One study shows that, paradoxically, during the 1968–9 and 1970–1 sessions the respective Labour and Conservative governments appeared more willing to accept amendments moved by backbench and opposition members in the Lords than in the Commons. A principal reason advanced for this phenomenon was that 'the less contentious, less partisan, atmosphere in the Lords makes amendments moved by those who are not Ministers more likely to be accepted'.[40]

The proportion of Lords' amendments subsequently accepted by the Commons varied according to the political complexion of the government. Thus in 1974–7 during the Labour administration, 1,813 amendments were made to bills in the Lords and 400 reversed by the Commons; in 1979–83 during the Conservative administration, 2,283

[36] D. Shell, *The House of Lords* (Philip Allan, 1988), pp. 123–4; M. A. J. Wheeler-Booth, in Griffith and Ryle, *Parliament, Functions, Practice and Procedures*, pp. 508–10.

[37] G. Drewry and J. Brock, 'Government Legislation: An Overview', in Shell and Beamish, *The House of Lords at Work* (Clarendon Press, 1999), p. 77.

[38] Based on Public Bill Office statistics.

[39] Shell, *The House of Lords*, quoting Baldwin; by contrast J. A. G. Griffith found relatively few examples of this in the 1968–9 and 1970–1 sessions.

[40] J. A. G. Griffith, *Parliamentary Scrutiny of Government Bills* (Allen & Unwin, 1974), p. 231.

amendments were made and six reversed.[41] The reason for this is not hard to see. Because of the relative strengths of the political parties, more amendments were carried against the wishes of Labour governments than Conservative governments and thus more were reversed. But it was also the case that Conservative governments were more reluctant—occasionally even powerless—to reverse outright amendments which their own supporters had favoured. Important amendments might be reversed, while amendments *in lieu* or concessions would be offered on those deemed to be of secondary importance.

What was the effect of the House of Lords' revision of legislation in the later part of the century? A detailed survey lies beyond the scope of this chapter but some noticeable examples spring to mind where successive governments—Labour and Conservative alike—were obliged to temper their policies in response to Lords scrutiny.[42] Under Edward Heath's administration, protracted debate on the Industrial Relations bill and Immigration bill in 1970–1 led to many concessions; and an amendment to the National Health Service (Reorganisation) bill 1972 provided free contraceptive services on the NHS. Under the Wilson–Callaghan administration which followed, amendments to the Aircraft and Shipbuilding Industries bill 1976 prevented the nationalisation of ship repair yards (see above); excluded the driving of vehicles on public roads from the provisions of the Dock Work Regulation bill in 1976; and provided that pupils with special needs be taught in ordinary schools, under the Education bill of that year.

The bills of the Thatcher administration were by no means immune. After 1979, Lords amendments to the Housing bill 1980, Housing and Building Control bill 1984 and Housing and Planning bill 1986 ensured that the 'right to buy' provisions did not extend to public housing which had been designated 'sheltered housing', or had been adapted for the elderly or disabled, or where the freeholds were held by charitable trusts. The academic freedom, opting out and religious education provisions of the Education Reform bill 1988 owed their final shape to amendments made, and compromises arrived at, in the Lords. On industrial relations, a Lords amendment to the Trade Union bill 1984 required postal ballots

[41] Shell, *The House of Lords*, p. 122.
[42] See Janet Morgan, *The House of Lords and the Labour Government 1964–1970* (Clarendon Press, 1975), pp. 231–2; Shell, *The House of Lords*, p. 133ff; Miers and Brock, in Shell and Beamish, *The House of Lords at Work*, pp. 103–36; Silk and Walters, *How Parliament Works*, p. 143; 1989 edn, pp. 143–4; 1998 edn, pp. 139–40; Home Report, pp. 54–6; House of Lords Information Office, Government Defeats 1970–97.

to be held for union elections. Perhaps the most widely known instance of Lords intervention in the 1980s was the amendment to the Local Government bill 1983 which prevented the government from cancelling the forthcoming Greater London Council elections until after the bill for abolition had passed. This threw abolition plans into turmoil, although the House's influence on subsequent local government legislation—including the 'poll tax'—was more muted. The Lords continued to exert influence on bills under the Major administration. After a savaging at second reading, provisions in the Police and Magistrates Courts bill 1993–4 on the appointment of police constables and police authorities were largely rewritten. And amendments to the Pensions bill 1995 and the Family Law bill 1996 provided for payment of pensions to remarried war widows and pension-splitting on divorce.

After the election of the Labour government in 1997, the House continued to make its mark in modifying the transitional arrangements for assisted places at preparatory schools in the Education (Schools) bill 1997, in requiring a review of the effect of tuition fees under the Teaching and Higher Education bill 1998, and in forcing the government to provide public funds for publicity about the candidates for election as mayor to be held under the Government of London bill 1999.[43] In 2000, the House took advantage of a crowded legislative programme to make its influence widely felt. A provision in the Child Support, Pensions and Social Security bill whereby an unproven allegation of a breach of a community penalty would have led to withdrawal of social security benefits was struck out; safeguards on privacy relating to e-mail interceptions were written into the Regulation of Investigatory Powers bill; government undertakings were secured that the Race Relations (Amendment) bill would be amended in the Commons so as to extend the indirect discrimination provisions of the 1976 Act to public authorities and to make it a duty for public bodies to promote racial equality; and privatisation of air traffic control in the Transport bill was delayed. The Criminal Justice (Mode of Trial) bill, which sought to restrict the use of trial by jury, was not proceeded with after a serious government defeat. Although the latter bill was reintroduced in the Commons as a 'No. 2' bill, it was then rejected by the Lords at second reading.

It is easy to explain, given the composition of the House, how the Lords might have sought to revise bills of a Labour government but it

---

[43] Although amendments to the bill were overturned in the Commons, the Lords eventually prevailed by rejecting the subsequent regulations.

is at first sight more surprising to find that the House successfully revised the bills of a Conservative government against the government's wishes. As we have seen, from the late 1960s the Conservative Party could not count on an absolute majority if crossbench peers and other parties voted against it. And party discipline was weaker in the Lords than in the Commons and backbench rebellion more frequent. There are a number of reasons for this: peers were not directly accountable to an electorate and a party manifesto; professional politicians or former politicians were a minority in the House and could on occasions be out of sympathy with certain aspects of their party's policy; and the payroll vote (of office-holders) was very small in the Lords while the need for circumspection in voting held little sway.

What, then, should be the final assessment of the Lords as a revising chamber in the twentieth century? So far as government amendments are concerned, the Lords were clearly an essential vehicle for the improvement—and not infrequently the rewriting—of bills. According to Richard Crossman in 1969, if no second chamber had existed at least two further stages would have been needed to deal with legislation in the Commons[44]—an assertion which could have been made with even greater conviction by 1999! So far as the modification of policy by scrutiny is concerned, the picture was much more complicated and depended on how successive administrations—for whatever reasons—responded, or had the will to respond, to pressure in debate on the floor and in the division lobby. In the face of determined government opposition, the Lords could often make little headway: yet in *relative* terms it was possible for one commentator to write that 'by 1987 the impact of the Upper House in amending the actual content of bills was widely recognised to be greater than that of the House of Commons'.[45] Subject to the post-1911 constitutional constraints and the convention on manifesto bills, the overall impact of House of Lords revision on legislation after about 1971 could certainly bear favourable comparison with the Commons.

Delegated legislation

A remarkable feature of twentieth-century legislation was the dramatic development in the scope, variety and quantity of delegation under

---

[44] Quoted by Shell, *The House of Lords*, p. 151.
[45] Miers and Brock, *The House of Lords at Work*, p. 136; Shell, *The House of Lords*, p. 151.

statutory procedures. Most of this delegation took the form of statutory instruments and some required the approval of both Houses of Parliament (affirmative instruments) or might be opposed by a prayer to annul in either House (negative instruments). In their earliest form, the procedures were determined by the Rules Publication Act 1893, replaced by the Statutory Instruments Act 1946. The number of statutory instruments of general, rather than local, application rose from 218 in 1910 to 733 in 1960 and 1,576 in 1998. In 1988–9, of 1,306 statutory instruments considered by the Joint Committee on Statutory Instruments, 130 required affirmative resolution and 868 were subject to negative procedure. Moreover, the instruments increased greatly in length and complexity. In 1955 the total length of all statutory instruments ran to some 3,240 pages: by 1988 there were 9,048 pages (A4 format).[46]

For most of the century the House exercised its powers in this area partly in committee and partly on the floor. Early delegated legislation was mainly local or private in character. In 1925 the House set up the Special Orders Committee to consider those which required affirmative resolution and to report whether they raised important questions of policy or principle; whether they accorded with precedent; and whether they could be passed without further inquiry. The recommendations of the Donoughmore Committee of 1932 that a committee be established in each House to inquire into every bill with delegation-making powers and into every regulation made was not taken up. Thus, until the establishment of the Joint Select Committee on Statutory Instruments in 1972, Lords scrutiny by committee extended only to affirmative instruments.[47]

Furthermore the scrutiny exercised was clearly unequal to modern needs. A select committee found in 1970 that the kind of scrutiny offered by the Special Orders Committee was 'generally of little value to the House'.[48] Following a modification of standing orders, the committee was thereafter required to consider the question of *vires*—a function assumed by the joint committee after 1972 as part of its wider remit of technical scrutiny.

The House's power on the floor to refuse to affirm affirmative instruments and to annul negative ones was, by contrast, in effect so considerable that up to 1972 'virtually no attempt' had been made to use

---

[46] Cm 4534, p. 68; R. L. Borthwick, 'Delegated Legislation', in Shell and Beamish, *The House of Lords at Work*, pp. 137, 157.
[47] Report from the Joint Committee on Delegated Legislation, 1971–2, HL 184, pp. xii–xvii.
[48] Report from the Select Committee on Proceedings in Relation to Special Orders, 1970–1, pp. iii–v.

it.[49] Indeed, until 1955 no division had ever taken place on a motion relating to a statutory instrument, although in 1937 some negative instruments had been withdrawn and relaid following a debate on a prayer to annul. Between 1955 and the end of the 1999–2000 session there were seventy-one divisions on statutory instruments. But such was the unease of the two major parties while in opposition of unleashing the full force of the House's powers that thirty of these divisions were on motions which would not, if carried, have proved fatal to the passage of the instrument in question. This nervousness led, in the 1970s and 1980s, to an understanding between the frontbenches of the two major parties that the opposition would not vote against delegated legislation. The understanding was never observed by the Liberal Party or by crossbench members. To the extent that it was of any effect, it seems to have been observed more in the breach and was declared dead by the leader of the opposition, Lord Strathclyde, in 1999. Only three times in the century was the government of the day defeated on a vote directly on an order. The motion to approve the Southern Rhodesian (UN Sanctions) Order 1968 was narrowly defeated in June 1968. Although the order was approved in virtually identical form a few weeks later, this caused the Labour government to call a halt to the inter-party talks on Lords reform that were then underway. The other occasions were both in February 2000 on a prayer to annul the Greater London Authority Elections Rules 2000 and a motion to approve the Greater London Authority (Election Expenses) Order 2000. In spite of the House's unease at applying its ultimate sanctions in this field and further hobbled by its inability to amend statutory instruments, some 3–5 per cent of sitting time was spent in debating delegated legislation in the last quarter of the century.[50]

Thus, while scrutiny of *vires* and other technical matters was satisfactorily exercised after 1972, the powers of approval and disapproval were such that the House could not comfortably use them and the effect of debates, often held after the Commons had held theirs, was very limited. This was recognised by the Royal Commission on Reform of the House of Lords in its recommendation that the Statutory Instruments Act 1946 be amended to enable the Commons to override a Lords rejection of an

---

[49] Report from the Joint Committee on Delegated Legislation, p. xiii.
[50] Divisions on Delegated Legislation in the House of Lords 1950–1999, House of Lords Library Note LLN2000/001; and data from the House of Lords Information Office.

affirmative or negative instrument.[51] By diminishing the theoretical powers over delegated legislation slightly, it was argued that the House might make more use of the powers that remained to it.

Towards the end of the century, the House began to look 'upstream' and showed increasing unease at features of primary legislation which gave inappropriate powers to ministers with regard to delegated legislation—so-called 'Henry VIII clauses' which allowed primary legislation to be amended or repealed by delegated legislation; 'framework bills', where the real operation of the bill was by the regulations made under it; and a general downgrading of the level of parliamentary control. In 1993 the House established its Delegated Powers Scrutiny Committee to review every bill to ensure that any delegation of legislative power was appropriate. The committee—foreseen as long ago as 1932 by the Donoughmore Committee and following the more recent example of the Australian Parliament—was a great success and inappropriate delegation of powers was swiftly curbed. Indeed, the Pollution Prevention and Control bill was recommitted to a Committee of the Whole House following a very critical report by the committee in 1998–9.[52] In some ways the House's success at scrutiny of delegated powers made up for its rather unsatisfactory role in relation to the instruments themselves.

Select committees

Turning now from the House's legislative functions to those relating to executive scrutiny, it is perhaps significant that the activities listed by Bryce made no specific mention of select committees, as distinct from his more generalised 'full and free discussion of large and important questions'. That may be because in the early years of the century the House set up relatively few committees, other than those on domestic, private or consolidation matters; and those that were set up were very different animals from those for which the House earned a deserved reputation in later years.

Before 1970, most Lords committees were set up to consider bills. Thus, between 1919 and 1939, of fifteen Lords select committees set up to consider public matters (that is, excluding matters relating to private legislation, utilities, or consolidation) thirteen were on bills, mostly

---

[51] Cm 4534, pp. 68–78.
[52] Silk and Walters, *How Parliament Works*, 4th edn, p. 152; 1998–9, HL 12.

private members' bills. Evidence might be taken but reports were usually very short even where the bill might be extensively amended. Only two committees sat on general policy issues, and only one of these—on prevention of road accidents in 1938–9—is recognisable as a serious assessment of public policy in the modern sense. Of the seven joint committees set up, five were to consider bills and two to consider issues. On the whole the quality of the proceedings of the joint committees was higher than the Lords only committees, particularly those dealing with Imperial questions—the Joint Committee on the Government of India Bill in 1919,[53] and the Joint Committees on Closer Union in East Africa in 1931 and on Indian Constitutional Reform in 1933–4. Indeed the report of the latter committee was in its length and scope quite unlike anything attempted by a joint committee before or since.

But the admirable work of the joint committees on colonial matters and of the Lords committee on prevention of road accidents does not seem to have been followed up in the decades immediately following the end of the Second World War. A joint committee considered aspects of reform—specifically disclaimer—in 1963, as a precursor to the Peerage Act of that year; and in 1966–7 a joint committee considered censorship of the theatre, producing a competent report recommending the abolition of the role of the lord chamberlain, implemented in the Theatres Act 1968.

By 1970 the Lords still had no settled tradition of committee work on issues of public policy. The establishment of the Select Committee on Sport and Leisure in 1971–2 represented a conscious attempt by the House, in the wake of the failure of the Wilson government's reform proposals, to branch out into serious scrutiny of public policy by select committee. Although the subject matter was anodyne, the committee's report was the first by a House of Lords select committee on public policy (with the sole exception of the committee on road accidents in 1938) to engage in a proper and thematic consideration of evidence leading to conclusions and recommendations. It represented a turning point by illustrating not only what might be achieved by the Lords but also the best way of achieving it.[54]

Not until 1974 did the Lords acquire a sessionally reappointed select committee when, following the recommendations of a Select Committee on European Instruments in 1973, the House set up the Select Com-

[53] 1919, HL 226.
[54] 1972–3, HL 84 and 193-I.

mittee on the European Communities to scrutinise draft EU legislation and other policy matters. This committee and its eventual six subcommittees was to form the core of a permanent Lords committee system. The establishment of a sessionally reappointed Science and Technology Committee in 1979 extended the scope and character of the House of Lords' committee work. In addition, the House began to set up committees as a matter of course to consider issues *ad hoc*, such as those on a Bill of Rights (1977–8), Unemployment (1979–82), Overseas Trade (1983–4), Murder and Life Imprisonment (1988–9), and the Monetary Policy Committee of the Bank of England (1997–9, reappointed 2000).

Public bills, chiefly controversial private members' bills, continued to be referred to select committees, beginning with the Anti-discrimination (No. 2) bill in 1972–3. The committee's report was effectively a review of sex discrimination and of policy relating thereto. It helped to focus the debate which eventually led to the passing of the Sex Discrimination Act in 1975. Other committees on bills followed, some with more obvious outcomes than others, like Parochial Charities (1983–4), Laboratory Animals Protection (1979–80), and Infant Life (Preservation) (1986–7).[55]

It is not easy to assess the impact of select committees but independent assessments of Lords committee work have on the whole been very favourable. Many of the committees on bills had an immediate effect. Others helped focus opinion in a manner which ultimately led to outcomes not far removed from the committees' findings. The European Union (formerly Communities) Committee was later imitated by the parliaments of other member states and its reports had a circulation beyond Whitehall, in the European institutions themselves. The Science and Technology Committee helped to influence the development of UK science policy and the organisation of the science base. As one commentator has written, 'The authority of the House of Commons derives from election, the authority of the House of Lords—and especially its committees—from its expertise.'[56]

As the century ended, a general consensus emerged that the House's committee work had added significantly to the ability of Parliament to contribute to the development of public opinion on major issues; and

[55] Wheeler-Booth, in Griffith and Ryle, *Parliament, Functions, Practice and Procedures*, pp. 490–4; C. Grantham, 'Select Committees', in Shell and Beamish, *The House of Lords at Work*, pp. 282–306; Report from the Select Committee on the Committee Work of the House, 1991–2, HL 35-I, pp. 10–11, 37.

[56] Grantham, in Shell and Beamish, *The House of Lords at Work*, p. 306.

that, subject to its continuing to be complementary to the work of the Commons, it should be expanded. Decisions had been taken to establish a sessional Select Committee on the Constitution and a Joint Committee on Human Rights; and it was agreed in principle to set up an Economic Affairs Committee in succession to the Committee on the Monetary Policy Committee in 2001. In addition, the Royal Commission recommended the establishment of a Treaties Committee. In 1968, the white paper on Lords reform had very tentatively suggested that following reform there might 'be scope for involving the Lords in specialist or Select Committees'. How different from the more confident tones of the Royal Commission some thirty years later when it stressed that 'specialist committee work should continue to be an important function of the reformed second chamber'.[57]

Debates and questions

The House was always a renowned forum of debate of public policy, though early debates exhibited characteristics that would not have been recognisable in the latter part of the century. While the procedure for debates—the forms of motion and the degree of precedence accorded them on the order paper—remained largely unchanged, the century saw great changes in the frequency with which they were held and the level of members' participation in them.

In the Edwardian House, routine occasions were 'little more than conversations between the two front benches'. While the set piece general debates could be 'authoritative' they involved only a small proportion of politically active members of the House.[58] Indeed, the House appeared to discourage wide participation. The Lords were a bad audience, interested only in the opinion of a few great men.[59] Nor were as many debates held—nine in 1909, twenty in 1912.[60] In some ways the House's reputation as a forum of debate was all that remained to it after the debacle of 1911. As Selborne wrote in 1932, 'The peers have felt humiliated and ashamed of themselves, and have lost all faith in themselves

---

[57] Cmnd 3799, p. 36; Cm 4534, p. 88.
[58] Smith, *The House of Lords in British Politics and Society*, p. 160.
[59] Adonis, *Making Aristocracy Work*, pp. 57–9. Bad acoustics and reporting were also discouraging.
[60] Bromhead, *The House of Lords and Contemporary Politics*, p. 228.

as a power of useful service to the nation except in the matter of academic debates.'[61]

After the Second World War, debating activity increased noticeably, no doubt reflecting the increased political diversity of the membership. Thus, in the late 1940s and the 1950s about fifty debates a session were held.[62] By 1998–9, the number had risen to seventy-five, twelve of which were on motions to take note of select committee reports—a rare occurrence before the 1970s. Although discussion of legislation took up proportionately more of the House's sitting time in the latter decades of the century, by sitting for longer and by time limiting debates the opportunities for initiating debate on a motion actually increased. Greater use of the 'unstarred' debatable question procedure from the early 1960s also gave further debating opportunities. Over the four sessions from 1995 to 1999 the House spent about 28 per cent of its time in debate: 18 per cent on general motions, 3 per cent on motions to take note of select committee reports and 7 per cent on unstarred questions.[63]

The practice of asking ministers questions for oral answer on the floor goes back to 1919 but questions did not have priority on the order paper and were not much used. In 1947 it was agreed that three would be given priority after private business on Tuesdays and Wednesdays, extended in 1954 to any sitting day. In 1959 the maximum was raised to four, a limit of two a day for any one member imposed, and priority over private business accorded.[64] Although to begin with not even the maximum number of three was always asked, demand for starred questions became so great in later years that by the end of the century a peer might have only one question on the order paper at any time, and a limit of thirty minutes had been imposed on question time. Topical questions—two questions each week drawn by lot—had been instituted to give greater currency to proceedings.

While competing claims for the attention of the House limited the opportunities for asking questions on the floor, for many years no constraints existed on the tabling of questions for written answer until a limit of six per day was instituted in 1989. In 1961–2, seventy-two questions for written answer were tabled: in 1998–9, 4,322. Interestingly, changes of

---

[61] Adonis, *Making Aristocracy Work*, p. 272.

[62] Bromhead, *The House of Lords and Contemporary Politics*, p. 228.

[63] Derived from statistics provided by the House of Lords Information Office.

[64] Wheeler-Booth, in Griffith and Ryle, *Parliament, Functions, Practice and Procedures*, p. 474.

administration seem to have caused the biggest step changes in the number of questions tabled.[65]

The purpose of debates and questions is to provide information and to require the government to justify its policies. They are, as procedures, ill-suited to the detailed analysis possible, say, in select committees. Nor can it be said that government policy changes solely because of a debate in the House of Lords; or that debates are in any sense educative of public opinion. It was ever thus. For all that, before 1945, the political one-sidedness of the House had severely compromised its capacity to review the policies of the executive in debate. Thereafter, and particularly after the arrival of life peers after 1958, the procedures were invested with new vigour, expertise and inclusivity.

Reform and legitimacy

No review of the House of Lords in the last hundred years would be complete without an assessment of the various projects for its reform, and of the baleful effect which the failure of the more far-sighted of those projects had on the reputation of the House.

The preamble to the Parliament Act 1911, somewhat disingenuously, had proclaimed the Liberal government's intention 'to substitute for the House of Lords as it at present exists a Second Chamber constituted on a popular instead of hereditary basis': but, it continued, 'such substitution cannot be immediately brought into operation'. It is open to question whether the Liberal Party under Asquith was really interested in dealing with the infinitely complex issues of composition of the House, once it had secured a curtailment of its powers of veto. A Cabinet committee was established in 1912 to consider further reform but no scheme for further change emanated.[66]

Towards the end of the First World War, Lloyd George established the Bryce Commission which, while it was agreed on the functions appropriate for the upper House, was divided on the question of the House's composition. A majority favoured a House of 246 members indirectly elected by MPs on a regional basis, with a further eighty-one members chosen from among hereditary peers and the bishops by a joint committee of both Houses (gradually reducing to thirty hereditary peers

---

[65] House of Lords Information Office.
[66] Jenkins, *Mr Balfour's Poodle*, pp. 279–81.

and fifty-one others). The law lords would remain, *ex officio*. Powers over financial legislation would remain circumscribed and differences between the Houses on other issues would be resolved by a 'Free Conference Committee' of up to thirty members of each House, so that bills might be passed without the agreement of the Lords. But times were not auspicious. Although reform was mentioned in the king's speeches of 1920, 1921 and 1922, another Cabinet committee set up in 1922 concluded that the Bryce proposals would not prove acceptable to the Commons or to the country at large. Instead some vague and incompletely developed ideas—a House of 350 members, part elected, part nominated and part hereditary, with the powers recommended by the majority of the Bryce Commission—were mooted by the government and not pursued.

The Baldwin government, elected in 1924, took reform seriously for a while and a further Cabinet committee was set up in 1925 which in 1927 reported a scheme not unlike that of the coalition government in 1922. But the proposals were criticised by both Labour and some Conservative members and once again were not pursued. Fatally, all these inter-war schemes would have left the Conservative majority in the Lords intact and so they found little favour with members of other parties. After 1927, Lords reform languished in the limbo of private members' business until after the Second World War.[67]

In the 1947–8 session, the post-war Labour government sought to reduce the suspensory veto introduced by the Parliament Act 1911 from three to two sessions. The chief reason for this was to facilitate the passage, within the lifetime of that Parliament, of the Iron and Steel bill which was to be introduced in the 1948–9 session.[68] Following pressure from the opposition parties, Lords consideration of the Parliament bill was broken off for a while in 1948 while an all-party conference discussed both powers and composition. The conference broke down, unable to agree on delaying powers. A special short session was held in the autumn of 1948 so that the Parliament bill was eventually enacted as it stood, following introduction for the third time in the 1949 session. But the conference issued an interesting statement of agreed principles on the future of a reformed House: that a second chamber 'should be complementary to and not a rival to' the lower House; that there should not be a permanent majority assured for any one political party; that heredity

---

[67] Jenkins, *Mr Balfour's Poodle*, pp. 279–81; Home Report, pp. 59–60; Cannadine, *Decline and Fall of British Aristocracy*, pp. 458–72.
[68] In the event, the bill was not rejected outright by the Lords.

should not by itself be a qualification for membership; that women should be admitted; that some remuneration should be provided; that membership should be partly hereditary and partly for life; and that a member who neglected, or was no longer fitted to perform, his duties might be disqualified.[69]

In the absence of any proposal for more radical change, over the next fifteen years or so a number of these ideas were acted upon piecemeal. The most far-reaching change was undoubtedly the introduction of life peerages, including women, in 1958. And the introduction of attendance allowances in 1957, the leave of absence scheme in 1958, disclaimer and women hereditary peers in 1963, were all foreshadowed in the 1948 statement. But, with the notable exception of the introduction of life peers, all these changes—while they may be seen as an attempt to make a mainly hereditary and largely absentee House more respectable—did little more than 'nibble at the ermine'.

In 1967 the Wilson government embarked on a reform of both powers and composition and an inter-party conference was convened. Although the conference was suspended following the Lords' rejection of the Southern Rhodesia (United Nations Sanctions) Order in June 1968, enough had been achieved to enable the government to publish a white paper setting out its proposals later that year and to introduce a bill in the 1968–9 session. The proposal was for a two-tier House of between 200 and 250 voting, created (mainly life) peers, plus law lords and a reduced number of bishops; and a non-voting remainder of hereditary peers, entitled to sit only for the rest of their lives. The voting peers would be expected to attend at least one-third of the sittings of the House. No one party would have an absolute majority, though the government of the day would have a small majority over opposition parties, with independent members holding the balance of power. Delaying powers on bills would be reduced to six months from the date of any disagreement between the Houses.[70] Although these proposals were approved in principle by a resolution of the Lords, the Parliament (No. 2) bill enacting the changes met strong opposition in the Commons from sections of both the Labour and Conservative parties, mistrustful of the patronage that would be placed in the hands of the prime minister and wary of the political power that it would place in the hands of the upper House,

[69] *Parliament Bill 1947 – Agreed Statement on Conclusion of Conference of Party Leaders*, Cmd 7380.
[70] Cmnd 3799.

and of the non-aligned voting members in particular. The bill was abandoned.

Once again, further discussion of the question of Lords reform was banished to the realm of the backbenches, principally in the Lords. A Conservative Party working group chaired by Lord Home of the Hirsel held meetings in 1977 and reported in 1978, but its proposals failed to capture the interest of Mrs Thatcher as prime minister. A Cabinet Committee set up in 1983 met but once. Meanwhile, between 1977 and 1989, the Labour Party espoused a policy of Lords abolition. By the 1990s this had metamorphosed into 'doing something about the hereditaries' and, following the return of a Labour government in 1997, reform returned to the political agenda.

As we have seen, the House of Lords Act 1999 disqualified all hereditary peers from sitting, save for the ninety-two 'excepted' by the Act; and a Royal Commission was set up with Lord Wakeham as chair to consider longer term proposals. The Commission, which reported in January 2000, confirmed most of the House's existing powers, including that of the suspensory veto. Its more interesting recommendations related to the composition of the House—a chamber of about 550 members, a 'significant minority' of which would be elected on a regional basis according to a list system of proportional representation. The majority would be appointed. Both elected and appointed members would serve fifteen-year terms. Existing life peers would become members for life of the new House. Finally, an 'Appointments Commission' established on a statutory basis would vet party nominations for membership of the new second chamber and make its own nominations, chiefly of independent members.[71]

While a House of Lords Appointments Commission with some of the functions recommended by the Royal Commission was established on a non-statutory basis in 2000, the introduction of elected members awaited legislation in a future Parliament; and a joint select committee to consider the parliamentary aspects of reform had yet to be set up.

Why did Lords reform prove so elusive after 1911? A number of reasons emerge. Lack of political will was perhaps the most enduring. Except for Harold Wilson in 1967, no prime minister after Baldwin showed any real commitment to the complexities of fundamental reform, and the abolition of the power of absolute veto by the 1911 Act had

---

[71] Cm 4534, pp. 8, 104–49. The Commission suggested three alternative figures for elected members—sixty-five, eighty-seven and 195.

removed the urgency. Second, there was insufficient cross-party support for the specifics—particularly on matters of composition. Third, while inter-party conferences might yield up proposals, one or other—or both—Houses of Parliament felt threatened by them and failed to identify with them. Thus, even the important reforms which were achieved—the abolition of veto in 1911 and the shortening of the suspensory veto to two sessions in 1949, the introduction of life peers in 1958 and the removal of hereditary peers in 1999—were each, in their day, an easier option to comprehensive change.

The failure of root-and-branch reform, especially of the composition of the House, cast a long shadow. The chimera of such a reform was used as a reason to prevent women peers taking their seats in the 1920s and 1930s. For much of the century it enabled those who disagreed with any action by the Lords—whether successive administrations, the principal political parties, the Commons, or individuals inside and outside Parliament—to question the very legitimacy of the House. This shadow, so far as it affected the behaviour of the House itself, paled somewhat after the failure of the Parliament (No. 2) bill in 1968—it was, many members felt, not their Lordships' fault that they still went unreformed. A new robustness in the exercise of power and in exploring new areas of activity, like select committee work, became apparent. The passage of the 1999 Act had a similar, stiffening effect on the 'transitional House' it left behind.

But further reform, whether on the lines of the proposals of the Wakeham Commission or no, will not be straightforward. In the twentieth century, would-be reformers faced two seemingly irresolvable problems. First, how to reconcile reform of membership with the heightened sense of legitimacy vis-à-vis the House of Commons that would inevitably result: and, second, how to reconcile a heightened sense of legitimacy with the exercise of an appropriate range of powers which, while retaining the practical utility of the upper House, nevertheless reflected the ultimate supremacy of the other place. It remains to be seen whether, in the twenty-first century, those problems can be resolved successfully.

Postscript

The House of Lords at the end of the century was quite clearly a very different place from the House of the early 1900s, engaged in different tasks and performing a different role, notwithstanding the failure of radical reform. Superficially, some things might have seemed the same—the parliamentary robes at state opening, the clerks in their wigs, the encaustic tiles, the smell of polish in committee rooms. But, under this veneer of changelessness, radical changes had in fact been wrought, partly by statute and in large measure by the House's own capacity to reinvent itself. Indeed, much of what was valued in the work of the House in the last decades was of much less antiquity than was generally supposed.

A hereditary and aristocratic chamber had, as a result of the Life Peerages Act and House of Lords Act, become largely nominated, pluto-cratic and, in some degree, more expert. A political complexion that was originally overwhelmingly Conservative and partisan had become more subtle when, after the late 1960s, the Conservatives had lost absolute control—a process hastened in 1999. And in the early 1960s the indepen-dent crossbench peers emerged for the first time as a force in the House.

In discharging its functions, a chamber of legislative veto had after 1945 evolved into a chamber of legislative scrutiny, handling legislation in a very different way. A chamber with practically no committee activity had, from the early 1970s, developed an elaborate system of select com-mittees on issues of public policy which owed little to anything the House had done before. And a House that had once been sparsely attended except on major occasions and which had been dominated in debate by the few, now sat oftener and longer than had ever previously been experienced, with record levels of participation.

For the House of Lords the century had been one of enormous change.

Bibliography

Government white papers etc.

Conference on the Reform of the Second Chamber, Cd 9038 (1918).
Parliament Bill 1947—Agreed Statement on Conclusion of Conference of Party Leaders, Cmd 7380 (1948).
House of Lords Reform, Cmnd 3799 (1968).
Modernising Parliament—Reforming the House of Lords, Cm 4183 (1999).
Report of the Royal Commission on the Reform of the House of Lords, Cm 4534 (2000).

Party and other review documents

Report of the Conservative Review Committee on the House of Lords (1978, Home Report).

Second Chamber: Some Remarks on Reforming the House of Lords, the Earl of Carnarvon, the Lord Bancroft, the Earl of Selborne, the Viscount Tenby and Douglas Slater (1995).

Report of the Conservative Party's Constitutional Commission on Options for a New Second Chamber (1999).

Reports of parliamentary committees

Report from the Select Committee on the House of Lords, 1908, HL 234.

Report from the Select Committee on Proceedings in Relation to Special Orders, 1970–1.

Report from the Joint Committee on Delegated Legislation, 1971–2, HL 184.

Report from the Select Committee on the Committee Work of the House, 1991–2, HL 35–I.

Books and other secondary sources

Adonis, Andrew, *Parliament Today* (Manchester University Press, 1990).

Adonis, Andrew, *Making Aristocracy Work* (Clarendon Press, 1993).

Bailey Sydney D., *The Future of the House of Lords: A Symposium* (Hansard Society, 1954).

Baldwin, N. D. J., 'The House of Lords: Its Constitution and Functions', Exeter Research Group Discussion Paper 9 (1982).

Baldwin, N. D. J., 'The House of Lords: A Study in Evolutionary Adaptability', Hull Papers in Politics 33 (1983).

Baldwin, N. D. J., 'Behavioural Changes: A New Professionalism and a More Independent House', in P. Norton (ed.), *Parliament in the 1980s* (Blackwell, 1985).

Baldwin, N. D. J., 'The House of Lords', Wroxton Papers in Politics (1990).

Bates, T. St J. N., 'Select Committees in the House of Lords', in Gavin Drewry (ed.), *The New Select Committees* (Clarendon Press, 1985).

Bromhead, P. A., *The House of Lords and Contemporary Politics 1911–1957* (Routledge & Kegan Paul, 1958).

Cannadine, David, *The Decline and Fall of the British Aristocracy* (Yale University Press, 1990).

Carmichael, Paul and Dickson, Brice (eds), *The House of Lords, Its Parliamentary and Judicial Roles* (Hart, 1999).

Dod's Parliamentary Companion.

Drewry, Gavin and Brock, Jenny, *The Impact of Women on The House of Lords*, Studies in Public Policy (University of Strathclyde, 1983).

Greenleaf, W. H., *The British Political Tradition* (Methuen, 1987), vol. 3.

Grantham, C. and Hodgson, C. M., 'Structural Changes: The Use of Committees', in P. Norton (ed.), *Parliament in the 1980s* (Blackwell, 1985).

Griffith, J. A. G., *Parliamentary Scrutiny of Government Bills* (Allen & Unwin, 1974).

Griffith, J. A. G. and Ryle, Michael (with M. A. J. Wheeler-Booth), *Parliament, Functions, Practice and Procedures* (Sweet & Maxwell, 1989).

Jenkins, Roy, *Mr Balfour's Poodle*, new edn (Heinemann, 1968).

Jennings, Sir Ivor, *Parliament*, 2nd edn (Cambridge University Press, 1959).

Jones, Clyve and Jones, D. L. (eds), *Peers, Politics and Power: The House of Lords 1603–1911* (Hambledon Press, 1986).

Lees-Smith, H. B., *Second Chambers in Theory and Practice* (Allen & Unwin, 1923).

May, Erskine, *Treatise on The Law, Privileges, Proceedings and Usage of Parliament*, 22nd edn (Butterworths, 1997).

Morgan, Janet, *The House of Lords and the Labour Government 1964–1970* (Clarendon Press, 1975).

Richard, Ivor and Welfare, Damien, *Unfinished Business, Reforming the House of Lords* (Vintage, 1999).

Rush, Michael (ed.), *Parliament and Pressure Politics* (Clarendon Press, 1990).

Shell, Donald, *The House of Lords*, 2nd edn (Harvester Wheatsheaf, 1992).

Shell, Donald and Beamish, David (eds), *The House of Lords at Work* (Clarendon Press, 1993).

Shell, Donald, 'The House of Lords and the Thatcher Government', *Parliamentary Affairs* (1995), 16–32.

Silk, Paul and Walters, Rhodri, *How Parliament Works* (Longman, 1987).

Smith, E. A., *The House of Lords in British Politics and Society 1815–1911* (Longman, 1992).

Vacher's Parliamentary Companion.

Vincent, J. R., 'The House of Lords', *Parliamentary Affairs* (1965–6), 475–85.

Windlesham, Lord, *Politics in Practice* (Jonathan Cape, 1975).

7.
The Civil Service

VERNON BOGDANOR

> The history of the permanent civil service would be one of the most instructive chapters in the long story of English constitutional development, but unfortunately it has never been written.
>
> A. L. Lowell, *The Government of England* (1908)

I

The creation of the civil service, so Graham Wallas believed, was 'the one great political invention in nineteenth-century England'. Its fundamental basis had been laid down in 1854 by the Northcote–Trevelyan Report which had proposed a permanent civil service, chosen by open competition with promotion by ability. It was indeed after publication of this report that the term 'civil service' had come into use.[1] Like all political institutions which have survived for any length of time, the civil service came to exemplify certain principles. It exemplified, in particular, four interrelated constitutional principles: *non-partisanship, ministerial accountability to Parliament, admission by open competition* and *promotion by ability.* These principles are not, however, enshrined in law, but are based largely on convention.

A non-partisan civil service implied a distinction between ministers who, in the twentieth century, were mostly elected, accountable to Parliament, and subject to ultimate dismissal by the electorate, and permanent officials, who would be required to serve governments of different political complexions. 'The nation', declared the American political scientist A. L. Lowell in 1908, 'has been saved from a bureaucracy such as

---

[1] Graham Wallas, *Human Nature in Politics*, 1st edn 1908 (Constable, 1948), p. 263; K. C. Wheare, 'The Civil Service', in Valerie Cromwell *et al.*, *Aspects of Government in Nineteenth-century Britain* (Irish University Press, 1978), p. 5.

prevails over the greater part of Europe, on the one hand, and from the American spoils system on the other, by the sharp distinction between political and non-political officials'.[2] There was, in Britain, no notion of the elected official as there is, for example, in France or Germany, while the non-elected politician—for example, the minister in the House of Lords—has been a declining species in the twentieth century. The distinction, both of personnel and of role between elected politicians and non-elected officials, seemed to most people in Britain obvious and fundamental. By the end of the twentieth century, however, the British civil service was almost alone, together with the Canadian, in remaining unpoliticised in its upper reaches.

The relationship in Britain between ministers and civil servants rested on the principle of ministerial responsibility which, by the beginning of the twentieth century, seemed already well established. This principle entailed that the executive powers of the Crown were in general exercised primarily by ministers and on the advice of ministers. Civil servants were responsible to ministers, not to Parliament. It was indeed ministers alone who were responsible to Parliament. This principle is entailed by the notion of a non-partisan civil service. For, if civil servants are to serve different political masters, they must be protected from attack, both in Parliament and in the country. Thus, the responsibility of civil servants is subsumed in that of ministers.

The last occasion on which MPs had suggested that a civil servant had any responsibility to Parliament was probably 1864.[3] By 1873, the principle seemed definitely to have been accepted. In that year, an official, Scudamore, at the Post Office, then a government department, had been accused in Parliament by his minister of various financial irregularities, from which he had not, however, personally profited. The minister was magisterially rebuked by a backbench MP, Bernal Osborne. 'This House has nothing to do with Mr Scudamore. He is not responsible to us . . . if we are to shuffle off these questions by saying that a clerk in the Post Office, however, distinguished and disinterested he may be, is to take the burden and the blame on his shoulders, there is an end to parliamentary government'.[4]

The principle of ministerial responsibility for official actions came to

---

[2] A. L. Lowell, *The Government of England* (Macmillan 1908), vol. 1, p. 144.

[3] Henry Parris, *Constitutional Bureaucracy: The Development of British Central Administration since the Eighteenth Century* (Allen & Unwin, 1969), p. 100.

[4] HC Debs, 3rd series, vol. 217, col. 1209. Quoted in Parris, *Constitutional Bureaucracy*, p. 104.

be accepted, since, by the time that the modern civil service came into existence, representative parliamentary institutions had already been firmly established. The development of the civil service in Britain has been profoundly influenced by the needs of parliamentary government, which requires ministers to defend their policies in great detail in the face of what are liable to be searching criticisms. It is for this reason that the British idea of a civil service was so different from the continental notion of a bureaucracy. Sir Warren Fisher, head of the civil service, declared to the Tomlin Commission in 1930:

> Essentially the two ideas are opposed . . . a service which is right in spirit and personnel realises that its sole *raison d'être* is to give service alike to its Government and to its country; a Bureaucracy, on the other hand, is the instrument of an Executive intent on forcing the citizen to digest the contents of the cornucopia so mystically associated with State action.[5]

In Britain, then, officials constituted a service rather than a bureaucracy. On the Continent, by contrast, the outlines of the bureaucratic state were already in existence before the development of representative institutions, and this bureaucratic state was grafted onto parliamentary machinery. But, in Britain, the character of the civil service was shaped by a particular understanding of parliamentary government.

Yet, already, at the beginning of the century, it was being alleged that the principle of ministerial responsibility served to shield civil servants from parliamentary inquiry, and consequently gave them immunity from criticism or punishment for error. 'The permanent official', so Lowell declared in 1908, 'like the King, can do no wrong. Both are shielded by the responsibility of the minister . . .'[6] During the early years of the twentieth century, the principle of ministerial responsibility could indeed have been said to shield the influence of such powerful civil servants as Sir Robert Morant of the Board of Education, Sir Anthony MacDonnell of the Irish Office, and Admiral Sir John (Jackie) Fisher at the Admiralty. Elie Halévy indeed called these three 'secret dictators', and dismissed their ministerial heads as 'the Parliamentary mouthpieces of these great men of action'.[7] It may be, indeed, that the convention of ministerial responsibility has always obscured the creative role of leading civil servants; and, to this extent, it misleads as to the real power relationships

---

[5] Minutes of Royal Commission on the Civil Service, 1929–31, Public Record Office, T 169/1.
[6] Lowell, *The Government of England*, vol. 1, p. 193.
[7] Elie Halévy, *A History of the English People in the Nineteenth Century*: vol. 6, *The Rule of Democracy, 1905–1914*, revised edn 1952 (Ernest Benn, 1961), p. 265.

between ministers and those who serve them. Perhaps, however, it is not an accident that the three 'secret dictators' were all eventually repudiated, either by their political masters or by Parliament.

The other two principles defining the civil service—admission by open competition and promotion by ability—had been proposed by Northcote–Trevelyan, but were being implemented only gradually and slowly. In 1855, the Civil Service Commission had been established, and in 1870, during Gladstone's first administration, an Order in Council had provided that a competitive test was obligatory for admission to positions in various scheduled departments. These did not, however, include the Home Office or the Foreign Office, which remained exempt until shortly before the First World War. For professional posts, moreover, the Civil Service Commission could dispense with an examination if requested to do so by the head of the department concerned and the Treasury. Nevertheless, Britain was the first nation to adopt competitive examinations for recruitment on a large scale, and this was to prove a powerful factor in the development of a unified civil service, and perhaps also of a public service ethos. Thus, the principle of open competition laid down in the Northcote–Trevelyan Report implied the unification of the civil service, while the principle of promotion by merit implied interdepartmental rather than departmental promotion.

In 1875, the Playfair Commission had indeed proposed a common method of recruitment for departments, each of which had, until then, been 'practically a separate organism with its own method of recruitment'.[8] During the latter half of the nineteenth century, the area of uniform regulation for the civil service was gradually extended to embrace conditions of employment such as hours of work, holidays, sick leave, and pay, while recruitment was made subject to Treasury approval. In addition, it seems to have been accepted that the permanent secretary of the Treasury held a certain pre-eminence in the civil service, deriving, of course, from the control of expenditure vested in the Treasury. Nevertheless, the two further principles, of a unified civil service and of interdepartmental rather than departmental promotion, were not fully accepted until the twentieth century, for uniform recruitment by competitive examination was not implemented until 1919.

The acceptance, however slow, of the principles of selection by open competition and promotion by ability, and the gradual diffusion of these

---

[8] Royal Commission on the Civil Service, MacDonnell Commission, 1st Report, Cd 6209 (1912–13), Qu. 1961.

principles throughout the civil service was to enable the Royal Commission on the Civil Service (the MacDonnell Commission) to conclude, perhaps complacently, in 1914, that:

> the fundamental principles upon which the civil service is based appear to us to be sound, and . . . in the main, its organisation is efficient.[9]

II

It was during the twentieth century that the civil service became both a unified and a career service. Before 1914, conditions varied so much between departments, each having its own traditions, procedures and organisation, that, in the words of Sir Henry Primrose, chairman of the Board of Inland Revenue between 1899 and 1907 and a member of the MacDonnell Royal Commission on the civil service, which sat between 1912 and 1914:

> there was no such single thing as the civil service, and . . . this should be recognised before discussing the proper methods of recruitment which might be found to vary.[10]

The civil service until after the First World War was thus more a conglomeration of departments than a unified service, and the administrative class was, until 1914, organised on a departmental basis, although in theory unified through Treasury control. Treasury control, however, was comparatively nebulous before 1919. Admittedly, the Treasury, through its responsibility for presenting the estimates to Parliament, had long been able to exercise some powers of control and co-ordination over other departments on matters involving finance; and, from 1910, it had powers to investigate the pay and numbers of staff employed in every government department. But, since the Treasury's powers were both limited and largely indirect, it could do little to help create a unified service. As Sir Robert Chalmers, permanent secretary to the Treasury, told the MacDonnell Commission in 1912:

> I do not think the Treasury is ever in a position to enforce changes on other departments against their will. I think the Treasury ought always to look for any change in organisation, which will increase efficiency or promote economy in the departments themselves. I think it is quite useless

[9] Cd 7338 (1914), p. 4.
[10] Minority Report of MacDonnell Commission (1913), cited in Richard Chapman and J. R. Greenaway, *The Dynamics of Administrative Reform* (Croom Helm, 1980), p. 17.

241

to attempt to force them upon departments who are not willing to accept them.[11]

The MacDonnell Commission agreed, stating in its fourth report that 'whatever may be its indirect influence, the Treasury does not, in practice, exercise a sufficiently effective control over the organisation of departments unless a question of finance is involved'. In its fourth report in 1914, the MacDonnell Commission echoed its predecessors, the Playfair Commission, and the Ridley Royal Commission, whose reports were issued between 1881 and 1892, in calling for a strengthened Treasury 'for the purpose of establishing a more effective control over the organisation of the civil service'.[12] This call was to be strongly reiterated by the Haldane and Bradbury committees after the First World War.

If, before the First World War, the civil service was far from being a unified service, it was also far from being a career service. One study of permanent secretaries discovered percentages of 'careerists', 'semi-careerists', and 'outsiders', in the civil service between 1870 and 1983 (see Table 7.1).

Table 7.1 Permanent secretaries, 1870–1983

	1870–99	1900–18	1919–45	1946–64	1965–83
Careerist*	52.1	66.7	85.5	86.6	83.5
Semi-careerist**	20.8	23.5	6.7	8.5	9.7
Outsider***	27.1	9.8	7.8	4.9	6.8
	100.0	100.0	100.0	100.0	100.0
	(N=48)	(N=51)	(N=90)	(N=82)	(N=103)
Not classified	1	2	1	1	1

* Someone who entered public service under the age of 27 and remained until becoming permanent secretary.
** Someone who entered the civil service after the age of 26 and who had followed another career for at least five years, but less than fifteen years before becoming a civil servant—or whose civil service career had been broken by a period of at least three years outside the civil service, including secondment.
*** Someone whose civil service employment prior to becoming a permanent secretary was less than seven years—or someone with at least fifteen years experience in another career.
Source: Peter Barberis, *The Career Civil Servant in Whitehall: An Historical Analysis*, Manchester Papers in Politics (1991), p. 12.

In the forty years after the Second World War, between 1945 and 1986, nearly three-quarters of the permanent secretaries had served over twenty-five years in Whitehall before appointment; but, in the years between 1900 and 1919, the figure was just 28 per cent, while 32 per cent

[11] Cd 6209, Qu. 1903.
[12] MacDonnell Commission, 4th Report, Cd 7338 (1914), p. 99.

had served for ten years or less.[13] It was not until the late nineteenth century that the careerist became the most common type of permanent secretary, and the final triumph of the careerist did not occur until the years between the wars.[14]

The years until 1914 were thus a period during which the civil service was gradually coming to be established on a unified and career basis through a process of 'gradual consolidation . . . without the process being in any way centrally directed or political initiatives taken'.[15]

III

The slow, evolutionary development of the civil service was, however, to be rudely interrupted by the social welfare reforms of the Liberal government elected in 1906, and by the demands of total war after 1914.

Legislation such as the Trade Boards Act of 1909, the Labour Exchanges Act 1909 and the National Insurance Act 1911 seemed to require the introduction of a new kind of public official, because they were concerned with offering a service to the citizen rather than with regulation. 'What was wanted', Halévy writes, 'was not so much special knowledge or a high standard of general education as acquaintance with industrial and labour circles'.[16] In the new regulatory state, which was coming to replace the nineteenth-century liberal state, it would no longer, so it seemed, be sufficient for civil servants to act purely as administrators and policy advisers. They would also have to become managers. Thus, the officials required to regulate labour exchanges and national insurance were selected, not by competitive examination, but by appointment following interview. This led Andrew Bonar Law, the leader of the opposition after 1911, to complain of a spoils system of the American type. He accused the Liberals of having created over 4,000 new administrative posts, most of which had been filled by procedures other than those of competitive examination. While there was little danger of the introduction of a spoils system, the MacDonnell Commission thought, nevertheless, that there was reason for concern:

This system of appointment has recently been adopted to some extent for

[13] Kevin Theakston, *The Civil Service since 1945* (Blackwell, 1995), p. 39.
[14] See Parris, *Constitutional Bureaucracy*; Chapman and Greenaway, *The Dynamics of Administrative Reform*, pp. 16–73; and P. Hennessy, *Whitehall*, revised edn (Pimlico, 2001), pp. 31–51.
[15] Chapman and Greenaway, *The Dynamics of Administrative Reform*, p. 55.
[16] Halévy, *The Rule of Democracy*, p. 265.

the purpose of recruiting officials under the National Health Insurance Act. It claims—and herein lies its essential character—to determine the comparative fitness of candidates by an appraisement, through personal interview, supplemented by testimonials, of their qualities of education and intelligence. Examination is often dispensed with, or, if used at all, is used only as a qualifying test. Substantially, the system of appointment is selection by patronage, the abuses of patronage, being, it is claimed, precluded by the substitution of a Board or Committee of Selection for the Patron. It makes a new departure in recruitment for the civil service, which calls for the most careful examination.[17]

The vast majority of posts in the civil service, however, and certainly posts in the higher 'administrative' grades, were by 1914 filled by competition, and exceptions had to be specifically justified on grounds of public policy. The MacDonnell Commission found that around one-third of the civil service, 20,000, entered through open competition. Around 2,000 entered through 'limited competition', candidates having first been nominated to compete by the department concerned, and a further 8,500 by nomination followed by a qualifying examination, for posts such as office-keepers, messengers, attendants etc. Around 250 posts—certain heads of departments or boards and HM inspectors of schools—were filled by 'nomination', that is by direct appointment from the Crown. Around 2,500 posts requiring professional or other qualifications remained exempt from competitive examination under section 4 of the Superannuation Act 1859, Finally, there were around 25,000 civil servants, mainly unskilled or subordinate, holding temporary or subordinate posts on a weekly wage.[18]

The civil service came to be transformed, not only by the social reforms of the 1905–15 Liberal government, but also by the First World War, especially after Lloyd George became prime minister in December 1916. New ministries, such as the Ministry of Munitions and the Ministry of Food were established, and they were staffed by 'a new class of professional administrator', who could combine the perspective of both the businessman and the official.[19] Some, indeed, were businessmen. Admittedly, most of the outsiders brought in during the war did not remain in the civil service after 1918, but other administrative reforms of the Lloyd George era were to prove more permanent.

[17] MacDonnell Commission, 4th Report, p. 235.
[18] MacDonnell Commission, 4th Report, pp. 24–6. See also Wheare, 'Civil Service', in Cromwell, *Aspects of Government*, pp. 28–9.
[19] E. H. Lloyd, *State Control* (Clarendon Press, 1924), pp. 393–5.

On entering Downing Street, Lloyd George established a Cabinet Secretariat, which he saw as a policy-making body, the nucleus indeed of a Prime Minister's Department. However, the first Cabinet secretary, Maurice Hankey, declared that the secretariat should not be a policy-making body, insisting that it be neutral between departments, 'neither an Intelligence Department nor a General Staff'; and he sternly reminded assistant secretaries 'that it is no part of their duties to do work which pertains to the Departments'.[20] Admittedly, Hankey himself hardly stuck to this dictum because he acted until 1918 as, in effect, strategic adviser to the prime minister on the problems of the war, and continued to advise on defence matters for much of his period as Cabinet secretary, until his retirement in 1938.

At its inception, moreover, the Cabinet Secretariat was not in a particularly strong position even to act as a co-ordinating body, let alone a policy-making one. For it was staffed not by career civil servants, but—like Lloyd George's personal secretariat, the so-called 'Garden Suburb', with which it was often confused—primarily by outsiders and by senior service personnel. Career civil servants did not enter it in any numbers until the 1930s.[21] In its early years, therefore, the Cabinet Secretariat was thought of as a rather temporary body, and it seemed somewhat isolated from the rest of Whitehall. In 1922, indeed, on the fall of the Lloyd George coalition government, Bonar Law, the new prime minister, and Sir Warren Fisher, permanent secretary at the Treasury and head of the civil service, sought to abolish it and absorb its functions into the Treasury.[22] Although they were unsuccessful in this endeavour, it was the Treasury and not the Cabinet Office which was to become the main co-ordinating department in Whitehall between the wars.

Gradually, and despite its founder, the Cabinet Secretariat came to follow the principles which Hankey had laid down. Unlike its predecessor, the secretariat of the Committee for Imperial Defence, the Cabinet Office would not pose as an expert critic of proposals put forward by the departments, but would confine itself to co-ordination. It remained faithful to this role until the end of the century when its role expanded and it came to fulfil functions of central support for the government, as

---

[20] Quoted in John Turner, 'Cabinets, Committees and Secretariats: The Higher Direction of War', in Kathleen Burk, (ed.), *War and the State: The Transformation of British Government, 1914–1919* (Allen & Unwin, 1982), p. 73.

[21] Stephen Roskill, *Hankey, Man of Secrets* (Collins, 1970), vol. 1, pp. 637–9.

[22] Eunan O'Halpin, *Head of the Civil Service: A Study of Sir Warren Fisher* (Routledge, 1989), p. 107.

well as co-ordinating functions. It had also begun to give policy advice to support the chairs of key Cabinet committees, and was involved in policy formulation through various units and task forces. Some even believed that the Cabinet Office might become the nucleus of a Prime Minister's Department, as had happened in Canada and Australia.

The First World War proved the catalyst for further major administrative reforms, designed to secure better co-ordination between Whitehall departments, and therefore greater unity in the civil service. During the war, the Treasury had lost control over both public spending and also the staffing of the new departments such as the Ministry of Munitions.[23] Co-ordination in the post-war years was to be restored in two ways: first, through the establishment of interdepartmental committees of officials and acceptance of the principle of interdepartmental transfer; and, second, through a firmer conception of Treasury control.

During the inter-war years, interdepartmental committees of officials were set up, parallel to Cabinet committees, to assist in the task of co-ordination. Such co-ordination would be easier to achieve if the civil servants doing the co-ordinating had experience of more than one department. Before 1914, this had rarely been possible, and civil servants tended to remain in the department to which they had originally been assigned or chosen to go at the start of their careers. It was not until after the First World War that interdepartmental transfer was to become the rule. Between 1900 and 1919, only one-quarter of permanent secretaries had worked in more than one department. Between 1945 and 1966, by contrast, the figure was two-thirds, and between 1965 and 1986 it was three-quarters.[24] Interdepartmental transfer was to be memorably anathematised by the Fulton Committee in its report of 1968, as marking the apotheosis of the nineteenth-century philosophy of the amateur. Yet it had been introduced in the twentieth century by modernisers, such as Sir Warren Fisher, permanent secretary to the Treasury and head of the civil service from 1919, with the purpose of creating both a more professional and a more unified civil service, analogous, on the civil side, to the armed forces of the state.

The post-war years also saw the introduction of a firmer conception of Treasury control. Indeed, one authority has declared that 'the formal strengthening of Treasury control was the most important administrative

[23] Kathleen Burk, 'The Treasury: From Impotence to Power', in Burk, *War and the State*, p. 86.
[24] Theakston, *The Civil Service since 1945*, p. 39.

change to come out of the First World War'.[25] In 1914, the MacDonnell Commission had declared that the influence of the Treasury fell well short of control, and proposed that a special section be established within the Treasury for the supervision and control of the civil service.[26] This call for firmer Treasury control was echoed after the war by three important committees. The first, the House of Commons Select Committee on National Expenditure, which reported in 1918, pointed out that the problem of control had become acute since many of the new 'mushroom' ministries established under the exigencies of wartime—for example, the Ministries of Labour, Food, and Shipping, and the Air Board—had not been subject to Treasury control over their numbers or organisation, the Acts setting up these ministries having left it to ministers themselves to determine the size of their staffs. Moreover, the Whitehall departments, so Sir Warren Fisher was to complain to the Tomlin Committee on the Civil Service in 1930, did not think of themselves 'as merely units of a complete and correlated whole; and in the recognition by each Department of the existence of others there was, from time to time, an attitude of superiority, of condescension, of resentment, or even of suspicion'.[27] The Haldane Report of 1918 echoed the House of Commons Select Committee on National Expenditure in calling for the Treasury to exercise oversight over the civil service. So also did the Committee of Inquiry into the Organising and Staffing of Government Offices—the Bradbury Committee—in its report of 1919.

In 1919, therefore, an Establishments Department was set up to ensure that the Treasury would be 'a powerful, strong central Department to be the Department of the Civil Service'.[28] At the same time, the permanent secretary to the Treasury was specifically designated head of the civil service, so that, as Lord Geddes, formerly Sir Auckland Geddes, reminisced in 1942, there would be 'a definite figure who would impersonate the Government as the employer in the vast extent of the civil service'.[29] In 1920, a Treasury circular provided that the consent of the prime minister, advised by the permanent secretary to the Treasury, would be required for all future appointments at upper and senior levels in departments. This would allow the permanent secretary to the Treasury

---

[25] Rodney Lowe, cited in Burk, *War and the State*, p. 4.
[26] MacDonnell Commission, 4th Report, para. xvi.
[27] Cmd 3909, Minutes of evidence.
[28] As remembered by Lord Geddes, formerly Sir Auckland Geddes, in the House of Lords, vol. 125, col. 286, 26 November 1942.
[29] Ibid.

to survey the whole of the civil service before recommending an appointment, rather than confining it to the department concerned. Thus, in 1922, Fisher successfully pressed for the appointment of Sir John Anderson, an under-secretary in the Irish Office, rather than a Home Office official, to the position of permanent secretary at the Home Office. 'Now for the premier posts in the public service', Fisher declared, 'the field of choice is the whole service, & unless each rare opportunity is seized as it arises, we shall not get the best men into the principal positions & departments so deprived will not become efficient. That was the motive of the Cabinet agreement that the final word was to be with the Prime Minister (and not with the departmental Minister) who would take a wider, more detached, and better informed view.'[30] An Order in Council in 1920 gave the Treasury legal authority over the civil service, and empowered it to make regulations for controlling the conduct of departments. There would be a common policy on pay, grading, recruitment and discipline in all Whitehall departments. The civil service would thus, it was hoped, become a genuinely unified body, a genuine service.

In 1926, a Treasury circular provided for the further strengthening of financial control by making the permanent head of each department its accounting officer. Fisher had told the Public Accounts Committee in 1920: 'I am very anxious indeed that it should not be open to any permanent head ... to say "please Sir, it wasn't me". That is what I am anxious for. Pin it on him in the last resort and you have got him as an ally for economy.'[31] Departmental heads, no less than the Treasury, were thus to be made financially accountable as trustees for the taxpayer.

In a lecture delivered in 1921 to the Society of Civil Servants, entitled 'The State and Finance', J. M. Keynes declared that 'Treasury control' was unique to the United Kingdom. In the United States, the Treasury had little authority 'beyond looking after the collection of taxes'. In France, also, it was 'more or less a tax-collecting institution', while the administration of the German Reich had been conducted by virtually independent departments, which had fought against each other almost as much as they had fought against the enemy.

In Britain, by contrast, the Treasury enjoyed a certain *esprit de corps* rather like a City livery company, an Oxbridge college, or the Church of England. It embodied 'the age of efficiency and incorruptibility in the civil service which was introduced in the Gladstonian epoch', and it

---

[30] O'Halpin, *Head of the Civil Service*, p. 73.
[31] O'Halpin, *Head of the Civil Service*, pp. 50, 54, 67.

would prove a 'bulwark against overwhelming wickedness'. 'I think', Keynes suggested, 'Treasury control might be compared to conventional morality'. Nevertheless, Keynes did not want to reform the system of Treasury control, but rather to convert the Treasury to his own ideas.

The trouble was, however, that the Treasury ethos stood essentially for continuity. But continuity had been disrupted by the war, when 'innumerable enthusiasts ... believed they could win the war if only they could spend unlimited sums of money'.[32] Would Treasury control prove an effective instrument for what Keynes saw as an era of discontinuity when the emphasis, in the view of many observers, ought to be less on saving candle-ends, and more on imaginative schemes of economic and social reconstruction?

The inter-war Treasury has been widely condemned for holding to the restrictive view that all public expenditure was wasteful, so rendering impossible both schemes for economic regeneration along Keynesian lines, and also much-needed measures of social improvement. Fisher himself, though by no means hostile to social reform, did little to encourage new thinking in economic and social affairs, for he was determined that there should be no independent or competing sources of advice to ministers. Nevertheless, the standard criticisms of the Treasury, which seemed so cogent during the high tide of the Keynesian revolution, appear less so perhaps today, when historians have become more sceptical as to the value of the alternative economic policies proposed during the inter-war years.[33]

It was, then, Sir Warren Fisher who helped ensure that the Cabinet Office was to be staffed by career civil servants rather than by outsiders or party appointees; he was responsible also for a massive reinforcement of the principle of Treasury control, acceptance of the principle of interdepartmental transfer, and the conception of permanent secretaries as accounting officers. He helped to create a civil service which was a genuinely integrated whole, a civil service whose collective advice would supplement the collective responsibility of the Cabinet. It was the reforms of the years immediately following the First World War which led to the creation of a recognisably modern civil service, based on the principles of unified control and interdepartmental transfer, and these reforms owe as much to Fisher, Haldane and Bradbury, and even perhaps to Lloyd

---

[32] A version of this lecture appears in the *Collected Writings of John Maynard Keynes* (Macmillan for the Royal Economic Society, 1971), vol. 16, pp. 296, 297, 299, 301.
[33] O'Halpin, *Head of the Civil Service*, pp. 77, 130.

George, as they do to Northcote-Trevelyan and Gladstone. The modern civil service is a product not only of the second half of the nineteenth century, as the Fulton Committee was later to believe, but also of the second decade of the twentieth, and, in particular, of the revolutionary changes wrought by the First World War.

IV

It has been suggested that it was during the inter-war period that 'the higher civil service in Britain probably reached the height of its corporate influence'.[34] Yet the achievement of an increasingly anonymous and career civil service did not inhibit those at the top of the civil service, such as Maurice Hankey, the Cabinet secretary, and Tom Jones, his assistant from political involvement. Tom Jones, for example, continued to work for Lloyd George in opposition and drafted electoral speeches for Stanley Baldwin in the tariff election of 1923, although Jones himself remained a free trader, voted Liberal, and the day after the election, wrote to Lloyd George to tell him to 'move to the Left'! 'I do not much like the disclosure', Sir Edward Bridges wrote to him in 1953, 'that, while a civil servant, you played so large a part in determining the political content of a series of speeches during a general election'. The two permanent heads at the Treasury between 1919 and 1942, Sir Warren Fisher and Sir Horace Wilson, have both been criticised—in the case of Fisher quite unjustly—for their involvement in the policy of 'appeasement'. Wilson, in particular, who travelled with Neville Chamberlain to Munich, was exposed to public opprobrium as one of the 'guilty men', of the 1930s, and in 1940, Attlee made his exclusion from Downing Street a 'condition' of the Labour Party joining Churchill's coalition government. Wilson, however, was not a policy-maker, but an executant, albeit an enthusiastic one, of appeasement.[35] All the same, it has been correctly pointed out that, 'None of the three giants of the inter-war Higher Civil Service [Hankey, Fisher and Wilson] fully observed the mores of the constitutional convention of ministerial responsibility.'[36]

[34] Max Beloff, 'The Whitehall Factor: The Role of the Higher Civil Service, 1919–1939', in Gillian Peele and Chris Cook (eds), *The Politics of Reappraisal, 1918–1939* (Macmillan, 1975), p. 210.

[35] E. L. Ellis, *T. J. A Life of Dr Thomas Jones CH* (University of Wales Press, 1992), pp. 247, 259, 465, 524.

[36] Geoffrey Fry, 'Three Giants of the Inter-war British Higher Civil Service: Sir Maurice Hankey, Sir Warren Fisher and Sir Horace Wilson', in Kevin Theakston (ed.), *Bureaucrats*

The behaviour of prima donnas such as Hankey, Fisher and Wilson should not of course be taken as representative of the higher civil service as a whole where the broad trend was towards a sharpening rather than a blurring of the dividing line between politics and administration. Nevertheless, it was not until the post-war period that the convention of anonymity, if it is a convention, came to be observed by those at the top of the civil service as well as their juniors, and perhaps it began to decline after 1979 under the impact of what one minister called 'a revolution in the whole management of the civil service'.[37] The period of genuine anonymity of top civil servants, then, may be shorter than is generally thought; lasting from 1939 to 1979, just forty years.[38]

If it was during the inter-war years that the civil service collectively enjoyed its greatest influence, it was during the 1940s, the years of the Second World War and the reforming Attlee administration, that its prestige reached its height. It emerged from the 1940s, as did so many British institutions, both self-confident and assured. Having helped to defeat Hitler, nationalised the major public utilities and created the welfare state, there was nothing, so it seemed, that it could not do; and it did not seem too incongruous for Douglas Jay to write in his book, *The Socialist Case*, published in 1947, that 'in the case of nutrition and health, just as in the case of education, the gentleman in Whitehall really does know better what is good for people than the people know themselves'.[39]

The Second World War, like the First, had seen an infusion of talented outsiders into the civil service. In their paper, 'How Adolf Hitler Reformed Whitehall', Douglas Hague and Peter Hennessy discuss the contribution of, amongst others, Oliver Franks, John Maud, William Penney, Harold Wilson, William Beveridge, J. M. Keynes, R. V. Jones and Norman Chester.[40] Only two of these, however—Oliver Franks and John

and Leadership (Macmillan, 2000), p. 63. See also on Sir Horace Wilson, Rodney Lowe and Richard Roberts, 'Sir Horace Wilson, 1900–1935: The Making of a Mandarin', *Historical Journal*, 30 (1981).

[37] William Waldegrave MP, minister for public service and science, HC 27, p. li.

[38] Even before 1979, there was a singular case of official identification with government policy, that of Sir William Armstrong, head of the home civil service from 1968 to 1974, who became so associated with the Heath government's statutory incomes policy, that he came to be known as the deputy prime minister.

[39] Douglas Jay, *The Socialist Case*, revised edn (Faber & Faber, 1947), p. 258. Prime Minister C. R. Attlee contributed a foreword to the book.

[40] Peter Hennessy and Douglas Hague, 'How Adolf Hitler Reformed Whitehall', *Strathclyde Papers on Government and Politics* (1985).

Maud—reached the rank of permanent secretary. Most of the outsiders left the civil service after the end of the war, so that, by the 1950s, it had become once again what it had been in the 1930s—a professional, career service. Later critics, such as Sir Philip Allen, permanent secretary at the Home Office in the 1960s, and a member of the Fulton Committee, were to argue that 'an opportunity had been missed of reforming the civil service after the war. We simply went back to the old order of things.'[41] That, however, was very much a hindsight view. For confidence in the civil service remained high during the 1950s, an era during which Britain's economic and social progress was compared favourably with her performance during the inter-war years. Even Crichel Down in 1954, seen at the time as casting doubt on both the efficiency and integrity of senior civil servants, did not give rise to any radical rethinking nor to any fundamental questioning of the role of the higher civil service.[42] In 1954, the same year as Crichel Down, Herbert Morrison ended his standard work, *Government and Parliament: A Survey from the Inside*, with a 'Tribute to the British Civil Service', claiming: 'The worst that can be said of them is that sometimes they are not quick enough in accustoming themselves to new ideas, but then it is up to the Minister to educate them.'[43]

In this new era of consensus and affluence, therefore, fundamental re-examination of the civil service seemed quite unnecessary. Thus the terms of reference of the Priestley Royal Commission on the Civil Service, established in 1953, which reported in 1955, excluded wider issues of principle and restricted it to a consideration of civil service pay and conditions. In 1954, the centenary of the Northcote-Trevelyan Report, Sir Edward Bridges, permanent secretary at the Treasury, observed that 'looking back over the last hundred years, the reforms of 1854 can be seen to have stood the test of time'; and he insisted that the service had adapted well to the challenges of the war and immediate post-war era.[44]

---

[41] In an interview with Geoffrey Fry. See Geoffrey K. Fry, *Reforming the Civil Service: The Fulton Committee on the British Home Civil Service, 1966–1968* (Edinburgh University Press, 1993), p. 2.

[42] Report of the Royal Commission on the Civil Service, Priestley Report, Cmd 9613 (1955). Report of the Public Inquiry ordered by the Minister of Agriculture into the Disposal of Land at Crichel Down, Clark Report, Cmd 9176 (1954). But see on Crichel Down the important work by I. F. Nicolson, *The Mystery of Crichel Down* (Oxford University Press, 1986).

[43] Reprinted without alteration ten years later, Herbert Morrison, *Government and Parliament: A Survey from the Inside*, 3rd edn (Oxford University Press, 1964), pp. 345–6.

[44] Sir Edward Bridges, 'The Reforms of 1854 in Retrospect', *Political Quarterly* (1954), 322.

In a lecture celebrating the centenary, K. C. Wheare, Gladstone professor of government and public administration at Oxford, remarked that the greatest change since the publication of the report 'consists not in the removal of patronage nor in the establishment of competition. It consists in the tremendous rise in the authority of the civil service.' This rise in authority had of course coincided with the rise of the state. Wheare argued that the critics were mistaken in thinking that the civil service had been unable to deal with the expanding state. On the contrary,

> One of the most fortunate things in the history of British government, as we look back on the hundred years since the Report was published, is seen to be this premature vision in the middle of the nineteenth century of the sort of civil service we need in the middle of the twentieth century.[45]

V

It was not until the end of the 1950s that the civil service came to be assailed, and that occurred primarily as a result of a change in the intellectual atmosphere. For, by the end of the 1950s, commentators were less impressed with the fact that Britain's economic performance was better than it had been in the 1930s, than with her relative decline compared to her main industrial competitors. If Britain were to increase her rate of growth, so it was argued, she would have to modernise her institutions; and, in particular, a major constraint on Britain's economic performance was the amateurism and lack of economic expertise of the civil service and, in particular, the Treasury. In the search for the reasons for Britain's poor economic performance, the alleged 'amateurism' of the civil service came to assume the position of prime scapegoat. 'Can any general conclusion be drawn as to who was mainly responsible for the course of Britain's financial policies in the 1950s and early 1960s?' one influential commentator asked. He replied to his own question: 'If the reader would like a one-word answer, before going on to the qualifications and complexities, it is: officials. For it is they who provided the framework of thought through which the Government acted.'[46]

The attack began with an essay, 'The Apotheosis of the Dilettante' by the economist Thomas Balogh, a fellow of Balliol College, Oxford,

[45] K. C. Wheare, *The Civil Service in the Constitution* (Athlone Press, 1954).
[46] Samuel Brittan, *The Treasury under the Tories* (Penguin, 1964), p. 303.

published in 1959, in a volume edited by Hugh Thomas entitled *The Establishment*. In this essay, Balogh declared that 'Britain's power has been declining at a rate unparalleled since the crash of the Spanish Empire, and the decline cannot be explained by the venality of the voters, or the folly of politicians acting in a democratic system, or even the harshness of the world.' Admittedly, Balogh went on to acknowledge that, 'Civil service reform alone will not restore parliamentary democracy or Cabinet responsibility in Britain. It cannot by itself create the basis for a successful Socialist Government.' Nevertheless, civil service reform was 'one of the most essential and fundamental pre-conditions of both . . . It is a challenge to Labour to achieve this and it dare not fail.'[47] The challenge was to replace a civil service which was ill-informed, insufficiently numerate and unaware of modern developments in economics, with a professional cadre of men and women properly qualified to undertake the quantitative analysis of economic and social problems.

The influence of Balogh's essay derived not only from his academic position, but from his closeness to leading figures on the Labour Left, and, in particular, Harold Wilson and Richard Crossman. The latter was indeed to declare, in 1967, as lord president of the Council and leader of the House of Commons, that 'before I became a Minister I had found Tommy Balogh's chapter on the Establishment the most important statement on the civil service. Now I had some experience I was even more impressed by it.'[48]

But the attack did not come only from the Labour Left. In 1964, the Fabian Society published a similar critique to that of Balogh in an influential report entitled *The Administrators*, the product of a group which included Anthony Crosland and Shirley Williams, as well as two permanent secretaries who remain anonymous to this day. The conclusions of this group were very much in line with the Fabian ethos. Admittedly, the early Fabians in *Fabian Essays* (1889) had strongly favoured the Northcote-Trevelyan civil service, which would, so they believed, undermine the contention of economic liberals that the state was incompetent at running public services. But, by the beginning of the twentieth century, the Webbs had come to favour the introduction of outside experts to combat the 'amateurism' and inefficiency of the permanent officials; and, in 1920, in

[47] Thomas Balogh, 'The Apotheosis of the Dilettante', in *The Establishment*, ed. Hugh Thomas (Anthony Blond, 1959), pp. 99, 125.
[48] Richard Crossman, *Diaries of a Cabinet Minister*: vol. 2, *Lord President of the Council and Leader of the House of Commons, 1966–8* (Hamish Hamilton, 1976), p. 200.

their *Constitution for the Socialist Commonwealth of Great Britain*, they called for 'a civil service of a new kind, capable of planning a socialist society'.[49] The Fabians of the 1960s followed the Webbs in their belief that the British civil service had been designed to administer a liberal but not an interventionist state, and suggested that reform of the civil service 'may be a prerequisite to enabling a Labour Government— or any other government—to carry through the modernisation of the country'.[50]

The Fabian critique took its place in the 'What's Wrong with Britain' literature, a favourite genre of the 1960s, much of which indicted the civil service; and it received popular support in the novels of C. P. Snow, one of whose themes was that civil servants lacked both scientific training and the technical expertise to make a success of economic planning. Like Balogh and Snow, the Fabians found the civil service amateurish, untrained in economics and quantitative matters, and dominated by public-school boys and arts graduates from Oxbridge. They concluded, in *The Administrators*, that there was 'a consensus of opinion in favour of reform of the Civil Service . . . emerging amongst those in all parties who are concerned with the problems of modernising Britain'.[51]

Harold Wilson, who became prime minister in 1964, responded to this consensus of opinion by setting up, in 1966, a Committee on the Home Civil Service, chaired by Lord Fulton. Its report was published in 1968. The Fulton Committee, unlike Priestley, was designed to secure reform. Its terms of reference required it 'to examine the structure, recruitment and management, including training, of the Home Civil Service and to make recommendations'. It was, however, precluded from considering constitutional matters. For, as Harold Wilson told the House of Commons, there was 'no intention . . . to alter the basic relationship between Ministers and civil servants . . . Civil servants, however eminent, remain the confidential advisers of Ministers, who alone are answerable to Parliament for policy; and we do not envisage any change in this fundamental feature of our parliamentary system of democracy.'[52] The committee was thus precluded from assessing the convention of ministerial responsibility, a crucial foundation of the twentieth-century civil service.

---

[49] Sidney and Beatrice Webb, *A Constitution for the Socialist Commonwealth of Great Britain* (Longmans Green, 1920), pp. 175–6.
[50] Fabian Society, *The Administrators* (1964), p. 1.
[51] Fabian Society, *The Administrators*, p. 43.
[52] HC Debs, vol. 724, col. 210, 8 February 1966.

This restriction, of course, begged two crucial questions. The first was that if, as Balogh and others had alleged, the civil service was a crucial factor in Britain's decline, ought not the very fundamentals, including the constitutional position of the civil service, be investigated, in addition to what might be seen as less fundamental, managerial features?

But, second, was it even possible to make such a separation between 'managerial' and 'constitutional' issues? Did it made sense to consider one set of issues in abstraction from the other; for might not seemingly 'managerial' reforms have constitutional consequences. Perhaps, indeed, the scope of managerial change might be constrained by the very constitutional relationships between ministers and civil servants which Fulton had been told to ignore.

The Fulton Report was characterised by one of its members, Sir Philip Allen, permanent secretary at the Home Office, as 'the worst report I have ever been concerned with (and I've sat on many committees in my time)'.[53] It represented, in a sense, the culmination of the Fabian critique, that the civil service was geared to managing a liberal rather than an interventionist state. 'The Home Civil Service today', the report began, 'is still fundamentally the product of the nineteenth-century philosophy of the Northcote-Trevelyan Report. The problems it faces are those of the second half of the twentieth century. In spite of its many strengths, it is inadequate . . . for the most efficient discharge of the present and prospective responsibilities of government'.[54] This dramatic opening, which attracted numerous press headlines, was in fact quite inaccurate. For what the committee stigmatised as 'the cult of the generalist' was, as we have seen, a product of the Warren Fisher era, not of Northcote-Trevelyan, and it had been encouraged by Fisher in order to increase the pool of talent available for senior posts.

The main recommendations of the Fulton Committee were, however, far less radical than its provocative opening implied, and not all of its proposals stood the test of time. For example, Fulton recommended the transference of the central management of the service from the Treasury to a new Civil Service Department. This department, in effect the establishment's side of the Treasury, was duly set up, only to be abolished in 1981, its functions being mainly returned to the Treasury. Fulton also recommended the establishment of a Civil Service College, which, it seems to have hoped, would become a British version of the *École*

---

[53] Symposium, 'Fulton: 20 Years On', *Contemporary Record*, 2 (1988), 50.
[54] Cmnd 3638 (1968), p. 1.

Nationale d'Administration. It favoured, in addition, the recruitment of more outsiders, and proposed that recruitment by competitive examination be supplemented by other procedures for special permanent or temporary appointments, especially for those with 'relevant' experience.

But perhaps the most influential recommendation of the Fulton Report was that executive work should be 'hived off' from the departments so as to separate management from policy-making, and improve management skills. Fulton believed that such 'hiving off' would encourage the civil service to emphasise the importance of management. To encourage this, the principle of 'accountable management' should be introduced. Civil servants would be given specific targets of achievement so that their successes or failures could be more objectively assessed, as was apparently the case with their counterparts in the private sector. This would give rise to a greater degree of personal responsibility in the civil service, and so act as an inducement to efficiency. Ironically, the Fulton recommendation for 'hiving off', which was to bear fruit in executive agencies in the 1990s, went beyond its terms of reference, which did not include machinery of government issues.

VI

Despite the Fulton critique, civil service confidence was not seriously dented until the mid-1970s. It was the economic and social collapse of the 1970s, which culminated in the International Monetary Fund crisis of 1976 and the winter of discontent in 1978–9, that led to a fundamental alteration in attitudes towards government. Having been seen as part of the solution, government henceforth came to be seen as part of the problem. Civil servants, it came to be argued, were like a closed corporation. They were too negative in their approach and insufficiently committed to the goals of the governments which they served. They saw themselves as being above politics and thus withheld that last ounce of commitment that was needed if Britain's deep-seated economic and social problems were to be resolved. 'There is', declared Nevil Johnson in 1977, 'a kind of deadness at the heart of the conventional doctrine defining the position of the civil service in British government. It denies commitment and encourages indifference; it sets the preservation of form far above the expression of purposes.'[55]

---

[55] Nevil Johnson, *In Search of the Constitution* (Pergamon, 1977), p. 96.

Thus, in the 1980s, the civil service found itself very much on the defensive. With the arrival of Margaret Thatcher in Downing Street in 1979, who found her first meeting with the permanent secretaries a 'dismal' occasion,[56] there was a culture shift in the direction of individualism and greater emphasis on the rights of consumers. Many began to question whether public services should continue to be delivered by the state and, inevitably, criticism came to be directed towards the public officials who delivered these services. The application of economic analysis to the activities of the state seemed to show that civil servants, far from being a Hegelian universal class whose central concern was the welfare of the community, were just as much concerned as everyone else to maximise their own welfare, which in their case meant maximising the size of their departments and the budgets under their control.[57]

Criticism of the civil service as sustaining an anti-industrial culture was intensified during the 1980s by the work of commentators such as Martin Wiener in his book *English Culture and the Decline of the Industrial Spirit* (1981), and Correlli Barnett in *The Audit of War* (1986), one of a series of works criticising British amateurism and incompetence, a result, so they claimed of the dominance of a civil service elite whose ethos was fundamentally anti-industrial. These works had considerable influence among politicians, even though their conclusions were vigorously contested by many scholars. By the end of the 1980s, indeed, it had become commonplace to claim that the civil service was a powerful hindrance to Britain's economic progress. In 1989, Peter Hennessy began his history, *Whitehall*, with a quotation by the economist-historian Sidney Pollard to the effect that 'The peculiar strengths and weaknesses of the civil service, and of the Treasury in particular, form a powerful contributory cause of our decline.'[58] Little empirical evidence, however, was given for this or similar assertions, and the call for 'reform' of the civil service perhaps symbolised a loss of self-confidence in British institutions. One need only contrast the tone of Sir Edward Bridges's magisterial Rede Lecture, *Portrait of a Profession*, delivered in 1950, with the later literature of 'modernisation', to appreciate the extent of the loss of national self-confidence during and after the 1960s. It was within this context that

---

[56] Margaret Thatcher, *The Downing Street Years* (HarperCollins, 1993), p. 48.

[57] See, for example, the very influential book by W. A. Niskanen, *Bureaucracy and Representative Government* (Aldine, Atherton, 1971).

[58] Hennessy, *Whitehall*, p. 1. The quotation is from Sidney Pollard, *The Wasting of the British Economy*, 2nd edn (Croom Helm, 1984), p. 159.

Margaret Thatcher determined to get a grip on what she regarded as Britain's failing institutions.

The managerial reforms proposed by Fulton thus came to be implemented, not in the context of an expanding state, but by the Thatcher and Major administrations which were seeking to reduce the scope of government. There came to be less concern with constitutional principles and procedures, the emphasis being placed instead on the effectiveness of the public sector, its output. Indeed, the dominant theme of the public management reforms of the 1980s and 1990s may be summed up in a phrase often used by John Major, the privatisation of choice. The aim was to give the consumer the same rights in respect of the public services as were enjoyed by the shopper at Marks & Spencer or Sainsbury's. To achieve this, the Thatcher and Major governments put in train the most radical changes in the structure of British administration since the Northcote-Trevelyan Report. The civil service was subject to more change in its structure and organisation between 1979 and the end of the century than at any time in the preceding 125 years.

There is an element of paradox, however, in the programme of reform. For, before 1979, it had constantly been asserted that the interventionist state needed a new civil service more properly attuned to interventionism, that it needed what Lloyd George had called 'men of push and go'.[59] The 'amateur', 'generalist' approach of Northcote-Trevelyan was, so it was argued, suitable for the nightwatchman state, but not for the interventionist state. Yet the period of the growth of the state corresponded—apart from the years 1911–22, the years dominated by Lloyd George—with the period when the orthodox civil service, born with Northcote-Trevelyan and nurtured to fruition by Warren Fisher, reached its apogee. By contrast, the years since 1979, when the interventionist state was in retreat, saw the greatest dissatisfaction with the qualities of the traditional civil service.

The reforms of the years after 1979 constituted a revolution in Whitehall. It was, however, a quiet revolution, and put into effect in a somewhat haphazard way. The reforms were implemented by ministers under prerogative powers, rather than through legislation. The revolution, moreover, did not come about as a result of the recommendations of a Royal Commission or similar body, and although the reforms were

---

[59] Cited in Hennessy, *Whitehall*, p. 52.

regularly evaluated by the House of Commons Treasury and Civil Service Committee, they were not the subject of a great deal of public debate.

The main principles of the revolution in Whitehall were the introduction of quasi-market structures into the public services, and the setting of performance objectives. This was to be achieved through market-testing, the contracting out of public services, and, above all, by the devolution of functions via the 'Next Steps' programme to new executive agencies outside Whitehall, which, through effecting the separation of executive activity from the rest of the work of the department, split the function of the purchaser from that of the provider. By the end of the century, around 60 per cent of civil servants were working in such agencies.[60] The *Citizen's Charter* of 1991 emphasised the consumerist orientation of the reforms by defining the standards of service which citizens were entitled to expect and providing some right of redress if those standards were not delivered.

'Next Steps' was a child of Fulton's 'hiving off'; indeed the agencies of the 1990s had been prefigured in Fulton's 'units of accountable management'. 'The basic case' for it was, in the words of Professor W. J. M. Mackenzie, 'the simulation of a business situation'.[61] The fundamental leitmotif of the reforms was that efficiency in the public services could be achieved by adapting the methods and practices of the private sector. This had been prefigured in the report of the Fulton Committee's Management and Consultancy Group, which, in the words of one of its members, had recommended 'the introduction into the civil service of the attitudes of mind and practices that were common in private industry and commerce and the adoption of which we believed would make for a more efficient civil service'.[62] By the 1980s, Britain had become a society dominated by the ethic of self-realisation and, in that culture, business inevitably enjoyed a special role, since only business seemed capable of producing the consumer goods upon which consumer satisfaction depended. It was, however, never made clear why, during a period of industrial decline, the practices of British industry and commerce, hardly noted for their efficiency, offered a better blueprint for the civil service than the traditions built up by Northcote-Trevelyan and Warren Fisher, which had made Britain's civil service a model for emulation in many other countries.

---

[60] *Improving Management in Government: The Next Steps*, Ibbs Report (HMSO, 1988).
[61] Quoted in Fry, 'Three Giants', p. 103.
[62] Interview by E. K. Ferguson with Geoffrey Fry in Fry, 'Three Giants', p. 66.

VII

The need to introduce business methods into government was seen by the Thatcher and Major administrations, and indeed by the Blair government which succeeded them, as a new idea. In reality, it was an echo of an old idea first heard amidst the mismanagement of the Crimean War which had led to the formation of an Administrative Reform Association in 1855 with the aim of bringing up 'the public management to the level of private management in this country.'[63] Similar mismanagement during the Boer War had revived the cry for business people in government. In 1901, for example, a committee investigating the working of the War Office discovered 'a general, if not a precise analogy ... between the conduct of large business undertakings and that of the War Office. There are certain well-defined principles of management in all well-conducted business corporations, and the more closely the War Office can be brought into conformity with such principles, the more successful will be its administration.'[64] A new Administrative Reform Association was duly established to put these principles into effect.

Exactly the same battle, to create a more 'open' civil service, and one more familiar with the realities of commercial life, had been waged at the beginning of the century as was to be fought at its end. It raised the same fundamental issue of whether the managerial reforms proposed to increase civil service efficiency were compatible with the constitutional principles regulating the relationships between ministers and civil servants.

One of the reasons why the agitation at the beginning of the century had failed was that the cry for business methods in government seemed to many to pose a threat to the parliamentary system. Similarly, at the end of the century, there seemed a degree of tension between managerial reform and constitutional principle. The analogy drawn by reformers with management in the private sector seemed to many to be fundamentally flawed. The board of a company, after all, did not have to defend its policies on a continuous basis before a body of critical shareholders constituted as a Parliament, with an official opposition determined to undermine the directors. The business of a government department would inevitably, so it seemed, be scrutinised in a different way from

---

[63] Quoted in G. R. Searle, *The Quest for National Efficiency: A Study in British Politics and Political Thought, 1899–1914* (Blackwell, 1971), p. 17.
[64] Ibid., pp. 89–90.

that in which shareholders of a public company judged the operations of their firm. In the latter case, the net financial outcome of all of the firm's operations over a period of time would be evaluated at the annual meeting of shareholders. Parliament, however, could scrutinise any single operation carried out by government at any time, and could do so some considerable time after the operation in question had occurred. This had obvious implications for record-taking and the avoidance of risk, and it seemed to make the conduct of public affairs by civil servants a profession rather than a branch of management. It also seemed to form the basis for the traditional contract by means of which civil servants would be offered job security in exchange for levels of pay generally lower than many of them could command elsewhere.

Thus, at the end of the twentieth century as at its beginning, the principle of ministerial responsibility seemed to limit the degree of devolved executive authority which could be accorded to civil servants. The constitutional principle, that responsibility for the decisions of civil servants is located uniquely in the office of the minister, seemed bound to restrict the degree of executive leadership which could be exercised by civil servants. There was thus, so it seemed, a constitutional obstacle to securing a wholly managerial civil service.

A further principle seemingly under threat from the new public management reforms was that of the unity of the civil service, so carefully built up by Warren Fisher after the First World War. The Efficiency Unit report, *Improving Management in Government: The Next Steps* (the Ibbs Report), declared in 1988:

> The Civil Service is too big and too diverse to manage as a single entity. With 600,000 employees it is an enormous organisation compared with any private sector company and most public sector organisations. A single organisation of this size which attempts to provide a detailed structure within which to carry out functions as diverse as driver licensing, fisheries protection, the catching of drug smugglers and the processing of Parliamentary Questions is bound to develop in a way which fits no single operation effectively.

Thus,

> the advantages which a unified Civil Service are intended to bring are seen as outweighed by the practical disadvantages, particularly beyond Whitehall itself. We were told that the advantages of an all-embracing pay structure are breaking down, that the uniformity of grading frequently inhibits effective management and that the concept of a career in a unified

Civil Service has little relevance for most civil servants, whose horizons are bounded by their local office, or, at most, by their department.[65]

Thus the devolution of authority to executive agencies was accompanied by provisions allowing agencies to recruit and pay staff at their own preferred rates. Chief executives of agencies were generally appointed on fixed-term contracts, a majority of them from outside the civil service. This, however, gave rise to the danger that, with pay and conditions determined by each agency separately, it would be much less easy for civil servants to move between agencies to departments. It therefore seemed to undermine the principle of transferability established by Warren Fisher. There seemed a danger that the establishment of agencies would give rise to a dual civil service: the first, a small core, enjoying job security and career prospects, relatively standard terms and conditions and transferability; the second, the periphery, with a wide and varying range of conditions of employment. With three-fifths of the civil service working in agencies, the majority of them on fixed-term contracts, and with the removal of central pay determination, what remained of the idea of a unified civil service? In 1989, the government declared that the civil service would be made up of 'a federal structure of more autonomous units', while in 1991, Sir Angus Fraser, the prime minister's adviser on efficiency, declared that 'a "unified Civil Service" really is not compatible with the way we are going'.[66]

In 1994, during the Treasury and Civil Service Committee inquiry into the civil service, John Garrett MP asked Sir Robin Butler, then head of the home civil service:

> Is it not the case that we are in the process of moving from a unified civil service of some 30 main departments to a civil service which consists of 30 Ministerial Head Offices, about 150 Executive Agencies and Units, hundreds of quangos, like TECs, trusts and corporate bodies, and thousands of contracts with private contractors, all of whom are trying to make a profit? Would you agree with that description?

Sir Robin replied:

> Yes, I do not think that is an inaccurate description; nor do I think there is anything that is contrary to the traditions of the civil service which is in it.[67]

---

[65] Paras 10, 12.
[66] *Developments in the Next Steps Programme: The Government Reply to the Fifth Report from the Treasury and Civil Service Committee*, Cm 841 (1988–9), p. 5: HC 495, 1990–1, p. xii.
[67] Treasury and Civil Service Committee, Fifth Report (1993–4), *The Role of the Civil Service*, HC 27, 1994, vol. II, p. 52.

Sir Robin was also insistent that the reforms did not undermine the unified nature of the civil service. The civil service, he was frequently to insist, remained unified but it was no longer uniform. Unity, however, was no longer to be secured by common standards of recruitment and common pay scales, but by certain moral attributes such as integrity and impartiality and by the constitutional principle of ministerial responsibility. The trouble was, however, that the moral attributes seemed hardly specific to the public service, but were desirable attributes in every walk of life. Thus, it did not seem that they could form part of a common civil service consciousness of the kind that men such as Fisher and Bridges had tried, so laboriously, to construct. In a world in which grading and pay structures had been delegated to agencies, and with different conditions of service for staff employed in the agencies, the civil service seemed to be becoming irredeemably fragmented. Indeed, in many, if not most of the agencies, staff were positively encouraged to identify with their own independent unit, their agency, rather than with the civil service as a whole.

The 'revolution in Whitehall' coincided with the longest period of one-party government which Britain had seen since the Napoleonic Wars—the years of Conservative rule between 1979 and 1997. It is perhaps hardly surprising that there were accusations that the civil service was becoming politicised, in the sense that reward or promotion was dependent upon commitment to the ideology of the government. Critics could point to a number of occasions during these years when, so it seemed, senior civil servants were removed or denied promotion because they did not suit Margaret Thatcher's style. In 1981, for example, when the Civil Service Department was abolished, its head, Sir Ian Bancroft, was not found alternative employment, and was, in effect, dismissed. There were other cases of senior officials who left the service when it became clear that Margaret Thatcher was not prepared to promote them.[68] Were such a practice to have become widespread, it could well have constituted a threat to the political neutrality of the civil service. However, an authoritative study carried out by the Royal Institute of Public Administration in 1986 rejected the view that the civil service had been politicised:

---

[68] The various instances are summarised in an admirable article by David Richards, entitled 'The Conservatives, New Labour and Whitehall: A Biographical Examination of the Political Flexibility of the Mandarin Cadre', in K. Theakston, *Leadership in Whitehall* (Macmillan, 1999), pp. 91–117.

To some extent the appointment process has become more personalised in the sense that at the top level 'catching the eye' of the Prime Minister (in a favourable or unfavourable manner) may now be more important than in the past . . . However, we do not believe that these appointments and promotions are based on the candidate's support for or commitment to particular political ideologies or objectives.[69]

But perhaps governments, both Conservative and Labour, were becoming more concerned that a civil servant was 'one of us' in the sense, as Sir Richard Wilson, Cabinet secretary between 1998 and 2002, told the Committee on Standards in Public Life (the Neill Committee) in 2000, that they wanted, 'somebody who will deliver what we want . . . get up and make sure it happens'.[70]

VIII

The 'new public management', and the 'revolution in Whitehall', were implemented by Conservative governments. But the defeat of the Conservatives in 1997, and the election of a Labour government led by Tony Blair, did not lead to any fundamental reappraisal. Labour was just as eager as the Conservatives had been to improve the managerial effectiveness of the civil service. 'Effective performance management', declared the Cabinet Office in 1999, 'is the key'.[71] This effectiveness was to be achieved by creating 'a well-functioning business planning system'.[72] In a modern civil service, performance management systems should both 'link individuals' objectives to business objectives'; and 'incentivise (*sic*) people to seek more challenging responsibilities, develop their competences and demonstrate leadership'.[73]

The Blair government intensified the policy, recommended by Fulton and implemented in part by the Conservatives, of increasing the number of outsiders in the civil service. In 1999, the proportion of senior civil service posts subject to open competition rather than being filled through internal promotion was between 20 and 25 per cent. A Cabinet Office report of 1999 to the prime minister proposed that 'This proportion

---

[69] Richards, 'The Conservatives, New Labour and Whitehall', in Theakston, *Leadership in Whitehall*, pp. 103–4.
[70] Evidence to the Committee on Standards in Public Life (Neill Committee), Sixth Report, Cm 4557 (2000), para. 5.14
[71] Cabinet Office, *Performance Management: Civil Service Reform* (HMSO, 1999), para. 3.
[72] Ibid., para. 4, i.
[73] Ibid., para. 12, i, ii.

would be expected to rise to 35 per cent.'[74] Some of the new appointees had little or no experience of civil service practice. They lacked, for example, the traditional pattern of experience, gained from being private secretary to a minister, which helped to socialise civil servants as neutral advisers. Moreover, an outsider recruited in virtue of relevant knowledge might well arrive with political baggage, policy commitments derived from his or her previous experience. There were worries, therefore, that a greater degree of open competition to senior policy positions might lead to politicisation or at least some degree of prior policy commitment, incompatible with traditional notions of political neutrality.

Moreover, a large infusion of outsiders into the civil service was hardly compatible with the notion of a career civil service. But that too might affect the political neutrality of the service, since this neutrality flowed fundamentally from its career basis. For, if one joined the service for life, one would inevitably be called upon to serve successive administrations of different political colours. Here, too, fears were raised that the civil service was in danger of being politicised. The Blair government sought to resolve this problem by making a clear distinction between political appointees such as special advisers, and career civil servants, but the proliferation of special advisers in Whitehall—whose numbers doubled under the Blair government, so that by the end of the century, there were around seventy special advisers—itself gave rise to concerns that civil service advice was coming to be overridden by political considerations. These concerns were, however, probably exaggerated. For civil service appointments continued to be made under the aegis of the Civil Service Commission, and there was no serious attempt by politicians to interfere with the principle of appointment by ability on the basis of fair and open competition. At the end of the century, in 1997, it remained the case that fewer senior positions changed hands following the change of government than would have been the case in almost any other democracy.

The reformers, both Conservative and Labour, had argued that a 'closed' civil service was an anachronism. Yet there was a sense in which a closed civil service was inevitable if it was to remain, as Warren Fisher and Edward Bridges had believed it to be, a profession. For professions are, almost by definition, closed; and it would not be very sensible to suggest to anyone who objected to unqualified doctors or lawyers that they favoured a 'closed' medical or legal profession. By the end of the

---

[74] Cabinet Office, *Bringing In and Bringing On Talent*, p. 30.

century, however, it was unclear whether the civil service would remain a profession, based on its own particular expertise of public administration, or whether it would come to be transformed, under the impact of managerialism, into something quite different.

The Blair government introduced a new element into the debate on civil service reform, one which was difficult to reconcile with the new public management of the Thatcher and Major years with their scepticism towards community values. This new element was that of joined-up or holistic government. The central idea behind holistic government was that many of the most deep-seated or intractable problems of modern government—such as, for example, crime, social exclusion and the fragmentation of communities—cut across the traditional demarcation lines of Whitehall departments. They required, therefore, a co-ordinated attack between departments at the centre, and between central government, local authorities and other local agencies. To this end, the Cabinet Office was strengthened and a number of units were attached to it, such as the Social Exclusion Unit, with a remit to secure co-ordination between different administrative bodies.

There was, however, some degree of tension between the idea of joined-up or holistic government and previous civil service reforms based on the idea of the new public management. For holistic government implied shared responsibility, both between civil servants at the centre and between civil servants and their counterparts at local level. The new public management reforms, on the other hand, had been intended largely to encourage the individual responsibility of civil servants.

It could be argued, and had indeed been argued by Sir Edward Bridges in his Rede Lecture of 1950, *Portrait of a Profession*, that the essence of civil service work was shared responsibility. Civil servants, Bridges had argued, were bound to have to consult more with their colleagues and with those outside Whitehall than members of other professions such as, for example, doctors, accountants or schoolteachers. 'Few of them [civil servants] are ever completely responsible for the work they are doing . . . Through the nature of his work, therefore, he [the civil servant] has much less consciousness than other professional men that the work he does is his own individual achievement, and is inevitably far more conscious than others that the work he does is part of something greater than himself.'[75]

[75] Sir Edward Bridges, *Portrait of a Profession: The Civil Service Tradition*, Rede Lecture 1950 (Cambridge University Press, 1950), pp. 26–7.

Holistic or joined-up government emphasised this element of shared consciousness. In dealing with highly intractable and difficult social problems, such as social exclusion, drugs and community health, it stressed the importance of re-creating social capital and restoring community ties. Success in such an endeavour would probably prove a long-term affair, and it was difficult to see how it could be made subject to a regime of incentivising or performance pay, as was proposed by the new public management. Moreover, holistic government implied an end to defensive compartmentalisation and turf wars. It implied co-operation between different parts of the governmental machine, between the departments of central government, and between central and local government and local agencies. Under such a dispensation, how would it be possible to distinguish and disentangle the various contributions made by different individuals so as to determine precisely how much each individual had contributed to the whole?

There seemed, then, a deep-seated conflict between the ethos of the new public management, which lay behind many of the proposals for civil service reform, by which government would be broken down into discrete or separate units of accountability, and the idea of holistic government whose central theme was that there was a context of interdependence to many of Britain's most intractable social problems.

IX

The revolution in Whitehall during the last two decades of the twentieth century transformed the civil service. Many of the public utilities nationalised by the post-war Attlee government had been privatised. The civil service had been reduced in size from around 750,000 in 1979, when Margaret Thatcher took office, to around 475,000 by the end of the century; and only a small part of this reduction had been due to privatisation. By the end of the century, around three-fifths of all civil servants were working in executive agencies. In addition, market disciplines were being applied to the civil service, which was made subject to contracting out, market-testing and performance targets.

By the end of the century, the notion of the anonymity of the civil servant, regarded, perhaps mistakenly, as a convention of the constitution, was coming to be undermined. That was, in part, inevitable because of the pressures of the media and the extension of the select committee system through the creation of departmentally related select committees in the House of Commons in 1979. Although the Osmotherly Rules required that civil servants giving evidence before these select committees did so on behalf of their ministers, and prohibited them from revealing what policy advice they had given, nevertheless the public and open cross-questioning of senior officials was bound to undermine their anonymity. The position of the Cabinet secretary, in particular, became more exposed during the last two decades of the century. The Westland crisis of 1986 and the litigation in Australia over the publication of a book by a former member of the secret service put Sir Robert Armstrong, Cabinet secretary from 1979 to 1988, in the public spotlight, and Sir Robert was, perhaps, the first Cabinet secretary to become widely known beyond the small circle of Whitehall watchers. Sir Robert's successors, Sir Robin Butler and Sir Richard Wilson, also took on a more public role, feeling the need to speak publicly in defence of the civil service against what they sometimes saw as unsympathetic ministers and a hostile press.

The principle of the anonymity of civil servants was further undermined with the creation of executive agencies. This had been foreseen in the evidence of Sir William Armstrong, then head of the home civil service, to Fulton, who had declared that 'the head of an executive board' would be 'a public figure in his own right'.[76] The chief executives of the more contentious agencies, such as Ros Hepplewhite, the first chief executive of the Child Support Agency, and Derek Lewis, the first chief executive of the Prison Service, did not hesitate to speak out publicly in their defence. Moreover, after being, in effect, dismissed as chief executive of the Prison Service, Derek Lewis wrote a book to defend his interpretation of the role of the Prison Service against that proffered by his political bosses.[77] It gradually came to be expected that chief executives of politically sensitive agencies would speak out in their defence when attacked. If they did not respond, then, so it was assumed, they accepted the criticisms. Because the responsibilities of chief executives, unlike those of civil servants working in the core, were clearly laid down in framework documents, they were likely to be held responsible for specific failures in services. Thus, although the 'Next Steps' programme sought to avoid altering the formal constitutional position of the civil servant, it seemed to undermine the *Carltona* doctrine in virtue of which civil servants acted only in the name of ministers, and possessed no

---

[76] Quoted in Fry, *Reforming the Civil Service*, p. 103.
[77] See Derek Lewis, *Hidden Agendas* (Hamish Hamilton, 1997).

constitutional personality of their own.[78] It seemed hardly possible to reconcile executive leadership by officials with the doctrine that responsibility for the actions of a civil servant working in an agency is located uniquely in the office of the minister.

This tendency towards the undermining of anonymity could in the future be accentuated by the effects of freedom of information legislation. The Scott Report of 1996 on the supply of defence-related equipment to Iraq had declared that it was the availability of information rather than the willingness of ministers to resign, which constituted the key to ministerial accountability. It was presumably for select committees to ferret out this information so that Parliament could discover who was at fault after some policy failure, and in particular whether ministers or civil servants were to blame.[79] Admittedly, civil service advice would be specifically exempted from the provisions of freedom of information legislation. It is difficult, however, to see how select committees could carry out the task assigned to them by the Scott Report unless they were able to ask civil servants what advice they had given to their ministers. They would then be asking civil servants to speak in their own names, not in the name of their minister. There is likely to be some tension, therefore, between freedom of information legislation and the *Carltona* doctrine, which could come under even greater pressure in the new century. This in turn would threaten the convention of ministerial responsibility; for, if the advice which a civil servant had given were to become known, it would always be open to Parliament to tell a minister that the advice given to him by his officials was better than the decision which he had taken. Thus, the attempt to delimit spheres of ministerial and official responsibility seemed to threaten a long-held doctrine of the constitution.

In moulding the twentieth-century civil service, both Warren Fisher and Edward Bridges had believed that the professionalism of the civil service, together with its high standards of integrity and incorruptibility, would be secured largely through continuity of experience. This continuity would yield a common ethical basis so deeply embedded in the culture of the service that there was no need for it to be codified, to be

---

[78] See Greene, MR, in *Carltona Ltd* v. *Commissioners of Works And Others* [1943], 2 All ER 560.
[79] HC 115 (1995–6). The Report of the James Tribunal, HC 133 (1971–2) on the collapse of the Vehicle and General Insurance Company had named, in para. 341, an individual civil servant guilty, in its judgement, of gross negligence.

put on paper. As a profession, the civil service would be, as many other professions were, self-regulated. The common ethical basis which held the civil service together seemed, however, to be under threat by the end of the century, and in part as a result of the introduction of outsiders into the civil service. In 1994, Sir John Bourn, the comptroller and auditor-general, told the Treasury and Civil Service Select Committee that there was 'a common feature' of many of the failings in the civil service which represented 'a departure from the standards of public conduct which have mainly been established during the past 140 years', and that this was the involvement of 'senior staff brought in from outside the public service unaccustomed to the standards required in the public service and the audit procedures associated with them, and not imbued with its ethos'.[80] In its report, the Committee recommended that a code be established to provide greater clarity about the role, duties and responsibilities of civil servants, and to act as a unifying force in an increasingly homogeneous civil service.[81] John Major's government introduced a Civil Service Code in 1996, updated in 1999 to take account of devolution, setting out the constitutional framework within which civil servants worked, and establishing a new complaints procedure for civil servants who believed that they were being required by their minister to act unethically. At the end of the century, there were calls for giving this code legal force through a Civil Service Act, entrenching the non-political status of the civil service. Such an Act was proposed by the Labour and Liberal Democrat parties in the report of their Joint Consultative Committee on Constitutional Reform published in 1997;[82] and also in the Sixth Report of the Committee on Standards in Public Life (the Neill Committee) in 2000, which declared that 'there now appears to be a political consensus that a Civil Service Act of some kind is desirable'.[83]

Thus, at the end of the twentieth century, there was a tension between the managerial reforms which governments, both Conservative and Labour, thought essential for the effective delivery of public services, and the constitutional principles which had for so long regulated the civil service. Nevertheless, the four fundamental constitutional principles—*non-partisanship, ministerial accountability to Parliament, admission by open competition* and *promotion by ability*—remained broadly intact.

[80] Treasury and Civil Service Select Committee, *The Role of the Civil Service* (1994), HC 27, p. xvii.
[81] Ibid., HC 27–I (1993–4), paras 103–7 and Annex 1.
[82] Para. 84.
[83] Para. 5.44.

It is easy, perhaps, to be over-impressed by 'the revolution in White-hall', and to underestimate the importance of what did not change. The 'revolution' did not undermine the constitutional framework of the civil service. The outworks surrounding the citadel, the idea of a unified civil service and the idea of a career civil service, were certainly threatened and perhaps undermined by 'the revolution'. But the inner citadel itself seemed to remain inviolate.

The tenacity of the hold of the fundamental constitutional principles regulating the civil service in the twentieth century is indeed very striking. In an account of the civil service published in 1947, and dedicated to Sir Warren Fisher, H. R. G. Greaves claimed that it was 'a study in relativity—an attempt to see the key principles of civil service organisation in relation to the administrative needs of the state existing at the time they were laid down, and to reconsider them in relation to present needs'.[84] It would seem reasonable to suppose that the changing role of the state would have fundamentally altered Greaves's 'key principles of civil service organisation'. And yet, looking at the long perspective of the twentieth century, it is the continuity of the basic assumptions that stands out. The reforms have altered the institutional machinery, the furniture, as it were, without altering the shape of the house. That the basic constitutional principles regulating the civil service have survived more or less intact during a century of such turbulence and change may strike some as an instance of the deep-seated conservatism of Britain's political culture. Others, however, may regard it as a reassuring instance of the dictum that the inner life of institutions can be resistant to the intentions of the men and women who seek to reform them.

Note. I am grateful to my colleagues, Dr Anne Davies, Fellow in Law at Brasenose, Professor Christopher Hood and Dr Christopher McKenna, Fellow in Management at Brasenose, and also to Sir John Bourn, for their most helpful comments on an earlier draft of this chapter. But they are not to be implicated in my arguments or conclusions.

---

[84] H. R. G. Greaves, *The Civil Service in the Changing State: A Survey of Civil Service Reform and the Implications of a Planned Economy on Public Administration in England* (Harrap, 1947), p. 18.

Bibliography

Official reports

From the time of the Northcote–Trevelyan Report in 1853 to the Fulton Report of 1968, it was almost an established convention that the civil service should be investigated by a Royal Commission or committee once every generation. In the twentieth century, the relevant commissions and committees and the dates when they reported are: MacDonnell (1914), Tomlin (1929), Priestley (1955), and Fulton (1968). The references are as follows:

- Reports of the Royal Commission on the Civil Service (MacDonnell Commission), 1st Report, Cd 6209 (1912–13); Appendix to 1st Report, Cd 6210 (1912–13); 2nd Report, Cd 6534 (1912–13); Appendix to 2nd Report, Cd 6535 (1912–13); 3rd Report, Cd 6739 (1913); Appendix to 3rd Report, Cd 6740 (1913); 4th Report, Cd 7338 (1914); Appendices to 4th Report, Cd 7339–40 (1914), 5th Report, Cd 7748 (1914–16); Appendix to 5th Report, Cd 7749 (1914–16); 6th Report, Cd 7832 (1914–16); Appendix to 6th Report, Cd 8130 (1914–16).

    The papers of the commission can be found in the Public Record Office (PRO) at T 100, while T 170/11 is devoted to Sir John Bradbury's memoranda on the commission, and T 170/16 gives the report of the government committee set up to consider the report of the commission.

- Report of the Royal Commission on the Civil Service, 1929–31 (Tomlin), Cmd 3909 (1931)

    The papers of the Tomlin Commission can be found in the PRO at T 169. T 164 has the papers of the committee set up by the government to consider the Tomlin report.

- Report of the Royal Commission on the Civil Service, 1953–55 (Priestley), Cmnd 9613 (1955).

- Report of the Committee on the Civil Service, 1966–68 (Fulton), Cmnd 3638 (1968).

    The papers of the Fulton Committee can be found in the PRO at BA 1/97. Thomas Balogh's evidence to Fulton is in CAB 147/78.

Also relevant are the following two reports:

- Report of the Machinery of Government Committee (Haldane Report), Cd 9230 (1918).

- Report of the Committee of Inquiry into the Organising and Staffing of Government Offices (Bradbury Report), Cmd 62 (1919).

    The papers of the Bradbury Committee can be found in the PRO at T 170.

Also worth looking at in the PRO are the papers of Sir Edward Bridges in T 273. The papers of Sir Warren Fisher are in the Library of the London School of Economics; those of Sir Maurice Hankey are in Cambridge University Library; and those of Sir Norman Brook in the Bodleian Library, Oxford.

The so-called Osmotherly Rules, the Memorandum of Guidance for Officials

Appearing Before Select Committees, was first published in the Report of the Select Committee on Procedure (1977–8), HC 588, Appendix D. This was superseded in 1997 by *Departmental Evidence and Response to Select Committees* (Cabinet Office, 1997), but is still colloquially referred to as the Osmotherly Rules.

In 1977, the report of the first inquiry by a House of Commons select committee into the civil service as a whole since 1942 was published. The report of the House of Commons Expenditure Committee on the Civil Service is HC 535 (1977). This report was to be followed, however, by many others. The government's response is at Cmnd 7117.

The following official and parliamentary reports from the 1980s and 1990s show the development of thinking on the so-called new public management and the problems associated with it:

- Third Report from the Treasury and Civil Service Committee, 1981–2, *Efficiency and Effectiveness in the Civil Service*, HC 236 (1982).
- *Financial Management in Government Departments*, Cmnd 9058 (1983).
- *The Duties and Responsibilities of Civil Servants in Relation to Ministers* (Armstrong Memorandum), Cm 2627 (1986).
- Seventh Report from the Treasury and Civil Service Committee, 1985–6, *Civil Servants and Ministers: Duties and Responsibilities*, HC 92 (1986). Government response, Cmnd 9841 (1986).
- First Report from the Treasury and Civil Service Committee, 1986–7, *Ministers and Civil Servants*, HC 62 (1986). Government response, Cm 78 (1987).
- K. Jenkins, K. Caines and A. Jackson, *Improving Management in Government: The Next Steps: Report to the Prime Minister*, Ibbs Report (HMSO, 1988).
- *The Financing and Accountability of Next Steps Agencies*, Cm 914 (1989).
- *Making the Most of Next Steps: The Reorganisation of Ministers Departments and their Executive Agencies: Report to the Prime Minister*, Fraser Report (HMSO, 1991).
- *The Citizen's Charter: Raising the Standard*, Cm 1599 (1991).
- *Competing for Quality: Buying Better Public Services*, Cm 1730 (1991).
- House of Commons Treasury and Civil Service Committee, 8th Report, *The Role of the Civil Service*, HC 390 (1992–3).
- House of Commons Treasury and Civil Service Committee, 5th Report, *The Role of the Civil Service*, HC 27 (1993–4).
- Cabinet Office Efficiency Unit, *Career Management and Succession Planning Study*, Oughton Report (1993).
- *Next Steps: Moving On*, Office of Public Service and Science, Trosa Report (1994).
- *The Civil Service: Continuity and Change*, Cm 2627 (1994).
- *The Civil Service: Taking Forward Continuity and Change*, Cm 2748 (1995).

The House of Commons Treasury and Civil Service Committee also produced four reports on the 'Next Steps' programme. They are:

- Eighth Report from the Treasury and Civil Service Committee, 1987–8, *Civil*

Service Management Reform: The Next Steps, HC 494 (1988). Government response, Cm 524 (1988).

- Fifth Report from the Treasury and Civil Service Committee, 1988–9, *Developments in the Next Steps Programme*, HC 348 (1989). Government response, Cm 914 (1989).
- Eighth Report from the Treasury and Civil Service Committee, 1989–90, *Progress in the Next Steps Initiative*, HC 481 (1990). Government response, Cm 1263 (1990).
- Seventh Report from the House of Commons Treasury and Civil Service Committee, *The Next Steps Initiative*, HC 496 (1991). Government reply, Cm 1761 (1991).

On the 'Next Steps' programme, the following reports are also relevant:
- The National Audit Office, *The Next Steps Initiative*, HC 410 (1989).
- Thirty-eighth Report from the Public Accounts Committee, 1988–89, *The Next Steps Initiative*, HC 420 (1989).
- Eighth Report from the Public Accounts Committee, *The Proper Conduct of Public Business*, HC 154 (1993–4).
- Third Report from the Home Affairs Committee, 1990–1, *Next Steps Agencies*, HC 177 (1991).
- Report of House of Lords Select Committee on the Public Service, HL 55 (1997–8).
- Cabinet Office, *Modernising Government*, Cm 4310 (1999).

Books and articles

Works by civil servants

A surprising number of civil servants have written memoirs, or offered reflections, on the changing civil service. Much of this literature is of merely ephemeral interest. Of permanent value, however, are:

Armstrong, Sir William, *The Role and Character of the Civil Service* (Oxford University Press, 1970).
Beveridge, Sir William, *The Public Service in War and Peace* (Constable, 1920).
Beveridge, Sir William, *Power and Influence* (Hodder & Stoughton, 1953).
Bridges, Sir Edward, *Portrait of a Profession: The Civil Service Tradition*, Rede Lecture 1950 (Cambridge University Press, 1950).
Bridges, Lord, *The Treasury*, 2nd edn (Allen & Unwin, 1966).
Bunbury, H. N., *Lloyd George's Ambulance Wagon* (Methuen, 1957).
Butler, Sir Robin, 'New Challenges or Familiar Prescriptions', *Public Administration* (1991).
Butler, Sir Robin, 'The New Public Management: The Contribution of Whitehall and Academia', Frank Stacey Memorial Lecture (1992).
Butler, Sir Robin, 'The Evolution of the Civil Service: A Progress Report', *Public Administration* (1993).

Butler, Sir Robin, 'Reinventing British Government', *Public Administration* (1994).

Butler, Sir Robin, 'The Themes of Public Service Reform in Britain and Overseas', *Policy Studies* (1995).

Clarke, Sir Richard, *New Trends in Government* (HMSO, 1971).

Demetriadi, Sir S., *A Reform for the Civil Service* (Cassell, 1921).

Franks, Sir Oliver, *The Experience of a University Teacher in the Civil Service* (Oxford University Press, 1947).

Grigg, P. J., *Prejudice and Judgment* (Jonathan Cape, 1948).

Jones, Thomas, *Whitehall Diary*, 3 vols, ed. Keith Middlemas (Oxford University Press, 1969–71).

Kemp, Sir Peter, *Beyond Next Steps: A Civil Service for the 21st Century* (Social Market Foundation, 1993).

Lewis, Derek, *Hidden Agendas* (Hamish Hamilton, 1997).

Meynell, Alix, *Public Servant, Private Woman: An Autobiography* (Gollancz, 1988).

Biographies of civil servants

Allen, Bernard, *Sir Robert Morant: A Great Public Servant* (Macmillan, 1936).

Chapman, Richard A., *Leadership in the British Civil Service* (a study of Sir Percival Waterfield) (George Allen & Unwin, 1984).

Chapman, Richard A., *Ethics in the British Civil Service* (a biographical account of Edward Bridges) (Routledge, 1988).

Ellis, E. L., *T. J. A Life of Dr Thomas Jones CH* (University of Wales Press, 1992).

Fry, Geoffrey, 'Three Giants of the Inter-war British Higher Civil Service: Sir Maurice Hankey, Sir Warren Fisher and Sir Horace Wilson', in Kevin Theakston (ed.), *Bureaucrats and Leadership* (Macmillan, 2000).

Hamilton, Sir. Horace P., 'Sir Warren Fisher and the Public Service', *Public Administration* (1951).

Harris, José, *William Beveridge: A Biography*, revised edn (Clarendon Press, 1997).

Lowe, Rodney and Roberts, Richard, 'Sir Horace Wilson, 1900–1935: The Making of a Mandarin', *Historical Journal* (1981).

Naylor, John, *A Man and an Institution: Sir Maurice Hankey, the Cabinet Secretariat and the Custody of Cabinet Secrecy* (Cambridge University Press, 1984).

O'Halpin, Eunan, *Head of the Civil Service: A Study of Sir Warren Fisher* (Routledge, 1989).

Roskill, Stephen, *Hankey, Man of Secrets*, 3 vols (Collins, 1970–4).

Wheeler-Bennett, John, *John Anderson, Viscount Waverley* (Macmillan, 1962).

General

A Fabian Group, *The Administrators, The Reform of the Civil Service*, Fabian Society Pamphlet 355 (1964).

Balogh, Thomas, 'The Apotheosis of the Dilettante', in Hugh Thomas (ed.), *The Establishment* (Anthony Blond, 1959).

Barberis, Peter, *The Elite of the Elite: Permanent Secretaries in the British Higher Civil Service* (Dartmouth, 1996).

Barberis, Peter (ed.), *The Whitehall Reader* (Open University Press, 1996).

Barberis, Peter (ed.), *The Civil Service in an Era of Change* (Dartmouth, 1997).

Beloff, Max, 'The Whitehall Factor: The Role of the Higher Civil Service, 1919–1939', in Gillian Peele and Chris Cook (eds), *The Politics of Reappraisal, 1918–1939* (Macmillan, 1975).

Brittan, Samuel, *The Treasury under the Tories, 1951–1964* (Penguin, 1964).

Burk Kathleen (ed.), *War and the State: The Transformation of British Government, 1914–1919* (George Allen & Unwin, 1982).

Butler, David, Adonis, Andrew and Travers, Tony, *Failure in British Government: The Politics of the Poll Tax* (Oxford University Press, 1994), ch. 9.

Chapman, Richard A., 'The Fulton Commission on the Civil Service', in Chapman (ed.), *The Role of Commissions in Policy Making* (George Allen & Unwin, 1973).

Chapman, Richard A. and Greenaway, J. R., *The Dynamics of Administrative Reform* (Croom Helm, 1980).

Cohen, Emmeline W., *The Growth of the British Civil Service, 1780–1939* (Allen & Unwin, 1941).

Contemporary Record, 2 (1988), 'The Changing Face of Whitehall'—includes symposium on 'Fulton, 20 Years On'.

Daintith, Terence and Page, Alan, *The Executive in the Constitution: Structure, Anatomy and Internal Control* (Oxford University Press, 1999).

Dale, H. E., *The Higher Civil Service of Great Britain* (Oxford University Press, 1941).

Davidson R. and Lowe, R., 'Bureaucracy and Innovation in British Welfare Policy, 1870–1945', in W. J. Mommsen (ed.), *The Emergence of the Welfare State in Britain and Germany* (Croom Helm, 1981).

Davies, Anne and Willman, John, *What Next? Agencies, Departments and the Civil Service* (IPPR, 1991).

The Development of the Civil Service, lectures delivered before the Society of Civil Servants (P. S. King, 1920).

Dunsire, A. (ed.), *The Making of an Administrator* (Manchester University Press, 1956).

Finer, Herman, *The British Civil Service* (Fabian Society and Allen & Unwin, 1927).

Foster, Christopher and Plowden, Francis, *The State under Stress* (Open University Press, 1996).

Fry, Geoffrey K., *Statesmen in Disguise: The Changing Role of the Administrative Class of the British Home Civil Service, 1853–1966* (Macmillan, 1969).

Fry, Geoffrey K., 'Some Weaknesses in the Fulton Report on the British Home Civil Service', *Political Studies* (1969).

Fry, Geoffrey K., *The Administrative 'Revolution' in Whitehall: A Study of the Politics of Administrative Change in British Central Government since the 1950s* (Croom Helm, 1981).

Fry, Geoffrey K., *Reforming the Civil Service: The Fulton Committee on the British Home Civil Service, 1966–1968* (Edinburgh University Press, 1993).

Fry, Geoffrey K., *Policy and Management in the British Civil Service* (Prentice Hall/ Harvester International, 1995).

Greaves, H. R. G., *The Civil Service in the Changing State: A Survey of Civil Service*

Reform and the Implications of a Planned Economy on Public Administration in England (Harrap, 1947).

Greenleaf, W. H., *The British Political Tradition*: vol. 3, *A Much Governed Nation* (Methuen, 1987), part 1, ch. 3.

Hennessy, Peter, *Whitehall*, revised edn (Pimlico, 2001).

Johnson, Nevil, *In Search of the Constitution* (Pergamon, 1977).

Kellner, Peter and Crowther-Hunt, Lord, *The Civil Servants: An Inquiry into Britain's Ruling Class* (Macdonald, 1980).

Laski, Harold, *Grammar of Politics* (Allen & Unwin, 1925).

Lee, J. M., 'The British Civil Service and the War Economy: Bureaucratic Conceptions of the "Lessons of History" in 1918 and 1945', *Transactions of the Royal Historical Society* (1980).

Lowell, A. L., *The Government of England* (Macmillan, 1908), vol. 1.

MacLeod, Roy (ed.), *Government and Expertise: Specialists, Administrators and Professionals, 1860–1919*, especially chapters by John Turner, 'Experts and Interests: David Lloyd George and the Dilemmas of the Expanding State, 1916–1919', and José Harris, 'William Beveridge in Whitehall: Maverick or Mandarin?'(Cambridge University Press, 1988).

Moses, Robert, *The Civil Service of Great Britain* (Longmans Green, 1914).

Muir, Ramsay, *Peers and Bureaucrats: Two Problems of English Government* (Constable, 1910).

Nicolson, I. F., *The Mystery of Crichel Down* (Oxford University Press, 1986).

Osborne, D. and Gaebler, T., *Reinventing Government: How the Entrepreneurial Spirit is Transforming the Public Sector* (Addison-Wesley, 1992).

Parris, Henry, *Constitutional Bureaucracy* (Allen & Unwin, 1969).

Plowden, William, *Ministers and Mandarins* (Institute for Public Policy Research, 1994).

Rhodes, R. A. W, 'The Civil Service', in Anthony Seldon (ed.), *The Blair Effect* (Little, Brown, 2001).

Richards, David, *The Civil Service under the Conservatives, 1979–1997* (Academy Press, 1997).

Robson, W. A. (ed.), *The Civil Service in Britain and France* (Hogarth Press, 1956). This symposium includes essays by C. R. Attlee on 'Civil Servants, Ministers, Parliament and the Public', and by Sir Edward Bridges on 'The Reforms of 1854 in Retrospect'.

Roseveare, Henry, *The Treasury: The Evolution of a British Institution* (Penguin, 1969).

Royal Institute of Public Administration, *Top Jobs in Whitehall: Appointments and Promotions in the Senior Civil Service* (1987).

Savage, Gail, *The Social Construction of Expertise: The English Civil Service and its Influence, 1919–1939* (University of Pittsburgh Press, 1996).

Searle, G. R., *The Quest for National Efficiency: A Study in British Politics and Political Thought, 1899–1914* (Blackwell, 1971).

Sisson, C. H., *The Spirit of British Administration* (Faber, 1959).

Theakston, Kevin, *The Labour Party and Whitehall* (Routledge, 1992).

Theakston, Kevin, *The Civil Service since 1945* (Blackwell, 1995).

Theakston, Kevin, 'The Heath Government and Whitehall', in Anthony Seldon and Stuart Ball (eds), *The Heath Government, 1970–74* (Longman, 1996).

Theakston, Kevin, 'A Permanent Revolution in Whitehall: The Major Governments and the Civil Service', in Peter Dorey (ed.), *The Major Premiership* (Macmillan, 1999).

Theakston, Kevin, *Leadership in Whitehall* (Macmillan, 1999).

Theakston, Kevin (ed.), *Bureaucrats and Leadership* (Macmillan, 2000).

Theakston, Kevin and Fry, Geoffrey K., 'The Conservative Party and the Civil Service', in Anthony Seldon and Stuart Ball (eds), *Conservative Century: The Conservative Party since 1900* (Oxford University Press, 1994).

Thomas, Rosamund, *The Philosophy of British Administration* (Longmans, 1978).

Turner, John, *Lloyd George's Secretariat* (Cambridge University Press, 1980).

Wheare, K. C., *The Civil Service in the Constitution* (Athlone Press, 1954).

Wheare, K. C., 'Crichel Down Revisited', *Political Studies* (1975).

Wheare, K. C., 'The Civil Service', in Valerie Cromwell *et al.*, *Aspects of Government in Nineteenth-century Britain* (Irish University Press, 1978).

Zifcak, Spencer, *New Managerialism: Administrative Reform in Whitehall and Canberra* (Open University Press, 1994).

8.
Ministerial Responsibility[1]
DIANA WOODHOUSE

Introduction

The convention of ministerial responsibility, which locates power in ministers and provides the mechanism by which they are accountable to Parliament, is central to Britain's constitutional arrangements. Yet, despite its political and constitutional importance, the requirements it imposes are uncertain. The convention has its origins in Parliament's need to act as a check on ministers, without having to resort to impeachment proceedings, and in the recognition by ministers that they required the support of the House of Commons for their policies. The principle that ministers were responsible to Parliament was well established prior to the nineteenth century, but the high point for ministerial accountability is traditionally seen as the middle of that century. This was a period when the Commons had the ability and determination to 'exercise a constant supervision of all government affairs'[2] and when successive governments recognised Parliament's right to censure ministers as part of the supervision process. The position was noted by Earl Grey, who in 1858 wrote: 'It is a distinguishing characteristic of Parliamentary Government that it requires the powers belonging to the Crown to be exercised through Ministers, who are held responsible for the manner in which they are used . . . and who are considered entitled to hold their office only while they possess the confidence of Parliament, and more especially the House of Commons'.[3]

The mid-century success of Parliament in its role as scrutineer of the

---

[1] Throughout this chapter 'responsibility' and 'accountability' are used in their everyday sense and not as terms of art.
[2] F. W. Maitland, *The Constitutional History of England* (Cambridge University Press, 1908), p. 380.
[3] Earl Grey, 'Parliamentary Government 1858', in H. J. Hanham, *The Nineteenth-century Constitution: Documents and Commentary* (Cambridge University Press, 1969).

executive fostered the belief, associated, perhaps mistakenly, with Dicey and other constitutional writers of the time,[4] that accountability through ministers to Parliament was practically and constitutionally superior to other forms of accountability, notably to the courts. This accorded with a Liberal view of the constitution, which placed Parliament at its centre, and it resulted in the convention of ministerial responsibility becoming the political rationale around which an expanding system of government was structured. Not only did ministers head the new departments of state, they became a 'protecting machine'[5] for the civil service, which, transformed into a permanent administrative body, needed to be insulated from political interference from Parliament. Hence the principle was established that civil servants were accountable to their minister, who alone was accountable to Parliament.

However, by the time the convention was consistently accepted, Parliament no longer had the ability, nor, necessarily, the inclination, to extract the accountability constitutionally required. The decline in parliamentary authority was linked directly to the increased importance of the electorate, as the prime source of government power, and to the development of party politics, evident by the latter part of the nineteenth century. This resulted in a transformation of the House of Commons from shifting alliances to stable party groups and its domination by the executive. It also meant that its main purpose became one of supporting the elected government and passing its legislation, the task of checking the executive being ceded to the opposition. As a consequence, administrations were increasingly able to rely on a highly disciplined party in Parliament for support. Moreover, as the party in Parliament became more important, so did collective responsibility, which became tied to the party machinery and could be used, when necessary, to provide an individual minister with collective cover.

The political actors of the twentieth century therefore inherited a version of ministerial responsibility, which had grown out of political conditions that no longer prevailed. Moreover, not all agreed with the model described, and to an extent prescribed, by Dicey and his contemporaries. They portrayed the convention as having two strands, requiring ministers, first, to subject themselves to parliamentary scrutiny and to account for their departments and, second, to tender their resignations

---

[4] A. V. Dicey, *Introduction to the Study of the Law of the Constitution*, 10th edn (Macmillan, 1959).

[5] Walter Bagehot, *The English Constitution* (1867, Fontana edn, 1963), p. 191.

when they lost Parliament's support. This second element, which was upheld by nineteenth-century constitutional writers as the central tenet of the doctrine, was particularly contested by those with a 'Whitehall'[6] view of the constitution, who argued that, as part of the elected government, ministers were 'ultimately answerable to the electorate'[7] and their position in that government should therefore be a matter for its leader, the prime minister, and for voters at a general election, not for Parliament. This view of ministerial responsibility could be expected to prevail, given that it is generally held, although seldom fully articulated, by governments of both political persuasions and by senior civil servants. The fact that it has not entirely done so and that the debate on ministerial responsibility continues to be debated in Diceyan terms, 'by those against as well as in favour of Liberal ideals',[8] demonstrates the force of this view. In a system where other forms of accountability are limited, the Liberal model would seem to have greater constitutional resonance than the Whitehall model, which might be seen—perhaps unfairly—simply as those in power protecting their position. Ministerial responsibility has not been replaced by any other principle. Despite its inadequacies and concerns about its effectiveness, which increased as the century progressed and government became larger and more complex, it continues to permeate the procedures and language of the House of Commons, underpin the structure of government and govern the relationship between ministers and civil servants.

The accountability of ministers to Parliament

Giving an account

The convention of ministerial responsibility stipulates that ministers, and ministers alone, are accountable to Parliament. The extent to which they are constitutionally required to explain or give an account (rather than being held to account) is not clear, although politically it is likely to be the minimum Parliament will accept. During the nineteenth century, when Parliament had the power to assert its right to explanations and justification, it 'had no conscious feeling that it was being starved of information or opportunities'.[9] However, by the 1920s, there was a recog-

---

[6] A. H. Birch, *Representative and Responsible Government* (Allen & Unwin, 1964), p. 166.
[7] Ibid.
[8] Ibid.
[9] J. P. Mackintosh, *The British Cabinet* (Stevens, 1962), p. 192.

nised decline in the ability of the House of Commons to act 'as an agency for effective criticism and containment of the executive'.[10] This was not only because of its loss of power in relation to the executive but because the ever-increasing size and complexity of government, together with the culture of secrecy which surrounded it, made it difficult for MPs to hold ministers to account for the workings of their departments.

Moreover, despite the Haldane Committee's support of the principle that all the activities of government should be conducted within departments and thus under the full responsibility of the minister,[11] the notion of full or direct responsibility 'seemed rapidly to lose its vitality'[12] and a range of agencies were established outside departments to carry out governmental functions. These quasi-autonomous government organisations (quangos) or non-departmental public bodies, as they are more accurately known, operate at arm's length from the minister, which means that, while the minister remains directly responsible for policy, where administration or operations are concerned, his or her responsibility is only indirect.[13] The limitation on direct responsibility was particularly contentious where the nationalised industries were concerned. Although they were not non-departmental public bodies, they operated under similar principles with similar consequences for accountability. These were set out by Herbert Morrison in 1947. He stated:

> A Minister is responsible to Parliament for actions which he may take in relation to a board, or action coming within his statutory powers which he has not taken. This is the principle that determines generally the matters on which a question may be put down for answer by a Minister in the House of Commons ... It would be contrary to this principle, and to the clearly expressed intention of Parliament, in the governing legislation, if Ministers were to give, in replies in Parliament or in letters, information about day-to-day matters.[14]

In the case of 'day-to-day matters' or administration, the accountability of ministers to Parliament was therefore limited to redirecting questions from MPs to the chair of the nationalised industry, giving rise to concern

[10] Mackintosh, *The British Cabinet*, p. 191.
[11] *Report of the Machinery of Government Committee* (Chairman, Lord Haldane), Cd 9230 (1918).
[12] D. L. Keir, *The Constitutional History of Modern Britain*, 9th edn (Black, 1969), p. 522.
[13] The number of such agencies has always been difficult to calculate. In 1980 Pliatzky estimated that there were 489 executive bodies, which included operational and regulatory agencies, and 1,561 advisory bodies (*Report on Non-departmental Public Bodies*, Cmnd 7797 (1980), paras 20–33).
[14] HC Deb., vol. 445, col. 566, 4 December 1947.

that ministers, who interfered in administrative matters, could evade responsibility for their own actions and that some issues of policy could be portrayed as administration. The privatisation of the nationalised industries, some forty years later, appeared to remove the problem. However, where the utilities, such as gas and water, were concerned, it resulted in the establishment of new regulatory bodies, which operate under the same model of accountability and thus have the same potential for allowing evasion.

The limiting of ministerial accountability to redirection increased with the establishment of Next Steps executive agencies. These agencies, named after the 1988 report, *Improving Management in Government: The Next Steps*,[15] are intended to improve service delivery and managerial accountability and owe much to the concept of 'management units', outlined by Fulton in 1968.[16] Unlike quangos or non-departmental bodies, they are sited within departments and thus technically remain the direct responsibility of ministers. It was not, therefore, felt necessary to modify the convention of ministerial responsibility to accommodate them. Nevertheless, the formal division of responsibilities between ministers and chief executives, as stipulated by framework agreements, has resulted in the practice whereby ministers redirect MPs' questions to chief executives, who answer in their own names, their replies being recorded in *Hansard* under a general ministerial heading. However, there is uncertainty as to whether a particular reply has come straight from the chief executive or has been approved or amended by the minister, the practice varying from agency to agency.[17] There is also uncertainty surrounding a minister's 'non-executive'[18] or informatory accountability for his or her agency. This concerns the responsibility to report to the House on matters outside his or her direct responsibility and, again, was initially applicable in the context of the nationalised industries, where it limited the extent to which the minister was required to give an account to that of relaying to Parliament what he or she has been told by the chair of the board. A similar procedure has been used in relation to Next Steps agencies although, given that these remain within departments and are

[15] Efficiency Unit, *Improving Management in Government: The Next Steps: Report to the Prime Minister* (1988).
[16] *Report of the Committee on the Civil Service* (Chairman, Lord Fulton), Cmnd 3638 (1968), vol. 1, para. 150.
[17] Public Service Committee, *Ministerial Accountability and Responsibility* (1995–6), HC 313-I, para. 93. The committee's specialist adviser was Vernon Bogdanor.
[18] G. Marshall, 'Parliamentary Accountability', *Parliamentary Affairs* (1991), 460.

still the direct responsibility of the minister, such limited accountability may not always be appropriate.

In situations where the minister has direct responsibility, he or she is required to explain or account for the department's actions and, where appropriate, to take amendatory measures. Explanatory responsibility is central to a minister's accountability to Parliament but, as the twentieth century progressed, it became increasingly apparent that the floor of the House of Commons was ineffective in securing the accountability required. Hence in 1979 the departmentally related select committee system was established, to shadow all government departments.[19] Such reform had previously been opposed on the dubious grounds that it challenged 'the vital doctrine of the responsibility of ministers to Parliament as a whole'[20] and the committees were soon in conflict with the government, which, paradoxically, sought to use ministerial responsibility to limit its accountability to them. It insisted that the committees only exercised 'their formal powers to inquire into policies and actions of departments by virtue of the accountability of Ministers to Parliament'.[21] Select committees, on the other hand, argued that these powers were exercised 'because Parliament is sovereign and has established the select committees to monitor Government Departments on its behalf'.[22]

The underlying tension between the two views—one which sees ministerial responsibility as grounding power in ministers, who should be free to govern with minimal interference until the next election, and the other, which sees it as the mechanism through which Parliament exercises its inherent right to hold ministers to account—has been particularly evident in the dispute over the giving of evidence by officials. Civil servants, who are servants of the Crown, are seen by the courts as an extension of the minister[23] and by the *Civil Service Code* as 'ow[ing] their loyalty to the duly constituted Government'.[24] They therefore have no legal or constitutional personality separate from that of the minister, in whom power is invested. Accordingly, when they appear before select committees they appear not on their own behalf but on behalf of their

---

[19] Except that of the Lord Chancellor.

[20] Herbert Morrison, *Government and Parliament* (Oxford University Press, 1954), p. 159.

[21] *The Government's Response to the Fourth Report from the Defence Committee on Westland plc; The Defence Implications of the Future of Westland plc: The Government's Decision-making*, Cmnd 9916 (1986).

[22] Treasury and Civil Service Committee, *First Report* (1986–7), HC 62.

[23] Known as the *Carltona* principle from *Carltona Ltd* v. *Commissioner of Works* [1943] 2 All ER 560.

[24] *Civil Service Code* (1996).

minister and 'on his instructions'. The rules relating to giving evidence are contained in the Osmotherly Rules, which, while telling officials to be 'as helpful as possible to Committees',[25] impose a number of restrictions, including limitations on the disclosure of advice given by civil servants to ministers, interdepartmental exchanges concerning policy, and alternative policy options. These are portrayed by the government as necessary to uphold the conventions of ministerial and collective responsibility. However, at times they are overly restrictive and, as far as select committees are concerned, may prevent effective accountability. Hence the Foreign Affairs Committee reported in 1980 that 'great difficulty was presented by a rigid interpretation of the so-called convention by which Ministers and officials are prohibited from informing the House about the way in which government decisions are made',[26] while the Trade and Industry Committee similarly complained in 1985 that its inquiry was frustrated by the instructions given to officials by the permanent secretary that 'they were to observe very carefully, in answers to questions put to them, the Memorandum of Guidance'.[27]

Select committees are also restricted in their inquiries by the stricture that they should not inquire into the conduct of officials, that is, 'explicitly or implicitly seek to assign criticism or blame to individual civil servants'.[28] This reinforces the principle that ministers are accountable to Parliament for all the actions of their department, 'even if officials have acted outside or contrary to the authorisation given to them by their Ministers',[29] and is intended as a protection for officials. However, the failure of ministers, on occasions, to fulfil their accounting obligations can undermine committee inquiries and thus, at times, ministerial responsibility acts to frustrate, rather than provide, the accountability required.

---

[25] The rules were named after the author of the guide to officials, *Memorandum of Guidance for Officials Appearing before Select Committees*, Gen. 80/38 (1980). This was superseded in 1997 by *Departmental Evidence and Response to Select Committees* (Cabinet Office, 1997), still colloquially referred to as the Osmotherly Rules.

[26] Third Report of the Foreign Affairs Committee (1979–80), HC 553, para. 16.

[27] Report of the Trade and Industry Committee (1985–6), HC 305-I, para. 10 and 305-II, q. 696.

[28] *Government's Response to the First Report of the Treasury and Civil Service Committee (HC 62) and to the First Report of the Liaison Committee (HC 100)*, Cmnd 78 (1986–7), para. 5.

[29] Ibid.

The provision of information

Crucial to the accountability of ministers is the requirement that they provide Parliament with accurate information: it may be detrimental to their careers if they fail to do so and, by such omission, mislead the House.[30] The obligation to provide information was given particular prominence by the 'Arms to Iraq' (Matrix Churchill) affair, where one of the key issues was whether ministers, through their failure to provide accurate answers to parliamentary questions, had misled Parliament about the government's policy on the export of defence-related materials after the end of the Iran–Iraq war in 1988. The inquiry by Sir Richard Scott concluded that the policy had changed and that, in both parliamentary questions and letters to the public, ministers had failed 'to disclose either the terms of the adjustment to the guidelines . . . or the decision to adopt a more liberal policy on defence sales to Iraq'.[31] The information they had provided about government policy was, according to Scott, 'by design incomplete and in certain respects misleading'.[32] Moreover, by their behaviour ministers had failed 'to comply with the standards set by paragraph 27 of *Questions of Procedure for Ministers*, which referred to "the duty to give Parliament, including its select committees, and the public as full information as possible about the policy decisions and actions of the Government, and not to deceive or mislead Parliament or the public"'.[33] Most important, as far as Scott was concerned, they had 'failed to discharge the obligations imposed by the constitutional principle of ministerial accountability'.[34]

This obligation had been confirmed by Prime Minister John Major, who, prior to Scott reporting, had stressed the importance of ministers giving accurate and truthful information to Parliament. However, he seemed to modify the requirement of resignation for misleading the House by his stipulation that this needed to be done 'knowingly' and, by so doing, to protect William Waldegrave, who had been a minister in the Foreign Office and, given Scott's conclusions, was particularly vulnerable. In the event, Scott accepted that Waldegrave and other ministers had no 'duplicitous intention'[35] and that, while Waldegrave was in

---

[30] As John Profumo found in 1963 (see section on resignations, below).

[31] *Report of the Inquiry into the Export of Defence Equipment and Dual-use Goods to Iraq and Related Prosecutions* (Chairman, Sir Richard Scott) (1995–6), HC 115, K8.1.

[32] Ibid., D4.10.

[33] This document, produced by the Cabinet Office, was first made public in 1992.

[34] *Report of Inquiry into Export of Defence Equipment*, HC 115, D4.63.

[35] Ibid., D3.124.

a position to know that his letters were 'apt to mislead readers as to the true nature of the policy on export sales to Iraq', he 'did not intend his letters to be misleading and did not regard them as so'.[36] Moreover, Scott maintained that there had always been an implicit requirement that a minister must have acted deliberately and that adding 'knowingly' into the equation did not change the requirement for resignation. However, in at least one important respect it did. It removed instances where the minister had been negligent or incompetent in what he said,[37] situations which might be seen to cover Waldegrave. Thus, despite grave misgivings from many members of his own party, the minister survived—just—and it seems that when it comes to misleading the House, ministers not only have to be caught in the act, they also have to be shown to have intention. In this respect ministerial culpability would seem to equate with criminal responsibility, requiring both *mens* and *actus reus* and a burden of proof which is beyond all reasonable doubt. However, unlike the criminal law there is no provision for recklessness.

Despite Waldegrave's survival, the emphasis on the 'obligation to give information'[38] which Scott considered the 'key to ministerial accountability', was taken up by Parliament, through the Public Service Committee. Scott sought to reverse the 'two vital elements' of the convention, that is 'clarity about who can be held to account and held responsible when things go wrong; and confidence that Parliament is able to gain the accurate information required to hold the Executive to account and to ascertain where responsibility lies'.[39] His reason for doing so was the belief that focusing too much on culpability and resignation could 'distract attention from the more important although less dramatic aspects' of the convention[40] and encourage ministers to conceal, rather than reveal, information for fear of giving their opponents political ammunition. The Public Service Committee accepted that 'proper and rigorous scrutiny and accountability may be more important to Parliament's ability to correct error than forcing resignation',[41] as did the

---

[36] *Report of Inquiry into Export of Defence Equipment*, D4.12.

[37] Vernon Bogdanor, 'Ministerial Accountability', in B. Thompson and F. F. Ridley, *Under the Scott-light: British Government seen through the Scott Report* (Oxford University Press, 1947), p. 74.

[38] Sir Richard Scott, 'Ministerial Accountability', in *Government Accountability* (CIPFA, 1996), p. 5.

[39] Treasury and Civil Service Committee, *Role of the Civil Service* (1993–4), HC 27-I, para. 132.

[40] Sir Richard Scott, 'Ministerial Accountability', *Public Law* (1996), 410.

[41] HC 313-I, para. 26.

government,[42] and it supported the move of the committee to seek Parliament's approval for a Resolution, which affirmed the obligation of ministers to provide information and to account to Parliament.

This Resolution was approved by the House of Commons on 19 March 1997.[43] It stated:

> It is of paramount importance that Ministers give accurate and truthful information to this House and its Committees. Any inadvertent error should be corrected at the earliest opportunity. If Ministers knowingly mislead the House, the House will expect them to offer their resignation to the Prime Minister.
>
> Ministers should be as open as possible with this House and its Committees, refusing to provide information only when disclosure would not be in the public interest, which should be decided in accordance with relevant statute and the government's Code of Practice on Access to Government Information.
>
> Similarly, Ministers should require civil servants who give evidence before Select Committees on their behalf and under their directions to be as helpful as possible in providing full and accurate information in accordance with the duties and responsibilities of civil servants as set out in the Civil Service Code.

The Resolution was a significant constitutional statement and a formalisation of previous positions. Moreover, its constitutional status was enhanced by its inclusion in 1997 in a revised version of *Questions of Procedure*, renamed the *Ministerial Code: A Code of Conduct and Guidance on Procedures for Ministers*.[44] However, the fact that it does not apply directly to civil servants means that its effect is likely to be limited.[45] In addition, much is left open to interpretation and it may be difficult to monitor compliance for, while a record is kept of the answers that are refused,[46] those that are incomplete or unsatisfactory may not always be apparent. The resolution therefore provides Parliament with some authority to which appeals can be made although, given the executive

---

[42] Public Service Committee, *Government's Response to the Second Report from the Committee (1995–6) on Ministerial Accountability and Responsibility* (1996–7), HC 67, p. vi.

[43] HC Deb., vol. 291, cols 1046–79, 19 March 1997; a Resolution was also passed in the House of Lords, HL Deb., cols 1055–62, 20 March 1997.

[44] Cabinet Office, 1997.

[45] Both the Conservative government and the Labour opposition rejected the Public Service Committee's submission that civil servants should be brought within the ambit of the resolution 'to underline the fact that as witnesses before a Committee . . . [they] are themselves bound by the obligation not to obstruct or impede members or Officers of the House in the performance of their duty'. (HC 313–I, para. 82.)

[46] Annual lists are kept by the Table Office.

dominance of the House, in practice, ministerial openness is still likely to depend on political factors rather than upon notions of constitutional obligation.

The Resolution was part of a move towards greater openness, evident in the publication in 1994 of the *Code of Practice on Access to Government Information* referred to in the Resolution. This has implications for ministerial responsibility, casting doubt indeed on its function of protecting officials from public accountability. There is, of course, a thin line between ministers reasonably disclaiming personal responsibility and unreasonably appearing to blame officials in order to distance themselves from culpability. The statement by Sir David Maxwell Fyfe in response to the Crichel Down affair in 1954, when he was home secretary, suggested that ministers were not required to support officials, who acted contrary to ministerial policy,[47] while Scott stated: 'If ministers are to be excused blame and personal criticism on the basis of the absence of personal knowledge or involvement, the corollary ought to be an acceptance of the obligation to be forthcoming with information about the incident in question. Otherwise Parliament (and the public) will not be in a position to judge whether the absence of personal knowledge and involvement is fairly claimed or to judge on whom responsibility for what has occurred ought to be placed'.[48] However, being 'forthcoming with information' may mean laying the blame on officials.

In an incident in 1998, which bore some similarities to the 'Arms to Iraq' affair, the foreign secretary Robin Cook found himself, initially, accused of doing just that and, subsequently, when he sought to protect his officials, of obstructing a select committee inquiry. The incident concerned allegations that officials in the Foreign Office had secretly sanctioned the supply of military equipment to Sierra Leone in breach of a United Nations embargo. Cook, who stated that he was 'trying to be frank and open about what happened',[49] moved quickly to deny any ministerial involvement and knowledge and to set up an independent investigation, chaired by Sir Thomas Legg. However, he was criticised for being too ready to accept allegations against his officials and for blaming them for the inconsistencies in the answers given by ministers to Parliament.

---

[47] HC Deb., 20 July 1954, vol. 530, col. 1290. His statement is discussed fully in the section on resignations, which follows.
[48] HC 115, K8.16.
[49] HC Deb., vol. 311, col. 726, 6 May 1998.

Legg reported some three months later[50] and his report was made public. He confirmed that there had been no policy to breach the arms embargo and no conspiracy by officials to undermine government policy. Like the Crichel Down inquiry in 1954, the Legg inquiry infringed the Maxwell Fyfe principle that the minister 'alone can tell Parliament what has occurred'. Legg confirmed that there had been misjudgements by named officials and that some of the briefings given to ministers had been deficient. The foreign secretary accepted all the recommendations of the report which were aimed at addressing the 'systematic and cultural factors', held by Sir Thomas to have been mainly responsible, and invited Parliament, through the Foreign Affairs Committee, to make sure that 'the Foreign Office and I are harried, pursued and kept up to scratch in putting in place the programme of reform'.[51] However, rather than being praised for his involvement of the committee in the accountability cycle, Cook was condemned for having failed to co-operate with the committee's inquiry until after Legg had reported[52] and for, subsequently, refusing to allow two of the three officials named in Legg's report to appear before it. Again the tension between government and select committees was evident. The select committee claimed the right to question officials, as part of the accountability process, and believed the minister was obstructing its inquiry; the minister claimed he was fulfilling his duty of protecting his officials from public accountability.[53]

Naming and blaming officials

The naming and blaming of officials in reports is not new. After the Crichel Down inquiry in 1954, five officials were named and one transferred to other duties,[54] while an under-secretary in the Department of Trade and Industry was named as having been negligent by the tribunal inquiring into the collapse of the Vehicle and General Insurance Company in 1972.[55] However, these instances, which can be explained by the level of incompetence displayed, were exceptional and did not

---

[50] *Report of the Sierra Leone Investigation* (1997–8), HC 1016.

[51] HC Deb., vol. 315, col. 19, 27 June 1998. The Maxwell Fyfe principle is at HC Deb., vol. 52, col. 1291, 20 July 1954.

[52] Foreign Affairs Committee, Second Report, *Sierra Leone* (1998–9), HC 116–I.

[53] The protection of his officials would seem to have been Cook's motivation. He allowed one of the three named officials to give evidence at that official's request.

[54] *Report from the Public Inquiry into the Disposal of Land at Crichel Down*, Cmnd 9176 (1954).

[55] *Report of the Tribunal of Inquiry on the Vehicle and General Insurance Company* (1971–2) HC 133, para. 8.

detract from the constitutional position, whereby, in cases of civil service error, the minister takes responsibility for instituting corrective measures, without naming those concerned. The same can be said of the conduct of named officials, two of whom were subsequently subject to disciplinary proceedings[56] by Sir Richard Scott's 1996 report on 'Arms to Iraq'. Parliamentary reports have similarly identified officials. In 1968 the report of the parliamentary ombudsman into the Sachsenhausen case attributed the failure of the Foreign Office to compensate twelve prisoners of war largely to maladministration and thus to officials,[57] much to the concern of the responsible minister, George Brown. He not only maintained that he, not his officials, had made the decision, but that, under the convention of ministerial responsibility, ministers, not officials, should be held responsible by Parliament for faults or errors within a department.[58] An inquiry by the Select Committee on the Parliamentary Commissioner, which revisited the case, reported that there had been shortcomings on the part of both ministers and officials.[59] Moreover, the committee subsequently concluded that, at least where inquiries by the ombudsman were concerned, the complete anonymity of civil servants was no longer part of ministerial responsibility.[60] It also seems no longer always part of the convention, where select committee inquiries are concerned. The Defence Committee was highly critical of particular officials in its report on Westland,[61] discussed below, and the Foreign Affairs Committee's inquiry into the Sierra Leone incident also blamed certain officials for failing to keep ministers informed,[62] although its findings were disputed by the government.[63]

In all these instances, blame was the consequence of an investigation which was independent of the minister. A different situation arises when ministers seek to defend themselves by naming and blaming officials. Attributing blame to nameless officials, on the basis that they gave ministers an incomplete brief or erroneous information, as the home secretary Jack Straw did when apologising to the House for giving wrong figures

---

[56] See Public Administration Committee, Minutes of Evidence (1997–8), HC 285, Appendix 2.

[57] (1967–8), HC 54.

[58] HC Deb., vol. 758, cols 107–11, 5 February 1968.

[59] (1967–8), HC 258, pp. ix–xi.

[60] (1967–8), HC 350, p. xii.

[61] Defence Committee, *The Defence Implications of the Future of Westland plc* (1985–6), HC 518, para. 172.

[62] HC 116-I.

[63] *The Government's Response to the Foreign Affairs Committee Report*, Cm 4325 (1999).

on police recruitment and asylum seekers,[64] may be acceptable as part of being forthcoming about what has happened. Similarly, telling Parliament that errors were made by officials and that new procedures have been established to prevent a repeat of the incident satisfies the requirement of explanation and also the need to take amendatory action, as does the setting up of an inquiry, or reporting that officials involved in serious departmental fault have been disciplined. Less acceptable are instances where the minister blames civil service advice in what seems to be an attempt to evade responsibility[65] for, as the Royal Commission on Mesopotamia noted in 1917, 'those who are political heads of departments . . . cannot be entirely immune for the consequences of their own actions. They have the option and the power of accepting or rejecting the advice of their expert subordinates.'[66] Instances where ministers have actually named officials are, in fact, rare, although the establishment of Next Steps agencies, which provide for a division of responsibilities between the minister and the chief executive, has increased the number of situations in which the minister may see the appropriate amendatory action to be the public disciplining of an official. Whether such action is appropriate or not is discussed below.

The requirement of resignation

Important though the requirements of information, explanation and amendatory action are, the second element of ministerial responsibility—namely the threat of resignation—'remains an essential component of the control of government'.[67] Resignation may be seen as the highest level of amendatory action, representing an apology or a punishment for the betrayal of public trust. As the Public Service Committee commented, 'It is, in effect, the final stage in the process of accountability.'[68] Thus, rather than seeing ministerial responsibility as composed of two

---

[64] HC Deb., vol. 336, col. 814, 26 October 1999.

[65] As seemed to be the case when Kenneth Baker sought to blame legal advice for his decision to ignore a court order and thus the finding that he was in contempt of court: see HC Deb., vol. 200, col. 31, 2 December 1991 and *M* v. *Home Office and Another* [1992] 2 WLR 7 (CA) and [1993] 3 WLR 333 (HL).

[66] From Sir Ivor Jennings, *Cabinet Government*, 3rd edn (Cambridge University Press, 1961), p. 498.

[67] HC 313-I, para. 33.

[68] Ibid.

elements—accountability to Parliament and resignation—it seems more appropriate to see it as based on a single principle.

Resignations are a product of the interaction between constitutional obligation and political practice. There is a temptation, when looking back to the mid-nineteenth-century resignations of Lord John Russell (1855), Lord Ellenborough (1858), Robert Lowe (1864), Lord Westbury (1865) and Spencer Walpole (1867),[69] to see them as a recognition of constitutional obligation, with political pressure playing no part. This, however, is a false perspective, for it was Parliament's ability to force resignation through the threat of a censure motion that gave substance to the belief that there was a resigning convention. Such a threat became less effective with the advent of tight party discipline and majority governments after 1867, which meant that censure motions were unlikely to be carried and could, if necessary, be made into votes of confidence in the whole administration to protect a valued minister. The chancellor of the Exchequer, Denis Healey, was, for instance, protected in 1978 from a motion to halve his salary by the prime minister's insistence that 'the House should make up its mind on the whole record of the Government'.[70] This ensured the support of government backbenchers and thus the continuation in office of the chancellor.

It is seldom necessary for the prime minister to go to such lengths. Making the issue a collective one will usually suffice. Thus, Shinwell survived criticism over his handling of the fuel crisis in 1947, although he was subsequently moved to the War Office; Bevin and Arthur Henderson remained in office after British Spitfires were lost over Israel in 1949, despite political attacks on them; and Strachey was shielded by the prime minister, Attlee, in the 1949 parliamentary debate on the failure of the ground-nuts scheme in Tanganyika. As Professor Finer comments, 'In such cases . . . the majority party have but two alternatives—to pursue their vendetta and turn out their own government (and, incidentally, themselves); or to drop the matter. They choose the latter.'[71] Collective cover was similarly used by John Major, when prime minister, to protect Norman Lamont, chancellor of the Exchequer, after Britain's withdrawal from the Exchange Rate Mechanism in September 1992. He made it clear in the House of Commons that Lamont was following agreed government policy. But in Spring 1993 Lamont left the government. On other

[69] See S. E. Finer, 'The Individual Responsibility of Ministers', *Public Administration* (1956).
[70] HC Deb., vol. 951, col. 1129, 14 June 1978.
[71] Finer, 'The Individual Responsibility of Ministers'.

occasions, the popularity of a minister with the party would seem to have been of importance. Thus Lennox-Boyd's survival, after revelations of the killing of prisoners at the Hola Camp in Kenya in 1959, was in part because he was 'nearing the end of a very distinguished political career' and was expected to retire from the Commons in the near future, which he, in fact, did;[72] and James Prior's continuation in office, after the escape of IRA prisoners from the Maze Prison in 1984 (see below), owed much to his popularity on both sides of the House.

Protection by the prime minister and the support of the party in Parliament have therefore limited the number of resignations in the twentieth century. Indeed, Finer suggests that resignation is only forthcoming 'if the Minister is yielding, his Prime Minister unbending, and his party out for blood'.[73] A minister's career may therefore depend on his or her ability to tough it out, the extent to which the prime minister gives protective cover, and standing with the party; in other words on political considerations. These considerations may have changed since the mid-nineteenth century, but the underlying principle remains—a minister is unlikely to resign if he or she retains political support. Thus constitutional and political requirements will usually need to coincide before a minister tenders a resignation.

Other factors also limit the number of resignations. By the time errors or misjudgements, which may have made resignation appropriate, come to light, a minister may have been moved to a different position in government or may no longer be part of the ministerial team. For instance, Lord Young, who, as secretary of state at the Department of Trade and Industry, was responsible for the sale of the Rover car company in 1989, no longer held a ministerial position when it became apparent that he had 'seriously misled'[74] the House of Commons over the cost of the sale to the taxpayer. He could not therefore be held to account. Moreover, the situation becomes even more difficult when several ministers have been involved, particularly if they were from different governments. This was evident when the Northern Ireland company, De Lorean car enterprises, collapsed in 1982 and it was revealed that most of the £80 million of taxpayers' money invested in the company had ended up in numbered Swiss bank accounts. The initial investment was made by a Labour minister, Roy Mason. The amount was topped up by

---

[72] Birch, *Representative and Responsible Government*, p. 148.
[73] Finer, 'The Individual Responsibility of Ministers', 393.
[74] Trade and Industry Committee, *Sale of Rover Group to British Aerospace* (1990–1), HC 34.

Humphrey Atkins, a Conservative minister and, by the time the company collapsed, James Prior was the responsible minister. However, as he had had nothing to do with the investment, he could not reasonably be held accountable.

Yet, despite a variety of factors limiting the occasions on which ministers will relinquish office, resignations do occur. However, of the twentieth-century resignations which can, with some degree of certainty, be attributed to ministerial responsibility, only a very small number belong in the category of departmental fault, most being broadly classified as personal fault resignations (see Table 8.1).

Resignation for personal fault

Ministerial responsibility is based on the premise that ministers are accountable for their own behaviour and the evidence of the twentieth century suggests that, when this falls below the standard accepted at the time, resignation may be required. Personal fault relates to both political misjudgement and private indiscretion and, while such a division is not precise, it distinguishes between situations which arise because of a minister's official position, and those which owe nothing to it. In the first category are resignations attributable to policy, which is seen as flowing from a particular minister rather than the government as a whole. For instance, Colonel Seely resigned in 1914 over the Curragh incident, after it became apparent that, in pursuing his policy in Ireland, he had bargained with army officers, who were refusing to obey orders, without the consent of the Cabinet. Indeed, he admitted that he had 'inadvertently and with honest intentions' misled his Cabinet colleagues'.[75] Birrell's resignation in 1916 also arose from his policy in Ireland, which was seen as partly responsible for the Easter Rising of that year. It seems that in his determination to maintain 'the picture of an unbroken unanimity in Ireland' he ignored advice from many quarters that he should seek out and disarm units of Sinn Fein. In an emotional speech to the House of Commons, Birrell stated that he had 'made an untrue estimate of this Sinn Fein movement . . . [regarding] the possibility of a disturbance of the kind that had occurred in Dublin, of the mode of the warfare . . . and of the desperate folly displayed by the leaders and their dupes'.[76] He told the House that, as a consequence, the moment he had been assured

---

[75] HC Deb., vol. 6, col. 402, 25 March 1914.
[76] HC Deb., vol. 82, cols 33–4, 3 May 1916.

Table 8.1 Ministerial resignations in the twentieth century

Resignations for departmental fault or political misjudgement*

Date	Minister(s)	Reason
6 March 1905	G. Wyndham	Ireland
30 March 1914	J. Seely	Curragh Mutiny
3 May 1916	A. Birrell	Irish Rebellion
12 July 1917	A. Chamberlain	Campaign in Mesopotamia
8 August 1917	N. Chamberlain	Ministry of National Service
25 April 1918	Lord Rothermere	Air Force
9 March 1922	E. S. Montagu	Turkey
18 December 1935	Sir S. Hoare	Laval Pact
12 May 1938	Earl Winterton	Strength of Airforce
16 May 1938	Viscount Swinton	Strength of Air Force
20 July 1954	Sir Thomas Dugdale	Crichel Down
5 June 1963	J. Profumo	Lying to Parliament
5 April 1982	Lord Carrington, H. Atkins and R. Luce	Invasion of Falklands
24 January 1986	Leon Brittan	Westland affair

Cases of departmental fault or political misjudgement where there was no resignation**

Date	Minister(s)	Reason
1947	E. Shinwell	Fuel crisis
1949	E. Bevin, A. Henderson	Loss of Spitfires over Israel
1949	J. Strachey	Groundnut scheme in Tanganyika
1959	A. Lennox-Boyd	Deaths at Hola Camp in Kenya
1964	J. Amery	Overpayment to Ferranti Ltd for defence contract work
1982	Sir John Nott	Invasion of Falklands
1982	William Whitelaw	Security at the Palace
1983	James Prior	Breakout from Maze Prison
1989	Lord Young	Sale of Rover
1991	Kenneth Baker	Escape of IRA remand prisoners from Brixton Prison
1995	Michael Howard	Prison security
1996	William Waldegrave	Misleading Parliament
1996	Sir Nicholas Lyell	Matrix Churchill prosecution
1998	Robin Cook	Sierra Leone
1999	Jack Straw	Passport Agency crisis

* This excludes cases of resignation which relate to a minister's behaviour or judgement in a private capacity.
** This list is not exhaustive nor is it meant to suggest that all the ministers contained within it should have resigned. It is simply illustrative of instances of serious departmental fault or political misjudgement where resignations, for a variety of reasons, were not forthcoming.

that the insurrection had been quelled, 'I placed my resignation in the hands of my right hon. Friend the Prime Minister, who accepted it. No other course of action was open to me or to him.'[77]

Like the resignations of Seely and Birrell, that of Sir Samuel Hoare in 1935 was made necessary by what was perceived to be a policy failure for which he was held responsible. In seeking to negotiate a settlement of the Italian–Abyssianian conflict, Hoare had suggested terms, which British politicians and the public saw as rewarding the aggressor Italy at the expense of the victim. He 'sincerely believe [d] that the course that [he] took was the only one possible in the circumstances' but considered that his loss of support in the country meant that he would 'not carry the weight and influence in the councils of the world'.[78] He therefore tendered his resignation, wishing his successor 'better luck than I have had in the last two weeks'.

The resignations of Austen and Neville Chamberlain (1917), Lord Rothermere (1918) and Edwin Montagu (1922) can also be broadly classified as resulting from a policy fault or dissatisfaction with the policy a minister was pursuing. Resignations on this basis were a feature of the first half of the century and not the second, although arguably such a classification could appropriately be used for Lord Carrington's resignation (see below). His resignation, like the others, arose because of criticism of his judgement in a conflict situation and it may be that popular opinion is more easily inflamed in such circumstances than at other times. It may also be that, as the century progressed, policy issues were invariably covered by collective responsibility, although this, of course, could still be withdrawn if the future of the government was threatened.

Still within the broad category of personal fault, both Jimmy Thomas (1936) and Hugh Dalton (1947) resigned, after it became apparent that they had revealed information on the Budget prior to its official disclosure, an unacceptable action by a minister, and John Belcher (1948) resigned after the Lynskey Tribunal found that he had accepted gifts while at the Board of Trade. For his part, Nicholas Fairbairn, solicitor-general for Scotland, relinquished office in 1982 for 'errors of judgement'[79] in his dealings with the press over a Glasgow rape case while Edwina Currie, minister for health, was forced to leave office in 1988 after her

[77] HC Deb., vol. 82, cols 33–4, 3 May 1916.
[78] Sir Samuel Hoare, HC Deb., vol. 307, col. 2016, 19 December 1935.
[79] Letter of resignation, reproduced in *The Times*, 22 January 1982.

statement that 'most of the egg production of this country, sadly, is now infected with salmonella'[80] resulted in a dramatic fall in egg sales. Her comment was taken to mean that most eggs were contaminated and she did nothing to correct this interpretation. Nicholas Ridley, secretary of state for trade and industry, resigned in 1990. He had used intemperate language to attack the European Community and express anti-German sentiments. In an interview published in *The Spectator*, he spoke of monetary union as 'a German racket designed to take over the whole of Europe', the European Commission as 'seventeen unelected reject politicians' and the French as 'poodles to the Germans'.[81] He also opined that giving up sovereignty to the European Community was akin to giving it to Adolf Hitler. Michael Mates (1993) was also required to resign, after he had publicly supported Asil Nadir, a businessman who had fled to Cyprus to avoid prosecution by the Serious Fraud Office. All these examples can be described as errors by ministers, acting in their official capacity but without departmental backing. They were embarrassing to the government and resulted in collective support being withdrawn. Resignation was therefore inevitable.

Other departures from office have related to a conflict, or perceived conflict, of interest. Thus Reginald Maudling's resignation from his position as home secretary in 1972 stemmed from the investigation of the affairs of an architect, John Poulson, with whom he had had dealings. Similarly, the resignation in 1998 of Peter Mandelson, secretary of state for trade and industry, became necessary when it was revealed that he had borrowed money from Geoffrey Robinson, a minister at the Treasury, whose business affairs were being investigated by his department. Mandelson had distanced himself from the inquiry but had failed to inform his permanent secretary of the loan and, while insisting that he had not behaved improperly, he accepted that it was imperative that ministers not only uphold high standards in public life but that they are 'seen to do so'.[82] He accepted that his behaviour did not accord with this requirement and that the public might perceive a conflict of interest. Robinson also resigned from his position as paymaster-general. The loan itself was not a resigning matter, but he had faced continuing allegations of a conflict between his ministerial role and his business interests, some of

[80] Agriculture Committee, First Report, *Salmonella in Eggs* (1988–9), HC 108-I, vol. 1, para. 96.
[81] Published in D. Lawson, 'Saying the Unsayable about the Germans: An Interview with Nicholas Ridley', *The Spectator*, 14 July 1990.
[82] Letter of resignation reproduced in *The Times*, 24 December 1998.

which he had inadvertently failed to declare in the Register of Members' Interests.[83]

The requirement that ministers should relinquish their positions for misjudgements made in their official capacity, or where there is a conflict of interest, relates to the need for the government to retain the confidence of the party in Parliament and the public. This became a particular issue for John Major's government of 1992–7, which was discredited by a string of instances of financial impropriety. These included the acceptance by Mates of gifts from his constituents, a contributory factor in calls for his resignation, and by Jonathan Aitken and Neil Hamilton of hospitality.[84] Hamilton, along with Tim Smith, was also found by the parliamentary commissioner of standards to have taken money for asking questions in Parliament,[85] and he was one of several ministers who had failed to register all his financial interests in the Register of Members' Interests. Such instances added to the impression of a government which was unfit to govern,[86] and even the resignations of those involved did not restore confidence in it.

Instances of financial impropriety clearly cast doubt on an individual's suitability and trustworthiness as a minister. This may also be the case where indiscretion or misjudgement in a minister's private life is concerned. The immediate resignation in 1998 of Ron Davies, secretary of state for Wales, following an incident on Clapham Common during which he was attacked and robbed, was a recognition of this. While denying impropriety, he admitted that his presence on the Common was a serious misjudgement.[87] Whether sexual impropriety or indiscretion provides sufficient grounds on its own to justify demands for resignation

[83] Committee of Standards and Privileges, *Complaint against Mr Geoffrey Robinson* (1997–8), HC 488 and *Complaint against Mr Geoffrey Robinson (No. 2)* (1997–8), HC 975. He was not the first minister to resign for this reason. For instance, Lord Brayley resigned in 1974 because of an inquiry into his former business interests.

[84] Jonathan Aitken resigned in 1995 to fight a libel action to clear his name against allegations of financial impropriety, including accepting hospitality. He ended up serving a prison term for perjury.

[85] Committee on Standards and Privileges, *Complaint from Mr Mohamed Al Fayed, the Guardian and others against 25 Members and Former Members* (1997–8), HC 30.

[86] The Conservatives had been in office since 1979 and, while there were no allegations of corruption, the media referred to 'a climate of sleaze'.

[87] Serious misjudgement also accounted for the resignation in 1990 of Patrick Nicholls, a junior environment minister. He had been arrested for drink driving the day after the home secretary had promised the Conservative Party conference new measures against drinking in public places. Likewise, Iain Stewart resigned in 1995 after a violent confrontation with motorway protestors.

is doubtful. The evidence suggests that, in the absence of a minister choosing to relinquish office for personal reasons, perhaps to protect his family from sustained publicity, there needs to be another factor which undermines the minister's reputation or embarrasses the government. In 1958 the scandal surrounding Ian Harvey's private life was sufficient to require him to relinquish office, while in 1963 the relationship of John Profumo, secretary of state for war, with a call girl not only had security implications[88] but resulted in Profumo lying about it to the House of Commons. Security was also a factor in the resignation of Thomas Galbraith in 1962, although he was exonerated and given a new post the following year, and in the resignations in 1973 of Lord Lambton, minister for defence, and Earl Jellicoe, lord privy seal, both of whom had entertained call girls, although the Security Commission subsequently found that, because Jellicoe had behaved 'discreetly',[89] his relationship presented no security risk.

Cecil Parkinson, secretary of state for trade and industry, survived the revelation in 1983 that his mistress, Sara Keays, was expecting his child, but not the subsequent release of details about their relationship. This coincided with the Conservative Party conference and distracted attention from it. Moreover, the details suggested that he was indecisive and unreliable, hardly commendable traits for a Cabinet minister. His private life therefore interfered with his ability to function as a minister and embarrassed his party. David Mellor's resignation, as secretary of state for national heritage, in 1992, followed extensive coverage by the tabloid press of his affair with an actress. However, it was not his sexual antics but two other factors which made his position untenable. The first was his handling of the press, which he accused of invading his privacy while, at the same time, using it to mount a public relations exercise. This undermined his credibility as a minister, whose portfolio included responsibility for the press and possible privacy legislation. The second was evidence, which emerged from a libel action, that Mellor and his family had accepted a free holiday in Spain from the daughter of an executive member of the Palestine Liberation Organisation. The holiday had coincided with the beginning of the Gulf War crisis and, despite the prime minister's denial that Mellor had acted in contravention of

[88] The woman, Christine Keeler, was also involved with a Russian intelligence officer, although Lord Denning's subsequent inquiry found there had been no security risk (1963, Cmnd 2152).
[89] Its members were Lords Diplock, Sinclair and Garner, Sir Philip Allen and General Sir Dudley Ward (1973, Cmnd 5367).

the rules of ministerial behaviour, contained in *Questions of Procedure*,[90] the minister's judgement was seen by many MPs as suspect.

It is notable that, prior to the 1960s, resignations that arose at least in part from sexual indiscretion were not a feature of the political scene. Thereafter, they became the most familiar type of resignation. This can be attributed largely to the rise in the tabloid press, which resulted in a less deferential attitude to those in public office and increased competition between newspapers. Editors and proprietors were no longer prepared to keep silent about ministerial misdemeanours, the exposure of which helped to sell their papers. The role played by the press in determining whether or not a minister should resign is uncertain. Suggestions that editors, rather than the prime minister, decides the fate of a minister are overstated.[91] However, through exposing and sensationalising ministerial misbehaviour, papers keep the matter in the public eye and, by so doing, may make it difficult for a minister to continue effectively with official duties and may undermine his or her credibility with the party.

This was evident when the government of John Major (1992–7) appeared to make private morality a political issue with his Back to Basics speech at the Conservative Party conference of 1993. Press exposure of their private lives resulted in a number of ministers resigning. They had failed to live up to the standards of personal behaviour which they and their colleagues had publicly proclaimed. Thus Tim Yeo (1994) resigned after an adulterous affair resulted in a child; the Earl of Caithness (1994) after his wife committed suicide; Michael Brown (1994) after allegations of a homosexual relationship; and Robert Hughes (1995) and Rob Richards (1996) after press claims of infidelity. The Blair government, which came to office in 1997, was careful to distinguish between financial impropriety— a matter of public concern and thus a resigning offence— and sexual indiscretion—which was neither; a distinction which seemed to be supported by the new Conservative leadership.[92] As a consequence, Robin Cook, the foreign secretary, stayed in office, despite sustained media coverage of his decision to leave his wife for his constituency

[90] Cabinet Office, 1992. Replaced in July 1997 by the *Ministerial Code: A Code of Conduct and Guidance on Procedures for Ministers*.

[91] Such allegations were made by Mellor, who argued that, despite the fact that he had the prime minister's support, the press had successfully hounded him from office.

[92] At the Conservative Party conference in 1997 Hague indicated that ministers should resign for gross hypocrisy and financial impropriety, implying that sexual indiscretion was not a resigning offence.

diary secretary.[93] There were no other grounds that might have required him to relinquish office, and he retained the necessary political support to carry on.

While resignation for personal fault may, on occasion, be self-imposed, it is more frequently a punishment imposed by the prime minister and the party. Either way, whether and when a minister returns to office depends on the seriousness of the offence, the extent to which he has redeemed himself while in exile, and, most notably, his indispensability. Both Parkinson and Mandelson were sufficiently valued by their prime ministers to be recalled, Parkinson after there had been a general election, Mandelson less than a year after relinquishing office. However, such recalls are the exception rather than the rule.

Resignation for departmental fault

The situations discussed above relate obviously to the personal behaviour of ministers, over which, it is assumed, they have control. This link between responsibility and control is an essential feature of ministerial responsibility and was evident in the simple doctrine of the early nineteenth century, whereby ministers were answerable for their departments to Parliament and resigned if they lost its support. The presumption was that they personally ran, or oversaw the running of, their departments and therefore had close control of them. This gave rise to a formulation of ministerial responsibility, which suggested that ministers were required to resign for all serious departmental errors.[94] However, even as the doctrine was being formulated, the link between responsibility and control was weakening. The increase in the size and complexity of government made it impossible for ministers to be involved in the detail of departmental activities. They were also distanced from administration by the establishment of a permanent civil service. Yet the constitutional responsibility they assumed for their officials, upheld by the Haldane Committee in 1918,[95] was seen by some to support the principle that ministers accepted the blame, as well as the praise, for their depart-

---

[93] Cook left his wife in 1997 and remarried the following year.
[94] Sir William Anson, *Law and Custom of the Constitution*, 4th edn (Clarendon Press, 1935); A. L. Lowell, *The Government of England* (Macmillan, 1908), vol. 1; Sir Ivor Jennings, *The Law and the Constitution*, 5th edn (Cambridge University Press, 1959).
[95] *Report of the Machinery of Government Committee*, Cd 9230 (1918).

ments.[96] They were therefore assumed to be vicariously liable, in terms of resignation, for the faults of their officials.

Such a notion is unsupported by precedent. Indeed, cases of resignation suggest that, rather than vicarious liability, there needs to be a direct connection between ministerial involvement and resignation. This was evident after the resignation of Robert Lowe, the vice-president of the Committee of the Council on Education, in 1864. Lowe resigned after a report from a school inspector had been altered by an official in his department. He claimed that his honour had been impugned by attacks on him in Parliament. However, a select committee subsequently reported to the House that his resignation had been unnecessary because he had not been involved in or aware of the alteration and had, in fact, taken steps to prevent such alterations being made.[97] It thus confirmed the need for some ministerial involvement before resignation was required.

The resignation in 1905 of George Wyndham, the Irish secretary, supports this view of departmental fault. Wyndham resigned following public and political criticism of a scheme for the devolution of power in Ireland. He had no involvement in, and no knowledge of, the scheme, which had been devised by the department's under-secretary, Sir Anthony MacDonnell, and it is therefore tempting to see his resignation as an example of a minister accepting vicarious liability. However, Wyndham's lack of knowledge resulted, in part, from his failure to read correspondence sent by Sir Anthony and to keep abreast of political developments while on holiday. By his own admission, he had 'paid no heed to the newspapers', 'neglected' his correspondence and his 'mind was not intent on politics at all'.[98] It also arose from the unusual degree of discretion accorded to Sir Anthony, such that he had felt it permissible to draft proposals for devolution, which he believed the minister supported, without actually obtaining Wyndham's approval. This action was repudiated by Wyndham and censured by the Cabinet, although Wyndham insisted that there was 'no charge against Sir Anthony Mac-Donnell of having in any way been disloyal to me or having in any word, written or said, done anything of which a man need to be ashamed'.[99]

Wyndham came under attack, both for his appointment of Sir

[96] Jennings, *The Law and the Constitution*, p. 146.
[97] For an interpretation of this and other nineteenth-century and early twentieth-century resignations, see Finer, 'Individual Responsibility of Ministers'.
[98] HC Deb., 4th series, vol. 141, col. 658, 22 February 1905.
[99] Ibid., col. 985.

Anthony, which had been made on the basis that he would be 'a colleague' and be able to influence policy, and for blaming him rather than accepting responsibility himself. As he observed, 'The charge against me is either that I appointed a distinguished public servant whom I had no business to appoint, and that I gave him powers I had no business to confer on him; or that I was right in doing so, but that the moment he put a foot wrong I threw him over.'[100] His resignation was not, therefore, an acceptance of responsibility for the action of an official but for departmental fault, in which he had played a part. He had failed to fulfil his overseeing or supervisory responsibility.

Wyndham's resignation is the only case in the first half of the twentieth century, which can be cited with certainty as attributable to departmental fault. It is therefore not surprising that doubt remained as to its requirements. Indeed, from the 1930s, there was doubt about whether a resigning convention existed at all.[101] Fifty years after Wyndham, the resignation of Sir Thomas Dugdale provided another example. Sir Thomas, who was minister for agriculture, resigned after criticism of his department's handling of the disposal of land, as revealed by the Crichel Down inquiry.[102] The land had been acquired in 1938 for use as a bombing range and, despite the understanding of neighbouring landowners that they would be able to bid for the land when it was no longer needed, they were given no chance to do so. Moreover, the request of a former owner to buy it back was refused.

The rhetoric surrounding the resignation suggested it was an example of a minister sacrificing his career as atonement for the errors of his officials, Sir Thomas telling the House: 'I, as Minister, must accept full responsibility to Parliament for any mistakes and inefficiencies of officials in my Department, just as, when my officials bring off any successes on my behalf, I take full credit for them.' As a result, his resignation was, for some time, seen as the classic example of ministerial responsibility and as a precedent for vicarious liability. In fact, not only was Dugdale paying the price for pursuing a policy which was unpopular with government backbenchers, but he and two of his junior ministers had played some part in the Crichel Down decision.[103] Thus, rather than Dugdale's

---

[100] HC Deb., 4th series, vol. 141, col. 648.

[101] Birch, *Representative and Responsible Government*, p. 148.

[102] *Report from the Public Inquiry into the Disposal of Land at Crichel Down*.

[103] For an analysis of Crichel Down, see I. F. Nicolson, *The Mystery of Crichel Down* (Oxford University Press, 1986) and the commentary by J. A. G. Griffith in *Contemporary Record* (1987).

resignation being a precedent for vicarious responsibility, it provided evidence for the principle that, for a resignation to be forthcoming, the minister must have had some personal involvement. As Lord Boyle subsequently noted:

> Sir Thomas Dugdale . . . did not resign because he accepted responsibility for an act of maladministration; he resigned because he was not prepared to abandon . . . the decision that his Department should retain and equip Crichel Down as a single farm unit—which was unacceptable to an influential section of his own party in Parliament, as well as individuals and interests outside.[104]

This need for ministerial involvement was implied by the home secretary, Sir David Maxwell Fyfe, in the debate on Crichel Down, although his speech lacked the necessary coherence for it to become a definitive statement on the requirements of ministerial responsibility. He distinguished between three situations. The first was where officials had carried out a minister's explicit order or acted completely in accordance with the policy laid down by the minister. In such an instance, the responsibility of the minister included that of protecting and defending the officials. The blame, if any, was the minister's. The second was where officials had made relatively minor errors in administration, of which the minister was unaware. Here 'the Minister acknowledges the mistake and he accepts the responsibility, although he is not personally involved. He states he will take corrective action in the Department.'[105] The third situation was where an official had taken an action 'of which the Minister disapproves and has no prior knowledge, and the conduct of the official is reprehensible'. In this case 'there is no obligation on the part of the Minister to endorse what he believes to be wrong, or to defend what are clearly shown to be errors of his officials . . . But, of course, he remains constitutionally responsible to Parliament for the fact that something has gone wrong, and he alone can tell Parliament what has occurred and render an account of his stewardship.'[106]

This third situation was somewhat 'ambiguous', for, as noted by the Public Service Committee some forty years later, Maxwell Fyfe appeared 'to argue that a Minister has no responsibility for the conduct of his officials when they are not explicitly or implicitly following his policy',

---

[104] Lord Boyle of Handsworth, 'Address to the Royal Institute of Public Administration', *Public Administration* (1980).
[105] HC Deb., vol. 53, col. 1290, 20 July 1954.
[106] Ibid., cols 1290–1.

while, at the same time, stating that he, and he alone, is responsible to Parliament when something goes wrong and that, as part of his responsibility to Parliament, he should 'take necessary action to ensure efficiency and the proper discharge of the duties of his department'.[107] Nevertheless, Maxwell Fyfe seemed to refute any principle of vicarious liability, suggesting that where serious errors were made by officials, in which the minister had no part and of which the minister was unaware, the responsibility of the minister was confined to telling Parliament what had happened and how he would put it right, and convincing the House that he was in effective command of his department.[108] Ministerial responsibility in such instances therefore required explanation and amendatory action not resignation. This requirement only arose when the minister was involved in or knew of serious errors or had been negligent in the running of the department. Two subsequent cases, those of Lord Carrington and Leon Brittan, support this view of ministerial responsibility.

In 1982 the foreign secretary Lord Carrington and two junior ministers resigned after the invasion of the Falklands by Argentina. Carrington denied that he or his department had been at fault, attributing his resignation to the need to respond to the 'feeling in the country that Britain's honour and dignity had been affronted'.[109] However, according to the Franks Report, both officials and ministers had misjudged the situation. The report, whose conclusions appeared to exonerate ministers from blame, in fact criticised officials for 'not attach [ing] sufficient weight . . . to the changing Argentine attitude' and for not giving 'sufficient importance to the new and threatening elements in the Argentine Government's position'[110] and Lord Carrington for his misjudgement of the situation and for failing to initiate a government review of policy on the Falklands. It noted that this failure meant that 'the Government were in a position of weakness, and that the effect of Lord Carrington's decision was to pass the initiative to the Argentine Government'.[111] There had therefore

---

[107] HC 313-I, para. 13.

[108] This line was endorsed by opposition spokesman, Herbert Morrison, HC Deb., col. 1278, 20 July 1954.

[109] HL Deb., vol. 35, col. 159, 25 January 1983; two junior ministers, Luce and Atkins, resigned with Carrington, although constitutionally, as junior ministers, they were under no obligation to accept responsibility for departmental fault.

[110] Report by Commission of Privy Councillors, *Falkland Islands Review*, Cmnd 8787 (1983), para. 302.

[111] Ibid., para. 290.

been departmental error, in which the foreign secretary was involved, and this had had very serious consequences.

A few years later, in 1986, the resignation of Leon Brittan provided a further precedent for resignation for departmental fault. Brittan, secretary of state for trade and industry, was a casualty of the Westland affair.[112] This concerned an open dispute between two government ministers about the future of a helicopter company, which was in financial difficulties. Brittan, backed by the prime minister, believed that Westland's fate should be left to the market, which meant that an American competitor would buy a controlling share. Michael Heseltine, secretary of state for defence, favoured a European solution in the form of a consortium of helicopter companies, which he sought to put together. In an attempt to discredit Heseltine's campaign, Brittan's department leaked extracts from a confidential letter, written to him by the solicitor-general. Brittan subsequently accepted 'full responsibility for the fact and the form of the disclosure',[113] and admitted that 'the disclosure of that information— urgent and important though it was—should not have taken place in that way'. Moreover, he insisted that his officials had in no way gone beyond what he 'authorised them to do'.[114] However, his acceptance of responsibility was marred by his failure to articulate it until after the Cabinet secretary, Sir Robert Armstrong, had conducted an inquiry and the names of the three officials involved had become public knowledge. His silence until that point 'might be thought to have fallen short of the backing which a Minister normally gives his officials'[115] and contrary to Maxwell-Fyfe's extrapolation of the convention. Moreover, his resignation was reluctant and was not accompanied by a full explanation.

Brittan maintained that he had authorised the leak but only 'subject to the agreement of Number Ten'.[116] Whether this agreement was forthcoming or what form it took is uncertain, as Brittan refused to answer questions relating to the part played by the Prime Minister's Office and the officials involved were not allowed to give evidence to the select

---

[112] As was Michael Heseltine, secretary of state for defence; for an account of the Westland affair, see D. Woodhouse, *Ministers and Parliament: Accountability in Theory and Practice* (Clarendon Press, 1994); D. Oliver and R. Austin, 'Political and Constitutional Aspects of the Westland Affair', *Parliamentary Affairs* (1987).

[113] HC Deb., vol. 90, col. 67, 27 January 1986.

[114] HC 169, q. 967.

[115] Defence Committee, Fourth Report, *Westland plc: The Government's Decision-making* (1985–6), HC 519, para. 205.

[116] The Defence Committee, *The Defence Implications of the Future of Westland plc* (1985–6), HC 169, Minutes of Evidence and Appendices, q. 933.

committee, the Cabinet secretary appearing instead. It seemed therefore that Brittan's concern was less constitutional convention than political damage-limitation and loyalty to the prime minister. Thus, if the constitutional character of a resignation is, in part, measured by the extent to which the political actors feel and express a moral obligation to resign, Leon Brittan's relinquishment of office barely registered on the constitutional scale. However, this does not prevent it being classified as departmental fault and joining the Dugdale–Carrington tradition. The fact that a resignation may be politically expedient does not affect the constitutional principle on which it is based.

The Dudgale, Carrington and Brittan resignations are precedents for a resigning convention in situations where the minister was involved in, or aware of, serious departmental fault. The position remains that there has been no clear instance of resignation for civil service fault, thereby enabling Geoffrey Marshall to say 'with confidence' that 'the convention of ministerial responsibility contains no requirement of any such vicarious accountability'.[117] This view of ministerial responsibility was reinforced in 1990 by the head of the civil service, Sir Robin Butler, when he stated: '[Ministers] cannot and should not be expected to shoulder the blame for decisions of which they know nothing or could be expected to know nothing.'[118] This raises the question of what a minister 'could be expected to know', a question which, with the employment by ministers of distinctions between 'policy' and 'administration/operations' and 'responsibility' and 'accountability', has remained largely unresolved. Indeed, rather than ministerial responsibility becoming clearer, it has become more confused and this confusion has been compounded by the structural and cultural changes in government, which took place during the final decades of the twentieth century.

The policy/administration (operations) division

In 1983, after thirty-eight IRA prisoners escaped from the Maze Prison, the secretary of state for Northern Ireland, James Prior, sought to limit his responsibility by the employment of the division between policy and administration and, by so doing, to extend its use from areas, such as

---

[117] G. Marshall, *Constitutional Conventions* (Clarendon Press, 1984), p. 65.
[118] Address to First Division Association of Civil Servants, reported in P. Hennessy, 'Whitehall Watch', *The Independent*, 14 November 1990.

the nationalised industries where ministerial responsibility was indirect, to the departmental context. The division, discussed above, had long been criticised on the basis that it enabled ministers to distance themselves from culpability, and Prior's use of it in an area within his direct responsibility suggested a similar motive. He stated that he would resign if the inquiry, chaired by Sir James Hennessy, found that government policy was to blame for the escape, or that the incident had resulted from his failure to implement something which it was his duty to implement.[119] He therefore accepted a narrow, specific responsibility, but implied that he was under no obligation to resign for administrative errors. To an extent, this was correct. Most administrative errors are too remote from the minister, either geographically or in hierarchical terms, to be within the minister's area of knowledge or control. Resignation would therefore be an unnecessary acceptance of vicarious responsibility. However, the phrasing used by Prior suggested that ministers should never resign for administrative errors, regardless of their scale, their centrality to policy, and the degree of ministerial involvement. His statement also took no account of situations where ministers should have been engaged in the administration of their departments, which was arguably the case in Northern Ireland.

While there was no move to force Prior's resignation, the distinction he made was contested in Parliament on the basis that the breakout from the Maze was not 'in a peripheral area of the responsibility of the Northern Ireland Department'. Rather 'it was a disaster that occupied an area which was quite clearly central to the department's responsibility . . . [it was] an administrative failure of the sort that goes from the bottom straight to the top'.[120] Moreover, although the Hennessy Report held the prison governor ultimately accountable,[121] it noted that concessions made to the prisoners by the government had resulted in low morale among the staff and that this had been a contributory factor in the escape.[122] Prior was therefore not absolved from constitutional responsibility and his continuation in office owed more to his popularity and to concerns about the effect of his resignation on the situation in

---

[119] HC Deb., 6th series, vol. 47, cols 23–4, 24 October 1983.
[120] HC Deb., 6th series, vol. 47, col. 1061, 9 February 1984.
[121] *Report on Security Arrangements at the Maze Prison* (Sir James Hennessy) (1984), HC 203, para. 10.12.
[122] Ibid., para. 9.27.

Northern Ireland than to acceptance of his reformulation of ministerial responsibility.[323]

Despite the fact that the division between policy and administration was strongly contested, both in the House of Commons and outside, in 1991, Kenneth Baker, the home secretary, cited Prior's continuation in office as a precedent for the principle that ministers never resign for administrative errors. He utilised the division after the escape of two IRA remand prisoners from Brixton Prison, telling the House: 'the Home Secretary is responsible for policy in prison matters. The administration, development and running of the prisons are the responsibility of the director-general [of the prison service] and of individual prison governors.'[124] While in general terms this may be true, Baker's definition of administration was so broad, encompassing, as it did, departmental policies, which gave effect to political preferences, and decisions about the housing of high-risk prisoners, that it confined his responsibility to matters of overall strategy. He was therefore automatically distanced from any culpability, unless it concerned government policy, in which case he would, in most instances, come under the protective umbrella of collective responsibility.

Baker's distinction was uncontested in Parliament,[125] an indication that constitutional change may happen by default or through the misinterpretation of a previous precedent, and the policy/administration division became part of the landscape of ministerial responsibility. This enabled a subsequent home secretary, Michael Howard, to use the division in 1995, again in the context of departmental responsibilities relating to prisons. Moreover, he asserted that such a division had 'been recognised for years, indeed generations',[126] thereby providing another demonstration that constitutional development may have more to do with misinformation than with sound analysis. It may also have more to do with ministerial interests than with those of accountability or the policy/administration division. For it enabled the lines of responsibility

---

[123] For a further example of the operation of ministerial responsibility in Northern Ireland, see HC Deb., 21 January 1998, where the secretary of state, Dr Mowlam, was asked whether 'political direction from the Northern Ireland Office contributed to the relaxation of security, which facilitated the escape of an IRA prisoner and the murder of Billy Wright [in the Maze Prison]' (vol. 304, col. 980). But few regretted the death of Wright, head of the LVF, or wanted Mowlam to resign, given her role in the peace process. MPs were therefore satisfied with the setting up of an inquiry.

[124] HC Deb., vol. 194, col. 657, 8 July 1991.

[125] Ibid., cols 650–7.

[126] HC Deb., vol. 252, cols 39–40, 10 January 1995.

to be blurred and allowed the minister to disclaim responsibility for serious departmental fault on the grounds that the fault was administrative, even if he knew, or should have known, what was happening. The lines were further blurred by the distinction between 'responsibility' and 'accountability'.

Accountability and responsibility

The meaning of 'responsibility' in the context of ministerial responsibility has been the subject of considerable discussion[127] but, until the 1990s, it tended to be used interchangeably with 'accountability' or 'answerability'. Where different meanings were attributed, it was to the extent that the responsibility of ministers to Parliament was described as requiring them to account or answer for their responsibilities. Accountability and responsibility were therefore inextricably linked. However, in a Memorandum to the Treasury and Civil Service Committee, which was inquiring into the role of the civil service, the Cabinet secretary, Sir Robin Butler, sought in 1993 to distinguish between the two words, arguing that, while accountability related to the constitutional obligation of ministers to account to Parliament for their departments and agencies, responsibility 'implies personal involvement in an action or decision, in a sense that implies personal credit or blame for that action or decision'.[128] It therefore followed that 'a Minister is *accountable* for all the actions and activities of his department, but not *responsible* for all the actions in the sense of being blameworthy'. It also followed that if responsibility did not reside with ministers, it must lie with officials, such that 'a civil servant is not directly accountable to Parliament for his actions but is responsible for certain actions'.[129]

The use of such a distinction to protect ministers 'from being seen as personally responsible for minor failings (an incorrect social security payment, for example)' was seen by the Public Service Committee as 'no more than a statement of the obvious; few would seriously advance the proposition that a Minister should resign in such circumstances'.[130] In this context it is therefore uncontroversial, seeking merely to restate the

---

[127] See, for instance, Nevil Johnson, *In Search of the Constitution* (Pergamon, 1977); Geoffrey Marshall and Graeme Moodie, *Some Problems of the Constitution* (Hutchinson, 1959).
[128] HC 27-II.
[129] Ibid.
[130] HC 313-I, para. 21.

position as understood since Crichel Down. However, when looked at in the context of the *Civil Service Code*, which implies that civil servants have no constitutional personality or responsibility separate from the duly constituted government of the day,[131] there appears to be some conflict. More important, the distinction can be used by ministers to escape responsibility (in the sense of blame) for a series of operational errors, which amount to mismanagement or negligence on the minister's part, on the basis that the mistake was not the minister's own and that he was not to blame.[132]

This was illustrated by its use by Sir Nicholas Lyell, the attorney-general, to defend himself from the findings of Sir Richard Scott's inquiry into 'Arms to Iraq'.[133] One of the issues under investigation was the use of public interest immunity certificates to prevent three men, who were on trial for exporting defence-related equipment to Iraq, gaining access to some government papers.[134] Michael Heseltine, president of the Board of Trade, had strong reservations about signing such a certificate and had only done so on condition that his reservations were made known to the trial judge. They were not. The prosecution counsel had not been adequately instructed and Sir Richard Scott concluded that the 'major responsibility' for this must be borne by the attorney-general, whose personal involvement had been made necessary by Heseltine's stance.[135] While Scott accepted 'the genuineness of [Sir Nicholas'] belief that he was personally, as opposed to constitutionally, blameless for the inadequacy of the instructions sent to Mr Moses [the prosecuting counsel]', he did not accept that, in fact, 'he was not personally at fault'. As far as he was concerned, 'the issues raised by Mr Heseltine's stand on the PII certificate did not fall into the category of mundane, routine, run of the mill issues that could properly be dealt with by officials in the treasury solicitor's department without the attorney-general's supervision'.[136] Thus, while accepting the responsibility/accountability distinction, he did not accept that they exonerated Lyell. Yet, despite the

---

[131] *Civil Service Code* (1996).

[132] HC 313-I, para. 19.

[133] HC 115.

[134] Michael Heseltine, Kenneth Clarke, Tristan Garel-Jones and Malcolm Rifkind had signed these on the advice of the attorney-general.

[135] HC 115, G13.123–4. He was also concerned that a letter from Heseltine to the attorney-general had been left unread for between three to seven weeks and that the attorney-general had not himself read the documents about which Mr Heseltine expressed concern.

[136] Ibid., G13.125.

implication that Lyell was negligent in the running of his department, the attorney-general remained in office.

The distinction between 'accountability' and 'responsibility', which was considered by Scott to clarify ministerial responsibility,[137] was also supported by a number of Whitehall commentators and academics.[138] However, the Public Service Committee was not convinced and concluded: 'It is not possible absolutely to distinguish an area in which a Minister is personally responsible, and liable to take the blame, from one where he is constitutionally accountable. Ministerial responsibility is not composed of two elements, with a clear break between the two.'[139] Indeed, '[p]roperly analysed, accountability is merely part of responsibility, a subset, something which makes it possible in practice to hold someone responsible'.[140] Responsibility and accountability are therefore part of the same process and inextricably linked. Yet the government persisted with the distinction, arguing that it described 'modern practice' and provided 'Parliament and the public with a broad and practical framework against which to judge government's continuing endeavours to remain properly accountable'.[141] This suggests a convention evolving to accommodate twentieth-century changes in political structures and practice and to improve accountability. However, in practice, it seemed to limit ministerial liability.

Part of the problem lay in attempts to specify the areas for which a minister was responsible in the context of the policy/operations division. This was evident in the government publication, *Taking Forward Continuity and Change*,[142] which stated that the minister was responsible for 'the policies of the department', 'the framework through which these policies are delivered', 'the resources allocated', 'such implementation decisions any agency framework document may require to be referred or agreed with the Minister', and for 'responding to major failures or expressions of Parliamentary or public concern'. However, it made no reference to the minister's responsibility for interventions, which were

[137] HC 115, K8.15.

[138] Lord Howe in evidence before the Public Service Committee, HC 313-III, q. 266; Brazier, HC 313-II, p. 12.

[139] HC 313-I, para. 21.

[140] G. Mather, 'Clarifying Responsibility and Accountability', in *Government Accountability* (CIPFA, 1996), p. 21.

[141] Public Service Committee, First Special Report, *Government's Response to the Second Report from the Committee (1995–6) on Ministerial Accountability and Responsibility* (1996–7), HC 67, p. vi.

[142] Cm 2748 (1994).

315

not included in the framework document, or for the minister's decision not to intervene when a matter was brought to his or her attention. Yet, unless agencies become completely free-standing,[143] ministers can neither escape responsibility for the way in which they exercise supervisory judgement nor claim that non-intervention removes responsibility. Nor was there any reference to mismanagement by the minister which results in a succession of errors, or in the department 'prevent [ing] a Minister knowing about things that he should have known about'.[144]

Indeed, there was no reference to the general supervisory responsibility, recognised some twenty-five years earlier by the home secretary Reginald Maudling when he said: 'Ministers are responsible not only for their personal decisions but also for seeing that there is a system in their Departments by which they are informed of important matters which arise. They are also responsible for minimising the dangers of errors and mistakes so far as is possible, and clearly, they are responsible for the general efficiency of their Department.'[145] Such supervisory responsibility seems just as appropriate at the turn of the century, particularly in the context of Next Steps agencies, where the distinctions between policy/operations and responsibility/accountability have given particular cause for concern.

Administrative reform

Next Steps agencies

Next Steps agencies, which formalise the policy/operations division, can and do generally provide greater clarity and transparency. However, even though responsibilities are delegated through framework documents, there may still be problems in 'determining what is an operational matter and what is policy, leading to confusion as to where responsibility lies'.[146] It may also be difficult to tell whether errors are 'operational' or the result of poor policy or erratic changes in policy direction, policy

---

[143] A number of commentators have suggested that for some agencies a statutory or contractual framework is more appropriate and the Public Service Committee recommended that the government should, at each agency review, consider whether the agency should be converted to a statutory body (HC 313-I, para. 122).

[144] Giles Radice MP, HC Deb., vol. 290, col. 274, 12 February 1997.

[145] HC Deb., vol. 836, col. 33, 1 May 1972.

[146] Sir John Woodcock, *Report on the Escape from Whitemoor Prison*, Cm 2741 (1994), para. 9.2.9.

success or failure frequently becoming apparent only at the operational level. Moreover, where politically sensitive agencies are concerned, there may 'be difficulty in defining precisely who takes what decisions or when the Secretary of State should be involved'[147] or, given the tendency for ministers to interfere in operational matters, when they have done so inappropriately or unofficially.

Confusion of this nature provides the opportunity for ministers to abdicate responsibility by classifying all failures as 'operational', and therefore falling within the responsibility of the chief executive. This was the case with both the Child Support Agency and the Prison Service. The chief executive of the Child Support Agency, Ros Hepplewhite, resigned in 1994, after a disastrous first year, which was attributed by ministers to operational mismanagement. The agency had failed by a long way to meet its performance targets, and maladministration had been widespread. However, the Committee on the Parliamentary Commissioner for Administration reported that maladministration 'could not be divorced from the responsibility of Ministers for the framework',[148] which gave a greater priority to saving money than to the quality of service. The ability of the agency to operate effectively had also been directly affected by the failure of ministers to ensure that the agency was properly established and adequately staffed and financed.[149] Thus it would seem that ministers had failed to fulfil their supervisory responsibilities and should at least have shared the blame.

The director-general of the Prison Service, Derek Lewis, was similarly held responsible for a number of prison escapes, after the Learmont Report into the Whitemoor and Parkhurst breakouts blamed operational and management errors.[150] In dismissing Lewis, the home secretary, Michael Howard, not only utilised the division between policy and operations, but also made a distinction between 'accountability' and 'responsibility', the effect of which was that ministerial responsibility was 'defined away almost to nothing'.[151] He argued that, while he was accountable to Parliament for the agency in the sense of 'giving an

---

[147] Derek Lewis, ex-director-general of the Prison Service, in evidence before the Public Service Committee, HC 313-III, q. 637.
[148] Select Committee on the Parliamentary Commissioner for Administration, Third Report, *The Child Support Agency* (1994–5), HC 199, para. 27.
[149] Social Security Committee, First Report, *The Operation of the Child Support Act* (1993–4), HC 69.
[150] *Review of Prison Service Security in England and Wales*, Cm 3020 (1995).
[151] Mather, 'Clarifying Responsibility and Accountability', p. 21.

account', the director-general was fully responsible for operations and therefore culpable when things went wrong.[152] For his part, Lewis claimed that many of the failures in the prison service were not operational but the result of policies that increased the prison population without providing additional resources and that, far from the agency being operationally independent, it was subject to extensive interference from the home secretary. His contentions were subsequently supported by the prisons minister, who told Parliament that 'important issues that were discussed in the House were in fact omitted from the minutes that [the home secretary] laid before it as a full account'.[153] These issues included the pressure that he had put on Lewis to sack the governor of Parkhurst Prison, which provided evidence of his interference in the prison service.

Lewis, who had been appointed by the previous home secretary from outside the civil service, claimed that his sacking was politically motivated and was not a reflection of his managerial competence. He subsequently secured an out-of-court settlement from the Home Office. He had, after all, met his performance targets, which seemed to prove his point, although it also brought into question the extent to which the success of an agency should be determined by quantifiable targets. Whether or not Lewis should have been required to resign his position, the effect of the policy/operations and responsibility/accountability distinctions seemed to be that, rather than ministerial responsibility protecting officials, it worked to shield ministers. Thus, distinctions, introduced in response to the tendency to blame ministers for everything that goes wrong in government, would seem to enable them to transfer the blame to officials.

This has implications for all Next Steps executive agencies, and particularly those likely to be subject to political scrutiny, although in practice any agency may find itself in the political spotlight, as the Passport Agency discovered in the summer of 1999. The crisis at the Passport Agency, another Home Office agency, gave the home secretary, Jack Straw, the opportunity to take the responsibility he had seemed to advocate upon assuming office in 1997. In the aftermath of the Howard–Lewis affair, Straw had stated that the 'so-called split between

---

[152] The subsequent director-general, Richard Tilt, found that his responsibility for operations required him to apologise publicly for the mistaken release of certain prisoners, while his minister Michael Howard sat silently at his side.

[153] The claim by Ann Widdecombe (HC Deb., vol. 294, col. 406, 19 May 1997) severely damaged Howard's chances of being elected leader of the Conservative Party.

operations and policy' was 'absurd and unworkable',[154] adding that he had a 'fundamental objection to this notion that you can have agencies detached from ministerial responsibility'.[155] He therefore said that he would be taking 'proper ministerial responsibility'.[156] As far as the Prison Service was concerned, he stressed that this did not mean that if a cell door had been left open by accident, he was assumed to be 'culpable, guilty of that act'. However, it did mean that he was 'responsible for checking whether the right procedures are in place and that effective management decisions have been made through the director-general of the Prison Service to ensure that that sort of thing doesn't happen again'.[157]

Straw was thus reasserting the responsibility that his predecessor, Michael Howard, had abdicated and, by so doing, was making a political point. He was also making a constitutional point, his outline of ministerial responsibility corresponding with the idea of the minister having a supervisory responsibility, rather than just a duty to account for what has happened. His statement did not, however, mean that he would resign over lapses in prison security—indeed home secretaries have never done so—nor that he would not have dismissed Lewis himself: his support of the director-general had been muted when he had been shadow home secretary. However, he could be expected to ensure that appropriate amendatory measures had been taken and so he might be seen as culpable if such lapses continued.

The crisis at the Passport Agency, which tested Straw's view of ministerial responsibility, arose after difficulties with a new computer system coincided with an upsurge in seasonal demand and a new requirement that children should be issued with their own passports. The resulting delays in the processing of passports led to a loss of public confidence, a 'run on the bank' and a backlog of over 50,000 applications. As an immediate response, the home secretary not only explained what had happened and apologised in person to those queuing at the Petty France Passport Office, he also ensured that appropriate amendatory measures were taken and that compensation was paid to those whose travel plans had been disrupted. He subsequently asked the chief executive designate

[154] HC Deb., vol. 294, col. 398, 19 May 1997.
[155] 'Inside Story', BBC2, 2 November 1997.
[156] HC Deb., vol. 294, col. 598, 19 May 1997.
[157] 'Inside Story'.

to take up his position early and, as a sign of the agency's failure, removed its Chartermark.

The incident was therefore portrayed as operational error, which arose from 'inadequate planning',[158] the permanent secretary telling the Home Affairs Select Committee that 'the agency was operating on a very fine margin in terms of whether it would get through this summer. In the end "the run on the bank" factor was more than it could cope with, and for that we are all deeply regretful.'[159] While insisting that he did 'not seek to slide away from anything that we in the Home Office should have done',[160] he was firm where the blame lay, stating: 'The chain of command in the Passport Office is very clear. It is an executive agency, and the home secretary is accountable to Parliament for its activities. The Chief Executive is accountable to the Home Secretary for his performance.'[161] As performance was at fault, the agency was blamed.

However, it is evident that the agency had informed the permanent secretary and ministers at the Home Office that there was a risk that demand might outstrip capacity and, according to the permanent secretary, there had been 'active management of this matter by ministers and the chief executive throughout'.[162] This included the decision not to publicise advice on possible delays in passport applications for fear of precipitating the very crisis which, in fact, arose. Arguably, therefore, it was not only the chief executive who miscalculated but also officials in the Home Office and, possibly, ministers. Attributing the poor performance of the agency entirely to its chief executive therefore seemed questionable and suggested that, while the home secretary might have had reservations about the split between policy and operations, he was not averse to blaming the operational arm of government. The difference was, however, that whereas his predecessor had used managerial responsibility as a substitute for constitutional responsibility, Straw used it as a spur to action.

Nevertheless, the problem for chief executives remains. They may find themselves publicly disciplined by the person, who, according to the convention of ministerial responsibility, is required to protect them. The issue is compounded by the application of the Osmotherly Rules to

[158] David Omand in evidence before the Home Affairs Select Committee, *Home Affairs Annual Report* (1998–9), HC 653, Minutes of Evidence, 118.
[159] Ibid.
[160] Ibid., q. 120.
[161] Ibid.
[162] Ibid., q. 138.

them. Despite recommendations from select committees that they should appear before committees on their own behalf,[163] the government has remained firm, not being 'prepared to breach the longstanding basic principle that civil servants, including the Chief Executives of Next Steps Agencies, give an account to Parliament on behalf of the Ministers whom they serve'.[164] Thus, chief executives, like all officials, remain theoretically 'subject to that Minister's instructions'.[165]

In reality, the conventional position is frequently ignored or forgotten, at least where non-contentious agencies are concerned, suggesting that the 'practice in this case has evolved considerably in advance of the theory'.[166] This may be an indication that ministerial responsibility will, by stealth, self-adjust to the new government structure. However, the refusal of ministers to accept a formal adjustment, or even the need for it, is disturbing. It enables them to evoke the theory as and when it suits their purpose. Thus, chief executives may be publicly criticised for the under-performance or errors of their agencies but, unless they are pre-pared to act contrary to the Osmotherly Rules and embarrass the minister, an unlikely scenario where career civil servants are concerned, they are unable to defend themselves before select committees by revealing the extent to which changes in policy, a lack of resources, or ministerial interference contributed to the agency's performance.[167]

Policy initiatives

The individual accountability of ministers becomes even more problem-atic where 'joined-up' government initiatives and public–private partnerships are concerned. The first can involve a number of depart-ments, as well as local government and voluntary agencies, in policy-making, but there has been little attempt to build new structures of accountability and it may therefore be difficult to determine where responsibility lies. The second, which revolve around contracts with the private sector, may result in commercial confidentiality obscuring the lines of accountability and in ministerial responsibility being sidelined.

---

[163] For example, see the report of the Treasury and Civil Service Committee, *Developments on the Next Steps Programme* (1988–9), HC 348, and its successor committee, the Public Service Committee, HC 313-I.

[164] HC 67, p. vii.

[165] Ibid.

[166] HC 313-I, para. 110.

[167] Derek Lewis, ex-director of the Prison Service, who did defend himself, was not a career civil servant but had come from the private sector.

Both types of venture are part of the entrepreneurial culture the government wishes to promote and there are indications that it sees political accountability as detrimental to this culture. In 1999 the Cabinet secretary stated: 'We need to look at our concepts of accountability and make sure they do not reward too highly the "safe" way of doing things.'[168] This line was supported in the government's paper, *Modernising Government*, which stated: 'The cultures of Parliament, Ministers and the civil service create a situation in which the rewards for success are limited and penalties for failure can be severe. The system is too often risk-averse.'[169]

The Performance and Innovation Unit in the Cabinet Office also argued that the current scrutiny arrangements gave departments a 'powerful incentive' to concentrate on 'their own internal performance and much less incentive to consider how they could improve the Government's overall performance by working with other organisations'.[170] It therefore sought to 'identify reforms to existing accountability arrangements and incentive structures which will encourage better cross-departmental policy-making and implementation' without weakening 'financial discipline or formal accountability to Parliament'.[171] To this end, it recommended that the government should 'signal the willingness of central Government departments to provide oral and written evidence to Parliamentary Committees on cross-cutting issues regardless of the terms of reference or ambit of the Committee', that the government should make available to select committees, 'at an early stage in the policy process, information about the factual and analytical basis of cross-cutting policies, including joint appraisals' and should be ready 'to agree to the appointment of *ad hoc*, cross-cutting Select Committees'.[172] In addition, it advised the government to 'welcome initiatives' by Parliament to have 'more hearings on cross-cutting policies and programmes, taking evidence jointly from responsible Ministers and/or Accounting Officers'.[173]

---

[168] Speech given by Sir Richard Wilson, *The Civil Service in the New Millennium* (Cabinet Office, 1999).

[169] *Modernising Government* (Cabinet Office, 1999).

[170] *Wiring it Up* (Cabinet Office, 2000), para. 10.4; and see also *Adding it Up* (Cabinet Office, 2000).

[171] Ibid., para. 2.4.

[172] Ibid., Conclusion 28.

[173] Ibid., Conclusion 29. A number of cross-cutting investigations have been heard. For example, the Education and Employment and Social Services Committees undertook a joint investigation into ONE, the single work-focused gateway to benefit, which involves

These recommendations suggest greater openness and a long overdue acceptance that policy information, as opposed to policy advice, should be open to scrutiny. As long ago as 1977, the head of the civil service, Lord Croham (then Sir Douglas Allen), wrote to the heads of departments: 'when policy studies are undertaken in future, the background material should as far as possible be written in a form which would permit it to be published separately'.[174] This has rarely happened. However, if the intention is to ensure the effective scrutiny of cross-cutting issues, the restriction on officials giving information on interdepartmental communications may need to be revised.[175] Moreover, ministers will have to be prepared to give evidence on their relevant responsibilities, 'regardless of their departmental label'.[176]

The report of the Performance and Innovation Unit, which included a statement from the prime minister that it 'formed a blue-print for action',[177] was warmly welcomed by the Liaison Committee, which, in turn, made recommendations to Parliament as to how committee membership and procedure could be modified to make cross-cutting committees effective. However, while stating that 'select committees must be able to adapt to the joined-up approach, which is an increasing priority within government',[178] it was concerned that joint inquiries should not interfere with other committee work, that is, with the responsibility of individual committees to hold particular departments to account. It would also seem important for the committees themselves to determine the inquiries they will undertake so that they do not become simply a mechanism by which the government forwards its agenda for managerial accountability. Arguments that accountability can better be secured through framework documents, that is, by holding agencies and departments accountable for their progress against objectives set by the government, have merit.[179] However, such accountability should sup-

---

the Department for Education and Employment, the Department of Social Security and their agencies—the Employment Service and the Benefits Agency—and local authorities. It invited responsible officials to attend a committee session together. See Education and Employment Committee, Sixth Report, *The One Service Pilots* (1998–9), HC 412.

[174] Croham Directive, 6 July 1977.

[175] *Departmental Evidence and Response to Select Committees*; 'Osmotherly Rules'.

[176] Liaison Committee, First Report, *Shifting the Balance: Select Committees and the Executive* (1999–2000), HC 300, para. 70.

[177] *Wiring it Up*, Foreword.

[178] HC 300, para. 66.

[179] Sir Christopher Foster, *Two Concepts of Accountability: Is a Bridge Possible between Them?* (Public Management and Policy Association, 2000).

plement, not replace, political accountability, which is concerned with wider issues, including the scrutiny of policy choices and outcomes and the overall supervision by the minister of his department.

The effectiveness of the convention

Throughout the twentieth century, the effectiveness of ministerial responsibility has been questioned, both in terms of ministers 'giving an account' and being 'held to account'. There has also been debate as to which of the strands of the convention is more important, although they are better understood as being interrelated and mutually supporting, the effectiveness of the convention in securing 'an account', depending on there being a sanction by which erring ministers can be held 'to account'. The problem lies in making the threat of imposing this sanction, namely resignation, meaningful.

With Parliament dominated by the executive, its ability to force a resignation is minimal. In 1996, in recognition of its impotence, the Public Service Committee sought to transfer the responsibility for ministerial behaviour from the House to the prime minister, arguing: 'A Minister has to conduct himself and direct the work of his department in a manner likely to ensure that he retains the confidence both of his own party and of the House. It is for the Prime Minister to decide whom he chooses for Ministers; but the Prime Minister is unlikely to keep in office a Minister who does not retain the confidence of his Parliamentary colleagues.'[180] It also sought to make the prime minister responsible for ensuring that 'ministers live up to the standards required of them',[181] and, by so doing, echoed the recommendation of the Nolan Committee that the *Ministerial Code of Conduct* should stipulate that it was for the prime minister to determine whether or not ministers had upheld the highest standards.[182] The government had refused to implement the Nolan recommendation, on the basis that it went 'too far towards suggesting that the Prime Minister's relationship with his ministerial colleagues is that of invigilator and judge. And it would not reflect the responsibility that ministers should have to justify their conduct to Parliament.'[183] It also rejected the

---

[180] HC 313, para. 32.
[181] Ibid., para. 52.
[182] Committee on Standards in Public Life, *First Report*, Cm 2850-I (May 1995).
[183] Cm 2931.

Public Service Committee's recommendation.[184] Ministerial responsibility therefore remains dependent on the integrity of ministers and the co-operation of government for its operation.

The vibrancy of the convention—in respect of informatory, explanatory and amendatory responsibility—is not easy to measure, hence the tendency of those concerned about accountability to focus on resignations. However, a number of high-profile incidents[185] suggest that, during the twentieth century, the half-told story became a feature of British government. The control of information by government has meant that members of Parliament are often unable to challenge ministerial evasions and, despite the *Code of Practice on Access to Government Information* introduced in 1994, and the parliamentary resolution of 1997, greater openness cannot be assumed where parliamentary questions are concerned. Moreover, although the government agreed that 'reasons should invariably be given when information is being refused in response to a Parliamentary Question and that . . . these reasons should relate to the exemptions laid down in the Code',[186] the practice has not always been followed. Hence, in November 1999 the Public Administration Committee reported: 'We continue to be disappointed by this failure by many departments to adopt a practice accepted by the Government.'[187]

The implementation of a Freedom of Information Act should provide better access to information. Despite its limitations, any reduction in the government's control of information is likely to reinforce the requirements of explanation and justification, as MPs, armed with information gathered by their own endeavours and those of others, become better equipped to probe the processes and policies of government and the actions of both ministers and officials.[188] The Act may make it more difficult for ministers to hide behind the policy/operations division or to use the responsibility/accountability distinction to escape culpability. Conversely, it may expose the misdemeanours of officials more obviously, further undermining the notion that one of the functions of ministerial responsibility is to protect officials from public accountability.

While Freedom of Information legislation seems likely, in some

[184] HC 67, p. viii.
[185] For example, Westland (1986), sale of Rover (1989), 'Arms to Iraq' (1994).
[186] HC 67, pp. xv–xvi and see HC Deb., vol. 312, col. 82W, 12 May 1998.
[187] Public Administration Committee, Fourth Report, *Ministerial Accountability and Parliamentary Questions* (1998–9), HC 821.
[188] Public Administration Committee, Fourth Report, *Ministerial Accountability and Parliamentary Questions* (1997–8), HC 820, para. 15.

measure, to improve the workings of a convention, the purpose of which is frequently frustrated by government's control of information, the effect of devolving responsibilities to Scotland, Wales and Northern Ireland[189] is less certain. Accountability in the new legislatures should be better than at Westminster. They may gain from the absence of single-party government, and the ability of their members to hold those who exercise power to account is likely to be aided by their closeness to decision-making and the scale and nature of decisions. Certainly the inquiries undertaken by two Scottish parliamentary committees into the examination results crisis of the summer of 2000[190] were effective in securing the accountability constitutionally required, even to the extent that their convenors, although not other committee members, were given 'sight' of papers, containing the advice of officials to ministers.[191]

However, in other respects accountability may be confused. The Scotland Act, for instance, protects ministers against 'double accountability', that is having to answer in two different Parliaments for the same responsibility.[192] However, it does nothing to cater for situations where ministers from both Scotland and Westminster disclaim responsibility, the former on the basis that the matter is 'reserved', and thus for Westminster, and the latter on the grounds that it is a 'general responsibility' and thus falls within the remit of the Scottish Parliament.[193] Such a situation would create an accountability gap. This is recognised in government guidance to civil servants on accountability and devolution, which states: 'As a general principle, the UK government will normally answer UK Parliamentary Questions purely on devolved matters of fact by making it clear that such questions should be addressed to the relevant devolved administration.'[194] This is in line with a statement on the issue made by the speaker in the House of Commons[195] and accords with the general practice when issues for which a minister is indirectly responsible are raised. However, the guidance accepts that in some cases 'a clear distinc-

---

[189] Through the Scotland Act 1998, Government of Wales Act 1998 and Northern Ireland Act 1999.

[190] Education, Culture and Sports Committee, *Exam Results Inquiry* (2000), SP Paper 234; Enterprise and Lifelong Learning Committee, *Inquiry into the Governance of the Scottish Qualifying Authority* (2000), SP Paper 232.

[191] Scottish Parliament, *Official Report*, 13 December 2000, vol. 9, no. 9, col. 867.

[192] Scotland Act 1998, s. 23(B).

[193] Thus, for instance, agriculture is a general responsibility of the Scottish Parliament, but to the extent that it is affected by the common agricultural policy it is a reserved matter, coming under 'foreign affairs', and is therefore for Westminster.

[194] DGN 1 (Cabinet Office, 2000).

[195] HC Deb., 12 July 1999, cols 21–2.

tion between respective responsibilities may not be possible', for instance, where policy remains with the UK government but implementation lies with the devolved administration. In such cases it states: 'consultation between administrations will be necessary to determine handling'.[196] When the issues are non-controversial, consultation will no doubt lead to a satisfactory arrangement for accountability. However, where issues are politically contentious, protecting the minister may prove to be the priority and accountability will be the loser.

Ministerial responsibility may also be tested in other respects. The failure of any one party to secure control of the Scottish Parliament or the National Assembly for Wales in the elections of 1999 raised the prospect of censure motions being resurrected to force resignation. Such motions were a feature of the nineteenth-century Westminster Parliament but, as discussed above, the advent of majority governments and party discipline meant that they fell into disuse in the twentieth century.[197] In October 1999 a censure motion was passed by the National Assembly for Wales against the agriculture secretary. In the nineteenth century this would have resulted in immediate resignation. Indeed, the threat of a censure motion was sufficient for a minister to relinquish office.[198] However, this was not the case in the Welsh Assembly, where the agriculture secretary, backed by the first secretary, Alun Michael, refused to resign. Opposition members of the Assembly took no further action, preferring to focus their attention on the first secretary himself, who subsequently resigned in February 2000 immediately prior to a vote of no confidence. As a consequence, ministerial (or secretarial) responsibility to the Assembly remains unclear. In what circumstances is a secretary required to resign? If errant ministers can only be removed along with the rest of their colleagues on a vote of confidence in the administration, the principle that ministers (or secretaries) are individually accountable to Parliament (or Assemblies) collapses.[199]

---

[196] DGN 1.

[197] This contrasts with the Australian experience, where during the period 1976–89 there were forty-one censure motions, although all but one was lost: see B. Page, 'Ministerial Resignation and Individual Ministerial Responsibility in Australia 1976–89', *Journal of Commonwealth and Comparative Politics* (1990).

[198] Lord John Russell (1855) and Lord Ellenborough (1858) resigned without waiting for the vote to be taken.

[199] In 2000 the Scottish Parliament debated a motion of no confidence against Sam Galbraith. He had been minister for education at the time of the Scottish Qualifying Authority crisis, which had resulted in some students receiving wrong results, but had been moved to the Department of the Environment some two months later. The motion was not passed: Scottish Parliament, *Official Report*, 13 December 2000, col. 841.

Conclusion

The twentieth century saw 'the decay of imperfect but working conventions'.[200] The divisions between 'policy' and 'operations' and 'accountability' and 'responsibility' may suggest a rationalisation of ministerial responsibility, which is more realistic and thus more workable in an age of big and complex government. However, at the beginning of the twenty-first century, the convention is confused and contradictory. Indeed, it is no longer clear in what sense 'responsibility' is used. Ministers remain constitutionally responsible to Parliament but what this requires is uncertain. They must provide information and explanation but it seems acceptable for them to mislead the House, so long as this is not done 'knowingly'. They may abdicate responsibility for anything other than government policy, for which they are likely to be covered by collective responsibility; and blame officials when things go wrong. Governments may argue that the attachment of such blame relates to managerial not constitutional responsibility, but the distinction confuses, rather than clarifies, the convention of ministerial responsibility.

Yet changes in the structure of government, most notably the establishment of Next Steps agencies, provided an opportunity to rethink ministerial responsibility. The separation of ministerial and official responsibilities could give the convention greater clarity,[201] while the direct responsibility of chief executives to ministers should mean that ministers are better able to exercise a supervisory responsibility. However, the insistence of governments of both political persuasions, that officials speak on behalf of ministers and not on their own behalf, has done nothing to illuminate ministerial responsibility and much to cast suspicion over governments' motives. Indeed, the convention at times has been used to provide protection for ministers, with Parliament, by its failure to insist on meaningful accountability, conniving in the use of ministerial responsibility for this purpose. Allowing officials to be constitutionally responsible, in terms of speaking before select committees on their own behalf for those responsibilities delegated to them, would not undermine ministerial responsibility, as ministers have

---

[200] Sir Christopher Foster, 'Reflections on the True Significance of the Scott Report for Government Accountability', *Public Administration* (1996).

[201] This may particularly be the case where framework agreements are renegotiated, for example the Prison Service's agreement was renegotiated in 1999 to make responsibilities clearer. There are now two levels of supervision—a strategy board and a management board.

claimed—policy advice, for instance, could still be protected—but, together with the Freedom of Information Act and the greater emphasis on providing Parliament with information, it could contribute to a more open interpretation of the convention, in which the myth that ministers are involved in the detail of departmental administration would be laid to rest and the role of the minister would be recognised as supervisory. Accountability would therefore be more realistic and honest, according more readily with the constitutional and managerial reforms of government, which took place in the final decades of the twentieth century.

For more than a century, ministerial responsibility has underpinned Britain's constitutional arrangements and the Westminster system of government. It has provided the rationale for the institutional structure of government and the basis for political relationships. The strength of the doctrine lies in its theoretical contribution to the democratic process, whereby it provides political accountability. Its weakness lies in the execution of the theory, in the gap between the expectation of accountable government and the reality. The existence of such a gap is perhaps inevitable, given that the convention operates in the political context and is, to an extent, aspirational. It is a mixture of description and prescription and, as such, contains principles with which ministers usually comply and those with which they should, but often do not. It also contains an inherent tension, for it not only provides the mechanism by which ministers are accountable to Parliament but, by its nature, elevates the ministerial role and ensures executive rather than parliamentary government. Thus, even if the balance between the executive and Parliament is redressed, political accountability will still be imperfect and, on occasions, disappointing and the effectiveness of ministerial responsibility will therefore continue to be questioned. This does not mean that its importance should be downplayed or that it is redundant for, in a system where powers are vested in ministers, political accountability is essential. The challenge for the new millennium is how to ensure that, despite its imperfections and contradictions, the convention of ministerial responsibility plays a meaningful part in securing that accountability which is constitutionally required.

Bibliography

Official documents

Report of the Machinery of Government Committee (Chairman, Lord Haldane), Cd 9230 (1918).

Report from the Public Inquiry into the Disposal of Land at Crichel Down, Cmnd 9176 (1954).

Report of the Committee on the Civil Service (Chairman, Lord Fulton), Cmnd 3638 (1968), vol. 1.

Report of the Tribunal of Inquiry on the Vehicle and General Insurance Company (1971–2), HC 133.

Report on Non-departmental Public Bodies, Cmnd 7797 (1980).

Memorandum of Guidance for Officials Appearing before Select Committees, Gen. 80/38 (1980), superseded by *Departmental Evidence and Response to Select Committees* (Cabinet Office, 1997).

Report by a Commission of Privy Councillors, *Falkland Islands Review*, Cmnd 878 (1983).

Report on Security Arrangements at the Maze Prison (Sir James Hennessy) (1984), HC 203.

Defence Committee, *The Defence Implications of the Future of Westland plc* (1985–6), HC 518.

Defence Committee, *The Defence Implications of the Future of Westland plc* (1985–6), HC 169, Minutes of Evidence and Appendices.

Defence Committee, Fourth Report, *Westland plc: The Government's Decision-making* (1985–6), HC 519.

The Government's Response to the Fourth Report from the Defence Committee on Westland plc; The Defence Implications of the Future of Westland plc: The Government's Decision-making, Cmnd 9916 (1986).

Treasury and Civil Service Committee, *First Report* (1986–7), HC 62.

Government's Response to the First Report of the Treasury and Civil Service Committee (HC 62) and to the First Report of the Liaison Committee (HC 100), Cmnd 78 (1986–7).

Efficiency Unit, *Improving Management in Government: The Next Steps: Report to the Prime Minister* (1988).

Treasury and Civil Service Committee, *Developments in the Next Steps Programme* (1988–9), HC 348.

Agriculture Committee, First Report, *Salmonella in Eggs* (1988–9), HC 108-I.

Trade and Industry Committee, *Sale of Rover Group to British Aerospace* (1990–1), HC 34.

Treasury and Civil Service Committee, *Role of the Civil Service* (1993–4), HC 27-I.

Sir John Woodcock, *Report on the Escape from Whitemoor Prison*, Cm 2741 (1994).

Social Security Committee, First Report, *The Operation of the Child Support Act* (1993–4), HC 69.

Select Committee on the Parliamentary Commissioner for Administration, Third Report, *The Child Support Agency* (1994–5), HC 199.

Committee on Standards in Public Life, *First Report*, Cm 2850-I (May 1995).

Report of the Inquiry into the Export of Defence Equipment and Dual-use Goods to Iraq and Related Prosecutions (Chairman, Sir Richard Scott) (1995–6), HC 115.

Public Service Committee, *Ministerial Accountability and Responsibility* (1995–6), HC 313.

Civil Service Code (Cabinet Office, 1996).

Public Service Committee, First Special Report, *Government's Response to the Second Report from the Committee (1995–6) on Ministerial Accountability and Responsibility* (1996–7), HC 67.

Ministerial Code: A Code of Conduct and Guidance on Procedures for Ministers (Cabinet Office, 1997).

Resolution of Parliament, HC Deb., 19 March 1997, cols 1046–7.

Public Administration Committee, Fourth Report, *Ministerial Accountability and Parliamentary Questions* (1997–8), HC 820.

Public Administration Committee, Fourth Report, *Ministerial Accountability and Parliamentary Questions* (1998–9), HC 821.

Foreign Affairs Committee, Second Report, *Sierra Leone* (1998–9), HC 116-I.

The Government's Response to the Foreign Affairs Committee Report, Cm 4325 (1999).

Sir Richard Wilson, *The Civil Service in the New Millennium* (Cabinet Office, 1999).

Modernising Government (Cabinet Office, 1999).

Performance and Innovation Unit, *Wiring it Up* (Cabinet Office, 2000).

Performance and Innovation Unit, *Adding it Up* (Cabinet Office, 2000).

Liaison Committee, First Report, *Shifting the Balance: Select Committees and the Executive* (1999–2000), HC 300.

Education, Culture and Sports Committee, *Exam Results Inquiry* (2000), SP Paper 234.

Enterprise and Lifelong Learning Committee, *Inquiry into the Governance of the Scottish Qualifying Authority* (2000), SP Paper 232.

Books and articles

Anson, Sir William, *Law and Custom of the Constitution*, 4th edn (Clarendon Press, 1935).

Barberis Peter, 'The New Public Management and a New Accountability', *Public Administration* (1998).

Barker, Anthony (ed.), *Quangos in Britain* (Macmillan, 1982).

Barker, Anthony, 'Political Responsibility for UK Prison Security: Ministers Escape Again', *Public Administration* (1998).

Birch, A. H., *Representative and Responsible Government* (Allen & Unwin, 1964).

Bogdanor, Vernon, 'Ministerial Accountability', in B. Thompson and F. F. Ridley, *Under the Scott-light: British Government seen through the Scott Report* (Oxford University Press, 1997).

Boyle, Lord of Handsworth, 'Address to the Royal Institute of Public Administration', *Public Administration* (1980).

Finer, S. E., 'The Individual Responsibility of Ministers', *Public Administration* (1956).

Foster, Sir Christopher, 'Reflections on the True Significance of the Scott Report for Government Accountability', *Public Administration* (1996).

Foster, Sir Christopher, *Two Concepts of Accountability: Is a Bridge Possible between Them?* (Public Management and Policy Association, 2000).

331

Fry, Geoffrey K., 'The Sachsenhausen Concentration Camp Case and the Convention of Individual Ministerial Responsibility', *Public Law* (1970).

Griffith, J. A. G., 'Comment on Crichel Down', *Contemporary Record* (1987).

Jennings, Sir Ivor, *The Law and the Constitution*, 5th edn (Cambridge University Press, 1959).

Jennings, Sir Ivor, *Cabinet Government*, 3rd edn (Cambridge University Press, 1961).

Johnson Nevil, *In Search of the Constitution* (Pergamon, 1977).

Keir, D. L., *The Constitutional History of Modern Britain*, 9th edn (Black, 1969).

Lewis, N. and Longley, D., 'Ministerial Responsibility: The Next Steps', *Public Law* (1996).

Mackintosh, J. P., *The British Cabinet* (Stevens, 1962).

Maitland, F. W., *The Constitutional History of England* (Cambridge University Press, 1908).

Marshall, Geoffrey and Moodie, Graeme, *Some Problems of the Constitution* (Hutchinson, 1959).

Marshall, Geoffrey, *Constitutional Conventions* (Clarendon Press, 1984).

Marshall, Geoffrey (ed.), *Ministerial Responsibility* (Oxford University Press, 1989).

Marshall, Geoffrey, 'Parliamentary Accountability', *Parliamentary Affairs* (1991).

Mather, Graham, 'Clarifying Responsibility and Accountability', in *Government Accountability* (CIPFA, 1996).

Morrison, Herbert, *Government and Parliament* (Oxford University Press, 1954).

Nicolson, I. F., *The Mystery of Crichel Down* (Oxford University Press, 1986).

Oliver, D. and Austin, R., 'Political and Constitutional Aspects of the Westland Affair', *Parliamentary Affairs* (1987).

Oliver, D. and Drewry, G., *Public Service Reforms: Issues of Accountability and Public Law* (Pinter, 1996).

Robinson, A., Shepherd, R., Ridley, F. F. and Jones, G. W., 'Symposium on Ministerial Responsibility', *Public Administration* (1987).

Scott, Sir Richard, 'Ministerial Accountability', in *Government Accountability* (CIPFA, 1996).

Scott, Sir Richard, 'Ministerial Accountability', *Public Law* (1996).

Theakston, K., *Junior Ministers in British Government* (Blackwell, 1987).

Tomkins, A., *The Constitution after Scott* (Clarendon Press, 1998).

Turpin, C., 'Ministerial Responsibility; Myth or Reality?', in J. Jowell and D. Oliver (eds), *The Changing Constitution*, 3rd edn (Oxford University Press, 1994).

Woodhouse, D., 'When do Ministers Resign?', *Parliamentary Affairs* (1993).

Woodhouse, D., *Ministers and Parliament: Accountability in Theory and Practice* (Clarendon Press, 1994).

Woodhouse, D., 'Ministerial Responsibility; Something Old, Something New', *Public Law* (1997).

9.
Government and the Judiciary
ROBERT STEVENS

For much of the twentieth century the judiciary has been thought of more as a dignified than an effective element in the constitution.[1] In part this categorisation is justified. The courts have an important role in the modern social or welfare state as the result of their responsibility for the maintenance of internal order, whether that is through their work in the criminal law or through the work of the civil courts in regulating markets. Historically, however, there is a residual but, in the end, more important remit for the courts, namely their role—and thus that of the judges—in the constitution. The twentieth century has been important in reminding the country of this residual jurisdiction.

No one doubted this constitutional function in the seventeenth century where the lawyers and the judges from Coke through *Ship Money* under Charles I to the *Bankers* case in the reign of William III were seen as allies of Parliament in resisting the Crown. The judges were also important players in the political arguments which underlay the intellectual bases of the Bill of Rights and the Act of Settlement. Indeed, if one stops the clock in 1701, the Act of Settlement not only provided independence and constitutional protection for the judiciary, but excluded the executive from sitting in the House of Commons. The separation of powers bore a lineal relationship to the concept incorporated in the United States constitution some ninety years later, although in 1701 the parliamentarians were more interested in protecting judges from royal influence rather than from parliamentary influence,[2] and

---

[1] The British constitution is served by three legal systems: England, Ireland (after 1922 Northern Ireland) and Scotland. This chapter is primarily about the English constitution and courts although the analysis is generally true of the other jurisdictions. Both Ireland and Northern Ireland, while common law jurisdictions, are inevitably influenced by the politics of those jurisdictions. Scotland has the additional element of being a civilian jurisdiction.
[2] David Lemmings, 'The Independence of the Judiciary in Eighteenth Century England', in *The Life of the Law*, ed. Peter Birks (Hambledon, 1993), p. 125.

rapidly abandoned the exclusion of placemen from the House of Commons.

The King's Council, which by then had been transformed into the Privy Council, had only limited functional specialisation, although legislature and judiciary had emerged without totally severing their links. The effort in 1701 to keep the executive out of the lower House was a step too far; by the time of the Offices of Profit Act in 1705, placeholders were back in the House of Commons and, by the 1720s, a partially non-resident and largely non-English-speaking monarch allowed a surprisingly modern form of Cabinet government, with Walpole as a relatively contemporary looking prime minister. With some perturbations during the reign of George III, the modern form of responsible government had been born.

The shadow of the Great Council was still there, however; the senior judge, the Lord Chancellor still presided in the House of Lords, which remained the final appeal court; Chief Justices Mansfield and Ellenborough sat in the Cabinet. Indeed, the concern was that Mansfield was far more politician than judge,[3] while Ellenborough was to be a force for reaction in the Cabinet waging war against Napoleon. The judges still received a call to Parliament; until the reign of George III, they had to be reappointed whenever there was a new monarch and such necessity sometimes led to non-renewal. Meanwhile lay peers voted in legal appeals to the Lords as late as 1844, while High Court judges still had a role in private members' bills. In the first half of the nineteenth century Denman and Campbell were active politicians and both had agreed to accept chief justiceships at salaries below that provided by statute.[4] It was perhaps not surprising that, in this privileged position, the utilitarian reforms in the nineteenth century, while they affected the courts, left the judges largely untouched.

In private law, the judges played a vital role in keeping the common law up to date. Mansfield brought modern mercantile law into the courts. His successors wrestled with the changes necessary to adapt medieval forms of action to the regulation of an economy undergoing the Industrial Revolution. Some public law or political issues the judiciary could not avoid in the eighteenth century—the *North Britain* outlawed the general warrant and *Somersett's* case probably outlawed slavery. By the end of

---

[3] Lemmings, 'The Independence of the Judiciary', p. 145.
[4] Robert Stevens, *The Independence of the Judiciary: The View from the Lord Chancellor's Office* (Clarendon Press, 1993), p. 50.

George III's reign, however, the courts' role in public law or political issues was declining. As Britain moved from oligarchy to democracy, and as utilitarianism and then liberalism became the fashionable order of the day, the Reform Acts of 1832, 1867 and 1884 (work completed with the enfranchisement of women in 1918 and 1928) made it appear increasingly inappropriate for the judiciary to intrude into the public law arena.

The Edwardian era

If one were to stop the clock in 1900, however, it would not have been obvious that the transformation to a depoliticised judiciary had occurred. The second Home Rule bill of 1893 and the decline of the Liberals in the 1890s left the Lord Chancellorship in the hands of Lord Halsbury who, in many ways, was the type of Tory who had thrived a hundred years earlier. Both in terms of appointments and decisions Halsbury saw the senior judiciary as part of a system of spoils that Prime Minister Walpole or President Jackson would have understood. The partial depoliticisation under Hatherley, Cairns, Selborne and Herschell in the 1860s, 1870s and 1880s had been quietly abandoned.

To Halsbury it seemed entirely normal that undistinguished Conservative backbenchers with indifferent practices at the Bar, should be appointed to the High Court bench. It was a view that was supported by Halsbury's prime minister, Salisbury:

> It is . . . the unwritten law of our party system; and there is no clearer statute in that unwritten law than the rule that party claims should always weigh very heavily in the disposal of the highest legal appointments. In dealing with them you cannot ignore the party system as you do in the choice of a general or an archbishop. It would be a breach of the tacit convention on which politicians and lawyers have worked the British Constitution together for the last two-hundred years.[5]

Assuming that Salisbury's view of the constitution was the correct one,[6] Halsbury fulfilled the expectation.

From the point of view of the Conservative Party there was logic to this position. Conservatives were not committed to the separation of powers; and they were ambivalent about the balance of powers. The

[5] R. F. V. Heuston, *Lives of the Lord Chancellors 1885–1940* (Clarendon Press, 1964), p. 52.
[6] On this see now Andrew Roberts, *Salisbury: Victorian Titan* (Weidenfeld & Nicolson, 1999), p. 684.

Salisbury–Halsbury wing of the party had re-established the House of Lords as the final appeal court, with the law lords sitting in the legislature, in the 1870s because, in Salisbury's words, since 'practically they have often to make law as judges, they will do it all the better from having also to make it as legislators'.[7] Political peers—although no longer those without legal training—still made up the quorum in panels in the Lords and the Privy Council. The attorney-general was still thought to have the right of reversion to the chief justiceship. The mystique of the King's Council was still not dead.

Halsbury was not, however, totally unaffected by the political philosophy of the times. Albert Venn Dicey's spirit was increasingly dominating legal thought. At least as expounded in his *Introduction to the Study of the Law of the Constitution* (1885), Dicey praised the absence of a distinctive constitutional and administrative law in England— arguing that the common law was sufficiently strong to protect citizens' rights and to hold individuals personally liable for administrative acts.[8] Moreover, in propounding his concept of the rule of law, Dicey seemed to leave no room for judicial discretion or creativity. This position was, in so many ways, the flowering of utilitarian thought, far closer to Austin than to Maine, superficially at variance with the Halsbury style. An intellectual state of mind which had led to reform of the franchise, the court structure and the civil service, left an intellectual tradition of mechanical formalism in substantive law. Democracy was to be protected by Acts of Parliament, but not by the judges.[9] This interpretation of Dicey's concept of the rule of law was to dominate legal thinking until the 1960s and to be important throughout the twentieth century.[10] A

---

[7] Robert Stevens, *Law and Politics: The House of Lords as a Judicial Body 1800–1976* (University of North Carolina Press, 1978), p. 55.

[8] See A. V. Dicey, *Law of the Constitution* (Macmillan, 1885), ch. 12.

[9] Richard A. Cosgrove, *The Rule of Law: Albert Venn Dicey, Victorian Jurist* (Macmillan, 1980), see especially chs 4 and 5.

[10] The irony was that by the end of his life Dicey had resiled from his earlier position. In 1898, in lectures delivered at Harvard (published in 1905 as *Lectures on the Relation between Law and Public Opinion in England during the Nineteenth Century*), Dicey expressed some alarm about the 'growth in collectivism'. And, whereas in 1885 he had talked of judge-made law in the past tense, by 1905 he assumed it was very much alive. By then, jurisprudentially, he accepted that 'the best part of the law of England is judge-made law . . . Nor let anyone imagine that judicial legislation is a kind of law-making which belongs wholly to the past, and which has been put an end to by the annual meetings and the legislative activity of modern Parliaments.' In fact by this time Dicey had given up his unqualified enthusiasm for parliamentary sovereignty, the rule of law and democracy. He by then welcomed the fact that judges are 'for the most part persons of a conservative disposition'.

Harold Laski or Ivor Jennings might rail against the canon, but Dicey ruled.

Dicey was, however, right that the judges could be relied on for a Conservative spirit. Halsbury had ensured that the High Court was overstocked with Conservative MPs manqués, but he also appointed Conservative lords of appeal. While Loreburn, when he became Lord Chancellor with the Liberal government in 1905, sought to lessen the importance of politics in appointments to the High Court bench, politics remained important in appointing lords of appeal. Under the Liberals, Lord Shaw, the lord advocate, and Lord Robson, the English attorney-general, were both appointed lords of appeal, for, as Robson put it, the Lords were handling 'disputes that are legal in form but political in fact'. He added: 'it would be idle to deny the resolute bias of many of the judges—there and elsewhere'.[11] It all sounded a little like Tocqueville writing of the new United States a hundred years earlier.

The interaction of utilitarianism, high toryism, and the collectivism of a Lib–Lab administration produced fascinating juxtapositions in decisions in the final court of appeal. Lord Halsbury had developed in *London Street Tramways* v. *London County Council* (1898) what appeared to be a formalistic view of *stare decisis*: 'a decision of the House once given upon a point of law is conclusive upon this House afterwards, and that it is impossible to raise that question again'.[12] Or as Halsbury announced in the *Earldom of Norfolk Peerage* case (1907): 'to alter it [the law] or even modify it is the function of the Legislature and not of your Lordships' House'.[13] Yet, while Halsbury seemed anxious to endorse a declaratory formalistic theory of law, that claim may have been more a political statement than at first sight appears. He did not hesitate to manipulate the composition of panels in the House of Lords, whether the matter was Scottish ecclesiastical history or charities.[14]

Halsbury had, however, more important matters to address. *Allen* v. *Flood*[15] was the first in a series of cases whereby he sought to weaken

---

He admired the *Taff Vale* decision and was shocked by the legislative politics of home rule for Ireland. Yet, it was his position on parliamentary sovereignty, based on a democratic franchise and the rule of law, defining a formalistic role for the judges, which dominated the twentieth century. Stevens, *Law and Politics*, p. 104.

[11] Heuston, *Lives 1885–1940*, p. 151.

[12] [1898] AC 375, 379.

[13] [1907] AC 10.12.

[14] See *General Assembly of Free Church of Scotland* v. *Lord Overtoun* [1904] AC 515 (Scot.); *IRC* v. *Pemsel* [1891] AC 531. See also Stevens, *Law and Politics*, pp. 87–8.

[15] [1898] AC 1 (1897).

the unions. The Court of Appeal held there was a tort of conspiracy where the unions pressed for the sacking of a worker even where no breach of contract was involved. In the Lords, Halsbury found that only two persons in the panel of seven law lords were willing to support him and uphold the decision of the Court of Appeal. Without consultation, he then called up the High Court judges to appear before the law lords and offer their advice—a constitutional device not used since the reform of the courts in the 1870s. Since many of the judges had been appointed for their Tory views, it is scarcely surprising that six of the eight sided with Halsbury. The law lords were not impressed. Of the nine law lords sitting, six voted to overrule the Court of Appeal.[16]

The point of law was, however, rapidly resurrected. Three years later, *Quinn* v. *Leatham*[17] raised the issue of whether *Allen* v. *Flood* had made all boycotting illegal. This time Halsbury chose the hearing panel more carefully—excluding the Liberals and including the Conservatives. Moreover Halsbury appeared to go back on the jurisprudential implications of *London Street Tramway*, announcing: 'A case is only authority for what it actually decides. I entirely deny it can be quoted for a proposition which may appear to flow logically from it.' Halsbury won this time, admitting it was a policy decision;[18] but he had more in store for the unions. In 1901 in *Taff Vale Railway* v. *Amalgamated Society of Railway Servants*, the Court of Appeal had held that an injunction was not available against the threat of a strike nor could the officers of the union be personally responsible for damages flowing from such a strike. Halsbury once again chose the House of Lords panel carefully and, to the horror of the unions, the Court of Appeal was overruled. The Lords decision in *Taff Vale*[19] drove many unions into affiliation with the Labour Party and was a significant element in the Liberal landslide of 1906.[20]

It was this election that helped change the form and substance of the English judiciary. From 1905 to 1915 the Lord Chancellorship was in the hands of Loreburn and Haldane. They were very much politicians, but politicians who saw that the Halsbury system could not survive in a democratic society, particularly one in which political power—at least a meaningful part of it—had passed to the working classes. It was necessary to remove the judges from trade union law and to keep them

---

[16] Stevens, *Law and Politics*, pp. 92–4.
[17] [1901] AC 495 (Ire.).
[18] Stevens, *Law and Politics*, pp. 93–4.
[19] [1901] AC 426.
[20] Stevens, *Law and Politics*, pp. 94–6.

out of the proposed welfare state. As a way of protecting the judiciary, the more formalistic view of the common law, which could be traced back to the reform of law, procedure and the courts between the 1850s and the 1870s, was re-emphasised. The more judges could appear to have no control over the outcome of decisions, the less the newly empowered Left could complain. Initially, however, it was the new legislation that attracted attention.

The Trade Disputes Act 1906, putting the unions to a very large extent outside the law, horrified Halsbury, who, in the legislative debates announced: 'the Bill is most unjust . . . it is contrary to the spirit of English liberty . . . [it was a] Bill for the purpose of legalising tyranny'.[21] The new Liberal Lord Chancellor Loreburn, however, was determined to see that the new legislation was interpreted neutrally and this was significantly achieved in 1909, *Conway* v. *Wade*.[22] While the more conservative law lords hit back by striking down the mandatory political levy that same year in *Amalgamated Society of Railway Servants* v. *Osborne*,[23] the government took legislative action to restore the power of the unions to raise funds for political purposes in the Trade Union Act 1913. Halsbury's legacy—and the reaction to it—was not a happy one as the country began to build a welfare state. Lloyd George, as the responsible minister, carefully excluded the judges from the National Insurance bill and related legislation, while the home secretary Winston Churchill told the House of Commons in 1911 that 'where class issues are involved . . . a very large number of our population have been led to the opinion that they [the judges] are, unconsciously no doubt, biased'.[24] A combination of legislation, self-protection and a change in legal style was removing courts and judges from the political arena.

Dicey had seen the absence of administrative law as a separate system as one of the great advantages of the English legal system; Loreburn and

---

[21] HL Deb., 4th series, vol. 166, col. 704, 4 December 1906. While Halsbury's response was an overreaction, the unhappy history of union disruption of the British economy was not unrelated to the 1906 Act.

[22] [1909] AC 506.

[23] [1910] AC 87 (1909).

[24] HC Deb., 5th series, vol. 26, col. 1022, 30 May 1914. In that same year, Churchill was reported in a TUC document to have said: 'statements have been made from the bench reflecting on the trade unions in language which is extremely ignorant and wholly out of touch with the general development of modern thought, and which has greatly complicated the administration of justice and created a sense of distrust in the ordinary administration of the law'. Stevens, *Law and Politics*, p. 97. See also David Pannick, *Judges* (Oxford University Press, 1988), ch. 2, 'Expertise and Bias'.

Haldane worked to ensure that the elements of administrative law would be excised. Lord Loreburn, who had a practical sense of politics denied to Haldane, set a balanced tone in *Board of Education* v. *Rice* in 1911[25] where he drew a distinction between procedural due process ('natural justice') where the courts had a vital role, and substantive due process, where the courts had none.[26] Haldane, who became Lord Chancellor in 1912, with a reputation of being more intellectual and, in theory at least, more of a radical than Loreburn, nevertheless destroyed the rational distinction in *Rice* in the case of *Local Government Board* v. *Arlidge*.[27] Haldane put together a panel of law lords, all of whom had been active Liberal politicians. As Lord Shaw put it, to require even procedural due process 'would be inconsistent, as I say, with efficiency, with practice, and with the true theory of complete parliamentary responsibility for departmental action . . . that the judiciary should presume to impose its own methods on administrative or executive officers is a usurpation'.[28] By denying the courts even a limited role protecting procedural due process, British administrative law was to sleep for the next fifty years.[29]

The idea of a cofidied constitution, or even fundamental laws, by which executive or legislative decisions might be judged, was alien to both the royal prerogative and parliamentary sovereignty. It is an absence which confuses—or mystifies—North American and continental lawyers, as well as being frustrating to some British reformers. The closest the English legal system came to a flirtation with such ideas was the Judicial Committee of the Privy Council which had taken on a new lease of life with the expansion of the British Empire in the nineteenth century. It was given even greater prominence as the dominions came into being, with British statutes serving as written constitutions in Canada in 1867, Australia in 1900, New Zealand in 1907 and South Africa in 1909. The sad thing was that the British judges showed little flair for constitutional matters and, from 1900 onwards, each successive imperial conference complained about the casual staffing of the Judicial Committee and the failure of the law lords to comprehend the nature of constitutional decisions.

It is perhaps not surprising that while the British North America Act

---

[25] [1911] AC 179.

[26] Stevens, *Law and Politics*, pp. 178–9.

[27] [1915] AC 120 (1914).

[28] Ibid., 137–8.

[29] And for this Dicey must take a significant share of the blame. Cosgrove, *The Rule of Law*, ch. 5.

(the Canadian constitution) allowed appeals in all matters, the Commonwealth of Australia Act restricted constitutional appeals and the South Africa Act virtually excluded them. The royal prerogative and parliamentary sovereignty had so permeated thinking that the idea that a parliamentary statute might be unconstitutional—the basis of the new dominions' constitutions—eluded some of the British judges. In *Webb* v. *Outrim*, an Australian appeal in 1906, Halsbury, faced with judicial review in the American sense—that is the ability to strike down statutes—recoiled in horror: 'That is a novelty to me. I thought an Act of Parliament was an Act of Parliament and you cannot go beyond it . . . I do not know what an unconstitutional act means.'[30] Halsbury therefore refused to listen to arguments based on American precedents going back to *Marbury* v. *Madison*. Even those law lords who were more conscious of the realities had little sense of the niceties of the organic nature of constitutions.

The war to end all wars, economic strife and the long weekend

Under Loreburn and Haldane then, Liberal Party policy came to be that High Court and Court of Appeal judges were appointed on the basis of success at the Bar to the general exclusion of party affiliation—a remarkable switch in which success in a private profession (albeit determined by a politician) was substituted for political claims. This policy was in general pursued by their Conservative successors, although political experience was still thought appropriate for law lords in the final court of appeal—witness the appointment of the Irish Protestant and Unionist politician Carson by Lloyd George. Lord Chancellors, however, remained very much politicians, presiding in the Lords as a legislative body, sitting in the Cabinet, running the Lord Chancellor's Office and still sitting frequently—some of them—as judges in both Lords and Privy Council. With the exception of the few politically weak Lord Chancellors, it was they who set the judicial tone.[31]

---

[30] [1907] AC 81 (Aus. 1906). And, on the quote, see Stevens, *Law and Politics*, p. 181.

[31] The chief justiceship was also used politically. Indeed, when that devious prime minister David Lloyd George was looking, in 1921, for a 'temporary' lord chief justice to 'stand in' until Sir Gordon Hewart, the attorney-general, was ready to take over, the job went to A. T. Lawrence (created Lord Trevethin)—yet another of Halsbury's dubious appointments to the High Court bench. It was perhaps not surprising that Lawrence gave Lloyd George

Outside the Privy Council, however, the public law element in the courts was increasingly irrelevant. *Arlidge* and *Rice* had left very little of English administrative law. In 1931, *Minister of Health* v. *R. ex p. Yaffé*[32] confirmed that this was the situation. Increasingly, delegated legislation operated under 'Henry VIII clauses', which, frequently coupled with clauses preventing challenges in the courts, meant that it was sacrosanct. Defects in an order once confirmed by a minister were automatically cured There was also a wide range of discretionary acts based on the exercise of the royal prerogative, which the courts were reluctant to question, as they were those of most administrative tribunals. Dicey's vision of a legal system devoid of administrative law was close to being accepted, but in the English context it meant that control of the administration was left to the vagaries of the parliamentary question rather than systematic control by the courts.

While the judges had been primarily responsible for the tepid state of UK administrative law, this did not prevent the chief justice, Lord Hewart, a former Liberal attorney-general, from complaining bitterly about the state of affairs, for example, in his book *The New Despotism* (1929). He detected 'a long-standing plot (hatched among part of the civil service and fostered by Royal Commissions) to alter the position of the judiciary'.[33] The civil service felt the pressure. Sir Claud Schuster, the powerful permanent secretary of the Lord Chancellor's Office, complained: 'In recent years . . . it has been difficult for the State to obtain justice from the judges of the High Court. It is not too much to say that in recent years, the weight of prejudice against the State in the minds of many members of the Court of Appeal and judges of the High Court has been such as seriously to affect the administration of justice.'[34] The conflict ultimately led to the establishment of the Committee on Ministers' Powers in 1929, which reported in 1932 (Cmd 4060).

The committee not surprisingly found that since 1905 an increasing amount of social legislation excluded the jurisdiction of the courts entirely, while disputes under such legislation were handled by tribunals outside the scope of the regular courts. Rather than urge reconciliation, however, the committee blessed the dichotomy between legal decisions

---

an undated letter of resignation and read of his own resignation in *The Times* the following year—1922—when the coalition collapsed. Stevens, *Independence of the Judiciary*, pp. 30–9.
[32] [1931] AC 494.
[33] Stevens, *Law and Politics*, p. 193.
[34] Stevens, *Independence of the Judiciary*, p. 27.

(the rightful province of the regular courts) and policy decisions (the domain of the executive and tribunals). It was Dicey's original concept of the rule of law carried to the outer limit. The committee apparently had no doubt that a line could be drawn between a judicial decision 'which disposes of the whole matter by a finding upon the facts in dispute and an application of the law of the land to the facts so found' and a quasi-judicial situation (not appropriate for the judges) where such process was replaced by 'administrative action' that might involve 'consideration of public policy' or 'discretion'. The report assumed the objectivity of legal rules and the feasibility of interpreting statutes 'impartially'.[35] Formalism (and in particular the declaratory theory of law) had achieved public and political respectability.

It was, in short, a sad period in British history and a petulant period for the judiciary. While deferring to the legislature—as Dicey had decreed[36]—the judges seethed. While Dicey demanded such deference, they retained the right to declare delegated legislation *ulta vires*. With the bloody memory of the First World War fading, in *Roberts* v. *Hopwood*,[37] the law lords struck down, with speeches loaded with class assumptions, Poplar council's minimum wage of £4 per week. As Harold Laski observed, the decision might be 'fatal to the esteem in which judges should be held ... It is an easy step from the *Poplar* judgment to the conclusion that the House of Lords is, in entire good faith, the unconscious servant of a single class in the community.'[38] The judiciary appeared increasingly out of touch with an England which was rent by class divides and economically in decline. The situation was not helped when Mr Justice Astbury decided that the General Strike was illegal.[39]

---

[35] 'Not only the ideas but the language of Dicey spiced the report; *Law of the Constitution* permeated every page. The Donoughmore Committee, as it was known, cited Dicey favourably so often that Sir Cecil Carr remarked that the committee investigated whether Britain had gone off the Dicey standard in regard to administrative law and, if so, what was the quickest way to return. The committee accepted Dicey as gospel, inquiring whether his constitutional teachings were being betrayed by delegated legislation heretics. In particular, the committee embraced Dicey's antithesis between *droit administratif* and English law. "In our opinion Professor Dicey's conclusion is no less true than it was in 1915." Recommendation XI of the Report exhorted that no system of administrative law in any guise should be established in England.' Cosgrove, *The Rule of Law*, pp. 95–6.

[36] Parliamentary sovereignty, said Dicey, was 'the dominant characteristic of our political institutions'. Dicey, *Law of the Constitution*, p. 71.

[37] [1925] AC 578.

[38] Stevens, *Law and Politics*, p. 204.

[39] *National Sailors and Firemen's Union of Great Britain* v. *Reed* [1926], ch. 536. J. A. G. Griffith, *Judicial Politics since 1920* (Blackwell, 1993), pp. 11–15.

As if to confirm the class basis of the appeal judges, the House of Lords, which under Loreburn had sought to take a balanced approach to tax statutes, became caught up with the idea that tax statutes must be construed narrowly to protect civil liberties. The high point of this was *IRC v. Duke of Westminster* (1935)[40] where the House of Lords, over the objections of Lord Atkin who wished to look to the substance of the transaction, held that by a series of formal arrangements the duke might pay his servants out of untaxed income. For the next forty years, Britain, even in the period of 'socialistic' taxation, was able to provide a way for the wealthy, with good tax advisers, to avoid much of their tax burden.

In that tawdry atmosphere, it was perhaps not surprising that the judges were not minded to join in the general sacrifice expected of all civil servants during the Depression. When the National Economy Act was passed in 1931, judges' salaries were cut. Stanley Baldwin, as lord president of the Council, unwisely wrote to the judges that he had not consulted them because 'it seemed to me best . . . to rely on the patriotism of the eminent and patriotic body to which you belong and to assume their acquiescence'. The judges had a legitimate concern; as Mr Justice Maugham put it, perhaps unfortunately, they had been treated 'as if they were policemen or postmen'. The judges published a memorandum and threatened a petition of right to challenge the cuts. The government understandably worried about who would hear the petition. In the end the government had a defensive bill drawn up. Schuster wrote to the parliamentary draftsman: 'Begin with a recital, which should be as long and pompous as possible, asserting the independence and all the rest of it and negating any idea that the Economy Act or the Order in Council affected that in any way . . . Then declare that notwithstanding all this, they are affected by the cut.'[41]

The interaction between the judiciary, the legislature and the executive in the 1920s and 1930s left much to be desired. The increasing judicial obsession with deference and status seemed to be in inverse proportion to the declining importance of the judiciary in constitutional and other disputes. The courts were increasingly limited to crime, property, tort and contract. While property matters still heavily involved the profession, much of social, commercial and industrial life was passing the courts by.

It would be wrong, however, to think that the judges had been completely excluded from the constitution. As judges became less

[40] [1936] AC 1 (1935).
[41] Stevens, *The Independence of the Judiciary*, p. 61.

important in hearing public law cases and in dealing with new areas in the courts they were used more frequently to chair commissions and committees. Judges were increasingly seen as 'impartial' and capable of 'objective' solutions. For most of the nineteenth century committees of one or other House of Parliament had investigated both narrow factual issues and general policy areas—hence the ubiquitous Blue Books. The Pigott forgeries in the 1880s, however, had led to a judicial inquiry, although one conducted by good Unionist judges. The norm, nevertheless, remained for Parliament to police itself; as for instance the investigation of the Marconi scandal (1913). By the end of the First World War, however, the tide turned and the Tribunals of Enquiry Act 1921 gave status and certain privileges to such judicial enquiries. Shaw, a law lord, had been used in 1919 to handle the dock strike; Sankey, a High Court judge was used to project the future of the coal industry (recommending a form of nationalisation); Scott finished the Committee on Ministers' Powers.[42] A regular new role for the judges had emerged.

Moreover the judges still had important constitutional roles in the Commonwealth, sitting as judges of the Judicial Committee of the Privy Council. It was probably with respect to Canada that the British judicial influence in constitutional interpretations was most obvious. Earlier in the century the formalistic pro-provincial views of Watson, Davey and Haldane contrasted with the more instrumental and balanced views of Loreburn. Sankey (Lord Chancellor 1929–35) returned to the broad approach: 'the British North America Act planted in Canada a living tree capable of growth and expansion within its natural limits ... their Lordships do not conceive it to be the duty of this Board—it is certainly not their desire—to cut down the provisions of the Act by a narrow and technical construction, but rather to give it a large and liberal interpretation'.[43] Sankey was dismissed as Lord Chancellor in 1935 to be replaced by Hailsham. In 1936 Hailsham was faced with a series of appeals testing the constitutionability of Ottawa's 'New Deal'. He tried to persuade Sankey to preside, but Sankey was still sulking as a result of his dismissal. Lord Atkin, a distinguished commercial lawyer, presided instead and disassociated the Judicial Committee from the Sankey view: 'while the ship of state now sails on larger ventures and into foreign waters she still retains the watertight compartments which are an essential part of

---

[42] Stevens, *The Independence of the Judiciary*, p. 61.
[43] *Edwards v. A-G for Canada* [1930] AC 124, 136 (PC 1929).

her original structure'.[44] The Canadian New Deal was struck down; responsible opinion in Ottawa was outraged; the Canadian Senate's O'Connor Report of 1939 recommended abolition of appeals, something which, with the intervention of the Second World War, was ultimately achieved in 1949.[45]

High formalism, world war and increasing irrelevance

The period from 1939 to the early 1960s marked the depths of the irrelevance of the courts in the development of the constitution. The workload of the House of Lords as a judicial body declined steadily. In 1953 only nineteen cases were heard—half as many as in 1939. They took, however, twice as long to hear; some four days rather than two; and almost half of them concerned tax.[46] Far from being a supreme court for the United Kingdom, the House had lost its way as a final court of appeal. With legal aid not at that point extended to the House of Lords, it was scarcely surprising that Gerald Gardiner, writing in 1963, the year before he became Harold Wilson's Lord Chancellor, recommended the abolition of the second appeal.[47]

Tax law itself had become an elaborate form of chess or crossword puzzle with the courts giving an appearance of joining in the game. Even the Lord Chancellors of the period—Lord Simon (1940–5), Lord Jowitt (1945–51) and Lord Simonds (1951–4)—took pleasure in emasculating anti-avoidance devices, with the result that Britain was increasingly seen by foreigners as a tax haven. In purely public law cases only the 18B case—allowing detention without trial—of *Liversidge* v. *Anderson*[48]— became well known and that chiefly for the vigorous dissent of Lord Atkin. Elsewhere public law was a wasteland. *Duncan* v. *Cammell Laird*[49] gave *carte blanche* to Crown privilege. In *Franklin* v. *Minister of Town and Country Planning*[50] the House of Lords denied that the law had any

---

[44] [1937] AC 326, 354 (PC).

[45] Coen G. Pierson, *Canada and the Privy Council* (Stevens, 1960), p. 69 ff.

[46] Louis Blom-Cooper and Gavin Drewry, *Final Appeal: A Study of the House of Lords in its Judicial Capacity* (Clarendon Press, 1972). For a study of the actual operation of the law lords, see Alan Paterson, *The Law Lords* (Macmillan, 1982).

[47] Stevens, *Law and Politics*, p. 415.

[48] [1942] AC 206 (1941). See A. W. Brian Simpson, *In the Highest Degree Odious: Detention without Trial in Wartime Britain* (Clarendon Press, 1992).

[49] [1942] AC 624.

[50] [1948] AC 87 (1947).

responsibility for procedural due process under the New Towns Act. The same response was given with respect to the Central Land Board—the epitome of central planning—in 1951 in *Earl Fitzwilliam's Wentworth Estates Co.* v. *Minister of Housing and Local Government.*[51] It could be argued that the massive majority of the Labour government in 1945 justified judicial caution. The depths of judicial abdication, however, were reached in *Smith* v. *East Elloe RDC,*[52] at a time when the Conservative Party was back in power. Then the House held there was no way the courts could entertain a case even if fraud had been alleged in making or confirming a compulsory purchase order.

The flight of the courts from public law was, in some ways, understandable. In one famous interchange, James Reid—who later became a law lord, but at that time was a Conservative MP—moved an amendment to the National Health bill concerning the Standing Committee of the NHS, which had the right to fire physicians or other employees of the service. The bill provided a final right of appeal to the minister. The Reid amendment suggested the appeal should go to a High Court judge. Aneurin Bevan, the health minister, opposed the change: 'we cannot admit that the courts should interpret whether the doctor has, in fact, been a good servant of the people . . . [this] would be real judicial sabotage of socialized services in which the functions of industrial dispute are entrusted to the judiciary'. Reid saw this as a charge that 'His Majesty's judges . . . desire to commit judicial sabotage on the introduction of Socialism.' While Bevan claimed he had been 'monstrously misconstrued', the exchange was scarcely an invitation to judicial activism; and, at the same time, it made it even odder that the Labour government should be willing to use judges so freely outside the courts to settle wage disputes and other industrial issues.[53] The charade of independence and irrelevance was taken to a remarkable degree. The Lord Chancellor Lord Jowitt was proud of the fact that he had never appointed a Labour man to the bench (he did eventually appoint Donovan) and he was clearly anxious to retain his Diceyan credentials, telling the American Bar Association: 'Never has there been a time when the rule of law has been more firmly entrenched in my country. Never has there been a time when the acts of the executive are

[51] [1952] AC 362 (1951).
[52] [1955] AC 736.
[53] Griffith, *Judicial politics since 1920*, p. 80.

more completely subject to the opinions of an entirely independent judiciary.'[54]

The Labour government (1945–51) was, in this sense, a study in contrasts. The judges did, however, continue to influence politics in other ways. It had always been a murky constitutional convention about which subjects it was appropriate for law lords to speak on in the legislative debates in the House of Lords. In the 1950s and 1960s Lord Goddard, the chief justice, defended capital punishment and supported flogging, two causes taken up by his successor Lord Parker. Goddard, a Conservative, although appointed by a Labour government, saw no reason to extend legal aid to criminal cases.[55] While the government was anxious to reform divorce law, such reform was vigorously (and largely successfully) opposed by Lord Merriman (and later Lord Hodson) in the legislative sessions of the Lords.[56]

Even more powerful was the role of the judges as chairs of Royal Commissions and departmental committees. Between 1945 and 1969, judges—mainly law lords—chaired seven of the twenty-four Royal Commissions and 118 of the 358 departmental committees. The law lords might increasingly be seen as eunuchs in legal appeals, but they were virile in investigation, advising and prescribing. Lord du Parcq, for instance, chaired the Royal Commission on JPs; Lords Cohen and Radcliffe shared the Royal Commission on the Taxation of Profits and Income; Lord Morton chaired the Royal Commission on Marriage and Divorce; Lord Uthwatt chaired the Committee on Leaseholds; Lord Donovan chaired the Royal Commission on Industrial Relations; Lord Asquith chaired the Royal Commission on Equal Pay; Lord Cohen chaired the Committee on Company Law; both Lord Evershed and Lord Devlin chaired committees on the Port Transport Industry; and Lord Jenkins chaired a Committee on Intermediaries. On a more controversial level, Lord Denning reported on the Profumo affair; Lord Devlin on the riots in Nyasaland; and Lord Radcliffe on the Vassall affair and 'D' notices. Pay disputes were increasingly referred to judicially chaired bodies. Lord Wilberforce dealt with electricity supply and the mines; Mr Justice Lloyd Jacob with the doctors. In a brief space of time, as the decline in the importance of the courts in public policy became obvious, the judges'

[54] Stevens, *Law and Politics*, p. 337.
[55] Ibid., p. 362.
[56] Stevens, *Judicial Independence*, pp. 114–15.

time was increasingly spent in activities which many societies would define as political.[57]

In the courts the work was inevitably primarily of a private nature, and it was approached in the most formalistic manner. While there were more imaginative judges—Reid, Denning, Radcliffe and Devlin—theirs was a voice little heard in the 1940s and 1950s. The tone was set by the Lord Chancellors who at that time still sat regularly in the judicial committees of both Lords and Privy Council—Simon, Jowitt and Simonds—and their view allowed little by way of judicial creativity in the common law or statutory interpretation. Jowitt was obsessed with the idea of certainty which may have insured technical competence in private law decisions at first instance; yet it was the antithesis of what was needed in public law cases in the final court of appeal. Jowitt, however, believed fixed rules 'an inevitable tendency in civilized society'. In talking of a possible appeal he emphasised that 'we should loyally follow the [earlier] decision of the House of Lords . . . it is not really a question of being a bold or timorous soul . . . we are really no longer in the position of considering what the law ought to be . . . the problem is not to consider what social and political considerations do today require, that is to confuse the role of the lawyer with the task of the legislator. It is quite possible that the law has produced a result which does not accord with the requirements of today. If so put it right by legislation, but do not expect every lawyer . . . to decide what the law ought to be . . . do not get yourself into a frame of mind of entrusting to the judges the working out of a whole new set of principles which does accord with the require-ments of modern conditions. Leave that to the legislature, and leave us to confine ourselves to trying to find out what the law is.'[58]

In short, judges should apply objective rules (to be determined by strict rules based on *stare decisis* and *ratio decidendi*) and interpret statutes according to their 'plain meaning'. How could a socialist government object to such a policy-neutral bench even if its members were public school and Oxbridge educated with an alleged conservative bias? More-over, Lord Simonds, who became Lord Chancellor when Churchill returned to power in 1951, continued the Jowitt approach. Even the mischief rule of statutory interpretation was offensive to him: 'it is suf-ficient to say that the general proposition that it is the duty of the court to find out the intention of Parliament—and not only of Parliament but

---

[57] Stevens, *Judicial Independence*, ch. 6.
[58] Stevens, *Law and Politics*, pp. 338–9.

of Ministers also—cannot by any means be supported. The duty of the court is to interpret the words that the legislature has used; these words may be ambiguous, but, even if they are, the power and duty of the court to travel outside them on a voyage of discovery are strictly limited.' To modern eyes the style was not helpful.[59]

Simonds' approach to developing the common law was similarly negative: 'I will not be led by an undiscerning zeal for some abstract kind of justice to ignore our first duty, which is to administer justice according to law, the law which is established for us by Acts of Parliament or the binding authority of precedent.' He was, moreover, firm about binding authority. In *Jacobs* v. *LCC* the law of invitees and licensees was pushed back some fifty years by an insistence on treating both reasons for an earlier decision as binding: 'There is in my opinion no justification for regarding as obiter dictum a reason given by a judge for his decision, because he has given another reason also . . . it would, I think, be to deny the importance, I would say the paramount importance, of certainty in the law to give less than coercive effect to the unequivocal statement of the law made after argument by members of this House . . . nor . . . are your Lordships entitled to disregard such a statement because you would have the law otherwise. To determine what the law is, not what it ought to be, is our present task.'[60] It was Simonds who had presided in *Smith* v. *East Elloe RDC*.[61] To administrative law he applied the same brand of formalistic deference to the status quo. It was scarcely surprising that public law was moribund in the 1940s and 1950s, with private law also approaching judicial catatonia.

The 1960s and 1970s: confusion and renewal

The period of high formalism was in the ascendant during the 1940s and 1950s; its demise was erratic. Periods in history are inevitably fuzzy. Some effort to make the courts more relevant and less formalistic can be traced back to Lord Kilmuir (Sir David Maxwell Fyfe) who was appointed

---

[59] Stevens, *Law and Politics*, pp. 342–4. In *IRC* v. *Ayrshire Employers Mutual Insurance Association* [1946] 1 All ER 637 (HL, Scot., 1945), Simonds opined: 'It is at least clear what is the gap that is intended to be filled and hardly less clear how it is intended to fill that gap. Yet I can come to no other conclusion than that the language of the section fails to achieve its apparent purpose and I must decline to insert words and phrases which might succeed where the draftsman failed.' At p. 641.

[60] [1950] AC 361, 368–9.

[61] [1956] AC 736. See especially on pp. 750–1.

Lord Chancellor by Churchill in 1954. Kilmuir was not a great lawyer, but he had common sense. He argued that the law 'must play its part in the modern scientific state . . . the law should be brought in to help in the solution of the great problems of the modern State'.[62] He was a law reformer. He changed the rules for occupiers liability, put in a retirement age for judges, began devolution of the courts, and even suggested that political service ought to be taken into account for appointments to the bench so that the judges had the experience to enable them to handle public law cases. (In this latter endeavour, however, he found he was far too late to turn back the tradition of choosing High Court judges on the basis of success in advocacy.) Yet he may have been the last Lord Chancellor to take Dicey at face value—establishing the Franks Committee on Administrative Tribunals. He also restated the rather platitudinous position on judicial objectivity and denied the need for rights to be entrenched, insisting that the common law and the judges were an adequate protection of civil liberties.[63]

Early in the Churchill administration, the president of the Board of Trade had wanted to appoint a judge as chair of the Monopolies' Commission, but he was thwarted by Sir George Coldstream, the permanent secretary to the Lord Chancellor, who did not want 'to ask the judiciary to descend into the arena of public affairs'. By the time the matter was raised again in 1955, Kilmuir had become Lord Chancellor. The permanent officials took the Diceyan position: 'public interest questions are not justiciable issues such as are appropriate for determination by a truly judicial body: the function is more nearly executive or administrative'. When later in the year a Cabinet committee opted for registering restrictive agreements and having them investigated by High Court judges, the civil servants were shocked. The deputy permanent secretary minuted the permanent secretary that 'the whole nonsense had been caused by the agitation about tribunals . . . a High Court Judge . . . is ill suited to decide the sort of cases that will be at issue here'. That same day, the permanent secretary, Sir George Coldstream, presented a paper to the Lord Chancellor, pointing out that the permanent secretaries of all the relevant departments were agreed that the proposals were 'thoroughly unsound' and should be 'remitted to officials'.

Kilmuir persevered and by 1956 the Restrictive Trade Practices bill was before Parliament. Sir Lynn Ungoed-Thomas (later a Chancery

---

[62] Stevens, *Law and Politics*, p. 421.
[63] See generally, ibid., pp. 420–5.

judge) argued for Labour that 'the function of a court is not that which is mentioned in the Bill; it is entirely different, namely to enforce and administer law, and not to make it. The Bill hands over to this court governmental and parliamentary power ... [its judgements] will [represent] a political and economic decision'. The government countered by arguing that 'the courts deal with many social and economic matters under the guidance of principles laid down by Parliament ... The real distinction is the level at which the subject is dealt with.' The Bill became law, but the judges rapidly allied themselves with the civil servants and the Labour opposition. The Chancery judges had 'grave objections' because of the 'political element'. The Queen's Bench Division was vigorously opposed, with the sole exception of Mr Justice Devlin, who was chosen as the first president of the new court. It was not an auspicious start for the regeneration of the courts.[64]

The 1960s saw more obvious changes. In 1962, Lord Reid—a former Scottish Conservative politician, who had been appointed a lord of appeal in 1948—became the senior law lord. His broad Scottish approach, coupled with his earlier political experience, made him eschew the formalism of the earlier period. In 1972 he wrote: 'There was a time when it was thought almost indecent to suggest that judges make law—they only declare it. Those with a taste for fairy tales seem to have thought that in some Aladdin's cave, there is hidden the Common Law in all its splendour and that on a judge's appointment there descends on him knowledge of the magic words Open Sesame. Bad decisions are given when a judge muddles the pass word and the wrong door opens. But we do not believe in fairy tales anymore.' Reid's was an approach which enabled the judges to regain the initiative in public law.[65] In 1964 in *Ridge* v. *Baldwin*[66] the House began the process of restoring procedural due process; in *Conway* v. *Rimmer* (1968)[67] they began taking back the initiative in Crown privilege; *Padfield* v. *Minister of Agriculture* (1968)[68] and *Anisminic* v. *Foreign Compensation Commission* (1969)[69] pointed towards re-establishing judicial review of administrative actions. Life was once again poured into the old prerogative writs. The courts not only restored procedural due process, but, with the restatement of the so-called *Wednes-*

---

[64] Stevens, *Judicial Independence*, pp. 101–13.
[65] Stevens, *Law and Politics*, pp. 466–88.
[66] [1964] AC 40 (1963).
[67] [1968] AC 910 (1967).
[68] [1968] AC 997.
[69] [1969] 2 AC 147 (1968).

bury doctrine, added, in the view of some, a hint of substantive due process.[70] While the House of Lords crafted a new role for the judges in public law, Lord Denning, by then installed as Master of the Rolls (the presiding judge for civil cases in the Court of Appeal) was, more flamboyantly, advertising the potential and real power of judges.[71]

In the 1960s, too, there was a fillip from an unexpected source. In 1964, Harold Wilson was returned as prime minister and the new Labour Lord Chancellor was Gerald Gardiner. While professionally conservative and, like so many intellectuals of the Left, an advocate of a formalistic role for the law, leaving the judges with precious little creative role, Gardiner was also a reformer. His Law Commission was designed to reform and restate black letter rules. Another reform, however, again originally with the internal logic of the law in mind, was to allow the House of Lords to overrule its own earlier decisions, the intention being that this would occur only when there had been logical inconsistency. The practical and psychological impact of the change was, however, broader and more dramatic. It was not long before overruling had moved well beyond internal logic.

Another of Gardiner's reforms had a similar unintended impact. He picked up the Kilmuir suggestion that the Privy Council should become a peripatetic court. The cruel rejection of the idea brought home the fact that English judges were not necessarily held in the Commonwealth in quite the high regard they had always assumed, but, more importantly, in different—sometimes inadequate ways—the Commonwealth countries reminded Britain that a legal system needed to take into account the economic and social conditions within which it operated and towards which the judges needed to develop doctrine.[72] At the same time, Gardiner allowed dissenting opinions in the Privy Council and this helped open up further opportunities for judicial creativity.

In the late 1960s, the political environment—and especially the unsatisfactory labour relations in the UK—had once more attracted the attention of the courts. In 1964 in *Rookes* v. *Barnard*[73] the House of Lords held that a person dismissed by an employer after a strike threat by the union might sue the union officials for conspiracy and, in the same year, in *Stratford* v. *Lindlay*[74] extended this principle to boycotts. This apparent

---

[70] David Robertson, *Judicial Discretion in the House of Lords* (Clarendon Press, 1998), ch. 7.
[71] Stevens, *Law and Politics*, pp. 488–505.
[72] Stevens, *Judicial Independence*, 160–1; Stevens, *Law and Politics*, pp. 418–19.
[73] [1964] AC 1129.
[74] [1965] AC 269 (1964).

expansion of the law led to the appointment of the Donovan Commission in 1965, and the Labour government's white paper, *In Place of Strife* (1968), which proposed the establishment of an Industrial Board to police labour relations with a limited power to impose sanctions. The government proposed legislation along these lines, but was forced to back down in the face of Labour and trade union opposition. The strikes continued and in 1970 the Conservatives, led by Edward Heath, were returned. Their solution to industrial unrest was the National Industrial Relations Court (NIRC) loosely based on the Restrictive Practices Court, with a requirement of registration of unions and openness about their rules for strikes as the basis for staying within the 1906 Act. Sir John Donaldson, a High Court judge and former Conservative candidate, was appointed president of the NIRC. He soon found his decisions apparently inconsistent with those of Lord Denning, presiding in parallel cases in the Court of Appeal. Heath's Lord Chancellor, Lord Hailsham of St Marylebone, in a remarkable act, appeared to attempt to pressure Denning, but it was to no avail. By this time the Heath government was caught up in the miners' strike, and the two elections of 1974 returned Labour with a small majority. The following year the new government abolished the NIRC—and later refused to appoint Donaldson as Master of the Rolls. Labour relations continued to deteriorate. Inflation was rampant; the International Monetary Fund was brought in; and after the Winter of Discontent, the Conservatives, now led by Margaret Thatcher, were returned in 1979.[75]

While there were law lords—particularly Lord Diplock (appointed a lord of appeal in 1968) and Wilberforce (appointed in 1964)—who accepted a positive role for the judiciary, they lacked the political acuity of Reid or the flamboyance of Denning.[76] The majority of judges in the Court of Appeal and House of Lords laboured under the weight of a strongly formalist tradition. Only in legislative debates in the Lords[77] and, more noticeably as chairs of commissions and committees, were

---

[75] J. A. G. Griffith, *The Politics of the Judiciary*, 5th edn (Fontana, 1997), pp. 63–102.

[76] Griffith, *Judicial Politics since 1920*, ch. 5.

[77] Between 1956 and 1967 the law lords took different sides on capital punishment, artificial insemination, adultery, majority verdicts, corporal punishment and damages for widows. During the period, Lord Hodson attacked the merits of a private member's bill to reform (and make more liberal) divorce law, intervening no less than sixteen times. On the Labour Relations (Amendment) bill, Lord Salmon made a somewhat emotional speech on communist influence in the unions.

judges heavily involved in public affairs.[78] Such activities inevitably, on occasion, led the judges into trouble. Wilberforce's 1972 foray into miners' wages was described by *The Economist* as 'incredible economic nonsense', while others thought the Heath government 'had set up this enquiry to produce a report which would enable them to yield to the miners' claim without total loss of face'.[79]

It was, however, in Northern Ireland that the judges were most obviously used—and potentially put in an increasingly impossible position politically. The first appointment was that of Mr Justice Scarman whose report, *Violence and Civil Disturbances in Northern Ireland 1969*, was much criticised because it was not published until 1972, by which time the Cameron Report had been published (Cameron was a Scottish judge). Then followed the Widgery Report on so-called Bloody Sunday, the loss of life in Londonderry in January 1972, which failed to satisfy most sections of the community. *The Independent* later commented that the enquiry was 'so blatantly biased in its findings that it brought British justice into contempt in many parts of the world'. Lord Parker, the next lord chief justice, chaired a Committee of Privy Councillors to look at interrogation methods. Then followed Lord Diplock's *Legal Procedures for Dealing with Terrorists* (1972), recommending curbing the traditional common law protection to prevent the intimidation of witnesses, which led to the so-called Diplock courts, sitting without a jury. Harold Wilson sent his former Lord Chancellor, Lord Gardiner, to look at *Civil and Human Rights in the Province* (1975) and Judge Bennett took a further look at *Police Interrogation Procedures* (1979).[80] To different segments in Ulster

---

[78] They were used in the 1960s and 1970s for the usual committees: Committee on Security in the Public Service (Radcliffe, 1961), the Security Service and Mr Profumo (Denning, 1963), the Port Transport Industry (Devlin, 1964), the Age of Majority (Latey, 1965), Legal Education (Ormrod, 1967), One Parent Families (Finer, 1969), Abuse of Social Security (Fisher, 1971), Ministerial Memoirs (Radcliffe, 1975), Recruitment of Mercenaries (Diplock, 1976) Police Pay (Edmund-Davies, 1977), Brixton Disorders (Scarman, 1981), Civil Service Pay (Megaw, 1981). At the same time in these two decades, there were Royal Commissions on Trade Unions (Donovan, 1965), Tribunals of Enquiry (Salmon, 1966), the Constitution (Kilbandon—Scottish judge, 1968), Civil Liability (Pearson, 1973), the Press (Finer co-chair, 1974), Standards of Conduct in Government (Salmon, 1974). In addition, under the 1921 Act, there was an enquiry into the Official Secrets Act and Vassall (Radcliffe, 1962), the Disaster at Aberfan (Davies co-chair, 1967) and the Vehicle and General Insurance Co (James, 1972). In addition to this, Lord Pearce was in 1972 made chair of a commission on Rhodesian opinion, to help settle the future of what became Zimbabwe.

[79] Griffith, *Judicial Politics since 1920*, pp. 132–3.

[80] Cmnd 566, NI (1972); *Report of the Tribunal Appointed to Enquire into the Events of Sunday, 30 January, 1972, which Led to a Loss of Life in Connection with the Processions in Londonderry*

all the reports were unacceptable and there is little doubt that they threw doubt on the impartiality and independence of the British judiciary.[81]

Since the English judges also are accustomed to being consulted by departments on bills and specific problems,[82] and in turn to give advice on the principles of damages and sentencing to lower courts, it is possible to see a surprising internal conflict in the way the English judges and courts saw their roles. It is true that in the 1960s and 1970s the judges both continued the process of pushing the courts slowly back into public law, as well as reclaiming some responsibility for keeping the common law in line with the needs of society, yet the tone of the approach was tentative. The courts in this sense remained, as a political force, largely insignificant in the constitution; and the judges' contribution to the constitution was significantly outside the courts.

The eleven Thatcher years

As the new leader of the Conservative Party, Margaret Thatcher came in without the clear political policies that were later attributed to her. As she moved to a more market-orientated approach than Britain had seen since the turn of the century, or perhaps even the mid-nineteenth century, she was also accused of moving to a more presidential style of government. Parliamentary sovereignty may already have been somewhat undermined—as was argued when Edward Heath finally took Britain into the Common Market in 1973. Mrs Thatcher's acceptance of the Single European Act confirmed that trend. With a seemingly more presidential system of government, coupled with the declining importance of Parliament, such developments occurred at the very moment when there appeared to be something of a vacancy by way of opposition. The Labour Party, after the economic disasters of the 1970s and the defeat of 1979, chose to lurch to the Left under Michael Foot rather than to seek a political formula likely to appeal to a majority of the electorate. These developments provided the background for a potentially dramatic change in the role of the judges.

The atmosphere had also been changed by the European Communi-

---

on that Day (1971–2), HL 101/HC 120 1972; Cmnd 4901 (1972); Cmnd 5185 (1972); *Report of a Committee to Consider the Context of Civil Liberties and Human Rights Measures to Deal with Terrorism in Northern Ireland,* Cmnd 5847 (1975); Cmnd 7497 (1979).

[81] Stevens, *Judicial Independence,* pp. 170–1.

[82] For recent examples see Griffith, *The Politics of the Judiciary,* pp. 45–6.

ties Act 1972—drafted under the guidance of the then solicitor-general, Sir Geoffrey Howe—which provided for a broad reception for European law; an invitation which the judges, with Lord Denning in the van, accepted. Judicial activism in this area accelerated in the 1980s and 1990s, and the power of the UK courts in enforcing European directives was underlined with the *Factortame* case[83] in 1991, when a British statute was suspended while its constitutionality was tested before the European Court. The final logical step was taken in 1995 when, in *R. v. Secretary of State for Employment, ex p. Equal Opportunities Commission*,[84] the House of Lords held that British legislation relating to part-time employees violated European directives and was therefore unenforceable. Lord Mackay—Mrs Thatcher's Lord Chancellor from 1987—explained the decision in conventional terms, namely that one British statute had been interpreted in the light of another (the 1972 Act). The press, however, was not convinced. *The Times* concluded that 'Britain may now have, for the first time in its history, a constitutional court'. In a paper to Cabinet, Michael Howard—the home secretary, and a Euro-sceptic—argued that British courts should be forbidden from enforcing Community law. The paper marked an important step in the ongoing fracturing of the Conservative Party over the issue of Europe.[85]

The European influence, however, was not limited to the broadening impact of EU law. The European Convention on Human Rights was increasingly influential. Drafted with the support of the Foreign Office in the late 1940s, it had been eschewed by the Labour government of 1945–51, significantly because Lord Chancellor Jowitt was sceptical of foreign entanglements, indeed of foreigners. The Conservatives adhered to the Convention, while not incorporating it into English law, in the 1950s. The atmosphere had changed significantly enough by the 1960s to allow Harold Wilson's government to permit individuals to petition the Commission, although the Convention was still not incorporated into English law. The UK then became a frequent litigant before the Commission and Court of Human Rights in Strasbourg. A rights-based

---

[83] *R. v. Transport Secretary ex p. Factortame (No. 2)* [1991] 1 AC 603.

[84] [1995] 1 AC (1994). Patricia Maxwell, 'The House of Lords as a Constitutional Court: The Implications of *Ex parte EOC*', in *The House of Lords: Its Parliamentary and Judicial Roles*, ed. Brice Dickson and Paul Carmichael (Hart, 1999), p. 197.

[85] Robert Stevens, 'Judges, Politics and the Confusing Role of the Judiciary', in *The Human Face of Law: Essays in Honour of Donald Harris*, ed. Keith Hawkins (Clarendon Press, 1997), p. 265. The paper by Michael Howard is referred to in 'Howard Splits Cabinet on Europe', *Independent*, 18 May 1996.

approach to law was increasingly accepted intellectually, partly because of the writings of scholars such as Rawls and Dworkin and through the influence of, for example, Lord Scarman's Hamlyn Lectures. Gradually a groundswell of academic support for incorporating the Convention into English law was heard. Not only politicians but judges, including two chief justices—Lords Taylor and Bingham—became active in pressing for incorporation; by the early 1990s, incorporation was the policy of both Labour and Liberal Democrats. Lord Mackay, on behalf of the Conservatives, resisted, insisting that incorporation would politicise the judiciary.[86]

During the Conservative administration, the most expansive (and notorious) area in the development of public law was the growth of judicial review. The developments of the 1960s were expanded exponentially. In a way unthinkable thirty years earlier, ministers and civil servants found a new partner in the public decision-making process—the judges. In 1987 the Treasury Solicitor's Department issued *The Judge Over Your Shoulder*, a guide for civil servants about this new presence. Moreover the presence was felt not only by the civil servants but by their political bosses. The home secretary found his efforts to reform sentencing and the Criminal Compensation Programme, as well as immigration and deportation decisions (and sometimes policies), increasingly circumscribed by the judiciary. Prime Minister John Major was prevented by a Scottish judge from appearing on Scottish television, interpreting the electoral provisions of the Broadcasting Act, while the foreign secretary had to restructure foreign aid after he was held to have acted unlawfully in the funding arrangements for the Pergau Dam. Judges took unheard-of interest in subjects like gays in the military and housing for asylum seekers.[87]

It was little wonder that the press played up the changing and more public role of the judges and sought to politicise it. The Beaverbrook press claimed there was 'a sickness sweeping through the senior judiciary—galloping arrogance'. The Rothermere press joined in: 'Now it seems that any judge can take on himself to overrule a minister, even though Parliament might approve the minister's action. This is to arrogate power to themselves in a manner that makes a mockery of Parliament.' The *Daily Mail* accused the judges of giving the impression that they were

---

[86] Stevens, 'Judges, Politics and the Confusing Role of the Judiciary', pp. 265–7.
[87] Ibid., pp. 263–4. But in order to get a remedy the members of the armed forces had to go to Strasbourg; while Parliament rapidly overrode the housing allowance for asylum seekers.

'acting on a political agenda of their own'. While Lord Hewart had not hesitated to fight public battles, his were mainly outside the courts; by the 1980s these battles were being fought inside the courts. As the lord chief justice (Lord Lane) put it in a legislative debate, 'as Parliament is increasingly liable to do what the government of the day [may] wish it to do . . . it is . . . becoming more and more necessary to preserve intact the courts' power of judicial review . . . the one thing that will stop a bullying government in its tracks'.[88]

There was, however, another force at work. The appeal judges of the 1980s and 1990s had grown up during the Second World War and the period of consensus politics that followed. Perhaps the wartime catchphrases of 'fairness' and 'decency' had been absorbed into their blood streams. As a class they were probably not comfortable with the growing market solutions sought by Mrs Thatcher, while more sympathetic to Europe than she. The Labour Party's abdication of the primary responsibility of an opposition—namely to oppose—left the judges in the firing line. Mrs Thatcher saw the judges, like permanent secretaries, as 'part of the problem' in her efforts to push the British economy towards market solutions. Judges, whose music-hall reputation was that of out-of-touch conservatives, were now reviled in the press as interfering woolly liberals out of touch with democracy and classical liberal solutions.[89]

There were increasing judicial hints that judges saw themselves—at least embryonically—as a separate branch of government along the lines of the American judiciary. Through the 1980s and early 1990s, there were remarks that set the Thatcher years apart from earlier decades. Lord Browne-Wilkinson argued for the courts to have greater control over their own funds and the court system—an idea rapidly shot down by Lord Hailsham. Lord Woolf delivered a public lecture in which he posited political situations where the judges would question parliamentary sovereignty. Then Lord Justice Laws talked of the 'higher law' which limited parliamentary sovereignty.[90] On a parallel theme, Lord Justice Sedley claimed that Dicey's concept of parliamentary sovereignty had given way to 'a bi-polar sovereignty of the Crown in Parliament and the Crown in the courts, to each of which the Crown's ministers are answerable—politically to Parliament, legally to the courts'. While two of

---

[88] Stevens, 'Judges, Politics and the Confusing Role of the Judiciary', pp. 274–6.
[89] Ibid., pp. 257–61.
[90] J. A. G. Griffith, 'The Brave New World of Sir John Laws', *Modern Law Review* (2000).

Mrs Thatcher's three Lord Chancellors—Lords Hailsham and Mackay—insisted that parliamentary sovereignty was sacrosanct and continued to reside in Westminster and not Brussels, and certainly not in the judges, the mantra was increasingly less convincing.[91]

Moreover, with the arrival of Lord Mackay, the Kilmuir Rules, which made it difficult for judges to speak out, were lifted. There was therefore a much greater willingness for judges to comment on all manner of issues, but psychologically the new regime seemed to give those judges with a seat in the legislative House of Lords a licence to oppose government policy as the custodians of the old consensus politics. Certainly, in penal policy, the judges found the policies of Michael Howard, John Major's home secretary, distasteful. The imposition of mandatory terms and the taking away of judicial discretion in setting sentences was upsetting; the 'two strikes and you're out' mentality abhorrent. Lord Taylor, the chief justice, did not hesitate to issue a statement disagreeing with speeches made at the Conservative Party conference and, when he resigned because of ill-health, he delivered a blistering attack on Conservative penal policy. It was a very different world from that of the immediate post-war years.[92]

It was not surprising to discover that some judges were not hesitant in continuing the more vigorous development of the common law which had by then become the norm. Nor was it even surprising that the law lords, in *Pepper* v. *Hart* (1993),[93] overthrew the accepted view of the centuries that legislative debates were not admissible in interpreting statutes. (Only Lord Chancellor Mackay dissented; some felt that he should not have sat.) While the law lords attempted to put some limits on the new system, in practice those limits have proved nugatory. The judges had been given a powerful new weapon in instrumental interpretation. From then on, the limited flexibility that had been theirs in interpreting statutes by using the literal, mischief or golden rules has been dramatically enhanced. The powers of judicial creativity seemed to know no bounds.[94]

By the 1970s, with the exception of New Zealand, the old Commonwealth had abolished appeals to the Judicial Committee of the Privy Council, but appeals by no means disappeared. While some newly inde-

[91] Stevens, 'Judges, Politics and the Conflicting Role of the Judiciary', pp. 267–9.
[92] Ibid., pp. 274–9.
[93] [1993] AC 593.
[94] See Kenny Mullan, 'The Impact of *Pepper* v. *Hart*', in *The House of Lords*, ed. Dickson and Carmichael, p. 213; Robertson, *Judicial Discretion in the House of Lords*, ch. 5.

pendent Commonwealth countries, particularly in Africa, rapidly abandoned appeals, Sri Lanka and Malaysia kept that court busy for far longer than had been predicted. By the 1990s, however, most of the appeals were from New Zealand, Hong Kong (until the handover in 1997) and the West Indies. Appeals from the latter included a series of decisions in the mid-1990s, the most famous of which was *Pratt* v. *Attorney-General for Jamaica* striking down, in that case under the human rights provisions of the constitution of Jamaica, sentences of death where there had been inexcusable delay.[95] While the decision and a number of related ones came close to ending appeals from the West Indies,[96] the cases reflect a very different view of the Judicial Committee's role from earlier decades. It was in this spirit that Lords Hoffmann and Nichols were seconded as members of the Hong Kong Court of Final Appeal after the 1997 handover.

Mrs Thatcher believed in governments taking decisions and she abhorred delegating them. There were, therefore, no Royal Commissions during her eleven years rule. With the arrival of John Major in 1990, there was once again some limited use of them. Lord Nolan, a law lord, was brought in to chair a Committee on Standards in Public Life after a series of particularly unfortunate incidents of Conservative Party sleaze. While there was some harassment of Lord Nolan by individual Tory MPs, and it is arguable that he failed to get the full support of the government to implement his recommendations, his treatment was generous when contrasted with that of Vice-Chancellor Sir Richard Scott, brought in to report on the 'Arms to Iraq' affair. While the procedure he adopted may have left something to be desired,[97] and Scott may have been rather naive about the nature of government with little sense of public relations,[98] the opposition believed that there was an officially orchestrated, mischievous, wilful campaign to undermine the judge who

---

[95] [1994] 2 AC 1 (PC, Jam.). With respect to Bahamas, see *Henfield* v. *A-G of Bahamas* [1997] AC 413. While the Privy Council came to live uneasily with capital punishment in the Caribbean, see *Reckley* v. *Minister of Public Safety and Immigration (No. 2)* [1996] AC 527 (PC, Bahamas), individual law lords continued to register their discomfort, for example dissents of Lord Nicholls, *Briggs* v. *Baptiste*, [2000] 2 AC 1 (PC, Trin. and Tob.); and Lords Steyn and Cooke in *Higgs* v. *Minister of National Security* [2000] 2 AC 228 (PC, Bahamas).

[96] This has not deterred the Privy Council from strong decisions with respect to the death penalty. *Lewis* v. *Attorney-General of Jamaica* [2000] 3 WLR 1785 (PC), with Lord Hoffman dissenting in favour of the death penalty. *Flowers* v. *The Queen*, 1 WLR 2396 (PC, Jam.).

[97] Lord Howe, 'Procedure at the Scott Inquiry', *Public Law* (1996).

[98] Joshua Rozenberg, *Trial of Strength: The Battle between Ministers and Judges over Who Makes the Laws* (Richard Cohen, 1997), p. 203, 'How Not to Publish a Report'.

had done no more than his public duty. As judges had taken on a more central role in political decision-making, their utility as outsiders, blessed with the cloak of independence and impartiality, was increasingly questioned.

More questions were being asked too about the 1876 compromise whereby the House of Lords remained as the final appeal court, with the law lords; with professional judges also remaining as legislators. The most dramatic conflict occurred when Lord Mackay introduced the green papers designed to begin the process of weakening restrictive practices in the legal profession. Led by Lord Lane, the lord chief justice, the Lord Chancellor was accused in legislative debates of authoritarian tendencies. Former law lords and Lord Chancellors—including Lords Ackner, Donaldson and Elwyn-Jones—were less charitable, accusing Lord Mackay of Nazi tendencies. While some claimed that former law lords were entitled to make 'political' speeches, the whole episode was a reminder of the murkiness of the separation of powers and constitutional conventions in Britain. The conventions were indeed vague. Lord Chief Justice Taylor supported the government bill to weaken an accused person's right to remain silent; Lord Browne-Wilkinson opposed the government on electronic surveillance; Lord Woolf opposed mandatory sentencing; while many of the law lords supported Lord Lester's bill to incorporate the European Convention on Human Rights, although it was contrary to government policy.[99] Some also found it uncomfortable that Lord Bingham, the then lord chief justice, spoke in favour of New Labour's controversial bill to curb trial by jury.

An argument in favour of law lords in the legislature, to be repeated after the establishment of the Royal Commission on the House of Lords in 1999, was the great merit of having law lords available to offer legal advice or at least advice on legal matters. Yet, for much of the century, in family and criminal law the law lords had been a force for reaction. Sometimes they were arguably wrong in law. The war crimes legislation was opposed by several law lords, including that distinguished international lawyer Lord Wilberforce, on the grounds of its being 'retrospective legislation', an argument questioned by leading international lawyers. It was the House of Commons, led by Margaret Thatcher and later John Major, which undid the erroneous position of

---

[99] On this see generally, Lord Alexander *et al.*, *The Judicial Functions of the House of Lords*, Written evidence to the Royal Commission on the Reform of the House of Lords by a JUSTICE working party (1999), pp. 6–7.

the law lords. The inherent confusion of the legislative and the judicial was highlighted in the *Fire Brigades Union* case (1995) where so many law lords had spoken legislatively against the government's proposed changes in the Criminal Injuries Compensation Scheme that it was difficult to find five law lords to sit judicially. Five were eventually found and they dutifully ruled that the home secretary had exceeded his powers.[100]

In all of this the role of the Lord Chancellor appeared to be changing. From the 1970s, the Lord Chancellor's Office had become the Lord Chancellor's Department with responsibility for running all the courts. By the mid-1980s the massive increase in legal aid had begun and the department was forced to look for ways of capping expenditure as every spending department of government was forced to do. It was a process, however, alien to the legal profession and the judiciary. When Lord Hailsham began efforts to rein in the legal aid budget the deference traditionally accorded to the head of the judiciary rapidly receded. It declined even further when Lord Mackay became Lord Chancellor in 1987. His green papers were seen by leading judges and practitioners as a sinister plot by the Treasury to bring market economics to the law by denying justice to the public and destroying the independence of the judiciary and the legal profession. The Lord Chancellor was harangued politically and sued in the courts. Leading legal figures led by Lord Steyn, one of the law lords, suggested it was time to have a judge as head of the judiciary and not a politician. The world seemed to be changing ever more rapidly.[101]

New Labour and new millennium

The landslide victory of New Labour under Tony Blair in May 1997 found the judges entering a period which was, by English standards, a revolutionary one. Overt hostility between judges and government was less obvious than it had been under John Major. This was significantly because Lord Bingham, as chief justice, was somewhat less confrontational than Lord Taylor, but also because he took a more conventional view of parliamentary sovereignty: 'if Parliament were clearly and unam-

---

[100] Rozenberg, *Trial of Strength*, pp. 99–100.
[101] Robert Stevens, 'Loss of Innocence? Judicial Independence and the Separation of Powers', *Oxford Journal of Legal Studies* (1999).

biguously to enact, however improbably, that a defendant convicted of a prescribed crime should suffer mutilation, or branding, or exposure in a public pillory, there would be very little a judge could do about it—except resign'. Lord Woolf, the new Master of the Rolls, did not repeat his flirtation with fundamental laws, but rather made an articulate defence of the British system of balance of powers rather than the separation of powers, in particular defending the role of the Lord Chancellor in much the terms Lord Schuster had done sixty years earlier. The context of the judiciary could, however, once again change, as a powerful prime minister faced a weak and divided opposition.[102]

There was little evidence, however, that judges were abandoning their new creative role; far from it. The *Pinochet* case (1999), where the former Chilean dictator was subject to a request for deportation to Spain, showed the strength of the continued independence of the judiciary.[103] The judicial willingness to be bold in public law cases was equally shown in the *Shah* case (1999) where the House of Lords, led by Lords Hoffmann and Steyn, effectively created a new 'social group' under the Geneva Protocol on Refugees in order to protect Pakistani women against the possibility of 'gender related violence' if they were deported home.[104] In the interpretation of statutes Lord Steyn remarked in a tax case that 'during the last 30 years there has been a shift away from the literalist approach to progressive methods of construction. When there is no obvious meaning of a statutory provision the modern emphasis is on a contextual approach designed to identify the purpose of a statute and give effect to it.'[105] The new judicial attitude to the common law was put by Lord Browne-Wilkinson in *Kleinwort Benson* v. *Lincoln City Council* (1998).[106] 'The theoretical position has been that judges do not make law or change law: they discover and declare the law which is thought the same. According to this theory, when an earlier decision is overruled the law is not changed; its true nature is disclosed, having existed in that form all along . . . In truth judges make and change law. The whole of the common law is

[102] Stevens, 'Loss of Innocence?', p. 393 ff.
[103] *R.* v. *Bow Street Stipendiary Magistrate, ex p. Pinochet Ugarte* [1998] 4 All ER 897 (HL); House of Lords, *Judicial Business and Consideration of the 11th Report from the Appeal Committee (Petition of Senator Augusto Pinochet Ugarte)* [1998] HLJ No 42 (QL); *R.* v. *Bow Street Stipendiary Magistrate, ex p. Pinochet Ugarte (No. 2)* [1999] 1 All ER 577 (HL).
[104] *R.* v. *Immigration Appeal Tribunal, ex p. Shah* [1999] 2 All ER 545 (HL).
[105] *R.* v. *McGuckian* [1997] 3 All ER 817 (HL).
[106] [1998] 4 All ER 513 (HL).

judge-made and only by judicial changes in the law is the common law kept relevant in a changed world.'[107]

The changes were, however, taking place amid a remarkable series of constitutional changes which had first been pressed by Blair's deceased predecessor as Labour leader, John Smith. Within the first two years, after their landslide victory in 1997, New Labour had established devolved Parliaments for Scotland and Wales; proposed a new form of devolution in Northern Ireland; introduced proportional representation for all but UK national and local elections; completed the first stages of reform of the House of Lords; produced a Freedom of Information bill; introduced the concept of elected mayors; and passed the Human Rights Act. In so many of these changes the courts were destined to play a significant role. The Judicial Committee of the Privy Council, despite its amateur system of selecting panels, was destined to be arbiter of disputes between Westminster and the Scottish Parliament. The judges, by the Human Rights Act, could not strike down Westminster statutes (although they could Scottish ones), but had the right to request fast-track legislation to remedy breaches—in some ways a more powerful solution. As Lord Browne-Wilkinson put it, 'The incorporation of the European Convention on Human Rights into English law will have a major impact on the methodology and reasoning of the judges. In large part the Convention is a code of the moral principles which underlie the common law . . . As these cases come before the courts in Convention cases the courts will be required to give moral answers to moral questions. Moral attitudes which have previously been the actual but unarticulated reasoning lying behind judicial decisions will become the very stuff of decisions on convention points. The silent true reason for decisions will have become the stated *ratio decidendi*.'[108]

Almost everything seemed 'up for grabs'. The Royal Commission on the House of Lords, while not radical in composition, was invited to consider whether the law lords should continue to be involved as legislators. While the evidence of both Labour and Conservative parties was in favour of their continued membership of the Lords, the Liberal Demo-

---

[107] More recently Lord Browne-Wilkinson has gone further: 'the features of current judicial reasoning are therefore as follows: First, the actual decision is based on moral, not legal factors. Second, these moral reasons are not normally articulated in the judgment. Third, the morality applied in any given case is the morality of the individual judge', Lord Browne-Wilkinson, 'The Impact of Judicial Reasoning', in Basil Markesinis (ed.), *The Impact of the Human Rights Bill on English Law* (Oxford University Press, 1998), p. 21.

[108] Browne-Wilkinson, 'The Impact of Judicial Reasoning', p. 22.

cratic Party, and particularly the Liberal Democrat lawyers, Lords Goodhart and Lester, argued for a separate constitutional court. It was not an argument that was totally out of bounds. After the *Pinochet* case, the *Daily Telegraph* commented 'we now seem to have a supreme court, just not a very competent one'. That paper also saw the implications of that case: 'This can only strengthen calls for greater public scrutiny over the way in which judges are appointed, most likely leading in the present climate to greater politicization.' *The Guardian* on 25 March 1999 looked at it rather differently, calling for a new look at the law lords, demanding a more open appointments process and a commitment to human rights on the part of appointees.

Lord Lester argued in the House of Lords on 28 October 1998 (col. 1968) that during his time at the Bar the judges had become a third branch of government. The parallel with the United States was obvious. While many would question his position, it was becoming increasingly difficult for the judiciary, and particularly the law lords, to fulfil all the complex roles they had come to play and were being invited to play within the constitution. Increasingly, active law lords—most recently Lords Mustill, Saville and Steyn—had consciously chosen not to participate in legislative debates. There was also a sense in which judges were finding their role as chairs of public commissions and committees increasingly hazardous. Lord Saville was invited, together with two Commonwealth judges, to revisit the Bloody Sunday events in Londonderry nearly thirty years after the Widgery Report. While this was intended to be basically a factual inquiry and therefore one that judges should be well equipped to undertake, the committee was vigorously attacked by the *Daily Telegraph* for being created at all: 'a mockery of the judicial enquiry system . . . this government . . . set up this unnecessary inquiry just to please the terrorists'.[109]

In some ways more open to attack was Mr Justice Macpherson's inquiry into the Stephen Lawrence murder—a tragic racist murder poorly investigated by the Metropolitan Police. Observers felt the judge—and his lay committee—did a good job analysing the facts and the police handling of the case. It was generally felt, however, that, as the committee moved on to analysing policies and making normative statements about the future, judges were in no better position than others to claim expertise. In particular the press cast doubt on the wisdom of

---

[109] 'A Shameful Inquiry', editorial, *Daily Telegraph*, 20 May 1999; and see editorial, 'Resign, Lord Saville', *Daily Telegraph*, 29 July 1999.

unspecific allegations of institutional racism in the police and suggestions which appeared to include curbing racial acts in the home.[110] The matters were highly charged and some of the claims unfair, but the attacks underlined that the judges may be coming to the end of their useful life as chairs of committees that go beyond the primarily factual and analytical.

It was perhaps inevitable that the Lord Chancellor—as the embodiment of the judicial, the legislative and the executive—should be the focus of much of the tension flowing from the political positions articulated by New Labour. Lord Irvine was, perhaps, more willing to be confrontational than his predecessor Lord Mackay and he was perhaps not always as politically circumspect. Moreover he was far more powerful politically. He was close to Prime Minister Blair, and perhaps some of the attacks on the Lord Chancellor were in effect attacks on the prime minister, who, like Margaret Thatcher, was thought to have a presidential style. Lord Irvine chaired significant Cabinet committees, not merely those relating to law, but also those charged with the extensive programme of constitutional reform.[111] He was also regarded as the instigator of successful government political moves, ranging from a deal with Lord Cranborne (the Conservative leader in the Lords) behind the back of Mr Hague (the Conservative Party leader) about the future of hereditary peers, to—whether fairly or not—the engineering of the dismissal of Lord Richard (the Labour leader in the Lords).

Lord Irvine was therefore in a delicate position made more difficult by the inexorable growth in the cost of legal aid despite the Mackay reforms. As Irvine produced the Access to Justice bill, he was vilified by the legal profession (although this time not by the judiciary) more vigorously than Mackay had been. The judges (especially the retired law lords) reserved their hostility for his plans to remove from the judiciary the power to determine rights of audience. Irvine's was not an easy political road. He was a partisan politician in reforming the House of Lords and was seen by some as an over-mighty subject; yet he had on other occasions, when not attempting to reform his spending department or the body of which he was speaker, to appear as head of the judiciary. In this last capacity he frequently sounded conservative, while his leader

---

[110] *Report of an Inquiry by Sir William Macpherson of Cluny advised by Tom Cook, the Rt Revd Dr John Sentamu, Dr Richard Stone*, Cm 4262-I (1999). See Charles Moore, 'Everyone Deserved Better', *Daily Telegraph*, 2 March 1999; editorial, 'Handcuffing the Police', *Daily Telegraph*, 24 April 1999.

[111] Dominic Egan, *Irvine: Politically Correct?* (Mainstream, 1999).

Tony Blair was castigating persons with such inclinations. While admitting that the Human Rights Act would transfer some political issues to the judges, he appeared opposed to a Constitutional Court and a Judicial Appointments Commission.[112] He opposed reform of the Lord Chancellorship and taking the law lords out of the legislature, and appeared to endorse the casual composition of the Judicial Committee of the Privy Council. The Lord Chancellor's role—together with that of the law lords—was supported by the 2000 report of the Royal Commission on the House of Lords,[113] but was possibly undermined by the *McGonnell*[114] decision in Strasbourg. A combination of New Labour, the political and personal views of the Lord Chancellor and the Cerberus-like nature of his office meant that Lord Irvine's tenure as Lord Chancellor was accompanied by a low rumble of controversy.

Irvine's insistence that parliamentary sovereignty has not been impaired by New Labour's constitutional reforms is understandable. The urge of many who would regard themselves as reformers is to see the judges as the incipient third branch of government, with Britain appearing to be on the edge of a codified constitution by which the democratic deficit might be judged. This, however, was still far from the case. The rank-and-file MPs of all parties were not about to abandon parliamentary sovereignty. They felt as strongly about that as if they were eighteenth-century Whigs. There had, of course, been a sea change in the role of the judges. The Privy Council may have to decide whether the Scottish Parliament has violated the letter (and, if the judges seek to be constitutional lawyers, the spirit) of the Scotland Act. As a result of EU directives, *de facto* judges may hold parliamentary legislation inoperative. The Human Rights Act means that judges have been given the right to flag violations of the Human Rights Act after hearings which require them to make difficult moral and political judgements in delicate areas. As if to remind the government of what they had wrought, as the century ended the Scottish Court of Session (a jurisdiction where the Human Rights Act came into force before England and where Scottish

---

[112] The dubious role of the House of Commons in the selection of Nicholas Bratza QC as the British judge on the European Court of Human Rights was not an encouraging precedent for such a commission. Labour MPs attacked his appointment because, as a barrister, he had represented the Thatcher government. But see now the Peach Report, *An Independent Scrutiny of the Appointment Processes of Judges and Queen's Counsel in England and Wales: A Report to the Lord Chancellor by Sir Leonard Peach* (1999).

[113] Royal Commission on the House of Lords, *A House for the Future*, Cm 4534 (2000), ch. 9.

[114] *McGonnell* v. *United Kingdom* (2000), 30 EHRR 289.

Acts—as opposed to Westminster Acts—may be struck down), decided that the system of temporary sheriffs violated the requirement of 'independent and impartial' judges under Article 6.[115] The implication for the system of recorders and deputy judges in England was obvious. Meanwhile the English Court of Appeal struck down ministerial involvement in planning decisions, a traditional cornerstone of the civil servant–minister relationship. While this decision was later struck down by the House of Lords, psychologically and practically the new Act was changing the way the public and politicians looked at judges.

Such changes were not the same, however, as a constitutional court or the end of parliamentary sovereignty. The Human Rights Act was fundamentally different from the US constitution's notion of judicial review of legislation or the power of the German Constitutional Court; it was even a considerable distance from the Supreme Court of Israel, which, with its president Mr Justice Barak, had taken the British system which it had inherited in 1948 and turned it into something akin to the American model.[116] At the same time, English judges were moving well beyond what had been thought of as the norm in reading one statute in the light of another. Whatever the public perceived, English judges were moving back to centre stage in constitutional law.

In determining where the story will end, it is important to remember that, even with devolution, Britain continued to be blessed with a legislature which normally speaks clearly, authoritatively and finally on difficult social issues. The social issues, which often lead to a murky half-life in the United States as the result of the tripartite system of government, the absence of strict party discipline, federalism, and perhaps a different political and social ethos, were spelled out clearly in the UK: abortion, the limits of ethical research, race discrimination, the death penalty, gun control. That did not mean that the courts were not involved on the periphery; it did mean that many of the policy issues were clearly settled publicly in a democratic forum. That could, of course, change. The independent commission on the electoral system, chaired by Lord Jenkins, recommended in 1998 a form of modified proportional representation, in place of first-past-the-post, in Westminster elections. This could lead to coalitions as the norm. If the legislature were to produce compromise legislation, then, even without the direct right

---

[115] 'Alarm Bells in Edinburgh', *Economist*, 20 November 1999.
[116] For example, *Public Committee Against Torture in Israel v. The State of Israel* (1999), not yet reported.

to strike down legislation, the courts could find themselves in a far more significant position in interpreting compromise wording. There is also talk of greater use of referenda. If introduced, and even if not as destructive as the California initiatives,[117] the courts might find even more political issues moving in their direction.

While Lord Irvine may well go down in history as a significant Lord Chancellor, the pressures evident in his tenure crystallised the difficulties faced by the British judges within the constitution. Expectations had changed. Despite the claims, the Diceyan concept of parliamentary sovereignty was changing in form and perhaps in substance. The House of Commons seemed less relevant in the total picture of governance, although in theory the power of members remained total. The premiership seemed to some to be moving away from responsible government towards a presidential model. The judges were being pushed and were pushing themselves more to centre stage. The nature of the bench had changed.[118] The mythology of the independence of the profession and judicial independence were in need of review. A radical rethinking of the separation or balance of powers was long overdue. While the Royal Commission on the House of Lords recommended that the law lords remain in the upper House, in *McGonnell* the European Court of Human Rights began a process which may make it difficult for such a system to survive. Historians normally resist artificial barriers like centuries and millennia, but the new millennium clearly began with a backlog of unresolved business in respect of the role of the judges and courts in the constitution. The first decade of the new century must resolve some of this unfinished business.

Note. The author would like to thank Bruce Ackerman, Vernon Bogdanor, John Eekelaar, Robert Gordon, John Langbein, John Griffith, Sir Thomas Legg, Kate Malleson, Sir Philip Otton and David Robertson for their perceptive observations and comments. Opinions and errors are those of the author.

---

[117] Peter Schrag, *Paradise Lost* (University of California Press, 1999), *passim.*

[118] In 1900, there were one hundred full-time professional judges; in 2000—excluding the district judges—some 1,100 full-time judges. The number of barristers and solicitors had roughly quadrupled in that same period.

Bibliography

For much of the twentieth century, the judiciary was not seen as an effective part of the constitution, so the literature on the judiciary is generally unhelpful. There are, of course, innumerable judicial biographies, but their contribution to a study of the role of the judiciary in the modern constitution is limited. Indeed, their contributions are chiefly by omission or unintended information. Sadly, the same is generally true of the standard constitutional law books, which assume no serious constitutional role for judges.

There are, however, exceptions. Harold Laski's *Studies in Law and Politics* (Allen & Unwin, 1932), and Lord Hewart's *The New Despotism* (Ernest Benn, 1929) are indeed revealing. By the 1960s there were increasingly important books by English judges, talking about the judicial process. Among them are Lord Radcliffe's *The Law and its Compass* (Northwestern University Press, 1960) and *Not in Feather Beds* (Hamish Hamilton, 1968). Lord Reid produced a series of thoughtful articles and lectures, for example 'The Judge as Law Maker', *Journal of the Society of the Public Teachers of Law* (1972), and Lord Denning a series of more polemical books and lectures, for example *The Changing Law* (Stevens, 1953), all of which helped to change the concept of what judges were about.

From the outside, matters began to change, from both right and left, in the 1960s. Robert Heuston with his *Lives of the Lord Chancellors*—R. F. V. Heuston, *Lives of the Lord Chancellors, 1885–1940* (Clarendon Press, 1964) *Lives of the Lord Chancellors, 1940–1970* (Clarendon Press, 1970)—while approaching the subject from a relatively conservative and sycophantic point of view, was nevertheless revealing about the politics of the judiciary generally. From the left, and far less deferentially, J. A. G. Griffith with his *The Politics of the Judiciary*, 1st edn (Manchester University Press, 1977), 5th edn (Fontana, 1995), opened up a whole new way of thinking about judges. The work of Alan Paterson on *The Law Lords* (Macmillan, 1982) began for the first time to look at the actual working of Britain's final appeal courts from a sociological viewpoint. Finally, for a sceptical political scientist's view of the judicial process, see David Robertson, *Judicial Discretion in the House of Lords* (Clarendon Press, 1998).

Modern history has been slowly catching up with what has been going on. See, for instance, K. D. Ewing and C. A. Gearty, *The Struggle for Civil Liberties: Political Freedom and the Rule of Law in Britain, 1914–1945* (Oxford University Press, 2000), and Robert Stevens, *Law and Politics: The House of Lords as a Judicial Body 1800–1976* (University of North Carolina Press, 1978), and *The Independence of the Judiciary: The View from the Lord Chancellor's Office* (Clarendon Press, 1993).

Slowly, during the century, writers on other areas of the law have begun to think about the judges in their constitutional role. While, in general, the leading figures in jurisprudence and legal philosophy have not addressed this issue, at least in the United Kingdom, the writings of William Twining, for example, his book *How to Do Things with Rules*, 4th edn (Butterworths 1999), certainly have. Similarly, those writing about the legal system have increasingly addressed the issue of the role of the judges. See, especially, the writings of Michael Zander, such as his book *The Law Making Process*, 5th edn (Butterworth 1999). Moreover, a number of recent books have highlighted specific issues in the role of the judiciary. See, for example, Brice Dickson and Paul Carmichael, *The House of Lords: Its Parliamentary and Judicial Roles* (Hart, 1999).

10.
Administrative Law

JEFFREY JOWELL

Attitudes toward governmental power in the twentieth century fluctu-
ated between deference and defiance. During the course of the century
a variety of principles and mechanisms were devised to control the
exercise of official discretion. The principles were largely decreed by
judges; the mechanisms by Parliament. Opinion was divided. One school
of thought held that public officials should not be constrained by the
'pathology of legalism'.[1] Another believed that unfettered discretion,
even in the hands of the most compassionate administrator, tempted
tyranny.[2] Judicial activism was variously applauded for properly controlling the state, or derided for its trespass into areas of public policy in
which the judges were said to lack competence.

The various encounters in pursuit of the appropriate balance between
law and administration were not a mere series of self-contained tussles
for power, won or lost on the form of the moment. They cloaked a
profound exploration of the relationship between government and the
individual in a constitutional democracy. That exploration was rarely
articulated and perhaps not even always understood. At the end of the
century, however, the very model of British democracy was, as a result,
fundamentally different from the one that prevailed at its start.

I shall in this chapter describe four stages of development of administrative law over the century. In stage one there is a concern for the rule
of law as a modest restraint on the exercise of official power. Soon,
however, both Parliament and the judiciary hold off, so that government
is permitted broad scope to exercise the powers necessary to conduct
two world wars and to erect the foundations of a welfare state. The
third stage, from mid-century, sees a growing concern for administrative

---

[1] Words used by Professor Richard Titmuss 'Welfare "Rights", Law and Discretion', *Political
Quarterly* (1971).
[2] See the works of Lords Hewart, Denning and others outlined below.

justice, giving rise to a number of measures, largely procedural in content, seeking to promote administrative accountability and to strike down the most flagrant abuses of power. The final stage, at the century's end, sees the establishment of fundamental standards, both procedural and substantive, which confer rights on individuals against the state and which aim to constrain all institutions wielding public power— including even Parliament itself.

Each stage was determined as much by a calculus of the temporal needs of modern government as by the prevailing view of the necessary requirements of constitutional democracy.

Stage one: Dicey and the rule of law

The twentieth century began securely in the tradition articulated fifteen years earlier, in 1885, by Professor Albert Venn Dicey in his seminal work, *Introduction to the Study of The Law of the Constitution*. It was accepted without much question that the central pillar of constitutional principle was the sovereignty of Parliament. As an aside, it bears recalling that when Dicey wrote his book that cast such a long shadow, Parliament, whose power he so exalted, was chosen by a population of which only around 60 per cent of male adults possessed the right to vote. Two-thirds of the members of Parliament were peers or their sons. Dicey himself opposed female franchise to the end of his life.[3] Yet it was not only Parliament that Dicey was willing to invest with authority. His abiding contribution to constitutional thinking was his insistence that Parliament's supremacy should be tempered, even though not ultimately controlled, by the rule of law. The fashioning of administrative law over the next century involved, effectively, the elucidation and practical implementation of the rule of law,[4] and its relationship with parliamentary sovereignty.

The central issue, then as now, was administrative discretion. Even in the nineteenth century, government's designs were becoming more and more complex. It was not possible to control safety on the railways,

---

[3] See Richard A. Cosgrove, *The Rule of Law: Albert Venn Dicey, Victorian Jurist* (Macmillan, 1980).

[4] For three particularly valuable accounts of Dicey's contribution to administrative law see Martin Loughlin, *Public Law and Political Theory* (Clarendon Press, 1992), ch. 7; I. Harden and N. Lewis, *The Noble Lie: The British Constitution and the Rule of Law* (Hutchinson 1986), ch. 1; and Paul Craig, *Public Law and Democracy in the United Kingdom and the United States of America* (Clarendon Press, 1990), ch. 2.

any more than it is today, by rule alone. Individual judgement was required to exercise that and other regulatory tasks, such as the provision of health and safety in factories and mines, the administration of the poor law, the provision of public health or the prevention and punishment of crime. For that reason Parliament conferred powers on administrators in the broadest terms: to act 'as they think fit', or 'in the public interest'. A frequent formula was that the minister/local authority/board/etc. *may* bring enforcement proceedings/grant permission for a licence/hear an appeal and so on. On its face, the degree of discretion under these formulae was infinite, unconstrained by any legal limits. Yet, despite Parliament's apparently open-ended grant of limitless power, could it be assumed that Parliament, or indeed the common law, implicitly intended that discretion to be controlled? And, if so, by what standards and what principles? Those were the questions.

In the early part of the nineteenth century, as the career civil service was developing, Bentham, who did not believe in rights against the state, warned against 'the licentiousness of interpretation' of legislation by judges.[5] Bentham's disciple Chadwick sought to exclude judicial review of factory inspectors and other administrative bodies.[6] Attempts to permit appeals from immigration officers to justices of the peace were rejected on the ground that they would lead to legal proceedings 'upon such simple questions as whether a cask of biscuits was good or bad'.[7]

That is not to say that there were, even then, no controls on the exercise of discretionary power. It was just that the controls were not on the whole exercised by judges or lawyers and that the techniques of control were not judicialised. Boards, inspectorates, ministries and commissions implemented policy not by formalised techniques of the courtroom but through persuasion, negotiation, admonition, education, compromise and other informal processes.[8]

Dicey did not even try to conceal his antipathy to broadly defined regulatory powers. For him discretionary power was by its very nature 'arbitrary' and had no place in a regime under the rule of law. The rule of law as he defined it did not allow the *ad hoc* implementation of

[5] L. J. Hume, *Bentham and Bureaucracy* (Cambridge University Press, 1981), p. 82.

[6] Henry Parris, *Constitutional Bureaucracy: The Development of British Central Administration since the Eighteenth Century* (Allen & Unwin, 1969), p. 82.

[7] Ibid., pp. 221–2.

[8] For a comprehensive and enlightening account of the tension between Diceyism and informal and increasingly centralised administration in the nineteenth century, see H. W. Arthurs, *'Without the Law': Administrative Justice and Legal Pluralism in Nineteenth-century England* (University of Toronto Press, 1985), esp. chs 5 and 7.

regulatory powers. It required, above all, certainty. Clear rules should be applied prospectively and enforced equally against the ordinary public and officials alike (unlike the situation in France which, Dicey believed, possessed a system of 'administrative law' which had no place in England).

It was this view that prevailed as the twentieth century broke. Courts were greatly influenced by the Diceyan approach that had been employed in cases such as *Cooper* v. *Wandsworth Board of Works*.[9] Mr Cooper had challenged the board's power to demolish a house he had recently built. The board claimed that the literal meaning of the law should be observed. Unrestricted power was conferred by Parliament on the board, in the interest of public health, to demolish any building for which notice of construction had not been given. The court, however, read down the broad power as requiring the board to listen to the complainant before the implementation of such a draconian remedy. It was true that the legislature had not provided for any hearing, but the 'justice of the common law' should supply the 'omission of the legislature'. Due process or natural justice so required, even outside the ambit of a judicial-type inquiry. No one should be condemned unheard. In similar vein, Lord Loreburn, the Lord Chancellor, in 1911, in the case of *Board of Education* v. *Rice*,[10] went so far as to say that the duty to provide a hearing, even in the absence of explicit statutory instruction, was a duty resting upon 'anyone who decides anything'.

Stage two: the retreat of law

Public decision-makers do not view with pleasure their subjection to legal fetters at the best of times. When war broke out in 1914 they were particularly concerned to preserve wide discretionary powers considered necessary to perform the military and defence tasks in hand. The Defence of the Realm Acts 1914–18 conferred unprecedented power on the executive to deal with the emergency. These powers flew in the face of Dicey's rule of law but few judges were then willing to confine their scope.

And so the second period of administrative law was ushered in—a period characterised by a willingness to permit governmental power

---

[9] [1863] 14 CB (NS) 180.

[10] [1911] AC 179. The case concerned the question whether schoolteachers in state schools should be paid the same salaries as those in church schools.

freely to be exercised in the public interest, relatively undisturbed by the constraints of legality. The case of *Local Government Board* v. *Arlidge*[11] confirmed the change of judicial approach. It was held that an inspector's report to the minister on the question of whether housing should be condemned need not be published. The right to natural justice, so broadly defined by Lord Loreburn in *Rice*, was suddenly truncated in situations that were considered to be 'administrative' rather than 'judicial', or where a 'privilege' was in issue, as opposed to a 'right'.[12] Generations of law teachers have had untold trouble explaining to students the logic of those distinctions. In fact they were pretexts; artificial barriers to judicial intervention in the new regulatory state where broad discretion should not be obstructed or distorted. Judges had suddenly become bureaucrats, with, as a later chief justice put it, 'a positive responsibility to be the handmaidens of the administration rather than its governor', and 'a duty to facilitate the objects of administrative action as approved and authorised by Parliament'.[13] The enforcement of the rule of law was now transmuted into an obligation, on the part of the courts and all officials, to secure Parliament's designs, free of any presumptions of the common law.

The critics of this new judicial passivity were by no means silent during this period. In his later years, Dicey himself became more and more overt in his opposition to state intervention. He bemoaned the existence of 'statutes passed under the influence of socialistic ideas',[14] a process which he felt 'saps the foundations of the rule of law which has been for generations a leading feature of the English constitution'.[15]

Courts were not always supine in the face of broad discretionary power,[16] but the exceptions were directed largely at the power of those

---

[11] [1915] AC 120.

[12] For a later case in the Privy Council, see *Nakkuda Ali* v. *Jayaratne* [1951] AC 66.

[13] Parker LCJ, quoted in D. G. T. Williams, 'The Donoughmore Report in Retrospect', *Public Administration* (1982), 291.

[14] In his 1914 introduction to the eighth edition of *The Law of the Constitution* (Macmillan, 1915), p. xliv. And see also his *Law and Public Opinion in England* (Macmillan, 1st edn 1905; 1962), where he warns that 'State help kills self help', at p. 258, and regards parliamentary sovereignty without the rule of law as 'an instrument well adapted for the establishment of democratic despotism', at p. 306.

[15] A. V. Dicey, 'The Development of Administrative Law in England', *Law Quarterly Review* (1915), 148–50.

[16] For example, where the decision-making decision was 'judicial' in character (such as a public inquiry into a housing clearance scheme), it was held that the inspector could not meet privately with any party after the end of the inquiry and before the decision had been reached. *Errington* v. *Minister of Health* [1935] KB 249. See, generally, de Smith, Woolf and Jowell, *Judicial Review of Administrative Action*, 5th edn (Sweet & Maxwell, 1989), ch. 7.

local authorities which, for the first time, were coming under the control of the Labour Party. The first Labour local authority was the London Borough of Poplar which, in 1921, sought to raise the wages of all its employees—at a time when the cost of living was falling—and to pay women salaries equal to those of men. The relevant statute gave the council the power to pay 'such salaries and wages as they may think fit'. The district auditor disallowed a proportion of the increased wages and imposed a surcharge upon the councillors concerned with the decision. The councillors appealed the decision before the Divisional Court, presided over by Lord Chief Justice Hewart (about whom see below) which upheld the auditor on the ground that the payment was 'so excessive as to go beyond the limits of legality and become an illegal or *ultra vires* payment'.[17] On appeal, the Court of Appeal upheld the councillors and deferred to their exercise of discretion, Lord Justice Scrutton saying:

> The question is not whether I should have sanctioned these wages; I probably should not; nor whether the Auditor or the Whitley Council would have sanctioned these wages; it is for the Poplar borough council to fix these wages which are not to be interfered with unless they are so excessive as to pass the reasonable limits of discretion in a representative body.[18]

The district auditor then appealed to the House of Lords,[19] where all five law lords found in his favour.

The *Poplar* case has often been assumed to have been decided on the basis of the personal prejudices of the conservative law lords who based their decisions on the 'unreasonableness' of the council's decisions. The speech of Lord Atkinson invites such a conclusion. He regarded the councillors as guided by 'eccentric principles of socialistic philanthropy and feminist ambition'.[20] These words were of course inappropriate, but they do hint, as the other judgements do not, that the case was highly charged politically and was the culmination of a number of previous legal and political encounters instigated by the overtly anti-capitalist and pro-socialist manoeuvres of the leader of Poplar council, George Lansbury.[21] Nevertheless, despite the overblown rhetoric of some of the

---

[17] *R.* v. *Roberts, ex p. Scurr* [1924] 1 KB 514.
[18] Ibid. [1924] 2 KB 695.
[19] Now under the name *Roberts* v. *Hopwood* [1925] AC 578.
[20] Ibid., at 594.
[21] Outlined in B. Keith-Lucas, 'Poplarism', *Public Law* (1962), 52. For example, 'We are

law lords in this case the decision itself, as has subsequently been recognised,[22] was based not upon the 'unreasonableness' of the council's actions, but on the ground that it had acted strictly outside its given powers. The statute permitted the council to pay 'salaries and wages'. What was effectively paid was considered to be a 'gratuity', because of the fact that the levels of payment were significantly out of line with those prevailing in the labour market.

Diceyism during this period by no means died a quiet death. Some judges were insistent upon their right to assert the rule of law. Dissenting from the majority in *R. v. Halliday*,[23] Lord Shaw said:

> The increasing crush of legislative efforts and the convenience to the Executive of a refuge to the device of Orders in Council would increase the danger [of arbitrary government after the war] tenfold were the judiciary to approach any such action by the Government in a spirit of compliance rather than of independent scrutiny. That way would also lie public unrest and public peril.

In that spirit, the lord chief justice, Lord Hewart, published a tract entitled *The New Despotism* in 1929. This work railed against the replacement of the ordinary law by statutes; against the growing practice of framework legislation (which delegated to government departments the power to fill out the gaps in the legislation), and against the evasion of judicial control of discretionary power.[24] Sir John Marriott, an Oxford academic who later became a Conservative member of Parliament,[25] and C. K. Allen[26] joined forces with Hewart, although to little avail. Diceyism in its raw form was in terminal decline. As the American Supreme Court

---

all clear class-conscious Socialists working together, using the whole machinery of local government and Parliament for the transformation of Capitalist Society into Socialism. We are under no delusions about our day by day work. We are only patching up and making good some of the evils of Capitalism.' Ibid., 57. Lansbury and some of his fellow councillors had been committed to Brixton Prison for contempt of court. Ibid., 59–63.

[22] In *Pickwell v. Camden LBC* [1983] QB 962.

[23] [1917] AC 260, 287.

[24] Lord Bingham has recently researched some of the lesser known writings and speeches of Lord Hewart in his Lionel Cohen Lecture at the Hebrew University of Jerusalem. See The Rt Hon. Lord Bingham of Cornhill, 'The Old Despotism', *Israel Law Review* (1999), 169. Perhaps the most characteristic is Lord Hewart's reply to the toast to the judges at the Mansion House in June 1928 where he parodied the coming of a 'new Eldorado' 'where there will be no judges at all' and 'all controversial questions will be decided in the third floor back of some or other Government Department'.

[25] J. Marriott, *The Mechanism of the Modern State* (Clarendon Press, 1927).

[26] C. K. Allen, *Law in the Making* (Clarendon Press, 1927), *Bureaucracy Triumphant* (Oxford University Press, 1931), and later *Law and Orders* (Stevens, 1950).

judge and former Harvard law professor, Felix Frankfurter, wrote a few years later: 'The persistence of the misdirection that Dicey has given to the development of administrative law strikingly proves the elder Huxley's observation that many a theory survives long after its brains are knocked out.'[27]

Two academics then at the London School of Economics, William Robson and Ivor Jennings, guided by a third, Harold Laski[28], probably had most influence in hastening the demise of Dicey's influence in the 1920s and 1930s. Robson's book, *Justice and Administrative Law*, published in 1928, sought to justify a system of public law in Britain. He argued convincingly that Dicey had misunderstood the French system, and that in England there was and had been in Dicey's time 'colossal distinctions' between the rights and duties of private individuals and those of public bodies. He showed how, increasingly, Parliament had conferred decision-making powers not on the courts (as Dicey required for his rule of law), but upon specialised bodies of adjudication. This was because these bodies were cheaper and speedier and had 'fewer prejudices against government' than the courts.[29] Robson proposed a separate system of administrative courts, outside of the ordinary courts, as the best means of endorsing judicial attitudes inside of the administration and of rationalising the 'labyrinthine' system of administrative adjudication.

The Donoughmore Committee into Ministers' Powers, established in 1929,[30] was set up by the Labour government to consider whether both administrative adjudication and the increasing resort to delegated legislation unduly offended the rule of law. The committee accepted Robson's view that there was no need for alarm in respect of either development, both of which were necessary for effective modern governance. Robson's prescription of a separate, specialised system of administrative courts was, however, roundly rejected.

---

[27] F. Frankfurter, Foreword to 'Discussion of Current Developments in Administrative Law', *Yale Law Journal* (1938), 515, 517.

[28] See H. Laski, *A Grammar of Politics* (Allen & Unwin, 1926); 'The Growth of Administrative Discretion', *Journal of Public Administration* (1923); 'Judicial Review of Social Policy in England', *Harvard Law Review* (1926), 839 (arriving at the conclusion that the *Poplar* case, above note 19, showed the House of Lords as 'the servant of a single class in the community', at 848).

[29] W. A. Robson, *Justice and Administrative Law* (1928), 2nd edn (Stevens, 1947), pp. 343–7. For a similar approach see J. Willis, *The Parliamentary Powers of English Government Departments* (Harvard University Press, 1933).

[30] *Report of the Committee on Ministers' Powers*, Cmd 4060 (1932).

Jennings' attack on Dicey was even less restrained. Like Robson, Jennings regarded the approach of public law to be distinct and requiring different attitudes from those of the private lawyer. In his *Law and the Constitution*, published in 1933, he equated Dicey's opposition to state regulation and administrative discretion with that of the 'manufacturers who formed the backbone of the Whig Party', who 'wanted nothing which interfered with profits, even if profits involved child labour, wholesale factory accidents, the pollution of the rivers, of the air, and of the water supply, jerry-built houses, low wages and other incidents of nineteenth-century industrialism'.[31] Jennings did not believe that the constitution should be based upon a system of individual rights which was suited to a system based upon individualism and the philosophy of *laissez faire*.[32]

The outbreak of the Second World War in 1939 resulted in unprecedented centralisation of power. The notorious Regulation 18B of the Defence (General) Regulations was made in 1939, conferring power on the home secretary to detain anyone whom he had 'reasonable cause to believe' to be of 'hostile origin or associations'. A number of recent refugees fleeing Hitler's Germany were detained under this provision, including Jack Perlzweig, alias Robert Liversidge, who challenged his detention on the ground that there was no evidence of any 'reasonable cause' for the home secretary's belief of any 'hostility' on his part to Britain (or of any 'associations' with the Hitler regime). The House of Lords, by an eight-to-one majority, interpreted the regulations as conferring virtually infinite power on the home secretary and upheld his actions despite the lack of any objective evidence against Liversidge. In his ringing dissent, Lord Atkin rebuked his fellow judges for permitting the home secretary to infringe a person's freedoms on a mere suspicion. He was appalled that his brethren, 'on a mere question of construction, when face to face with claims involving the liberty of the subject, show

[31] Sir Ivor Jennings, *The Law and the Constitution* (University of London Press, 1933), pp. 309–10.

[32] These views were also shared by others associated with Robson and Laski, especially through the journal *Political Quarterly*. They included Leonard Woolf, John Maynard Keynes (see his pamphlet, published by Leonard and Virginia Woolf at the Hogarth Press in 1926, entitled *The End of Laissez Faire*), and George Bernard Shaw, who is quoted by Greenleaf as saying: 'The ocean of Socialism cannot be poured into the pint pot of a nineteenth-century parliament.' *The British Political Tradition*, vol. 2, p. 369. See, further, Loughlin, *Public Law and Political Theory* (Methuen, 1987), pp. 165–74, who also mentions the contributions of Tawney and Malinowski. See also C. Glasser. 'Radicals and Refugees: The Foundations of the *Modern Law Review* and English Legal Scholarship', *Modern Law Review* (1987), 688.

themselves more executive minded than the Executive'. Just how executive-minded the judges had become was displayed in their hostile attitude to Lord Atkin himself for daring to dissent in so forthright a manner during what he referred to as the 'clash of arms'.[33] However, the majority of the Lords made it clear that their deferential attitude to ministerial authority was not confined to times of war. As Lord Macmillan put it, their approach was 'in accordance with a general rule applicable to the interpretation of all statutes or statutory regulations in peace-time as well as in war-time'.

Later in the war a seven-judge House of Lords refused to require the Crown to reveal evidence that was sought by the victims of a tragic submarine accident.[34] And even after the war ended the courts continued to allow public authorities free reign, for example, by upholding statutory clauses seeking to avoid the jurisdiction of the courts.[35] 'Ouster clauses' thus became a legitimate means of shielding official powers from judicial control. Even without such blatant protection, however, the judges developed a doctrine to avoid interference in the substance of administrative decisions. In 1948, the court refused to strike down the decision of the Wednesbury council which forbade children under the age of 16 attending cinema performances on a Sunday (whatever the context of the film showing and whether or not accompanied by an adult). The court refrained from striking down the decision and allowed a very wide margin of discretion to the council. Lord Greene said that courts should not interfere with such decisions on the ground that the body had acted merely unreasonably. In order to summon the court's intervention the body had to act in a way which was 'so unreasonable that no reasonable body could so act'.[36] This tautologous definition is not easy to comprehend in the abstract. In practice, what has come to be known as 'Wednesbury unreasonableness' signalled yet a further green light to public authorities possessed of discretionary power.[37] Henceforth courts

---

[33] For an account of Lord Atkin's ostracisation by his fellow law lords see Robert Stevens, *Law and Politics* (Weidenfeld & Nicolson, 1979), p. 287.

[34] *Duncan* v. *Cammell Laird & Co.* [1942] AC 736.

[35] *Smith* v. *East Elloe Rural District Council* [1956] AC 736. The terms of the clauses varied. Some provided that the decision of the administrative body should be 'final and conclusive'. Others precluded any legal challenge of the body's determination. Others precluded legal challenge after a period of time (usually six weeks).

[36] Per Lord Greene MR in *Associated Provincial Picture Houses Ltd* v. *Wednesbury Corporation* [1948] 1 KB 22, at 229–30.

[37] See the 'green light' and 'red light' approaches drawn by Harlow and Rawlings. C. Harlow and R. Rawlings, *Law and Administration* (1984), 2nd edn (Butterworth, 1997).

would only interfere with such power if the arguments in favour of so doing were 'overwhelming'[38] or if the body had 'taken leave of its senses'.[39]

The radical programme of public services, regulation and nationalisation introduced by the Labour government, elected in 1945, clearly required for its implementation a range of discretionary powers. Two influential voices at the London School of Economics had foreseen that the habit of draconian wartime powers could tempt the architects of socialism into adapting them to their cause. F. A. Hayek had passionately warned against that route, pleading for a return to the rule of law, for fear of what he called *The Road to Serfdom*.[40] Harold Laski, much earlier even, had by contrast spotted the opportunity with delight, writing that: 'Anyone who studies the record of war-control of industry from 1914 to 18, will be amazed at the mass of material we possess upon the necessary mechanisms of regulation.'[41]

The opportunity was not lost. Few avenues of legal challenge were built in to the procedures of the new bodies, whether those of the National Health Service, or those of local authorities (for example, to grant or refuse permission to develop land) or those of the new public corporations governing the nationalised industries such as coal and the railways. Such controls as were provided over the discretion or performance of these bodies relied for their implementation upon parliamentary scrutiny, or upon weak overseeing boards, or administrative tribunals (often containing lay or industry representation), or public inquiries (conducted by an inspectorate who would report to the minister to take the ultimate decision). Even within the seemingly more judicialised bodies, such as the tribunals and inquiries, procedures were informal. As William Robson wrote in the second edition of *Justice and Administrative Law* in 1947, the avoidance of judicial control of administration was not due to any 'fit of absentmindedness'. The primary motive was

---

[38] Lord Greene in *Wednesbury*, above note 36.

[39] Per Lord Scarman in *R. v. Secretary of State for the Environment ex p. Nottinghamshire CC* [1986] AC 240, 247–8. Judicial review is not equivalent to review on the merits of a decision. Nevertheless, the extent of deference accorded by the *Wednesbury* approach is broader than is absolutely necessary. See for example the more restricted approach towards substantive discretion adopted by Lord Justice Scrutton in the *Poplar* case, above note 17, and that adopted in the nineteenth century by the chief justice (Lord Russell of Killowen) in *Kruse v. Johnson* [1889] 2 KB 291. See, generally, J. Jowell and A. Lester, 'Beyond *Wednesbury*: Substantive Principles of Judicial Review', *Public Law* (1987).

[40] Published in 1943. See also F. A. Hayek, *The Constitution of Liberty* (Routledge & Kegan Paul, 1960).

[41] Laski, *A Grammar of Politics* (1925), in the 1967 edn, p. 489. Quoted by Loughlin, *Public Law and Political Theory*.

revealed by Aneurin Bevan, health minister in the 1945 Labour government and architect of the National Health Service, during a debate in the House of Commons on the subject of legal controls over the myriad of new health bodies he was about to create. Bevan stoutly defended the fact that the proposed tribunals, established to resolve disputes, would be divorced from the 'ordinary courts'. He candidly admitted the reason, namely the likelihood of 'judicial sabotage [of] socialist legislation'.[42]

Stage three: towards administrative justice

Reaction against government unconstrained during a time of relative peace was probably predictable. From the late 1950s consumers were flexing their muscles everywhere, whether to protest against urban renewal schemes which rendered thousands homeless, without much consultation, or to assert the 'welfare rights' of recipients of state benefits. Complacency about the wisdom of our civil service to exercise its discretion unimpeded by law was somewhat shaken by the Crichel Down affair,[43] which then prompted the establishment in 1955 of the Franks Committee into tribunals and inquiries dealing with land. Franks firmly insisted that the locus of the system of tribunals and inquiries was in the sphere of justice, rather than administration.[44] Franks both troubled and pleased Robson. Robson was disappointed that Franks did not recommend a separate system of administrative courts, which he had always promoted. Franks preferred to integrate the tribunal and inquiry system into those of the courts. But Robson had always argued for controls over discretion (to a far greater extent than Jennings), and was concerned at the 'hegemony of the executive'. He therefore welcomed the greater judicialisation which Franks proposed for the system of tribunals and inquiries and lauded Franks' attempt to strengthen their 'fairness, openness and impartiality'.[45]

The procedural protections recommended by Franks were achieved by means of a general statute,[46] and by administrative codes and regulations aimed principally at the procedures of planning inquiries (for

---

[42] HC Deb., 23 July 1946, col. 1983.

[43] Peter Hennessy refers to the 'moral panic' induced by that incident, *Whitehall* (Secker & Warburg 1989), p. 502. And see Loughlin, *Public Law and Political Theory* p. 179.

[44] Report of the Committee on Tribunals and Inquiries, Cmnd 218 (1957).

[45] See Robson's account of Franks, 'Administrative Justice and Injustice: A Commentary on the Franks Report', *Public Law* (1958).

[46] The Tribunals and Inquiries Act (now 1992).

example, requiring the publication of those inspectors' reports previously protected by cases such as *Arlidge*).[47]

Before moving to consider how the courts changed their deferential attitude to administration—and that is a remarkable chapter in the history of the common law of the UK—it should be noted that the enterprise of fashioning the development of administrative law during this phase did not only involve the judiciary. The impetus for a variety of controls over official power came equally from Parliament, and indeed even the executive (through planning inquiry regulations, for example, which were drafted in Whitehall). It was Parliament which introduced into the UK a distant relative of the Scandinavian ombudsman, known here as the parliamentary commissioner for administration, and charged with the task of rooting out 'maladministration' in areas not normally amenable to recourse through the courts or tribunals.[48] In the 1960s laws were passed prohibiting, first, race discrimination, and, then, sex discrimination (in 1964 and 1966 respectively), which established positive statutory rights to equality in those areas. Mention should also be made of the fact that in 1952 Britain acceded to the European Convention on Human Rights. We were the first signatory. Although the Convention was not made subject to mandatory interpretation by English judges until the very end of the century, in 1966 the right of direct petition to the Court of Human Rights at Strasbourg was permitted to UK citizens. In international law, at least, human rights against the state were thus recognised.[49]

What of the judges? We have seen that they had been 'leaning over backwards almost to the point of falling off the Bench to avoid the appearance of hostility [to the government]'.[50] But in the mid-1960s a number of key cases were decided which ushered in a radically altered approach. Those artificial barriers to procedural justice introduced in

---

[47] [1915] AC 120.

[48] Parliamentary Commissioner Act 1967. Extensions of the powers of the parliamentary commissioner to the NHS followed under the National Health Services Reorganisation Act 1973. Commissioners for local administration were established under the Local Government Act 1974.

[49] The Convention is based to a large extent upon the Universal Declaration of Human Rights. The UK is also a signatory to other later international human rights instruments such as the International Covenant of Civil and Political Rights.

[50] J. A. G. Griffith in Morris Ginsberg (ed.), *Law and Opinion in England in the Twentieth Century* (Stevens, 1959), writing more particularly about the attitude of judges to the Labour government of 1945–51.

Arlidge were dismantled by the House of Lords in *Ridge* v. *Baldwin*.[51] It would no longer matter whether a person was denied a privilege or a right, or whether the situation was judicial or administrative. If an important interest was at stake, such as reputation or livelihood, a person should be afforded a fair hearing. In *Conway* v. *Rimmer*,[52] the Lords refused to shelter the Crown from the duty to produce documents for inspection. In future it would be for the court to decide whether those documents should be privileged. In 1968 the Lords held that a statute, which on a literal interpretation conferred an unfettered discretion upon the minister to hold an inquiry into farmers' complaints, should be interpreted purposively. Despite the words of the statute on its face (which contained the well-known formula 'the minister *may* [hold an inquiry into complaints]'), the failure to investigate genuine grievances ran counter to the 'objects and purpose' of the statute.[53]

In 1969 a tried and tested method employed by Parliament to protect its administrators from judicial intervention was mauled by the courts. The device was the 'ouster clause'—a provision in a statute that provides that no decision of the body in question could be challenged in any court of law. In the case of *Anisminic*[54] such a clause sought to protect a decision of the Foreign Compensation Commission from judicial review. The House of Lords was not, however, deterred from intervening in this case. It was held, robustly, that the ouster clause did not protect the commission from being reviewed when its decision went outside its jurisdiction, having been infected by an error of law. Most legal errors would qualify as jurisdictional errors.

Anisminic seemed to amount to a direct challenge to parliamentary sovereignty. Despite Parliament's apparently clear words to the contrary, the courts insisted on their right to review. By later standards, the reasoning of *Anisminic* is cautious and tortuous—scant attention was paid, at least overtly, to the principle of access to justice which the ouster clause would offend. Nevertheless, the courts had significantly flexed their muscles, and Parliament and public bodies took notice of the fact that 'judge-proof' clauses were not easy to sustain.

---

[51] [1964] AC 40. The case concerned the dismissal of a chief constable without a hearing. The tenure of the chief constable could be terminated virtually at will, therefore there was no right to a continuation of his appointment and there was no duty on the committee to hold any judicialised hearing on the matter.

[52] [1968] AC 910.

[53] *Padfield* v. *Minister of Agriculture, Fisheries and Food* [1968] AC 997.

[54] *Anisminic* v. *Foreign Compensation Commission* [1969] AC 147.

In the space of just five years the attitude of the courts to the administration turned dramatically. Power conferred broadly was no longer read as necessarily conferring unfettered discretion. In *Padfield* it was even said that unfettered discretion is not recognised in law.[55] There were of course cases the other way. Where national security was involved, the courts would tend to defer to the executive,[56] but the position had been reached where virtually no statutory power was unreviewable. And the courts were increasingly ready to extend their categories of review. For example, the situations in which a fair hearing could be provided were being expanded. Even where a person's mere expectations were disappointed, without any right or even interest adversely affected, the courts required a hearing on the matter to be held. The notion of the 'legitimate expectation' was endorsed by the House of Lords in the *GCHQ* case,[57] in 1984, where it was held that the minister for the civil service (who was the prime minister, Margaret Thatcher) could not withdraw the rights to membership of a trade union from workers at the Cheltenham security headquarters without a hearing. Although the civil servants had no rights to union membership, they had a legitimate expectation of a continuation of their membership, and of being consulted if membership was withdrawn. That case was significant too for the fact that it accepted that even a prerogative power could be reviewed by the courts. (Civil servants' conditions of employment are made under the prerogative power.) The Civil Servants Union was deprived of victory in the case because the court accepted the prime minister's claim that her decision was justified on the grounds of national security. (She feared that strikes at GCHQ could impede important communications.) However, the Lords held (and this too was new law) that the mere assertion by the government that national security was imperilled would no longer act as an automatic barrier to further inquiry by the court. The court had to be furnished with at least some evidence of that assertion.

In the 1980s and 1990s the Conservative government sought to roll back the boundaries of government. Executive agencies were created,[58] such as the Employment Service under the Department of Employment, the Benefits Agency under the Department of Social Security, or the

---

[55] See especially Lord Upjohn in *Padfield* [1968] AC 997.

[56] See *R. v. Secretary of State for Home Affairs ex p. Hosenball and Agee* [1977] 1 WLR 766.

[57] *Council for the Civil Service Unions v. Minister for the Civil Service* [1985] AC 374.

[58] These were established broadly along the lines proposed by members of the prime minister's Efficiency Unit in a paper entitled *Improving Management in Government: The Next Steps* (1988).

quasi-independent Planning Inspectorate—all operating at arm's length from ministers and headed by chief executive officers and operating under 'framework documents'. From 1991 it was government policy to 'market test' functions with a view to contracting them out to the private sector where appropriate. Prisons and health services were 'hived off' to the private sector companies and health trusts. 'Government by contract' replaced the 'command and control' model of public administration in many areas.[59] Most of the nationalised industries were privatised during this time.

It is important to note that the divesting of state ownership and some governmental functions during that period did not result in the abandonment of government regulation. One offshoot of the privatisation of a number of natural monopolies (water, gas, etc.) was the creation of new bodies to regulate the new industries and to protect the consumers from monopolistic practices. Thus, the new Office of Gas (OFFGAS) and Office of Water (OFFWAT) and others came into being.[60] The executive agencies and other bodies were controlled by a new Citizen's Charter initiative,[61] which required that a number of bodies which had public or quasi-public functions should produce particulars of their services and establish complaints procedures for aggrieved 'customers'.[62] The Higher Education Funding Councils were given powers to ensure the quality of teaching and research in the universities. Central control over local authority financing and other powers was greatly increased.[63] In addition, various bodies were created to seek financial accountability[64] and to avoid corruption at all levels of government.[65] A convincing argument could be made that the Thatcher and Major years, from 1979 to 1997,

---

[59] See Ian Harden, Norman Lewis and Cosmo Fisher, *The Contracting State* (Open University, 1992).

[60] See A. Ogus, *Regulation, Legal Form and Economic Theory* (Clarendon Press, 1994); Tony Prosser, *Law and the Regulators* (Clarendon Press, 1997).

[61] *The Citizen's Charter*, Cm 1599 (1991).

[62] See Norman Lewis and Patrick Birkinshaw *When Citizens Complain: Reforming Justice and Administration* (Open University Press, 1993).

[63] See Martin Loughlin, *Local Government in the Modern State* (Sweet & Maxwell, 1986).

[64] The Local Government Finance Act 1982 established the Audit Commission to attempt to control local authority expenditure. The National Audit Office performs a similar role for central bodies. See J. McEldowney, 'The National Audit Office and Privatisation', *Modern Law Review* (1991); 'The Control of Public Expenditure' in J. Jowell and D. Oliver, *The Changing Constitution*, 4th edn (Oxford University Press, 2000).

[65] The House of Commons Committee on Standards in Public Life. See its first report establishing 'Seven Principles of Public Life', Cm 2850. A parliamentary commissioner for standards was established in 1995.

resulted in a significant strengthening of state power and more rather than less regulation.[66]

The long reign of a Conservative government pledged to privatisation and deregulation (whatever the reality) by no means stemmed the tide of judicial activism. The protective walls around the government continued to crumble. Prompted by the European Court of Justice, the Lords issued an injunction against the Crown, first where Community law was directly in issue,[67] later when domestic law was in issue as well.[68] Then the House of Lords assumed the jurisdiction to make a finding of contempt against a minister of the Crown who disobeyed an undertaking given during the course of judicial review proceedings.[69] A duty to give reasons for an administrative decision, although not yet general, was being progressively imposed.[70] The reach of judicial review extended. Increasingly, review was undertaken of powers exercised under the residual royal prerogative.[71] Even self-regulatory bodies, such as the Panel on Takeovers and Mergers of the Stock Exchange, were considered amenable to judicial review[72] on the ground that, although strictly private in structure, they were considered in effect to be performing a public, regulatory function.

As was the case under the second stage of judicial review, the new principles of control were largely confined to procedural matters. In a notable case, the National Union of Journalists challenged the home secretary's ban on the broadcasting of the direct words of the spokespersons of certain Northern Ireland terrorist organisations. The House of Lords held that the ban was not unreasonable in the *Wednesbury* sense (in the sense of being 'absurd') and declined to lower that high threshold of review in favour of the continental principle of 'proportionality', with its more intense scrutiny of the administrative decision.[73]

Nevertheless, in that case and one or two others at that time, we do

---

[66] An argument convincingly made by Simon Jenkins, *Accountable to None: The Tory Nationalisation of Britain* (Hamish Hamilton, 1995).

[67] *R. v. Secretary of State for Transport, ex p. Factortame (No. 2)* [1989] 1 AC 374.

[68] *R. v. Secretary of State for Employment, ex p. Equal Opportunities Commission* [1995] 1 AC 1.

[69] *M. v. Home Office; sub nom. Re M* [1994] 1 AC 377.

[70] *R. v. Secretary of State for the Home Department, ex p. Doody* [1994] 3 WLR 154.

[71] *R. v. Secretary of State for the Home Department, ex p. Fire Brigades Union* [1995] 2 WLR 1 (HL). Even the power of (retrospective) pardon for a person sentenced to death thirty-nine years earlier was reviewed in *R. v. Secretary of State for the Home Departments, ex p. Bentley* [1994] QB 349.

[72] *R. v. Panel on Takeovers and Mergers, ex p. Datafin plc* [1987] 1 QB 815.

[73] *R. v. Secretary of State for the Home Department, ex p. Brind* [1991] AC 696 (HL), especially Lords Ackner and Lowry.

see the beginnings of a recognition by the courts that infringements upon fundamental human rights by officials require some special attention. Where the right to life was at issue, in an asylum case,[74] or the right of expression, as in the broadcasting ban case, the courts were willing at least to provide more 'anxious scrutiny' of the decision. While not yet explicitly abandoning the *Wednesbury* reserve, it was said by Lord Bingham MR in a case upholding the defence secretary's ban on homosexuals in the armed forces: 'the more substantial the interference with human rights, the more the court will require by way of justification before it is satisfied that the decision is reasonable . . . in the sense that it is beyond the range of responses open to a reasonable decision-maker'.[75]

Stage four: constitutional limits on governance

At the end of what I have called the third stage, the notion of administrative law is clearly established and in general accepted. Various influential judges have commented that administrative law exists and is desirable.[76] Even Lord Diplock, who stood against judicial intervention in some of the notable cases in the 1960s, exhibited all the zeal of a convert when he pronounced that the development of a system of administrative law was one of the greatest developments of his judicial lifetime.[77] Claims of a 'system' of administrative law were probably overblown, insofar as the notion of a system imports connotations of unity and coherence. Nevertheless, following reports of the Law Commission,[78] the procedures for hearing 'public law' cases were consolidated in 1978, through the introduction of an 'application for judicial review'.[79] From then on, relatively specialised judges nominated to the 'Crown Office list' of the High Court, would hear the applications for judicial review and related cases, by means of a procedure more simplified than

[74] R. v. *Secretary of State for the Home Department, ex p. Bugdaycay* [1987] AC 514, at 531.
[75] R. v. *Ministry of Defence, ex p. Smith* [1996] QB 517, at 554.
[76] Whereas even Lord Reid could say in 1964: 'We do not have a system of administrative law, because up until fairly recently we did not need it', in *Ridge v. Baldwin* [1964] AC 40, at 72. Lord Denning said: 'It may truly now be said that we have a developed system of administrative law.' *Breen v. Amalgamated Engineering* [1971] 2 QB 175, at 189.
[77] '. . . progress towards a comprehensive system of administrative law . . . I regard as having been the greatest achievements of English courts in my judicial lifetime', R. v. *Inland Revenue Commissioners, ex p. National Federation of the Self-employed and Small Businesses Ltd* [1982] AC 617, at 641.
[78] *Remedies in Administrative Law,* Cm 6407 (1976).
[79] *Rules of the Supreme Court* 1977, Order 53. See also Supreme Court Act 1981.

the normal writ procedures. The stage was set for a more coherent set of public law principles to be developed.

Strangely enough, during the great expansion of judicial review and other controls over administrative decision-making in that period, the overall purpose of administrative law was rarely considered. Does it exist to heighten the accountability of officials to the public? Or to ensure 'good administrative practice'? Is its purpose to promote responsiveness of public bodies to those they serve? To ensure that they keep within the bounds of their conferred powers? Or simply to promote fairness? In all this, are we concerned to enforce the duties of administrators or to protect the rights of individuals against the state?

On the whole, the expansion of public law case-law took place without much philosophical justification. The courts determine the scope of official power by reference to seemingly neutral principles of fairness or reasonableness, specified only by an empirically determined list of administrative sins, such as the failure to take into account relevant considerations; acting for an improper purpose; lack of a fair hearing or natural justice; manifest unreasonableness, and so on. In the *GCHQ* case Lord Diplock helpfully categorised three 'grounds' of judicial review: illegality, procedural impropriety and irrationality.[80] It is noteworthy that none of these grounds is explicitly justified by any particular constitutional imperative, or by reference to any overriding purpose. The rules of bad (or good) public administration hang in suspended animation, not grounded in any fundamental purpose or explicit constitutional context.

It was only in the 1990s that the theoretical basis of judicial review was engaged in any depth. Two theses heatedly vied with each other.[81] The first, known as the *ultra vires* theory,[82] contends that, when the courts strike down the action of officials acting under broad powers conferred by Parliament, they are enforcing the intent of Parliament, express or implied. This theory holds passionately that courts cannot do other than enforce Parliament's will, as Parliament is the supreme source of constitutional authority.

The second thesis advances a justification for judicial review that is based upon the quasi-autonomous authority of the common law.[83] This thesis contends that to ascribe the growing restraints upon official action

---

[80] See [1985] AC 374, at 410.

[81] The various contributions to the debate have been collected in one volume. See C. Forsyth (ed.), *Judicial Review and the Constitution* (Hart, 2000).

[82] See the articles in Forsyth, *Judicial Review*, by Forsyth and Elliott.

[83] See the articles in Forsyth, *Judicial Review*, by Oliver, Craig, Laws and Dyzenhaus.

to parliamentary intent is a fiction or fig leaf. It also points out that some official power does not rest upon Parliament's statutes (prerogative power, or contractual power, for example). Judicial review is fashioned by the judges, in accordance with the inherent principles of the common law. Both sides of this debate have recently made concessions to the other. (For example, the *ultra vires* camp assumes that Parliament by implication accepts the creative role of judges, and the common law protagonists in the main accept that the standards of judicial review should yield to parliamentary provision to the contrary.)

In the mid-1990s the judges themselves answered the question about the proper basis for judicial review. For the first time, a justification was provided for judicial intervention—a justification based neither upon *ultra vires*, nor upon the common law. Instead of pretending that the common law contained, and had always contained, principles to restrain the state, the courts rested their decisions upon the constitutional foundations of a properly democratic state and invoked principles of democracy (other than parliamentary sovereignty alone) upon which to ground their decisions.

In the *Leech* case[84] the Court of Appeal struck down a prison rule, made under legislation which conferred broad discretionary power upon the home secretary to regulate and manage prisons. The rule in question permitted the governor to censor correspondence between a prisoner and solicitor. Lord Steyn held that a prisoner's right to communicate in confidence with his or her solicitor was a 'constitutional right'—that of access to justice—even where no specific litigation was contemplated.[85] It could only be interfered with where there was a 'pressing need' and the intrusion even then should be the minimum necessary to ensure that the correspondence was bona fide. The home secretary, it was held, had not in that case discharged the onus of satisfying that test.

A similar approach was taken in the *Witham* case,[86] where the Divisional Court struck down an order of the former Lord Chancellor who, under a very wide enabling power, imposed substantial court fees, even upon litigants in person. Laws J. held that this order interfered with the constitutional right of access to a court.

In the case of *Pierson*,[87] a prisoner serving a life sentence had been

---

[84] R. v. *Secretary of State for the Home Department, ex p. Leech (No. 2)* [1994] QB 198.
[85] In *Raymond* v. *Honey* [1983] AC 1, Lord Wilberforce had endorsed the 'basic right' of a prisoner of access to the court.
[86] R. v. *Lord Chancellor, ex p. Witham* [1997] 1 WLR 104.
[87] R. v. *Secretary of State for the Home Department, ex p. Pierson* [1998] AC 539.

told that a tariff period (minimum period of incarceration) of fifteen years would be applied in his case. The former home secretary then raised the tariff to twenty years. The majority of the House of Lords held the home secretary's decision unlawful, for differing reasons. Lord Steyn held that to increase the tariff retrospectively was to offend the rule of law, which had substantive effect as well as procedural. He also held that the courts were entitled to assume that:

> Parliament does not legislate in a vacuum. Parliament legislates for a European liberal democracy based upon the principles and traditions of the common law . . . and . . . unless there is the clearest provision to the contrary, Parliament must be presumed not to legislate contrary to the rule of law.[88]

The above cases justify judicial intervention specifically on the basis of the constitutional principle of the rule of law. Unless Parliament speaks clearly to the contrary the rule of law is expected to prevail. But the rule of law is just one of a number of constitutional principles that may be invoked. Another is freedom of expression, endorsed in the case of *Simms*,[89] where a unanimous House of Lords held unlawful the home secretary's blanket ban on prisoners giving oral interviews to journalists in the cause of the protestations of their innocence.

We see here that at the century's end the courts shift the boundaries of administrative law into the constitutional realm by explicitly endorsing a higher order of rights inherent in our constitutional democracy. These rights apply both to the procedures of public bodies and to the substance of their decisions. They emanate not from any implied parliamentary intent, nor from any general principles hidden in the interstices of the common law, but from the framework of modern democracy within which Parliament legislates. They are 'not a consequence of the democratic process but logically prior to it'.[90] Parliament can exclude these

---

[88] *R. v. Secretary of State for the Home Department, ex p. Pierson* [1998] AC 539, at 575 and Lord Browne-Wilkinson said: 'A power conferred by Parliament in general terms is not to be taken to authorise the doing of acts by the donee of the power which adversely affects the legal rights of the citizen or the basic principles on which the law of the United Kingdom is based unless the statute conferring the power makes it clear that such was the intention of Parliament.'

[89] *R. v. Secretary of State for the Home Department, ex p. Simms* [1999] 3 All ER 400.

[90] Sir John Laws, 'Law and Democracy', *Public Law* (1995), 72, citing R. Latham, *The Law and the Commonwealth* (1949), p. 523. Laws was one of several judges who, writing extra-judicially, sought to place judicial review within the context of democratic rights. See, for example, Lord Browne-Wilkinson, 'The Infiltration of a Bill of Rights', *Public Law* (1992); Lord Scarman, 'The Development of Administrative Law: Obstacles and Opportunities',

rights but it must do so in clear language. Silence or ambiguity will not suffice. There is a presumption in favour of the rights operating which may only be rebutted by express statutory language or necessary implication. The mere conferral of broad discretionary power on the decision-maker will not necessarily be sufficient to rebut that presumption.

This approach is a far cry from the mere assertion of tenets of good administration, based on general notions of fairness writ large. It challenges the notion of democracy as being the equivalent of majority rule. It asserts that in any democracy properly so-called certain fundamental rights must be assumed to be entrenched, even against the power of the majority. It contends that such a limitation does not impair democracy, but constitutes its full realisation.

It was not only the judges, at the end of the century, who fashioned that approach to constitutionality and democracy. Parliament itself concurred. One of the first acts of the Labour government, elected in 1997, was to enact the Human Rights Act 1998, which held that all acts of public officials should in future comply with most of the provisions of the European Convention on Human Rights.[91] In addition to any constitutional rights already inherent in the law, express Convention rights now reinforce the limitations of government officials. Most significant, however, is the fact that the Act permits the courts to review not only the acts of officials but also primary and subordinate legislation for conformity with Convention rights. In respect of legislation, the courts are limited to issuing a 'declaration of incompatibility', which will not affect the validity, continuing operation or enforcement of the provision of the incompatible statute.[92] The device of the declaration of incompatibility affords an accommodation between parliamentary sovereignty and the rule of law. The courts may review the legislation and speak if it is held to be deficient by the standards of the newly defined, limited democracy. Yet it is up to Parliament in the end to decide whether to

---

Public Law (1994); Sir Stephen Sedley, 'The Sound of Silence: Constitutional Law without a Constitution', *Law Quarterly Review* (1994); Lord Woolf, 'Droit Public: English Style', *Public Law* (1995). For a comprehensive account of the application of human rights in the courts see Murray Hunt, *Using Human Rights in English Courts* (Hart, 1997), ch. 5.

[91] For a comprehensive record of the debate in the last third of the twentieth century in favour and against the incorporation in domestic law of a bill of rights see Robert Blackburn, *Towards a Constitutional Bill of Rights for the United Kingdom* (Pinter, 1999). Particularly influential proponents of a bill of rights were Lord Scarman, Anthony Lester and Michael Zander. Ronald Dworkin's works, especially *Taking Rights Seriously* (Duckworth, 1977), provided the philosophical justification for a model of limited government.

[92] Human Rights Act 1998, section 4.

accede to the court's declaration. The Act helpfully provides the machinery for speedy amendment so as to bring legislation in conformity with Convention rights.[93]

Some speculation and conclusion

We have seen over the century different attitudes towards the exercise of state power and its legal control. The century began with a concern for procedural justice and a particular concept of the rule of law. It ended with judicial constraints upon both the procedures and the substance of official decisions, justified by constitutional rights. In the middle part of the century government was left relatively free of legal constraints. Why did these various swings between deference and defiance take place? What justified what the distinguished American legal historian Lawrence Friedman calls a 'zone of immunity'[94] around government in the middle part of the century; and the invasion of that zone in the 1960s? To what needs or demands were the judges and Parliament responding? Was the new activism from the 1960s appropriate to the judicial role? Certainly some critics thought that the judges had over-stepped their mark; that they were close to deciding public policy, which is the proper preserve of politics; and that they were, by training and inclination, conservative and prone to strike disproportionately at the designs of the political Left, as in *Poplar* days, on matters with which they were out of tune.[95]

It is certainly true that the target of the first wave of judicial activism in the mid-1960s was largely ministers in the then Labour government. However, ministers in the Conservative government from 1979 to 1997 received more than their share of judicial drubbing. In the late 1990s there broke out what *The Economist* described as a 'turf war'[96] between

[93] Human Rights Act, section 10 and Schedule 2. Section 3(1) of the Act provides that: 'So far as it is possible to do so, primary legislation and subordinate legislation must be read and given effect in a way which is compatible with convention rights.' This provision is likely to have the same effect as the approach of Lord Steyn in *Pierson* [1998] AC 539, which was endorsed also in *Simms* [1999] 3 All ER, namely, that there is a presumption that the constitutional (or convention) right will apply in the absence of clear language or necessary implication.

[94] Lawrence M. Friedman, *Total Justice* (Russell Sage Foundation, 1985).

[95] See particularly J. A. G. Griffith, *The Politics of the Judiciary*, 4th edn (Fontana 1991), pp. 87–93; *Judicial Politics since 1920* (Blackwell, 1993). See also Lord Devlin, *Samples of Lawmaking* (Oxford University Press, 1962), p. 23.

[96] *The Economist*, 16–22 December 1995, p. 34.

the executive (and particularly the then home secretary, Michael Howard) and the courts.

One way to explain the increasing intervention by the courts is to focus on the judicial personalities involved. Two judges stand out in the 1960s as leading the way: Lord Reid and Lord Denning. Lord Reid, as senior law lord, presided in all the groundbreaking cases of the 1960s mentioned above. Lord Denning, as Master of the Rolls, headed the Court of Appeal below. He too participated in all but one of those cases.[97] Interestingly, in all those cases Lord Denning was the sole dissenter in the Court of Appeal but his view prevailed in the Lords. Denning had already set out his approach in his Hamlyn Lectures in 1949 entitled *Freedom under the Law.* Those lectures contain the germ of the 'grounds' of judicial review that were later developed. They drew liberally from French administrative law.[98] In 1953 he wrote *The Changing Law* in which he expressed anxiety about the 'growing powers of the executive' and staked a role for the judges (sometimes called 'upright' or 'independent' judges) as arbiters of the constitution and protectors of freedom against the abuse of power. Even before *Ridge* v. *Baldwin* Lord Denning had been paving the way for a broader duty to provide procedural protections in relation to the powers of domestic tribunals and in some judgements bearing his hand in the Privy Council.[99] After his retirement, a number of his dissenting views, regarded as far ahead of their time, were adopted as orthodoxy.[100]

Textbooks assist the development of a field of law. They provide a subject with the aura of a recognised discipline. Doctrine is facilitated by the assembled precedent and the exposition of guiding principle. Two major treatises assisted the legitimacy of administrative law and pointed the way forward. In 1959 Professor Stanley de Smith published his massive thesis on the subject of judicial review of administrative action.

[97] *Ridge* v. *Baldwin* [1964] A C 40.

[98] Denning was friendly with Professor Jack Hamson of Cambridge, who was an expert in the principles of French administrative law. See C. J. Hamson, *Executive Discretion and Judicial Control* (Stevens, 1954).

[99] For an account of Lord Denning's influence generally as a judge in different fields of law see Jeffrey Jowell and Patrick McAuslan, *Lord Denning: The Judge and the Law* (Sweet & Maxwell, 1994).

[100] See Jeffrey Jowell, 'Administrative Law', in Jowell and McAuslan, *Lord Denning*, p. 209, at 250. Other of his dissenting views which were later accepted were the applications of the principles of equality and proportionality, the duty to give reasons, the requirement that a decision be supported by evidence and the requirement of substantive (as well as procedural) fairness. Not all of his judgements were 'progressive', especially in relation to national security.

Although he regarded judicial review as 'sporadic and peripheral' in the context of public administration as a whole, he cited 1,800 cases on the subject, thus proving even to the positivist that administrative law existed—whatever Dicey may have said—and was ripe for application and development.[101] In 1961 Professor (now Sir William) Wade published a work entitled *Administrative Law*.[102] Its clarity, elegance and authority coaxed the judges into citing it with approval with increasing frequency.

Another explanation for the increased resort to law to challenge administration contends that traditional British habits of deference were dissolving.[103] No longer were the orders of the officer class obeyed without question. So too would welfare recipients no longer gratefully accept the allocation of their benefits without the possibility of challenge. Welfare was seen as equivalent to a property right and not mere largesse.[104] Urban dwellers also would demand a say in the rebuilding of their communities. The way these political demands are translated into legal principle is subtle. Public law became the instrument by which the extent of public participation in a democracy was evaluated, endorsed and required.

Then there were the influences from abroad. In the United States, at least in mid-century, law was seen to be a legitimate instrument of social change, spearheading the civil rights revolution. Mention has been made of the European Convention on Human Rights. In addition, Britain's membership of the European Community from 1972 meant that, in cases before the European Court of Justice in Luxembourg, principles were applied that were extrapolated from a variety of jurisdictions. Three fundamental principles of European Community law emerged: legal certainty (akin to our rule of law), equality and proportionality. English judges could review not only administrative action for conformity to European Community law but even primary legislation. In the mid-1970s European Community law incorporated into its jurisprudence that

---

[101] S. A. de Smith, *Judicial Review of Administrative Action* (1959), now in its 5th edn as de Smith, Woolf and Jowell.

[102] Now in its 8th edn as Wade and Forsyth. In 1983 Paul Craig published his influential *Administrative Law*, now in its 4th edn.

[103] J. A. G. Griffith, 'The Political Constitution', *Modern Law Review* (1979).

[104] As advocated by Professor Charles Right in 'The New Property', *Yale Law Journal*; Jeffrey Jowell, 'The Legal Control of Administrative Discretion', *Public Law* (1973). Welfare rights were opposed by Professor Richard Titmuss, see Titmuss, 'Welfare "Rights", Law and Discretion'.

of the European Convention.[105] So the Convention came to be applied in all directly effective European Community law.

All the above explanations may have contributed to the development of administrative law but none, in my view, is sufficient to explain the profound changes that took place. The century began secure in the notion of sovereignty of Parliament as a basic constitutional principle and the one and only constitutional rule. The middle part of the century graphically demonstrated the potential consequences of unrestrained majoritarianism. Sir Isaiah Berlin wrote this about the twentieth century in an essay in *The Crooked Timber of Humanity*:

> There are, in my view, two factors that, above all others, have shaped human history in this century. One is the development of the natural sciences and technology, certainly the great success story of our time—to this great and mounting attention has been paid from all quarters. The other, without doubt, consists of the great ideological storms that have altered the lives of virtually all mankind: the Russian Revolution and its aftermath—totalitarian tyrannies of both right and left and the explosions of nationalism, racism, and, in places, of religious bigotry, which, interestingly enough, not one among the most perceptive social thinkers of the nineteenth century had ever predicted.
>
> When our descendants, in two or three centuries time (if mankind survives until then), come to look at our age, it is these two phenomena that will, I think, be held to be the outstanding characteristics of our century, the most demanding of explanation and analysis.

The 'ideological storms' passed by Britain, to its eternal credit. But the unpredictable totalitarian tyrannies nearby provided a stark lesson in the potential consequences of unrestrained majoritarianism. The growth of administrative law over the century has been more than a diverse collection of court cases and structures to promote fairness, reasonableness and accountability. Its development steadily carved, from crooked timber, a new model of democracy which accepts the necessary power of the state—but insists too upon its necessary limits.

Bibliography

Books

Allen, C. K., *Law in the Making* (Clarendon Press, 1927).
Allen, C. K., *Bureaucracy Triumphant* (Oxford University Press, 1931).

[105] In the case of *Nold* v. *Commission*, Case 4/73 [1974] ECR 491.

Allen, C. K., *Law and Orders* (Stevens, 1945).

Arthurs, H. W., *'Without the Law': Administrative Justice and Legal Pluralism in Nineteenth-century England* (University of Toronto Press, 1985).

Berlin, Isaiah, *The Crooked Timber of Humanity* (Fontana, 1991).

Cosgrove, Richard A., *The Rule of Law: Albert Venn Dicey, Victorian Jurist* (Macmillan, 1980).

Craig, Paul, *Public Law and Democracy in the United Kingdom and the United States of America* (Clarendon Press, 1990).

Craig, Paul, *Administrative Law*, 4th edn (Sweet & Maxwell, 1999).

De Smith, S. A., *Judicial Review of Administrative Action* (Stevens, 1959).

De Smith, S. A., Woolf, Sir Harry and Jowell, Jeffrey, *Judicial Review of Administrative Action* (Sweet & Maxwell, 1999).

Devlin, Lord, *Samples of Lawmaking* (Oxford University Press, 1962).

Dicey, A. V., *Law and Public Opinion in England* (Macmillan, 1959).

Forsyth C. (ed.), *Judicial Review and the Constitution* (Hart, 2000).

Friedman, Lawrence M., *Total Justice* (Russell Sage Foundation, 1985).

Griffith J. A. G., in Morris Ginsberg (ed.), *Law and Opinion in England in the Twentieth Century* (Stevens, 1959).

Griffith, J. A. G., *Judicial Politics since 1920* (Blackwell, 1993).

Griffith, J. A. G., *The Politics of the Judiciary*, 5th edn (Fontana, 1997)

Hamson, C. J., *Executive Discretion and Judicial Control* (Stevens, 1954).

Harden, Ian and Lewis, Norman, *The Noble Lie: The British Constitution and the Rule of Law* (Hutchinson, 1986).

Harden, Ian, Lewis, Norman and Fisher, Cosmo, *The Contracting State* (Open University Press, 1992).

Harlow, Carol and Rawlings, Richard, *Law and Administration*, 2nd edn (Butterworths, 1984).

Hayek, F. A., *The Constitution of Liberty* (Routledge & Kegan Paul, 1960).

Hayek, F. A., *The Road to Serfdom* (Routledge & Kegan Paul, 1964).

Hennessy, Peter, *Whitehall* (Secker & Warburg, 1989).

Hume, L. J., *Bentham and Bureaucracy* (Cambridge University Press, 1981).

Jenkins, Simon, *Accountable to None* (Hamish Hamilton, 1995).

Jennings, Sir Ivor, *The Law and the Constitution* (University of London Press, 1933).

Jowell, Jeffrey and McAuslan, Patrick, *Lord Denning: The Judge and the Law* (Sweet & Maxwell, 1984).

Jowell, Jeffrey and Oliver, Dawn (eds), *The Changing Constitution*, 4th edn (Oxford University Press, 2000).

Keynes, John Maynard, *The End of Laissez Faire* (Hogarth Press, 1926).

Laski, H. J., *A Grammar of Politics* (Allen & Unwin, 1925).

Lewis, Norman and Birkinshaw, Patrick, *When Citizens Complain: Reforming Justice and Administration* (Open University Press, 1993).

Loughlin, Martin, *Local Government in the Modern State* (Sweet & Maxwell, 1986).

Loughlin, Martin, *Public Law and Political Theory* (Clarendon Press, 1992).

Marriott, J., *The Mechanism of the Modern State* (Clarendon Press, 1927).

Ogus, A., *Regulation, Legal Form and Economic Theory* (Clarendon Press, 1994).

Parris, Henry, *Constitutional Bureaucracy: The Development of British Central Administration since the Eighteenth Century* (Allen & Unwin, 1969).

Prosser, Tony, *Law and the Regulators* (Clarendon Press, 1997).

Robson, W. A., *Justice and Administrative Law* (Macmillan, 1928).

Stevens, Robert, *Law and Politics: The House of Lords as a Judicial Body, 1800–1976* (Weidenfeld & Nicolson, 1979).

Wade, H. W. R. and Forsyth, C., *Administrative Law*, 8th edn (Oxford University Press, 2001).

Willis, J., *The Parliamentary Powers of English Government Departments* (Harvard University Press, 1993).

Articles

Bingham of Cornhill, Rt Hon. Lord, 'The Old Despotism', *Israel Law Review* (1999).

Dicey, A. V., 'The Development of Administrative Law in England', *Law Quarterly Review* (1915).

Frankfurter, F., Foreword to 'Discussion of Current Developments in Administrative Law', *Yale Law Review* (1938).

Glasser, C., 'Radicals and Refugees: The Foundations of the *Modern Law Review* and English Legal Scholarship', *Modern Law Review* (1987).

Griffith, J. A. G., 'The Political Constitution', *Public Law* (1979).

Jowell, Jeffrey and Lester, Anthony, 'Beyond *Wednesbury*: Substantive Principles of Judicial Review', *Public Law* (1987).

Keith-Lucas, C., 'Poplarism', *Public Law* (1962).

Laski, H., 'The Growth of Administrative Discretion', *Public Administration* (1923).

Laski, H., 'Judicial Review of Social Policy in England', *Harvard Law Review* (1926).

Laws, Sir John, 'Law and Democracy', *Public Law* (1995).

Robson, W. A., 'Administrative Justice and Injustice: A Commentary on the Franks Report', *Public Law* (1958).

Titmuss, Richard, 'Welfare "Rights", Law and Discretion', *Political Quarterly* (1971).

Williams, D. G. T., 'The Donoughmore Report in Retrospect', *Public Administration* (1982).

11.
Civil Liberties[1]

DAVID FELDMAN

In the first edition of his classic work on the constitution in 1885,[2] Dicey argued that it was an essential feature of the rule of law that the common law, rather than special constitutional rules or procedures, protected the freedom of subjects of the Crown. He did not idealise this position, but recognised that its strength depended on the sentiments of judicial institutions:

> Freedom of discussion is, then, in England little else than the right to write or say anything which a jury, consisting of twelve shopkeepers, think it expedient should be said or written. Such 'liberty' may vary at different times and seasons from unrestricted license [sic] to very severe restraint . . .[3]

The essential point was that freedom was worth nothing unless it could be vindicated, even against the state, through reliable and impartially administered legal remedies. By 1908, he regarded this as a matter of fundamental constitutional significance. Contrasting the position in England with that in Belgium, he wrote:

---

[1] The term 'civil liberties' is anachronistic when used in relation to 1900. The idea that some liberties were specially important, deserving the attachment of the adjective 'civil', did not emerge significantly in legal thinking until rather later. I use the term here as a convenient shorthand, understood from the perspective of our own time, to include freedom from arbitrary detention and interference with personal integrity, freedom from degrading treatment, autonomous choice in relation to lifestyle, movement, expression, enjoyment of property, and some positive rights to privacy and equality. The chapter does not deal with positive social rights to social security, education, or health care, which lie outside the field of classical civil liberties. They are essential to the full enjoyment of liberties in modern society. At the same time, provision for such rights through the welfare state justified incursions on traditional civil liberties. They are therefore present in the background, without attracting direct attention here.

[2] A. V. Dicey, *Lectures Introductory to the Study of the Law of the Constitution* (Macmillan, 1885).

[3] A. V. Dicey, *Lectures Introductory to the Study of the Law of the Constitution*, 2nd edn (Macmillan, 1886), p. 261.

> If it be allowable to apply the formulas of logic to questions of law, the difference in this matter between the constitution of Belgium and the English constitution may be described by the statement that in Belgium individual rights are deductions drawn from the principles of the constitution, whilst in England the so-called principles of the constitution are inductions or generalisations based upon particular decisions pronounced by the courts as to the rights of given individuals . . .
>
> The declaration of the Belgian constitution, that individual liberty is 'guaranteed', betrays a way of looking at the rights of individuals very different from the way in which such rights are regarded by English lawyers. We can hardly say that one right is more guaranteed than another . . . [Freedoms] seem to Englishmen all to rest upon the same basis, namely, on the law of the land . . . The matter to be noted is, that where the right to individual freedom is a result deduced from the principles of the constitution, the idea readily occurs that the right is capable of being suspended or taken away. Where, on the other hand, the right to individual freedom is part of the constitution because it is inherent in the ordinary law of the land, the right is one which can hardly be destroyed without a thorough revolution in the institutions and manners of the nation.[4]

Dicey probably did not mean to imply that such a revolution was impossible. A highly political man, he was well aware that the means used to relieve suffering may cause suffering of a different kind. He saw the nineteenth century as an era of growing collectivism. He wrote of a leading humanitarian:

> Lord Shaftesbury, in short, was in practice, though not in theory, the apostle of governmental interference, and this, in part at least, because his intellectual limitations prevented him from realising the difficulty of reconciling paternal government with respect for individual freedom.[5]

In 1900, then, it was plausible, and among lawyers orthodox, to see the constitution as based on freedom, secured by effective remedies in ordinary legal proceedings. However, Parliament could limit freedom, and the bias in favour of individual liberty was under pressure from humanitarian and collectivist values. For example, in the field of labour relations and working conditions, both humanitarianism and socialism provided arguments against unfettered individualism, and in favour of state intervention to improve the lot of under-privileged groups.

During the twentieth century, Parliament regarded humanitarian col-

[4] A. V. Dicey, *Introduction to the Study of the Law of the Constitution*, 7th edn (Macmillan, 1908), pp. 197–8, 201.
[5] A. V. Dicey, *Lectures on the Relation between Law and Public Opinion in England during the Nineteenth Century* (Macmillan, 1908), p. 230.

lectivism, together with war and sporadic industrial and political unrest, as justifying greater intervention in individuals' lives. Many, including judges, lost faith in the ability of the negative freedoms of the common law, enforced through ordinary legal procedures, to protect people's basic interests. A growing movement saw positive rights, expressly enshrined in legislation, as essential to protect the vital core of individuals' basic interests. The Human Rights Act 1998, coming fully into effect on 2 October 2000, gave special status to a selection of important rights and provided certain new remedies to allow citizens to enforce them against public authorities. This indicates a change of attitude of seismic proportions, the revolution of which Dicey wrote in 1908. Common law freedoms continue to operate alongside rights, but municipal law, following international human rights instruments, has identified certain freedoms as more fundamental than others. They were still to be enforced through courts, and subject to parliamentary sovereignty, but the impression is of a move from a constitutional culture based on liberty in 1900 to one based on positive rights in 2000.

However, this simple account masks changes of great complexity in underlying political and legal structures. Throughout the century, circumstances simultaneously produced pressures towards both greater protection for freedom and an increase in state regulation and control over people's lives. The growing importance of human rights was to some extent a reaction to the increasing power of state agencies to interfere with liberty, backed by Acts of Parliament, against which ordinary law provided only limited protection. The idea of human rights was not new. There was a strongly Lockean thread in the common law which had led to some rights, particularly the right to property, being treated as fundamental in law. The Declaration of the Rights of Man and the Citizen in France and the first ten amendments to the Constitution of the United States of America in the late eighteenth century, like treaties to abolish slavery in the nineteenth century, can be seen as being based on human rights. But the twentieth century saw the idea of human rights exerting a huge impact on international and constitutional law in many countries. The treaty provisions protecting the religious rights of ethnic and religious minorities in the parts of Europe which the victorious powers were carving up and reassigning, willy-nilly, to new masters at the end of the First World War[6] were part of an accelerating trend.

---

[6] See Malcolm D. Evans, *Religious Liberty and International Law in Europe* (Cambridge University Press, 1997), ch. 2.

Events in the United Kingdom were affected by many factors, including wars, economic boom and bust, the universal adult franchise, the decline of the British Empire, a steadily weakening respect for authority in all its social forms, the organisation of labour, the growth and decline in trust in the police, the development of international human-rights instruments and institutions, and technological innovation. Political, legal and regulatory institutions reacted in diverse ways. Sometimes they made far-reaching changes in response to transient problems. At other times they seemed paralysed in the face of major, long-term changes. Nevertheless, it seems possible to identify some broad trends which help to impose order on a chaotic century.

The century can be divided into four periods: the growth of the power of the state at the expense of the liberty of the individual until 1945; the growth of the welfare state in post-war Britain, matched by growing state regulation, between 1945 and 1960; growing freedom of lifestyle accompanied by some attempt to control state power between 1960 and 1990; and the establishment of a human rights rhetoric coupled with a further growth in state power between 1990 and 2000. These periods are not, of course, watertight. Within each period, there are currents and counter-currents, and reality was inevitably more complicated than this schema will make it appear. There was nothing inevitable about the way things developed, and nothing here should be taken to suggest that people generally had more liberty (as a matter of law) in 2000 than they had in 1900.

The growth of state power, 1900–45

The legal power of the agents of the state to interfere with the lives of subjects increased markedly between 1900 and the end of the Second World War. Successive governments faced, or thought that they faced, both external and internal threats to national security, and responded defensively. The revolutionary movements in Russia—anarchist and later socialist, leading ultimately to the revolutions of 1917—fostered paranoia about their effect on internal stability and industrial relations in the United Kingdom.[7] In the period before the outbreak of the Second World

---

[7] Richard Deacon, *A History of the British Secret Service* (Granada Publishing, 1980), pp. 152–8; Bernard Porter, *The Origins of the Vigilant State: The London Metropolitan Police Special Branch before the First World War* (Weidenfeld & Nicolson, 1987), ch. 7; K. D. Ewing and C. A. Gearty, *The Struggle for Civil Liberties: Political Freedom and the Rule of Law in Britain, 1914–1945* (Oxford University Press, 2000), ch. 3 and *passim*.

War, fears of German economic and territorial expansion were coupled with deep concern about espionage by German agents and their British sympathisers in the United Kingdom.[8] During the First World War, security measures were put in place through subordinate legislation which was only fitfully policed by courts, and which survived the war to affect police powers and labour relations in the inter-war years. The political and military conflict in Ireland in the years leading up to partition provided an additional reason for increasing the powers of the police there, and when Fenian violence spilled over to the mainland it provided a reason for extending the role of the police Special Branch and its undercover techniques of surveillance and use of *agents provocateurs*.[9] It was through Ireland that some of the powers routinely used to maintain control over subject peoples in the Empire were imported to mainland Britain.[10] In the 1920s and 1930s, the effect of economic depression on labour relations combined with the emergence of fascist politics to generate public-order problems which justified significant attacks on civil liberties by Parliament, the police and the courts. The Second World War then permitted or required the state to reinforce its already powerful hold over liberty, and weakened people's willingness to question authority too strongly.

At the same time, there were some movements towards equality in public and private life. The attempt to settle the Irish question in the period of partition produced a devolved legislature and executive in the six counties of Northern Ireland which left extensive autonomy to the Stormont Parliament. In order to protect the Catholic minority of the province, the Local Government (Ireland) Act 1919 instigated a system of proportional representation for elections to local authorities, and the Government of Ireland Act 1920, which took effect in the north in 1922, extended the system to elections to the Stormont Parliament. Section 5 of the 1920 Act limited the legislative power of the Stormont Parliament in the interests of religious equality, making void any law to establish, endow, restrict the practice of, or give any advantage or impose a disadvantage on, a religion, or make a religious test a precondition of

---

[8] Christopher Andrew, *Secret Service: The Making of the British Intelligence Community* (Heinemann, 1985), pp. 34–49; Deacon, *History of British Secret Service*, ch. 14; Porter, *Origins of the Vigilant State*, pp. 166–73; Robert K. Massie, *Dreadnought: Britain, Germany, and the Coming of the Great War* (Jonathan Cape, 1992), 213–31, 351–69, 630–9.

[9] Porter, *Origins of the Vigilant State*, chs 2, 3 and 4.

[10] Charles Townshend, *Making the Peace: Public Order and Public Security in Modern Britain* (Oxford University Press, 1993), ch. 3; Ewing and Gearty, *Struggle for Civil Liberties*, ch. 7.

marriage or schooling, or deprive any person of property except for limited purposes and on payment of compensation. This section repealed existing enactments imposing any penalty, disability or disadvantage on people by reason of religious belief or membership of a religious order. Nevertheless, this cautious step towards legislative protection for certain rights was more or less a dead letter in practice. The Stormont Parliament had power to repeal and amend the Government of Ireland Act. It abolished proportional representation for local government in 1922, entrenching a Unionist stranglehold on political power in the province which lasted for fifty years and did much to ensure support for the activities of the IRA. Proportional representation for Stormont was removed in 1929, reinforcing a Protestant and Unionist hegemony which continued until direct rule of the province from Westminster was reimposed in 1972. Stormont proceeded to pass legislation which legalised a segregated society, notwithstanding section 5 of the 1920 Act. Challenges in the courts of Northern Ireland were unsuccessful, and the Westminster Parliament took no remedial action, despite having reserved the power to do so in section 75 of the 1920 Act.[11] One cannot dissent from the conclusion that '[m]ost of these innovations ... were to be removed or proved to be a dead letter'.[12] The political will to establish genuine religious equality in the province was absent both in Belfast and Westminster.

In mainland Britain, there was much more toleration of racial and religious differences. The United Kingdom had a good record, compared to that of most countries other than the USA, in accepting refugees. It was generally accepted until the passage of the British Nationality Act 1948 that it was wrong to impose racially discriminatory entry requirements. This is not to say that immigrants were accepted unconditionally, or on equal terms.[13] The Aliens Act 1905 for the first time gave statutory power to immigration officers to refuse entry to foreigners who were deemed undesirable, and imposed obligations on carriers to ensure that

[11] Full treatments of these matters can be found in Harry Calvert, *Constitutional Law in Northern Ireland* (Sweet & Maxwell, 1968); Brigid Hadfield, *The Constitution of Northern Ireland* (SLS, 1989). For a brief introduction, see Brigid Hadfield, 'The Northern Ireland Constitution', in Brigid Hadfield (ed.), *Northern Ireland: Politics and the Constitution* (Open University Press, 1992), ch. 1.

[12] John Morison and Stephen Livingstone, *Reshaping Public Power: Northern Ireland and the British Constitutional Crisis* (Sweet & Maxwell, 1995), p. 124.

[13] Ann Dummett and Andrew Nicol, *Subjects, Citizens, Aliens and Others: Nationality and Immigration Law* (Weidenfeld & Nicolson, 1990), ch. 6.

they did not land people who were not entitled to enter the country.[14] These provisions did not stop the acceptance of people fleeing from the pogroms and wars which racked central and eastern Europe early in the century, and from the Nazi persecution of the 1930s.[15] Nevertheless, there was a significant level of casual racism and anti-Semitism in everyday life. It appears for example, in the 1930s novels of Dorothy L. Sayers. Yet only the far right exploited it politically both in the 1930s, and again from the 1960s. Anti-Semitism was a weak force in British politics at the start of the twentieth century unlike France. There, the Dreyfus affair in the 1890s, focusing attention on anti-Semitism in the French establishment, had provided a crucible in which French radicals and socialists defined their politics in terms of religious toleration, linked to anti-clericalism and a move to separate the State from the Church. This influenced the whole shape of French policy under the Third Republic, ensuring in the process that anti-Semitism and racism remained a political issue. As Zeldin comments:

> The [Dreyfus] case did indeed serve the purpose of freeing the socialists of their anti-Semitism, and turning this into an exclusively right-wing phenomenon; but it also exacerbated anti-Semitism and chauvinism into far larger proportions. It was one of the great failures of the republic, precisely because it impeded advance beyond the disputes of the nineteenth century.[16]

The distaste in Britain for making a big issue of such matters was, on the whole, benign.

Some steps were taken during this period to advance equal treatment for women who had already been given a measure of equality and autonomy in the nineteenth century. Married women were able to hold property on relatively equal terms with men after the Married Women's Property Act 1882, and to enter into contracts and sue and be sued in their own names, but their separate property was held on a statutory trust until the Law Reform (Married Women and Joint Tortfeasors) Act 1935. Women could petition for divorce, like men, after the Matrimonial Causes Act 1857, although conduct which justified a man in divorcing his wife would not always allow a wife to divorce her husband. It was

[14] Dummett and Nicol, *Subjects, Citizens, Aliens and Others*, pp. 160–9 on this, and on moves to repatriate immigrants.
[15] See Louise London, *Whitehall and the Jews* (Cambridge University Press, 1999).
[16] Theodore Zeldin, *France 1848–1945*: vol. 1, *Ambition, Love and Politics* (Clarendon Press, 1973), pp. 681–2.

not until the Matrimonial Causes Act 1923 that Parliament provided for the same conduct to constitute a matrimonial offence for either sex. Divorce became marginally easier when A. P. Herbert, the independent MP for Oxford University, piloted the Matrimonial Causes Act 1937 through Parliament as a private member's bill, making desertion a ground for divorce, but a spouse who had committed adultery before the end of the period of a decree nisi could not obtain a decree absolute until the idea of a matrimonial offence as the basis for a divorce was removed in the Divorce Reform Act 1969. On the educational and professional fronts, women achieved access to a far wider range of opportunities during this period, with many legal disabilities being swept away by the Sex Disqualification Removal Act 1919.

On the political front, Parliament recognised the contribution which women had made at home during the First World War by conceding the principle of women's suffrage in the Representation of the People Act 1918, but women could not vote at the same age as men until 1928. The first woman to be elected to Parliament, in 1918, Constance Gore-Booth, Countess Markiewicz, was a member of Sinn Fein, and did not take her seat; but in 1919 Lady Astor was elected as a Unionist, and became an active parliamentarian.

In sexual matters, male homosexuality remained a criminal offence. So did abortion, unless to save the life of the mother.[17] Barrier contraception was legal but not much used. Even when made relatively respectable by Dr Marie Stopes, advice on methods was not widely available. Sheaths tended to be delivered by post in plain covers. Women could take a measure of control by using a diaphragm, invented in Holland in 1919, and later increase its effectiveness by using contraceptive jelly (invented in 1932). However, not until the invention of the contraceptive pill in the 1960s did most ordinary women control their sexual activity and its consequences.[18]

Freedom of thought, association and expression, as Dicey observed, changed with the times. In the early years of the century, Parliament took steps to protect the freedom of workers to join trade unions and to strike after the courts had tried, in a series of cases, to emasculate those freedoms.[19] In wartime, freedom of expression was severely limited, as one would expect. Even in the USA, the crime of seditious libel survived

[17] *R. v. Bourne* [1939] 1 KB 687.
[18] A. J. P. Taylor, *English History 1914–1945* (Clarendon Press, 1965), pp. 165–6.
[19] See, for example, Trade Disputes Act 1906, and Trade Union Act 1913.

review under the First Amendment during the First World War,[20] and one could expect little sympathy for opponents of the war effort in Britain. Freedom of conscience and belief fared a little better. It was held in 1917 that a bequest to a society which aimed to propagate atheism was not unlawful.[21] When conscription was introduced during the First World War, the conscientious objector was a social pariah, but, in an unusually liberal gesture, local tribunals were established to assess people's objections and to allow genuine conscientious objectors to perform services as non-combatants. The practical effect of this provision was mixed, and several ministers (notably Lloyd George) did all they could to place obstacles in the way of conscientious objection. In this they were, of course, very much in tune with public sentiment. At the end of the war, the same Representation of the People Act which gave women the vote disfranchised conscientious objectors for five years. Yet by the end of this period, in the Second World War, social attitudes to conscientious objectors were far more tolerant, and they did not suffer post-war disabilities.[22] On the other hand, the common-law crime of blasphemy, although rarely invoked, remained available to protect the feelings of Anglicans against offence.[23]

While the right to strike and universal adult suffrage made major advances in this period, both threatened established interests. Officials responded to the campaigns with a forcefulness which threatened a wide range of civil liberties. First, new institutions were created to exercise control in ways which would previously have been suspect. For example, the period before the First World War saw the birth of the Security Service (later MI5) and Special Branch. Second, the substance of the law was altered by legislation, a process made easier by the primacy of Dicey's model of parliamentary supremacy. The growing use of subordinate legislation meant that Parliament exercised less real control over incursions on civil liberty than would have been possible had primary legislation been used. Third, the courts were generally reluctant or unable to provide an effective level of scrutiny of the increasing use which government and police made of their political, physical and legal power, or adequate remedies for abuse of power. All these developments were

---

[20] See the unsatisfactory discussion by the US Supreme Court in *Abrams* v. *United States*, 250 US 616 (1919).
[21] *Bowman* v. *Secular Society* [1917] AC 406, HL.
[22] Taylor, *English History 1914–1945*, pp. 54–5, 116, 457.
[23] See *R.* v. *Gott* (1922) 16 Cr. App. R. 87, CA; *R.* v. *Lemon* [1979] AC 617, HL.

more or less contemporaneous, and each affected public sensitivity to civil-liberty issues in ways which made it easier for others to take root.

The effect of threats on institutions and their control

One immediate effect of concern about hostile activities of anarchists, bolsheviks and foreign powers was to stimulate the government to establish a counter-espionage agency, MO5, which was later to become MI5, the Security Service.[24] Initially consisting of only one person, Captain Vernon Kell, it expanded during the First World War and had some notable successes. It regularly intercepted mail on an authority issued by the home secretary. Initially each interception had to be authorised by warrant from the home secretary and had to be carried out in the presence of Royal Mail officials, but the procedure changed when it became clear that this compromised security. In 1911, Winston Churchill, as home secretary, started to issue general warrants to intercept the correspondence of anyone on a list of suspected spies supplied by Kell, in place of the individual warrants which had previously to be sought for each suspect.[25] However, the service was not publicly recognised, and as its staff were not constables they had no legal power to interfere with people's freedom. In order to take overt action, such as making arrests and searching premises, they depended on the regular police.

To facilitate counter-espionage activity, Kell worked closely with the Metropolitan Police Special Branch, headed by Basil Thomson. Special Branch had been established in the 1880s as one of a series of measures aimed at combating Fenian terrorism, and had well established intelligence networks.[26] One of the reasons for the initial success of counter-espionage operations leading up to the First World War was the capable leadership of the heads of MI5 and Special Branch, and their ability to co-operate with each other. The secrecy necessary to successful counter-

[24] Deacon, *History of British Secret Service*, ch. 13; Andrew, *Secret Service*, pp. 51–64. The early history of the Security Service is well documented. Many of the files relating to it were declassified in 1997, and published by the Public Record Office on a CD-ROM entitled *MI5: The First Ten Years 1909–1919*. The official histories of the work of MI5 during the First World War were also declassified and published with an introduction by Christopher Andrew as *MI5: The First Ten Years 1909–1919* (PRO Publications, 1997). The PRO has also published *The Security Service 1908–1945: The Official History*, prepared by John Curry in 1944–6, with an introduction by Christopher Andrew (PRO Publications, 1999), although this work concentrates on the work of MI5 during the Second World War.
[25] See Deacon, *History of British Secret Service*, pp. 191–2, 196, 214; Porter, *Origins of the Vigilant State*, pp. 168, 176–7.
[26] Porter, *Origins of the Vigilant State*, chs 2–8.

espionage operations was helped by making them accountable to the home secretary rather than to a chief constable or commissioner of police.

The head of MI5 found that the law on official secrecy made it very difficult to prosecute foreign agents for information-gathering activities. Matters became easier when Parliament passed the Official Secrets Act 1911. Section 2 was a catch-all provision which criminalised a huge range of dealings with official information in a way which was to bedevil the law of civil liberties until it was replaced by the Official Secrets Act 1989, but it served the purposes of MI5.[27] Even then, no special legal powers were conferred on MI5 or Special Branch, so it is likely that some surveillance and information-gathering had to be carried on outside the law.

There were, however, a number of legal provisions which interfered with civil liberties. The Aliens Act 1905 established an inspectorate with power to exclude undesirable foreigners from the country, a measure aimed initially at anarchists but later applied to bolsheviks and others. A secret police register of aliens was instigated in 1910, and became official when the First World War began. The legal requirement on all aliens to register with the police was initially a security measure, but continues in force today for the purpose of immigration control. Restrictions on the movement of aliens included internment of 'enemy aliens' during both world wars, on grounds which, as the classic study by Professor Brian Simpson[28] has shown, were sometimes exiguous. The work of Special Branch and MI5 in gathering information by a variety of means and taking action to detain or deport suspects was and remains significant, and interferes with privacy and sometimes with personal liberty. The model for the counter-espionage function was in many respects that which had been used against Irish separatists in Ireland, and against anti-colonial agitators in the Empire, particularly in India.[29]

Special Branch was an unusual institution, as was MI5. The well-established police structure was also used to enforce order in ways which were both political and out of tune with previously accepted policing practice. The police met suffragette demonstrations before the First World War with notable severity. Professors Ewing and Gearty have shown[30] how, after the war, the police exercised their discretionary powers principally against meetings and publications organised by communists and

---

[27] Andrew, *Secret Service*, pp. 64–73.

[28] A. W. B. Simpson, *In the Highest Degree Odious: Detention without Trial in Wartime Britain* (Clarendon Press), 1992.

[29] Townshend, *Making the Peace*, chs 2–4.

[30] Ewing and Gearty, *Struggle For Civil Liberties*, pp. 100–8, 112–21, 184–92, and ch. 5 *passim*.

the National Unemployed Workers Movement in the 1920s, and against communists more rigorously than against Mosleyites in the 1930s. The law was seen as acting, through its agents, in a politically discriminatory way, doing much to bring it into disrepute, particularly as there were signs that magistrates and judges were sometimes applying the law to communists with scant regard for the proprieties of due process.[31] Excessively violent policing was bolstered, as a matter of law, by the Emergency Regulations which continued many of the special wartime powers in peacetime. In the 1920s, they were used (together with military aid to the civil power) against labour activists and strikers, helping to defeat the General Strike in 1926. The procedural model in which civilians could be tried before military tribunals for certain offences was also imported to mainland Britain from Ireland during the First World War under the Defence of the Realm Regulations. To these matters we now turn.

The effect of threats on the type and content of legislation

It will by now be clear that legislation was increasingly used as an instrument of social control as well as to protect security. Several features of this type of legislation deserve to be noted. First, an increasing number of very broadly drawn provisions created offences which were potentially far more restrictive of liberty than the government of the day acknowledged. Second, the enforcement of the legislation became increasingly a matter for official discretion. Discretion was introduced to the system expressly, for example by the Public Order Act 1936, in relation to the control of processions. It also arose incidentally, as proliferating restrictions and over-broad offences made liberty dependent on the discretion of enforcers and prosecutors. Third, a great deal of anti-libertarian legislation was introduced by subordinate legislation, instead of being contained in parliamentary bills. This reduced the scope for Parliament to scrutinise and control the legislation (although it has to be admitted that most parliamentarians showed little inclination to challenge legislation even when given the opportunity to do so).

The scope and nature of such legislation can best be illustrated by looking at the Official Secrets Act 1911, the Defence of the Realm Regulations, and the Public Order Act 1936. All were responses to threats of disruption of one kind or another.

---

[31] Ewing and Gearty, *Struggle for Civil Liberties*, pp. 194–200.

412

The Official Secrets Act 1911 was hurried through Parliament with almost indecent haste, largely unhampered by opposition. This happy state of affairs was fostered by some misleading statements by the government, which claimed that the bill was largely a clarifying and consolidating measure and did not threaten the liberty of loyal subjects.[32] Yet it gave extensive new powers of search and seizure; section 1 created a new offence of gathering information about military and naval matters; and section 2 was a criminal provision of extraordinary breadth, making it an offence to pass or receive official information without authorisation, unless the action was in the interests of the state. It allowed civil servants and journalists to be prosecuted over ensuing decades, and in the 1970s it became the focus of attention for freedom-of-information campaigners who saw it as symptomatic of the secretive nature of the state.[33] Eventually the *Ponting* case[34] made it a broken reed, and forced the government to review the position. The Act was a prime illustration of the culture of secrecy which dominated British public life for much of the century.[35]

The Defence of the Realm Acts 1914–15 were the main, but not the only, pieces of legislation which restricted liberty. The freedom of foreigners was limited by the Aliens Restriction Act 1915, and the liberty of subjects was affected by the National Registration Act 1915, which required everyone between the ages of 15 and 65 to register. This was a natural precursor to the Military Service Act 1916, which introduced conscription with only limited exceptions to take account of conscientious objection when the supply of volunteers for the slaughter was in danger of drying up. The Defence of the Realm Act 1914 was a framework Act, giving very wide powers to the government to make regulations by Order in Council concerning the powers and duties of the Admiralty and Army Council 'for securing the public safety and the defence of the realm'. Alleged breaches by civilians of certain regulations were to be triable by court-martial, provisions widened in the Defence of the Realm (No. 2) Act 1914 to include spreading 'reports likely to cause disaffection or alarm'. The Defence of the Realm (No. 3) Act 1914, although mainly a consolidating measure, widened the power to make regulations. This

---

[32] Ewing and Gearty, *Struggle for Civil Liberties*, pp. 40–1.
[33] See D. G. T. Williams, *Not in the Public Interest* (Hutchinson, 1965); David Hooper, *Official Secrets: The Use and Abuse of the Act* (Secker & Warburg, 1987).
[34] *R. v. Ponting* [1985] Crim. LR 318.
[35] See David Vincent, *The Culture of Secrecy: Britain 1832–1998* (Oxford University Press, 1998), chs 4, 5, 6, 7.

bill, and particularly the provisions which deprived British civilians of the right to trial by jury, led to opposition and the government reinstated the right, subject to a power to suspend it by proclamation in an emergency.

The regulations made under the Acts gave power to enter, search, and take private property including land, to clear people from designated areas, to restrict freedom of movement, to introduce deportation and internment of aliens, to extend criminal sanctions against collecting or communicating information without authority, to create offences of interfering with military duties and supplies, and to arrest suspects and try some of them in military rather than civil courts. As Keith Ewing and Conor Gearty write, 'The regulations . . . gave the authorities an extensive range of powers and consequently imposed restrictions on personal and civil liberties of a quite extraordinary scope, so much so that it is impossible to cover them all here or indeed even to give a full account of their range.'[36] It is questionable whether the range of largely uncontrolled official discretion was really necessary for the purposes of the war effort. As Ewing and Gearty have shown, the use of the powers against communists both during and after the war demonstrated that the provisions were capable of being interpreted overly broadly. What is more, there was no appeal against, or effective legal scrutiny of, several of the powers, most notably that of internment of aliens, which were accordingly often used on grounds which could not be sustained as objectively acceptable.[37]

While this sort of regime is acceptable in wartime, it is harder to justify in peacetime. Yet most of the powers which the executive had under the Defence of the Realm Regulations, other than the power to intern aliens, were retained after the end of the wartime emergency, on account of fear of communist subversion following the Russian revolutions of 1917. Some regulatory structures were incorporated into public general Acts shortly after the end of the war. These included the Firearms Act 1920, the Shops (Early Closing) Act 1920, the Dangerous Drugs Act 1920, and the Official Secrets Act 1920. Others could be invoked by the executive in time of emergency under the Emergency Powers Act 1920.[38] These powers were employed to powerful political effect against communists, who were the target of Special Branch attention following the

---

[36] Ewing and Gearty, *Struggle for Civil Liberties*, p. 51.
[37] Ewing and Gearty, *Struggle for Civil Liberties*, chs 3–5.
[38] Ewing and Gearty, *Struggle for Civil Liberties*, p. 93.

formation of a communist government in Russia,[39] and against supporters of the General Strike in 1926, when a state of emergency was declared by proclamation. While some parliamentarians recognised that the legislation of 1920 affected civil liberties, there was relatively little opposition to it, and it became law without difficulty. When the legislation was invoked at the time of the General Strike, Parliament failed to exercise control over the government's continuation of the powers. Theoretically needing parliamentary approval for proclamations declaring or renewing a state of emergency, the government was able to renew the emergency regulations eight times. Although the General Strike ended after nine days, the regulations continued to be used against the miners who remained on strike in a dispute with the private owners of mines. The regulations were not allowed to lapse until December 1926, after the last of the miners had returned to work at the end of November. While these renewals of the emergency powers were increasingly challenged in Parliament, the opposition failed to force their withdrawal at the end of the genuinely national emergency.[40]

The greatly increased statutory powers of the executive under this legislation were buttressed by older legislation, and by common-law powers and offences of uncertain extent. When an article appeared in *The Syndicalist* in 1912 urging troops not to fire on strikers, the printer and publisher were convicted of contravening the Incitement to Mutiny Act 1797.[41] The same charge awaited J. R. Campbell, acting editor of the *Workers' Weekly* in 1924, after the paper published a letter urging soldiers, sailors and airmen to organise against capitalism and to refuse to go to war or to fire on strikers. In this case the prosecution caused a political storm among the supporters of Ramsay MacDonald's Labour government, and was withdrawn. But by then Special Branch had been able to study a considerable haul of papers taken away from the premises of the paper during a search.[42] The prosecution of nine British communists on a charge of sedition in 1925 produced a conviction and substantial terms of imprisonment for all defendants. Meanwhile, the police developed techniques of preventing communists from addressing meetings on the basis of a power to prevent apprehended breaches of the

---

[39] Even before the First World War, the UK's secret intelligence service had been more developed in spying against Russia than against Germany: see Deacon, *History of British Secret Service*, p. 180.

[40] Ewing and Gearty, *Struggle for Civil Liberties*, pp. 175–83.

[41] *R. v. Bowman* (1912) 76 JP 271.

[42] Ewing and Gearty, *Struggle for Civil Liberties*, pp. 121–7.

peace which was later upheld by the courts. The law became a tool of industrial and political control.

In the 1930s, the powers of the police were used against the National Unemployed Workers' Movement, and new legislation was passed to outlaw publications aiming to persuade the police not to act against strikers: the Incitement to Disaffection Act 1934 did for the police what the Incitement to Mutiny Act 1797 had done for the armed forces. These measures were of a type appropriate in time of war or a major national emergency, but they were enacted to combat purely domestic upheavals and, as Ewing and Gearty have demonstrated,[43] they were used, and calculated for use, against those on the Left. From the perspective of the end of the century, this seems hard to justify. However, the fear of communist insurrection was real, and made to seem more immediate by the economic difficulties and high level of unemployment which beset the country in the 1930s.

The economic problems, coupled with the rise of fascism in Europe, also provided the background against which it was judged expedient to legislate against the disorder caused by Blackshirt rallies and socialist counter-demonstrations in the mid-1930s. The Public Order Act 1936, sections 1 and 2, banned quasi-military drilling and the wearing of uniforms signifying association with a particular political movement. Sections 3 and 4 also gave statutory power to the police to impose conditions on processions, and to local authorities with the consent of the home secretary (or, in London, to the home secretary) to ban processions of a specified class for a period, on the application of the police, in order to prevent serious disorder. In fact, much of the statutory power proved to overlap with common-law powers which the courts conferred on the police in a series of cases to which we will turn in the next section. Section 5 of the Public Order Act 1936 put on a national footing an offence which had existed in various local by-laws for many years, namely the use of threatening, abusive or insulting words or behaviour in a public place with intent to cause a breach of the peace or whereby a breach of the peace was likely to be occasioned. Initially, the Act was seen as an emergency measure for use against violent political demonstrations. However, it was not repealed when the fascist threat receded. It came to be employed as a general tool against public disorder of all kinds, and impacted on a wide range of political activities and social behaviour in public.

---

[43] Ewing and Gearty, *Struggle for Civil Liberties*, ch. 5.

Against this background, one looks almost in vain for evidence of Parliament asserting itself at all to protect or extend civil liberties. There was one major legislative extension of a civil liberty: the extension of the franchise. Apart from this hard-won and initially very limited victory for the suffragette movement, it has to be said that Parliament did little in the first period under review to protect civil liberties, and indeed acted mainly to restrict them. The first period ended with the Second World War, during which the restrictions imposed during the first World War were reintroduced with some additional elements.

The effect of threats on the courts

If the orthodox political process failed to protect civil liberties adequately in the first forty-five years of the century, how did the other self-proclaimed protectors of the liberty of the subject, the courts, perform? The answer has to be: 'Patchily.' It will be convenient to consider the courts' approach to subordinate legislation; their attitude to rights to personal integrity; their concern for due process, particularly in relation to internment; their approach to powers of arrest and questioning and search and seizure; and their attitude to public order in political contexts.

One of the most important civil liberties for people who are concerned to maintain the rule of law is freedom from secret laws. Whether citizens or subjects, we are entitled to know the legal rules which govern our lives. Indeed, the law presumes us to know the law, so that ignorance of it does not normally excuse a contravention of it. Three principles follow from this. First, courts, when applying legislation to an act or omission, should not interpret any law in a way which would not have been reasonably foreseeable when the act or omission took place. Second, legislators and courts should ensure that the only law which is applied to someone's disadvantage is that which was reasonably accessible to that person when he or she did the act in question. Third, uncertain or inaccessible legislation should not be used by courts to justify incursions on people's civil liberties, either by the executive or by courts themselves. These principles are central to that aspect of the rule of law which is sometimes called the principle of legality.

Subordinate legislation presents special problems in relation to accessibility. Even today, there is no general requirement that all subordinate legislation should be published, despite the impact which it can have on civil liberties, for example in relation to rights of public assembly and freedom from arbitrary arrest and detention. In the early part of the twentieth century, the position was governed (so far as it was governed at all) by the Rules Publication Act 1893. This required forty days' pre-legislative publicity for ministerial orders, but did not deal with the vast bulk of orders at all, and was silent as to the effect of failure to publicise. In *Johnson* v. *Sargent*,[44] Bailhache J. held that subordinate legislation could not take effect until it 'became known'. He cited no authority, but perhaps felt that he needed none: the proposition flowed ineluctably from the constitutional principles set out above. On the other hand, Parliament does not seem to agree. Section 3(2) of the Statutory Instruments Act 1946 (which replaced the 1893 Act in the light of criticisms made most notably by the Donoughmore Committee on Ministers' Powers in 1932) provides a defence against a criminal charge based on a statutory instrument which had not been published by the Stationery Office at the time of the alleged offence, subject to various provisos. This express provision, which would have been unnecessary if the decision in *Johnson* v. *Sargent* had been considered to be correct, implies that subordinate legislation can take effect before being published.[45] As section 3(2) of the 1946 Act applies only to criminal proceedings, it implies that people's private-law rights and liabilities may lawfully be interfered with by subordinate legislation which was not in the public domain and of which no attempt had been made to inform them. In respect of the exercise of sub-delegated legislative powers, whether by way of by-laws, codes of practice, guidance or circulars, the procedures and publicity requirements were (and remain) virtually non-existent, despite criticism from courts,[46] Parliament,[47] and distinguished commentators.[48]

If the courts were generally unable to provide adequate protection against unpublished subordinate legislation, the protection which was offered against the executive exploiting broadly drafted legislative powers was patchy. One can say that, even during the First World War, the courts were relatively vigilant to protect property rights, but were far less attuned to protecting other civil and personal liberties. The courts

---

[44] [1918] 1 KB 101.

[45] Streatfield J. therefore held in *R.* v. *Sheer Metalcraft Ltd* [1954] KB 586 that statutory instruments come into force when they are made and express procedural requirements are complied with, unless a later date is set in the instrument.

[46] *Blackpool Corporation* v. *Locker* [1948] 1 KB 349, CIA, *per* Scott L.J.; *Lewisham Borough Council* v. *Roberts* [1949] 2 KB 608, CA, *per* Scott L.J., dissenting.

[47] Select Committee on Statutory Instruments, Special Report for Session 1945–6 (HMSO, 29 Oct. 1946).

[48] See, for example, C. K. Allen, *Law and Orders*, 2nd edn (Stevens, 1956), pp. 204ff; *Law in the Making*, 7th edn (Oxford University Press, 1964), ch. 7.

regularly asserted the right to review both Orders in Council under the prerogative and subordinate legislation made under statute on the ground of *ultra vires*. Even during the First World War, in a case concerning the scope of a power to legislate for internment, Lord Shaw could say:

> In so far as the mandate has been exceeded, there lurk the elements of a transition to arbitrary government and therein of grave constitutional and public danger. The increasing crush of legislative efforts and the convenience to the Executive of a refuge to the device of Orders in Council would increase that danger tenfold were the judiciary to approach any such action of the Government in a spirit of compliance rather than of independent scrutiny.[49]

None the less, as that case itself showed, interned aliens had little success during the war in challenging the adequacy of the grounds for their detention: the applicant failed to convince the House of Lords that the rhetoric of judicial control of arbitrariness should be translated into effective action. Lord Atkinson rejected the argument that legislation which invades the liberty of the subject should be interpreted more restrictively than other legislation.[50] Faced by a state of national emergency, the judiciary interpreted the conditions for detaining aliens in a spirit, if not of compliance, at least of deference to the executive. The very broad terms in which the Defence of the Realm Regulations were drafted, and in particular the lack of any express requirement in the notorious Regulation 14B that the minister should have reasonable grounds for believing that the person to be detained or deported represented a threat to national security or welfare, constituted a stumbling block for judges who wanted to exercise independent scrutiny. Yet even when a requirement for reasonable grounds was inserted in the legislation, as had happened by the start of the Second World War, the courts were unwilling to act according to its natural meaning. The famous dissenting speech of Lord Atkin in *Liversidge* v. *Anderson*[51] was (it has since been held) correct as a matter of law,[52] but it was deeply unpopular at the time both in the country and among Lord Atkin's fellow judges, who ostracised him for it.

It is understandable that in time of war the courts should have been

---

[49] *R.* v. *Halliday, ex p. Zadig* [1917] AC 260, at 287.
[50] *R.* v. *Halliday, ex p. Zadig* [1917] AC 260, at 274.
[51] [1942] AC 206, HL.
[52] See *Inland Revenue Commissioners* v. *Rossminster Ltd* [1980] AC 952, HL; *R.* v *Secretary of State for the Home Department, ex p. Khera and Khawaja* [1984] AC 74, HL.

unwilling to challenge the executive's view of what was expedient in the national interest, and perhaps even felt a patriotic duty to support the executive. This applied to due-process rights as well as to freedom from arbitrary detention. When a submarine of new design sank on its trials, killing all hands, relatives of the crew sought to sue the builders, alleging that a design or construction fault had caused the disaster. The government refused to disclose the plans for the submarine, claiming what was then called Crown privilege for them on the ground that disclosure would damage defence security. The House of Lords laid down a very sweeping general principle that the Crown could never be required to disclose evidence if it made a claim for Crown privilege in the proper form.[53] Judicial scrutiny of the claim was entirely excluded, understandably on the facts of the case but a dangerous precedent for non-sensitive information and peacetime.

When the immediate pressures of war were lifted after 1918, the judges were able to have a little more regard for the rights of subjects. This did not generally lead to decisions that acts done during the war had been unlawful (although occasionally the relevant regulation was in effect reinterpreted to make retrospectively unlawful a requisition which would almost certainly have been treated as lawful had it been litigated during the war).[54] It was far more common for courts to hold that requisitioning, albeit lawful, had to be accompanied (under either legislation or the prerogative) by compensation for the owner, and that interference with or imposts on property had to be clearly justified by the terms of legislation.[55]

The judges were less active when dealing with freedom from arbitrary detention, freedom from physical assault, freedom from searches and seizures, freedom of movement, and freedom of speech and assembly. Here, as elsewhere, the courts were influenced by the exigencies of situations involving significant public disorder, and seem to have felt obliged to support the executive against the forces of lawlessness. When suffragettes were arrested and imprisoned during their campaign of civil disobedience, several of them went on hunger strike. When the prison authorities force-fed them, they brought proceedings to challenge the legality of feeding against their will. Despite the normal principle that

---

[53] *Duncan* v. *Cammell Laird & Co. Ltd* [1942] AC 624, HL.
[54] See *Chester* v. *Bateson* [1920] 1 KB 829; *Newcastle Breweries Ltd* v. *R.* (1920) 36 TLR 276.
[55] See *Attorney-General* v. *De Keyser's Royal Hotel Ltd* [1920] AC 508, HL; *Attorney General* v. *Wilts United Dairies Ltd* (1921) 37 TLR 884, CA.

touching a person without consent constitutes a battery, the courts held that force-feeding was permissible in order to preserve life, notwithstanding the absence of evidence that the women's capacity to make decisions about their welfare was compromised.[56] This decision stood until 1994.[57]

Similarly, foreigners had little joy when attempting to challenge their arrest and detention by the police under the regulations, although this resulted largely, if not entirely, from the very expansively permissive form in which the powers of the police had been drafted in the regulations and approved by Parliament.[58] On the other hand, the High Court judges were sufficiently concerned about what were then seen as abuses by the police of their powers of arrest to issue a direction to the police as to the way in which detained suspects were to be treated. These 'Judges' Rules'[59] included the requirement that suspects should be informed of their right to remain silent. This 'caution' survived virtually unchanged until the erosion of the right in the late 1980s and 1990s. The Judges' Rules also laid down the extent to which, and the way in which, suspects might be questioned. The Judges' Rules were rules of practice, not of law. The only way of enforcing them was for judges to express their disapproval of breaches, usually by excluding evidence obtained through breaches of them. However, judges were (and to a great extent still are) reluctant to exclude otherwise admissible and probative evidence merely on account of police errors or minor sins. The general rule is that all relevant evidence should be available; if the courts exclude evidence to discipline the police, the public interest in rational decision-making and the conviction of the guilty suffers. As a result, the effectiveness of the rules depended largely on the willingness of the police to internalise them as operational rather than presentational principles. By the 1970s, as we shall see, it had become clear that (at least among some police officers) they were more honoured in the breach than the observance.

If the courts were concerned about police treatment of suspects in terms of arrest and questioning, they had no such qualms about extending the powers of the police in relation to search and seizure and

---

[56] *Leigh* v. *Gladstone* (1909) 26 TLR 139.

[57] See *R.* v. *Secretary of State for the Home Department, ex p. Robb* [1995] 1 All ER 677.

[58] See *R.* v. *Inspector of Lemon Street Police Station, ex p. Venicoff* [1920] 3 KB 72, DC.

[59] These were a set of guidelines issued by the Home Office to the police, originally in 1912, with additions in 1918 and a new version produced in 1968 which remained in force until the Police and Criminal Evidence Act 1984 took effect. See Peter Mirfield, *Silence, Confessions and Improperly Obtained Evidence* (Clarendon Press, 1997), p. 111ff.

the control of public meetings where that seemed desirable in order to facilitate the control of the perceived communist threat. This became clear in the 1930s in a series of decisions, which depended entirely on extensions of the common law and not at all on the emergency regulations or other legislation. The judges developed the legal powers of the police in several ways, always in cases involving communists.

With regard to search and seizure, the authorities established that, on making an arrest for a serious offence, the police were entitled to search for and seize material evidence in relation to that offence which was in the possession or under the control of the person arrested at the time of the arrest. The purpose of the power was to preserve evidence against the person arrested and people implicated with that person, thus advancing the public interest in convicting the guilty, since an accused could rely on the privilege against self-incrimination to defeat a *subpoena duces tecum*.[60] In 1934 in *Elias* v. *Pasmore*,[61] a case involving a search by police of the premises of the headquarters of the National Unemployed Workers' Movement (NUWM), Horridge J. decided that the power extended also to seizing any documents or other materials which were evidence of any crime committed by anyone. The legality of such a seizure would depend on the use which was subsequently made of the material. If it were introduced as evidence in a trial of anyone, a seizure made without reasonable grounds would be retrospectively legalised. The unsatisfactory nature of this decision led to criticism at the time and subsequently,[62] and it no longer represents the law[63] (if it ever did). However, it indicates the extent to which judges were prepared to bend the law in order to facilitate police action and prosecutions for sedition against the NUWM.[64]

The police also took action to prevent crowds gathering to hear leaders of the NUWM making speeches, and to discourage the expression of anti-police views at meetings. In two important cases, the courts extended police powers at common law to accommodate pre-emptive action by the police, in ways which anticipated and went beyond the powers to control processions given by the Public Order Act 1936. In

---

[60] *Mellor* v. *Leather and Clough* (1853) 1 E&B 619; *Dillon* v. *O'Brien* (1887) 20 LR Ir. 300, a case concerning police action against the Irish Land League.
[61] [1934] 2 KB 164.
[62] E. C. S. Wade, 'Police Search', *Law Quarterly Review* (1934); David Feldman, *The Law relating to Entry, Search and Seizure* (Butterworths, 1986), pp. 243–5.
[63] See *Ghani* v. *Jones* [1970] 1 QB 693, CA; Police and Criminal Evidence Act 1984, ss. 32, 19.
[64] Ewing and Gearty, *Struggle for Civil Liberties*, pp. 232–4.

1935, the Divisional Court, in short, unreserved and badly argued judgements, held that a police officer was entitled to use reasonable force if necessary to enter a meeting in a private hall, to which the general public had been invited, notwithstanding the organiser's withdrawal of the invitation from the officer concerned. The case, *Thomas* v. *Sawkins*,[65] concerned a meeting held by the NUWM, and the police claimed to have reasonable cause to suspect that seditious speeches would be made. The judgements have been interpreted as giving a power to the police to enter private premises whenever they reasonably anticipate an imminent breach of the peace or seditious speech on those premises. The court failed to subject the grounds and motives of the police to any proper scrutiny, or to provide any satisfactory legal rationale for the decision.[66] In practice, the power was applied differentially: the police were far more reluctant to enter Mosleyite meetings than NUWM ones, suggesting a political bias.[67]

In 1936, in *Duncan* v. *Jones*,[68] the Divisional Court held that the police had power to require a person to move away from the place near an employment exchange in a cul-de-sac where they were about to hold an open-air meeting, if an officer had reasonable grounds for suspecting that a breach of the peace might result. Again, the power had been used against the NUWM, and Mrs Duncan had been charged with wilfully obstructing a constable in the execution of his duty. The decision allowed the police to criminalise speech or assemblies merely by telling the organisers or speakers to stop, whenever there was a reasonable apprehension of a breach of the peace. This was not the purpose for which the offence of wilful obstruction was created. It makes free speech and criminal liability depend on police discretion, an approach which would today be regarded as objectionable by reference to human-rights and rule-of-law standards and which even then attracted sharp criticism from a distinguished constitutional lawyer.[69] The power was also (needless to

---

[65] [1935] 2 KB 249. For the factual background, see D. G. T. Williams, *Keeping the Peace* (Hutchinson, 1967), pp. 142–4; Ewing and Gearty, *Struggle for Civil Liberties*, pp. 216–34.

[66] Feldman, *Entry, Search and Seizure*, pp. 324–31.

[67] Ewing and Gearty, *Struggle for Civil Liberties*, pp. 289–311.

[68] [1936] 1 KB 218, DC.

[69] E. C. S. Wade, 'Police Powers and Public Meetings', *Cambridge Law Journal* (1936–9). See also Williams, *Keeping the Peace*, pp. 120–3; T. C. Daintith, 'Disobeying a Policeman: A Fresh Look at *Duncan* v. *Jones*', *Public Law*, (1966); David Feldman, 'Protest and Tolerance: Legal Values and the Control of Public-order Policing', in Raphael Cohen-Almagor (ed.), *Liberal Democracy and the Limits of Tolerance: Essays in Honor and Memory of Yitzhak Rabin* (University of Michigan Press, 2000), pp. 43–69.

say) used far more often against left-wing than right-wing speakers,[70] but just as worrying was the court's wilful blindness to civil-liberties issues: Lord Hewart C.J. denied that any freedom of assembly was implicated in the case.[71]

We can now draw some conclusions about the first forty-five years of the century. There were some small gains for civil liberties, but many incursions on them. These incursions were significant, and were the result of official indifference to liberties when faced with what were seen as greater and more pressing evils: anarchism, German espionage, communism, social and industrial disruption, and a challenge to the existing order. The voices which were raised against the erosion of liberty were isolated and generally unsuccessful in holding back the tidal advance of state control, led by successive governments of different political complexions, the police, the security service, and the courts.

However, the fact that campaigns for civil liberties were maintained, and that even in times of war and disruption voices were raised against the pervasive anti-liberal tendency of the establishment (which, it must be said, was probably shared by a majority of voters if not of the public as a whole), indicates that the roots of a civil liberties revolution were in place. In this respect, one of the most significant developments of the period was the foundation, in 1934, of the Council for Civil Liberties, later to become the National Council for Civil Liberties (NCCL) and now known as Liberty. This was formed in an attempt to oppose what was seen as the excessive use or abuse of power by the police against left-wing organisations, and the attempt by government (initially in the Incitement to Disaffection Act 1934) to introduce new legal restrictions on free speech and political campaigning. It also supported litigation, and became an increasingly respected expert body as the century progressed, although its reputation and sense of purpose was temporarily damaged by disputes over the approach it should take to freedom of speech for neo-Nazis and the rights of miners who continued to work during the strike of 1983–4.[72]

---

[70] Ewing and Gearty, *Struggle for Civil Liberties*, pp. 262–74.

[71] *Duncan* v. *Jones* [1936] 1 KB 218, DC, at 221–2.

[72] On the founding and work of the NCCL, and the role of D. N. Pritt KC in particular, see Carol Harlow and Richard Rawlings, *Pressure through Law* (Routledge, 1992), pp. 54–9. On the disputes of the 1980s, and a comparison with the approach of the American Civil Liberties Union to the rights of those regarded as having unacceptable opinions, see Larry Gostin in Gostin (ed.), *Civil Liberties in Conflict* (Routledge, 1988), pp. 7–20, 117–21.

The welfare state, the European Convention, and British nationality, 1945–60

In 1945, the United Kingdom and its allies had won two major wars in thirty years, and were determined that the later peace should not generate stresses like those which, after the Treaty of Versailles, had brought the Nazis to power in Germany. Part of the plan was to establish the Council of Europe, to preserve democracy and peace in Europe (the two were seen as going hand in hand).

Shock at the level of systematic inhumanity practised by the Nazis, which had been revealed by the liberating troops in Europe towards the end of the war, together with concern for the plight of the huge number of displaced persons at the end of the war, spurred the nations of the world to act to protect both human rights and the interests of refugees. The United Nations General Assembly approved the Universal Declaration of Human Rights (a non-binding instrument) in 1948, encompassing civil, political and social and economic rights. This spawned numerous binding multilateral treaties which were concluded under the aegis of the United Nations over the succeeding decades. In Europe, the member states of the newly established Council of Europe quickly took up the challenge of converting the general principles of the Universal Declaration into a binding treaty for the states of western Europe. After about two years of negotiations and drafting to which lawyers from the United Kingdom contributed greatly, the text of the European Convention on Human Rights (ECHR) was opened for signature in 1950. The United Kingdom was among the first to sign, and the Convention entered into force in 1953.

It is noteworthy that the Labour Party was prepared to sign and ratify the Convention and, more than a decade later, to grant the right of individual petition. Socialists were historically opposed to the idea of human rights or constitutional rights which might restrict the ability of an elected socialist government to give effect to collective economic and social goals. They also opposed subjecting essentially political disputes to judicial decision, viewing judges (with some justification) as temperamentally and professionally unreceptive to collectivist values and objectives. The UK's ratification of the Convention can be explained on the basis that the Cabinet saw it principally as an exercise in the field of foreign affairs, exporting to continental Europe values which were thought to be inherent in the British way of life. Although the chancellor of the Exchequer, Sir Stafford Cripps, feared that the Convention might undermine a socialist economic policy, and the Lord Chancellor, Lord Jowitt, thought that it might necessitate changes to municipal law, most ministers did not expect it to affect law or politics significantly. Concerns about the impact on domestic affairs seemed either exaggerated or trivial. Outside government, few politicians or organs of popular opinion took much interest in such matters.[73] However, it grew in importance, particularly after Harold Wilson's government granted people the right to petition the Strasbourg organs directly from 1965. Two characteristics of the European Convention on Human Rights were new and distinctive. It was the first international treaty to attempt to codify a wide-ranging set of rights in an instrument which bound its parties in public international law; but also it was the first international instrument to allow (initially subject to each state's discretion) ordinary people to bring their grievances against states before an international tribunal for binding arbitration. Between these two factors, we can see with the benefit of hindsight how likely it was that the Convention, and the Commission and Court which were its main organs, would come to exercise a major influence over the protection of civil liberties and human rights in all member states of the Council of Europe, including the United Kingdom.

In domestic affairs, humanitarian paternalism held sway, socially reformist, but not morally liberal. Perhaps because those who had fought in the Second World War were more concerned in the late 1940s and 1950s with rebuilding their lives and the country's economy, serious and critical interest in enhancing freedom tended to be seen in the younger generation, whose growing prosperity led them to be interested in a greater variety of lifestyle choices than had been available to their elders. In Parliament, attention concentrated on providing the means of securing social and economic rights—education, health, social security and housing—and economic freedom rather than civil liberties. Administrative law proved to have limited power to protect individuals' interests against the burgeoning power of state bureaucracy. One reason why courts often proved unable to bolster individual interests against official attack was the common law's assumption that it was safe to allow those in power to have considerable discretionary authority over their subjects, because the powerful would feel a strong sense of responsibility for the

---

[73] See Anthony Lester, 'Fundamental Rights: The United Kingdom Isolated', *Public Law* (1984); Elizabeth Wicks, 'The United Kingdom Government's Perceptions of the European Convention on Human Rights at the Time of Entry', *Public Law* (2000).

welfare of all subjects which would act as a brake on abuse of power. This sense of responsibility for people, and particularly the worst off, underlay the great social developments of the 1940s, the National Health Service, Beveridge, and the extension of education as of right. It relied on a consensus as to basic values which held up throughout this period, but which started to collapse in the 1960s, triggering a resurgence of administrative law which continues today.

There was a degree of complacency about the protection of freedom, an assumption (strengthened by the conflict with Germany) that the United Kingdom enjoyed a uniquely happy state of legal affairs. George Orwell identified 'the respect for constitutionalism and legality, the belief in "the law" as something above the State and above the individual, something which is cruel and stupid, of course, but at any rate *incorruptible*', as 'an all-important English trait' in his 1941 essay 'England your England'. It was an illusion, but 'An illusion can become a half-truth, a mask can alter the expression of a face.'[74]

> Even hypocrisy is a powerful safeguard. The hanging judge, that evil old man in scarlet robe and horsehair wig, whom nothing short of dynamite will ever teach what century he is living in, but who will at any rate interpret the law according to the books and will in no circumstances take a bribe, is one of the symbolic figures of England. He is a symbol of the strange mixture of reality and illusion, democracy and privilege, humbug and decency, the subtle network of compromises, by which the nation keeps itself in familiar shape.[75]

It is not a coincidence that Miss Emma Warburton Hamlyn, who died in Torquay in 1941, should have bequeathed the residue of her estate to trustees on charitable trusts which, as settled by the Chancery Division of the High Court, were for:

> The furtherance by lectures or otherwise among the Common People of the United Kingdom of Great Britain and Northern Ireland of the knowledge of the Comparative Jurisprudence and the Ethnology of the Chief European Countries, including the United Kingdom, and the circumstances of the growth of such Jurisprudence to the intent that the Common People of the United Kingdom may realise the privileges which in law and custom they enjoy in comparison with other European Peoples and realising and appreciating such privileges may recognise the responsibilities and obligations attaching to them.

[74] George Orwell, *Inside the Whale and Other Essays* (Penguin, 1962), pp. 63–90 at 71. I am grateful to Professor Vernon Bogdanor for this reference.
[75] Ibid., p. 72.

All very *1066 And All That*, but the result was to establish a prestigious annual series of published lectures which continues today. The first series of lectures was delivered in 1949 by Sir Alfred Thomas Denning, then a lord justice of the Court of Appeal and already on his way to being recognised as a formative influence on twentieth-century public law. His lectures showed that, while he strongly respected the common law's tradition in protecting liberty, he was not complacent about the state of the law. In particular, the fourth lecture on 'The Powers of the Executive' ended with a bugle call to awake administrative law from its long sleep:

> Our procedure for securing our personal freedom is efficient, but our procedure for preventing the abuse of power is not . . . This is not a task for Parliament. Our representatives there cannot control the day to day activities of the many who administer the manifold activities of the State; nor can they award damages to those who are injured by any abuses. The courts must do this. Of all the great tasks that lie ahead, this is the greatest.[76]

Although the late 1940s and 1950s saw little innovation in the law of civil liberties, this was the stirring of an administrative law revival (although its roots can be traced back to Lord Chief Justice Hewart's book *The New Despotism* more than twenty years earlier). The 1950s also witnessed some important developments on moral matters which set the tone for the socially liberal 1960s. A Royal Commission on Capital Punishment was established in 1949, chaired by Sir Ernest Gowers. Its report, published four years later, reviewed the moral issues relating to capital punishment and the evidence for and against its value as a deterrent, and recommended its abolition.[77] This was a step too far and too fast for the Conservative government, but a campaign for abolition led by figures like the criminologist Terence Morris and the barrister and author Louis Blom-Cooper ensured that the subject was not forgotten. *The Report of the Committee on Homosexual Offences and Prostitution*,[78] chaired by Lord Wolfenden, placed J. S. Mill's harm principle, together with the idea of personal autonomy and choice of lifestyle, at the centre of the discussion of legal regulation of morality, and made a major contribution to the ascendancy of liberalism as the dominant moral creed. It led to a relaxation of the law against prostitution in 1957, and set the tone for the discussion which ultimately led to the progressive decrimi-

---

[76] Lord Justice Denning, *Freedom under the Law* (Stevens, 1949), p. 126. The relevant terms of the scheme settled for the Hamlyn Trust are set out at pp. vii–viii.
[77] *Report of the Royal Commission on Capital Punishment*, Cmd 8932 (HMSO, 1953).
[78] Cmnd 247 (HMSO, 1957).

nalisation of homosexuality from 1967. And literature became more free with the passing of the Obscene Publications Act 1959, which substituted a statutory test of tendency to deprave and corrupt the likely readership for indecency as the standard for criminal liability under the statute, and gave a new defence of social merit which might excuse the publisher even of a work which tended to deprave and corrupt.

The full impact of these developments was felt later. For the fifteen years after 1945, the scene was dominated by a drive to improve social conditions by collective measures, and a consensus between the main parties on basic values even when they disagreed markedly about individual policies. Civil liberties were not generally considered to be a problem. Managing the break-up of the Empire was a more significant concern. The need to sort out the nationality of the inhabitants of newly independent dominions, and the extent of the United Kingdom's continuing responsibility for them, produced the British Nationality Act 1948. This created British Commonwealth citizenship, which gave all Commonwealth citizens a right of entry to the United Kingdom, but did nothing to define the nationality or citizenship of inhabitants of the United Kingdom itself. It thus did nothing to foster a sense of citizenship, but led to fears of uncontrolled immigration which set the scene for political wrangling over succeeding decades.[79]

Freedom of lifestyle, commissions of inquiry, and checks on the power of the state, 1960–90

In the 1960s, lifestyles began a period of rapid change, and immigration began to produce an ethnically and racially diverse and increasingly multicultural society. Demands grew that the state should tolerate, or even celebrate, different lifestyles. The United Kingdom accordingly entered a phase in which respect for civil liberties and, as they were increasingly called, human rights became a touchstone for the acceptability of policies and governmental initiatives at home, and recognition of regimes abroad. At the same time, it was a period in which social and technological developments would make it increasingly easy to interfere with liberties. The rapid development of the welfare state required procedures for administering and co-ordinating benefits involving state agencies in holding a fast-growing volume of information

---

[79] Dummett and Nicol, *Subjects, Citizens, Aliens and Others*, pp. 133–42.

about individuals. The methods of communicating and processing this information multiplied and accelerated. The rapid development of computers, and their progressive improvements in power, speed, miniaturisation and incorporation in a vast number of different technologies, presented great opportunities to government but also great threats to liberty. The same applied to the technologies of cameras, television, microphones and recording devices. These offered new ways in which people, their homes and offices, and their communications could be monitored. The move from an economy based on cash and written orders for the transfer of funds and sale of assets to the electronic economy, although slower, gathered pace in the last decade of the century. The law of civil liberties was left behind in the exploding technical capacity of the state to know about people.

For various reasons, public faith in the ability of many public institutions to deal properly and fairly with their new capabilities was undermined. Growing cultural diversity and the decline of social deference indicated that cracks were appearing in the consensus over political values. Governments attempted to rebuild the consensus. The Labour governments of 1964–70 and 1974–9 developed links with the trade unions in making policy, particularly on economic and employment matters. All governments until 1979 made extensive use of Royal Commissions. But it was only a matter of time before the underlying conflicts in society broke through. Under Margaret Thatcher, the government stopped trying to paper over the cracks. Ideological divisions turned politics into an extension of a highly competitive market-place, eroding the belief that those in power had a special obligation to safeguard those who were unable to participate, or who had lost out, in market competition.

> Resort to public choice theory as a form of participatory democracy marginalised both Parliament and traditional government as channels for legitimate policy-making ... Recent recognition that there is no longer a clear, ethical consensus as to how public bodies and public figures should discharge their obligations to the public for whom they work has led to the creation of bodies such as the Committee on Standards in Public Life.[80]

To maintain public faith in the state in these conditions, new institutions had to be put in place to regulate the use of power. Some of these, like the Police Complaints Authority, resulted from domestic pressure. Some

---

[80] David Feldman, 'The Human Rights Act and Constitutional Values,' *Legal Studies* (1999).

430

flowed from international pressures: the European Convention on Human Rights and the EEC were particularly fertile sources of pressure for change. Others again, such as the growing body of anti-discrimination law, were consequences of a growing willingness (both within the United Kingdom and in Europe) to place substantive equality in the forefront of political and legal discourse, and of a new recognition of the problems and needs of an increasingly multicultural and multi-ethnic society.

This had some apparently contradictory effects. As the United Kingdom became more outward-looking in relation to its public law, international influences gave rise to, or encouraged, concern for a growing range of interests. More significantly, people started to ask questions about how those interests could be effectively protected against arbitrariness and abuse. In administrative law, this generated considerable strides, particularly in the protection of economic interests against state collectivism.

The Thatcher government's commitments to economic individualism and minimal government (except in the areas of crime and public order) left reduced scope for respecting personal freedom in non-economic matters, but the courts were unable to protect the area of individual liberty against assault by Act of Parliament. The political ethos had changed, but the common law was unable to adapt to provide effective protections in the new political environment. This resulted in an absence of legal and political protection for important non-economic interests. There was relatively little legislation protecting rights between 1979 and 1990. This may have been partly the result of the prime minister's reluctance to allocate parliamentary time to non-government business. Many important legislative steps to advance civil liberties in the 1960s and 1970s had come in the form of private members' bills on matters such as abortion and homosexuality. There was little time for private members' bills in the 1980s. (It may also explain the relative dearth of civil liberties legislation in the late 1940s, when the Labour government with a large majority and a busy legislative agenda was similarly loth to allow time to private members: in 1945, private members' time was reduced, over the protests of A. P. Herbert MP and others, being restored only in 1949.)[81]

When the judiciary grasped the scale of the change, it began to develop the common law in ways which offered some protection to traditional civil liberties. Many of these halting steps were concerned with

---

[81] An account of this is given by A. P. Herbert, *Independent Member* (Methuen, 1950), pp. 374–6.

chipping away at state secrecy in one form or another, and at extending judicial scrutiny to executive and administrative behaviour in relation to which it would previously have been impossible to obtain an effective legal remedy. For example, the very wide doctrine of Crown privilege, described in the 1900–45 section above, was replaced by 'public interest immunity from disclosure', with defined grounds for seeking the immunity and at least some power for the courts to make their own evaluation of the adequacy of the grounds advanced by bodies claiming to represent the public interest.[82] A growing range of royal prerogatives were brought within the scope of judicial review, and the grounds for their exercise subjected to some, albeit not very extensive, scrutiny.[83] In the litigation arising from the government's attempts to stop people in the UK from finding out about allegations being made by a former MI5 officer, Peter Wright, in his book *Spycatcher*, based on his experiences in MI5, the government brought to bear the civil law of breach of confidence to restrain publications, rather than the criminal law which provided no means of prior restraint. Despite initially granting very wide injunctions restraining publication pending a full trial of the action, the House of Lords eventually discharged them on the ground that the government had no private interest to protect, and had failed to show that there remained a public interest in restraining publication of allegations which were already in the public domain.[84]

However, it was too little, too late. Many people had lost confidence in the domestic legal system, with its emphasis on liberty, as a way of protecting vital interests, and had started to talk instead about human rights, enforceable against the state by the international procedure of the European Commission and Court of Human Rights. This disenchantment with judicial protection for liberties was accelerated by the Ponting affair.[85] Believing that the government had misled the House of Commons in the account which it had given of the sinking of the Argentinian battleship *General Belgrano* during the Falklands War, a civil servant, Clive Ponting, leaked relevant material to Tam Dalyell MP. When Ponting

---

[82] *Conway* v. *Rimmer* [1968] AC 910, HL; *Rogers* v. *Secretary of State for the Home Department* [1973] AC 388, HL; *D* v. *National Society for the Prevention of Cruelty to Children* [1978] AC 171, HL.

[83] *Council of Civil Service Unions* v. *Minister for the Civil Service* [1985] AC 374, HL.

[84] *Attorney-General* v. *Guardian Newspapers (No. 2)* [1990] 1 AC 109, HL; and see also *Lord Advocate* v. *The Scotsman Publications Ltd* [1990] 1 AC 812, HL.

[85] *R.* v. *Ponting* [1985] Crim. LR 318. See Rosamund M. Thomas, 'The British Official Secrets Acts 1911–1939 and the *Ponting* Case', *Criminal Law Review* (1986); Clive Ponting, '*R.* v. *Ponting*', *Journal of Law and Society* (1987); Hooper, *Official Secrets*, ch. 12.

was prosecuted under the Official Secrets Act 1911, he argued that his disclosure had been made to 'a person to whom it is in the interest of the State his duty to communicate it', and so was not an offence under section 2(1)(a). McCowan J. disagreed, and directed the jury that the interest of the state was whatever the government for the time being decided that it was, so that only officially authorised disclosures were protected. Despite this, the jury acquitted Ponting. The verdict was widely seen as having upheld freedom of expression and parliamentary accountability against an attempt by the judge to stifle it. It sounded the death-knell for section 2 of the Act, and dented public faith in the judges as upholders of freedom under law. The government reacted by introducing the Official Secrets Act 1989, which identified a more limited range of circumstances in which people could be criminally liable for making disclosures, but also withdrew the 'interest of state' defence from serving and former members of the security and intelligence services.

Some other important institutions of social control and national protection, such as the police and the security service, faced a loss of public support and legitimacy, forcing the state to change arrangements in order to protect rights. More generally, the state proactively encouraged the development and enjoyment of human rights, through participation in international treaties and by taking action to regulate potential interferences with rights. On the other hand, the state responded to threats, or perceived threats, from terrorism and particular types of non-political crime, by radically reducing protection for people's liberties, either generally or for particular purposes. The remainder of this section briefly examines each of these areas.

The great, the good, and the search for legitimacy through consensus

The earlier part of the period was the great age of the Royal Commission, in a search for rationality and objectivity. The assumption, which underlay all forms of corporatism in political life, was that people's shared interests were more important than their factional interests, and that a satisfactory and legitimate solution could be found by bringing together representatives of different interest groups to discuss problems, ameliorating potential clashes through the influence of a chair of recognised independence, often with the addition of a strong dash of academic expertise and rigour. The mechanism gave 'the great and the good' the task of achieving solutions to problems which, because of their moral or political intractability, stumped the ordinary political process. It was the pattern for the work of standing bodies such as the Criminal Law Revision Committee, the Law Commission (established under the Law Commission Act 1967), and of committees or commissions established to report on particular issues of current importance.

Some earlier reports produced notable effects on civil liberties. Capital punishment for murder was suspended under a Labour administration in 1965, a decision made permanent in 1970, but the pro-hanging lobby remained vociferous. Only in 1999, following a free vote in the Commons during debate on the Human Rights bill, did the United Kingdom sign the Sixth Protocol to the European Convention on Human Rights and abolish capital punishment for all offences in peacetime, completing the process of reform begun half a century earlier.[86] The decriminalisation of some male homosexual acts was finally achieved in 1967. Committees and commissions were active in many other important areas. A committee chaired by the archbishop of Canterbury achieved consensus on reforming the grounds for divorce to banish the notion of the matrimonial offence and replace it with that of irretrievable breakdown, in response to which a Law Commission report led directly to the Divorce Reform Act 1969 and no-fault divorce. The *Report of the Committee on Obscenity and Film Censorship*,[87] chaired by the philosopher Bernard Williams, made clear evidence of harm to identifiable individuals the threshold test for legal interference with liberty, helping to protect liberal individualism against a backlash in the 1970s. The importance to the ethos of civil liberties is inestimable.

Inquiries and reports were also pivotal in gaining acceptance for the idea that suspects' rights in the criminal process needed and merited protection. The weakness of the Judges' Rules as a means of achieving this was made clear in a series of cases in the 1970s and 1980s, many of them involving offences of terrorism in connection with the affairs of Northern Ireland. The case which had the most widespread influence, however, and ultimately persuaded most politicians, lawyers and police officers that legal rules to protect the welfare and due-process rights of suspects would ultimately lead to more reliable decision-making in the criminal process, was that of three teenagers who were convicted of the murder of Maxwell Confait. They had confessed after being subjected

[86] See Gavin Drewry, 'The Politics of Capital Punishment', in Gavin Drewry and Charles Blake (eds), *Law and the Spirit of Inquiry: Essays in Honour of Sir Louis Blom-Cooper* (Kluwer, 1999), pp. 137–59.

[87] Cmnd 7772 (HMSO, 1979).

to detention and interrogation without legal advice, despite their limited mental capacities. Other evidence later made it clear that they were innocent. An inquiry into the case[88] produced a backbench amendment to the Criminal Justice bill 1977 which for the first time gave suspects a right to legal advice at police stations, but without any means of enforcement. Eventually, the Labour government, bowing to pressure from civil liberties groups, established the Royal Commission on Criminal Procedure in 1979, chaired by a sociologist, Sir Cyril Phillips. When it reported to a Conservative government in 1981, its comprehensive review of the criminal process, its intelligent use of well planned and executed sociological research, and its balanced recommendations[89] made it impossible for the government not to legislate. Despite opposition from the police, the Police and Criminal Evidence Act 1984 came into force on 1 January 1986. This provided a codified law of investigation, arrest, search, seizure, detention and questioning which broadly gave the police the powers they need to do their job while protecting the fundamental rights of people in police custody and in possession of material evidence of offences. The Act also established the Police Complaints Authority, a body independent of the police to oversee the investigation by police officers of serious complaints against other officers. The 1984 Act was followed by the Prosecution of Offences Act 1985, also based on the recommendations of the Phillips Commission, which established the Crown Prosecution Service (CPS) and removed responsibility for conducting prosecutions from the police. Although criticised by the Police Federation as a villain's charter, by the NCCL as giving the police powers they had never had before, and by those who complain about the performance of the CPS, the scheme has broadly stood the test of time and won over most of its detractors.

Inquiries also affected social and official attitudes to multiculturalism and the policing of public order. Members of some ethnic minorities suffer from differential application of the criminal law and criminal procedure, including stop and search, arrest and bail, the probability of conviction at trial, and the likelihood of receiving a custodial sentence after conviction.[90] Addressing this challenge to the principle of equality

---

[88] *Report of an Inquiry by the Hon. Sir Henry Fisher into the Circumstances leading to the Trial of Three Persons on Charges arising out of the Death of Maxwell Confait and the Fire at 27 Doggett Road, London SE5* (1977), HC 90.

[89] *Report of the Royal Commission on Criminal Procedure*, Cmnd 8092–I (HMSO, 1981).

[90] See, for example, Roger Hood (in collaboration with Graca Cordovil), *Race and Sentencing* (Clarendon Press, 1992).

before the law and the right to equal protection of the law, and identifying its root causes, will be major tasks for the twenty-first century. In our period, politicians increasingly accepted that racism was a problem for policing, as a result of several important inquiries into a series of outbreaks of violence which were said to have been sparked by insensitive policing of ethnic minority communities. The Scarman reports on the Red Lion Square and Brixton disorders established that the problems existed, and indicated ways forward through changing techniques of policing in order to achieve essential community co-operation.[91] It is taking a long time to achieve the goal, as the recent report of the Stephen Lawrence inquiry by Sir William Macpherson (who, unlike Lord Scarman, had never previously been regarded as a liberal) demonstrates.[92]

There were many other important inquiries during the second half of the century. The report by Kenneth Younger's committee on privacy[93] did much to hold up the enactment of a statutory tort of interference with privacy, which was later held not to exist at common law either in England and Wales (despite having been established at common law in the USA, on the basis of English precedents, for nearly a century).[94] Nevertheless, the Younger committee made clear the threats posed to civil liberties by the increasingly powerful technologies of surreptitious surveillance, data tracking and processing. The further review of data protection by the Lindop committee[95] set the scene for the introduction of the Data Protection Act 1984, which (*inter alia*) gave rights to data-subjects to know what computerised personal files were being held on them and to correct errors, and established the office of the Data Protection Registrar to maintain a register of people holding personal information on computer and to enforce observance of statutory data protection principles. This regime is currently being extended, under the

---

[91] *Report of an Inquiry by the Rt Hon. Lord Justice Scarman, OBE: The Red Lion Square Disorders of 15 June 1974*, Cmnd 5919 (HMSO, 1975); *Report of an Inquiry by the Rt Hon. Lord Justice Scarman, OBE: The Brixton Disorders, 10–12 April 1981*, Cmnd 8427 (HMSO, 1981).

[92] *The Stephen Lawrence Inquiry: Report of an Inquiry by Sir William Macpherson of Cluny, advised by Tom Cook, the Rt Revd Dr John Sentamu, Dr Richard Stone*, Cm 4262–I (Stationery Office, 1999).

[93] *Report of the Committee on Privacy*, Cmnd 5012 (HMSO, 1972).

[94] *Malone* v. *Metropolitan Police Commissioner (No. 2)* [1979] Ch. 344; David Feldman, *Civil Liberties and Human Rights in England and Wales*, 2nd edn (Oxford University Press, 2002), ch. 9.

[95] *Report of the Committee on Data Protection* (Chairman, Sir Norman Lindop), Cmnd 7341 (HMSO, 1978).

influence of international and Community law,[96] to offer similar protection to personal information held in paper files via the Data Protection Act 1998.

On the whole, inquiries of this sort exercised a liberalising influence. They could make recommendations more liberal than those which governments—with one eye on an electorate which was relatively intolerant towards the rights of suspects of crime and social or ethnic minorities—would have been willing to make. Their perceived independence gave their recommendations an unusual degree of legitimacy among the general public, and weight with government. Inquiries, committees and commissions did much to provide fora, beyond the heat of day-to-day politics, in which contentious issues could be considered with due regard to the freedoms of people affected, as well as wider social interests. Although they became less popular within government for a time under the premiership of Margaret Thatcher, who was less concerned to seek consensus than most previous prime ministers since 1939, we shall see that the treatment of parades in Northern Ireland under John Major and Tony Blair provides another example of this process.

A variant on the inquiry model is the semi-independent commissioner: a member of 'the establishment', albeit sometimes an idiosyncratic member, brought in from outside government to keep under review state activities which have a significant impact on civil liberties but which involve matters of secrecy or security that the government will not open to fully independent review. Where, however, the scheme of the legislation seems calculated to avoid rather than to instantiate effective review, and when the commissioner's reports are not published in full, while those parts which are published give little confidence that he or she has been given access to the necessary information to enable him or her to perform the review function with any great rigour, this method can seem like a sop to public concern rather than a genuine instrument of accountability. The reviews under the Interception of Communication Act 1985 are cases in point. On the other hand, there are some reviews which seem to be more rigorous, and which make proposals for reform which sometimes go beyond anything the government is prepared immediately to implement. This has been true of the annual reviews of the operation of powers under the prevention of

---

[96] See David Feldman, 'Information and Privacy', in Jack Beatson and Yvonne Cripps (eds), *Freedom of Expression and Freedom of Information: Essays in Honour of Sir David Williams* (Oxford University Press, 2000).

terrorism legislation, of the work of the independent commissioner for the holding centres in Northern Ireland (the first of whom, Sir Louis Blom-Cooper, was appointed in 1993),[97] and the sometimes vitriolic reports of Judge Stephen Tumim and his successor General Sir David Ramsbotham as chief inspector of prisons. The value of such reviews depends largely on the personality and independence of the person conducting them but, where the right person brings his or her talents to bear, it can give great weight to the resulting recommendation, significant gains can be achieved, and the outcome carries a moral and rational legitimacy which no mere democratic accountability could confer.

All these forms of inquiry and reporting contributed to establishing an ethos in government, and to some extent among the judiciary and the general public, which was conducive to a growing respect for the values which underpin human rights and civil liberties.

The influence of international human rights

After 1965, when the Labour government allowed individuals to petition the Strasbourg institutions directly to complain of violations of the ECHR by the United Kingdom, the government's confidence that the law in the United Kingdom complied with Convention rights was shown to be misplaced. Thereafter, the Convention has had a significant impact on our law, and our lawyers have had a significant impact on the interpretation and development of the Convention. Once the European Court of Human Rights had decided that the Convention was a living instrument, to be interpreted dynamically in the light of changing social, economic, moral and technological conditions, it became inevitable that the meaning of the rights under the Convention would have to be understood by reference to the case-law of the Commission and the Court as well as the text itself. Lawyers from the common-law systems of the United Kingdom were particularly well suited by training and experience to advance arguments in the context of a developing case-law. It is therefore not surprising with hindsight (although it surprised most people at the time) that many of the early cases to go to the Strasbourg organs after 1965 came from the United Kingdom, or that the lawyers representing applicants against the United Kingdom were able to advance particularly

---

[97] See Clive Walker and Ben Fitzpatrick, 'The Independent Commissioner for the Holding Centres: A Review', *Public Law* (1998).

ingenious and rigorous arguments which helped both protect their clients and push forward the Strasbourg case-law.

Within government, there were further signs that a human-rights ethos was developing. The United Kingdom ratified the International Covenant on Civil and Political Rights and the International Covenant on Economic, Social and Cultural Rights, which impose reporting obligations to various United Nations human rights committees; the Convention on the Rights of the Child, which similarly requires periodic reports to be lodged; and a range of anti-discrimination instruments. Joining the EEC, although not initially a body concerned with human rights, soon involved complying with directives on equal pay and equal opportunities for men and women, as well as a raft of economic rights, including freedom of establishment and freedom of movement for workers, goods, and services. Admittedly governments, especially the Conservative administrations of 1979 to 1997, employed anti-European rhetoric which deprecated both the efforts of the EEC (and subsequently the EC and the EU) in the field of social engineering, and particularly the power of the European Court of Justice to make law by interpreting the treaties without reference to the intentions of the member states. This aversion to supra-national or international judicial law-making extended, by late 1996, to the European Court of Human Rights, to which the Lord Chancellor, Lord Mackay of Clashfern, was dispatched to explain the importance of respecting sovereign states' legitimate sphere of discretionary action coupled with democratic accountability. Nevertheless, governments went on signing and ratifying treaties, and loyally complying with decisions of the courts even when they were unfavourable. If this does not unequivocally demonstrate a commitment to human rights, it does at least show a degree of respect for the rule of law, even at international level.

The effect of the treaties in municipal law took some time to stabilise, for reasons relating to the dualist nature of the United Kingdom's constitution. In Scotland, the judges long refused even to consider rights under the Convention in domestic proceedings, holding to a very pure form of dualist theory. In England and Wales, and Northern Ireland, the position was rather different. Unlike customary international law,[98] treaties have never been regarded as giving rise to directly enforceable legal rights and obligations in municipal law. A strict dualism as to treaties saves

---

[98] See *Trendtex Trading Corporation* v. *National Bank of Nigeria* [1977] QB 529, at 553ff. *per* Lord Denning MR, and *cp.* 578f. *per* Shaw L.J., and 571f. *per* Stephenson L.J.

Parliament from being forced to accept, or the government and citizens to comply with, changes to municipal law over which Parliament has no control, because the government alone exercises the royal prerogative of treaty-making. Parliament has only limited oversight of treaty-making, unless it has restricted the treaty-making power of the Crown by statute.[99] The so-called 'Ponsonby Rule' (a constitutional convention) requires the government to lay treaties before Parliament before ratifying them, but parliamentary approval is not a legal condition precedent to ratification, let alone signing. Nor is the treaty-making prerogative justiciable.[100]

However, there were circumstances in which the courts would have regard to international treaties. When interpreting legislation, there was a rebuttable presumption that Parliament did not intend to legislate in a manner inconsistent with the United Kingdom's international obligations, although this came into play only where the legislation was ambiguous. The courts also began to take account of rights under the European Court of Human Rights when developing the common law, often claiming that the rights were already well entrenched in English law. This was a convenient way of legitimising a process of legal reasoning which gave weight to international law within a dualist system, but was sometimes a fiction, as the number of occasions on which the United Kingdom was held to have violated Convention rights showed. After the United Kingdom acceded to the Treaty of Rome and joined the EEC (later the EC), the values underlying human rights had some effect indirectly. In response to a challenge from the German courts to the primacy of Community law over national law, the European Court of Justice introduced fundamental rights as 'general principles of Community law'. This enabled the Court to apply human-rights standards when reviewing the legality of the actions of Community organs, particularly the European Commission and the Council of Ministers, and that in turn allowed the German courts to concede primacy to Community law without undermining protection offered to the fundamental rights of Germans under the *Grundgesetz*. Because of the primacy of Community law, this injection of human-rights values to it affected the systems of all member states. Although the European Court of Justice later held that the Community lacked the legal capacity to become a

---

[99] For a rare example of such a restriction, see European Parliamentary Elections Act 1978, section 6(1).

[100] See, for example, *R. v. Foreign Secretary, ex p. Rees-Mogg* [1994] QB 552; Select Committee on Procedure, Second Report, *Parliamentary Scrutiny of Treaties* (26 July 2000), HC 210.

party to the European Convention on Human Rights, the impact of the rights on the Community was put on a treaty footing by Article F2 of the Maastricht Treaty, and made justiciable as Article 6(2) by the Treaty of Amsterdam.

The direct and indirect impact of the European model of human rights on the United Kingdom has been inestimable. A series of important decisions from the European Commission and Court of Human Rights made it necessary to introduce changes to English law in a number of fields. For example, a major part of the Contempt of Court Act 1981 was the result of the decision in *Sunday Times Ltd* v. *United Kingdom*.[101] The decision in *Malone* v. *United Kingdom*[102] led to the enactment of the Interception of Communications Act 1985. The decision in *X* v. *United Kingdom*[103] led to radical changes in the Mental Health Act 1983. A series of decisions about treatment of prisoners' correspondence and Article 8 led to major changes in the prison rules.[104] Decisions about the way in which local authorities took decisions about child care in suspected abuse cases were among the considerations which led to changes in the procedures under the Children Act 1989,[105] although Dame Elizabeth Butler-Sloss's *Report of the Inquiry into Child Abuse in Cleveland*[106] was also hugely influential. And there were many other cases.

The government's response to such decisions was not always enthusiastic. In a number of cases, including the enactment of the Interception of Communications Act 1985, the approach seemed to be to change the law by the minimum amount to give a reasonable prospect of not being held to be in violation of rights in the future, rather than to put the law on a comprehensively and securely Convention-compliant footing. In the case of the 1985 Act, indeed, a large part of the legislation was devoted to ensuring that people would be unable to discover that their communications had been intercepted, or to obtain an effective remedy. The drafting of the Act has made interpretation and application very diffi-

---

[101] Series A, No. 30, Judgment of 26 April 1979, 2 EHRR 245.

[102] Series A, No. 82, Judgment of 2 August 1984, 7 EHRR 14.

[103] Series A, No. 46, Judgment of 5 November 1981, 4 EHRR 188.

[104] *Golder* v. *United Kingdom*, Series A, No. 18, Judgment of 21 February 1975; *Silver* v. *United Kingdom*, Series A, No. 61, Judgment of 25 March 1983; *Boyle and Rice* v. *United Kingdom*, Series A, No. 131, Judgment of 27 April 1988; *McCallum* v. *United Kingdom*, Series A, No. 183, Judgment of 30 August 1990; *Campbell* v. *United Kingdom*, Series A, No. 233, Judgment of 25 March 1992.

[105] *O* v. *United Kingdom*, Series A, No. 120, Judgment of 8 July 1987, 10 EHRR 82; *W, R, and B* v. *United Kingdom*, Series A, No. 121, Judgments of 8 July 1987, 10 EHRR 29, 87, 74.

[106] Cm 412 (HMSO, 1988).

cult,[107] and ensured that violations would continue in cases not covered by the Act.[108] What is most worthy of note, however, is that the government has made an attempt (even if sometimes half-heartedly) to give effect to adverse judgements of the Court in all cases save one. In that case, concerned with the period for which terrorist suspects could be detained without being brought before a judicial officer, the United Kingdom entered a derogation from Article 5 which was subsequently upheld by the Court.[109] By and large, it cannot be doubted that the Convention and its jurisprudence began to exercise a significant influence over municipal law-making during this period, perhaps planting the germs of a *Rechtsstaat*. Legislation came to be assessed within departments for compatibility with the Convention even when there had been no decision establishing a violation. For example, a good deal of care was taken in the Home Office to ensure that the Police and Criminal Evidence Act 1984 and its associated codes of practice would be likely to comply with the requirements of the Convention.

Meanwhile, the political process of European Community law-making was fleshing out some concrete rights in ways which went beyond the European Convention on Human Rights. As befits the origin of the European Community as a common market, the rights developed by it were economic in origin. They included rights to the free movement of goods and services between member states, and rights of establishment in member states. At an early stage, the requirement that there should be, as far as possible, a level playing field for economic actors in different member states led to legislation which could be seen to be social- and individual-rights based in the employment field. This ensured that a member state could not establish a trading advantage against other member states by adopting rules which failed to give proper protection to employees' rights. On this basis, the provisions of Article 119 of the Treaty of Rome, the Equal Pay Directive and the Equal Treatment Directive were applied by the European Court of Justice in ways which went significantly beyond the protection provided in municipal law, and which were capable of complementing municipal law to the extent that it fell short of the European standard.

In all these ways, developments on the international and supra-

---

[107] See now *Morgans* v. *Director of Public Prosecutions* [2000] 2 WLR 386, HL.
[108] *Halford* v. *United Kingdom*, Judgment of 25 June 1997, RJD 1997–III No. 39, 24 EHRR 523.
[109] See *Brogan* v. *United Kingdom*, Series A, No. 145, Judgment of 29 November 1988, 11 EHRR 107; *Brannigan and McBride* v. *United Kingdom*, Series A, No. 258-B, Judgment of 26 May 1993, 17 EHRR 539.

national stage came to influence the protection of civil liberties and human rights in the United Kingdom.

Proactive law-making and the concern for equality and autonomy

Quite apart from the international dimension, there was a growing body of support within the United Kingdom for making certain values central to domestic law-making. Among the most important of these were equality and autonomy. A formal notion of equality underlies the doctrine of the rule of law, which would be impossible without the idea of equality before the law in the sense of the equal application of legal rules to all. English law in the second forty-five years of the century marked two significant advances on this formal notion. First, there was a distinct hardening in the common law's recognition that differential treatment of members of different groups required special justification, irrespective of the classes of people involved. This benefited members of groups with little or no political power who had previously been regarded as being naturally entitled to fewer rights than most people: for example, prisoners and immigrants. In *Raymond* v. *Honey*[110] the House of Lords, holding that a prison governor committed contempt of court when he stopped a prisoner's letter which attempted to institute court proceedings against a prison officer, stressed that prisoners retained all their rights and civil liberties (including the right to have access to a court) save those which were expressly taken away by statute or necessarily held in abeyance by reason of the very fact of imprisonment. Prisoners were no longer regarded as people without rights, and could expect the courts to provide at least some protection against the arbitrary exercise of state power.[111] After a brief hiccup,[112] the House of Lords asserted its power to use habeas corpus to require the home secretary to show that he had objectively acceptable grounds to justify detaining people for deportation as illegal immigrants[113] In doing so, their lordships interpreted the relevant legislation in accordance with the dissenting judgement of Lord Atkin, rather than that of the majority, in *Liversidge* v. *Anderson*.[114] People who had previously been legally invisible were coming to enjoy the protection

---

[110] [1983] 1 AC 1, HL.
[111] *Leech* v. *Deputy Governor of Parkhurst Prison* [1988] AC 533, HL.
[112] See *Zamir* v. *Secretary of State for the Home Department* [1980] AC 930, HL.
[113] *R.* v. *Secretary of State for the Home Department, ex p. Khera and Khawaja* [1984] AC 74, HL., disapproving *Zamir*.
[114] [1942] AC 206, HL.

of law alongside, if not yet on a par with, less disfavoured groups, in a process which went hand in hand with the post-war rebirth of administrative law.

Second, there was growing pressure for legislation to outlaw discrimination on certain grounds, including sex, race (on the British mainland) and religion (in Northern Ireland). This pressure was a response to the perceptible personal, social, political and economic problems which discrimination engendered. The advocates of anti-discrimination legislation were influenced by their awareness of these problems both nationally and internationally. Lawyers who were critics of apartheid in South Africa observed the treason trials there in the 1950s, and on their return founded JUSTICE, which since then has been a respected organisation functioning as the British arm of the International Commission of Jurists, acting alongside other organisations to raise the profile of civil liberties and human rights generally and of equality in particular. Not only were some of the observers to become dedicated campaigners for civil liberties, but a growing number of the South African advocates who had appeared in the treason trials ended up in the United Kingdom and became influential academics and barristers whose views have shaped a generation. The form of proposals for anti-discrimination legislation was also influenced by developments in the USA, where federal courts led the nation into desegregation through constitutional decisions under the Equal Protection clause of the Fourteenth Amendment in the 1950s and 1960s, bolstered by federal legislation in the form of the Civil Rights Act of 1964. Subsequently, European Community law moved in to complement to some extent the United Kingdom's municipal legislation. Anti-discrimination law in the United Kingdom displayed both a capacity to adopt and accommodate initiatives from elsewhere, adapting them where necessary to local needs, and a willingness to develop remedies from a wider range of discriminatory practices than had been commonly recognised by law in other systems.

The Race Relations Act 1965 was ground-breaking albeit limited legislation which provided judicial remedies but little other support for victims of some discrimination on the ground of race. The Sex Discrimination Act 1975 was equally ground-breaking and more far-reaching. It protects people against discrimination on the ground of sex in the fields of employment, housing, education, and the provision of goods and services. It outlaws both direct discrimination (where a person is treated less favourably than another simply on the ground of sex) and indirect discrimination (operating a criterion for allocating employment, or associated promotion, remuneration, benefits, or dismissal, or housing, education, goods or services, which members of certain groups definable by sex would find it more difficult to meet than others). As well as providing for remedies for individuals in ordinary tribunals and courts, it established the Equal Opportunities Commission (EOC) to encourage good employment practices, monitor performance, conduct investigations, bring proceedings of its own motion, and support private litigants. The new Race Relations Act 1976 (which did not extend to Northern Ireland) was modelled on the 1975 Act, prohibiting direct or indirect discrimination on the ground of race, colour, nationality, and ethnic or national origin in respect of employment, housing, education, and provision of goods and services, and allowing civil actions to be brought for alleged breaches. It created the Commission for Racial Equality (CRE) with powers parallel to those of the EOC.

Although these steps were widely unpopular at the time, and attracted some ridicule as well as opposition, they gave rise to changes of attitude which have passed into the main stream of British life and language. The Race Relations Act 1976 presented problems in interpreting terms like 'race' and 'ethnic origin'. A sign outside a pub prohibiting 'travellers' is not unlawful discrimination, although a sign prohibiting gypsies or Roma would be. Sikhs but not Muslims are treated as forming an ethnic group: the latter are regarded as being only a religious group, and there is no law in mainland Britain forbidding religious discrimination. In Northern Ireland, by contrast, there was not (until much later) legislation against racial discrimination, but the fair employment legislation sought to protect people (particularly Roman Catholics) from entrenched discrimination by employers (particularly in the Protestant majority) on the ground of religion. Despite the oddities, the legislation gradually changed attitudes over the next quarter of a century.

The period should not be seen as one of continuous advance for the value of equality. The courts, in accordance with the principles of liberty from official arbitrariness, interpreted the powers of the CRE and EOC in a restrictive way which, commentators have suggested, removed at least some of their efficacy, while there is a limit to the extent to which litigation by individuals can produce large-scale changes in society.[115]

---

[115] See Evelyn Collins and Elizabeth Meehan, 'Women's Rights in Employment and Related Areas', and Christopher McCrudden, 'Racial Discrimination', both in Christopher McCrudden and Gerald Chambers (eds), *Individual Rights and the Law in Britain* (Law Society/Clarendon Press, 1994), chs 12 and 13 respectively.

However, the period laid the foundations for a sea-change in social attitudes, so that by the end of the century differential treatment of one person by another came to be seen not as an exercise of the latter's liberty of choice but as a presumptively unfair act in need of justification. The presumption in favour of equal treatment contributed to an ethos of citizenship constituted by rights, in place of the old idea of people as subjects of the Crown. The idea of a UK or British nationality became part of the foundation of immigration law after the Immigration Act 1971, and particularly following the British Nationality Act 1981, although (like most immigration law) the object was to exclude people from elsewhere rather than to encourage a sense of citizenship or belonging among natives of England, Northern Ireland, Scotland and Wales, and there were regular complaints that the immigration rules were racist in operation, although not on their face. Nevertheless, the idea of citizenship and its associated rights attracted increasing attention from organisations such as Charter 88 and from constitutional theorists.[116]

If the value of equality was making gradual and modest advances, to some degree at the expense of individual liberty of choice, the value of autonomy (which underpins liberty) was also being treated more seriously and more systematically. The legal system increasingly respected people's capacity to make choices about how they should lead their lives. For most people, this was most obvious in relation to the extent of legal intervention in choices about lifestyle. Between 1950 and 1980, something of a liberal consensus emerged among the political and intellectual elite. It was antipathetic to state paternalism in respect of people of full age and capacity. It was influenced by burgeoning democracy, a better educated citizenry, and an approach to utilitarianism which treated thwarting people's choices as a harm which needed to be justified, if possible, by showing that an appreciably greater good would follow. Towards the end of the period, the dominant liberal philosophy came to include an influential element whose exponents, particularly John Rawls and Ronald Dworkin, argued that there were some rights so significant to individual choice and flourishing that it would normally be impermissible for the state to interfere with one person's right in order to produce a benefit, however great, for someone else, unless to protect the latter's own rights. In other words, people should be taken to be free to use their rights as they would, excluding paternalism, and

---

[116] See Paul Craig, 'Public Law, Sovereignty and Citizenship', in Robert Blackburn (ed.), *Rights of Citizenship* (Mansell, 1993), pp. 307–30.

individual rights trumped nearly all countervailing social interests. This strong view of rights has never had much of a following in Europe (including the United Kingdom) except, during the 1980s and 1990s, in economic matters. However, the growing acceptance by politicians of a philosophy of liberalism, accelerated by the social turmoil and scientific advances of the 1960s, helped to undermine some restrictions on choices of lifestyle which had previously seemed self-evidently good and sound.

The most obvious examples of this relate to the control of sexuality, reproduction, health, and popular culture. The prohibition of all homosexual acts between males, through the offences of buggery and gross indecency, was partially relaxed in this period by the Sexual Offences Act 1967, introduced as a private member's bill sponsored by Leo Abse MP and Lord Arran to deal with a matter which was morally too sensitive for the government to feel able to handle. Section 1(1) of the Act provided that homosexual acts between consenting parties who were both aged at least 21 years, 'in private'—that is, where not more than two people were present—were no longer to be criminal (with certain exceptions to protect vulnerable people and good order and discipline in the armed forces and merchant navy). Male homosexuals remained less free than female homosexuals, whose consensual activities were not criminal as long as the parties were aged at least 16, and heterosexuals, to whom the same applied (although heterosexual buggery was, and remained, illegal). Nevertheless, the legislation established that sexual activity was a matter in which the law should respect individual choice unless there were empirically supportable reasons for not doing so. This cautious relaxation of the law was largely the result of the Wolfenden Report,[117] which had treated the criminalisation of prostitution and homosexuality as civil liberties issues and argued for the application of J. S. Mill's 'harm principle' to its justification. Although the approach had been heavily criticised by Sir Patrick Devlin,[118] who argued that the law had a responsibility to preserve the essential core of shared morality which held society together, the prevailing tone of the era was set by Professor H. L. A. Hart,[119] whose response to Devlin placed liberty alongside the harm principle at the centre of the policy of criminal law in the area. Subsequent relaxations of the remaining law on sexuality have turned as much on arguments of equality between people of different sexual orien-

---

[117] *Report of the Committee on Homosexual Offences and Prostitution*, Cmnd 247 (HMSO, 1957).
[118] Sir Patrick Devlin, *The Enforcement of Morals* (Oxford University Press, 1965).
[119] H. L. A. Hart, *Law, Liberty, and Morality* (Oxford University Press, 1963).

tations as on the need to establish respect for personal autonomy as a basic principle.

The growing importance of personal choice in social morality was also reflected in changes to the law on abortion, for which the Liberal MP, David Steel, whose private member's bill became the Abortion Act 1967, deserves much credit. Again, government was unable or unwilling to grasp the nettle of a morally and politically contentious issue, but a member of a minority party could take the risk of introducing legislation to deal with an acknowledged social problem. The legislation, now amended by the Human Fertilisation and Embryology Act 1990, section 37, made termination of pregnancy lawful for certain purposes other than saving the mother's life, and led to the procedure becoming available on a large scale through the National Health Service. Besides aiding women's mental and physical health and controlling the dangerous industry of back-street abortionists, the measure advanced respect for women's autonomy in decisions about childbirth (a development also fostered by the pharmaceutical development of a relatively safe contraceptive pill). Between them, contraception and abortion contributed to the safety of (if they did not actually encourage) the revolution in sexual morality which the 1960s and 1970s witnessed.

In England and Wales, theatre, cinema and literature were also significantly freed from legal controls in the late 1950s and 1960s. The Obscene Publications Act 1959, as amended by the Obscene Publications Act 1964, amended the law of obscenity by defining 'obscene' in terms of the probable effect of a publication ('likely to deprave or corrupt') on those likely to come in contact with it. This distanced criminal liability from locally prevailing standards of decency. The effect of a publication was to be judged when taken as a whole, rather than by concentrating on particular passages out of context. The legislation also introduced a defence of public good, which can save the publisher of an obscene article from criminal liability. The 1960 trial of Penguin Books for publishing *Lady Chatterley's Lover* by D. H. Lawrence showed the power of this defence. Expert evidence as to the book's literary merit led to an acquittal, and made the director of public prosecutions very careful about future prosecution decisions.[120] By the 1970s, it was clear that juries were unwilling to convict where there was any tolerable claim to literary merit, as the acquittals of *Inside Linda Lovelace* and *Last Exit to Brooklyn* made

---

[120] See C. H. Rolph, *The Trial of Lady Chatterley* (Penguin, 1961); Bernard Levin, *The Pendulum Years: Britain and the Sixties* (Pan, 1972), pp. 280–92.

clear. The regime of the Obscene Publications Act 1959 was subsequently extended (*mutatis mutandis*) to the theatre,[121] and, in a watered-down form, with extensive additional regulation, to the cinema, videos, and the broadcast media.[122]

These were ways in which the law was adapted to the growing significance of lifestyle choices for ordinary people. This was not principally a legal phenomenon. Legal protection for autonomous choice became more important to people as society became more prosperous and science and technology (particularly in medicine and communications) made more opportunities readily available to more people. Not only did safer contraception and abortion allow people to avoid unwanted pregnancies and parenthood, but antibiotics seemed to offer protection against sexually transmissible diseases (at least until the appearance of HIV/AIDS). In relation to the freedom to receive and impart information and ideas, increased democratisation of politics allowed more people to become actively involved in mainstream politics, and the explosion of cheap paperback books, radio and television channels, and specialised magazines put ideas, art, literature and music within the reach of millions, and made legal protection for that access important to them, often for the first time.

Respect for autonomy had its limits, however. The common law, being inherently less capable of accommodating revolutionary ideas than statute, was much slower to respond to the new ethos. By a majority, the House of Lords even tried to put the process of liberalisation into reverse in *Shaw* v. *Director of Public Prosecutions*,[123] when they discovered (or rediscovered) common-law crimes of conspiring to corrupt public morals and conspiring to outrage public decency, which the defendant had committed by publishing details of prostitutes and the services they offered in a book called *The Ladies' Directory*. The historical role of the judiciary as *parens patriae* went beyond concern for the welfare of wards of court and lunatics and led to an attempt to enshrine 1940s public morality into the common law, influenced by the approach of Lord Devlin (as he had by then become) to morality.

In relation to the proper subjects of paternalism, children and mental-health patients, Parliament and the judges gradually came to respect

---

[121] Theatres Act 1968, bringing to a close the lord chamberlain's role in censoring plays, which had given rise to many entertaining stories.
[122] Video Recordings Act 1984; Cinemas Act 1985; Broadcasting Act 1990.
[123] [1962] AC 220, HL. See also *Knuller* v. *DPP* [1973] AC 435, HL; *R.* v. *Gibson* [1990] 2 QB 619, CA.

449

their liberty and autonomy when satisfied that they had the capacity to make their own decisions. The Mental Health Act 1983 instituted a system for reviewing the continued need to detain people compulsorily admitted to hospital for treatment. This reflected growing concern about the implications of medical paternalism for patients' liberties, heightened by awareness of the abuse of psychiatry for the purpose of social and political control in the Soviet Union. Courts, too, began to acknowledge that people might be able to make some decisions for themselves, even if they were not capable of taking responsibility for all decisions. In a landmark case on the right of children to make decisions about taking medical advice and treatment, a majority of the House of Lords decided that doctors would not act unlawfully in advising Mrs Victoria Gillick's children about contraception, without her knowledge or consent, as long as a doctor was satisfied that the child was of an age and mental capacity to understand and cope with the consequences of the advice.[124] This idea of the '*Gillick*-competent child' had a major impact on the legal capacity of children under the age of 16 to obtain confidential advice from their doctors, and established that parental rights over their children are there to benefit the children and not to allow the parents to interfere with the autonomy of children when they are capable of exercising it.

Nevertheless, the *Gillick* case was not purely a recognition of children's rights. Judges were concerned to protect the professionals who look after the interests of children. The *Gillick* decision protected them against legal liability for advice given in good faith to children who appeared to be capable of seeking, understanding and acting on it. Doctors were legally free to act in what they reasonably conceived to be the best interests of the child. Sometimes this meant that children were held to be able to consent to treatment recommended by doctors, but had their views overridden when they tried to refuse treatment which doctors considered to be in their best interests.[125] In a similar vein, the courts have shown themselves willing to extend the power of doctors to make decisions in the best interests of patients who are suffering from learning difficulties or mental-health problems. In some cases, courts have gone so far as to make declarations, without statutory authority, that non-therapeutic sterilisation would be permissible,[126] although there

---

[124] *Gillick* v. *West Norfolk and Wisbech Area Health Authority* [1986] AC 112, HL.

[125] See, for example, *Re R (A Minor) (Wardship: Medical Treatment)* [1992] Fam. 11, CA.

[126] *In re B (A Minor) (Wardship: Sterilisation)* [1987] AC 199, HL; *In re F (Mental Patient: Sterilisation)* [1990] 2 AC 1, HL.

are signs that this is being rather more carefully regulated by the courts now than in the past.[127] Courts also sometimes declared that Caesarian sections conducted to save the baby but without the mother's consent would be lawful, on the ground that refusal of treatment was said to demonstrate that the mother lacked mental capacity to make decisions. Recently, however, the Court of Appeal has re-established the orthodox position based on the idea of patient autonomy: an adult who is not at the time suffering from a recognised mental illness affecting his or her capacity to make health-care decisions is entitled to refuse treatment, either at the present time or prospectively, and it will then be unlawful for treatment to be inflicted subsequently in disobedience to the patient's earlier direction.[128] On the other hand, where the patient is a child, or suffering from a learning difficulty or mental illness, or is unable to make or communicate a decision, paternalism overrides autonomy. The courts then make decisions on the basis of what are objectively considered to be the patient's best interests (which may involve ceasing to be treated for fatal conditions), rather than by seeking to establish what the patient would subjectively have chosen had he or she been in a condition to do so.[129] On this basis, courts have authorised doctors to cease to treat babies when further treatment would be likely to confer no benefit,[130] and to perform a heart transplant operation on a fifteen-year-old patient who was refusing to consent to it,[131] and to separate conjoined twins by surgery which was certain to cause the death of one of them.[132]

Many of the problems faced in these cases are the direct result of medical or scientific advances which allow intervention in people's lives which would not previously have been possible. Parliament has sometimes provided a regulatory framework which seeks to guide the way in which new developments can affect people. In the case of new technologies for assisted reproduction and human genetic engineering, the Human Fertilisation and Embryology Act 1990 established a special body, the Human Fertilisation and Embryology Authority, to oversee the oper-

---

[127] *In re S (Adult Patient: Sterilisation), The Times,* 26 May 2000, CA.
[128] *St George's Healthcare NHS Trust* v. *S* [1999] Fam. 26, CA. See also *In re C (Adult: Refusal of Treatment)* [1994] 1 All ER 819; *Secretary of State for the Home Department* v. *Robb* [1995] Fam. 127; *In re AK,* 10 August 2000, Hughes J., unreported.
[129] *In re B (A Minor) (Wardship: Medical Treatment)* [1981] 1 WLR 1421, CA; *Airedale NHS Trust* v. *Bland* [1993] AC 789, HL; *B* v. *Croydon Health Authority* [1995] Fam. 133, CA.
[130] *In re B (A Minor) (Wardship: Medical Treatment)* [1981] 1 WLR 1421, CA; *In re (A Minor) (Wardship: Medical Treatment)* [1991] Fam. 33, CA.
[131] *R.* v. *M,* unreported, 15 July 1999, Johnson J.
[132] *Re A, (Children), (Conjoined Twins: Surgical Separation)* [2001] 2 WLR 480, CA.

ation of the new technologies. Any such framework can only be as good as its founding legislation, and, by taking a view of how public interests should be weighed against individual autonomy, may limit people's freedom to benefit from new developments. After initial suspicion (noted above) of intrusion by (for example) the CRE and EOC on the commercial freedom of business enterprises, the recent tendency has been for courts to treat decisions of such regulatory bodies with considerable respect.[133] Autonomy is important, but will always be weighed against relevant public interests.

Growth of state power in response to crime, terrorism and disorder

While courts and the legislature moved gradually more under the influence of values such as equality, rights-blindness remained in a number of areas. In *Home Office* v. *Harman*,[134] a solicitor (who later became a Labour Cabinet minister) was held to have committed contempt of court. She had shown papers about a special prison regime, disclosed by the Home Office pursuant to a court order in the course of proceedings brought against it by a prisoner,[135] to a journalist. The papers had been read in open court, and the journalist wanted to check his notes against the originals. Despite this limited purpose, and ignoring the interest in open justice and press freedom, the House of Lords held that it was contempt of court to use papers disclosed during discovery for any purpose other than the conduct of the litigation. Lord Diplock astonishingly characterised the case as involving no issue of freedom of speech or of the press,[136] a view which echoed the approach of Lord Hewart C.J. in *Duncan* v. *Jones* nearly fifty years earlier. In relation to public order, the policing of the miners' strike in 1984–5 reminded anyone who had forgotten just how dependent were the freedom to travel, assemble and protest in public places on the discretion of the police, and how reluctant the courts were to second-guess the judgements made by police officers on the spot.[137]

---

[133] See, for example, R. v. *Radio Authority, ex p. Bull* [1998] QB 294, CA ; R. v. *Human Fertilisation and Embryology Authority, ex p. Blood* [1999] Fam. 151, CA ; R. v. *Broadcasting Standards Authority, ex p. British Broadcasting Corporation* [2000] 3 WLR 1327, CA.

[134] [1983] 1 AC 280, HL.

[135] *Williams* v. *Home Office* [1981] 1 All ER 1151; *Williams* v. *Home Office (No. 2)* [1982] 2 All ER 564, CA, affirming [1981] 1 All ER 1211.

[136] *Home Office* v. *Harman* [1983] 1 AC 280, HL, at 299.

[137] See *Moss* v. *McLachlan* [1984] IRLR 76, D–C, and the discussions of these issues in Bob Fine and Robert Millar (eds), *Policing the Miners' Strike* (Lawrence & Wishart, 1985); Sarah

One of the most potent catalysts of draconian provisions was the violence and terrorism which erupted in the late 1960s and 1970s in Northern Ireland in connection with the conflict between Irish republicans and unionists in Northern Ireland. Parliament passed pieces of legislation which were (and largely remain) the linear descendants of the emergency powers legislation described in the first section of this chapter. In Northern Ireland itself, new arrangements included the introduction of internment without trial for people with links to terrorist organisations; criminalisation of membership of proscribed organisations; the making of exclusion orders preventing named people from mainland Britain going to Northern Ireland; the institution of new, jury-free criminal courts (the 'Diplock courts', named after Lord Diplock, on whose recommendations they were based) to hear serious cases where some suspected link with terrorist organisations gave rise to a fear that jurors would be intimidated; powers to arrest people without the need to suspect that they had committed an offence; a positive obligation to inform the police about terrorism; and, after limits to detention for questioning and rights to legal advice and assistance at police stations had been introduced to Northern Ireland, longer than usual periods for detention without charge and denial of legal advice in terrorism cases. On the mainland, provisions included exclusion orders to prevent people from Northern Ireland coming into Britain, and longer than usual periods for detention without charge and denial of legal advice in terrorism cases. In the 1990s, these provisions were bolstered with legislation to allow seizure of assets believed to be bound for proscribed or terrorist organisations, arrangements for international co-operation in the fight against organised and terrorist crime, and provisions which allowed a police officer's stated suspicion that a person is a member of a proscribed organisation to be admissible evidence that the suspicion is correct. All this put orthodox notions of the rule of law and respect for civil liberties under strain. Some valuable work was done by the independent reviews of the operation of

---

McCabe, Peter Wallington *et al.*, *The Police, Public Order and Civil Liberties: Legacies of the Miners' Strike* (Routledge, 1988); Roger Geary, *Policing Industrial Disputes, 1893–1985* (Methuen, 1985); Richard de Friend and Steve Uglow, 'Policing Industrial Disputes', in John Baxter and Laurence Koffman (eds), *Police, the Constitution and the Community* (Professional Books, 1985), pp. 62–71; Gerry Northam, *Shooting in the Dark: Riot Police in Britain* (Faber, 1988); P. A. J. Waddington, *The Strong Arm of the Law: Armed and Public Order Policing* (Clarendon Press, 1991), ch. 6; Michael King, *Public Order Policing: Contemporary Perspectives on Strategy and Tactics* (Perpetuity, 1995); Feldman, 'Protest and Tolerance', in Cohen-Almagor (ed.), *Liberal Democracy.*

the terrorism legislation,[138] but the recommendations were not binding and were often ignored by government.

Parliament also acted against particular sorts of crime, restricting the rights of suspects in police custody on suspicion of drug-trafficking offences and a growing number of other serious crimes. Legislation to allow proceeds of crime to be seized put people under an obligation to disclose details of their assets, and required banks and other financial institutions to provide the authorities with details of transactions involving £10,000 or more. Lawyers and others who suspected that their clients were concerned in money laundering had to disclose their suspicions, on pain of severe penalties. The Serious Fraud Office was empowered to demand self-incriminating information from people whose affairs it was investigating, and only in 1999, in response to adverse rulings of the European Court of Human Rights, did statute provide that such coerced disclosures could not be used in criminal proceedings against the person making them.

The courts showed a certain lack of sympathy with the rights of suspects, given freest rein in cases concerning the investigation of crime and the treatment of criminals. Some attempt was made to regulate arbitrary arrests by insisting on clear and positive legal authority[139] and reasonable grounds for suspicion[140] before any arrest could be made, and by requiring the arresting officer to tell the detainee why he or she was being arrested.[141] Nevertheless, for much of the period the courts placed considerable trust in the good faith and professionalism of all, or at least the overwhelming majority of, police officers. Refusing to contemplate the possibility of either serious or widespread police misbehaviour, the courts failed to recognise the need to provide adequate protection against abuse of power by the police. There had been little legislation to extend the powers of the police (unlike the very extensive statutory powers which were given to other investigators, such as the customs and excise commissioners and the inland revenue commissioners). Nor had police powers been regulated by statute in the light of new investigative technologies and techniques and new kinds of crime. The judges therefore tended to interpret questions about police

---

[138] See for example Lord Colville, *Report on the Operation in 1990 of the Prevention of Terrorism (Temporary Provisions) Act, 1989.*

[139] *Gelberg* v. *Miller* [1961] 1 All ER 291, DC; *Wershof* v. *Metropolitan Police Commissioner* [1978] 3 All ER 540.

[140] *Shaaban Bin Hussien* v. *Chong Fook Kam* [1970] AC 942, PC.

[141] *Christie* v. *Leachinsky* [1947] AC 573, HL.

powers as issues about how the police could be protected from legal liability when doing the job which society had given them, but for which the legislature had failed to provide adequate legal authority. A combination of acceptance of the police service's own rhetoric of fairness and (increasingly) professionalism,[142] with public concern about mounting crime, encouraged the courts to allow pragmatism to overcome constitutional principle in a number of cases.

This manifested itself in a number of ways. In relation to arrest, the courts refused to imply a requirement for reasonable grounds for suspicion into statutes which appeared to permit arrest without any such grounds. Instead, the courts assumed that the arrest was lawful unless it could be shown to have been so completely irrational that no reasonable officer, properly understanding the law and the facts, could have thought it reasonable.[143] Where the statute required reasonable grounds for suspicion, either before an arrest or before a search, the courts placed heavy reliance on the officer's own assessment of the evidence, so that the reasonable suspicion test came to represent a form in which the officer had to present his or her story to the court, rather than anything restricting or structuring the officer's operational decision-making.[144]

Where the police entered and searched (or conducted other investigative activities in) private premises, the judges were prepared to give a certain amount of protection against excess of power, particularly when the premises were a dwelling.[145] However, in cases of serious crime the courts extended rather than controlled rights of seizure, and even seemed to countenance illegality where necessary to obtain evidence. As Lord Denning MR said, commenting on the fact that before the Police and Criminal Evidence Act 1984 there was no power to issue a warrant to search for evidence of homicide in England and Wales:

> The police have to get the consent of the occupier to enter if they can: if not, do it by stealth or by force. Somehow they seem to manage. No decent

---

[142] Robert Reiner, *The Politics of the Police*, 3rd edn (Oxford University Press, 2000), ch. 2.
[143] *Mohammed-Holgate* v. *Duke* [1984] AC 437, HL.
[144] *McKee* v. *Chief Constable of Northern Ireland* [1984] 1 WLR 1358, HL; *O'Hara* v. *Chief Constable of Royal Ulster Constabulary* [1997] AC 286, HL (although cp. *Riley* v. *Director of Public Prosecutions* (1989) 91 Cr. App. R. 14, DC); David Dixon, Keith Bottomley, Clive Coleman, M. Gill and David Wall, 'Reality and Rules in the Construction and Regulation of Police Suspicion', *International Journal of the Sociology of Law* (1989).
[145] See *Great Central Railway Co.* v. *Bates* [1921] 3 KB 578, CA; *Davis* v. *Lisle* [1936] 2 KB 434, DC; *Morris* v. *Beardmore* [1981] AC 446, HL; *Clowser* v. *Chaplin*, *Finnigan* v. *Sandiford* [1981] 2 All ER 267, HL (but see Road Traffic Act 1972, s. 76 as substituted by Transport Act 1981, s. 25 and Sch. 8).

person refuses them permission. If he does he is probably implicated in some way or other. So the police risk an action for trespass. It is not much risk.[146]

In this mood, the Court of Appeal held that a constable with a warrant to search for specified stolen goods could lawfully seize other goods on the premises which he reasonably believed to be stolen, or which implicated the person in possession of them in some other offence.[147] Police could also seize evidence of serious crime even without a warrant or an arrest, if they reasonably suspected that the person in possession was implicated in the crime or his refusal to hand over the material was quite unreasonable.[148] The public interest in detecting criminals was held to justify seizing confidential items, even those covered by legal professional privilege.[149] It was left to Parliament to put the law of search and seizure on a rational footing, and to give procedural protection for confidential interests which had been lacking at common law, in the Police and Criminal Evidence Act 1984, Part II and Schedule 1. Even then, the courts interpreted the protective provisions in such a way as greatly to reduce their practical value.[150]

In a series of other cases, judges invented or extended common-law principles in order to allow people's property to be taken from them permanently if it appeared to represent the proceeds of a crime. The decisions usually failed to provide a proper legal basis for the move,[151] and a highly unsatisfactory situation developed until Parliament enacted draconian but formally proper proceeds-of-crime legislation. Judges also displayed a deferential attitude to the executive which made them reluctant to question the grounds on which decisions said to affect national security had been made.[152] This is a continuation of the story familiar from the earlier account of the legal treatment of internees during the two world wars. Before and during the Gulf War, there were few signs that judges were prepared to review executive decisions about deport-

---

[146] *Ghani* v. *Jones* [1970] 1 QB 693, CA, at 705.
[147] This was the combined effect of *Chic Fashions (West Wales) Ltd* v. *Jones* [1968] 2 QB 299, CA, and *obiter dicta* in *Ghani* v. *Jones* [1970] 1 QB 693, CA.
[148] *Ghani* v. *Jones* [1970] 1 QB 693, CA.
[149] See, for example, *Frank Truman Export Ltd* v. *Metropolitan Police Commissioner* [1977] Q.B. 952.
[150] See Feldman, *Civil Liberties and Human Rights in England and Wales*, 2nd edn, pp. 629–59.
[151] Occasionally a foundation could be found in the law of restitution, as in *Attorney-General* v. *Blake* [2000] 3 WLR 625, HL.
[152] David Feldman, 'Public Law Values in the House of Lords', *Law Quarterly Review* (1990).

ation, detention and exclusion at all rigorously, so the liberties of foreigners were left at the mercy of the executive and its advisers.[153]

The period 1960–90 thus saw the work of European bodies and Royal Commissions and similar bodies lead to a modest but steady extension of tolerance to new lifestyles and a systematisation of police powers by the legislature. Parliament and the European Communities developed important new laws protecting aspects of the right to equal treatment in respect of sex, race in Britain, and religion in Northern Ireland. Courts became more liberal in some respects, but were strongly disinclined to offer much protection to suspected criminals or to fetter the freedom of the executive to act as it saw fit in relation to foreigners and Irish people whom the executive considered to be a threat to security. The idea of human rights penetrated the consciousness of both judges and politicians, but showed few signs of dominating public discourse.

The growth of a human rights culture and the growing power of the state, 1990–2000

The 1990s saw human rights established as central to municipal law in the United Kingdom. The literature of the subject exploded. The postwar period had produced a classic but small-scale treatment of civil liberties by Professor Harry Street, *Freedom, the Individual and the Law*,[154] which was taken on by Geoffrey Robertson in 1989. Although not the first book on the law of civil liberties in this country,[155] it combined legal scholarship with popular accessibility, and influenced a generation of law students, within a brief compass. There were two books of cases and materials on the subject for students,[156] various books on particular aspects of the law, some for general readers and others for lawyers, often produced by non-governmental organisations, and a growing number of collections of essays. This indicates the growing interest in civil liberties and human rights as a field of political controversy, study and practice before 1990. But the absence of attempts at large-scale, comprehensive

---

[153] Feldman, *Civil Liberties and Human Rights in England and Wales*, ch. 8, esp. pp. 493–506.

[154] Penguin, 1963. Professor Street revised the book up to its fourth edition, published in 1983.

[155] The distinction may belong to W. H. Thompson, *Civil Liberties* (Victor Gollancz, 1938).

[156] Paul O'Higgins, *Cases and Materials on Civil Liberties* (Sweet & Maxwell, 1980); D. J. Harris, S. H. Bailey and B. L. Jones, *Civil Liberties Cases and Materials* (Butterworths, 1980; 5th edn, 2001).

monographs shows that there was as yet no agreement on the boundaries of the field, and the hold it had on the law curriculum was as yet tenuous. By contrast, the 1990s saw the publication of several substantial treatments of civil-liberties and human-rights law for students, and the passage of the Human Rights Act 1998 spawned a plethora of works aimed at the legal practitioner. These were accompanied by a mass of more or less scholarly critiques of the law and politics of civil liberties, monographs on international human rights treaties, the launch of two new journals dealing with civil liberties and human rights, aimed at and written by both academics and practitioners, and the publication of huge numbers of books on specialised topics within the field.

This reflected a major change of legal ethos, in both universities (where many new courses on civil liberties and human rights were established at undergraduate and postgraduate levels) and legal practice. Notwithstanding encouraging rhetoric, the courts had previously done relatively little to provide leadership in the protection of civil liberties and human rights. They could justifiably claim that it was not their role to provide such leadership: in a parliamentary democracy, any new fundamental values should be injected via the political rather than judicial process. But judges were losing faith in the ability of the political system to protect important freedoms. Extra-judicially, more and more judges were declaring themselves to be in favour of incorporating the European Convention on Human Rights.[157] On the bench, senior judges had stressed that they would scrutinise executive interference with fundamental rights and liberties particularly anxiously;[158] and cases in the 1990s established that non-compliance with rights guaranteed under the ECHR would require strong justification if the executive was not to be held to have acted unreasonably and so outside its powers.[159] It was also held that there were fundamental common-law rights which could not be taken away, even by statute, without clear words. These included

---

[157] See, for example, Sir Thomas Bingham, 'The European Convention on Human Rights: Time to Incorporate', *Law Quarterly Review* (1993); Lord Woolf, *'Droit Public*—English Style', *Public Law* (1994); Sir Stephen Sedley, 'Human Rights: A Twenty-first Century Agenda', *Public Law* (1995); Lord Steyn, 'The Weakest and Least Dangerous Branch of Government', *Public Law* (1997); Sir John Laws, 'The Limitations of Human Rights', *Public Law* (1998).

[158] *Bugdaycay* v. *Secretary of State for the Home Department* [1987] AC 514, HL, esp. at 537 *per* Lord Templeman.

[159] *R.* v. *Ministry of Defence, ex p. Smith* [1996] QB 517, DC and CA.

a right to have access to courts[160] and a right to public relief from destitution.[161]

The judges were becoming more suspicious of claims by public officers, whether government or police, to be sufficiently trustworthy not to need careful legal scrutiny. The greater scepticism about claims to official immunity from legal accountability stemmed partly from a series of cases (mostly but not exclusively relating to convictions for terrorism offences) in which it was shown that the police and prosecuting authorities had gathered and dealt evidence either incompetently or improperly,[162] and partly as a result of the Scott inquiry into the 'Arms-to-Iraq' affair.[163] In relation to the former, the quashing of the convictions of a large number of people convicted of terrorist bombings in the 1970s had a devastating effect on judicial faith in the police. When the 'Birmingham Six', convicted of the Birmingham pub bombings in 1974, tried to re-litigate their cases by suing the police for alleged brutality in interrogations, their action was struck out, ultimately on the ground of issue estoppel. In the Court of Appeal, Lord Denning MR said:

> If the six men win, it will mean that the police were guilty of perjury, that they were guilty of violence and threats, that the confessions were involuntary and were improperly admitted in evidence, and that the convictions were erroneous. That would mean that the Home Secretary would have either to recommend that they be pardoned or he would have to remit the case to the Court of Appeal ... This is such an appalling vista that every sensible person in the land would say: 'It cannot be right that these actions should go any further.' ... This case shows what a civilized country we are. Here are six men who have been proved guilty of the most wicked murder of 21 innocent people. They have no money. Yet the state lavished large sums on their defence. They were convicted of murder and sentenced to imprisonment for life. In their evidence they were guilty of gross perjury. Yet the state continued to lavish large sums on them, in their actions against the police. It is high time that it stopped.[164]

---

[160] R. v. Lord Chancellor's Department, ex p. Witham [1998] QB 575, DC.

[161] R. v. Secretary of State for Social Security, ex p. Joint Council for the Welfare of Immigrants [1996] 4 All ER 385, CA.

[162] See the often excellent essays in Clive Walker and Keir Starmer (eds), Justice in Error (Blackstone Press, 1993). See also The Stephen Lawrence Inquiry, Cm 4262–I.

[163] See, for example, Return to an Address of the Honourable the House of Commons dated 15th February 1996 for the Report of the Inquiry into the Export of Defence Equipment and Dual-use Goods to Iraq and Related Prosecutions (HMSO, 1996), HC 115, 5 vols and index; Adam Tomkins, The Constitution after Scott: Government Unwrapped (Clarendon Press, 1998), esp. ch. 5.

[164] McIlkenny v. Chief Constable of the West Midlands [1980] QB 283, CA, at 323–4.

The result was upheld by the House of Lords,[165] but the manner in which Lord Denning expressed himself in the Court of Appeal and the ideas expressed were indicative of an attitude towards the police which could not survive the embarrassment when, in 1989, the case was referred back to the Court of Appeal and the convictions were quashed.

With regard to the fall-out from the Scott inquiry, the increased scepticism revealed itself in improvements to the common law on public interest immunity introduced judicially by the House of Lords,[166] and in cases where some judges looked towards the adoption of proportionality as one of the tests for the lawfulness of executive action in detaining people and restricting their movements for security purposes.[167] This scepticism had an indirect effect on other rights for underprivileged groups. In *R. v. Secretary of State for the Home Department, ex p. Simms*,[168] the House of Lords held that the prison authorities could not refuse to allow a prisoner to communicate with a journalist who was taking up the prisoner's campaign against his conviction, because miscarriages of justice had shown that investigative journalists are often the only hope for prisoners to establish their innocence.

The judges also increasingly cited human rights treaties and the case-law of the European Court of Human Rights in their judgements to elucidate and illuminate principles of the common law.[169] The House of Lords regularly expressed the view that English common law already encapsulates the rights in the Convention, particularly freedom of expression.[170] At the end of the decade, when judges were starting to come to terms with the impending implementation of the Human Rights Act 1998, the right to respect for one's home under Article 8 of the ECHR was directly applied in the Court of Appeal in relation to people in residential homes,[171] and in *Fitzpatrick v. Sterling Housing Association Ltd*,[172]

---

[165] *Hunter v. Chief Constable of the West Midlands* [1982] AC 529, HL.

[166] *R. v. Chief Constable of West Midlands Police, ex p. Wiley* [1995] 1 AC 274, HL.

[167] *R. v. Secretary of State for the Home Department, ex p. Gallagher, The Times*, 16 February 1994, DC; *R. v. Secretary of State for the Home Department, ex p. Adams* [1995] All ER (EC) 177, DC; *R. v. Secretary of State for the Home Department, ex p. McQuillan* [1995] 4 All ER 400, DC.

[168] [1999] 3 WLR 328, HL.

[169] See regard to the right to freedom of expression under Article 10 in relation to the level of damages for defamation in *John v. MGN Ltd* [1997] QB 586, CA.

[170] See *Derbyshire County Council v. Times Newspapers Ltd* [1993] AC 534, HL, holding that it would stifle free political debate to allow an elected local government body to sue critics for libel.

[171] *R. v. North and East Devon Health Authority, ex p. Coughlan* [2000] 2 WLR 622, CA.

[172] [1999] 3 WLR 1113, HL.

a majority of the House of Lords accepted that same-sex couples in a stable and loving relationship could be regarded as forming a family for the purpose of succession to a tenancy of a house. In such cases, judges are expanding their awareness of the potential of fundamental rights both in the common law and in international law.

This new rights-consciousness had effects in widely diverse areas. In relation to patients' autonomy, the Court of Appeal at last affirmed the right of a mentally competent patient to refuse medical treatment, even if it put at risk an unborn child or, indeed, the patient.[173] In relation to the freedom to gather on roads and to protest, it led to a ground-breaking decision on the offence of trespassory assembly under the Criminal Justice and Public Order Act 1994, in which the House of Lords held that it was not necessarily unlawful per se for people to gather by the side of a main road to protest about the closure of Stonehenge to the general public, as long as the gathering was reasonable, peaceable and did not obstruct other road users.[174] On the other hand, the fact that even this very circumscribed freedom of assembly in public was established only by a three-to-two majority shows how meagre people's rights in public places are. Another decision of the House of Lords made it clear that the way in which public demonstrations are controlled is a matter for the largely unfettered discretion of the police, unless their action constitutes a violation of Community law, such as an unlawful restriction on free movement of goods.[175] In the continued subjection of freedom of assembly to official discretion, the spirit of *Duncan* v. *Jones* survives in England and Wales.

There were therefore few grounds for confidence that such freedoms and rights would be reliably protected by the courts. There remained a reluctance to extend remedies to suspected criminals for violations of their rights during investigations. In particular, there was no keenness to use the discretion under section 78 of the Police and Criminal Evidence Act 1998 to exclude evidence (other than confessions) even when exclusion was the only effective way of vindicating the right. Trial judges stuck to their view that it was their job to ensure a fair trial, and that this should not be sacrificed to the rather different goal of protecting defendants' rights.[176] Even victories in the courts were likely to be

---

[173] *St George's Healthcare NHS Trust* v. *S* [1999] Fam. 26, CA.
[174] *Director of Public Prosecutions* v. *Jones (Margaret)* [1999] 2 AC 240, HL.
[175] *R.* v. *Chief Constable of Sussex, ex p. International Trader's Ferry Ltd* [1999] 2 AC 418, HL.
[176] Se *R.* v. *Khan (Sultan)* [1997] AC 558, HL.

reversed quickly by legislation, with government taking advantage of the legislative supremacy of Parliament to give itself authority to do things which the courts had held to be insupportable on general principles of civil liberties and human rights, as occurred when legislation was passed to reverse the effect of *R. v. Secretary of State for Social Security, ex p. Joint Council for the Welfare of Immigrants.*[177]

Government and Parliament, too, had a mixed record on civil liberties and human rights in the 1990s. There were some notable steps forward. For example, the value of equality was advanced in the law by the Disability Discrimination Act 1995, and the implementation of non-discrimination rights took a step forward with the passage of the Disability Rights Commission Act 1999. In Northern Ireland, the violent clashes during the marching season, which came to a head around Drumcree in 1996, finally convinced the government that the police lacked the community support necessary to make or participate in decisions about imposing conditions on marchers and ultimately banning marches. An independent review of parades and marches in the province was established, chaired by Dr (later Sir) Peter North, an eminent public-law academic and vice-chancellor of the University of Oxford. Its report,[178] published in 1997, set the problem in a framework of democracy, tolerance, and respect for the human rights of all parties. It recommended removing the discretion to control marches from the police, and allocating it to an independent commission, which would have to act according to principles established in the light of those values. The Parades Commission which was subsequently established in Northern Ireland by the Public Processions (Northern Ireland) Act 1998 has had its problems, but at least the principles on which it makes its decisions are now public and transparent.

There were improvements in prison conditions during the 1990s, sparked by the report of Lord Justice Woolf and Judge Tumim,[179] reinforced by a finding by the European Committee for the Prevention of Torture that conditions in some prisons in the UK amounted to inhuman or degrading treatment of prisoners, and given added urgency by adverse reports from successive chief inspectors of prisons. Towards the end of the decade, devolution to Scotland, Wales and Northern

---

[177] Above, n. 161.

[178] *Report: Independent Review of Parades and Marches 1997* (Stationery Office, 1997).

[179] Lord Justice Woolf and Judge Stephen Tumim, *Prison Disturbances April 1990*, Cm 1456 (HMSO, 1991).

Ireland spread the force of human rights ahead of the coming into force of the Human Rights Act 1998 (of which more is said below), as the powers of the devolved legislatures and executives were limited by reference to Convention rights (among other matters). In Northern Ireland, a Human Rights Commission was established to oversee the implementation of the legislation.

In relation to criminal law and procedure, there were some positive steps. Concern about miscarriages of justice, and the time taken to rectify them through the Home Office, led to the establishment of the independent Criminal Cases Review Commission under the Criminal Appeal Act 1995. But in the 1990s the political desire to show that one's own party was tougher on crime than the others often led to legislation which severely compromised human rights and civil liberties. The controls on protest in public places under the Criminal Justice and Public Order Act 1994 have already been mentioned. Other examples include the assault on the right of silence in England and Wales in the same Act (the provisions allowing adverse inferences to be drawn from silence having already been introduced in Northern Ireland in 1988); the limitation by statute of extensions to the duty of prosecution disclosure which the courts had developed in the light of cases where miscarriages of justice had resulted from failure to disclose relevant material;[180] the introduction in the Crime and Disorder Act 1998 of orders which could in effect impose a long-term curfew on troublemakers with precious little regard for the rights of them or their families; provisions contained in the same Act allowing personal information to be shared between agencies without any clear framework of law to govern the use and disclosure of the information; and a growing number of statutes allowing the police, as well as the security and intelligence services, to undertake human surveillance, interception of communications, bugging, covert entry to premises and removal of goods, with a minimum of judicial oversight, prior or subsequent.[181] The consultation paper which preceded the latter innovations failed to deal with their human-rights implications.[182] Neither party in government had a monopoly of ill-conceived and illiberal ideas. The same failure of concern for the human-rights implications

---

[180] See *R. v. Ward (Judith)* [1993] 2 All ER 577, CA, and contrast Criminal Procedure and Investigations Act 1996.

[181] See, for example, Police Act 1997, Part III; Electronic Communications Act 2000; Regulation of Investigatory Powers Act 2000 (which at least had the merit of introducing regulation to investigative practices which had previously lacked any legal framework).

[182] See the editorial by Andrew Ashworth, [1997] Crim. LR, 769–70.

of recommendations was manifested by the Royal Commission on Criminal Justice, which was established by the Conservative government in the early 1990s.[183] There was a general sense that governments were excessively responsive to pressure from the police to have their jobs made easier regardless of the effect of, or on, civil liberties. To make matters worse, the political climate, the strong government majorities in the House of Commons, and the lack of a systematic procedure for scrutinising legislative proposals for human-rights implications, meant that Parliament was poorly equipped to subject the proposals to rigorous and principled scrutiny from a human-rights and civil-liberties standpoint.

Yet at the same time, the Labour Party, as it prepared for government and sought co-operation with the Liberal Democrats in the run-up to the 1997 general election, gave official support to the notion of introducing at least some of the rights under the European Convention on Human Rights in municipal law, a step opposed by the Conservatives under Margaret Thatcher and John Major. This marks an interesting reversal of attitudes. In 1957, the Conservatives had been notably open-minded about the desirability of reforming the constitution to give additional protection (political and legal) to liberty.[184] While the Labour Party opposed incorporation of the ECHR in the 1960s and 1970s because it might interfere with the pursuit of a collectivist governmental programme, the Conservatives when in opposition favoured the idea of a justiciable bill of rights, probably based on the ECHR, for the same reason.[185] When the House of Lords Select Committee on a Bill of Rights reported in 1978, all three Conservative peers were in the majority of six which favoured a bill of rights; three of the four Labour peers on the committee were opposed to it.[186] The Conservatives became less keen on a bill which might constrain government when they were themselves in government: Lord Hailsham, when Lord Chancellor, expressed no enthusiasm for the idea, and by 1997 opposition to a bill of rights, and disquiet about the ECHR, were settled elements of Conservative Party policy. The Labour Party, by contrast, was moving away from collectivism

---

[183] The Royal Commission on Criminal Justice (Chairman, Viscount Runciman of Doxford), *Report*, Cm 2263 (HMSO, 1993).
[184] Conservative Political Centre, *Liberty in the Modern State: Eight Oxford Lectures* (CPC, 1957). See especially the Foreword by Peter Goldman at pp. 7–10.
[185] See Sir Keith Joseph, *Freedom under Law* (CPC, 1975); and Lord Hailsham in four major articles in *The Times* on 2, 16, 19, and 20 May 1975.
[186] HL 176 of 1977–8.

in a move to relieve itself of electoral liabilities. It would not be unreasonable to see Labour's commitment to incorporating the ECHR from 1993 as a way of reassuring middle England that socialist or collectivist ideals no longer dominated the party.

For whatever reason, Labour in government felt able to accommodate the campaign for incorporation which had been fought long and hard by liberally minded peers and others.[187] Human Rights bills had been introduced to the House of Lords by Lord Wade, Lord Scarman and Lord Lester. Sometimes, as in the case of Lord Lester's bill which failed to reach the House of Commons before the dissolution of Parliament for the 1997 general election, the House of Lords approved them. However, they never had governmental support until the new Labour government pressed ahead with the Human Rights bill in the 1997–8 session.

The impact of the Human Rights Act 1998, as the bill became, is likely to be profound.[188] In formal, constitutional terms, it is a relatively conservative measure. It enacts rights, which bind public authorities, but allows Parliament to legislate inconsistently with the rights. In this way, it avoids threatening the traditional legislative supremacy of Parliament. Judges are not empowered to disapply or hold invalid primary legislation, although superior courts may make declarations of incompatibility in respect of such legislation which bring the incompatibility to the attention of the relevant minister and facilitate amending legislation. Nevertheless, in some ways the Act is revolutionary. Among its most significant provisions is section 3, which requires all legislation to be read and given effect so far as possible so as to make it compatible with Convention rights. While some legislation was amended before the Act came into force in order to avoid predictable incompatibilities, government was content to leave the courts to resolve as many potential incompatibilities as possible by way of robust interpretation of other legislation. This should avoid both the need for extensive legislative rewriting of earlier statutes and the danger of frequent declarations of

---

[187] For an account of the bills which had been unsuccessfully introduced to Parliament between 1968 and 1997, see Michael Zander, *A Bill of Rights?* 4th edn (Sweet & Maxwell, 1997), ch. 1.

[188] The Act has already generated a huge literature. For an introduction, see, for example, Keir Starmer, *European Human Rights Law: The Human Rights Act 1998 and the European Convention on Human Rights* (Legal Action Group, 1999); John Wadham and Helen Mountfield, *Blackstone's Guide to the Human Rights Act 1998* (Blackstone Press, 1999); Jack Beatson, Stephen Grosz and Peter Duffy, *Human Rights: The 1998 Act and the European Convention* (Sweet & Maxwell, 2000); David Feldman, 'The Human Rights Act 1998 and Constitutional Principles'.

incompatibility, which would demand further ministerial and parliamentary attention.

By virtue of sections 3 and 6, subordinate legislation will be invalid, and administrative action unlawful, to the extent of any incompatibility, unless incompatibility is absolutely required by primary legislation which cannot be interpreted so as to allow Convention-compatible action, decisions or subordinate legislation. The Act thus makes compatibility with Convention rights central to the interpretation of all legislation, the validity of subordinate legislation, and the lawfulness of the acts or omissions of public authorities. Through sections 7, 8 and 9, it also gives new statutory remedies to those who have suffered injury or loss as a result of action by public authorities which is incompatible with a Convention right, regardless of whether or not the behaviour in question would have given rise to a cause of action previously. The remedies may include damages, injunctions, declarations, etc. Furthermore, while the main focus of the Act is on relations between public authorities and citizens (the so-called 'vertical effect' of the Convention rights), there may also be some indirect effects on the rights and obligations of private parties in relation to each other. This 'horizontal effect' may flow from the duty to interpret all legislation compatibly with the Convention rights, whatever the matter in connection with which it is being interpreted, and also from the fact that courts and tribunals are themselves public authorities, and so have an obligation to act compatibly with Convention rights.[189] The extent (if any) of horizontal effect is highly uncertain and controversial, however; but, even if it proves to be very limited, the Act represents a huge move from the very limited scope for giving effect to human rights under the previous law.

Moreover, the Act enhances both the responsibilities and the powers of Parliament in terms of securing respect for human rights. Section 19 requires a minister introducing a government bill to either House to make a written statement (in practice, printed on the front of the bill) either that in his or her opinion the bill is compatible with Convention rights, or that he or she is unable to make such a claim but that the government wishes the House in question to consider the bill notwithstanding. The government has by concession extended this approach to

---

[189] For an introduction to horizontal effect, see Andrew Clapham, 'The European Convention on Human Rights and the British Courts: Problems Associated with the Incorporation of International Human Rights', in Philip Alston (ed.), *Promoting Human Rights through Bills of Rights* (Oxford University Press, 1999), ch. 4 at pp. 39–146, 152–6. The literature on the subject is now vast.

some subordinate legislation, and now gives its view of the compatibility of private members' bills, private bills, and local bills. Parliamentary procedure is being developed to respond to the human-rights imperative. A joint select committee has been established with a wide-ranging remit to consider and report on matters relating to human rights in the United Kingdom, and to report specifically on remedial orders.[190] There are a number of other institutions which have been set up to oversee the implementation of the Act, notably the Human Rights Commission in Northern Ireland and the Home Office Human Rights Task Force in London. The overall impression is of a growing commitment to human rights as the bedrock of politics and law. However, it remains to be seen how successfully this will be converted into everyday practice within Parliament.

Conclusion

The law and practice of civil liberties have pulled in many directions at the same time during the twentieth century. At the constitutional level, the doctrine of parliamentary supremacy gave Parliament the opportunity either to extend effective protection for rights or to interfere with them more extensively. Some rights, such as those derived from the ideal of equality, have been advanced by Parliament. At the same time, Parliament has restricted others, notably freedom of the person, freedom from oppression in the criminal process, and freedom of assembly. Long blind to the shortcomings of the executive branch in relation to civil liberties, the judges began to wake up late in the century, and have come to regard parliamentary supremacy in this field as something for which they need to compensate rather than something to be embraced. All this may have been turned on its head by the Human Rights Act 1998, which seems to bring Parliament and the judges onto the same side of the pitch, seeking to respect and vindicate civil liberties and fundamental rights. We probably cannot make sense of all this, but I offer the following suggestions by way of a tentative conclusion.

First, neither Parliament, the executive nor the courts have been generally proactive in seeking to identify and protect significant liberties

---

[190] For discussion of methods of pre-legislative scrutiny, see David Kinley, *The European Convention on Human Rights: Compliance without Incorporation* (Kluwer, 1993); David Kinley, 'Parliamentary Scrutiny of Human Rights: A Duty Neglected?', in Alston (ed.), *Promoting Human Rights through Bills of Rights: Comparative Perspectives*, pp. 158–4.

and rights. Human rights treaties have been signed and ratified without a systematic process for monitoring compliance with obligations, apart from the periodic reports which government submits to the international monitoring bodies under the treaties. The greatest strides have been taken where there has been a body charged with overseeing a specific field of endeavour, such as the Equal Opportunities Commission in relation to sex discrimination. Otherwise, most changes have been reactions to events, sometimes mediated through a review by a Royal Commission or similar inquiry, and sometimes (as in the case of the Human Rights Act 1998) a direct response to international influences. At no time until the present has government or Parliament had a human rights strategy. If the judges have had one, it has been unstated. So far as there have been advances, they have mostly been *ad hoc*. Even at the end of the century, the task of auditing protection of rights was discharged not by an official body, but by the Democratic Audit team at Essex University.[191] It will be interesting to see whether the next century produces a more systematic approach from government and Parliament.

Second, without prejudice to the generality of the first point, certain values have been newly injected into the politico-legal culture during the century, or have attained previously unsuspected weight within it. Examples are equality, both electoral and social; democracy, both electoral and as a value underpinning a free press and free expression; privacy in relation to personal information; and autonomy as to lifestyle and physical integrity, including that of children and patients. These values have become embedded in the institutional structure of the state as well as its law and politics, and we can expect their influence to continue to increase beneficently. Other forms of privacy have acquired less weight. Human dignity has strong support internationally but has not so far figured large in domestic civil-liberties law, although this may be a value to watch in the Human Rights Act era.[192] We can expect that greater attention will be paid to basic values of civil liberties and human rights when making and applying policy and law in years to come. This should make it possible for all institutions to adopt a more strategic and prin-

---

[191] The Democratic Audit, led by Professor Stuart Weir, produced two volumes surveying the scene in the 1990s: Francesca Klug, Keir Starmer and Stuart Weir, *The Three Pillars of Liberty: Political Rights and Freedoms in the United Kingdom* (Routledge, 1996) was followed by a volume on democratic rights.

[192] David Feldman, 'Privacy-related Rights and their Social Value', in Peter Birks (ed.), *Privacy and Loyalty* (Clarendon Press, 1997), pp. 15–50; *id.*, 'Human Dignity as a Legal Value', *Public Law* (1999, 2000).

cipled approach to civil liberties and human rights. The result is that there is now scope to develop a model of citizenship based on something more inclusive than the property-based, white-male-centred approach which dominated politics, law and society at the start of the twentieth century. A tension remains between liberal individualism and collective humanitarianism, but the ECHR and the Human Rights Act 1998 offer an opportunity to resolve it by reference to more coherent and clearly articulated criteria than were available one hundred years ago. The shift from liberty to human rights does not solve all, or perhaps any, of the problems, but it provides a clearer frame of reference for the debate.

Third, legal culture has become more self-confident and less deferential to the executive than it was. This is partly the result of European influence, both from the Council of Europe and from the European Community and their various institutions. Like it or not, constitutional law has become a supra-national, if not international, business, always influenced and sometimes controlled by developments elsewhere. But the lower level of deference reflects a similar trend in society as a whole. It is encouraged by the growing number of legal practitioners and judges who have now had a formal education or training in human rights law and feel comfortable about speaking of and balancing basic values. This process is likely to continue as judges get to grips with the implications of the Human Rights Act 1998, in preparation for which the Judicial Studies Board provided intensive seminars to familiarise courts and tribunals with the new elements in the legal system. Courts are more willing to scrutinise the reasons which public authorities give for their actions and decisions than at any previous time in the century, although this does not mean that they are terribly enthusiastic about it, having a sense of their restricted role as a constitutional institution. Even that limited change seems to me to be a healthy development. It makes the constitution more robust, and holds out the hope that, in the twenty-first century, it will develop a properly prescriptive aspect which will be capable of benefiting ordinary people in their ordinary lives.

Finally, although the House of Commons is now infinitely more representative of the population than it was in 1900, and steps are being taken to reduce the more obviously anti-democratic elements in the House of Lords, Parliament and government have been prime victims of the decline of social deference. Increasingly it is recognised that Parliament, with its almost unfettered legislative power, and government, which takes powers from Parliament, are at least as likely to threaten basic liberties as to protect them. In the past, Parliament has too often failed to protect people, and courts have been willing to trust the good faith of the executive or take refuge from confrontation in the idea of parliamentary supremacy. The institutional significance of the Human Right Act 1998 is that, for the first time, it places a joint responsibility on Parliament and public authorities, including the executive and courts, to work together to protect civil liberties and rights. Parliament must try to discharge that responsibility, and government must give it the freedom to do so. Otherwise, the authority of Parliament will decline still further, and the only check on government will be the judiciary. Legal accountability for excess or abuse of power is important, but it is not sufficient. It will be interesting to see whether Parliament has the will to develop the mechanisms for monitoring liberty in the twenty-first century, and whether governments will allow it to use them.

Note. This is a revised version of a paper originally prepared for a colloquium on the constitution in the twentieth century which took place at the British Academy in September 2000. I am grateful to the organiser, Professor Vernon Bogdanor, for his encouragement and assistance, and to all the participants at the colloquium for their helpful comments and criticisms. Remaining errors and eccentricities are my own.

Bibliography

Primary materials

Public records

Many of the files held in the PRO which seem to be potentially most useful are closed for 100 years: for a list, see Ewing and Gearty, pp. 419–26.

PRO, *MI5: The First Ten Years 1909–1919* (London: PRO, 1997) (a CD-ROM containing declassified material on the early operation of MI5).

PRO, CAB 16/8, Report of the Sub-Committee on Imperial Defence, 24 July 1909 (on decision to introduce the bill which became the Official Secrets Act 1911).

PRO, CAB 23/48, Cabinet 27 (24), 15 April 1924 (establishment of Cabinet Committee on Industrial Unrest).

PRO, CAB 24/166, CP 273 (24), Cabinet Committee on Industrial Unrest, 30 April 1924; CAB/175, CP 42 (25), Memorandum by the Attorney-General on the Present Law in Regard to Sedition and Strikes, 9 October 1925; CAB 23/51, Cabinet 48(25), 13 October 1925; CAB/179, CP 136 (26), Report of the Public Order Committee, 25 March 1926 (on approaches to counteracting perceived threats from the Communist Party of Great Britain).

PRO, HO 144/20158, 4 July 1934 (background to the Public Order Act 1936 with information about Home Office attitudes to proposals for extending the power of local authorities to control public assemblies during the period of Fascist campaigning in the mid-1930s).

PRO, HO 144/21086, 9 June 1937 (note by metropolitan police commissioner to home secretary on banning of Mosleyite march to prevent an apprehended breach of the peace).

PRO, FO 371/88753 (note by Boothby, Foreign Office, to Wallace, Colonial Office, 8 July 1950); CAB 128/18 (minute of Cabinet meeting, 1 August 1950); CAB 130/64 (memorandum by Lord Chancellor Jowitt for discussion at ministerial meeting on 18 October 1950, on ratification of the European Convention on Human Rights).

PRO, FO 371/184367, FO 371/184368, FO 371/184369, FO 371/190591, WUC 1735/43 (papers relating to the decision to grant the right of individual petition to the European Commission of Human Rights in 1965).

Parliamentary debates (Hansard)

HC Debs, 16 February 1998, 20 May 1998, 3 June 1998, 17 June 1998, 24 June 1998, 2 July 1998, 21 October 1998 (House of Commons debates on the Human Rights bill).

HL Debs, 3 November 1997, 18 November 1997, 24 November 1997, 27 November 1997, 19 January 1998, 29 January 1998, 5 February 1998, 29 October 1998 (House of Lords debates on the Human Rights bill).

Official publications

Curry, John, *The Security Service 1908–1945: The Official History*, with an introduction by Christopher Andrew (PRO Publications, 1999).

House of Lords Select Committee on a Bill of Rights, *Report* (1977–8), HL 176.

Lord Justice Woolf and Judge Stephen Tumim, *Prison Disturbances April 1990*, Cm 1456 (HMSO, 1991).

PRO, *MI5: The First Ten Years 1909–1919*, with introduction by Christopher Andrew (PRO Publications, 1997).

Report of an Inquiry by Rt Hon. Lord Justice Scarman, OBE: The Brixton Disorders, 10–12 April 1981, Cmnd 8427 (HMSO, 1981).

Report of an Inquiry by the Rt Hon. Lord Justice Scarman, OBE: The Red Lion Square Disorders of 15 June 1974, Cmnd 5919 (HMSO, 1975).

Report of an Inquiry by the Hon. Sir Henry Fisher into the Circumstances leading to the Trial of Three Persons on Charges arising out of the Death of Maxwell Confait and the Fire at 27 Doggett Road, London SE5 (1977), HC 90.

Report of the Committee on Data Protection (Chair, Sir Norman Lindop), Cmnd 7341 (HMSO, 1978).

Report of the Committee on Homosexual Offences and Prostitution, Cmnd 247 (HMSO, 1957).

Report of the Committee on Obscenity and Film Censorship, Cmnd 7772 (HMSO, 1979).

Report of the Committee on Privacy, Cmnd 5012 (HMSO, 1972).

Report of the Inquiry into Child Abuse in Cleveland (Chair, Dame Elizabeth Butler-Sloss), Cm 412 (HMSO, 1988).

Report of the Royal Comission on Capital Punishment, Cmd 8932 (HMSO, 1953).

Report of the Royal Comission on Criminal Justice (Chair, Viscount Runciman of Doxford), Cm 2263 (HMSO, 1993).

Report of the Inquiry into the Export of Defence Equipment and Dual-use Goods to Iraq and Related Prosecutions, HC 115 (HMSO, 1996), 5 vols and index (the Scott Report)

Report of the Royal Commission on Criminal Procedure, Cmnd 8092-I (HMSO, 1981).

Report: Independent Review of Parades and Marches 1997 (Stationery Office, 1997) (the North Report).

Select Committee on Procedure, Special Report, *Parliamentary Scrutiny of Treaties*, HC 210 (26 July 2000).

Select Committee on Statutory Instruments, Special Report for Session 1945–6 (HMSO, 29 October 1946).

The Stephen Lawrence Inquiry: Report of an Inquiry by Sir William Macpherson of Cluny, advised by Tom Cook, the Rt Revd Dr John Sentamu, Dr Richard Stone, Cm 4262-I (Stationery Office, 1999).

Statutes, statutory instruments, etc.

Abortion Act 1967

Aliens Act 1905

British Nationality Act 1948

Broadcasting Act 1990

Children Act 1989

Cinemas Act 1985

Crime and Disorder Act 1998

Criminal Justice and Public Order Act 1994

Criminal Procedure and Investigations Act 1996

Dangerous Drugs Act 1920

Defence of the Realm Acts 1914–15

Defence of the Realm Regulations, SR & O 1914 No. 1231, and subsequent amendments and consolidations

Disability Discrimination Act 1995

Divorce Reform Act 1969

EC Equal Pay Directive

EC Equal Treatment Directive

Electronic Communications Act 2000

Emergency Powers Act 1920

Firearms Act 1920

Human Rights Act 1998

Incitement to Disaffection Act 1934

Incitement to Mutiny Act 1797

Interception of Communications Act 1985

Law Reform (Married Women and Joint Tortfeasors) Act 1935

Married Women's Property Act 1882
Matrimonial Causes Act 1857
Matrimonial Causes Act 1923
Matrimonial Causes Act 1937
Mental Health Act 1983
Obscene Publications Acts 1959 and 1964
Official Secrets Acts 1911 and 1920
Police Act 1997
Police and Criminal Evidence Act 1984
Prevention of Terrorism (Temporary Provisions) Act 1974
Public Order Act 1936
Public Order Act 1986
Public Processions (Northern Ireland) Act 1998
Race Relations Acts 1965 and 1976
Regulation of Investigatory Powers Act 2000
Representation of the People Act 1918
Rules Publication Act 1893
Sex Discrimination Act 1975
Sex Disqualification Removal Act 1919
Sexual Offences Act 1967
Shops (Early Closing) Act 1920
Statutory Instruments Act 1946
Terrorism Act 2000
Theatres Act 1968
Trade Disputes Act 1906
Trade Union Act 1913
Treaty establishing the European Economic Communities (Treaty of Rome) 1957
Video Recordings Act 1984

Case-law

Abrams v. *United States*, 250 US 616 (1919) (US Supreme Court on crime of sedition).

Airedale NHS Trust v. *Bland* [1993] AC 789, HL (authorising withdrawal of feeding and hydration from PVS patient).

Attorney-General v. *Blake* [2000] 3 WLR 625, HL (restitutionary remedies for Crown in relation to disclosure of official secrets).

Attorney-General v. *De Keyser's Royal Hotel Ltd* [1920] AC 508, HL (on the prerogative power to requisition property and the duty to compensate).

Attorney-General v. *Guardian Newspapers (No. 2)* [1990] 1 AC 109, HL (the final judgement in the *Spycatcher* cases).

Attorney-General v. *Wilts United Dairies Ltd* (1921) 37 TLR 884, CA (prerogative powers).

In re B (A Minor) (Wardship: Sterilisation) [1987] AC 199, HL (authorising sterilisation of young person with mental disability).

Blackpool Corporation v. *Locker* [1948] 1 KB 349, CA (controls over subordinate legislation).

Bowman v. *Secular Society* [1917] AC 406, HL (on atheism, blasphemy, and related matters).

Boyle and Rice v. *United Kingdom,* Eur. Ct HR, Series A, No. 131, Judgment of 27 April 1988 (prisoners' correspondence).

Brannigan and McBride v. *United Kingdom,* Eur. Ct HR, Series A, No. 258-B, Judgment of 26 May 1993, 17 EHRR 539 (detention before charge in terrorism cases; validity of the UK's derogation).

Brogan v. *United Kingdom,* Eur. Ct HR, Series A, No. 145, Judgment of 29 November 1988, 11 EHRR 107 (detention before charge in terrorism cases).

Bugdaycay v. *Secretary of State for the Home Department* [1987] AC 514, HL (standard of review where fundamental rights are at risk).

In re C (Adult: Refusal of Treatment) [1994] 1 All ER 819 (right of lucid adult to give directions that he is not to be treated for physical illness in the event of further bout of mental illness).

Campbell v. *United Kingdom,* Eur. Ct HR, Series A, No. 233, Judgment of 25 March 1992 (prisoners' correspondence).

Chester v. *Bateson* [1920] 1 KB 829 (requisitioning in wartime).

Christie v. *Leachinsky* [1947] AC 573, HL (requirements for an arrest).

Conway v. *Rimmer* [1968] AC 910, HL (public interest immunity from disclosure of evidence).

Council of Civil Service Unions v. *Minister for the Civil Service* [1985] AC 374, HL (extending judicial review to the scrutiny of some prerogative powers).

D v. *National Society for the Prevention of Cruelty to Children* [1978] AC 171, HL (public interest immunity from disclosure of evidence).

Davis v. *Lisle* [1936] 2 KB 434, DC (limited power of police at common law to enter premises).

Derbyshire County Council v. *Times Newspapers Ltd* [1993] AC 534, HL (public authorities cannot sue for libel).

Dillon v. *O'Brien* (1887) 20 LR Ir. 300 (search related to arrest).

Director of Public Prosecutions v. *Jones (Margaret)* [1999] 2 AC 240, HL (developing right to assemble on land adjacent to a highway).

Duncan v. *Cammell Laird & Co. Ltd* [1942] AC 624, HL (Crown privilege).

Duncan v. *Jones* [1936] 1 KB 218, DC (police powers in respect of meetings on highways; no recognition of right to freedom of assembly).

Elias v. *Pasmore* [1934] 2 KB 164 (search and seizure in relation to suspected sedition).

In re F (Mental Patient: Sterilisation) [1990] 2 AC 1, HL (authorising sterilisation of young adult woman with mental disability).

Ghani v. *Jones* [1970] 1 QB 693, CA (common law power to seize items for evidential purposes).

Gillick v. *West Norfolk and Wisbech Area Health Authority* [1986] AC 112, HL (children's rights and parents' powers).

Golder v. *United Kingdom*, Eur. Ct HR, Series A, No. 18, Judgment of 21 February 1975 (prisoners' correspondence).

Great Central Railway Co. v. *Bates* [1921] 3 KB 578, CA (limited power of police at common law to enter premises).

Halford v. *United Kingdom*, Eur. Ct HR, Judgment of 25 June 1997, RJD 1997-III No. 39, 24 EHRR 523 (telephone tapping).

Hunter v. *Chief Constable of the West Midlands* [1982] AC 529, HL.

Inland Revenue Commissioners v. *Rossminster Ltd* [1980] AC 952, HL (meeting statutory preconditions to the exercise of powers).

John v. *MGN Ltd* [1997] QB 586, CA (levels of libel damages).

Johnson v. *Sargent* [1918] 1 KB 101 (limits on powers to implement subordinate legislation).

Knuller v. *DPP* [1973] AC 435, HL (common law offence of conspiracy to cause a public mischief).

Leech v. *Deputy Governor of Parkhurst Prison* [1988] AC 533, HL (on judicial protection for prisoners' rights).

Leigh v. *Gladstone* (1909) 26 TLR 139 (forced feeding of suffragettes on hunger strike in prison).

Lewisham Borough Council v. *Roberts* [1949] 2 KB 608, CA (controls over subordinate legislation).

Liversidge v. *Anderson* [1942] AC 206, HL (on internment powers under the Defence of the Realm Regulations).

Lord Advocate v. *The Scotsman Publications Ltd* [1990] 1 AC 812, HL (refusing to prevent publication of official information on confidentiality grounds).

McCallum v. *United Kingdom*, Eur. Ct HR, Series A, No. 183, Judgment of 30 August 1990 (prisoners' correspondence).

McIlkenny v. *Chief Constable of the West Midlands* [1980] QB 283, CA.

McKee v. *Chief Constable of Northern Ireland* [1984] 1 WLR 1358, HL (requirements for use of force to arrest).

Malone v. *United Kingdom*, Eur. Ct HR, Series A, No. 82, Judgment of 2 August 1984, 7 EHRR 14 (telephone tapping).

Mellor v. *Leather and Clough* (1853) 1 E&B 619 (search following arrest).

Mohammed-Holgate v. *Duke* [1984] AC 437, HL (requirements for an arrest).

Morgans v. *Director of Public Prosecutions* [2000] 2 WLR 386, HL (interpretation of Interception of Communications Act 1985).

Morris v. *Beardmore* [1981] AC 446, HL (limited power of police at common law to enter premises).

Moss v. *McLachlan* [1984] IRLR 76, DC (use of powers to prevent breaches of the peace).

Newcastle Breweries Ltd v. *R.* (1920) 36 TLR 276 (requisitioning in wartime).

O v. *United Kingdom*, Eur. Ct HR, Series A, No. 120, Judgment of 8 July 1987, 10 EHRR 82 (parents' rights in child care decision-making).

O'Hara v. *Chief Constable of Royal Ulster Constabulary* [1997] AC 286, HL (requirements for an arrest).

Re R (A Minor) (Wardship: Medical Treatment) [1992] Fam. 11, CA (authorising treatment against wishes of minor).

Raymond v. *Honey* [1983] 1 AC 1, HL (prisoners retain certain rights, including right of access to court).

R. v. *Bourne* [1939] 1 KB 687 (criminal liability of doctor for terminating pregnancy).

R. v. *Bowman* (1912) 76 JP 271 (newspapers and incitement to mutiny).

R. v. *Chief Constable of Sussex, ex p. International Trader's Ferry Ltd* [1999] 2 AC 418, HL (police discretion in preserving public order).

R. v. *Chief Constable of West Midlands Police, ex p. Wiley* [1995] 1 AC 274, HL (public interest immunity).

R. v. *Foreign Secretary, ex p. Rees-Mogg* [1994] QB 552 (limits on power to review exercise of prerogative power to enter into treaties).

R. v. *Gibson* [1990] 2 QB 619, CA (relationship between common law conspiracy offences and statutory offences under Obscene Publications Acts 1959 and 1964).

R. v. *Gott* (1922) 16 Cr. App. R. 87, CA (blasphemy).

R. v. *Halliday, ex p. Zadig* [1917] AC 260, HL (power to legislate for internment).

R. v. *Inspector of Lemon Street Police Station, ex p. Venicoff* [1920] 3 KB 72, DC (limits on protection for detained foreigners).

R. v. *Khan (Sultan)* [1997] AC 558, HL (illegal bugging in breach of Convention rights does not necessarily lead to the exclusion of evidence gained as a result).

R. v. *Lemon* [1979] AC 617, HL (on blasphemous libel and gay expression).

R. v. *Ministry of Defence, ex p. Smith* [1996] QB 517, DC and CA (limitations of judicial review as a way of protecting fundamental rights).

R. v. *Ponting* [1985] Crim. LR 318 (on section 2 of the Official Secrets Acts 1911–20 and the leaks following the sinking of the *General Belgrano*).

R. v. *Secretary of State for Social Security, ex p. Joint Council for the Welfare of Immigrants* [1996] 4 All ER 385, CA (common law right not to be left destitute).

R. v. *Secretary of State for the Home Department, ex p. Khera and Khawaja* [1984] AC 74, HL (requirement for secretary of state to show that preconditions for detention of immigrants have been satisfied in habeas corpus proceedings).

R. v. *Secretary of State for the Home Department, ex p. Robb* [1995] 1 All ER 677 (forced feeding of prisoners against their will presumptively unlawful).

R. v. *Secretary of State for the Home Department, ex p. Simms* [1999] 3 WLR 328, HL (recognition that prisoners retain freedom of expression).

R. v. *Sheer Metalcraft Ltd* [1954] 1 KB 586 (when subordinate legislation takes effect).

R. v. *Ward (Judith)* [1993] 2 All ER 577, CA (disclosure of evidence to defence).

Riley v. *Director of Public Prosecutions* (1989) 91 Cr. App. R. 14, DC (requirements for an arrest).

Rogers v. *Secretary of State for the Home Department* [1973] AC 388, HL (public interest immunity from disclosure of evidence).

In re S (Adult Patient: Sterilisation), The Times, 26 May 2000, CA (court's oversight of decisions to sterilise adults with mental incapacity).

St George's Healthcare NHS Trust v. *S* [1999] Fam. 26, CA (woman's right to be free of enforced Caesarian operation).

Shaaban Bin Hussien v. *Chong Fook Kam* [1970] AC 942, PC (requirements for an arrest).

Shaw v. *Director of Public Prosecutions* [1962] AC 220, HL (on the judicial assertion of a power to create or reinstate the common law offence of conspiracy to corrupt public morals).

Silver v. *United Kingdom,* Eur. Ct HR, Series A, No. 61, Judgment of 25 March 1983 (prisoners' correspondence).

Sunday Times Ltd v. *United Kingdom,* Eur. Ct HR, Series A, No. 30, Judgment of 26 April 1979, 2 EHRR 245 (freedom of expression and contempt of court).

Thomas v. *Sawkins* [1935] 2 KB 249, DC (entry powers to monitor activities on private premises for reasonably anticipated breaches of the peace).

Trendtex Trading Corporation v. *National Bank of Nigeria* [1977] QB 529, CA (on the relationship between national and customary international law).

W, R, and B v. *United Kingdom,* Eur. Ct HR, Series A, No. 121, Judgments of 8 July 1987, 10 EHRR 29, 87, 74 (parents' rights in child care decision-making).

Wershof v. *Metropolitan Police Commissioner* [1978] 3 All ER 540 (no power to arrest without clear legal authority).

X v. *United Kingdom,* Eur. Ct HR, Series A, No. 46, Judgment of 5 November 1981, 4 EHRR 188 (detaining mental patients).

Zamir v. *Secretary of State for the Home Department* [1980] AC 930, HL (restriction on use of habeas corpus to challenge detention of immigrants).

Secondary materials

Books

Allen, C. K., *Law and Orders,* 2nd edn (Stevens, 1956).

Allen, C. K., *Law in the Making,* 7th edn (Oxford University Press, 1964).

Alston, Philip (ed.), *Promoting Human Rights through Bills of Rights: Comparative Perspectives* (Oxford University Press, 1999).

Andrew, Christopher, *Secret Service: The Making of the British Intelligence Community* (Heinemann, 1985).

Baxter, John and Koffman, Laurence (eds), *Police, the Constitution and the Community* (Professional Books, 1985).

Beatson, Jack and Cripps, Yvonne (eds), *Freedom of Expression and Freedom of Information: Essays in Honour of Sir David Williams* (Oxford University Press, 2000).

Blackburn, Robert (ed.), *Rights of Citizenship* (Mansell, 1993).

Calvert, Harry, *Constitutional Law in Northern Ireland* (Sweet & Maxwell, 1968).

Cohen-Almagor, Raphael (ed.), *Liberal Democracy and the Limits of Tolerance: Essays in Honor and Memory of Yitzhak Rabin* (University of Michigan Press, 2000).

Conservative Political Centre, *Liberty in the Modern State: Eight Oxford Lectures* (CPC, 1957).

Deacon, Richard, *A History of the British Secret Service* (Granada Publishing, 1980).

Denning, Lord Justice, *Freedom under the Law* (Stevens, 1949).

Devlin, Sir Patrick, *The Enforcement of Morals* (Oxford University Press, 1965).

Dicey, A. V., *Lectures Introductory to the Study of the Law of the Constitution*, 1st edn (Macmillan, 1885); 2nd edn (Macmillan, 1886); 7th edn (Macmillan, 1908).

Dicey, A. V., *Lectures on the Relation between Law and Public Opinion in England during the Nineteenth Century* (Macmillan, 1908).

Drewry, Gavin and Blake, Charles (eds), *Law and the Spirit of Inquiry: Essays in Honour of Sir Louis Blom-Cooper* (Kluwer, 1999).

Dummett, Ann and Nicol, Andrew, *Subjects, Citizens, Aliens and Others: Nationality and Immigration Law* (Weidenfeld & Nicolson, 1990).

Evans, Malcolm D., *Religious Liberty and International Law in Europe* (Cambridge University Press, 1997).

Ewing, K. D. and Gearty, C. A., *The Struggle for Civil Liberties: Political Freedom and the Rule of Law in Britain, 1914–1945* (Oxford University Press, 2000).

Feldman, David, *The Law Relating to Entry, Search and Seizure* (Butterworths, 1986).

Feldman, David, *Civil Liberties and Human Rights in England and Wales* (Clarendon Press, 1993); 2nd edn (Oxford University Press, 2002).

Fine, Bob and Millar, Robert (eds), *Policing the Miners' Strike* (Lawrence & Wishart, 1985).

Geary, Roger, *Policing Industrial Disputes, 1893–1985* (Methuen, 1985).

Gostin, Larry (ed.), *Civil Liberties in Conflict* (Routledge, 1988).

Hadfield, Brigid, *The Constitution of Northern Ireland* (SLS, 1989).

Hadfield, Brigid (ed.), *Northern Ireland: Politics and the Constitution* (Open University Press, 1992).

Harlow, Carol and Rawlings, Richard, *Pressure through Law* (Routledge, 1992).

Harris, D. J., Bailey, S. H. and Jones, B. L., *Civil Liberties Cases and Materials* (Butterworths, 1980; 5th edn, 2001).

Hart, H. L. A., *Law, Liberty, and Morality* (Oxford University Press, 1963).

Herbert, A. P., *Independent Member* (Methuen, 1950).

Hood, Roger (in collaboration with Graca Cordovil), *Race and Sentencing* (Clarendon Press, 1992).

Hooper, David, *Official Secrets: The Use and Abuse of the Act* (Secker & Warburg, 1987).

Joseph, Sir Keith, *Freedom under Law* (CPC, 1975).

King, Michael, *Public Order Policing: Contemporary Perspectives on Strategy and Tactics* (Perpetuity, 1995).

Kinley, David, *The European Convention on Human Rights: Compliance without Incorporation* (Kluwer, 1993).

Levin, Bernard, *The Pendulum Years: Britain and the Sixties* (Pan, 1972).

London, Louise, *Whitehall and the Jews* (Cambridge University Press, 1999).

McCabe, Sarah and Wallington, Peter *et al.*, *The Police, Public Order and Civil Liberties: Legacies of the Miners' Strike* (Routledge, 1988).

McCrudden, Christopher and Chambers, Gerald (eds), *Individual Rights and the Law in Britain* (Law Society/Clarendon Press, 1994).

Massie, Robert K., *Dreadnought: Britain, Germany, and the Coming of the Great War* (Jonathan Cape, 1992).

Mirfield, Peter, *Silence, Confessions and Improperly Obtained Evidence* (Clarendon Press, 1997).

Morison, John and Livingstone, Stephen, *Reshaping Public Power: Northern Ireland and the British Constitutional Crisis* (Sweet & Maxwell, 1995).

O'Higgins, Paul, *Cases and Materials on Civil Liberties* (Sweet & Maxwell, 1980).

Northam, Gerry, *Shooting in the Dark: Riot Police in Britain* (Faber, 1988).

Porter, Bernard, *The Origins of the Vigilant State: The London Metropolitan Police Special Branch before the First World War* (Weidenfeld & Nicolson, 1987).

Reiner, Robert, *The Politics of the Police*, 3rd edn (Oxford University Press, 2000).

Rolph, C. H., *The Trial of Lady Chatterley* (Penguin, 1961).

Simpson, A. W. B., *In the Highest Degree Odious: Detention without Trial in Wartime Britain* (Clarendon Press, 1992).

Simpson, A. W. B., *Human Rights and the End of Empire: Britain and the Genesis of the European Convention* (Oxford University Press, 2001).

Street, Harry, *Freedom, the Individual and the Law* (Penguin, 1963).

Taylor, A. J. P., *English History 1914–1945* (Clarendon Press, 1965).

Thompson, W. H., *Civil Liberties* (Victor Gollancz, 1938).

Tomkins, Adam, *The Constitution after Scott: Government Unwrapped* (Clarendon Press, 1998).

Townshend, Charles, *Making the Peace: Public Order and Public Security in Modern Britain* (Oxford University Press, 1993).

Vincent, David, *The Culture of Secrecy: Britain 1832–1998* (Oxford University Press, 1998).

Waddington, P. A. J., *The Strong Arm of the Law: Armed and Public Order Policing* (Clarendon Press, 1991).

Walker, Clive and Starmer, Keir (eds), *Justice in Error* (Blackstone Press, 1993).

Williams, D. G. T., *Not in the Public Interest* (Hutchinson, 1965).

Williams, D. G. T., *Keeping the Peace* (Hutchinson, 1967).

Zander, Michael, *A Bill of Rights?* 4th edn (Sweet & Maxwell, 1997).

Zeldin, Theodore, *France 1848–1945:* vol. 1, *Ambition, Love and Politics* (Clarendon Press, 1973).

Chapters in books

Collins, Evelyn and Meehan, Elizabeth, 'Women's Rights in Employment and Related Areas', in McCrudden and Chambers (eds), *Individual Rights and the Law in Britain*, ch. 12.

Craig, Paul, 'Public Law, Sovereignty and Citizenship', in Blackburn (ed.), *Rights of Citizenship*, pp. 307–30.

de Friend, Richard and Uglow, Steve, 'Policing Industrial Disputes', in Baxter and Koffman (eds), *Police, the Constitution and the Community*, pp. 62–71.

Drewry, Gavin, 'The Politics of Capital Punishment', in Drewry and Blake (eds), *Law and the Spirit of Inquiry*, ch. 8.

Feldman, David, 'Information and Privacy', in Beatson and Cripps (eds), *Freedom of Expression and Freedom of Information*, ch. 19.

Feldman, David, 'Protest and Tolerance: Legal Values and the Control of Public-order Policing', in Cohen-Almagor (ed.), *Liberal Democracy and the Limits of Tolerance*, pp. 43–69.

Gostin, Larry, 'Towards Resolving the Conflict' and 'The Conflicting Views of Two National Civil Liberties Organisations', in Gostin (ed.), *Civil Liberties in Conflict*, pp. 8–20 and 117–12.

Hadfield, Brigid, 'The Northern Ireland Constitution', in Hadfield (ed.), *Northern Ireland: Politics and the Constitution*, ch. 1.

Kinley, David, 'Parliamentary Scrutiny of Human Rights: A Duty Neglected?', in Alston (ed.), *Promoting Human Rights through Bills of Rights*, pp. 158–84.

McCrudden, Christopher, 'Racial Discrimination', in McCrudden and Chambers (eds), *Individual Rights and the Law in Britain*, ch. 13.

Journal articles

Bingham, Sir Thomas, 'The European Convention on Human Rights: Time to Incorporate', *Law Quarterly Review* (1993).

Daintith, T. C., 'Disobeying a Policeman: A Fresh Look at *Duncan* v. *Jones*', *Public Law* (1966).

Dixon, David, Bottomley, Keith, Coleman, Clive, Gill, M. and Wall, David, 'Reality and Rules in the Construction and Regulation of Police Suspicion', *International Journal of the Sociology of Law* (1989).

Feldman, David, 'Public Law Values in the House of Lords', *Law Quarterly Review* (1990).

Feldman, David, 'The Human Rights Act and Constitutional Principles', *Legal Studies* (1999)

Hailsham, Lord, *The Times*, 2, 16, 19, and 20 May 1975.

Laws, Sir John, 'The Limitations of Human Rights', *Public Law* (1998).

Lester, Anthony, 'Fundamental Rights: The United Kingdom Isolated', *Public Law* (1984).

Lester of Herne Hill, Lord, 'UK Acceptance of the Strasbourg Jurisdiction: What Really Went on in Whitehall in 1965', *Public Law* (1998).

Marston, Geoffrey, 'The United Kingdom's Part in the Preparation of the European Convention on Human Rights', *International and Comparative Law Quarterly* (1993).

Ponting, Clive, '*R*. v. *Ponting*', *Journal of Law & Society* (1987).

Sedley, Sir Stephen, 'Human Rights: A Twenty-first Century Agenda', *Public Law* (1995).

Steyn, Lord, 'The Weakest and Least Dangerous Branch of Government', *Public Law* (1997).

Thomas, Rosamund M., 'The British Official Secrets Acts 1911–1939 and the *Ponting* Case', *Criminal Law Review* (1986).

Wade, E. C. S., 'Police Search', *Law Quarterly Review* (1934).

Wade, E. C. S., 'Police Powers and Public Meetings', *Cambridge Law Journal*. (1936–9).

Walker, Clive and Fitzpatrick, Ben, 'The Independent Commission for the Holding Centres: A Review', *Public Law* (1998).

Wicks, Elizabeth, 'The United Kingdom Government's Perceptions of the European Convention on Human Rights at the Time of Entry', *Public Law* (2000).

Woolf, Lord, '*Droit Public*—English Style', *Public Law* (1995).

12.
The Electoral System

JOHN CURTICE

When scholars write about electoral systems what they most commonly analyse are the mechanisms by which ballots cast by voters are translated into seats won by parties and candidates.[1] Yet this is but one of a range of matters for which constitutional and/or legal provision needs to be made in order to conduct an election. Rules need to be laid down about who is entitled to vote. And it is often also thought desirable to regulate how candidates and parties conduct themselves in their efforts to seek votes.

Moreover, a country may have more than one electoral system. Electoral laws and regulations may vary between different parts of the country as well as between different bodies. Both kinds of variation certainly existed in twentieth-century Britain. Ireland was often an exception to the rule, while the electoral system for local and devolved institutions was often at variance with that for the House of Commons.

In this chapter we focus primarily on elections to the House of Commons. For, throughout the twentieth century, it is elections to the House of Commons that have far and away been the most influential in determining who holds power in Britain. In so doing we concentrate on the position in Great Britain and mostly only refer to separate developments in Ireland when they help to illuminate what happened in the rest of the United Kingdom. After all, following partition in 1922, MPs from across the Irish Sea constituted but a small and sometimes marginalised portion of the membership of the Commons.

We also concentrate upon the franchise and the translation of votes into seats, and leave aside the rules governing campaigning. This is because, while there were important developments and debates during

---

[1] Arend Lijphart, *Electoral Systems and Party Systems: A Study of Twenty-seven Democracies* (Oxford University Press, 1994); Rein Taagepera and Matthew Shugart, *Seats and Votes: The Effects and Determinants of Electoral Systems* (Yale University Press, 1989).

the course of the twentieth century on these matters until the end of the century at least, the rules about election campaigning were both largely uncontentious and were little changed, though this is not to say that they were uninfluential.[2]

We begin by looking at the franchise. We then turn to the two key features of the process by which votes are translated into seats, that is how constituencies are distributed and drawn and then how votes within them are cast and counted. For each we undertake three tasks. First, we delineate and describe the main features and the principal changes that occurred during the course of the twentieth century. Second, we attempt to explain why the electoral system came to have the characteristics it did. And third, we ask what have been the major consequences of the decisions that have been made.

One leitmotif runs through our tale. This is that over the course of the twentieth century there seems to have been a fundamental change in the principles that appear to underlie the British electoral system. At the beginning of the century, British elections were still very much about the representation of place. But by the end of the century a very different principle had come to predominate, the right of citizens to an equal say in the nation's affairs. True considerations of place still had some influence, but arguably for the most part they did so only in so far as they could also be justified by this second principle. And it certainly seems the case that the role of place in twenty-first century Britain will depend on whether it can continue to be defended successfully in terms of the new principle.

The franchise

The franchise bequeathed by the Reform Act of 1884 was a patchwork quilt sown together by incremental change rather than any consistent rationale. There were in fact no fewer than seven different ways in which a man could qualify for the vote.[3] Even so the importance of place in

---

[2] The Political Parties, Elections and Referendums Act 2000 introduced a system of national limits on campaign expenditure for the first time in British elections and gave the task of supervising these and other new regulations (though not electoral registration) to a new Electoral Commission. Provision was also made for the first time in 1998 for the registration of political parties.

[3] Neil Blewett, *The Peers, The Parties and the People: The General Elections of 1910* (Macmillan, 1972); Duncan Tanner, *Political Change and the Labour Party, 1900–1918* (Cambridge University Press, 1990).

Table 12.1 Key dates for the franchise

1918	Nearly all men over 21 and most women over 30 enfranchised. Residency qualification reduced to six months. Electoral registration placed in the hands of local government officials. Plural voting limited to two votes.
1926	Residency qualification reduced to three months.
1928	Vote extended to nearly all women aged over 21.
1948	Residency qualification and plural voting abolished. Significant extension of postal and proxy voting.
1969	Voting age reduced to 18.
1985	Vote first granted to British citizens living overseas.
2000	Introduction of rolling registration and vote extended to the homeless.

determining who could exercise the franchise is clear. Most of the seven ways of getting on to the electoral register required that someone be either an owner or a tenant of property or land in a constituency. In fact over four out of five people acquired the right to vote through just one of the seven ways, that is by virtue of being a householder. But it was a right that was only acquired after a period of twelve months continuous residence. As the register was only compiled once a year and there was also a six-month gap between compilation and registration, in practice there was a two-year gap on average between someone attaining the status of being the householder at an address and their securing the right to vote. Moreover, anyone who moved lost his right to vote though an exception was made if the move was within the same constituency or borough.

True, many of those without such a clear stake in a place could also be registered. Both lodgers and servants living rent-free in separate properties could qualify for the franchise. But lodgers had to be 'separately occupying' accommodation valued at more than £10pa unfurnished and, unlike householders, they had to make an annual application to appear on the register. Moreover, any change of address, even within the same constituency, cost them their residence qualification. Thus, in practice, securing the franchise as a lodger was far harder than as a householder or owner of property.

Thanks to this emphasis on having a demonstrable stake in a place, pre-First World War Britain had something considerably less than universal male suffrage. No more than two-thirds of men aged twenty-one actually appeared on the register at any one point in time. Those most likely to be excluded were the young (many of whom would still be living at home with their parents and thus not be householders) and

485

the geographically mobile.[4] Meanwhile women were barred from the parliamentary franchise entirely.

Moreover not only were one-in-three men effectively denied the franchise because they lacked an apparent stake in a place, other men who had stakes in more than one place were allowed to vote more than once. Each business premise with a rateable value of at least £10 brought its occupant an additional vote, though this right could be exercised only once in any particular borough or county. As voting in general elections was spread over a period of some three weeks, those with multiple business interests had the opportunity if they wished to travel around the country in order to exercise their plural franchise.

However, one other group that also had the opportunity to vote more than once enjoyed this right for a different reason. These were university graduates and teaching staff at universities who were granted a vote in addition to any other franchise to which they might be entitled. This university franchise was exercised not in territorial constituencies, but rather in separate functional university constituencies that between them elected nine MPs.

Nothing changed until the passage of the Representation of the People Act 1918. This Act was the product of a Speaker's Conference chaired by Speaker Lowther, a conference that, as we shall see, made important recommendations about boundaries and the counting of votes as well as the franchise. The Act swept away the patchwork quilt of seven different franchises and replaced them with just three—residency at an address, occupation of business premises worth £10pa or more, and the university franchise. So, place still mattered, but its role was attenuated. While not abolished, plural voting was limited such that no person could exercise more than two votes although these could now be exercised in different constituencies within the same borough.[5] More importantly for the majority of the population, the residency requirement was relaxed. Six rather than twelve months continuous residence was now all that was required to establish the right to be registered in a constituency. In addition, the register itself was to be compiled every six months rather than only every twelve, thereby reducing the gap between fulfilling the residence requirement and being placed on the register. Moreover,

[4] Martin Pugh, *The Evolution of the British Electoral System, 1832–1987* (Historical Association, 1988); Tanner, *Political Change*.
[5] Since all constituencies also normally voted on the same day after 1918, a practical limit was also effectively imposed on the degree to which someone could engage in plural voting in geographically disparate constituencies.

someone who moved could be registered straight away at their new address not only if they had moved from within the same borough or county but also if they had come from an adjacent county or borough. Soldiers could even be registered after just one month's residence.

A further indication of a decline in the role of place was that it was no longer the case that the only way someone could vote was to do so at their local polling station. The 1918 Act permitted limited postal and proxy voting when someone was unable to attend the polls for reason of employment. Arrangements were also made for the 1918 election for soldiers in Belgium and France to vote in person abroad while those soldiers stationed elsewhere were given an entitlement to a proxy vote. And, in an implicit recognition that the right to vote was coming to be determined by notions of citizenship, conscientious objectors were denied the right to vote for five years.

The 1918 Act also took registration out of the hands of poor law overseers and revising barristers and instead made it the responsibility of local government officers who were financed by the state. This ensured a more efficient and far less disputatious registration process. As a result, the overall effect of the Act was to introduce near though not complete universal suffrage for men over twenty-one. At the same time women aged over thirty who were either themselves eligible for the local government franchise or whose husbands were (a franchise that continued to be similar to the pre-1918 parliamentary franchise albeit with a six- rather than a twelve-month residency requirement) also became eligible for the vote. The practical effect was to give the vote to a little under four out of five women aged over thirty.[6] Together, the widening of the male franchise and its extension to women produced the single biggest expansion in the size of the electorate (from well over seven million to over twenty-one million) in the history of the franchise in Britain.[7] For the first time ever the majority of Britain's adult population had the right to vote.

It did not prove long before 'the majority' became 'nearly all'. In 1928 the vote was granted to women aged over twenty-one on the same basis as men. Otherwise there were but minor changes made to the rules during the inter-war period. Because of administrative difficulties, postal votes could no longer be exercised from an overseas address after 1920. Meanwhile in 1926 electoral registration again became only an annual

---

[6] Tanner, *Political Change.*
[7] Pugh, *Evolution of the British Electoral System.*

process, though at the same time the residence qualification was reduced once more to just three months.

But, like its predecessor, the Second World War was followed by important changes to the franchise. Between them these changes could be said to implement the principle of 'one man, one vote' for the first time in Britain.[8] The Representation of the People Act 1948, by eliminating the business and university franchises, entirely abolished plural voting, which had already been further limited in 1944 by denying the business vote to the wives of owners of business premises. Also abolished was the residency period (except that a person had to be resident for three months in Northern Ireland before being eligible to appear on the register anywhere in the province). A person simply had to be resident at a particular address on the 'qualifying date' in order to be eligible for inclusion on the next electoral register. Meanwhile there was a significant extension of postal and proxy voting which could now be exercised by invalids and those who had moved from the address at which they were currently registered as well as by those whose occupation necessitated their absence from home on polling day.

Thereafter there was again a lull. Indeed, until its very end at least, the second half of the twentieth century saw no change in the franchise as radical as in the first half. But there were some developments of note. When the Labour government of 1964–70 decided in 1969 that adulthood should begin at eighteen rather than twenty-one, the franchise was extended to eighteen year olds as part of the package.[9] One result of this change was to bring on to the register many university students who lived for part of the year near their place of study and for part in the parental home, thereby raising a question about where they could be considered resident. In *Fox* v. *Stirk*,[10] judgement was passed to the effect that they could be registered at both addresses although they could only actually vote in a general election in respect of one of those addresses. This right to plural registration, which extends to anyone who has two or more homes, thus gives some voters the opportunity to choose in which constituency they vote even if it has not restored a form of plural voting.

---

[8] David Butler, *The Electoral System in Britain since 1918*, 2nd edn (Oxford University Press, 1963), p. 124.

[9] The new law also made it possible for 18 year olds to vote as soon as they became 18. The previous regulations enacted in 1949 had in effect meant that typically no one acquired the vote until at least some months after their twenty-first birthday.

[10] [1970] 2 QB 463.

More controversial, but again further eroding the significance of place in the exercise of the franchise, was the decision of the Conservative government in 1985 to allow British citizens resident abroad for no more than five years to register to vote in respect of the last address at which they were resident in the UK. They were also allowed to vote by proxy. In 1989 the period of five years was extended to twenty, though in 2000 it was cut back to fifteen years. Members of Britain's expatriate population could now if they wished exercise their right to vote even though they were no longer resident anywhere in the country at all. The 1985 legislation also extended postal voting to those temporarily away from home on holiday.

But, although the legal framework of registration law changed little between 1948 and the end of the century, one existing provision gained a new import. Citizens of the Empire who took up residence in the UK have always had the right to vote in British elections, and, thanks to the provisions of the British Nationality Act 1948, this right was retained when the Empire gradually became the Commonwealth. (As members of the Commonwealth, Irish citizens were also granted the right to vote after partition in 1922, a right they then retained even after the Irish Republic left the Commonwealth in 1949.) So, when in the 1950s and 1960s, Britain admitted significant numbers of immigrants from Commonwealth countries, these new immigrants came with the right to vote. This put them in a politically more powerful position than their counterparts in many other West European countries where they had only the status of aliens. In contrast, despite Britain's membership of the European Union (EU), citizens of other EU countries (apart from Ireland) had still not been granted the right to vote in parliamentary elections by the end of the century, although EU-wide regulations did oblige the British government to grant EU citizens the right to vote in local and European elections.

However, after fifty years of little change, at the very end of the century Britain's franchise law underwent its most radical overhaul since 1918. Nearly all of the remaining vestiges of place in determining who could vote were set aside by the Representation of the People Act 2000. The most significant change was the introduction of a 'rolling register'. Although the 1948 Act had substituted a qualifying date for a qualifying period, someone who moved just after the qualifying date could still have to wait sixteen months before they were eligible to vote in respect of their new address. This was because the register was compiled only once a year and then actually came into force only four months after the qualifying date. But these delays were all but eliminated by the new system of rolling registration under which the register was updated nearly every month. As a result someone could now usually be registered at their new address within no more than six weeks of moving.[11] In addition, the new rules not only ensured that remand prisoners and persons in mental hospitals were able to vote, but they even made it possible for someone of no fixed abode to register. All they had to do was to show some connection with the area in which they wished to be registered. Meanwhile, anyone who wished to do so could ask to vote by post rather than appear in person at the polling station. While place might still determine where people's votes were counted, it no longer determined who had the right to vote. That right was conferred by citizenship.

But why did this change come about? Two forces suggest themselves—social change and partisan advantage.

Let us consider, first of all, social change. While it might have made sense in late Victorian Britain to believe that someone should demonstrate that they had a stake in a place in order to be entitled to vote, such notions of desert were destroyed by the upheaval of war. For the war required soldiers to fight abroad and civilians to move to munitions factories or other essential employment. As a result they might no longer have a stake in a place, but few could deny that they had a stake in their country. Yet, with electoral registration suspended during the war, these were precisely the kinds of people whose chance to vote appeared to be put at risk under the pre-1918 rules. Thus, the 1918 Act introduced a number of special measures to enable soldiers to vote as well as a more permanent reduction in the residency requirements. Indeed it even included a temporary measure that gave the vote to all soldiers aged nineteen and over rather than just those aged twenty-one plus.

Equally, the First World War resulted in increasing numbers of women being mobilised into the civilian effort. There was little doubt that they too had demonstrated their stake in their country, thereby making it difficult to continue to deny them the franchise. True, an entirely artificial age barrier of thirty was imposed initially to ensure that women did not constitute a majority of the electorate, but as we have seen it was only

---

[11] However, it continued to be the case that someone had to be resident in Northern Ireland for three months before they could be entered on the electoral register anywhere in the province.

a matter of a few years before the franchise for men and women was equalised.

In 1939–45 war again forced the pace of change. The normal registration process had to be suspended once again. But at the same time rationing had required the creation of a National Register. So it is perhaps little surprise that in 1943 the National Register, for which of course there was no residency requirement, should be used as the basis for compiling a new electoral register. Only those who wanted a business vote and those not covered by the National Register (such as soldiers) had to make a claim to be put on the register. These emergency provisions were in force for the 1945 election making this the first election in Britain to be fought on a register that did not demand a residency requirement. The 1948 Act merely ensured the permanent abolition of such a requirement.

In the absence of any war, in the second half of the twentieth century social change had a more gradual impact on the registration process. But from 1966 comparisons of the electoral register with the results of the decennial census revealed that the registration process was failing to capture an increasing proportion of the adult population entitled to vote. In 1966 the figure stood at 3–4 per cent, but by 1991 it had risen to somewhere between 7 and 9 per cent.[12] This increase occurred despite the fact that in 1983 legislation was passed that enabled people to apply to have their names added to the register even after it was published so long as they had in fact been resident in the constituency on the qualifying date. In part the rise in non-registration reflected the growing difficulty of keeping an accurate tally of an increasingly mobile population. But in part it was also the product of a sudden drop in the level of registration following the introduction in the late 1980s of a new and highly unpopular method of local government taxation. Known officially as the Community Charge but colloquially as the 'poll tax', this tax was a flat-rate annual charge payable by each adult living in a local authority's area. Some people attempted to avoid becoming liable for the charge by failing to declare their existence to the electoral registration officer.

So, much as in the First and Second World Wars, the apparent inability of the existing registration process to ensure that those whom it was felt were entitled to vote could actually do so brought about change. By the end of the twentieth century, a once-a-year only process of electoral registration seemed increasingly anachronistic given that the advent of ubiquitous computing made it relatively straightforward to update any

---

[12] Stephen Smith, *Electoral Registration in 1991* (HMSO, 1991).

list of persons. The only reason for still having some delay between someone moving and their names appearing on the register at their new address was to have some time to enable potentially fraudulent claims to be checked.

But, if social change sometimes appears to have forced politicians to act, on other occasions it is clear that calculations of partisan advantage have shaped the choices that have been made. Nowhere is this clearer than in respect of the plural voting occasioned by the occupancy of business premises, a vote that was universally regarded as a predomi- nantly Conservative one. Thus it was a Liberal government that made the first attempt to abolish plural voting, an attempt that was abandoned only because of the outbreak of the First World War. It was a Conservative government that in 1928 extended the business vote to the husbands of women with business premises. And it was eventually a Labour govern- ment that abolished the business vote in 1948 in the face of claims that in so doing it was breaking a bargain between the parties made in the 1944 Speaker's Conference.[13] Certainly the retention of the business vote in 1918, while at the same time limiting it to one additional vote, had been part of the compromise hammered out in the 1917 Speaker's Conference.

Equally, the impact of perceived partisan interest also revealed itself in the second half of the century in the decisions made about the exten- sion of the franchise to those who lived outside the United Kingdom. Those who could afford to live abroad were widely thought to be Con- servative voters. And it was a Conservative government that made the first provision for them to be able to vote in the 1980s and it was also a Conservative government which then extended the group covered to those who had been abroad for as long as twenty years. Equally it was a Labour government which at the very end of the century decided to limit the right once again to those who have been abroad for no more than fifteen years. Similarly, it was widely believed (though far from proven, see below) that those who were failing to appear on the electoral register in the 1990s were disproportionately Labour supporters, and thus it took the election of a Labour government in 1997 before proposals for a rolling register were enacted.[14]

---

[13] The 1931 Representation of the People bill introduced by Ramsay MacDonald's Labour government also made provision for the abolition of plural voting. That bill fell with the collapse of MacDonald's government in August 1931.

[14] Equally, the decision to facilitate voting by soldiers in the 1918 election and to allow soldiers as young as 19 to vote was urged by Unionist MPs because they believed that sol- diers would be sympathetic to their cause.

But what impact did the changes that were made to the franchise really have? By far and away the most important changes were of course those made in 1918, introducing universal male suffrage and giving the vote to a majority of women. It has been argued that by ensuring that all of the working class was enfranchised for the first time the 1918 reform made a significant contribution to Labour's eventual success in replacing the Liberals as the principal opposition to the Conservatives.[15] Indeed, one of the reasons why the Liberals—who were aware that they had been able to win a thumping victory in 1906 on the existing Third Reform Act franchise—made little attempt to widen the franchise until shortly before the First World War was a belief that perhaps Labour might benefit more than themselves. However, others have suggested that the patchwork quilt franchise of the Third Reform Act only differentially excluded working-class rather than middle-class people from the register, and that in any event the pre-1918 electorate was already a predominantly working-class one.[16] So, while Labour may have been helped by an increase in the proportion of the electorate belonging to the section of society that the party sought to represent, it cannot be considered a determining factor in its success in displacing the Liberals after 1918, a process that was also significantly assisted by the split in the Liberal Party between the followers of Asquith and those of Lloyd George.

But, if the extension of the franchise to all men may have given some limited assistance to Labour, granting the franchise to women proved to be a bonus for the Conservatives. Evidence for the inter-war period, prior to the advent of regular survey research, is inevitably patchy but even then it appears likely that women gave more support to the Conservatives than did men.[17] They certainly did so in the post-war period, even if there were signs towards the end of the century that perhaps the gender gap was narrowing.[18] At least one post-war Conservative victory (1951) and perhaps as many as three others (1955, 1959 and 1970) would not have happened if the franchise had been confined to men. In short, the enfranchisement of women played a significant role in ensuring

---

[15] H. C. G. Matthew, Ross McKibbin and John Kay, 'The Franchise Factor in the Rise of the Labour Party', *English Historical Review* (1976).

[16] Tanner, *Political Change*.

[17] James Ross, *Elections and Electors: Studies in Democratic Representation* (Eyre & Spottiswoode, 1955).

[18] Pippa Norris, 'Gender–Generation Gap', in Geoffrey Evans and Pippa Norris (eds), *Critical Elections: British Parties and Voting in Long-term Perspective* (Sage, 1999).

that the twentieth century proved to be predominantly a Conservative century.

Other developments in the franchise during the course of the century inevitably had a relatively minor impact compared with these two developments. The business vote undoubtedly benefited the Conservatives, but hardly to the degree that might have been anticipated given the degree of contention it aroused. After 1918 it never comprised much more than 1 per cent of the electorate.[19] Butler estimates that on average it helped the Conservatives win between seven and eleven seats, but that it never affected the overall outcome.[20] Postal voting, significantly extended in 1948 such that around 2 per cent of votes were usually cast that way,[21] appears to have benefited the Conservatives, typically proving decisive in up to a dozen seats. In its absence the Conservatives may well have failed to secure an overall majority in 1951.[22] However, by the end of the century it was no longer clearly the case that the Conservatives were better able to organise the postal vote.[23]

In contrast, Conservative attempts to derive benefit from the extension of the franchise to Britons living abroad proved to have little impact. Just 11,000 such voters were registered in the first year of the scheme's operation, a figure that then proceeded to decline to a little over 1,000 in four years. It then rose once more to 32,000 voters when the right was extended to those who had been out of the country for up to twenty years, but the number had fallen away again to fewer than 14,000 by the century's end.[24]

Meanwhile, it was widely believed that the increasing inefficiency of the electoral register towards the end of the century, particularly the losses occasioned by the poll tax, were hurting Labour.[25] However, survey research on the political preferences of those not on the electoral register has largely failed to support this belief. The 1997 British Election Study found that the proportion of Labour identifiers among those not on the

[19] F. W. S. Craig, *British Electoral Facts, 1832–1987* (Parliamentary Research Services, 1989).

[20] Butler, *Electoral System in Britain*.

[21] In the inter-war period the proportion of absent voters on the electoral register was less than 0.1 per cent.

[22] David Butler, *The British General Election of 1951* (Macmillan, 1952).

[23] David Butler and Dennis Kavanagh, *The British General Election of 1997* (Macmillan, 1997).

[24] Colin Rallings and Michael Thrasher, *British Electoral Facts, 1832–1999* (Parliamentary Research Services, 2000).

[25] Iain McLean and J. Smith, 'The Poll Tax and the Electoral Register', in Anthony Heath, Roger Jowell and John Curtice, with Bridget Taylor (eds), *Labour's Last Chance? The 1992 Election and Beyond* (Dartmouth, 1994).

register was in fact no higher than it was among those who were on the register.[26] After all, one of the principal causes of non-registration, geographical mobility, is more common among those in middle-class than among those in working-class occupations. Meanwhile, Labour certainly did receive disproportionate support from Commonwealth and Irish citizens,[27] though it should be remembered that by the end of the century many of the members of Britain's ethnic minorities were second-generation immigrants who had British rather than Commonwealth citizenship. Labour may also have benefited marginally from the extension of the franchise to eighteen year olds,[28] but the most important feature of those aged between eighteen and twenty was their consistent reluctance to vote at all.[29]

The twentieth century, then, saw Britain finally become a mass democracy in which all of its citizens had the right to vote, a change that had important consequences for the shape of its democracy. But even when that principle was accepted and implemented there still proved to be room for decisions about the exercise of the franchise that were politically motivated and which could have an impact on electoral outcomes. And it took the whole of the century before citizenship rather than residency was the only requirement for voting.

Constituencies

We now turn from who voted to how votes were translated into seats. As we indicated earlier, we can identify two separate aspects of this process. The first of these is the drawing of boundaries, the second how votes are cast and counted. We consider each of these in turn.

At the beginning of the century parliamentary representation was still primarily the representation of counties and boroughs. True, in most cases where a county or borough contained more than one seat, it was usually subdivided, but no parliamentary constituency crossed a county

[26] See also Peter Lynn and Bridget Taylor, 'On the Bias and Variance of Samples of Individuals: A Comparison of the Electoral Register and Postcode Address File as Sampling Frames', *The Statistician* (1995).

[27] Mohammed Anwar, *Race and Politics* (Tavistock, 1986), and Anthony Heath *et al.*, *Understanding Political Change: The British Voter, 1964–1987* (Pergamon, 1991).

[28] Heath, *Understanding Political Change*.

[29] Ivor Crewe, J. Fox and James Alt, 'Non-voting in British General Elections: 1966–October 1974', in Colin Crouch (ed.), *British Political Sociology Yearbook*: vol. 3, *Participation in Politics* (Croom Helm, 1977); Kevin Swaddle and Anthony Heath, 'Official and Reported Turnout in the British General Election of 1987', *British Journal of Political Science* (1989).

Table 12.2 Key dates for boundary drawing

1918	First boundary distribution to be undertaken using nationwide criteria for determining constituency sizes.
1922	Founding of Irish Free State. Number of Northern Irish MPs reduced.
1944	System of permanent boundary commissioners and regular reviews instituted.
1945	Twenty-five extra seats created to reduce size of the largest seats.
1948	First boundary distribution to be formulated by new boundary commissions implemented.
1954	First periodical review of boundaries.
1958	Frequency of boundary reviews reduced.
1969	Labour government delays implementation of second periodical review until after 1970 election. Over-representation of rural seats in England ended.
1983	Third periodical review reflecting extensive local government reform of the 1970s. Northern Irish seats increased to seventeen.
1992	Frequency of boundary reviews increased.
1995	Fourth periodical review.
1998	Scotland Act makes provision for reduction in number of MPs.
2000	Formation of Electoral Commission to which responsibility for boundary drawing will eventually pass.

or borough boundary (except where boroughs were joined together to form a single seat or where a borough was amalgamated with its surrounding county). True, also, the last redistribution in 1885 had resulted in less variation in the size of constituencies than had been tolerated hitherto. But there was no permanent machinery for redrawing boundaries to ensure that changes in the geographical distribution of the population were regularly accommodated, let alone rules to determine how many seats a county or borough might be entitled to. Significant differences in the size of constituencies had emerged since 1885, with some small boroughs having as few as 3,000 electors while Romford had over 50,000. The average English seat was far larger than its Irish counterpart[30] and also somewhat larger than seats in Scotland and Wales. The representation of place clearly predominated over any notion that every vote should have the same value irrespective of where it was cast.

And in truth even at the end of the century considerations of place were still far from absent in the process of drawing and redistributing parliamentary constituencies. But gradually notions of one vote, one value, implemented through having constituencies of roughly equal size, have come to exercise greater influence.

The first key step was taken at the 1917 Speaker's Conference. It agreed that any constituency with a population of fewer than 50,000

[30] Pugh, *The Evolution of the British Electoral System.*

should be abolished while new constituencies should be created on the basis of one for every 70,000 voters. While local government boundaries were still to be respected 'as far as practicable' and the recommendation did not apply to Ireland, it was the first time that a set of rules for redistribution was adopted that could be said to recognise the desirability of similarly sized seats. A boundary commission was appointed to implement the conference's recommendation and its eventual proposals were largely accepted without controversy. Rather late in the day redistribution also took place in Ireland but, whereas there was little difference between the average size of English, Scottish and Welsh constituencies, the average Irish constituency was still less than two-thirds the size of seats in the rest of the United Kingdom.

Eventually this disparity was removed when the partition of Ireland and the founding of the Irish Free State in 1922 meant that most of Ireland was no longer represented in the House of Commons. But in recognition of the creation of a devolved parliament in Belfast a new inequality was created when the Government of Ireland Act 1920 provided for just twelve territorial seats in Northern Ireland rather than the eighteen to which the electorate might have suggested it was entitled. But, more important, in the rest of the United Kingdom, the scheme first used in 1918 gradually became out of date as the population moved and no provision was made for any periodic review of constituency boundaries. By the end of the Second World War significant disparities had arisen. At one extreme Romford contained over 220,000 voters while at the other Southwark North had just 14,000. So, in practice the principle of one vote, one value was allowed to wither on the vine.

Only in 1944 did Parliament finally establish permanent machinery for the regular review of constituency boundaries. This followed the recommendations of the Vivian Committee in 1942 and the Speaker's Conference in 1944 which, *inter alia*, had suggested that in future constituencies should be redrawn every three to seven years. The 1944 Act required the boundary commissioners to calculate the average electorate per constituency, to retain more or less the existing number of constituencies and, while respecting local government boundaries where possible, to create constituencies that were no more than 25 per cent above or below the average. The one exception to these stipulations was the retention of a separate seat in the City of London.

This would appear to constitute a clear move towards ensuring that constituencies should be of an equal size. There was, however, one important breach of this principle: there was to be no reduction in the number of constituencies in Scotland or Wales, seventy-one in the former and thirty-five in the latter. This was despite the fact that the electorate of neither country had grown as fast as it had done in England in the inter-war period. By 1939 the average English MP was representing around 7,500 more voters than the average Welsh MP and no fewer than 10,000 more than the average Scottish one. But a mixture of political expediency and poor reasoning persuaded the Speaker's Conference to recommend against any cut in Scottish or Welsh representation.[31] In order to deliver this, the average electorate per constituency used in the redistribution was to be calculated separately in each of the four constituent parts of the United Kingdom, and the redistribution in each part undertaken by its own separate commission. At the same time Northern Ireland was to remain significantly under-represented because it had its own devolved parliament.

So far as the 1945 election was concerned the English commission was simply required to subdivide those constituencies which contained more than 100,000 voters (almost twice the English average) and as a result twenty-five new constituencies were put in place in time for the 1945 election. Meanwhile, before the commissioners produced their first full report in 1948, they successfully requested a relaxation of the rules on equality, because they had found it impossible to respect local boundaries, maintain approximately the current number of seats and keep within the maximum deviation rule of 25 per cent. Instead of a fixed rule the commissioners were simply required, much as they had been in 1917, to produce electorates as close to the average 'as is practicable' bearing in mind the value of respecting local government boundaries.

Despite the relaxation of the rules, the 1948 redistribution produced the most equal set of electorates yet. The ratio of the population of the largest to the smallest constituency was roughly two to one compared with three to one at the 1918 review.[32] Even so, the English commission still recommended the retention of eight borough seats with more than 80,000 electors, well above the average of 56,000. Rather controversially the government asked the commission to revisit these proposals and also to create an extra seat in nine other English boroughs, and the resulting amendments were implemented as part of the 1948 scheme.

In fact there was a wider issue behind this controversy about some large borough seats. Both this review and its two immediate predecessors

[31] Iain McLean, 'Are Scotland and Wales over-represented?', *Political Quarterly* (1995).
[32] Butler, *Electoral System in Britain*.

had in fact produced a redistribution in which the average borough constituency was larger than the average county seat. Indeed in its 1947 report the English Boundary Commission had indicated that it felt that urban seats could accommodate larger electorates more easily than could rural ones. This policy was retained in the next review completed in 1954. It was, however, never explicitly implemented by the other three commissions who appear to have interpreted their right to take into account special geographical considerations more narrowly, using it only to create smaller constituencies in particularly remote areas such as the Highlands & Islands.[33] And by the time of the second periodical review published in 1969 the English commission also decided to abandon the practice.

Other changes to the boundary review process also helped ensure that the tension between place and equality of electorate size came increasingly to be resolved in favour of the latter. The radical redrawing of local government boundaries in the 1970s, a redrawing that produced fewer bigger authorities, meant that the impact of the requirement on the boundary commissions to respect local government boundaries became less of a constraint. This was even more so thanks to the fact that following this reorganisation the English and Welsh boundary commissions were expected only to respect London borough and county boundaries and not those of districts within counties, while the equivalent requirements for Scotland and Northern Ireland were weakened even more significantly. Moreover, in its final review of the century, published in 1995, the commission even chose to cross the boundaries of seven pairs of London boroughs in order to produce more equally sized constituencies.

Indeed, analysis of the outcome of all the post-war reviews by Rossiter *et al.*[34] indicates that each one produced less variation in the size of constituencies than did its predecessor. This was despite the fact that in the Redistribution of Seats Act 1958 the commissions were given an additional instruction to take into account the disadvantages of disturbing existing constituency boundaries. True, the 1958 Act also reduced the frequency of reviews from once every three-to-seven years to once every ten-to-fifteen years thereby making it more likely that inequalities of electorate size would grow between reviews. But the time period was

---

[33] David Rossiter *et al.*, *The Boundary Commissions: Redrawing the United Kingdom's Map of Parliamentary Constituencies* (Manchester University Press, 1999).
[34] *The Boundary Commissions.*

cut back again in 1992 to every eight-to-twelve years. Moreover, by the end of the century some of the differences between the average size of English constituencies and those in the rest of the UK had been or were about to be reduced. Following the prorogation of the Northern Ireland Parliament in 1972 and the subsequent failure to put anything back in its place, the under-representation of Northern Ireland in the House of Commons was ended in 1983, the province being given seventeen seats.[35] Meanwhile, under the terms of the Scotland Act 1998, which established the Scottish Parliament, provision was made for a cut in the number of Scottish seats at the next boundary review so that the average Scottish constituency would be of the same size as its English counterpart. Thus, by the end of the century only Wales was still to be treated favourably.[36]

So, over the course of the twentieth century Britain developed a non-partisan method for the regular review and determination of constituency boundaries that were approximately equal in size. Once the principle of the equal franchise was accepted, so the principle of one vote, one value in the drawing of boundaries was perhaps an almost unavoidable corollary. This did not stop party interest from still playing some role at the edges. Perhaps the most notable examples of this were Labour's decision in 1948 to increase the number of borough seats, the same party's decision in 1969 to stall implementation of a review that would cost it seats, and the Conservatives' decision in 1992 to speed up a review that it thought would be to its advantage. And, of course, the parties could also hope to influence the work of the commissioners by participating in the local inquiries that were a regular feature of the review process. But it appears to have been recognised by all parties that decisions about constituency boundaries were potentially so explosive politically, and apparent attempts at gerrymandering potentially so harmful to public perceptions of the electoral system, that such decisions were best taken outside the political arena.

But the decisions that were made did have political consequences. The impact of the 1917 redistribution is impossible to discern because it

---

[35] This was indeed the number to which the province was entitled at that time if its seats were to be of the same size as those in England, though the new rules stated that Northern Ireland could have between sixteen and eighteen seats. The number was increased to eighteen in the final review of the century implemented in 1997.

[36] The provisions of the Scotland Act will, however, only deliver a once and for all cut in Scottish representation. If England continues to grow more quickly than Scotland after the next review, then Scotland will gradually become over-represented once more. See John Curtice, 'Reinventing the Yo-Yo? A Comment on the Electoral Provisions of the Scotland Bill', *Scottish Affairs* (1998).

was implemented at the same time as a threefold expansion of the electorate. But, so far as the remaining distributions are concerned, there are four clear points that can be made.[37] First, each boundary review cost Labour seats. This was because the cities, where Labour was stronger, were continually losing population to the suburbs and rural areas where the Conservatives tended to fare better. Moreover this became more true between the 1950s and the 1980s.[38] So, while the more regular review of constituencies in the post-war period helped avoid what might otherwise have been an ever growing pro-Labour bias, the boundary commissions were still always running to keep up with population movements, especially because they were not allowed to take into account future population projections.

Second, the decision in the 1969 review no longer to treat rural areas more favourably than urban ones meant that reviews no longer hurt Labour as much as they might have done. Third, the decision in 1944 to maintain the over-representation of Scotland and Wales proved to be of increasing benefit to Labour as it came increasingly to dominate representation in those two parts of the UK.[39] And fourth, Labour demonstrated in the 1995 review that a party which adopted a systematic approach to the submissions it made to local inquiries could reap a marginal partisan benefit.[40]

So, despite the increasing tendency for the boundary commissions to draw constituencies of a similar size, the British electoral system was still unable to provide a set of boundaries that was equitable between the two main parties. Rather, thanks to the growing concentration of Labour's support in areas with small and declining electorates, the determination of boundaries gradually became kinder to Labour as the century drew towards its close. This was at least one of the reasons why Labour won more seats but fewer votes than the Conservatives in the February

---

[37] Butler, *Electoral System in Britain*; Rossiter, *The Boundary Commissions*; and Roger Mortimore, 'The Constituency Structure and the Boundary Commission: The Rules for the Redistribution of Seats and their Effect on the British Electoral System, 1950–1987', D.Phil. thesis (Oxford, 1992).

[38] John Curtice and Michael Steed, 'Proportionality and Exaggeration in the British Electoral System', *Electoral Studies* (1986).

[39] The decision to increase Northern Ireland's representation in 1983 from twelve seats to seventeen did not, however, prove to be of particular long-term advantage to the unionist parties. See John Curtice and Michael Steed, 'The results analysed', in David Butler and Dennis Kavanagh, *The British General Election of 1992* (Macmillan, 1992).

[40] David Rossiter *et al.*, 'Redistricting and Partisan Bias in Great Britain', *British Journal of Political Science* (1997); Rossiter, *The Boundary Commissions*.

1974 election. And it was also one of the reasons why the Conservatives' majority was insufficient to withstand all the losses the party suffered during the course of the 1992–7 Parliament despite having an eight point voting lead.[41] One vote, one value has proved a rather elusive goal.

Counting

Table 12.3 Key dates for counting the votes

1911	Parliament Act reduces normal length of parliaments to five years.
1910	Royal Commission on Systems of Election recommends introduction of AV.
1917	Speaker's Conference proposes STV in larger boroughs and university seats and AV elsewhere.
1918	Apart from STV in some university seats, neither AV nor STV implemented in deadlock between Commons and Lords. STV introduced to Scottish local education authority elections until their abolition in 1929.
1920	Following introduction into all Irish local elections the previous year, Government of Ireland Act bequeaths STV to Irish Free State and devolved Northern Ireland Parliament.
1922	Asquithian Liberals become first party to back electoral reform in election manifesto.
1929	Northern Ireland Parliament abolishes STV.
1930	Minority Labour government proposes AV and abolition of university and double-member seats. Bill falls with collapse of government in 1931.
1948	Abolition of university seats and remaining double-member seats.
1973	Northern Irish Assembly elected by STV. System brought into regular use in Northern Irish elections thereafter.
1974	February election fails to deliver overall majority and gives Labour most seats despite not having most votes. Highest Liberal vote since 1929. Debate about electoral reform reignited.
1976	Influential Hansard Society report recommends additional member system.
1977	Regional open party list system rejected for European elections.
1997	Labour enters office with promise to hold referendum on electoral system for House of Commons.
1999	Scottish Parliament and Welsh Assembly elected using additional member system. European Parliament elections held using closed regional party lists system. Independent Commission on the Voting System proposes 'AV+' for House of Commons.
2000	Greater London Assembly elected using additional member system. London mayor elected using supplementary vote. Scottish Executive working group recommends STV for Scottish local elections.

[41] John Curtice, 'The British Electoral System: Fixture without Foundation', in Dennis Kavanagh (ed.), *Electoral Politics* (Clarendon Press, 1992); John Curtice and Michael Steed, 'Neither Responsible nor Accountable: First Past the Post in Britain', Paper presented at the Annual Workshops of the European Consortium for Political Research (1998); and David Rossiter *et al.*, 'Changing Biases in the Operation of the United Kingdom's Electoral System, 1950–97', *British Journal of Politics and International Relations* (1999).

If there is anything that supposedly lies at the heart of the British system of government, it is that elections take place using the single-member plurality electoral system. So, when we look at how people voted and how their votes were translated into seats we will surely find that little changed during the course of the twentieth century. Not so. Only after the Second World War did the single member plurality system become the only method by which MPs were elected. Meanwhile, in the first third of the century there were two serious attempts to scrap the system entirely. And by the end of the century Britain had become something of a hothouse of electoral experimentation from which not even the Commons itself could assume it was immune.

It was, indeed, only in 1884 that first past the post had become the method by which most MPs were elected. Before that, two-member rather than single-member seats had been the norm. Thus, for example, between 1867 and 1885 just 200 of the 658 MPs in the House of Commons were elected in single-member seats. Moreover, during this period the limited vote was used in the fourteen three- or four-member seats with each voter having one vote less than there were seats to be elected. It had been hoped that the limited vote would promote minority representation in these seats, but in practice this aim was frustrated by the ability of the largest party in each constituency to spread its vote evenly among its candidates.[42]

This failure of the limited vote to deliver more minority representation persuaded MPs to look to the single-member district as a means of achieving that end.[43] For the Conservatives, Salisbury took the view that dividing up boroughs into single-member seats improved his party's chances of winning seats in what were predominantly Liberal areas. Under the existing arrangements the Liberals either organised the limited vote or claimed both double-member seats. On the Liberal benches Gladstone concurred, arguing that single-member districts went 'a long way towards that which many Gentlemen have much at heart—namely, what is roughly termed the representation of minorities', and that, 'by means of one-Member districts you will obtain a very large diversity of representation'.[44] Thanks to this consensus between the two main party leaders, all but twenty-seven of the 634 constituencies created under the 1885

[42] Vernon Bogdanor, *The People and the Party System: The Referendum and Electoral Reform in British Politics* (Cambridge University Press, 1981).

[43] Michael Steed, 'The Constituency', in Vernon Bogdanor (ed.), *Representatives of the People? Parliamentarians and Constituents in Western Democracies* (Gower, 1985).

[44] HC Deb., 3rd series, vol. 294, col. 380, 1 December 1884.

distribution were single-member seats, the remainder being two-member divisions where each voter had two votes.

In practice, the single-member plurality system failed to deliver 'fairer', that is more proportional, representation. Rather, in late Victorian and Edwardian Britain the system exhibited the tendency for which it was to become well known in the twentieth century, that is exaggerating relatively small leads in votes into large leads in terms of seats. Indeed it was in evidence to the Royal Commission on Systems of Election in 1909 that James Parker Smith formulated what was to become known as the cube law. This stated that if two parties win votes in the ratio A:B then under the single-member plurality system they will win seats in the ratio $A^3:B^3$. In simple terms the law meant that a party with a small lead in votes would have that lead tripled when it came to seats.[45]

Not only did single-member districts not have the effect that had been intended but, by the time the First World War approached, members of all parties had reason for some doubt about whether they could continue to prosper under the single-member plurality system. The Liberals had to worry about the rise of Labour while Labour could not be sure that it would ever be able to establish itself as an independent party. Unionists meanwhile had to contemplate the experience of three defeats in a row between 1906 and 1910. At the same time, thanks to the activities of the Proportional Representation Society and in contrast to continental Europe, the single transferable vote had clearly established itself as the method of proportional representation that was most widely contemplated as an alternative to the existing system.

Indeed, Asquith's decision in 1908 to appoint the Royal Commission on Systems of Election to which James Parker Smith gave evidence in 1909 was a clear indication that the future of the system was not being taken for granted in Edwardian Britain. The Commission's eventual report affirmed the view that single-member plurality had not delivered the fairer representation that had been anticipated in 1885. But, rather than recommending the introduction of some form of proportional representation, the Commission proposed instead the use of the alternative vote. The Commission's report made little impact, appearing as it did just three days after the king's death and in the middle of the Lords crisis. But its recommendation in favour of the alternative vote proved

---

[45] M. Kendall and A. Stuart, 'The Law of Cubic Proportions in Election Results', *British Journal of Sociology* (1950); Graham Gudgin and P. J. Taylor, *Seats, Votes and the Spatial Organisation of Elections* (Plon, 1979).

a prescient reminder that there was more than one possible way of reforming the existing system.

A far more serious challenge to the continued use of single-member plurality came from the results of the 1917 Speaker's Conference which recommended the elimination of the single-member plurality system. But, crucially, it did not come out clearly in favour of one alternative rather than another. It unanimously suggested that, as an experiment in proportional representation, the single transferable vote should be used in boroughs that returned three or more MPs and also in the university seats. But for the rest of the country the Conference recommended that MPs should be elected using the alternative vote, though this recommendation was passed by only eleven votes to eight.

The Speaker's Conference proposals were incorporated into a Representation of the People bill. But, in contrast to the rest of the Conference's proposals that had been agreed unanimously, the government allowed MPs a free vote on the proposal for limited use of the single transferable vote as well as on the Conference's more disputed recommendation in respect of the alternative vote. This decision led to a game of constitutional ping-pong between the Commons and the Lords. The House of Commons repeatedly voted against the use of proportional representation in the borough seats and voted to use the alternative vote everywhere. The House of Lords in contrast insisted on some use of proportional representation. First, it proposed that rather than simply being conducted as an experiment in some boroughs, over 90 per cent of Commons seats should be elected that way. Then, it voted for a more limited scheme similar to that proposed by the Speaker's Conference while deleting the alternative vote. Eventually, in order to save the rest of the bill, the Lords accepted the offer of a Royal Commission charged with the task of developing an experiment in the use of proportional representation while the Commons was persuaded to drop its attempts to introduce the alternative vote. Of the proposed reforms, only the use of the single transferable vote in five university constituencies that were to elect more than one MP remained.[46] The existing system thus survived by default.

But, if it proved difficult to get Parliament to change the method by which it itself was elected, it proved easier to introduce innovation

---

[46] The total number of university seats was also increased from nine to fifteen though this fell back to twelve again following the creation of the Irish Free State, a change that also reduced the number of multi-member university constituencies from five to four.

elsewhere in the inter-war period, especially where new institutions were being created. In 1918 the single transferable vote (STV) was introduced for elections to local education authorities in Scotland and in 1919 for all local elections in Ireland.[47] Then the Government of Ireland Act 1920 provided for the use of STV in the two new home rule Parliaments that were envisaged by that Act in the belief that this would help protect the position of minority communities on the island.[48] As a result, the Westminster Parliament bequeathed STV to both the new Irish Free State and the devolved Parliament in the North. Stormont, however, then promptly abandoned the use of STV in Northern Irish local elections in 1922 and for itself in 1929.

Meanwhile, so far as the Commons itself was concerned, the issue of electoral reform reasserted itself in the wake of the indecisive result of the 1923 election. In 1924 the Liberal Party, the Asquithian branch of which had in 1922 become the first party to propose proportional representation in an election manifesto,[49] presented a bill for the introduction of proportional representation. However, it failed to secure Labour as well as Conservative backing. But, after the 1929 election Labour once again found itself dependent on Liberal support to remain in office and, following an inconclusive Conference on Electoral Reform, introduced a bill that provided for the use of the alternative vote everywhere.[50] Once again the Lords demonstrated its aversion to the alternative vote by attempting to limit its introduction to the larger boroughs. But in the event the bill was lost with the collapse of MacDonald's Labour government in August 1931. So, for a second time the status quo survived by default.

So far as the Commons is concerned, the electoral system was never to get so close to being changed again. Indeed, in 1948 single-member plurality finally became the only route to becoming an MP as the last

---

[47] Scottish education authorities were abolished in 1928, their responsibilities being taken over by county councils. As in Ireland, the use of STV helped ensure representation for the religious minority. See Enid Lakeman and James Lambert, *Voting in Democracies* (Faber, 1955).

[48] Some limited provision for the use of STV had also been included in the Government of Ireland Act 1914 which was not implemented following the outbreak of war.

[49] Though the party failed to repeat the proposal in its 1923 manifesto, probably because of the continuing reluctance of Lloyd George, who by then had rejoined his forces with Asquith, to back the idea. See Jenifer Hart, *Proportional Representation: Critics of the British Electoral System, 1820–1945* (Clarendon Press, 1992).

[50] To facilitate this the remaining two-member seats would be divided while the university seats would be abolished.

double-member seats together with the university seats were abolished. But the debate about proportional representation re-emerged following the outcome of the two 1974 elections. Neither of those two elections produced a clear overall majority while the third party vote was the highest since 1929. Particularly influential was a report of a commission brought together by the Hansard Society and chaired by Lord Blake which recommended the use of a variant of the electoral system used in West Germany known as the additional member system.[51] An important feature of this system was that it still allowed a significant proportion of MPs to be elected by single-member plurality, thereby making it appear a less radical break with the past. The report's recommendation helped transform the debate about electoral reform in Britain, for no longer was it assumed that the only alternative to the existing system was the single transferable vote.

But, equally important, four defeats in a row between 1979 and 1992 saw new interest in electoral reform within the Labour Party. The party established a commission chaired by Lord Plant to re-examine the issue. The commission failed to agree on a recommendation for an electoral system for the Commons but its report and the associated debate within the party was enough to persuade John Smith, then Labour leader, to commit his party to holding a referendum on electoral reform.[52] The 1997 Labour government under Tony Blair came to office retaining that commitment though the referendum was to be preceded by the creation of a commission charged with the task of establishing which alternative system should be put before the public in the referendum. That commission, under Lord Jenkins, proposed a variant of the additional member system under which 80–85 per cent of MPs would be elected using the alternative vote while the remaining 15–20 per cent would be county-wide top-up members.[53] This new system could hardly be described as proportional and was evidently designed to be a minimal change that the Labour government might be persuaded to swallow. In the event the government opted not to hold its promised referendum during its first term of office. Meanwhile, some of its leading lights

---

[51] Lord Blake, chair, *Report of the Hansard Society Commission on Electoral Reform* (Hansard Society, 1976).

[52] Lord Plant, chair, *Report of the Working Party on Electoral Systems* (Labour Party, 1993).

[53] Lord Jenkins, chair, *The Report of the Independent Commission on the Voting System*, Cm 4090 (Stationery Office, 1999).

floated the idea of holding a referendum on introducing the alternative vote rather than the scheme proposed by Lord Jenkins.[54]

But, if the renewed interest in electoral reform failed yet again to penetrate the House of Commons, then, as in the 1920s, it did percolate through elsewhere. Ireland again led the way. The outbreak of the Troubles in 1969 persuaded the UK government to find structures that would accommodate the political aspirations of the province's nationalist minority. One of these, just as it had been in the 1920s, was electoral reform. As a result, the single transferable vote became the norm in the province's elections in the last thirty years of the century. In 1973 a Northern Ireland Assembly was elected using STV, but the resulting body collapsed the following year. At the same time STV was also reintroduced for local government elections in Northern Ireland. STV was again used to elect another assembly in 1982 but this also ran into the sands in 1986. In 1996 yet another system of proportional representation—a two-tier closed party list system—was used to elect a Peace Forum, a body charged with establishing a new constitutional framework for the province. This forum eventually lead to the successful negotiation of the Belfast Agreement and the creation in 1998 of yet another devolved assembly for the province, elected once again by STV.

But electoral innovation was far from confined to Northern Ireland. In 1977 the then Labour government, lacking an overall majority and dependent on the Liberals for support, gave MPs a free vote on a proposal to use a regional open party list system of proportional representation in direct elections to the European Parliament. However, insufficient Labour MPs supported the measure and single-member plurality was used instead in the first four rounds of European elections held between 1979 and 1994 (except in Northern Ireland where a three-member STV seat was created). But, when Labour returned to power in 1997, then, following the recommendations of the Plant Commission, it introduced a closed regional party list system for the direct elections held in 1999.

The introduction of devolution to Scotland and Wales saw yet further electoral change. The first devolution proposals, passed by Parliament in the 1970s but not implemented following their failure to secure the necessary endorsement in referendums held in 1979, envisaged the use of the plurality rule although the Lords did attempt to introduce proportional representation for the Scottish Assembly. But by the time Labour returned to power in 1997 it had been persuaded, primarily as a

[54] Peter Mandelson and Roger Liddle, *The Blair Revolution* (Faber, 1996).

result of negotiations in the 1990s with the Liberal Democrats in the Scottish Constitutional Convention, that the new devolved bodies to which it was now committed should be elected by proportional representation.[55] But rather than STV the system introduced in the first devolved elections in both Scotland and Wales in 1999 was a variant of the additional member system, a further indication of the influence of the 1976 Hansard Society report. Equally, an additional member system was used to elect the first members of the Greater London Assembly in 2000 while a variant of the alternative vote, known as the supplementary vote, was used to elect the capital's first directly elected mayor. Meanwhile, at the century's end the new devolved administrations in Scotland and Wales were both contemplating the introduction of some form of proportional representation for local government elections.[56] Westminster's continued use of the plurality rule was in danger of becoming the exception rather than the rule.

But, how do we account for the survival of the plurality rule in elections to the House of Commons? There can be no doubt that perceptions of party interest played a key role. From the 1920s until towards the end of the century at least, there seemed little doubt where each party's interest lay. By 1924 it was evident that Labour was managing to replace the Liberals as the principal opposition to the Conservatives, while the latter had demonstrated to their own satisfaction their ability to win elections under the mass franchise. In short, both Labour and the Conservatives could look forward to the prospect of periods of power. So, by the time that the Liberals made their first serious attempt in 1924 to introduce proportional representation they had lost all chance of persuading any more than a handful of members of the other two parties to join them in support. Proportional representation had come to be seen purely to be a Liberal cause.[57] Thereafter, Labour and the Conservatives only wavered in their support for the current system when their prospects for power appeared to be in question. This happened to the Conservatives after October 1974 when they had lost four elections out of five and, as we have already noted, to Labour in the 1990s when they lost four elections in a row. In both cases, however, eventual restoration to office unsurprisingly helped restore faith in the current system.

[55] Scottish Constitutional Convention, *Scotland's Parliament: Scotland's Right* (COSLA, 1995).
[56] R. Kerley, chair, *Report of the Renewing Local Democracy Working Group* (Scottish Executive, 2000).
[57] Butler, *The British Electoral System*; and Andrew Chadwick, *Augmenting Democracy: Political Movements and Constitutional Reform during the Rise of Labour, 1900–1924* (Ashgate, 1996).

But, at the end of the First World War when electoral reform came closest to being implemented, matters were far less clear cut, as evidenced by the fact that all of the divisions on the subject cut across party lines.[58] The complex manoeuvring surrounding the 1917 Speaker's Conference and the Representation of the People Act 1918 can only be understood by bearing in mind three complexities that can arise when members of a party consider what might be in their interest. First, sometimes politicians fail to perceive what is in their interest, not least because such calculations may well be surrounded by considerable uncertainty about what the future will bring. Second, what is in a party's interest may depend on whether it is trying to maximise its chances of winning or minimise the dangers of its losing. And, third, different sections of the same party may well have different interests.

Misperception and uncertainty certainly surrounded the decisions made in 1917–18. Many Liberals either failed to understand how the single transferable vote worked at all, and even if they did they clearly failed to appreciate the calamity that was about to befall them. They still had, after all, the victories of 1906 and 1910 to lull them into a false sense of security. As Lloyd George admitted to C. P. Scott in 1925, 'Someone ought to have come to me in 1918 and gone into the whole matter. I was not converted then.'[59] Indeed, he had allowed himself to become ill disposed to reform simply because it would cost the Liberals seats in Wales.[60] Lloyd George's failure to appreciate the importance of electoral reform was one thing at least that he shared in common with his rival Asquith who remarked in the Commons in 1917: 'The matter is not one which excites my passions, and I am not sure it even arouses any very ardent enthusiasm.'[61] Indeed Asquith failed to vote in any of the key votes on the electoral system in 1917–18. Meanwhile, many Liberal MPs simply took a dislike to proportional representation from the moment that the Unionist-dominated House of Lords expressed its support for it.

In any case Liberal MPs had in front of them the possibility of an even bigger benefit, the alternative vote. This method of election had had its attractions for many Liberals and Labour supporters ever since Labour's emergence at the beginning of the century. The two parties had come to accommodate each other by forming a secret electoral pact in

---

[58] Bogdanor, *The People and the Party System*; Martin Pugh, *Electoral Reform in War and Peace 1906–18* (Routledge & Kegan Paul, 1978).

[59] Trevor Wilson, *The Political Diaries of C. P. Scott, 1911–1928* (Collins, 1970), pp. 484–5.

[60] Pugh, *Electoral Reform in War and Peace.*

[61] HC Deb., vol. 95, col. 1169, 4 July 1917.

which each stood down for the other in some constituencies so that the Conservatives would not win on a split vote. Introducing the alternative vote would allow both parties to stand where they wanted without running the danger of handing the seat to the Conservatives. This argument assumed of course that Liberal supporters would give their second preference vote overwhelmingly to Labour and vice versa.

It was an argument that many Unionists accepted, and it explains why they opposed the introduction of the alternative vote. But, even within Labour and Liberal ranks, the alternative vote could seem a two-edged sword. For Liberals the potential problem was that it might encourage more Labour candidates to stand (as indeed proved to be the case when it appeared that the system would be used in 1918). Better perhaps to keep the infant under control than give it a lifeline to independence. This at least in part explains why the Liberals made no attempt to implement the recommendation of the Royal Commission on Systems of Election in 1910 to introduce the alternative vote. Meanwhile, so far as Labour was concerned it was not clear that the party needed Liberal help to win working-class seats. The alternative vote might instead make it more difficult for Labour to supplant the Liberals as the main opposition to the Conservatives.

In short, whether or not the alternative vote was in the Liberals' or Labour's interests depended on whether they wanted to maximise their prospects of winning or minimise the danger that they might lose. The alternative vote might help avoid handing victory to the Conservatives but it could make it more difficult for either party to win a majority on its own. Moreover, its introduction was also associated with uncertainty. While it might have appeared likely at the beginning of the century that Liberals would favour Labour with their second preferences as well as vice versa, there was of course no guarantee that this would remain the case. Certainly there seems little reason to believe that this is what would have happened during much of the second half of the century if the alternative vote had been in place then.[62] Even so, it was striking that as well as being resurrected in 1930 the alternative vote was advocated once more as a means of helping to keep the Conservatives out of power

---

[62] Butler, *The British General Election of 1951*; David Butler, *The British General Election of 1955* (Macmillan, 1955); David Butler and Richard Rose, *The British General Election of 1959* (Macmillan, 1960); Butler, *The British Electoral System*; Heath *et al.*, *Understanding Political Change*, p. 292.

when Labour and Liberal Democrat relations were relatively warm once again at the very end of the century.

But confusion and doubt about what was in their parties' best interests were not confined to Labour and Liberal ranks in 1917–18. They were just as prevalent amongst Unionists where different wings of the party had very different views about what was in their long-term interest. Prior to the war Unionist free traders had developed an interest in STV because they hoped it would mean their party would put up representatives from both sides of the argument in each constituency, whereas with predominantly single-member seats free traders were being denied nominations.[63] But by 1917–18 there was also a clear difference between the perceptions of Unionist MPs and those of their colleagues in the Lords. Unionist MPs were increasingly confident of being able to win the next election on the back of a wave of war-induced 'khaki' patriotism. They thus saw little need for the introduction of proportional representation even though they might have hoped to profit from the minority representation it would have provided in many boroughs. Rather, they were concerned that the larger constituencies that would be needed to implement proportional representation in the larger boroughs would curtail the opportunities for exercise of the business vote.[64]

The perspective of Unionist peers was rather different. They were more inclined to look at the party's apparent prospects beyond the next election and were still concerned about the possible impact of the expansion of the franchise on their party's prospects in the long term. Meanwhile, peers also had an interest in avoiding the election of another radical government backed by a majority in the Commons. Such a government might be inclined to launch a further attack on the powers of the Lords just as the last one had done in 1910. Moreover, the Lords might even find its influence enhanced if no single party had a majority in the Commons, as would seem more likely to be the case if STV were introduced. But what Unionist peers did share with their colleagues in the Commons was an abhorrence of the alternative vote and, despite the passage of the Parliament Act, in practice they had the power to block it.

---

[63] Pugh, *Electoral Reform in War and Peace*.

[64] Pugh, *Electoral Reform in War and Peace*, p. 158. No voter was allowed to vote twice in the same constituency so the business franchise could be exercised only in a constituency where the business owner was not also a resident. The larger constituencies were, the less likely was this possibility to arise.

Some of the uncertainties surrounding the debate about electoral reform in 1917–18 were again present towards the end of the century when, as we have seen, Labour once more toyed with reform for the Commons and actually introduced varieties of proportional representation for European and devolved elections. For the most part these decisions were made in opposition when the party's faith in being able to win under the single-member plurality system had been shaken. The party certainly did not expect to secure the record majority it did in 1997. Given the difficulties it had faced in securing the passage of devolution legislation with little or no majority in the 1970s, it thus anticipated that it would need the support of the Liberal Democrats to secure passage of its second attempt. The price for securing that support was accepting that the new institutions should be elected by proportional representation. In any case, in Scotland at least, introducing proportional representation had the advantage of making it less likely that the nationalists would ever win an overall majority. In short, the new system was also a way of minimising the dangers to Labour of losing.[65]

But it would be a mistake to suggest that the debate about electoral reform in twentieth-century Britain was simply determined by considerations of party advantage. Intellectual argument about the impact of the system had a role too. Part of the reason for the renewed interest in electoral reform after 1974 was a belief that Britain's system of adversarial government was at least partly responsible for the country's economic difficulties in the 1960s and 1970s.[66] Others have criticised the system for exaggerating the country's regional and class differences.[67] But the kernel of the debate throughout the century was an argument about the role of elections in Britain's democracy. Looking at this debate we can see that, although considerations of place still formally played as important a role in the translation of votes into seats at the end of century as it had done at its beginning, much of the justification for the electoral system came to rest on arguments about the benefits that it had for the country's political system as whole.

As we noted earlier, James Parker Smith had pointed out as early as 1909 that the electoral system seemed to exaggerate the winning party's

[65] John Curtice, 'Why the Additional Member System has Won Out in Scotland', *Representation* (1996).
[66] David Stout, 'Incomes Policy and the Costs of the Adversary System', and Tom Wilson, 'The Economic Costs of the Adversary System', in S. E. Finer (ed.), *Adversary Politics and Electoral Reform* (Anthony Wigram, 1975).
[67] Bogdanor, *The People and the Party System.*

lead in seats. This of course made it quite likely that one party would have an overall majority in the Commons. On this apparent quality of the system an important intellectual case could be developed.[68] What mattered most about elections was not that votes were translated proportionately or fairly into seats so that the House of Commons represented a microcosm of the nation. Rather, elections should determine who wins office and then ensure that whoever holds office provides 'strong' rather than 'weak' government. And, it was argued, these desirable qualities are best provided by an electoral system that delivers a clear overall majority to the winning party even if it does not have a majority of the votes, while leaving open to the principal opposition party the prospect that it would be treated equally favourably should it secure a plurality of the votes in future.

Variants of this argument were used to defend the plurality system from the very beginning of the century. They can be found in the evidence given to the Royal Commission in 1909, during the debates in 1917–18,[69] and thereafter in discussion of the bills on electoral reform that were introduced during the 1920s. They acquired major intellectual reinforcement after the Second World War following the rediscovery of Parker Smith's cube law by David Butler immediately prior to the 1950 general election.[70] Butler's work did much to refute the argument that the relationship between seats and votes under single-member plurality was simply the product of 'chance'.

One of the key assumptions of this argument was of course that power alternated between the two largest parties. Yet in Ireland the deep cleavage between unionists and nationalists meant there was little or no prospect of such alternation. Nationalists would always predominate in the south, unionists in the north. Even the House of Commons recognised that what was desirable in these circumstances was a system, such as STV, that guaranteed the minority some representation. In fact, the abolition of STV in elections to the Stormont Parliament in 1929 had relatively little impact on the balance of unionist and nationalist representation because nationalists predominated in enough constituencies to ensure that they were represented in approximate proportion to their share of the Northern Irish electorate. What the change did do was to ensure that

---

[68] Curtice, 'The British Electoral System'.
[69] Hart, *Proportional Representation*, pp. 157, 193.
[70] Butler, *The British General Election of 1951*; Kendall and Stuart, 'The Law of Cubic Proportions'.

unionist representation did not fragment.[71] In short, when applied in the circumstances of Northern Ireland single-member plurality failed to deliver either alternating government or exaggerated majorities.[72]

But in practice even across the UK as a whole the record of the plurality system during the twentieth century has not lived up to the claims that have been made by its advocates. The first requirement for a system of alternating two-party government is that voters should be discouraged from voting for third parties,[73] and that when third parties do win votes they should secure little reward. Of the twenty-six general elections held in twentieth-century Britain, in only just over half, that is fourteen, did the two largest parties garner 80 per cent or more of the votes cast. True, the failure of this to happen between 1918 and 1929 could be accounted for by the fact that the party system was in transition from a Conservative/Liberal duopoly to a Conservative/Labour one. But the failure of the two largest parties to hit the 80 per cent target in all but one election from 1974 onwards cannot be explained away so simply.

The system did of course consistently give the Liberals little reward from 1924 onwards. But other third parties whose vote was geographically evenly concentrated had much less difficulty securing seats in proportion to votes. Prior to the First World War Irish Nationalists never won more than 2.5 per cent of the UK vote. But, aided by Ireland's over-representation, they managed to win no fewer than 12 per cent of the seats. Sinn Fein received a similar bonus in 1918. Equally, Northern Ireland's principal political parties had no difficulty in securing more or less proportionate representation after the divorce of Northern Irish parties from the mainland party system in 1974. Plaid Cymru ended the century over-represented in the Commons despite winning less than 0.5 per cent of the UK-wide vote. The Scottish Nationalists too were able to maintain at least a minimal presence in the Commons continuously from 1967 onwards.

The second requirement for a system of alternating two-party government is that it should normally provide the government with a safe

---

[71] Vernon Bogdanor, *Devolution in the United Kingdom* (Oxford University Press, 1999); John Curtice and Michael Steed, 'Electoral Choice and the Production of Government: The Changing Operation of the Electoral System in the United Kingdom since 1955', *British Journal of Political Science* (1982).

[72] Meanwhile one of the arguments against the use of single-member plurality in the Scottish Parliament and Welsh Assembly was that in both countries the system would appear more likely to result in Labour hegemony rather than alternating government.

[73] Maurice Duverger, *Political Parties* (Methuen, 1964).

overall majority. Yet this again was delivered in only just over half the elections held. No party managed to secure an overall majority on five occasions (both 1910 elections, 1923, 1929 and February 1974) while on five other occasions the government had a majority of fewer than twenty-five (1950, 1951, 1964, October 1974 and 1992). Safe overall majorities are better described as a tendency of twentieth-century British elections rather than a norm.

Detailed analysis of the operation of the electoral system in the second half of the twentieth century has revealed why overall majorities were only a tendency rather than a norm. Between 1955 and 1987 a growing bipolarisation of party support between the north and the south of the country, and between urban and rural areas, meant that the number of seats that were marginal between Labour and the Conservatives actually halved. Even thereafter the figure only recovered somewhat.[74] As a result while the cube law might once have been a reasonable summary of the exaggerative qualities of the electoral system, this was not the case after 1974. No longer could the system be relied upon to turn small leads in votes into large leads in seats. In short, the exaggerative quality of single-member plurality was shown by these trends to be contingent on the geography of party support rather than being an inherent feature of the system.

A third requirement of any system that claims to put the power to determine who holds office in the hands of voters is that it should deliver most seats to the party that wins most votes. Yet on five occasions this was manifestly not the case. On four occasions the Conservatives were the apparent losers. In both 1910 elections the Liberals won fewer votes than the Conservatives but marginally more seats, while in both 1929 and February 1974 Labour won fewer votes than the Conservatives but more seats. The roles were reversed on just one occasion, in 1951, when Labour won more votes but the Conservatives secured an overall majority of seats. True, on four of these occasions the apparently anomalous result could be accounted for by the fact that one party fought fewer seats than the other and/or was caused by unopposed returns. However, no such rationalisation can be provided for the outcome in February 1974.

[74] Curtice and Steed, 'Proportionality and Exaggeration', Curtice and Steed, 'Analysis', in David Butler and Dennis Kavanagh, *The British General Election of 1987* (Macmillan, 1988); Curtice and Steed, 'The Results Analysed', in David Butler and Dennis Kavanagh, *The British General Election of 1997* (Macmillan, 1997); and Curtice and Steed, 'Neither Responsible nor Accountable'.

In any event the failure of the two main protagonists to fight every seat at all elections simply raises another difficulty with the traditional defence of Britain's electoral system. If elections are intended to be an opportunity to choose between alternative governments then every voter ought to have the opportunity to express his or her preference. But it was only from 1945 onwards that both main parties routinely fought all or nearly all the seats, thereby giving all or nearly all voters the chance to express their views on the merits of the two principal candidates for governmental office. Even then Labour never fought all the constituencies in Northern Ireland.

Concern that the system could not be relied upon to treat both main parties equally even if they did fight all of the seats returned after the 1997 election. At that election Labour's vote was more efficiently distributed than that of the Conservatives. Together with imbalances in the size of constituencies (see above), differences in level of turnout and the fact that the Conservatives were more vulnerable to Liberal Democrat challenges, this pattern generated a clear bias in Labour's favour. This bias made a significant contribution to Labour's overall majority of 179. More importantly, if it persisted, there was a clear prospect that in future the Conservatives could win more votes than Labour but end up with significantly fewer seats.[75]

So, when it comes to the translation of votes into seats, place has continued to play an important role in twentieth-century elections. Formally, British elections continue to be 650 or so entirely separate local contests. And in practice the relationship between seats and votes across the country as a whole depends on where votes are won as well as how many are won. But the most important justification of the single-member plurality system has come to be about how it supposedly facilitates a system of alternating two-party government for the country as a whole. Moreover, in the second half of the century at least, British elections were fought as national contests with the two main parties contesting seats almost everywhere. Even so, as the century drew to a close it was still far from clear whether the system was a sufficiently reliable instrument for delivering a system of alternating two-party government.[76]

[75] Curtice and Steed, in Butler and Kavanagh, *The British General Election of 1997*; Curtice and Steed, 'Neither Responsible nor Accountable'; and Rossiter, 'Changing Biases in the Operation of the United Kingdom's Electoral System'.
[76] We might also note, for example, that government changed hands before the electorate had their say on two occasions in peacetime (1905 and 1931) as well as during both world wars.

Conclusion

At the beginning of the twentieth century a majority of Britain's adult population were denied the vote while a favoured few could vote more than once. Those who could vote did so in unequally sized constituencies. And none of the parties fought anything like all of the constituencies. Place made a difference to who could vote, the value of a vote, and for whom one could vote.

By the century's end the picture was very different. The franchise was based on the principle of 'one person, one vote' and tried to ensure that even those with no address at all retained the right to vote. The drawing of constituencies increasingly reflected the principle of 'one vote, one value', with many of the constraints and rules that resulted in unequally sized constituencies gradually being eased. And elections had come to be regarded as national contests where, in Great Britain at least, all the parties fought all of the seats and voters were able to determine who governed.

Three crucial decisions were taken during the course of the century that stand out as being the most important in shaping the changing character of Britain's electoral system. The first was the expansion of the franchise such that nearly every adult aged over twenty-one had the right to vote. The second was the decision to retain single-member plurality as the mechanism for translating seats into votes. And the third was the development of a system of regular non-partisan redistricting.

The expansion of the franchise in 1918 turned Britain into a mass democracy, thereby finishing the process of franchise reform that had begun in 1832. Although there remained room for some significant argument about how the mass adult franchise should be implemented, the principle that the right to vote was one that should be accorded to most citizens was never contested. Many of the subsequent more minor decisions that were made about the franchise in the rest of the century were simply about how best to put that principle into effect.

The decision to retain the single-member plurality system in 1918 meanwhile did much to determine what kind of mass democracy Britain became, that is a system that rested on the merits of alternating single-party government. True the reality did not always live up to the rhetoric but there is no doubt that single-party governments would have been at most rare events if a system of proportional representation had been in place.[77] Meanwhile the introduction of a regular non-partisan system of boundary review in 1944 was essential if citizens were to have the appearance of an equal say in the future government of the country.

Yet by the end of the century the issue of the future of Britain's electoral system was the subject of considerable debate and dispute, more so indeed than had been the case in the middle of the century. The ability of single-member plurality to continue to deliver a fair system of alternating government was in doubt. Its exaggerative quality had been shown to be variable, its ability to stop third parties winning seats uncertain and, despite an apparently increasingly fair system of boundary drawing, its treatment of the two largest parties was not guaranteed to be fair. Democracy might have become a principle from which few in Britain would dissent, but what it should mean in practice was still a subject of lively constitutional debate.

Bibliography

The most accessible summary of and commentary on the whole range of electoral law and regulation in late-twentieth-century Britain is R. Blackburn, *The Electoral System in Britain* (Macmillan, 1995). It does not, however, cover the significant changes made at the very end of the century. Facts and figures about election outcomes are to be found in C. Raillings and M. Thrasher, *British Electoral Facts, 1832–1999* (Parliamentary Research Services, 2000). For details of the Third Reform Act franchise see N. Blewett, 'The Parliamentary Franchise in the UK, 1885–1918', *Past and Present* (1965). For the development of the franchise between 1918 and the middle of the century, see D. Butler, *The Electoral System in Britain since 1918*, 2nd edn (Oxford University Press, 1963). The process of boundary drawing throughout the twentieth century is well described in D. Rossiter, R. Johnston and C. Pattie, *The Boundary Commissions: Redrawing the United Kingdom's Map of Parliamentary Constituencies* (Manchester University Press, 1999). The political manoeuvring about the voting system in the period up to 1918 is extensively analysed in M. Pugh, *Electoral Reform in War and Peace 1906–18* (Routledge & Kegan Paul, 1978), and for the period thereafter in Butler, *Electoral System in Britain since 1918*. The implications of the changes in the way that single-member plurality operated in the second half of the century are discussed in John Curtice, 'The British Electoral System: Fixture without Foundation', in

---

[77] This however is not true if the alternative vote had been in place, Butler, *The British Electoral System*.

Dennis Kavanagh (ed.), *Electoral Politics* (Clarendon Press, 1992). Meanwhile the debate about electoral reform in the first two-thirds of the century is well summarised in Vernon Bogdanor, *The People and the Party System* (Cambridge University Press, 1981).

13.
The Demise of Local Government
MARTIN LOUGHLIN

In 1888, Gladstone observed of local government that it was hard to find a subject in which there was 'greater difficulty in bringing into focus such a multitude of topics, so necessary to be connected and yet presenting so many difficulties in establishing a connection'.[1] Gladstone's warning is one which the most astute commentators on local government have taken to heart.[2] But, although one must tread carefully, the implicit injunction to stick to the highways of thick description provides little assistance if an assessment is to be made of the constitutional role of local government in the British system.[3] The impact of twentieth-century developments on local government cannot be appraised unless connections are drawn and generalisations formulated. Nevertheless, I start with Gladstone's sound observation not only because I shall sketch on a broad canvas but also because I intend to promote a radical thesis.

My thesis is that the cumulative impact of twentieth-century developments has resulted in a disintegration of the constitutional tradition of local government. To some, this argument might seem untenable; after all, local authorities exercised a broad range of governmental functions

[1] Cited in C. H. Wilson, 'The Foundations of Local Government', in Wilson (ed.), *Essays on Local Government* (Blackwell, 1948), p. 2.
[2] See, for example, J. A. G. Griffith, *Central Departments and Local Authorities* (Allen & Unwin, 1966), p. 1: 'The working relationship between central departments and local authorities in England and Wales can be regarded in terms which are formal, informal, statutory, non-statutory, legal, extra-legal, financial, official, personal, political, functional, tragical-comical-historical-pastoral. Seneca cannot be too heavy nor Plautus too light. Any generalization evokes shouts of protest. Every example can be shown in some way to be unrepresentative and ill-chosen ... Everything is true about local government and so nothing is true.'
[3] The tradition of local government I examine is essentially English, though many of the main principles and practices of the modern statutory system are shared throughout England, Wales and Scotland. The role of local authorities in Northern Ireland during the twentieth century, being bound up with more basic issues concerning the governance of the province, defies simple comparison.

throughout the twentieth century and, notwithstanding the shifts which were effected during the century, arguably remain major institutions of governance. Even if it is conceded that local authorities have lost some of their autonomy over the last one hundred years, others might argue that this is part of the general ebb and flow of the system; since local government may be rejuvenated in the twenty-first century, this contention therefore cannot be sustained. And there are those who will claim that this thesis can be maintained only by one who is seeped in that brand of sentimentality exemplified by the writings of Joshua Toulmin Smith.[4] I hope to distance my position both from those of romantic sentimentalism and technocractic functionalism. My thesis can be sustained only if we take seriously the injunction to assess local government from a constitutional perspective, and for that purpose an understanding of the nineteenth-century reformation in local government is as important as an appreciation of the character of the twentieth-century settlement. Whether this constitutional perspective retains much value today requires further discussion, but one which I reserve for the concluding section of the chapter.

The constitutional question

At the end of the nineteenth century the British still expressed considerable satisfaction over the state of their constitution. Through force of circumstance, other nations had come to rely on pieces of paper to define and allocate the functions of government; the British, by contrast, could congratulate themselves on the fact that their constitution was 'a living Constitution', a constitution 'that is in actual work'.[5] While others had been obliged to construct their constitutions, 'that of England has been allowed to grow'.[6] The British constitution remained in 'a state of constant development',[7] able continuously to adapt to changing circumstances without the need for formal changes in structure. The British constitution was therefore a distinctively political constitution. According to British sensibilities, the business of governing is a thoroughly practical activity,

---

[4] See, for example, J. Toulmin Smith, *Government by Commissions Illegal and Pernicious* (Sweet, 1849).
[5] Walter Bagehot, *The English Constitution* (1867), ed. R. H. S. Crossman (Collins, 1963), p. 267.
[6] Sidney Low, *The Governance of England* (T. Fisher Unwin, 1904), pp. 5–6.
[7] Ibid., p. 12.

one in which the craft of being able to set institutions to work should never be overlooked in favour of rationalist pretensions of institutional design.

Within this evolutionary political constitution the value of local government was universally acknowledged. When Edward Jenks noted in 1894 that 'England is pre-eminently the country of local government'[8] his remark was commonplace. It expressed the belief that the existence of local institutions exercising the responsibility of 'good rule and government' of their areas[9] was built into the foundations of authority of the British state. Commenting on the nineteenth-century reforms which had placed local government on a statutory foundation, Josef Redlich in his magisterial work, *Local Government in England*, noted that 'the ancient sub-divisions of government have not been sacrificed to system'.[10] Care had been taken to preserve 'local traditions and historical associations at the expense of scientific geography and, to a certain extent, of administrative convenience'.[11] The system of local government was complicated precisely because it remained rooted in historic communities rather than departments based on rational principles. The character of the nineteenth-century reforms, to Redlich's mind, constituted 'an expression of the English idea of the state as an association or federation of self-governing communities'.[12] Local institutions reflecting historic communities and exercising a voice at the centre through the workings of the parliamentary system were a central aspect of British constitutional arrangements.

One hundred years on and such claims seem fanciful. Redlich's themes express many of the issues with which those seeking to reform local government during the twentieth century were obliged to grapple. But although local authorities remain important agencies—being charged with the responsibility of ensuring the provision of major services relating to education, transport, housing, welfare and the environment—the notion that the institutions of local government at the beginning of the twenty-first century express basic constitutional values seems almost incomprehensible. The standard texts on constitutional law and practice continue to include some sketch of local

[8] Edward Jenks, *An Outline of English Local Government* (1894), 5th edn (Methuen, 1921), p. 9.
[9] Municipal Corporations Act 1835, s. 90; Local Government Act 1888, s. 16.
[10] Josef Redlich, *Local Government in England*, ed. Francis W. Hirst (Macmillan, 1903), vol. 2, p. 9.
[11] Ibid.
[12] Ibid.

government. But beyond some inchoate idea that the sharing of executive power is a positive value, few—if any—manage to convey a sense of how local government fits into the constitutional order of things. Local authorities are now generally conceived as being part of an extensive administrative system in which, notwithstanding a nod in the direction of local accountability through periodic elections, the primary lines of control and accountability run to central government. How and why did local government lose its constitutional role?

In addressing this question, we must unravel some of those many connections which Gladstone recognised as contributing to the formation of the institution of local government. This account must be as much concerned with developments affecting the centre as the localities. Consequently, in addition to the issues of local government areas, authorities and functions, changes that have been effected in the role of government within society and of the manner of its authorisation should also be considered. Of course, the scale and functions of government today are of a different order to those undertaken at the end of the nineteenth century. Further, with the institutionalisation of representative democracy and the emergence of party government in the twentieth century, the practices of aristocratic rule, bolstered in the nineteenth century by those of local commercial oligarchies, and which sustained the ancient compact between local government and the centre have been severely strained. But the consequences of this transformation in the role of government have often been obscured by the tendency of twentieth-century constitutional scholars to address the impact of these changes rather elliptically, thereby causing observers to complain that 'many English scholars understate their constitution, seem to make a particular point of not being helpful, and leave the alien reader with the feeling that the British constitution really amounts to the fact that, in the final analysis, the British people are clever and fine people who know how to go about in politics'.[13] Unless we bear in mind the notion that a constitution implies limitations on what government is able to achieve and restraints on how it may achieve its objectives, we are unlikely to appreciate the impact of twentieth-century developments on the constitutional role of local government.

---

[13] Giovanni Sartori, 'Constitutionalism: A Preliminary Discussion', *American Political Science Review* (1962), 854.

The ancient tradition

The claim to a distinctive tradition of local government is rooted ultimately in one simple historical fact: that the institutions of local government, rather than being centrally constructed prefectures, are based on the territorial divisions of ancient communities. This has meant not only that the institutions represent the interests, but also claim the allegiance, of their areas. And this point was one which did not fail to register with the centre. From the earliest days, the counties and incorporated towns were acknowledged to be the only official territorial divisions of the kingdom and the Crown found it advantageous, not least in preventing the build up of political feudalism, to work within the grain of these historic communities. Justices of the peace, drawn from these areas and appointed by the Crown to discharge governmental responsibilities, were the embodiment of a workable compromise between the centralising tendency of the Crown and the desire to keep alive local institutions.[14] A basic tension between central government and the claims of the localities thus became the characteristic feature of our system, causing Redlich to note that a 'fundamental antithesis between centralisation and "autonomous" decentralisation runs through the whole history of English government and its organisation'.[15]

While the Crown's policy of working with these local institutions is of decisive importance in determining the character of the system of local administration, the constitutional value of local government is largely a consequence of the growth in the power of Parliament. Since parliamentary constituencies were based on these local territorial divisions, membership of the Commons consisted essentially of the representatives of these counties and towns. The ancient divisions had always formed the key units of government for executive, judicial and military purposes. With the growth of Parliament, and in particular the arrangements for parliamentary representation, the localities also had the ability to exercise a powerful legislative voice at the centre over issues affecting their interests.

It is essentially because of the growth in the power of Parliament that there never emerged in Britain a hierarchical and undifferentiated concept of 'administration' through which the central government could

[14] For a concise overview see C. Foster, R. Jackman and M. Perlman, *Local Government Finance in a Unitary State* (Allen & Unwin, 1980), pp. 21–3.
[15] Redlich, *Local Government in England*, vol. 1, p. 12.

exercise an inherent superior jurisdiction over local agencies. It is precisely because local institutions exist not simply as creatures of the Crown but as representations of historic communities within a structure of national laws to which both the Crown and the localities are bound that we are able to call the English inheritance a tradition of local government rather than a system of local administration. And it is because of this tradition of local government that no system of 'administrative law' developed. The common law, as an undivided system of national laws, could not be altered by the Crown alone, but only with the consent of the people expressed in Parliament. The Crown-in-Parliament, as a supreme legislature, came to exercise absolute authority over internal administration.

The Act of Parliament thus became the form through which was framed, not only all new laws but also all the ordinances which regulate the conduct of administrative activity. When new needs made themselves felt through the demand for new services in local areas, these demands took the form of petitions to Parliament. Parliament preserved control over this jurisdiction primarily through the private bill procedure, in which bills presented on the petition of local bodies were deliberated upon mainly by the representatives of the localities concerned. When dealing with matters of internal local administration the Commons often felt itself 'to be scarcely more than a legislative "clearing house" of the several Courts of Quarter Sessions' and the 'Knights of the Shire who sat at Westminster habitually regard themselves as the spokesmen of these Courts, from which they received instructions as to Bills to be promoted, supported, amended or opposed'.[16] Local institutions thus became answerable not solely, or even mainly, to central government, but also to the courts and, ultimately, to Parliament. Consequently, the relationships between the centre and the localities were not primarily worked out through arrangements between central departments and local authorities, but through a network of relationships involving local and central government, Parliament and the courts.

The two defining characteristics of the ancient tradition of local government are the existence of local institutions based on historic communities, which were thus able to forge a strong sense of locality, and the arrangement of providing executive authority to local institutions in the form of statutes, thereby keeping under the control of a Parliament in which the localities were fully represented what in continental systems was the preserve of administrative law functioning under the

---

[16] Sidney and Beatrice Webb, *English Local Government* (Longman, 1922), vol. 4, p. 388.

control of the central authority. But although a tradition of local self-government can be discerned in these arrangements, it would be an error to overstate its significance. These local bodies formed a complex mosaic of parochial, manorial, borough and county institutions, originating in a jumble of local customs, common law, royal charters and Acts of Parliament.[17] The arrangements were haphazard, elitist and often corrupt, and 'the anarchy of local autonomy was heightened by the fact that there was nothing that could be regarded, either in theory or practice, as a system of Local Government'.[18] When faced with the major challenges presented by industrialisation and urbanisation in the nineteenth century they were seen to be hopelessly deficient.

Reformation

New agencies were needed and these—the special bodies such as sewer commissions, improvement commissions and turnpike trusts established under local Acts—threatened to displace the traditional arrangements. The threat was seen most clearly in the poor law reforms of 1834, when responsibility for the administration of the poor law was removed from 15,000 parishes and vested in new units operated by elected boards of guardians assisted by salaried officials and operating in accordance with precise rules and orders laid down by a central board. At this stage, it seemed likely that, although the ancient institutions might continue to represent the locality in a ceremonial sense, new special-purpose bodies operating under central direction would undertake the utilitarian functions of government. What was required, the Benthamites argued, was not veneration of the ancient, complex structure of local government but a simple, clear, understandable, efficient and centralised system.[19]

Nevertheless, radical reform of the system along strict Benthamite lines did not occur. The 'new rich', the industrialists and merchants who found themselves excluded from the county commission of the peace and the municipal corporation, eventually demanded reform of these institutions. The breakthrough came with the Municipal Corporations Act of 1835 which converted the corporations into institutions of government and began to reverse the tendency to split off function after function

[17] See B. Keith-Lucas, *The Unreformed Local Government System* (Croom Helm, 1980).
[18] Webb, *English Local Government*, vol. 4, p. 353.
[19] See N. L. Rosenblum, *Bentham's Theory of the Modern State* (Harvard University Press, 1978), ch. 6.

to special authorities. The 1835 Act established the principle of democracy in local government and restored the principle that a general authority should assume responsibility for the governance of the locality. This process of municipalisation was gradually extended to the other institutions of local government.[20] The Local Government Act of 1888 created elected county councils to undertake the governmental functions previously assigned to the justices in quarter sessions and established the councils as corporate bodies with a constitution and franchise similar to that of the municipal corporation. And with the Local Government Act of 1894, which replaced the ancient system of parish government by vestries with a network of urban and rural district councils, the process of modernisation of the institutions was complete. The nineteenth-century reformation put local government on a statutory foundation. However, 'by its careful patching up and renovation of old areas', Redlich argued that 'Parliament has created a territorial system built on history and consecrated by custom, which is far more valued, and therefore far more valuable, than those mathematical departments into which a centralised government, working from above and guided by purely rational and *a priori* principles, has cut and carved the land of France'.[21]

Although the centre worked with the grain of tradition, the restored local councils possessed few powers to tackle the major problems of industrialisation and urbanisation and new powers could be granted only by central authorisation. Responsibility initially was left with local authorities to take initiative and promote local Acts.[22] Subsequently, permissive legislation was framed; that is, public general legislation which left local authorities free to adopt the powers conferred.[23] But eventually the model of public general legislation which generally empowered, although occasionally also required, authorities to undertake particular tasks was utilised.[24] And with the enactment of public general legislation

[20] See B. Keith-Lucas, *The English Local Government Franchise: A Short History* (Blackwell, 1952).

[21] Redlich, *Local Government in England*, vol. 2, pp. 7–8.

[22] See, for example, Derek Fraser, *Power and Authority in the Victorian City* (Blackwell, 1979), chs 2–4.

[23] See John Prest, *Liberty and Locality: Parliament, Permissive Legislation, and Ratepayers' Democracies in the Nineteenth Century* (Clarendon Press, 1990).

[24] This impetus came about mainly through the public health movement and then later through educational reform: see W. C. Lubenow, *The Politics of Government Growth: Early Victorian Attitudes Toward State Intervention 1833–1848* (David & Charles, 1971), ch. 3 (public health); Redlich, *Local Government in England*, vol. 1, pp. 134–73 (development of a sanitary code); vol. 2, pp. 224–36 (organisation of education).

providing powers and duties to local authorities to provide services, central supervision, which lay at the heart of the poor law reforms,[25] assumed a more prominent position in the general arrangements.

One consequence of this legislative action was that an administrative relationship between the central department and the local authority was established. But the character of this relationship was not a simple one of superior and inferior. The statutory arrangements continued to ensure that the initiative in promoting and developing a service lay with the local authority. No effective method was devised of directing a council to exercise its powers; even the enforcement of duties involved an incredibly cumbersome process which required judicial proceedings to be instigated. So, although local authorities became bound to the central department by many administrative ties, the Local Government Board possessed no general right to issue administrative commands which compelled obedience. The board, Redlich noted, 'is a Board of controls, but not a Board of control'; it is 'not a motor engine; it does not supply power to set in motion the machinery of local government; and in practice the Board takes the initiative even less than the letter of the law might lead one to suppose'.[26]

By the end of the century, local government had been placed on a statutory foundation, with the powers of local authorities being generally contained in public general legislation. Of itself, this implied no great restriction on local autonomy, although those unable to appreciate the relationship between politics and law in British governmental arrangements might wrongly have assumed that local government was a creature of the centre. The real change stemmed mainly from the character of this legislation, three aspects of which might be highlighted. First, because of the need to maintain flexibility in responding to events, local government legislation took the form of framework legislation, and this resulted in central departments acquiring power to put flesh on the skeleton of the primary legislation and thereby influencing the manner in which the general powers of local authorities could actually be exercised. Second, because of the need to rationalise the growing volume of parliamentary

[25] See S. E. Finer, *The Life and Times of Sir Edwin Chadwick* (Methuen, 1952), p. 88: 'the administrative proposals of the [Poor Law] Report are worthy of the highest praise. They have proved the source of nearly all the important developments in English local government, viz. central supervision, central inspection, central audit, a professional local government service controlled by local elective bodies, and the adjustment of areas to administrative exigencies.'

[26] Redlich, *Local Government in England*, vol. 2, pp. 257, 300.

business, petitions for extensions to local powers came to be channelled through central departments and, with the streamlining of private bill procedure through the use of provisional orders, local authorities began to lose their channel of direct access to Parliament. Third, by vesting a range of administrative powers of supervision, the legislation ensured that central departments became a critical factor in local government.

The impact of these changes meant that Parliament became displaced and central government took over supervisory tasks, a trend which was reinforced by a growing differentiation, during the latter half of the nineteenth century, between local authorities and parliamentary constituencies.[27] This shift in the degree of control over local affairs was not inevitable. After the reformation of local government, Parliament could have moved beyond its practice of sanctioning specific grants of power to local authorities and entrusted them with general powers of local government.[28] The refusal to do so reflects the growing impact of a centralising political ethos.

Nevertheless, this centralising tendency should not be misunderstood. Although the language of partnership does not adequately express the relationship between the central authority and local government, it is equally evident that the centre was not authorised, and did not act, strategically to direct local authorities and transform them into its agents. Most of the centre's energies were directed towards defining and patrolling the boundaries of the central–local divide. The centre was much more concerned to limit the incursions of the localities into matters of high politics, especially by limiting the demands of local authorities on the national Exchequer and the money markets, than to give strategic direction to local authorities on the manner in which their tasks should be carried out.[29] The system of central controls which was established was thus much more in the nature of an emerging system of administrative law than one which sought to guide and promote service

---

[27] See Foster, Jackman and Perlman, *Local Government Finance*, pp. 12–13.

[28] Proposals to vest in local authorities a power of general competence were the subject of a number of unsuccessful bills during the 1920s. See W. A. Robson, *The Development of Local Government* (Allen & Unwin, 1931), pp. 206–11. On the question of parliamentary representation, Foster, Jackman and Perlman, *Local Government Finance*, p. 13, speculate that, had there not already been a House of Lords, it is conceivable that Britain could have followed the American model with 'one chamber based on parliamentary representation and the other representing local governments'.

[29] See Christine Bellamy, *Administering Central–Local Relations 1871–1919: The Local Government Board in its Fiscal and Cultural Context* (Manchester University Press, 1988), ch. 6.

development by local government.[30] The central authority saw itself mainly as a checking agency to ensure that the interests of individuals and sectional groups were properly considered and that local majorities did not abuse their powers. This role is manifest in a number of practices including the adoption of the principle of inspectability[31] and in the appellate jurisdiction acquired by the central departments. And this informal system of administrative law was acquiesced in by the judiciary which possessed neither the resources nor adequate working methods to exert effective supervision over local decisions affecting individual interests.[32]

Accommodation

The process of reforming local government which had been set in train during the 1830s did not reach the final stages of completion until the early decades of the twentieth century. The nineteenth-century reforms established the basic structure of modern local government, with single-tier county boroughs forming the urban authorities and the rest of the country being based on a two-tier, country–district division. As a result of these reforms, the Local Government Act 1933 was for the first time able to enact a common set of organisational rules governing all local authorities. The principle of municipalisation—that a single local council rather than a range of special purpose bodies should assume responsibility for all locally provided public services—was extended in the early decades of the twentieth century, notably with the absorption of the school boards in 1902[33] and the administration of the poor law in 1929.[34] By the 1920s, a modern statutory framework for a system of elected, multi-purpose local authorities had been established, although it was not until 1948 that the democratic character of local government was fully

---

[30] See H. W. Arthurs, *'Without the Law': Administrative Justice and Legal Pluralism in Nineteenth-century England* (University of Toronto Press, 1985), ch. 5.

[31] Redlich noted that inspection 'is an invention characteristically English' since it provided the channel through which the centre 'perform[ed] its functions as a guardian of public rights and interests without resorting to the imperative mood' and was 'designed to obtain the advantages of efficiency without the incubus of bureaucracy'. Redlich, *Local Government in England*, vol. 2, pp. 247, 251.

[32] For examples of such acquiesence see *Pasmore* v. *Oswaldtwistle UDC* [1898] AC 997; *Board of Education* v. *Rice* [1911] AC 179; *Local Government Board* v. *Arlidge* [1915] AC 120. See W. J. L. Ambrose, 'The New Judiciary', *Law Quarterly Review* (1910); A. V. Dicey, 'The Development of Administrative Law in England', *Law Quarterly Review* (1915).

[33] Education Act 1902.

[34] Local Government Act 1929.

established.[35] And although central government now exercised an important supervisory responsibility and a break had been made between local authority and parliamentary constituencies, it was a system that generally respected the constitutional values underpinning the tradition of local government.

Throughout the twentieth century this framework was continuously adjusted in the search for an appropriate role for local government within the modern administrative state. The main issues that have occupied official attention were those of functions, structure and finance. What are the appropriate tasks for local authorities? Can efficiency in the exercise of these tasks be reconciled with local government areas patterned on historic communities? How are the resources needed to provide local government services to be acquired? And underpinning discussion of these matters was the question of the appropriate relationship between central departments and local authorities. By briefly considering each of these issues something of the character of the twentieth-century system might be revealed.

Restructuring of functions

Although the objective of establishing local authorities as the sole agencies of local administration was maintained after 1930, it was promoted in conjunction with a policy of nationalising certain services previously undertaken by local government. This adjustment was made for three main reasons. First, as in the case of unemployment assistance (removed in 1934) and trunk roads (removed in 1936) it was generally accepted that local administration of these national responsibilities was inefficient and anachronistic.[36] Second, as is illustrated in the case of the removal of local authority hospital services through the formation of the National Health Service in 1946, it was recognised that, although local control was possible in principle, the existing areas rendered the exercise administrat-

---

[35] The 1835 Act principle of the ratepayer franchise had by the end of the nineteenth century been extended to all institutions of local government, but it was only in the Representation of the People Act 1948 that the most basic principle of representative democracy—vesting the right to vote in every person of full age living in the area—was permanently extended to local government. See Keith-Lucas, *The Local Government Franchise*, p. 224.

[36] The precise reasons for inefficiency nevertheless differ between the two cases, with the former case providing an illustration, *avant la lettre*, of the Tiebout hypothesis and the latter resulting in large part from technological change and the growth of long-distance traffic: see Foster, Jackman and Perlman, *Local Government Finance*, pp. 45, 51–2.

ively impractical.[37] Finally, local authorities lost responsibility for their gas and electricity trading services in 1947–8 as a result of the Labour government's policy of nationalisation of public utilities.

The loss of these responsibilities did not result in a diminished status for local government. With the formation of the welfare state, local services such as education, housing and personal social services grew in importance and local government continued to increase the share of total public expenditure which it consumed. But the loss of production-orientated services did give local government a distinct social service orientation and this restructuring had a major impact on the character of the central–local government relationship. By taking on a greater proportion of services which are redistributive in nature, local government not only became heavily dependent on the centre for financial support but, given the limited ability of any local agency independently to pursue policies of income redistribution,[38] it ensured that central government would continue to have a major role to play in regulating and co-ordinating local authority action.

Local government reorganisation

The nineteenth-century reformation reflected the traditional organic link between shire and borough and resulted in the establishment of a local government system which was divided along urban–rural lines. While the nexus between shire and borough may once have formed an integral unit, continuing urbanisation meant that, as towns and cities grew beyond their administrative boundaries, the structure provided a source of conflict. Since local authorities were engaged in a zero-sum game for territory, tax-base and status, there could never be consensus among the various groups of local authorities over the need for, and certainly the form of, any reorganisation. And if reorganisation as functionally effective units broke the link with the ancient communities, local authorities would lose their historic claims to be independent governing bodies

---

[37] See, for example, Charles Key, parliamentary secretary to the minister of health, HC Deb., vol. 422, cols 209–10, 1 May 1946: '[I]t has been asked: "Why not take over the local authority hospitals? Why not use the local government geographical distribution, the local government managerial machine, for what, in fact would become a greatly improved local government service?" I answer: Because of existing geographical areas and functional distribution that is administratively impossible . . . We have not made its sphere of operations grow with the character of the services we have developed, nor with the means and needs for wider areas of administration.'

[38] See, Foster, Jackman and Perlman, *Local Government Finance*, pp. 42–5.

and might eventually be treated as emanations of central government. Consequently, 'the conflict that was built into the local government system in the nineteenth century created *immobilisme* in the twentieth'.[39] Although the need for reorganisation had been widely recognised by the 1930s, these difficulties ensured that it was not until the 1960s and 1970s that local government reforms were enacted.

The reforms of this period, which followed a spate of official reports highlighting the importance of local government to the machinery of government, were part of a technocratic movement which treated institutional modernisation as the key to the reversal of Britain's economic decline. Reform of local government in London in the 1963 Act marked the watershed since it revealed to the centre that 'it was possible to effect quite radical change without allowing the local authorities affected to take any part in the formulation of the terms of reference of the inquiry preceding change, or in the process following the inquiry but preceding Ministerial decision'.[40] The subsequent establishment of the Redcliffe-Maud Commission to examine local government in England thus implied 'the total rejection of the principle that local authorities had a right to define the scope and nature of the change themselves'.[41] The processes of implementation were not without their difficulties.[42] Thus, although the Redcliffe-Maud Commission, noting that the failure of the existing structure 'to recognise the interdependence of town and country' was its 'most fatal defect',[43] had recommended the establishment of large unitary authorities, the Local Government Act 1972 introduced a two-tier system which, though more closely tied to the ancient divisions, simply perpetuated antagonism within local government and 'ensured that local government would be ill-equipped to resist the rapid increase in the pressure for centralization'.[44]

Although the official line was that by restoring local authorities as functionally effective units the reforms would reverse the trend towards

---

[39] Alan Alexander, 'Structure, Centralization and the Position of Local Government', in Martin Loughlin, David Gelfand and Ken Young (eds), *Half a Century of Municipal Decline 1935–1985* (Allen & Unwin, 1985), p. 52.

[40] L. J. Sharpe, ' "Reforming" the Grass Roots: An Alternative Analysis', in D. Butler and A. H. Halsey (eds), *Policy and Politics: Essays in Honour of Norman Chester* (Macmillan, 1978), p. 103.

[41] Jane Morton, *The Best Laid Schemes?* (Charles Knight, 1970), p. 117.

[42] See Bruce Wood, *The Process of Local Government Reform 1966–1974* (Allen & Unwin, 1976).

[43] *Report of the Royal Commission on Local Government in England* (Chair, Lord Redcliffe-Maud), Cmnd 4040 (1969), vol. 1, para. 85.

[44] Alexander, 'Structure, Centralization and Position', p. 64.

centralisation, critics argued that, particularly since effective central control and co-ordination required a significant reduction in the overall number of local authorities, reorganisation should be viewed as a facet of a process of centralisation.[45] It was argued in particular that the equation of functional effectiveness with the enhancement of local democracy[46] erroneously conflated system (functional) capacity with governmental (democratic) capacity.[47] Developing this analysis, Sharpe contended that the essence of local government is that it is local and therefore that the 'number of local units must be a function of the needs and conditions of the sub-national communities whose existence justifies the creation of a local government system in the first place'.[48] Consequently, '[i]f the structure of local government is ... to be determined by the needs of central government then it is difficult to see the justification for a local government system, as opposed to some form of deconcentrated central administration'.[49]

Financing local government

Having generally established ratepayer democracies in local government, the nineteenth-century reformation ensured that authorities were heavily dependent for their revenues on the rates. Given the restricted franchise, the limits of what was politically acceptable were soon reached and this often inhibited the implementation of imaginative responses to urban problems. Only at the turn of the century were these restrictions loosened, in part through a gradual extension of the franchise, but also because of the alleviation of the rate burden by the introduction of Exchequer grants.[50] Until the 1870s, Exchequer grants had accounted for about 5

---

[45] Sharpe, ' "Reforming" the Grass Roots', pp. 104–5. Foster, Jackman and Perlman conclude that throughout British history 'the reasons for enlarging jurisdictions to achieve redistributive ends have probably been its great convenience, in producing fewer but larger agents for central government to deal with'; *Local Government Finance*, p. 580.

[46] See, for example, Redcliffe-Maud Report, Cmnd 4040, vol. 1, para. 272: 'If, as we have said, a minimum population of around 250,000 is necessary for the efficient administration of services it seems to us an inescapable corollary that local democracy will be ineffective unless organized in units of at least that size.'

[47] L. J. Sharpe, 'The Failure of Local Government Modernization in Britain: A Critique of Functionalism', *Canadian Public Administration* (1980), 92, 106–8.

[48] Ibid., 104–5.

[49] Ibid., 105–6.

[50] Each of these factors had a significant impact on the emergence of Poplarism in the 1920s, as local authorities, coming under Labour control for the first time, experimented in the use of rates for redistributive purposes. See B. Keith-Lucas, 'Poplarism', *Public Law* (1962); Noreen Branson, *Poplarism, 1919–1925: George Lansbury and the Councillors' Revolt* (Lawrence & Wishart, 1979).

per cent of local government expenditure, but by 1900 around one-fifth of local government expenditure was grant-aided.[51] The growth in grant-aid caused concern on both sides. The centre was worried at the increasing proportion of tax revenues which were being absorbed by local grants. But there was also an apprehension that the use of grant-aid, especially in conjunction with the imposition of duties on local authorities, would transform them into instruments of central policy. The Goschen reforms of 1888, which scrapped most specific grants and replaced them with an assigned revenue system, was touted as the solution. By placing the burden directly on the general taxpayer, central government was removed as an active player in the process. But how were these revenues to be distributed between authorities? Allocation in proportion to rateable value or population was rejected, since the greater proportion would go to the richer authorities, but major problems were experienced in finding an adequate measure of need. This difficulty has afflicted the allocation of grant ever since.

The financial relationship between central and local government was transformed during the twentieth century. Local government expenditure steadily increased; from 4.5 per cent of GNP in 1890 it rose to 18.4 per cent in 1975.[52] But when expressed as a proportion of personal disposable income, the rate burden remained remarkably stable. The gap was met by central grants; by the mid-1970s over half of local expenditure was being provided by central government grants.[53] Since the Goschen reforms had been undermined by a proliferation of specific grants, a major attempt at rationalisation occurred in the 1929 Act with the replacement of many specific grants with a block grant designed to assist poorer authorities in meeting their spending needs. However, this general grant did not incorporate grants for the main services of education, housing and the police and it was only after 1958, when education was absorbed into the system, that the general grant covered the allocation of the majority of grant aid to local government. Block grant was an admirable attempt to reconcile the legitimate interests of central government with the preservation of local autonomy.[54] But the establishment of the block

---

[51] M. Schulz, 'The Development of the Grant System', in Wilson, *Essays on Local Government*, pp. 116, 127; Foster, Jackman and Perlman, *Local Government Finance*, ch. 7.
[52] Richard Jackman, 'Local Government Finance', in Loughlin, Gelfand and Young, *Half a Century of Municipal Decline*, p. 147.
[53] See Foster, Jackman and Perlman, *Local Government Finance*, ch. 7.
[54] For a sophisticated analysis of this issue, examining the co-efficient of variation in

grant principle did not alleviate the tensions, which now are buried in the complex and detailed formulae used to govern grant distribution.

Entrenchment of the principle of equalisation in grant distribution exposed certain additional difficulties with the system. Since it implied that standard services should be capable of being provided at standard rate poundages, it emphasised anomalies in the system of property valuation on which local rates were based and thus exposed weaknesses in the rating system. But the equalisation principle also highlighted the rather vexed question of the relationship between local government and redistribution. In the first half of the century, the bulk of the rate yield fell on households which, since the incidence of rate burden among households was regressive, provided a general restraint on the use of local powers for redistributive purposes. Since the 1950s, however, the position has changed with households first being given rate-relief through central grants; then, as a result of the introduction of the rate rebate scheme in 1966, the regressive nature of the system was modified. The combined effect of these measures to equalise and to alleviate the burden on the less wealthy meant that in certain authorities rating could be used as a mechanism of redistribution, particularly since the restructuring of local government functions had increased the incidence of redistributive local services. The existence of these local powers to implement redistributive policies provided a strong justification for active central supervision.

Central–local government relations

Although local government became a powerful agency within the twentieth-century administrative state, the price of this power was that the affairs of local government became inextricably bound up with those of the centre. This meant that in the twentieth century the pattern of central–local government relations provided an important indication of the constitutional status of local government. How then were arrangements between the centre and the localities co-ordinated? In a major study published in 1966, John Griffith identified three basic factors which condition the central–local relationship.[55] The first is that it is the local authorities which provide the services and therefore, although the centre

---

expenditures as a proxy for local autonomy, see Foster, Jackman and Perlman, *Local Government Finance*, pp. 352–6

[55] Griffith, *Central Departments and Local Authorities*, pp. 17–18.

may encourage, forbid or frustrate, the local authority is generally both the first and last actor. Second, that it is a misdescription to characterise the relationship as one of control since, although departments impose controls, local authorities also make their impact on departments: the relationship is two-way. The third factor is the general acceptance of a national minimum standard for most services which central departments will insist on local authorities attaining. Since one consequence of the last factor is that the rules and regulations are generally drafted with weaker authorities in mind, the legal framework of the central–local relationship tends to present a distorted view of actual relations. Furthermore, although the relationship is not essentially one of principal and agent, Griffith also considered that the language of partnership was 'a pleasant and comforting evasion'.[56] Although departments and authorities each exist to promote the public welfare, in many situations their interests differ. And while the power relations are invariably unequal, central departments and local authorities recognise that they are locked in a network of interdependency which requires a degree of mutual understanding, co-operation and compromise.[57]

During the nineteenth century, mutuality was rooted in a shared culture based on the fact that from top to bottom Britain was governed by a class of wealthy landowners who performed unpaid service not only as members of the Lords and Commons but as justices of the peace who administered the counties. It was precisely because of this shared culture that a tradition of local autonomy could continue to flourish alongside the assertion of a strong central will expressed by the doctrine of parliamentary sovereignty. With the break-up of the great estates after the First World War, however, the landowners gradually abdicated from local politics[58] and eventually the 'social leaders' came to be replaced by less exalted 'public persons'.[59] Also, after 1918 the Labour Party began to gain a significant strength in local government and this often led to anti-socialist alliances between Liberals, Conservatives and ratepayer organisations.[60] After 1945, when the first local elections under

---

[56] Griffith, *Central Departments and Local Authorities*, p. 18.

[57] See also R. A. W. Rhodes, *Control and Power in Central–Local Government Relations* (Gower, 1981).

[58] David Cannadine (ed.), *Patricians, Power and Politics in the Nineteenth Century* (Leicester University Press, 1982), esp. pp. 2–15.

[59] J. M. Lee, *Social Leaders and Public Persons: A Study of County Government in Cheshire* (Clarendon Press, 1963); G. W. Jones, *Borough Politics: A Study of Wolverhampton Town Council, 1888–1964* (Macmillan, 1969).

[60] Ken Young, *Local Politics and the Rise of Party* (Leicester University Press, 1975).

universal adult suffrage were held, the party contest rapidly became institutionalised in local government. And during this post-war period, local politics were assimilated into the national contest between the major parties.[61] This process of what might be called the 'nationalisation of local politics' had one feature in common with the nineteenth-century arrangements: it depended less on institutional mechanisms than on the shared assumptions and values of local and national politicians.[62]

Among these common political assumptions was the acceptance of a division between local and central matters, and this worked mainly because local politics took the form of 'administrative politics', in which officers exerted great influence over the decision-making processes.[63] The practice of administrative politics thus went hand-in-glove with an emerging tradition of 'managerial professionalism', in which a highly professionalised staff delivered services through a hierarchically structured, departmentally organised local authority.[64] The political and professional networks of central–local relations which emerged in the twentieth century were built on the foundations of these practices. These networks became of vital importance for the achievement of central co-ordination of policy development.[65] The emergence and institutionalisation of these policy and professional communities led in effect to the establishment of a 'national local government system'.[66] The network has facilitated two-way communication between local and central government through the development of a common technical language, the recognition of a common 'operating ideology'[67] and shared membership of professional associations. The network, within which the role of the

---

[61] This process was reinforced by the tendency since the nineteenth century of using local government as a training site in executive skills for aspiring national politicians. See Foster, Jackman and Perlman, *Local Government Finance*, pp. 564–5.

[62] John Gyford and Mari James, *National Parties and Local Politics* (Allen & Unwin, 1983).

[63] See M. Hill, *The Sociology of Public Administration* (Weidenfeld & Nicolson, 1972), ch. 11.

[64] J. D. Stewart, 'The Functioning and Management of Local Authorities', in Loughlin, Gelfand and Young (eds), *Half a Century of Municipal Decline*, ch. 5. See also Griffith, *Central Departments and Local Authorities*, p. 534: 'The professionalism of local government officers is the greatest single force which enables local authorities to carry out, with much efficiency, the considerable tasks entrusted to them.'

[65] See L. J. Sharpe, 'Central Coordination and the Policy Network', *Political Studies* (1985).

[66] P. Dunleavy, *The Politics of Mass Housing in Britain, 1945–1975* (Clarendon Press, 1981), pp. 123–4; R. A. W. Rhodes, *The National World of Local Government* (Allen & Unwin, 1986).

[67] L. J. Sharpe, 'Instrumental Participation in Urban Government', in J. A. G. Griffith (ed.), *From Policy to Administration* (Allen & Unwin, 1976), ch. 6.

local authority associations is central,[68] has been of particular importance in establishing norms of conduct which are not specified by law, has thus enabled administrative law arrangements to remain relatively informal, and has respected the constitutional status of local government.

Griffith had acknowledged that the 'antagonism which from time to time arises between the groups [central departments and local authorities] is an indulgence which each can afford because both recognize this necessary inter-dependence'.[69] But what sustained this network of interdependency? The twentieth-century accommodation was rooted in a nineteenth-century statutory framework which had made efforts to respect the ancient tradition of local government. But the twentieth-century settlement was also founded on the assumption that the centre and the localities shared a basic mutuality of objective and could be trusted not to interfere in one another's primary sphere of competence. And underpinning this 'necessary inter-dependence' were certain economic and political conditions, notably, continuous economic growth and a political consensus concerning the welfare state. Once these basic economic and political conditions were challenged, the tension points in the system were exposed. And once this occurred the assumptions about the constitutional position of local government were placed in question.

Disintegration

Widespread strains in the system first became publicly exposed as a result of political conflicts in the 1960s and 1970s over the Labour government's policy of promoting comprehensive schooling through administrative mechanisms.[70] But the most severe stress stemmed from the economic crisis of the 1970s as economic stagnation and fiscal retrenchment exposed those tensions which had been concealed by continuous economic growth, the political consensus over the welfare state and an acceptance of the ability of the professional communities to overcome narrow conceptions of self-interest and act in the public

[68] Of the local authority associations, Griffith, *Central Departments and Local Authorities*, p. 33 comments that it 'is difficult to exaggerate their importance in influencing legislation, government policies and administration and in acting as co-ordinators and channels of local authority opinion'. See further Rhodes, *National World of Local Government*.

[69] Griffith, *Central Departments and Local Authorities*, p. 506.

[70] See D. E. Regan, *Local Government and Education* (Allen & Unwin, 1977), pp. 46–53; Richard Buxton, *Local Government* (Penguin, 1970), pp. 202–15.

interest. This economic crisis contributed to the re-emergence of ideological politics within both the major parties and this exacerbated the differences not only between, but also within, the parties as radicals on each wing challenged the post-war consensus over the welfare state. It was to have a major impact on local government which during the twentieth century had enjoyed an almost continuous growth in expenditure relative to GDP.[71]

When in 1979 a Conservative government was elected on a radical programme based on the need to shift the boundaries between public and private, to promote market processes over planning techniques, and to assert the principle of consumer sovereignty, the consequences for local government seemed evident. The collectivist delivery arrangements of local services came to be seen as an impediment to the government's objective of extending the sphere of market relations. Since professionals were viewed not as disinterested promoters of the public interest but as self-serving status groups which had erected barriers against innovation, the government sought to challenge both the organisational structure of local government and the influence of professional communities within the central–local network. Furthermore, although the resulting strains were felt throughout local government, in many of the conurbations the economic and political circumstances caused local Labour parties to redefine the relationship between local authorities and local communities and, by exploiting the redistributive potential in the system of local government finance,[72] to rebuild a distinctive municipal socialist policy in which local government could provide an arena for opposing the capitalist state.[73] These new forms of ideological politics on both right and left thus sought not only to challenge existing policies but also to alter the basic operating methods and decision-making processes in both central and local government. It seemed obvious that the central–local co-ordination network, which ultimately was based on a congruence of values, would not be able to withstand the upheaval.

---

[71] See Foster, Jackman and Perlman, *Local Government Finance*, ch. 4.

[72] See Ken Livingstone, 'Interview' in Martin Boddy and Colin Fudge (eds), *Local Socialism? Labour Councils and New Left Alternatives* (Macmillan, 1984), p. 265: 'The way that housing, transport or education are funded by local government does directly challenge capital. The rating mechanism is the best method of redistributing wealth that the labour movement has ever had its hands on . . . That's why the Tories have woken up to the importance of centralising the state.'

[73] See Boddy and Fudge, *Local Socialism*; John Gyford, *The Politics of Local Socialism* (Allen & Unwin, 1985); Stewart Lansley, Sue Goss and Christian Wolmar, *Councils in Conflict: The Rise and Fall of the Municipal Left* (Macmillan, 1989).

The key Conservative policies for restructuring the welfare state were to reduce public sector employment, to shift expenditure away from social welfare services, and to reconstruct social policy on the principle of individualistic action rather than collectivistic organisation. These policies had a profound impact on local government: first, because, owing to the labour-intensive nature of their services and central government's lack of executant responsibility, local authorities employed more people than central government; second, because many local government services were collectively organised; third, because, as a result of functional reallocation in the twentieth century, local government had become heavily social-welfare orientated; and, finally, because of local government's dependency on central government grants for its finances. Over four successive terms the Conservatives were able to transform the character of local government. In order to assess the impact on the constitutional position of local government, the issues of finance, functions, structure and accountability should be sketched.

Local government finance

Being committed to the reduction of public expenditure, the Conservatives introduced changes to the grant system to provide an incentive to economy.[74] When this block grant mechanism failed to deliver reductions speedily, a system of expenditure targets was engrafted on to the mechanism[75] and then, in the Rates Act 1984, power was acquired to control the amount of finance which local authorities could raise through the rates. This measure, a direct attack on 'the foundation stone upon which is built the whole structure of local taxation in England'[76] constituted an unprecedented centralisation of political power. Far from achieving central control, however, rate-capping simply threatened 'to undermine what remain[ed] of financial accountability in local government'.[77] The

[74] Local Government, Planning and Land Act 1980, Part VI.

[75] Local Government Finance Act 1982, Part I.

[76] Redlich, *Local Government in England*, vol. 1, p. 24.

[77] Richard Jackman, 'The Rates Bill: A Measure of Desperation', *Political Quarterly* (1985), 161, 170. The Rates Act also raised the possibility of an unbridgeable gap developing between the expenditure of the local authority and the revenues available to it to meet its obligations, an issue which had never entered into the design of the financial security of supervisory arrangements: see Malcolm Grant, *Rate-capping and the Law*, 2nd edn (Association of Metropolitan, Authorities, 1986), chs 11–14. This issue was highlighted by the actions of Liverpool City Council during the mid-1980s. See Martin Loughlin, *Legality and Locality: The Role of Law in Central–Local Government Relations* (Clarendon Press, 1996), pp. 185–99.

government responded to this unstable situation by proposing the most radical reform to the system of local government finance ever countenanced in modern times, including nationalisation of the non-domestic rate and replacement of domestic rates with a 'community charge' or poll tax.[78]

Although ostensibly 'designed to ensure that local democracy and local accountability are substantially strengthened'[79] the reforms had the effect of greatly weakening the financial autonomy of local authorities and of undermining one of the basic pillars of the modern institution of local government. The nationalisation of the non-domestic rate had the effect of increasing the proportion of central funding of local government to around 80 per cent. This gave the regressive poll tax an extremely high gearing effect which, given the technical volatility of grant payments from one year to the next, destroyed the apparent objective of linking poll tax levels to voter preferences. Further, its highly regressive impact, together with the retention of capping powers, made it almost impossible for local authorities to diverge from central government spending assessments. The poll tax's subsequent dismantling and replacement with the council tax, within only a year or two of the scheme's implementation,[80] had all the elements of grand tragedy and offers a singular instance of 'a government putting a single piece of legislation at the forefront of its programme, forcefully implementing it, and then ignominiously abandoning it in the course of a single Parliament'.[81] The experiment not only destroyed the integrity of the local tax system but also 'came close to undermining the whole structure of local government'.[82]

After the poll tax reforms, any attempt to restore the taxing capacity of local government proved difficult. Further, with 80 per cent of local authority expenditure being centrally provided and universal capping being introduced in 1992, local authority expenditure was effectively determined by central assessments.[83] Consequently, we now have a system in which local authorities assume a degree of formal responsibility

---

[78] Abolition of Domestic Rates etc (Scotland) Act 1987; Local Government Finance Act 1988.
[79] Department of the Environment, *Paying for Local Government*, Cmnd 9714 (1985), para. 1.51.
[80] Local Government Finance Act 1992.
[81] D. Butler, A. Adonis and T. Travers, *Failure in British Government: The Politics of the Poll Tax* (Oxford University Press, 1994), p. 1.
[82] Ibid., p. 2.
[83] See Audit Commission, *Passing the Bucks: The Impact of Standard Spending Assessments on Economy, Efficiency and Effectiveness* (London HMSO, 1993); First Report of the House of Commons Environment Committee, *Standard Spending Assessments* (Session 1993–4), HC 90.

out of all proportion to their ability actually to control services. The constitutional implications were clearly signalled in the nomenclature: by designating the new local tax a 'community charge' the government indicated that local councils did not constitute a tier of government vested with a governmental power of taxation but were administrative agencies providing certain services for which the principle of direct charging could not efficiently be applied.

Functional change

The primary target of the Conservative attack was on the welfare state model of the local council as a self-sufficient, corporate authority vested with broad discretion to provide services. The main objective of the government's many reforms to local functions after 1980 was, so far as possible, to restructure the collective organisation of such services and place them in a market framework and to eliminate their redistributive dimension. A systematic attempt was thus made to convert collectively organised redistributive services into trading services (or quasi-trading services) and then to subject these trading services—together with local public goods provided by local authorities—to market testing. Operating under the slogan 'enabling not providing',[84] the government intended that the local council should withdraw entirely from direct service provision and assume the role of a monitoring and regulatory agency, with any redistributive issues being dealt with through national schemes for income transfers.

This pattern of reform was replicated across the major services of public transport, housing and education, where the objective was to set up the activity (for example, bus undertakings, council housing, schools and colleges) at arm's length from the council, to require that activity to be operated in accordance with commercial or competitive principles, to provide incentives for the operating units to break from local authority control and to alter the authority's duty from that of planning for a comprehensive system for meeting the needs of the area to that of bolstering a system operating on commercial/competitive lines. These principles were then applied in 1988 to a rolling programme of compulsory competitive tendering for a range of local services, including refuse

---

[84] See, for example, Nicholas Ridley, *The Local Right: Enabling not Providing* (Centre for Policy Studies, 1988).

collection, catering and cleaning services which, after 1992, was extended to professional services.[85]

The general effect of these reforms was to reverse the early twentieth-century trend of institutional integration and replace it with the principle of institutional differentiation. Three main dimensions to this movement can be distinguished: differentiation *within* the local council (for example, the changing relationship between maintained schools and the local education authority); differentiation as a result of a statutorily prescribed contractualisation of relationships between the local authority and private bodies over the provision of public services (for example, bus operators providing tendered services); and differentiation occasioned by the government's promotion of specific-purpose bodies to undertake tasks which previously had been the responsibility of local government. These latter agencies (such as urban development corporations, training and enterprise councils, housing action trusts, further education colleges) were either specially established public bodies subject to central government control or bodies which, though technically private, existed essentially to perform public functions. Because of their local character and essentially public functions, such bodies became part of an institutionally differentiated structure of local governance and were part of the process by which local government was being replaced by a complex local governance network in which the local council would simply be one—and not necessarily the most prominent—agency on the local scene.[86]

Structural reforms

Initially, the Conservative government expressed no significant interest in the appropriate structures of local government. Although the strategic authorities in London and the metropolitan areas were abolished in 1985, this action was essentially a response to the fact that all the abolished authorities were under Labour control and many were pursuing public transport, economic development and expenditure policies which central government opposed.[87] The government's attention turned to the ques-

---

[85] For an overview, see Christopher D. Foster and Francis J. Plowden, *The State Under Stress* (Open University Press, 1996), ch. 7.

[86] See Keiron Walsh, *Public Services and Market Mechanisms: Competition, Contracting and the New Public Management* (Macmillan, 1995).

[87] Consequently, the government's claim to be streamlining local government was subsequently shown not to be vindicated: see S. Leach, H. Davis, C. Game and C. Skelcher,

tion of local government structure only after implementing functional reforms which had the effect of undermining the rationale of the 1970s structure, rooted in assumptions about the need for a self-sufficient, corporate local authority. A simpler framework suggested itself and in 1996 local government in Wales and Scotland was streamlined through the establishment of unitary authorities while in England the Local Government Commission, established under the 1992 Act, recommended that unitary authorities be established in twenty-one of the thirty-nine county areas.

There can be no ideal solution to the question of local government structure: tensions will always exist between centralism and localism, between unity and diversity, and between functional requirements and community identities. However, it is precisely because of the existence of such tensions that the process through which local government reform is considered matters. From a constitutional perspective, then, what is most significant about the recent structural reforms is that in no case were the general principles evaluated by independent inquiry. The case for the metropolitan reforms was outlined in ten paragraphs of a white paper, the Welsh and Scottish reforms were introduced in legislation after a short period of official consultation, and only the English proposals were based on the workings of an independent commission, though one which operated in highly contentious circumstances.[88] The processes through which these reforms were proposed and implemented did nothing to acknowledge the principle that local government maintained a constitutional status such that its basic structure should be modified only after extensive deliberation and broad-based consensus.

Accountability

During the twentieth century, local councils were constituted as multi-functional authorities equipped with discretionary powers to enable them to provide services to meet the needs of their communities. Within this tradition, political mechanisms of accountability, whether to the local electorate or to ministers (and through ministers to Parliament) were primary. One major theme in the Conservative government's agenda was to extend the forms of accountability: institutional differentiation, value-

---

After Abolition: The Operation of the Post-1986 Metropolitan Government System in England (INLOGOV, University of Birmingham, 1991).
[88] See Steve Leach (ed.), *The Local Government Review: Key Issues and Choices* (INLOGOV, 1994).

for-money (VFM) audit, specification of service objectives through the use of performance indicators, transforming the inspectorial role from one of professional support to efficiency oversight, and vesting rights in service beneficiaries were all elements of this process. These mechanisms subjected local authorities to a comprehensive regime of accountability, and one which was much more extensive than for any other type of public body. By confining, structuring and checking within a highly restrictive financial framework, they also considerably reduced the local authorities' freedom of action. Cumulatively, these functional, financial and structural reforms signalled the end of local government's constitutional status.

It might be objected that this is not death but rejuvenation: that the last twenty years of the twentieth century marked the replacement of the welfare-bureaucratic model, dominated by producer interests, with the strategic-responsive model of local government focused on the maintenance of efficiency incentives to promote consumer interests. Who knows? What is clear is that this public policy argument is to be distinguished from constitutional analysis. In the tradition of local government which has emerged since the nineteenth century, the notion of a public service has always had an intrinsically political dimension; being complex packages of heterogeneous products, responsibility for decision-making about public services has under our governmental arrangements always been vested in elected representatives. Once such services are subjected to strict market disciplines, they rapidly lose their peculiarly political and hence public character and, if those basic attributes are relinquished, such services also lose their local character. Once local services are required to be provided in accordance with formal and testable market criteria of economy and efficiency they lose the sense of variety which lies at the heart of the justification of local government. If local services are to be provided according to market criteria then the tradition of tolerance—the acceptance of some degree of technical inefficiency—within the central–local government relationship rapidly disappears. The Redcliffe-Maud view that local councils 'can decide for themselves . . . what kind of services they want'[89] is replaced by the belief that central government 'has a duty to intervene to ensure that local government provides services for the people who live in the area in the

---

[89] Redcliffe-Maud Report, Cmnd 4040, p. iii.

most efficient and economical way'.[90] Rather than being concerned with ensuring national minimum standards, central government now promotes uniformity. Once this point is reached, the central–local compact which in the twentieth century sustained the constitutional status of local government has been dissolved.

Juridification

The constitutional implications of recent developments are highlighted by focusing on the issue of law. As part of the nineteenth-century reformation, local councils were placed on a statutory foundation and the judiciary then extended the doctrine of *ultra vires*, limiting the powers of a corporation to its statutory purposes, to local authorities. But because the reformation accorded respect to the ancient tradition, it would be wrong thereafter to treat local government simply as a product of statutory action by the centre. Local government, as Gladstone had implicitly recognised, was no purely legal phenomenon: although local government had been placed within a statutory framework, that framework did not define the practice. The framework was facilitative, establishing a structure 'enabling local authorities to experiment with the provision of new services, to keep the public-service frontier moving, and to order their priorities for themselves as they judged best for their localities'.[91]

The framework established an essentially permissive regime, with even the formal duties cast on local authorities being drafted in broad, often highly subjective, and therefore non-justiciable, terms. The basic objective, it would appear, was to marginalise the potentially restrictive effect of the *ultra vires* doctrine. It would be similarly distortive to extrapolate from the extensive statutory powers of supervision vested in ministers, most of which were rarely used. The effect of the legal framework was to displace Parliament and the courts as active supervisory agencies of local government and to establish the central–local network as a relatively closed administrative regime. Within this network of interdependency, conventional practices provided a more authoritative guide to behaviour than legal formalities. And through these conventional practices, the centre acknowledged the claims of local councils to repre-

[90] Michael Howard (minister for local government), Official Report HC Standing Committee A, col. 48, 21 October 1987.
[91] Prest, *Liberty and Locality*, pp. 219–20.

sent the interests of their communities and maintain their capacity of local initiative.

While these practices fulfilled conditions of both efficiency and legitimacy, their constitutional significance could remain indeterminate. Problems arose at the end of the twentieth century because, in pursuit of efficiency, the centre felt obliged to act contrary to many of the assumptions of this network. Once the conventional practices were undermined, law was dragged from the background into the foreground to fill the normative gulf. This brought both Parliament and the courts back into the mediation of the central–local relationship. The constitutional consequences of these late-twentieth-century developments, however, have not been positive.

Although the Conservative government sought to govern by way of central direction, it gradually realised that the existing legal framework, not having been drafted for such purposes, contained too many gaps and ambiguities to be susceptible to conversion into an instrument of command-and-control regulation. Consequently, the government's strategy required the establishment of a more explicit hierarchical structure of superior and subordinate and this necessitated a programme of local government legislation on an unprecedented scale; it has been estimated that, between 1979 and 1992, 143 Acts having a direct application to local government in England and Wales were enacted, of which fifty-eight contained major changes to the system.[92] Although this meant that Parliament was once again performing a pivotal role in the central–local relationship, this was not a happy experience for any of the parties involved, with the government both failing adequately to consult local government about proposed changes and generally riding roughshod over parliamentary procedures.[93] Rather than enabling that institution once again to act as the voice of the localities at the centre, the episode simply highlighted the degree to which Parliament had become an instrument of government.

The process of transforming the legal framework into a regime which defines the character of the relationship between central and local government also imposed pressures on the courts. The judiciary was, almost for the first time, drawn into the process of acting as an umpire in central–local disputes. But since the traditional framework was devised

[92] Report of the Hansard Society Commission on the Legislative Process, *Making the Law* (Hansard Society, 1992), pp. 19, 291.
[93] See Loughlin, *Legality and Locality*, pp. 382–99.

on the implicit understanding that the conduct of central–local relations was an internal rule-game, this shift often served only to confound the judiciary. The complexity of the system in combination with the ambiguities and lacunae within the statutory framework presented the courts with considerable difficulties. But one point is clear: all of the major central–local disputes proceeding through the courts during this period were resolved in favour of central government.[94] The government's control of Parliament together with the judiciary's lack of experience in handling complex regulatory disputes combined to ensure that the courts would not in any way act to curb the government's programme of change.

Juridification, the process by which law rather than convention becomes determinative of the status of local government, is symptomatic of the destruction of the twentieth-century central–local compact. Once the centre becomes wedded to the single-minded pursuit of technocratic efficiency, tolerance of local ways—a feature of the compact—disappears and the centre is obliged to take action. But attempts at central control have been frustrated largely because of the gaps and ambiguities in the legal framework, features which were not the product of oversight but reflect the attempt to express in law our historic traditions of local government. Central action destroys the compact and neither the courts nor Parliament have been able to develop a formal regulatory framework which expresses the basic values of a system of local government.

Modernisation

By the mid-1990s, wide-ranging concern was being expressed about local government's ability, in the face of such changes, to maintain its capacity for initiative and innovation.[95] A number of these concerns were taken up after the election in 1997 of a Labour government. The new government officially recognised that local councils are uniquely placed to provide leadership to their local communities and committed itself to a policy of ensuring that councils were empowered to take on this role.[96] But Labour had no desire to return to the model of the self-sufficient authority;

[94] See Loughlin, *Legality and Locality*, pp. 408–9.
[95] See, for example, Select Committee on Relations between Central and Local Government, *Rebuilding Trust* (Session 1995–6), HL 97.
[96] *Modern Local Government: In Touch with the People* (HMSO, 1998).

rather, it adopted a programme of modernisation which generally accepted, and in certain respects built on, the functional reforms of the Conservatives. Labour's policy seemed to envisage further limitations on the local authority's role in service areas such as education, housing and the social services and, although compulsory competitive tendering was abolished, it was replaced with the imposition of a duty on local authorities to achieve 'best value' which promoted local initiative but subject only to tight central supervision.[97] Since Labour also maintained restrictive and comprehensive central financial controls, there were many continuities in central government policy in relation to local government which were carried into the twenty-first century.

The main difference between Labour and the Conservatives was that the new administration specifically sought to reaffirm the traditional value of local government as an institution which expresses the needs and interests of the local community. Labour also recognised implicitly that, because of juridification, such aspirations must be placed within a formal framework of positive law. But on implementation Labour wavered: in opposition it seemed committed to the necessity of vesting local government with a power of general competence;[98] in government this initially was expressed as a foundational duty on local authorities to promote the social, economic and environmental well-being of their areas,[99] though latterly this duty was transformed into a power.[100] This was an important symbolic step in the rejuvenation of local government which, alongside proposals to restore local political leadership by enabling local councils to experiment with executive mayors and cabinet regimes,[101] could lead to renewal of local initiative. But given the general functional and financial regime under which local authorities were now obliged to operate, and given the government's intention to give greater autonomy only to those local authorities which responded 'constructively' to Labour's modernisation agenda, Labour's proposals were not sufficient to alter the general assessment that, by the end of the twentieth

---

[97] Local Government Act 1999, Part I.

[98] Labour Party, *Rebuilding Democracy, Rebuilding Communities* (Labour Party, 1995). And see note 28 above.

[99] *Modern Local Government*, para. 8.9.

[100] Local Government Act 2000, s. 2(1). See Ian Leigh, *Law, Politics and Local Democracy* (Oxford University Press, 2000), ch. 2.

[101] Local Government Act 2000, Part II. For discussion, see Leigh, *Law, Politics and Local Democracy*, ch. 7.

century, local authorities had effectively become agencies of central policy.

Conclusions

When in the nineteenth century local government was placed on a modern statutory foundation, the reformation respected the authority of the ancient tradition of local government, which was based on the fact that local authorities, being founded on ancient territorial divisions, were able both to claim the allegiance of their communities and, through parliamentary representation, to exercise a powerful influence over local affairs at the centre. The local council, being established as a multi-purpose institution responsible for the provision of public services at the local level, was vested with the powers needed to maintain a spirit of continuous initiative. By the beginning of the twentieth century, Parliament had lost much of its direct influence over local government, the link between local council and parliamentary constituencies had been broken, and the central–local arrangement was established as an essentially closed administrative relationship. But the informal norms which emerged respected local government's distinctive status and the system evolved as much because of the gradual adoption of the fruits of local experimentation in public legislation as from central initiatives.

During the twentieth century, this central–local compact, being the product of the workings of Britain's peculiar political constitution, was sustained by a set of understandings and underpinned by particular political and economic conditions. These understandings were adapted to twentieth-century circumstances, as professional networks replaced the common culture of the governing class in the emerging welfare state. But the basic changes in government, generated by the emergence of party government, the institutionalisation of big government, functional differentiation rooted in the growing complexity of governmental tasks and the growing demand of citizens for universalised service provision, all imposed strains on central–local arrangements and set the scene for creeping centralisation. When, during the last quarter of the century and as a product of the growing economic burden, the political consensus over the welfare state disintegrated, the hollowness of the claim to possess a robust system of local government was quickly exposed. The demise of local government's constitutional role, it should be emphasised, is not simply a function of capacity. It is primarily the product of governmental action which has shifted the distribution of political authority and altered the character of representative democracy: the pluralist notion of democracy as 'an acknowledgement of shared fallibility and shared vulnerability' has thus been supplanted with the idea that it is now essentially 'a boast of [central] political capacity'.[102] By the end of the twentieth century, local authorities had been transformed essentially into agencies of the central government.

Some may find this assessment too neat: the nineteenth-century framework, it may be argued, is presented in a rosy light and the analysis of twentieth-century adjustments fails to take full account of the impact of those basic social, economic and technological developments which have inexorably worked to diminish the importance of locality as a primary factor of political life. But such criticism misses the point about constitutional analysis. Constitutional analysis must try to explicate the value assumptions which put flesh on those legal and institutional frameworks of government; this may be a contestable exercise, but it is one that must inevitably make use of ideal-types.[103] This is no longer a fashionable exercise; indeed, part of our difficulty rests on the fact that although this type of immanent constitutional analysis no longer carries much weight, alternative authoritative methods of assessing constitutional arrangements have yet to be devised. It simply did not prove possible during the twentieth century to stimulate commentaries as incisive as those which such foreign constitutional scholars as Boutmy, Gneist, Halévy and Redlich were able to produce for nineteenth-century local government. But unless the notion of constitutional discourse is altogether abandoned in favour of positivist legal analysis and empiricist political science, normative models of assessment, however contestable, must be devised as a benchmark against which the impact of change is evaluated.

Finally, there are those who, having accepted the relevance of this type of constitutional discourse, detect within recent reforms the glimmerings of a renewal of local government. It certainly is possible that, from the emerging multi-layered governance structures of the twenty-

---

[102] John Dunn, *Interpreting Political Responsibility* (Polity Press, 1990), p. 214.

[103] See Montesquieu, *The Spirit of the Laws*, book II, ch. 6: 'It is not for me to examine whether at present the English enjoy their liberty or not. It suffices for me to say that it is established by their laws, and I seek no further.' See also Alexis de Tocqueville, *Democracy in America*, vol. 1, Introduction: 'I confess that in America I saw more than America; I sought there the image of democracy itself, with its inclinations, its character, its prejudices, and its passions, in order to learn what we have to fear or to hope from its progress.'

first century, local authorities can be reinvented as institutions vested with a constitutional role. In order for this to be achieved, however, local authorities will have to be treated not only as agencies for service delivery but also as institutions of community governance. And it is difficult to see how this can now happen without both drawing on the assistance of documents such as the European Charter of Local Self-government and taking seriously its guiding principles. Such a charter, requiring that the basic principles of local autonomy be inscribed in positive law, would provide a further signal to the effect that Britain's peculiar political constitutional tradition has now reached its terminus and incrementally is being replaced by a formal constitution founded on the bedrock of enforceable law.

Bibliography

Official reports

Report of the Royal Commission on Local Government, Cmd 2506 (1925).

Report of the Committee on Ministers' Powers (Donoughmore), Cmd 4060 (1932).

Report of the Royal Commission on Local Government in Greater London (Herbert), Cmnd 1164 (1960).

Report of the Committee on the Management of Local Government (Maud) (HMSO, 1967).

Report of the Royal Commission on Local Government in England (Redcliffe-Maud), Cmnd 4040 (1969).

Ministry of Housing and Local Government, *Reform of Local Government in England*, Cmnd 4276 (1970).

Report of the Committee of Inquiry on Local Government Finance (Layfield), Cmnd 6453 (1976).

Department of the Environment, *Paying for Local Government*, Cmnd 9714 (1985).

Report of the Select Committee on Relations between Central and Local Government, *Rebuilding Trust* (Session 1995–6), HL 97.

Modern Local Government: In Touch with the People (HMSO, 1998).

Secondary sources

Bellamy, Christine, *Administering Central–Local Relations 1871–1919: The Local Government Board in its Fiscal and Cultural Context* (Manchester University Press, 1988).

Branson, Noreen, *Poplarism, 1919–1925: George Lansbury and the Councillors' Revolt* (Lawrence & Wishart, 1979).

Butler, D., Adonis, A. and Travers, T., *Failure in British Government: The Politics of the Poll Tax* (Oxford University Press, 1994).

Buxton, Richard, *Local Government* (Penguin, 1970).

Chester, D. N., *Central and Local Government: Financial and Administrative Relations* (Macmillan, 1951).

Finer, H., *English Local Government*, 4th edn (Methuen, 1950).

Foster, C. D., Jackman, R. A. and Perlman, M., *Local Government Finance in a Unitary State* (Allen & Unwin, 1980).

Foster, Christopher D. and Plowden, Francis J, *The State under Stress* (Open University Press, 1996).

Griffith, J. A. G., *Central Departments and Local Authorities* (Allen & Unwin, 1966).

Gyford, John, *The Politics of Local Socialism* (Allen & Unwin, 1985).

Gyford, John and James, Mari, *National Parties and Local Politics* (Allen & Unwin, 1983).

Jennings, Ivor, *Local Government in the Modern Constitution* (Knight, 1931).

Jones, G. W., *Borough Politics: A Study of Wolverhampton Town Council, 1888–1964* (Macmillan, 1969).

Keith-Lucas, B., *The English Local Government Franchise: A Short History* (Blackwell, 1952).

Keith-Lucas, B., 'Poplarism', *Public Law* (1962).

Keith-Lucas, B. and Richards, P. G., *A History of Local Government in the Twentieth Century* (Allen & Unwin, 1978).

Laski, H. J., Jennings, W. I. and Robson W. A. (eds), *A Century of Municipal Progress* (Allen & Unwin, 1935).

Leach, S., Davis, H., Game, C. and Skelcher, C., *After Abolition: The Operation of the Post-1986 Metropolitan Government System in England* (INLOGOV, University of Birmingham, 1991).

Lee, J. M., *Social Leaders and Public Persons: A Study of County Government in Cheshire* (Clarendon Press, 1963).

Leigh, Ian, *Law, Politics and Local Democracy* (Oxford University Press, 2000).

Loughlin, Martin, *Legality and Locality: The Role of Law in Central–Local Government Relations* (Clarendon Press, 1996).

Loughlin, Martin, Gelfand, David and Young, Ken (eds), *Half a Century of Municipal Decline 1935–1985* (Allen & Unwin, 1985).

Prest, John, *Liberty and Locality: Parliament, Permissive Legislation, and Ratepayers' Democracies in the Nineteenth Century* (Clarendon Press, 1990).

Redlich, Josef, *Local Government in England*, ed. Francis W. Hirst (Macmillan, 1903), 2 vols.

Regan, D. E., *Local Government and Education* (Allen & Unwin, 1977).

Rhodes, R. A. W., *The National World of Local Government* (Allen & Unwin, 1986).

Robson, W. A., *The Development of Local Government* (Allen & Unwin, 1931).

Robson, W. A., *Local Government in Crisis* (Allen & Unwin, 1966).

Sharpe, L. J., 'Theories and Values in Local Government', *Political Studies* (1970).

Sharpe, L. J., 'Central Coordination and the Policy Network', *Political Studies* (1985).

Stewart, John, *Local Government: The Conditions of Local Choice* (Allen & Unwin, 1982).

Webb, Sidney and Beatrice, *English Local Government*, 4 vols (Longman, 1922).

Wilson, C. H. (ed.), *Essays on Local Government* (Blackwell, 1948).

Wood, Bruce, *The Process of Local Government Reform: 1966–1974* (Allen & Unwin, 1976).

Young, Ken, *Local Politics and the Rise of Party* (Leicester University Press, 1975).

14.
The Police

CLIVE EMSLEY

Policing in Britain developed in a piecemeal fashion. Outside London, the nineteenth century saw a series of Acts of Parliament enabling, and then obliging, local authorities to establish their own police organisations; layers of central supervision and financial support by the Treasury were superimposed as time went on. The police officer thus had local links, but tasks, supervision and funding were not uniquely local, and this contributed to an ambiguity over the officer's constitutional position. During the twentieth century there was a reduction in the number of individual police forces. Closely linked with this was a marked increase in uniformity between the forces and, at the same time, senior officers acquired a greater autonomy within their jurisdictions and much closer links with the Home Office. The police officer's constitutional role was clarified, to some extent, by legal ruling and legislation, and this loosened local ties still further. While it is probably the case that, since the beginning of modern bureaucratic police in Britain, government ministers and officials in the Home Office have had a dislike of small police forces and an increasing preference for centralisation, the changes wrought in the twentieth century were not part of a grand scheme but resulted rather from a mixture of causes and the pressure of events. Nevertheless, it is worth emphasising from the outset that the twentieth century witnessed a significant transformation from largely local policing to centrally directed policing, and that this transformation occurred with relatively little public debate.

Police and policing can be catch-all terms. If policing is concerned with the prevention of crime, the detection and pursuit of offenders, and the maintenance of order in its widest sense, then it has to be recognised that there are many more institutions involved with these tasks than simply those labelled 'police'; gamekeepers and customs officers, for example, provide two examples drawn respectively from the private and public spheres. Furthermore, there have been institutions labelled 'police' that have never been attached to central or local government; at the beginning of the twentieth century, for example, both railway companies and docks could have their own police institutions. In the last quarter of the century particularly, sociologists argued over the defining characteristics of the police officer.[1] Eschewing these debates this chapter takes 'police officer' to mean simply an agent of the state, central or local, belonging to an institution labelled 'police'. A second caveat: while this volume addresses the British constitution, what follows focuses primarily on the police institutions of England and Wales with only passing reference to the similar organisations to be found in other parts of the United Kingdom. Finally, the nature of the exercise here leaves little space to explore the social forces instrumental in police development. The requirement for policing should not be taken for granted. The police may have been created as a result of legislation, but pressure from below and from a variety of social forces have been as significant in policy and operational activity as have directives from government and judicial rulings.

In 1900 there were just under 200 separate police forces in England and Wales. Fifty-nine of these could be classified, more or less, as county forces, though the Isle of Ely and Peterborough Liberty were not counties in the strict sense; 127 were borough forces; in addition, there were two police forces in London—the Metropolitan Police and the City of London Police. In Scotland there were thirty-four county and thirty-five borough forces. There were some independent island police institutions on Jersey, Guernsey and the Isle of Man.[2] Ireland had just two police institutions, the Dublin Metropolitan Police and the Royal Irish Constabulary. All of these police institutions fell largely into two types— those directly responsible to the central state and those responsible to local government.[3] Only three fell into the former category. The Metropolitan Police of London, the oldest of the professional, bureaucratic police institutions in the country, had been established by Sir Robert Peel in 1829 and was responsible to the home secretary through its centrally appointed chief officer, the commissioner. The two other centrally con-

---

[1] See, *inter alia*, Egon Bittner, *The Functions of the Police in Modern Society* (National Institute of Mental Health, 1970); David H. Bayley, *Patterns of Policing: A Comparative Analysis* (Rutgers University Press, 1985); Carl B. Klockars, *The Idea of Police* (Sage, 1985); Jean-Paul Brodeur, 'Police et coercion', *Revue française de sociologie* (1994).

[2] Martin Stallion and David S. Wall, *The British Police: Police Forces and Chief Officers 1829–2000* (Police History Society, 1999), ch. 5 for a checklist of English, Welsh and Scottish forces.

[3] Clive Emsley, 'A Typology of Nineteenth-century Police', *Crime, histoire & sociétés* (1999).

trolled forces were the Dublin Metropolitan Police and the Royal Irish Constabulary (RIC). Central control had been established and maintained in Ireland because of the concerns over internal security, and the RIC, charged with the policing of the whole of Ireland outside the capital, had many of the attributes of the military gendarmeries that policed the countryside of much of continental Europe. Many of the provincial forces had been established in the second quarter of the nineteenth century, but the County and Borough Police Act of 1856 had made it obligatory for counties and boroughs to establish such institutions. The Act also established an inspectorate (Her Majesty's Inspectorate of Constabulary, HMIC) that reported annually to Parliament. Similar legislation was passed for Scotland in 1857, though by this time most burghs had a police force and Lanarkshire was the only significant county without one.

The provincial police forces at the beginning of the twentieth century varied considerably in size. The police of populous cities and counties such as Birmingham, Liverpool, Manchester and Lancashire were substantial institutions with 800, 1,730, 1,000 and 1,700 men respectively. But, at the other extreme, towns like Tiverton and Truro and the tiny county of Rutland each possessed only a dozen or so officers. The appointment of the chief constable of a county had, since the enabling legislation of 1839 and 1840, always required the approval of the home secretary although police authority was situated in the county. The Local Government Act of 1888 not only ended the Quarter Sessions' administration of counties together with the police committees composed of members of the county bench that went with it, but it also created standing joint committees (SJCs) made up of an equal number of new county councillors and county magistrates. The SJCs were *ad hoc* statutory bodies which, although in practice serviced by county councils, were in law wholly separate and independent bodies that effectively precepted on the county councils. In 1888 magistrates also lost their power to appoint chief constables, subject to home secretary approval, when, although the government had initially proposed otherwise, that power became vested similarly in the whole SJC acting together. Most SJCs met quarterly and continued the practice of not seeking to intrude on the considerable managerial and operational autonomy of the chief constables. This autonomy was greater than in the case of borough chief officers and was reflected in the fact that the chief constables of the counties were commonly recruited from the same social class as the magistracy and many had served as military officers or officers in paramilitary colonial police forces. In the boroughs, the Municipal Corporations Act of 1835 had required each town council to establish a watch committee that was to appoint and supervise local police. In some instances these committees appear to have given their senior officers a relatively free hand, but elsewhere they met weekly and maintained a close supervision of their police, passing direct orders to the head constable, as the senior officers in the boroughs were commonly known. Head constables in the larger boroughs were recruited from men similar to those appointed as chief constables of the counties. In the smaller boroughs, however, it was possible for a tractable career policeman, originating like the majority of his peers from the working class, to rise from the ranks to be a head constable.

Provincial police forces were funded partly by local rates and partly by Treasury grant. The grant had been introduced as part of the 1856 Act, but it was payable only when a force received its annual certification as 'efficient' from inspectors of constabulary (HMIC). Initially some boroughs had refused this Treasury funding and had sought to maintain their own police as a matter of municipal pride. Occasionally, a force lost its grant following a critical assessment by an inspector, though the definition of 'efficiency' was not particularly penetrating and the inspections of the late nineteenth and early twentieth centuries were often peremptory. The measurements used by the inspectors seem rarely to have involved much more than an assessment of the size of the force in relation to the population and acreage of its jurisdiction, the good order of police buildings, the smartness of men on parade, and the answers that men provided to the occasional question. Although the Metropolitan Police had received a measure of Exchequer subsidy since 1833, its financing, with one exception, became aligned with all other forces from 1856. The exception was the statute of 1909 which provided for an additional Exchequer contribution in recognition of the force's imperial and national functions such as the protection of the royal family, government ministers and government buildings. The financial arrangements in London had given rise to complaints from the beginning, one of the reasons for the early arrival of the Exchequer contributions in 1833. It was objected that ratepayers were required to contribute to the upkeep of an institution over which they had neither control nor any say in its deployment and management. These complaints were to recur in the twentieth century, but they were confined to the Metropolitan Police. In the square mile of the City of London the police remained, under the local act of 1839, wholly financed by the Common Council and under its own police committee.

Police work at the beginning of the twentieth century involved not much more than patrolling a beat at a steady pace, and more often by night than by day. In urban areas, particularly at night, the patrolling officer was expected to check that doors and windows were securely fastened. If he found anything loose or open, he was expected to contact the owner or proprietor. If he missed anything loose or open, and especially if an offence was committed as a result, he was liable to disciplinary action and a possible fine. The principal task of the police officer, as spelled out in the Metropolitan Police orders of 1829 and repeated in the orders of other forces, was the prevention of crime. But police officers were also required to maintain order and preserve the king's or queen's peace and, while the Victorian English prided themselves on their civilisation and decorum, there continued to be turbulent scenes at parliamentary elections, and the growth of trades unions and worker activism gave rise to fears of serious labour unrest. Demonstrations and industrial disorder were, generally speaking, not something that could be handled by the solitary police officer on the beat. Nor were some of the smaller forces capable of dealing with any large-scale demonstration within their jurisdiction. There was the facility, but a reluctance, to swear in special constables in case of trouble; the problem was that any such constables were untrained, moreover they had to be funded out of the rates. There was also a reluctance to use the army, not least because men armed with lethal weaponry were inclined to use it if the situation seemed desperate. At a West Riding colliery in September 1893, troops, called in because the bulk of the county constabulary was involved with supervising the Doncaster races, shot dead two strikers and wounded fourteen others. From the mid-nineteenth century, police forces had co-operated with each other on an *ad hoc* basis to confront serious disorder, and the 1890 Police Act recommended mutual aid agreements between any counties and boroughs likely to be the scene of disturbances. However, by 1908 only thirty counties and twenty-seven boroughs had such agreements and this was just as a wave of industrial unrest was to sweep the British Isles.

The industrial unrest in the years immediately before the First World War highlighted several of the contradictions and potential for conflict within the British policing system. Enforcing the law so as to protect the right to work of blackleg labour can lead to a situation where the maintenance of the public peace is threatened. A dock strike in Newport,

Monmouthshire, in May 1910 witnessed the head constable, in close consultation with his watch committee, opting for the preservation of the peace rather than the protection of blackleg labour. The decision was made easier by the aggressive and uncompromising attitude of the company which, new to the port, was the object of the strike. A few months later, however, a lock-out in Swansea brought a very different response. Here the local police chief acted in support of the company and its blackleg workers. Order was restored only after several baton charges and assistance was requested from neighbouring police forces. The watch committee took a different view of how the incident should have been handled, but it was never consulted by its chief police officer.[4] The south Wales coal strike of 1910–11 led to Winston Churchill, the aggressively interventionist home secretary, taking the initiative and sending to the district large numbers of Metropolitan Police supported by troops and under the overall command of an army officer, but accompanied by a Home Office official. At the same time police were deployed in considerable numbers to deal with strikes in Cardiff, Hull and Liverpool and, in 1912, in the London docks. The interpretation of Home Office behaviour and police deployment generated controversy at the time and, subsequently, among historians. Jane Morgan argued that these events boosted the idea of a centralised policing structure within the Home Office.[5] Barbara Weinberger stressed, in contrast, that once the interventionist home secretary, Winston Churchill, had left, the Home Office easily slipped back into a customary passivity regarding provincial policing. Weinberger quotes Prime Minister Asquith's statement to Parliament regarding the policing of these strikes as a 'perfect summary' of the traditional Liberal concept of the state and, it might be added by extension, of the management of the police:

> The Home Secretary is head of the Metropolitan Police. As such he has the same responsibility within that area for the control and management of the police as in municipal boroughs the Watch Committee has, as has the standing Joint Committee of a county, neither more nor less. In the next place, as Home Secretary he has an authority which has gradually grown up and developed for which it is difficult to find any legal or even constitutional origin. He has a conventional authority . . . which has no legal sanction, of giving advice to the local authorities of the country with

---

[4] Barbara Weinberger, *Keeping the Peace? Policing Strikes in Britain 1906–1926* (Berg, 1991), ch. 2.

[5] Jane Morgan, *Conflict and Order: The Police and Labour Disputes in England and Wales 1900–1939* (Clarendon Press, 1987), pp. 276–8.

whom . . . by the law of England, responsibility for the preservation of order rests. It does not rest with central government. The central government is not responsible for the preservation of order.[6]

Yet there were changes. It is difficult to conceive of the events of 1910 to 1912 failing to leave some legacy. Moreover, from the late nineteenth century there was also a growing bureaucratic professionalism within the Home Office, and it appears that the young administrators here were prepared to bypass local police committees and deal directly with senior police officers, who could be considered as the experts in policing matters. In their relations with the Metropolitan Police these bureaucrats had a model for more direct operational involvement with police. Informally too there was communication via the inspectors of constabulary, and all of this could be justified by the increasing complexity of an urbanised, industrial society with a burgeoning population. The First World War was to intensify these developments.

War has commonly been a spur to the strengthening of state power and administrative centralisation, not least with the total wars of the twentieth century. The exigencies of war required the police to undertake a range of new tasks on behalf of central government.[7] The police acquired, for example, duties with respect to military mobilisation and the surveillance of servicemen's wives who were in receipt of separation allowances. The collection of much of the information demanded by government under the Defence of the Realm Acts fell to the police, while police involvement in political surveillance and investigation, which had been increasing immediately before the war, was given a new impetus. All of this occurred as police numbers were significantly depleted by the military's demand for men. Police rest days were reduced and the Police (Emergency Provisions) Act 1915 included a section suspending a man's right to retire except with the authority of his chief constable. Special constables were deployed to plug some of the gaps, while concerns about the supervision of increased numbers of women workers and about the morality of young women in the vicinity of military camps led to the creation of women police patrols, though these women did not have the same powers as policemen and were not sworn in as constables. The Metropolitan Police Women Patrols were formally established in October 1918, but women were not to be fully integrated into the police

---

[6] Weinberger, *Keeping the Peace?*, p. 112.
[7] The following two paragraphs draw heavily on Clive Emsley, *The English Police: A Political and Social History*, 2nd edn (Longman, 1996), pp. 121–36.

service for more than another half-century. In 1948 they were grudgingly accepted into the Police Federation, and the Sex Discrimination Act 1975 led to the formal integration of women into the same units as male officers, though they still faced considerable prejudice and resentment.[8]

In March 1918, against a background of anxiety about public order, the District Conference system was inaugurated to facilitate the flow of information between the Home Office and those charged with maintaining the peace. The country was divided into eight districts, each with its own 'conference' that was periodically to discuss matters relating to public order and to appoint members to a central committee of chief constables that conferred, in turn, with representatives of the Home Office and the armed forces. The District Conference system established, for the first time, a formal forum for borough and county police chiefs to meet and discuss matters of common interest, and, through the link with the Home Office, tied these meetings in directly with central government. But even before the District Conference system was set up, the Home Office had been urging that senior police officers and their local civilian administrations should meet together, with Home Office advice, to decide on an increase in police pay and to bring some uniformity to pensionable pay

Police pay was determined locally but was uniformly frozen during the war. Men in some forces received small bonuses, but these were not linked to pensions. Occupational self-awareness was present among policemen from the mid-nineteenth century. Significant pressure had built up for the creation of a police union by 1914 and dissatisfaction resulting from increased duties and a reduction in holidays and rest days encouraged many wartime policemen to give support to the nascent police union. In August 1918 the dismissal of a Metropolitan Police constable for union activities was the spark which ignited a police strike in the capital. The strike lasted less than a week. It involved both the Metropolitan and City forces; it was almost total, and it achieved almost all of its ends. The dismissed constable was reinstated, a pay rise and other benefits were promised. The government gave ambiguous recognition to the police union, and, in March 1919, established a committee, under Lord Desborough, to examine methods of recruiting, conditions of service, and rates of pay, pensions and allowances in the police

---

[8] See, *inter alia*, John Carrier, *The Campaign for the Employment of Women as Police Officers* (Avebury, 1988); Frances Heidensohn, *Women in Control? The Role of Women in Law Enforcement* (Clarendon Press, 1992).

forces of England, Wales and Scotland. The committee presented its first report at the beginning of July.[9] It drew attention to the strains that the war had imposed on the police and recommended a pay increase which put the police constable significantly above the common labourer with whom he was generally equated. Moreover it urged that pay and conditions of service should be standardised and put under the control of the home secretary. To facilitate such standardisation a Police Council, including representatives of police authorities and men from all ranks of the police, was to be established to advise the home secretary. At the same time the committee considered that there ought to be a formal 'right to confer' within the police. The government used the latter to challenge the police union that had burgeoned following the successful strike in London. In August 1919 a second strike was provoked over the existence of the union. Probably because so many men were satisfied by the promises made in the Desborough Committee's first report and because of an increasing split between radicals and moderates within the union, the strike was a failure, though on this occasion it affected Birmingham and Liverpool as well as London. The union was destroyed; all strikers were dismissed, never to be reinstated; and in the autumn of 1919 what was to become known as the Police Federation was established providing the 'right to confer'.

The Desborough Committee rejected the idea of reorganising the police into a single, national organisation in the belief that this could prejudice relations between the police and the public they served. However, in its second report, published on 1 January 1920,[10] the committee recommended that a distinct Police Department be created within the Home Office; that co-operation between forces be formalised; that training be systematised; that some of the smaller forces be abolished; and that some watch committee powers be delegated to chief constables. Several local authorities objected to the overall standardisation. 'I think it is wicked' the mayor of Stalybridge told his town council,

> that a Policeman in Stalybridge, where rents are so low and where they can live so near their work, should have to be paid the same as London Constables, who have a long distance to travel from home to their work, and where rents are much higher.[11]

[9] *Report of the Committee on the Police Service of England, Wales, and Scotland, Part 1*, Cmd 231 (1919).
[10] *Report of the Committee on the Police Service of England, Wales, and Scotland, Part 2*, Cmd 574 (1920).
[11] *Police Review*, 9 May 1924, 254.

But, though often with reluctance, local authorities went along with most of the suggestions that emerged from the Desborough Committee. The one issue on which they did stand firm was their refusal to countenance the abolition of the smaller forces. Occasionally, governments considered taking steps to encourage or even enforce amalgamations; the Home Office and the inspectors of constabulary considered these would be beneficial and, above all, economical. But such proposals faced concerted opposition from threatened boroughs and from the Association of Municipal Corporations. Local police forces, subject to local control, suited local pride and they were in the tradition of English local government.[12] Responding to an inquiry about whether he considered his powers over the country's police forces were sufficient in November 1926 the home secretary, Sir William Joynson-Hicks, spoke of 'a combination of central and local authority which seems rather complicated, but . . . is well understood by those most concerned and, in practice, gives satisfactory results on the whole'.[13]

Yet even if 'those most concerned' understood the system, they still found it necessary to explain and justify it, and problems occurred from time to time about the relationship between police officers, police authorities and central government. Sir Edward Troup, who served as permanent under-secretary of state in the Home Office from 1908 to 1922, situated English police administration between the centralisation found on much of continental Europe and the practice in the United States which presented 'a picture of local autonomy and democratic control gone mad'. The English system, he maintained, made local authorities responsible for efficiency, chief constables and magistrates responsible for action, but dependent on the police regulations of the home secretary, supervision by the inspectorate, and constant advice and direction from the Home Office which, in turn, drew on the collected wisdom of all the interested and participating parties. Troup urged the necessity of 'team work' in a society that was becoming more and more complex.[14] Unfortunately team work did not help untangle the complexity of several constitutional issues regarding police officers and police committees. Two years before Troup's article, the journal, *Justice of the Peace*, had raised the issue of whether or not a constable was the 'servant' of a local authority. The journal suspected that he was, but considered the question 'not altogether

---

[12] Emsley, *English Police*, pp. 162–3.
[13] HC Deb., 5th series, vol. 199, col. 1224.
[14] Sir Edward Troup, 'Police Administration, Local and National', *Police Journal* (1928), 5–18.

free from doubt'.[15] In 1928 the issue was aired again by O. F. Dowson, barrister-at-law and assistant legal adviser to the Home Office. Dowson declared the police officer to be much more a servant of the Crown than of any local authority:

> Apart from the public character of his office he is clothed with functions and powers which, though exercisable locally only, are not dependent upon or under the complete control of the authority under whose management he is placed and at whose cost he is paid (apart from the Exchequer grant).[16]

In 1930 Justice McCardie gave his important ruling in the case of *Fisher v. Oldham Corporation* which appeared to confirm that the policeman was not the servant of a local authority. This judgement arose out of an incident in which a man, wrongly identified as wanted by two Oldham policemen, sought to sue Oldham Corporation as their employer for wrongful arrest. McCardie's ruling was based on precedents which some have argued relate to the question in very odd ways and, if it was rapidly accepted by politicians and Home Office administrators, others have continued to question its validity.[17] In addition to the constable's status there were other areas of policing and police management in which the definition of jurisdiction was such that it could be, and consequently was, queried by interested parties. Some queried whether, for example, watch committees were committees of, and therefore answerable to, town councils. Early in 1925 the town clerk of Manchester explained to local council members that they were not the police authority and that 'during the year for which the [watch] committee were appointed, the council must submit to the committee's decisions, whether they liked them or not'. The *Justice of the Peace* concurred, though it believed that, in practice, in smaller towns the minutes of the watch committee were generally submitted to the town council for confirmation.[18] Related issues could generate friction between local authorities and the Home Office.

In London there was trouble at the beginning of the 1920s when some Labour-controlled boroughs sought, among other things, to withhold their police precepts. Initially the tactic was proposed to force the reinstatement of men dismissed for their participation in the second

---

[15] *Justice of the Peace*, 6 March 1926, 158, and 15 May, 303.
[16] *Justice of the Peace*, 13 October 1928, 663, and see also 20 October, 679–80, 27 October, 695–6 and 3 November, 710–11.
[17] [1930] 2 KB 364. Geoffrey Marshall, *Police and Government: The Status and Accountability of the English Police Constable* (Methuen, 1965), ch. 2; Laurence Lustgarten, *The Governance of Police* (Sweet & Maxwell, 1986), esp. pp. 50–65.
[18] *Justice of the Peace*, 17 January 1925, 36.

police strike. By the close of 1921, Stepney and Islington councils had revived the complaint of having to pay a police precept without any say in how that money was to be spent. The situation became most acute in Poplar where the protest was widened by a council which argued that it would prefer spending money on schemes to assist the unemployed; several councillors were gaoled as a result.[19]

The home secretary enjoyed the privilege of being able to tell Parliament that he was not the police authority and therefore could not be involved when questions were asked about provincial police behaviour, particularly towards strikers and the unemployed. Nevertheless, during the inter-war period the Home Office was dragged into several clashes between chief constables and their police committees. In these instances the Home Office declined, metaphorically, to wash its hands, and commonly sided with the chief constable. The most notable instances concerned three chief constables in south Wales who argued bitterly with their police committees over the handling of industrial troubles,[20] and the head constable of St Helens who the town's watch committee sought to dismiss in 1927.[21] In these instances the critics of the police chief were generally from the political Left. V. F. Bosanquet, the chief constable of Monmouthshire, spoke disparagingly of the 'little lot of communists' on his police committee, while the inquiry that exonerated Head Constable A. R. Ellerington in St Helens, expressed concern about senior police officers 'at the mercy of a temporary majority of a Watch Committee acting perhaps on party lines'. The unspoken assumption within the Home Office, regarding such instances and inquiries, indeed the unspoken assumption among the political elite in general, appears always to have been that, while politicians, and especially men of the Left, were, by definition, 'political', chief policemen were police experts and, by definition, 'non-political'. But it must not be assumed that chief constables and police authorities with a Labour majority were always divided over the policing of strikes and political demonstrations during the inter-war period. While there were some senior officers who were highly suspicious of strikers and left-leaning organisations such as the National Unemployed Workers Committee and, while the National Council for Civil Liberties was established in part because of concerns

---

[19] *Bull's Eye*, 7 January 1921, 7 and 1 April 1921, 8; *Justice of the Peace*, 17 December 1921, 587.
[20] Morgan, *Conflict and Order*, pp. 133–4 and 192–201.
[21] *St Helen's Police Force: Reports of Inquiries held in November, 1927, and in March and April, 1928*, Cmd 3103 (1928).

over police bias against left-wing demonstrators, there were also a few chief constables who went out of their way to maintain good relations with strikers during the General Strike and who showed a singular hostility toward the British Union of Fascists.[22]

Constitutional anomalies that did not occur in the context of serious industrial unrest or have an overt political element were always less contentious, but they could excite keen debate. At the beginning of 1930, D. J. Vaughan, Labour MP for the Forest of Dean and chairman of the Monmouthshire SJC, expressed his alarm at the lack of democratic accountability of such police committees. 'At each quarterly meeting of the County Council', he explained in an article first published in *The Gloucester Citizen*,

> I 'present' (note the word) the minutes [of the SJC], stating among other things that we require £25,000 (£100,000 a year) from the Council Fund. As chairman, I carefully explain that even the 'presentation' of our minutes is only an act of grace, that we are a statutory body, that we need answer no questions, and that we are altogether outside such mundane matters as democratic rule. Our minutes are the minutes of the Medes and Persians, which alter not. No control, no cash, has no meaning in our philosophy.[23]

Three years later the chief constable of Warwickshire refused to send his force's accounts to the county council for audit. After a year's consideration, a Home Office investigation found in favour of the chief constable. To the *Police Review*, the weekly journal which claimed to speak for the rank-and-file police officers, this was another example of the autocratic powers possessed by the chief constables of the counties. The *Review* spoke up for democratic accountability though principally, perhaps, because it had long been critical of the disciplinary autonomy of county chief constables. It urged that the borough watch committee system be replicated in the counties. 'What answers so well in Birmingham City would succeed in Warwick County, and to the great advantage of Police administration.'[24] However, given the ruling of the town clerk of Manchester regarding the accountability of watch commit-

---

[22] Emsley, *English Police*, pp. 138–43.

[23] *Police Review*, 28 March 1930, 230.

[24] *Police Review*, 3 February 1933, 83 and 2 February 1934, 76. See also, *inter alia*, the *Review*'s comments on the chief constable of Monmouthshire, 1 April 1926, 211: 'let the powers of County Chief Constables be limited in like manner as those possessed by Borough Chiefs. This is not the age for autocrats.' A similar case was made in *The Countryman* in July 1935, see *Justice of the Peace*, 6 July 1935, 434.

tees to town councils, the situation in the boroughs was probably not quite the clear-cut contrast that the *Police Review* believed.

Criticism of the autocratic behaviour of chief constables was commonly linked with criticism of the military backgrounds of many chiefs, especially in the counties, and with fears of a 'militarisation' of the police. Such fears were recurrent in the short-lived journal *Bull's Eye* that was published in the aftermath of the failed strike of 1919 as the mouthpiece of the banned union.[25] But the appointment of Captain Athelstan Popkess—a former army intelligence officer in Ireland, an officer of the Palestine gendarmerie, and subsequently assistant provost-mashal at Aldershot—to be chief constable of Nottingham brought a protest from the Labour group on the city council. Popkess's 'experience and outlook', it was noted, 'are purely military in character, and differing fundamentally from those demanded in the civil Police'.[26] The *Justice of the Peace* believed that the appointment of military men to senior police posts should not become the rule.[27] Labour MPs raised questions in Parliament about such appointments; and George Lansbury, among others, protested that the proposal, made by Viscount Trenchard as Metropolitan Police commissioner, for a police college to train senior officers was just another step toward militarisation.[28] There were related concerns about the way in which the police handled political demonstrations. The Left was particularly critical and complained persistently of police sympathy towards the British Union of Fascists. But press and public concerns about the police generally focused elsewhere. In the inter-war years, for the first time, ordinary police began regularly to come into conflict with respectable members of the middle classes as a result of burgeoning car ownership.[29] Also during the 1920s, there were a series of scandals involving the bribery of policemen by bookies and nightclub owners, and allegations of police snooping and high-handedness towards members of the public while investigating infringements of public decency. Public unease led, in 1928, to the creation of the Royal Commission on Police Powers and Procedure, chaired by Viscount Lee of Fareham.

[25] See, for example, *Bull's Eye*, 11 August 1920, 3–4; 2 August 1920, 2; 1 October 1920, 3, 6 and 7; 29 October 1920, 1–4.

[26] *Police Review*, 13 December 1929, 1944; see also, PRO HO 45/24711.

[27] *Justice of the Peace*, 15 May 1927, 362; 30 July 1932, 513; 4 March 1933, 126.

[28] See, *inter alia*, HC Deb., 5th series, vol. 265, cols 845 and 873, vol. 278, col. 958, vol. 283, cols 1806–7, and vol. 304, cols 938–9.

[29] Clive Emsley, ' "Mother, what *did* policemen do when there weren't any motors?" The Law, the Police and the Regulation of Motor Traffic in England, 1900–1939', *Historical Journal* (1993).

The report of the Royal Commission gave the police a clean bill of health.[30] There were occasional 'black sheep', but then policemen were, like everybody else, 'prone on occasion to human infirmities, and more beset than most . . . by problems and temptations'. Indeed, in its introductory observations, the Commission went out of its way to stress how similar policemen were to ordinary citizens:

> Despite the imposition of many extraneous duties on the Police by legislation or administrative action, the principle remains that a policeman, in the view of the common law, is only 'a person paid to perform, as a matter of duty, acts which if he were so minded he might have done voluntarily'.

As the secretary of a subsequent Royal Commission was to note, this is a slight misquotation from Sir James Fitzjames Stephen's authoritative *A History of the Criminal Law of England*. It is a statement based on no legal standing, and appears to run completely counter to what the nineteenth-century police reformers had in mind when they established the institution.[31] Nevertheless, it fitted well with a desire to maintain a distinction between the police of the United Kingdom and those of continental Europe. It was to underpin the work of Charles Reith, one of the most prolific of police historians who began publishing his histories of the English police on the eve of the Second World War,[32] and it was to be quoted and endorsed by the Royal Commission that reported in 1962.[33]

The police were better organised and better prepared for war in 1939 than they had been a quarter of a century before. Once again war meant additional duties, reductions in manpower, a closer relationship between senior police officers and central government and a corresponding loosening of links with local government. In October 1942 the home secretary Herbert Morrison presented regulations to Parliament under the Emergency Powers (Defence) Act to enable him to amalgamate police forces if he considered it necessary for military operations. The proposal was criticised and Morrison gave assurances that any such measures would last only as long as the demands of war required. A series of amalga-

---

[30] *Report of the Royal Commission on Police Powers and Procedure*, Cmd 3297 (1929).

[31] T. A. Critchley, *A History of Police in England and Wales*, revised edn (Constable, 1978), pp. 20–2. Critchley was a career civil servant who served as secretary to the Royal Commission on Police which met from 1960 to 1962, and as a senior member of the Police Department in the Home Office.

[32] Reith published five books on the history of the police between 1938 and 1952. See also O. Hjellemo, 'A Tribute to an Unusual Historian of Police: Charles Edward Williams Reith (1886–1957)', *Police College Magazine* (1977).

[33] *Royal Commission on the Police: Final Report*, Cmnd 1728 (1962), para. 30.

mations, generally uniting borough forces with their surrounding counties, was made under these regulations early in 1943. When peace came, Morrison and Chuter Ede, his successor at the Home Office, were reluctant to see a return to the *status quo ante*. Much to the annoyance of the Association of Metropolitan Corporations, the Police Act 1946 provided for the amalgamation of forces in counties and county boroughs with populations of fewer than 100,000. By 1948 the number of forces in England and Wales had been reduced from 183 to 131, and another six disappeared before 1960.

Police pay had been significantly boosted as a result of the Desborough Committee. There were pay cuts during the Depression but the wage of the police officer remained comfortably above that of unskilled workers. New pay scales were introduced in April 1945 and a further increase followed the next year, but neither brought in sufficient recruits to restore the decline in numbers that had begun with the exigencies of war. The employment situation after 1945 meant that the pension and job security of police officers were no longer the draws that they had been during the 1930s. A committee chaired by Lord Oaksey presented two reports on pay and conditions in April and November 1949,[34] but neither these, nor the new negotiating body, the Police Council of Great Britain—set up as a result of the committee's recommendations—solved the problem of low pay which continued through the next decade. At the end of the 1950s a series of high-profile scandals involving chief constables charged with corruption and/or clashing with their police authorities, together with cases suggesting high-handed and/or brutal behaviour by officers of lower rank, led to the creation of a Royal Commission chaired by Sir Henry Willink QC, master of Magdalene College, Cambridge.

The Willink Commission was given a wide remit. It was to consider the constitution and function of local police authorities, the status and accountability of all police officers, police public relations with particular attention to the ways in which complaints might most effectively be handled, and the broad principles that ought to govern the remuneration of the police. It tackled the final issue first with an interim report in November 1960 declaring the pay situation to be serious, and proposing a significant increase that was as welcome to the Police Federation as it

[34] *Reports of the Committee on Police Conditions of Service, Part 1*, Cmd 7674, and *Part 2*, Cmd 7831 (1949).

was annoying to local authorities.[35] But, if the local authorities were irked by this, they were to find that far worse was to follow. The final report of the Willink Commission, published in May 1962, accepted without question McCardie's ruling in *Fisher* v. *Oldham Corporation*. It was open-minded on the issue of a national police force; a minority report by Dr A. L. Goodhart urged the creation of such, though the majority felt that local forces worked well enough. As a whole, however, the Commission agreed that the role of local authorities should essentially be one of offering advice and guidance to chief constables and it advocated a greater role for the home secretary in policing outside London, particularly with reference to the boroughs. Most of the Commission's recommendations were incorporated into a bill presented in November 1963 which attempted to define the roles of the various components of the tripartite system—home secretary, police authority and chief constable—and which completely revised the legislation on provincial police administration. The police authorities of both county and borough forces were to be uniformly drawn from councillors (two-thirds) and magistrates (one-third) and their task was to maintain and equip an efficient force. Henceforth chief constables were to have sole responsibility for all operational matters.

The Association of Municipal Corporations was strongly opposed to this proposal. It considered the home secretary to be misreading history:

> The historical anomaly is that when county councils were established in 1888 it was decided to make the administration of police in counties a joint function of county councils and quarter sessions—a compromise to retain for the justices some of their administrative functions. We believe in the principle of democratic control over the police, which means that all members of the watch committee should be elected members of the council. If uniformity between counties and boroughs is to be achieved at all costs then it is the existing county system which should be altered.[36]

It suspected that the real reason for the proposal was the notion that watch committees were not impartial bodies because they were largely composed of local politicians. This, however, was to confuse politics with party politics: 'Many decisions are made "politically" but are not necessarily thereby partisan or biased against individuals.' The association pointed out that the home secretary was the police authority for

---

[35] *Royal Commission on the Police: Interim Report*, Cmnd 1222 (1960).
[36] Birmingham University Library, Special Collections, Association of Municipal Corporations Records, Box 25, Minutes 1963, fol. 514.

the Metropolitan Police and was himself a politician. Moreover, there was no reason to suppose that magistrates were untainted by party politics, but they were not necessarily the worse for that. There were protests that the Royal Commission, and the proposed legislation, were moving the country in the direction of a 'police state', a term used by several speakers at a conference of representatives of the Borough Police Authorities. 'We do not want Gauleiters in our towns,' declared a speaker from Manchester, 'we want Chief Constables, and we want control by representatives'.[37] The proposed legislation was condemned as 'radical change'.

> The effect . . . would be to place full responsibility for efficient policing of the area on the chief constable, who would be directly accountable to no one: he would not be subject to any instructions from any elected body in the way in which he enforced the law. At present if a watch committee form the view that their force has acted with unnecessary violence in dealing with a political demonstration, they can require their chief constable to use gentler methods in future, or if they are not satisfied that he is sufficiently energetic in dealing with crime they can call on him to act more vigorously or to adopt new methods, for example the use of police dogs. A chief constable ought not to be permitted to be a law unto himself.[38]

In spite of this hostility the bill passed with relatively little opposition in Parliament. It did not lead to the kind of 'police state' that members of the Association of Borough Corporations professed to fear, but the problems of police accountability and control were not resolved as events of the last third of the century were to show.

The Royal Commission's assertion that greater efficiency was to be achieved through larger units was picked up in the 1964 Act which provided a more certain means for obtaining amalgamations. The real impetus for amalgamations, however, came when Roy Jenkins took up the policy on his arrival at the Home Office in 1966. The logical outcome of the policy would have resulted in forty-four police forces for England and Wales, but the boundary reorganisations resulting from the Local Government Act 1972 effectively resulted in the number of regional police forces being reduced further to forty-one. Robert Reiner's assessment of the chief constables of these forces published at the beginning of the 1990s suggests that most of these officers sought to establish good working relationships with their police authorities. This would suggest

---

[37] Association of Municipal Corporations Records, Box 25, fol. 64.
[38] Ibid., fol. 514.

that the chief constables were trying to provide the kind of service that the local representatives sought, though it was also apparent that chief constables generally preferred those authorities that essentially 'acted as a sounding-board for local opinion' and disliked those which questioned their decisions.[39] Reiner has also argued that the Police Act 1964 effectively emasculated police authorities.[40] These authorities were required to share police costs with the Treasury and, in the words of the legislation, to maintain an 'adequate and efficient police force' for their area. But their powers of appointment and dismissal of chief constables were circumscribed by the home secretary and, if the chief constable declined to submit any report requested by the authority, the home secretary was to arbitrate.

The legislation of 1964 gave chief constables complete authority over operational matters. Yet the concept of 'operations' was not, and is not, readily defined. Police operations can easily overlap with policing policy, and policy involves political and financial implications which, it has forcefully been argued, in a democratic society should be more properly decided by elected representatives.[41] In 1968, Raymond Blackburn, a moral entrepreneur, challenged the directives of the commissioner of the Metropolitan Police regarding the policing of clubs which he, Blackburn, quite rightly, saw as reducing the effectiveness of the enforcement of the laws against illegal gaming. The case was fought all the way to the Court of Appeal and resulted in a judges' ruling that was subsequently seen as underpinning the doctrine of constabulary independence. Constables, it was maintained, were responsible only to the law, with no account being taken by the judges of the police discretion to act, or not to act, in certain instances. Moreover, the assumption by the judges appears, once again, to have been that the democratic control of the police by political representatives could mean only the favouring of those representatives' supporters. Like the earlier ruling by McCardie the ruling in *R. v. Metropolitan Police Commissioner, ex p. Blackburn* has not gone unchallenged. '[S]eldom have so many errors of law and logic been compressed into one paragraph', concluded one professor of law on Lord Denning's judgement in the case.[42] Nevertheless, at the turn of the century, it was

[39] Robert Reiner, *Chief Constables* (Oxford University Press, 1991), p. 251.
[40] Robert Reiner, *The Politics of the Police*, 3rd edn (Oxford University Press, 2000), pp. 188–9.
[41] Lustgarten, *The Governance of Police*, pp. 20–2 and 172–3.
[42] [1968] QB 118. Lustgarten, *The Governance of Police*, p. 64.

Denning's judgement that was considered to define and to clarify the situation.

Proposals were made at the close of the 1970s for some increase in the influence of the provincial police authorities, and in 1980 for some democratic input into the running of the Metropolitan Police. However, during the 1970s the Police Federation and senior police officers appeared to become more and more closely identified with the law-and-order policies of the Conservative Party. Following their electoral victory in 1979, the Conservatives were inherently suspicious of those radical Labour politicians in the inner cities who demanded a greater measure of police accountability to the police committees. These demands were especially noticeable in London where the Greater London Council established groups to monitor police policy and behaviour. The industrial unrest and turbulence within the inner cities during the 1980s brought tensions between chief constables and police authorities to a head on several occasions, especially in Greater Manchester and on Merseyside.[43] In the miners' strike of 1984–5 some police authorities objected vociferously to their districts being denuded of police officers who were bussed to the coalfields for long periods to police picket lines. Their protests were overridden, sometimes rudely, by chief constables, though it would be wrong to suppose that the chief constables themselves were acting under orders from the Home Office. Rather, the mutual aid rendered during the strike was co-ordinated by officers from the Association of Chief Police Officers (ACPO) operating from the National Reporting Centre (NRC) within, but not part of, the Home Office. Furthermore, some requests for mutual aid were denied during the strike when chief constables considered that their local commitments would have been too compromised; and the chief constables in Wales remained determined to confine the policing of the Welsh pits to Welsh police.[44] The police role in the miners' strike led to accusations that they were becoming the strong arm of Margaret Thatcher's Conservative government. This, together with increasing media and public criticism, concerned many officers of all ranks.[45] The miners' strike witnessed the climax of what might be termed heavy policing and, in the aftermath, there was a

---

[43] Barry Loveday, *The Role and Effectiveness of the Merseyside Police Committee* (Merseyside County Council, 1985); Eugene McLaughlin, *Community, Policing and Accountability* (Avebury, 1994).

[44] Reiner, *Chief Constables*, pp. 186–8.

[45] Reiner, *Chief Constables*, pp. 183–6; Roger Graeff, *Talking Blues* (Collins, 1989), pp. 74–5.

significant degree of bridge building between senior police officers and the political opposition.

In the early 1990s, the Conservative government, still firmly wedded to policies of law and order, resolved upon a further reorganisation of police authorities. The avowed intention of the bill introduced by Michael Howard as home secretary was, in keeping with the political ideology of the time, to make them more 'businesslike'. The more rigorous elements of Home Office supervision of the authorities proposed in the bill were removed under pressure from the House of Lords. Nevertheless the effect of the Police and Magistrates' Courts Act 1994, confirmed by the Police Act 1996, was to reduce still further the democratic element within the police authorities, though it did provide them with a new, if very limited, degree of involvement in policy-making. The authorities were required to draw up annual policing plans for their area in conjunction with their chief constable and in the light of national objectives and performance targets set by the home secretary. The authorities themselves, however, were reduced from memberships of between thirty and forty to a uniform seventeen individuals, of whom nine were drawn from democratically elected councillors, three from the magistracy and the remaining five, including the chair, from a complex process that involved considerable input from the Home Office. The election of a Labour government in May 1997 brought no changes to the system in spite of the fact that the new Labour home secretary, Jack Straw, had been the principal advocate of greater local authority influence nearly twenty years before. However, the Greater London Authority Act 1999 established a degree of formal local government influence over the Metropolitan Police by establishing, for the first time in the capital, a police authority with similar powers to those elsewhere.

The overall strengthening of ties between the police and the Home Office was apparent, not only in the reduction of the police authorities but also through the development of HMIC and the increasing authority of the ACPO. Most notably from the early 1980s, inspections by the HMIC became more rigorous and more uniform. There was a gradual change in the personnel appointed to the inspectorate from senior officers at the end of their careers to somewhat younger chief constables who still had time to serve. Moreover, chief constables were now all career police officers; it was no longer acceptable to bring in commanders from the armed forces and, whatever their educational qualifications or speed of their promotion, by the 1980s all chief constables had begun their police service as lowly beat officers. Greater uniformity in HMIC inspections, exemplified by the computer-based management information system (the Matrix of Police Indicators) which was used to plan them, increasingly directed policing into the channels prepared by the Home Office. The ACPO—formed in 1948 as an amalgamation of the County Chief Constables Club and the Chief Constables' Association (Cities and Boroughs)—first gained significant public prominence for its centralised organisation of police mutual aid during the miners' strike of 1984–5. In 1989 its funding was enhanced by the Home Office specifically to develop a proper secretariat charged with establishing a policy analysis unit. Yet, to be fair to the Home Office, the policies of centralisation were not simply concocted within its own corridors for its own benefit and aggrandisement. It found itself under pressure to take greater control of policing, and from unlikely quarters. In 1991, for example, the influential House of Commons Public Accounts Committee was critical of the Home Office for its lack of control of provincial police forces when these forces absorbed so much public expenditure. The most vocal of the critics tended to be Labour MPs, some of whose local government colleagues had been those most determined to weaken central government influence over the police in the previous decade.

Another issue of concern during the closing years of the century was the system of investigating complaints against the police. Here the problem highlighted by critics was not central government involvement, but the lack of independent investigation and adjudication for such complaints. Section 49 of the Police Act 1964, following the recommendation of the Willink Commission, codified the existing situation—the police were responsible for investigating themselves, though in cases involving the most serious complaints officers from another force could be brought in. In 1976 the Police Complaints Board was established; it was to receive the report of the senior officer investigating a complaint and any other relevant papers. But the board did not provide independent, in the sense of non-police, investigations, and this continued to concern critics. Following Lord Scarman's report into the Brixton riots, the recommendations of the House of Commons Select Committee on Home Affairs, and the withdrawal of opposition to independent investigations by both the Police Federation and some chief constables, a new body, the Police Complaints Authority (PCA), was established by the Police and Criminal Evidence Act 1984. The new complaints procedure, like the old, did not distinguish between complaints that a police officer had committed a criminal offence and complaints that he or she was not properly carrying out his or her duties. The PCA was required to supervise all complaints connected with death or injury and was authorised to supervise all investigations. This constituted a significant step towards the independent scrutiny of complaints, but the PCA remained dependent on police officers for investigations, and a series of inquiries in the last decade of the century questioned whether the system enjoyed public confidence.[46]

Policing in twentieth-century Scotland followed a pattern similar to that in England and Wales. There was a reduction in the authority of local representatives on police committees and a series of amalgamations that left just eight large forces in Scotland by the close of the century. Yet the senior police officers of Scotland, unlike those of Northern Ireland, were not members of the ACPO. In Ireland the troubles of 1919–22 resulted in partition; the RIC was disbanded and the northern counties, which remained part of the United Kingdom, were henceforth policed by the Royal Ulster Constabulary (RUC). The RUC, with its various special constabulary adjuncts, was the only police force in the UK whose officers carried firearms as a rule. Given the continuing friction between the dominant, essentially Protestant politicians and their supporters, who sought to preserve the union, and Irish nationalists, the RUC acquired a partisan and sectarian tinge. At the turn of the century, however, Northern Ireland was the first region of the United Kingdom to have a fully independent official appointed whose task was to investigate and adjudicate on complaints against the police. At the same time an independent commission under a former Conservative minister, Chris Patten, recommended the creation of a policing board aimed at bringing a degree of local control over the force and a renaming of the institution to appease nationalist opposition.[47]

In conclusion, and looking forward, it is important to recognise that, at the close of the twentieth century, influences from a new direction were beginning to have an impact on policing in Britain.[48] Membership

---

[46] *Report of the Royal Commission on Criminal Justice*, Cm 2263 (1993), p. 48; *First Report of the House of Commons Home Affairs Committee on Police Disciplinary and Complaints Procedures*, HC 258 (1997); *The Stephen Lawrence Inquiry: Report of an Inquiry by Sir William Macpherson of Cluny*, Cm 4262-I (1999), ch. 46. For an important perspective on police complaints that has rarely figured in the debates, see Graham Smith, 'Police Complaints and Criminal Prosecutions', *Modern Law Review* (2001), 372–92.

[47] Independent Commission for Policing in Northern Ireland, *A New Beginning: Policing in Northern Ireland* (1999).

[48] Paul Swallow, 'The Effects of Europeanisation on the British Police', unpublished paper presented to the CESDIP/GERN-CNRS seminar, 'Questions de Police: Les enjeux nationaux de l'unification européene dans le domaine policier', Paris, March 2001.

of the European Community and initiatives emanating from Europe exposed weaknesses in the policing system and brought new pressures for centralisation. The ACPO sought to represent British policing with reference to European police co-operation. But, at times, individual forces could find themselves left to their own devices. The most obvious example here was the Kent Constabulary having to develop its own response to the Channel Tunnel and the necessary liaison with French, Belgian and Dutch police institutions. On the national level, however, principally as a result of government responses to European directives the National Criminal Intelligence Unit (NCIS) was established in 1992. Six years later the National Crime Squad (NCS) was created out of the former regional crime squads. The latter was equal to NCIS but served also as its operational arm. The directors of both NCIS and NCS were given ranks equivalent to that of chief constable and, since the organisations were granted 'agency' status, they acquired financial and operational independence, together with the ability to employ staff on their own account rather than borrow them from police forces. These organisations have the potential to present a challenge to the autonomy of chief constables. Moreover NCIS, through its links with Europol, also has the potential to develop a leading role in bringing together a variety of policing organisations some of which have hitherto been considered to be separate from the 'police', namely the sections of Customs and Excise involved with the suppression of drugs trafficking, of the Immigration Service responsible for dealing with illegal immigration, and the former MI5 and MI6 intelligence agencies which, with the end of the Cold War, were given new responsibilities concerning international terrorism and organised crime.

The new developments, which have not been widely aired in public debate, might further reduce the vestiges of local policing as it has been understood in England, though the extent to which any of this constitutes a threat to liberty is a moot point. When questions of the centralisation of the police have been raised, as for example in the early 1960s and during the 1980s, rational argument has commonly been swamped by emotion, and utopian visions of the English past or potential police–community relations. But centralised and/or militarised police systems do not automatically lead to a reduction in civil liberty. The Garda Siochana in the Republic of Ireland and the Rigspolitie of Denmark provide two examples of single state police forces functioning within democratic societies, and there are others. The French Gendarmerie Nationale and Italy's Arma dei Carabinieri are proud of their military heritage and are no more perceived by the population as a threat to liberty and democracy than is the traditional English bobby. It is at least arguable that it is neither centralisation nor militarisation that constitutes a threat to civil liberties, but political philosophies and the uses to which institutions are put.

Bibliography

Archival sources

Archival sources for the English police during the twentieth century tend to be scattered and often poorly catalogued and preserved. There is material in the Public Record Office, particularly in the Home Office files (especially HO 45) and in the Metropolitan Police files (MEPO). But the sources for provincial police forces are scattered between county and municipal record offices, and some still remain in police hands. Ian Bridgeman and Clive Emsley, *A Guide to the Archives of the Police Forces of England and Wales*, Police History Society Monograph No. 2 (Cambridge, 1989) provides information on the archives that remained in police hands, but the situation is known to have changed in several forces since publication. Some forces have handed over material to local record offices (Cambridgeshire, for example), while others have taken rather less interest and less care than could have been wished.

Printed sources

Primary

The annual reports of HMIC and of the commissioner of the Metropolitan Police, both of which are essential for any historical work on the police, are printed as parliamentary papers. The twentieth century also witnessed a series of parliamentary inquiries and Royal Commissions into the police and policing. Especially important are:

Report of the Royal Commission upon the Duties of the Metropolitan Police, Cd 4136 (1908), vol. 1.
Evidence, Cd 4260 (1908), vol. 2.
Evidence, Appendices, Cd 4261 (1908), vol. 3.
Report of the Committee on the Police Service of England, Wales and Scotland, Part 1, Cmd 253 (1919) (the Desborough Committee); *Part 2*, Cmd 574 (1919); *Evidence*, Cmd 874 (1920).
Report of the Royal Commission on Police Powers and Procedure, Cmd 3297 (1928–9).
Report of the Committee on Police Conditions of Service, Part 1, Cmd 7674 (1948–9) (the Oaksey Committee); *Part 2*, Cmd 7831 (1948–9).
Royal Commission on the Police: Interim Report, Cmnd 1222 (1960) (the Willink Commission); *Final Report*, Cmnd 1728 (1962).

The Stephen Lawrence Inquiry: Report of an Inquiry by Sir William Macpherson of Cluny, Cm 4262–I (1999); *Appendices*, Cm 4262-II.

Some journals also contain valuable material, notably the 'trade' paper *Police Review*, *Parade Gossip*, the periodical published by the strikers dismissed in 1919, *Bull's Eye*, and the semi-official *The Police Journal* (see below, Articles) and *Justice of the Peace*.

Books

Ascoli, David, *The Queen's Peace: The Origins and Development of the Metropolitan Police 1829–1979* (Hamish Hamilton, 1979).

Carrier, John, *The Campaign for the Employment of Women as Police Officers* (Avebury, 1988).

Critchley, T. A., *A History of Police in England and Wales*, revised edn (Constable, 1978).

Emsley, Clive, *The English Police: A Political and Social History*, 2nd edn (Longman, 1996).

Geary, Roger, *Policing Industrial Disputes, 1893–1985* (Cambridge University Press, 1985).

Heidensohn, Frances, *Women in Control? The Role of Women in Law Enforcement* (Clarendon Press, 1992).

Jefferson, Tony and Grimshaw, Roger, *Controlling the Constable: Police Accountability in England and Wales* (Frederick Muller, 1984).

Jefferson, Tony, *The Case Against Paramilitary Policing* (Open University Press, 1990).

Jones, David J. V., *Crime and Policing in the Twentieth Century: The South Wales Experience* (University of Wales Press, 1996).

Loveday, Barry, *The Role and Effectiveness of the Merseyside Police Committee* (Merseyside County Council, 1985).

Lustgarten, Laurence, *The Governance of Police* (Sweet & Maxwell, 1986).

McLaughlin, Eugene, *Community, Policing and Accountability* (Avebury, 1994)

Marshall, Geoffrey, *Police and Government: The Status and Accountability of the English Police Constable* (Methuen, 1965).

Morgan, Jane, *Conflict and Order: The Police and Labour Disputes in England and Wales 1900–1939* (Clarendon Press, 1987).

Reiner, Robert, *Chief Constables* (Oxford University Press, 1991).

Reiner, Robert, *The Politics of the Police*, 3rd edn (Oxford University Press, 2000).

Stallion, Martin and Wall, David S., *The British Police: Police Forces and Chief Officers 1829–2000* (Police History Society, 1999).

Waddington, P. A. J., *The Strong Arm of the Law* (Clarendon Press, 1991).

Wall, David S., *The Chief Constables of England and Wales: The Socio-legal History of a Criminal Justice Elite* (Dartmouth/Ashgate, 1998).

Weinberger, Barbara, *Keeping the Peace? Policing Strikes in Britain 1906–1926* (Berg, 1991).

Weinberger, Barbara, *The Best Police in the World: An Oral History of English Policing from the 1930s to the 1960s* (Scolar Press, 1995).

Articles

Allen, V. L., 'The National Union of Police and Prison Officers', *Economic History Review* (1958–9).

Cohen, Paul, 'The Police, the Home Office and Surveillance of the British Union of Fascists', *Intelligence and National Security* (1986).

Emsley, Clive, ' "Mother, what *did* policemen do when there weren't any motors?" The Law, the Police and the Regulation of Motor Traffic in England, 1900–1939', *Historical Journal* (1993).

Englander, David, 'Police and Public Order in Britain 1914–1918', in Clive Emsley and Barabara Weinberger (eds), *Policing Western Europe: Politics, Professionalism and Public Order, 1850–1940* (Greenwood Press, 1991).

Jones, Inspector W., 'The Scope and Functions of Local and Central Government in Police Administration', *Police Journal* (1932).

Marshall, Geoffrey, 'Police Accountability Revisited', in D. Butler and A. H. Halsey (eds), *Policy and Politics* (Macmillan, 1978).

Smith, Graham, 'Police Complaints and Criminal Prosecutions', *Modern Law Review* (2001).

Stevenson, John, 'The BUF, the Metropolitan Police and Public Order', in K. Lunn and R. C. Thurlow (eds), *British Fascism: Essays on the Radical Right in Inter-war Britain* (Croom Helm, 1980).

Taylor, Howard, 'The Politics of the Rising Crime Statistics of England and Wales, 1914–1960', *Crime, histoire & sociétés* (1998).

Troup, Sir Edward, 'Police Administration, Local and Central', *Police Journal* (1928).

Weinberger, Barabara, 'Police Perceptions of Labour in the Inter-war Period: The Case of the Unemployed and of the Miners on Strike', in Francis Snyder and Douglas Hay (eds), *Labour, Law, and Crime: An Historical Perspective* (Tavistock, 1986).

Unpublished manuscript volumes

Dixon, Sir A. L., 'The Emergency Work of the Police Forces in the Second World War', copy in the Police Staff College Library, Bramshill.

Dixon, Sir A. L., 'The Home Office and the Police between the Two World Wars', copy in the Police Staff College Library, Bramshill.

15.
The United Kingdom as a Territorial State
BRIGID HADFIELD

Introduction

Edmund Burke wrote, in a different context, that 'it is in the nature of all greatness not to be exact',[1] but in a chapter such as this, of potentially immense proportions, a certain amount of precision is required. First, the 'United Kingdom' of the title is being used here in its strict legal sense of Great Britain and (Northern) Ireland,[2] thus excluding from consideration the Isle of Man and the Channel Islands.

Second, the reach of the word 'territorial' has to be limited. This is more problematic, but a pragmatic choice has been made based on a constitutional leitmotif of at least half, probably more, of the twentieth century.

Home rule/devolution/independence—debated, introduced or not, successful or otherwise—has, in these various guises, focused primarily, although not exclusively, on the national component portions of the United Kingdom, by which is meant England, Scotland, Wales and Ireland/Northern Ireland. The exact constitutional description of such entities while a part of the United Kingdom is not itself free of controversy or debate. The Speaker's Conference on Devolution, which reported in 1920, used the term 'component portions'.[3]

Some fifty years later, the Kilbrandon Commission on the Constitution, reporting in 1973, referred to Scotland and Wales as (arguably)

---

[1] Edmund Burke, *On American Taxation* (1775), p. 26.
[2] Union with Ireland Act and Act of Union (Ir) 1800, First Article; Government of Ireland Act 1920, section 1(2); Irish Free State (Agreement) Act 1922; Irish Free State (Consequential Provisions) Act 1922; Royal and Parliamentary Titles Act 1927, section 2 (2); and the Interpretation Act 1978, schedule 1. For Great Britain, see the Anglo-Scottish Act and Treaty of Union 1707.
[3] Cmd 692 (1920), Terms of Reference (3).

possessing 'separate national identities',[4] although by the end of the century the Labour government, on introducing devolution, referred to Scotland as 'a proud historic nation'[5] in the United Kingdom, whereas Wales became a European 'economic region'.[6] The post-1920 Northern Ireland has received a variety of constitutional labels, employed with varying degrees of approval or opprobrium: from quasi-dominion status and province to statelet or sub-state to (not a) 'coconut colony'.[7] Its status in this regard cannot be isolated from the important distinction to be drawn between 'state' and 'nation'[8] in both its Irish and British manifestations. The 1937 Irish Constitution, in its opening Articles, draws a distinction between the Irish nation and the Irish state, a distinction at the heart of the original and amended Articles 2 and 3, to be considered further below.[9]

Nonetheless, in broad terms, it can be accepted that within the United Kingdom there are (excluding the 'European') six territorial identities:

[4] Cmnd 5460, vol. 1, para. 328. The commission's Terms of Reference referred to the 'several countries, nations and regions' of the United Kingdom. In para. 326, it is stated that it is 'possible to argue endlessly about the meaning of the word "nation", . . . The factors which have to be taken into account include the geography, history, race, language and culture.'

[5] The prime minister, Tony Blair, in the Preface to *Scotland's Parliament*, Cm 3658 (July 1997).

[6] The secretary of state for Wales, Foreword to *A Voice for Wales*, Cm 3718 (July 1997).

[7] A phrase used by the last prime minister of Northern Ireland, then Brian (later Lord) Faulkner, after direct rule had been imposed under the terms of the Northern Ireland (Temporary Provisions) Act 1972. Quoted in S. Elliott and W. D. Flackes, *Northern Ireland: Political Directory 1968–1999* (Blackstaff Press, 1999), p. 253. Also quoted in the significantly titled *Ulster—A Nation* by Ulster Vanguard 1972, available on www.cain.ulst.ac.uk.

[8] See, for example, Ernest Gellner, *Nations and Nationalism* (Cornell University Press, 1983): 'nations and states are not the same contingency. Nationalism holds that they were destined for each other; that either without the other is incomplete, and constitutes a tragedy. But before they could become intended for each other, each of them had to emerge, and their emergence was independent and contingent. The state has certainly emerged without the help of the nation. Some nations have certainly emerged without the blessings of their own state'. Gellner identified two incomplete, provisional definitions of the idea of the nation, the cultural and the voluntaristic, pp. 6–7. See also E. Gellner, 'Nations, States and Religions', in *The State: Historical and Political Dimensions*, eds R. English and Charles Townshend (Routledge, 1999). See also Neil MacCormick, *Questioning Sovereignty* (Oxford University Press, 1999), ch. 11, 'A Kind of Nationalism', esp. p. 170 on 'Civic Nationalism'.

[9] Amended Article 2, inserted in the Irish Constitution in 1999, reads, 'It is the entitlement and birthright of every person born in the Island of Ireland, which includes its islands and seas, to be part of the Irish Nation . . . Furthermore, the Irish nation cherishes its special affinity with people of Irish ancestry living abroad who share its cultural identity and heritage'.

British,[10] English, Irish, Northern Irish (or Ulster),[11] Scottish and Welsh. They are not necessarily exclusive identities. These identities constitute the focus of the 'territorial' in the title of this chapter, thus excluding consideration of regional or sub-national questions, such as the Cornish, the Shetlanders and Orcadians,[12] the relationships between Gael and Scot, or South, North or West Wales. Crucially, what this stance preludes is a detailed consideration of the regional answers to what is increasingly being termed the 'English question',[13] although in the context of 'home rule all round' or of devolution, the question is not a new one. The question itself is addressed broadly—as it inevitably must be—but the regional answers are not substantively considered.[14] Regionalism, on one level at least, addresses issues of better or decentralised government rather than the need for 'national' government.

The two major territorial questions, posed primarily in the first and last quarters of the twentieth century, may be broadly put. The first is: What should be done with Ireland, and later specifically Northern Ireland? For the Irish, at least, the question has been what should be done with Britain? The questions are phrased thus to indicate underlying attitudes of mind as much as a respect for constitutional niceties. Too often the Irish/Ulster question is avoided in consideration of the United Kingdom constitution—(often unacceptably) through resort to the evasive and bald epithet that it is 'different'.[15] It is argued here, however,

---

[10] For two recent and very different considerations of aspects of this identity, see the Runnymede Trust, *Commission on the Future of Multi-ethnic Britain*, chaired by Lord Parekh (Profile Books, October 2000), arguing, *inter alia*, for a movement from the debate concerning liberal and nationalist views of society to one between liberal (a community of citizens) and pluralist (a community of communities) theories of Britain, and Brian Feeney 'UUP haven't a Clue about UK Identity', *Irish News*, 8 October 2000.

[11] This adjective may be used to refer either to the ancient province of Ireland, thus including the six Northern Ireland counties and the counties of Cavan, Donegal and Monaghan, or Northern Ireland specifically, especially in its Unionist/Protestant context. It is used here in the latter—and later, but not generally accepted sense.

[12] How many now recall the existence of the debate which led to the inclusion of sections 41 and 84 in the Scotland Act 1978? See the Annotations to the Act by A. W. Bradley and D. J. Christie (Current Law Statutes Annotated, 1978).

[13] See, for example, *The English Question*, eds S. Chen and T. Wright (Fabian Society, 2000).

[14] See, for general reading covering this issue throughout the latter part of the century, G. Stoker, 'Is Regional Government the answer to the English Question?', J. Tomaney, 'The Regional Governance of England', in R. Hazell (ed.), *The State and the Nations* (Imprint Academic, 2000); and J. Tomaney and P. Hetherington, 'Monitoring the English Regions', Report 1 (Constitution Unit, 2000).

[15] For wider lessons to be drawn from Northern Irish constitutional innovations, see J. Hayes and P. O'Higgins (eds), *Lessons from Northern Ireland* (SLS Legal Publications, 1990).

that explanation of these issues is fundamentally pertinent to any real consideration of the territoriality of the United Kingdom constitution.

The second major territorial question concerns the relationships between the component parts of the United Kingdom, and specifically Great Britain.[16] Consideration of this enables an exploration of the move from a centre-driven or top down constitutional agenda to what may be termed grass-roots constitutionalism—or, to phrase it alternatively, it enables an exploration of the debates concerning the United Kingdom as a nation state or as a multinational state. The Speaker's Conference on Devolution had as one of its major concerns the desirability of facilitating Westminster in its consideration of national, imperial and foreign affairs and hence of delegating or devolving the regional and the local. The Kilbrandon Commission, by contrast, was at least partially driven by discontent with the workings of an over-centralised government, as expressed particularly within Scotland and Wales and manifesting itself in increased support for the nationalist parties.

This, it is accepted, is to posit the discreteness both between and within the two major questions too starkly. This is rectified below. The purpose of such a formulation at this stage is as a (partial) explanation for the threefold division of this chapter. The first section deals with 1900–25, home rule (all round?) and the Irish and Ulster questions. The second deals with 1925–65 and the dominance of constitutional homogeneity. The third deals with 1965–2000 and the constitutional reconfiguration of the United Kingdom. The two major questions were asked and answered differently in the first and last quarters of the century and largely ignored during the middle period. It is the purpose of this chapter to consider why.

Territoriality and the rule of recognition

Throughout the whole of the twentieth century, the constitution's dominant legal principle, its very keystone, has been the doctrine of

---

[16] Both the Speaker's Conference and the Kilbrandon Commission concentrated on Great Britain. The former felt itself 'absolved from the necessity of considering the special problems raised by Ireland' because of the introduction of the Government of Ireland bill (the 1920 Act), see Cmd 692, p. 3. The latter 'suspended' its work on Northern Ireland, in light of the onset of 'the Troubles' and no recommendations were made. See Cmnd 5640, vol. 1, paras 1246 and 1248.

parliamentary sovereignty,[17] although it has not been universally accepted in its absolute or 'pure' form, concerning the absence both of any legal restraints on its legislative competence and also of any other competing law-making power.[18] From the doctrine of sovereignty, the unitary nature of the state inevitably follows: 'Unitarianism, in short, means the concentration of the strength of the state in the hands of one visible sovereign power',[19] here Parliament. Professor Neil Walker has percipiently shown that the 'unitary constitutional conception of the British State' is actually 'a very flexible notion, capable of embracing a wide range of different constitutional structures and visions'.[20] He argues that even those fundamental limits, imposed by the unitary nature of the constitution, on this capacity to embrace diversity are less constraining than is often assumed; but that, anyway, the development of 'multi-dimensionality'[21] in public law itself means that the unitary conception of political community can now be transcended through the transcendence of the constitutional state itself.[22]

The aim of this chapter, being a historical review of the twentieth century in which current constitutional developments inevitably play but a small part, is to explore an hypothesis which in fact relates to the

---

[17] Dicey's *Law of the Constitution*, 9th edn (Macmillan, 1950); 'The Sovereignty of parliament is (from a legal point of view) the dominant characteristic of our political institutions ... Parliamentary sovereignty is ... an undoubted legal fact ... This doctrine of the legislative supremacy of parliament is the very keystone of the laws of the constitution. But it is, we must admit, a dogma which does not always find ready acceptance ...', at pp. 39, 68 and 70.

[18] With regard to the argument, for example, that the Westminster Parliament is not free to legislate contrary to the fundamental terms of the (constituent) Acts of Union, the issue of the 'justiciability' of a breach has been the harder element to address. See, most famously, the *dictum* of Lord President Cooper in *MacCormick v. Lord Advocate* (1953) SC 396. By contrast, arguments against the traditional doctrine based on the impact of EC law in the United Kingdom have, given the jurisdiction and jurisprudence of the European Court of Justice, more effectively addressed both limbs of the doctrine.

[19] Dicey, *Law of the Constitution*, n. 17, p. 157. See also Neil Walker, 'Beyond the Unitary Conception of the United Kingdom Constitution?', *Public Law (2000)*, 387: 'The unitary conception ... is parasitic upon the doctrine of parliamentary sovereignty, which, in formal terms at least, is the "top rule" of the constitution', and at 390: ' ... the unitary legal state ... has a single centre of authority from which all other authority flows, in the British case the Queen in Parliament'.

[20] Walker, 'Beyond the Unitary Conception?', 388.

[21] Walker, 'Beyond the Unitary Conception?', 388: 'Where there once prevailed a monist conception of public law, of state constitutions as the single and largely unrivalled sources of public legal authority within the world order ... the state [now] is increasingly in competition with other authoritative sites'.

[22] Walker, 'Beyond the Unitary Conception?', 388–9: 'Or, in other terms, the new pluralism *of* legal orders to some extent compensates for the limits of pluralism *within* a particular legal order.'

middle stage of Professor Walker's argument, the nature of the fundamental limits set by the unitary conception.[23]

Dicey, in comparing the sovereign Westminster Parliament and non-sovereign legislatures, quoted de Tocqueville as writing of Westminster as being 'at once a legislative and a constituent assembly'.[24] Dicey, while not accepting the total accuracy of the terms, accepted their descriptive convenience thus: 'Being a "legislative" assembly [Westminster] can make ordinary laws, being a "constituent" assembly, it can make laws which shift the basis of the constitution'.[25] In that light this chapter pursues what may be termed the 'externalised' and 'internalised' exercises of the constituent power in the territorial domain.

In the former case, Westminster exercises the constituent power with regard to a part of the United Kingdom, which part is then *de jure* or *de facto* externalised out of the territory (and in many ways out of the constitution) so that the principle of sovereignty remains undiminished, in essence simply becoming more territorially confined. (This may also be called the 'dominion option' without necessarily equating a part of the United Kingdom with a dominion. In this scenario, the Westminster Parliament essentially 'wills' the fundamental nature of the constitutional reconfiguration—although the underlying facts to which it is responding may or may not have been welcome.)

In the latter, the internalised, situation, the power is exercised by Westminster as a delegation of power *simpliciter*, subject at all times to its sovereignty. Westminster does not thereby intend to create a *fundamental* constitutional reconfiguration nor does it intend to create any competing centres of authority. It is, however, argued here that a constituent (territorial) power, even when exercised in an internalised fashion, cannot be exercised again by Westminster in the same way as theretofore

Professor H. L. A. Hart, in addressing the question of uncertainty in the rule of recognition and hence of 'the ultimate criteria used by the courts in identifying valid rules of law',[26] distinguishes between *continuing* and *self-embracing* omnipotence. The former means that Parliament is sovereign 'in the sense that it is free, at every moment of its existence as a continuing body, not only from legal limitations imposed *ab extra*, but

---

[23] Walker, 'Beyond the Unitary Conception?', 388–9.

[24] Dicey, *Law of the Constitution*, n. 17, p. 88. The quotation is from *Oeuvres complètes*, 14th edn (1864).

[25] Dicey, *Law of the Constitution*, n. 17, p. 88.

[26] *The Concept of Law*, 1st edn (Clarendon Press, 1961), p. 144.

also from its own prior legislation'.[27] The latter means that 'Parliament should *not* be incapable of limiting irrevocably the legislative competence of its successors but, on the contrary, should have this wider self-limiting power'.[28] Thus, taking a hypothesis to be tested throughout the twentieth century: when Westminster legislates in a way which de Tocqueville and Dicey describe as constituent, as shifting the basis of the constitution, its sovereign power ceases to be continuing[29] and becomes self-embracing. It irrevocably denies itself the power to legislate for the new dispensation in the same way, that is, on the same principles, as before.

1900–25: Home rule all round, devolution and independence

Within the first quarter of the twentieth century, several arguments were in play concerning the desirability of introducing at least some measure of devolution[30] within the United Kingdom. Obviously some of these arguments had arisen during the last decades of the nineteenth century. More pertinently here each argument received varying emphasis both in time and of place throughout this period. Crucially too, the interplay and interaction between these arguments influenced the nature and outcome of the devolution debate itself.

The first factor was the *imperial* concern, namely the desire to ensure or secure imperial unity, federation even[31] (and indeed to prevent any United Kingdom 'fragmentation' imperilling the Empire itself). At one level, this concern could be expressed as a desire to facilitate Westminster in its imperial role binding the Empire together at a time when centrifugal tendencies might have become stronger.[32] In order to do this, Westminster

---

[27] Hart, *Concept of Law*, p. 145.

[28] Ibid., emphasis in original.

[29] Given the almost universal acceptance, at least in the courts, of this definition of Westminster's sovereignty at the start of the twentieth century, no justification for its application here will be provided.

[30] Federalism, home rule (all round) and devolution were sometimes used interchangeably, sometimes not during this period. Technically, of course, federalism and devolution are not the same and where possible the former word will not be used here unless used by the proponents themselves.

[31] The then recent success of the Canadian and Australian federations was also, perhaps, a small factor influencing the debate on internal United Kingdom constitutional reform.

[32] See, for sample, Richard J. Finlay, *A Partnership for Good? Scottish Politics and the Union Since 1880* (John Donald, 1997), pp. 47–8, and P. Jalland, 'United Kingdom Devolution 1910–1914: Political Panacea or Tactical Diversion?', *English Historical Review* (1979), 759.

needed to be free of those responsibilities which might have tended to militate against it. At a time when the demands upon Westminster were increasing concomitant upon the arrival of an expansionist state, the need to 'decongest' Westminster had some force not solely with regard to imperial concerns but also with regard to those aspects of the state's responsibilities which, it was argued, belonged more suitably to regional legislatures, assemblies or councils. It may be stated, parenthetically, that this argument contains two recurring elements within the twentieth-century British constitution: (a) there is the concern to utilise Westminster's time more effectively and (consequently) not to make undue demands upon it, an argument repeated with greater or lesser justification on subsequent occasions,[33] although rarely by governments in the context of the imperative need to modernise Parliament and overhaul its own procedures; (b) the argument on imperial/national/regional affairs foreshadows, albeit in inchoate form and not identically, the 'best level' or subsidiarity debates in the last quarter of the twentieth century stemming from the Europeanisation, or even globalisation, of the constitution. It is thus possible to present the internal aspects of the decongestion of Westminster as a second and separate argument from those relating to the imperial concerns.

Third, there was the need to resolve the Irish question itself, including its conjunction with the Ulster question. This will be returned to as the only issue (the only issues) to be reflected in United Kingdom (and Irish) legislation at this time.

Fourth, there was the need, often overlooked in the light of subsequent events concerning Ireland, but an important element at the time, to secure equality of treatment for Scotland and Wales with regard to whatever measure of home rule was granted to Ireland—the need for 'home rule all round'. There was certainly a feeling, in the first twenty years of the twentieth century (and earlier)—how widespread and deep

---

Jalland here quotes a letter from Asquith to Rosebery written in 1892: 'continued centralisation [at Westminster] means congestion, decay and ultimately death; devolution is essential to free activity and permanent vitality . . . It is only from this point of view that (as I think) HR can be shown to be both imperial (in the true sense) and democratic.'

[33] In this context, see what is in fact a reversal of this point concerning the prorogation (later abolition) of the Northern Ireland Parliament in 1972 (1973) and the refusal of successive Westminster governments totally to integrate laws for Northern Ireland into its primary law-making procedures: '. . . it would [*inter alia*] impose a substantial new legislative burden on the Westminster Parliament'. *The Future of Northern Ireland: A Paper for Discussion* (NIO, HMSO, 1972), para. 44 (a), p. 21.

is hard to quantify—that elements within Scotland and Wales (and within the national political parties)[34] were resentful of the prospect of priority being given, and substantially so, to Ireland's demands. The (re-) introduction of the office of secretary for Scotland in 1885 was highly significant when compared with the provisions of the (Irish) Home Rule bills of 1886 and 1893 and of the later (never implemented) Government of Ireland Act 1914.[35]

A fifth element in the argument for devolution was the need, especially here for Scotland and Wales (essentially non-separatist in their aspirations), to secure parity of treatment with England—that is, as it were, to render the British constitution truly British.

There is, perhaps, a final argument, although it is the internal decongestion of Westminster argument looked at from the regional rather than Westminster perspectives—and that is the need for enhanced 'local' efficiency.

Clearly these factors were likely to interact upon each other, one being counterposed against another in the evolving debates. The search for a feasible formula for devolution all round, as an answer to the congestion of Westminster or the need for national parity within the constitution, could be perceived as a stratagem (intended or otherwise) to postpone or block resolution of the Irish question. The mode of accommodating England in a devolved settlement 'all round'—as one region or as several[36]—could be seized on as a parallel by Unionists keen to exclude Ulster from any all-Ireland constitutional answers. Ultimately, fears that the search for a solution to the Irish question only might imbalance the

---

[34] See, for example, Finlay, *Partnership for Good?*, pp. 44–6 and 'United Kingdom Devolution', 761. See also D. George Boyce, 'Wales and the British State: The Outer Form of Subjugation', in English and Townshend (eds), *The State.*

[35] See Finlay, *Partnership for Good?*, p. 44: 'The demands for the post had been fuelled by a considerable amount of Scottish national sentiment and the campaign, orchestrated by Rosebery, had attracted a significant amount of cross party support [footnote reference omitted]. Compared to home rule, the creation of a junior (Westminster) cabinet post was small beer indeed. At a stroke, the concessions given to Scotland were seen to be of little consequence.' See also Vernon Bogdanor, *Devolution in the United Kingdom* (Oxford University Press, 1999), p. 111, quoting both Lord Salisbury ('The whole object [of the office] is to redress the wounded dignities of the Scotch *(sic)* people—or a section of them— who think that enough is not made of Scotland') and Gladstone, during the Irish home rule debates in 1886, calling the recreation of the post 'a little mouthful of Home Rule'.

[36] See, for example, Winston Churchill's 'Heptarchy' solution to England, March 1911, discussed in Jalland, 'United Kingdom Devolution', 965–6.

constitution as a whole[37] did not prevent this becoming the dominant item on the constitutional agenda. Ireland's increasingly separatist aspirations and intentions were reflected crucially, in its insistence, manifested in a variety of ways, that its national identity and statehood lay not at the grant of Westminster but in the hands of the Irish people themselves.[38] The increasing circumscriptions, at least within Ireland, of the Irish identity (largely) by the adjectives 'Gaelic' and 'Roman Catholic'[39] meant ultimately that both Ireland and Britain would have to formulate the means of constitutionally accommodating the people (the 'British' and the 'Protestant') who, living largely but by no means exclusively in the north-eastern part of Ireland, regarded Irishness (as so defined) as inappropriate for their sense of national identity—if not anathema.

Westminster's two-stage response to the Irish and Ulster questions, as will be seen, effectively meant that the issues concerning the broader constitutional reconfiguration of Great Britain lay unaddressed for at least another fifty years. Westminster first decided to isolate the issue of home rule for Ireland from home rule all round,[40] thus removing much but not all of the dynamic for the latter (or at least the dynamic at Westminster to address the latter), especially when coupled with the absence of popular and political support for devolution for England *per se*. Second, Westminster at least *pro tempore* addressed the issues by resort to dominion status, *de jure* for what became the Irish Free State and *de facto* for what became Northern Ireland. Ironically, therefore, the Empire, whose unity was regarded by some as of sufficient interest as to (seek to) free Westminster of regional concerns more easily to concentrate on

---

[37] See, for example, F. S. Oliver, writing in *The Times*, 6 May 1918 and quoted in John D. Fair, *British Interparty Conferences: A Study of the Procedure of Conciliation in British Politics 1867–1921* (Clarendon Press, 1980.), p. 223: '. . . it would be an entirely unworkable arrangement—open to every form of confusion and intrigue—if the Parliament of the Union stood in a different relation to Ireland on the one hand, and to England, Wales and Scotland on the other'. It it interesting to wonder whether he would, *mutatis mutandis*, have expressed the same reservations about late-twentieth-century asymmetrical devolution.

[38] This significant factor will be returned to below, for example, with regard to Scotland at the end of the century: see the Scottish Constitutional Convention, *Claim of Right for Scotland*, its inaugural declaration, 30 March 1989; the Constitution Unit's *Issues Around Scottish Independence*, by David Sinclair (1999); and Neil MacCormick, 'Is There a Constitutional Path to Scottish Independence?', *Parliamentary Affairs* (2000).

[39] See Roy Foster, *Paddy and Mr Punch* (Penguin, 1993), p. 13 and chs 1, 2 and 13 generally.

[40] The fact is that home rule all round involved consideration of Scotland along with Ireland, both for parity reasons and with regard to Scotland in its own right. No general equation is being made between Ireland on the one hand and Wales and Scotland on the other hand, at this stage at least, in terms of how, and in accordance with what principles they sought to reflect their national identities in constitutional change.

the imperial, became in the immediate post-war years a vehicle of distance for the partial disintegration of the United Kingdom.[41] The best place for a lawyer to begin a detailed consideration of these two stages is with the enactment (and with events preceding its enactment) by Westminster of its first ever enacted devolution measure, the Government of Ireland Act 1914.[42]

The essence of the 1914 Act—it is not necessary to rehearse the details—is that it provided for one all-Ireland Parliament to be established, the whole of Ireland remaining within the United Kingdom subject to the sovereignty of the Westminster Parliament as 'saved' by section 1(2) of the Act. The Liberal government, at the inception of the bill, which had a prolonged parliamentary passage being enacted under the terms of the Parliament Act 1911, was still committed to a wider application of home rule, even though dealing here solely with Ireland. An original draft of the bill (at that stage, consequently, to be entitled, with accuracy if not brevity, the Government of Ireland and House of Commons (Devolution of Business) bill) contained Lloyd George's 'Grand Committee Scheme' to cater for the inequitable consequences of introducing home rule for Ireland in isolation from other parts of the United Kingdom:

> In order to obviate the inconvenience and injustice which would arise in the interregnum owing to Irish members interfering in purely English, Scottish and Welsh affairs a system of Grand Committees must be set up simultaneously with Irish HR Bill with full and final legislative powers in English, Scottish and Welsh affairs of same character as those delegated to Irish Parliament.[43]

This suggestion was eventually deleted from the bill as finally published (it thus much more closely, but not totally, reflected the 1893 Home Rule

---

[41] It should not be assumed that, throughout this time, all Ireland itself was against the Empire. One point was well put by the Irish nationalist leader and MP, John Redmond, who (in 1893) pointing out the Irish contribution to the Empire added that 'the one spot' where the Irish could not make a full (political) contribution was 'the land of their birth and affection'. Quoted by Norman Davies, *The Isles: A History* (Macmillan, 2000), p. 757.

[42] This was, however, the third Irish Home Rule measure, the first two bills, of 1886 and 1893, never receiving the royal assent. For a comparison of their provisions, see Brigid Hadfield, *The Constitution of Northern Ireland* (SLS Legal Publications, 1989), ch. 1. Although this present chapter is about twentieth-century territoriality, it would be remiss not to consider in passing the impact of Gladstone on the Irish question. See Peter J. Jagger (ed.), *Gladstone* (Hambledon Press, 1998), especially ch. 6 by D. George Boyce, 'Gladstone and Ireland'.

[43] Pencilled Cabinet note, 27 February 1911. Quoted and discussed by Jalland, 'United Kingdom Devolution', 766–7.

bill)—not least in the face of fears that that principle, if included, would stymie home rule for Ireland itself. Nonetheless H. H. Asquith, in introducing the bill into the House of Commons for the first time in April 1912, indicated that it would be carried through 'with the distinct and direct purpose of . . . further and fuller applications of the principle of devolution'.[44] This did not in fact materialise from the government, although parliamentary interest in Scottish home rule did not fade as quickly.[45] What ultimately mattered more, however, was not the 'devolution all round' dimensions (or lack of them) of what became the 1914 Act, but the appositeness both of one single 'all-Ireland' Parliament and, eventually also, of Irish devolution as opposed to independence. Ironically, the 1914 Act was by 1920 shorn of all its dimensions, standing since 1914 solely as a paper reminder of an inchoate and incomplete stage in the home rule debate. Why did this happen? Developments within Ireland, as the bill proceeded towards its enactment, rendered imperative a resolution, not solely of the Irish question, but also of the Ulster question; the question of how to accommodate within Irish home rule (if at all) the distinct identity[46] and political preferences of the majority of the population in the north-eastern part of Ireland[47], who opposed home rule, first in the hope of preventing it altogether, latterly with the intent of securing for themselves—and others within the region[48]—the non-application of the Home Rule bill. There was a not inconsiderable amount of support at Westminster for the Unionist cause,[49]

---

[44] Jalland, 'United Kingdom Devolution', 770 (quoting from HC Hansard of 11 April 1912). For the sequel, see ibid., 770–1.

[45] Ibid., and Finlay, *Partnership for Good?*, ch. 2.

[46] There is much history, on both sides, behind the debate as to whether Irishness within Ireland embraces or excludes the Protestant and the British identities and the extent to which sections within either community even desire such an inclusion or, even, coexistence.

[47] The aims and aspirations of Southern Unionists (Protestants outside the nine-county province of Ulster constituting in the 1911 census only just over 9 per cent of the population) increasingly diverged from Northern Unionists. See R. B. McDowell, *The Fate of Southern Unionists: Crisis and Decline* (Lilliput Press, 1997).

[48] Limitations of space prevent any detailed consideration here of the debate concerning the selection of the ultimately six Ulster counties which, from 1920–1, constituted Northern Ireland, to the omission of Monaghan (25.3 per cent Protestant), Donegal (21.1 per cent) and Cavan (18.5 per cent). See P. Buckland, *A History of Northern Ireland* (Gill & Macmillan, 1981); D. Harkness, *Ireland in the Twentieth Century* (Macmillan, 1996); and Bogdanor, *Devolution*, ch. 3.

[49] But after the December 1910 general election, the balance of power in the House of Commons was held by John Redmond's Irish Nationalist Party, which made the enactment of the bill more rather than less likely.

but events within Ulster had greater impact, as the provisions of the Parliament Act 1911 bore their double consequence: a lengthy parliamentary passage giving greater time for opposition within Ulster to mobilise, conjoined with the certainty that the House of Lords was no longer able to veto the passage of the bill into law.

On 28 September 1912, 'Ulster Day' or 'Covenant Day', the Ulster Solemn League and Covenant[50] was signed by the Ulster Unionist leaders and eventually by a total of nearly half a million men and women. These signatories, convinced that home rule 'would be disastrous to the material well-being of Ulster as well as the whole of Ireland, subversive of our civil and religious freedom, destructive of our citizenship and perilous to the Empire', pledged themselves to:

> stand by one another in defending for ourselves and our children our cherished position of equal citizenship in the United Kingdom and in using all means which may be found necessary to defeat the present conspiracy to set up a Home Rule Parliament in Ireland.

'All means' included, by January 1913, the Ulster Volunteers/the Ulster Volunteer Force, a force of some 90,000 men formed to fight home rule, by force of arms if necessary. They were, in fact, essentially unarmed, at least until the Larne gun-running expedition brought them, illegally, from Germany in April 1914, some 25–35,000 rifles and four million rounds of ammunition—an event of considerable political if not military significance. An 'Ulster Provisional Government' was also prepared for, from September 1913, to take over, at least in Unionist areas, in the event of all-Ireland home rule. The raising of the Ulster Volunteers was matched by the formation in November 1913 of the Irish (National) Volunteers of some 160–180,000 men, called upon, to stand by all means necessary in defence of home rule.[51]

The Government of Ireland bill received the royal assent on 18 September 1914 with no special provision made for Ulster but against the background, both inside and outside Parliament, of attempts ultimately to make provision for the exclusion of Ulster from home rule. The 1914 Act was enacted on the same day as the Suspensory Act 1914, which suspended the operation of both the Irish Act and the Welsh Church Act 1914. The latter Act, also passed under the terms of the Parliament Act 1911, disestablished the (Anglican) Church of Wales, it becoming

---

[50] See significantly, and for comparative purposes, the 1643 Solemn League and Covenant.
[51] Guns and ammunition for the Irish Volunteers also arrived from Germany in August 1914, being brought ashore at (particularly) Howth, near Dublin.

in 1920 the Church *in* Wales,[52] a change of immense significance for nonconformist Wales, and the Church lost all the benefits of establishment. The significance of this Act in securing for Wales a central element in its search for full recognition within the United Kingdom of its cultural and religious identity should not be underestimated. Nevertheless Welsh Church disestablishment and indeed the search for Scottish home rule were, at that time, both rendered of minimal import on the outbreak of the First World War. During the war years, however, the Irish and Ulster questions did not disappear, and 1916 was to become a watershed year, from that day to this, for both nationalist and unionist Ireland.

On the outbreak of the war, the 36th (Ulster) Division was formed from the Ulster Volunteer Force,[53] which played a leading part in the Battle of the Somme, losing 5,500 officers and men on the first two days of July 1916. Tens of thousands of Irish men also responded to Lord Kitchener's call, enlisting for example in the tenth (Irish) Division. Of the Irish Volunteers who responded to Redmond's call to support the war effort (probably 30,000 men) many enlisted in the sixteenth (Irish) Division which itself suffered about 4,500 casualties during the war.[54] Most of the remaining Irish National (that is, pro-Redmond) Volunteers, essentially found that, through military recruitment on the one hand and the lack of purpose (fighting for home rule) on the other, the organisation became defunct. A small number of dissident Irish Volunteers, however, (probably 3,000 initially, but rising to 15,000 by 1915) opposed Redmond's call and a handful of them, with the collaboration of the supreme council of the Irish Republican Brotherhood (an Irish revolutionary body which up until this moment had been subordinate to the constitutional home

---

[52] The Church of Ireland, on its disestablishment under the Irish Church Act 1869, kept its title.

[53] The Ulster Volunteer Force name reappeared in 1966 as the name of a loyalist paramilitary organisation.

[54] The sacrifice of the thirty-sixth (Ulster) Division has gone deep into (particularly) the Protestant Ulster Unionist 'psyche', and in any consideration of the history of Northern Ireland from a unionist perspective should not be underestimated. See the Somme Association and the literature cited on www.pitt.edu/unovose/ulster on 'Ulster and the Great War'. By contrast, the sacrifice of Irish men and women in the First World War was largely ignored in the Irish Free State/Republic of Ireland until relatively recently, as being too much a part of the 'British' history of Ireland. This was most clearly symbolised by the neglect of the Lutyens Irish national war memorial in Dublin to the estimated 49,000 Irishmen who died in the 1914–18 war. The site, including the surrounding gardens, was almost completely neglected until the Irish Office of Public Works restored it during the 1980s.

rule movement) planned the Easter Rising of 1916.[55] The General Post Office in Dublin having been seized on Easter Monday, 24 April, by about 1,000 volunteers, the Proclamation of the Irish Republic was issued, on behalf of its 'Provisional Government':

> ... we declare the right of the people of Ireland to the ownership of Ireland and to the unfettered control of Irish destinies, to be sovereign and indefeasible. The long usurpation of that right by a foreign people and government has not extinguished the right, nor can it ever be extinguished except by the destruction of the Irish people ... [We] hereby proclaim the Irish Republic as a sovereign independent state ... The Irish Republic is entitled to, and hereby claims, the allegiance of every Irishman and Irishwomen. The Republic guarantees religious and civil liberty, equal rights and equal opportunities to all its citizens, and declares its resolve to pursue the happiness and prosperity of the whole nation ... oblivious of the differences carefully fostered by an alien Government, which have divided a minority from the majority in the past.

The (over) reaction of the British authorities to the Rising, explicable at least in part in the context of the ongoing First World War, is often regarded as the (sole or main) cause for the Rising's success. Be that as it may, what is clear is that in the general election of December 1918, Sinn Fein, the party most associated with the Rising and its aims, won seventy-three of the 105 Irish Westminster constituencies, symbolically and in reality eclipsing the Irish Parliamentary Party which won only six. Sinn Fein, a party implacably opposed to the division of Ireland and committed to independence, had replaced the Irish Nationalist Party, a party of evolutionary constitutional change incorporating a willingness to discuss reaching an accommodation with Unionists. The Unionists themselves won a total of twenty-six seats, most notably concentrated in the only four Irish counties with a Protestant majority, Antrim, Armagh, Down and Londonderry.[56] One way and another the people of Ireland and of Ulster had spoken. The supreme legal powers of the Westminster

---

[55] The proclamation itself refers to the IRB (a 'secret revolutionary organisation'), and to the 'open military organisations', both the Irish Volunteers and the Irish Citizens Army. For details of the last-mentioned, see the *Oxford Companion to Irish History*, ed. S. J. Connolly (Oxford University Press, 1998). Sinn Fein (a 'radical nationalist party' founded in 1905 — for fuller details also see Connolly, *Oxford Companion to Irish History*) was, given its aims, widely associated with the Easter Rising, but was not as such mentioned in the Proclamation.

[56] In the 1911 census, Antrim had a 79.5 Protestant population; Armagh, 54.7 per cent; Down, 68.4 per cent; and Londonderry, 58.5 per cent. The cities of Belfast and Londonderry respectively had figures of 75.9 per cent and 43.8 per cent.

Parliament as contained in the Government of Ireland Act 1914 encountered political reality and were replaced.[57] The profundity and extent of
the changes which had taken place over the few years since the introduction of the third home rule bill by Asquith in April 1912 were immense.
A simple enumeration of the post-war developments illustrates this profundity far more than any complex exposition might do—and also
illustrates the price which many paid for the right to have their national
identity embodied in legal and constitutional structures.[58]

1. The Sinn Fein members of the Westminster Parliament refused to
take their seats.[59] On 21 January 1919 the first Dail Eireann (Assembly
of Ireland) met in the Mansion House in Dublin, confirmed the 1916
Proclamation and established a new government. The significance of the
absence of the Irish Republican MPs from Westminster as the Government of Ireland Act 1920 went through its parliamentary stages should
not be overlooked.

2. On 21 January 1919, the Anglo-Irish War (or the War of
Independence) began and lasted until 11 July 1922. It was essentially
waged between the Irish Volunteers (from 1919 known as the Irish
Republican Army) and the 'British Forces' in Ireland, including the Royal
Irish Constabulary and the 'Black and Tans'. During these eighteen
months, 'over 500 soldiers and policemen and over 700 IRA volunteers
were killed. Over 700 civilians died.'[60]

3. In March 1920, the Government of Ireland bill, which received
the royal assent in December 1920, had its second reading in the House
of Commons. It established that the whole of Ireland would remain
within the United Kingdom, with one Parliament for the twenty-six

---

[57] For reasons of space, this account has not considered the considerable number of attempts
made during the war to resolve the question of the (non-) exclusion of Ulster from home
rule. See on this, Buckland, *History of Northern Ireland*; Nicholas Mansergh, *The Unresolved
Question: The Anglo-Irish Settlement and its Undoing 1912–1972* (Yale University Press, 1991),
chs 3 and 4; D. George Boyce, 'Northern Ireland: The Origins of the State', in P. Catterall
and S. McDougall (eds), *The Northern Ireland Question in British Politics* (Macmillan, 1996);
Fair, *British Interparty Conferences*, chs 5, 6 and 10.

[58] It is appreciated that considerable argument lies latent in this sentence, both with regard
to the use of the word 'right' and with regard to the relationship between national identity
and the law.

[59] Mansergh, *Unresolved Question* at p. 109 quotes Churchill as writing that the 'two supreme
services which Ireland rendered Britain . . . are the accession to the Allied cause and the
withdrawal from the House of Commons at its close'.

[60] P. Taylor, *Provos, the IRA and Sinn Fein* (Bloomsbury, 1998), p. 12. The figures given in the
Oxford Companion to Irish History are 405 police, 150 'military', and an estimated 750 IRA
and civilians.

counties of Southern Ireland and one for the six counties of Northern Ireland, in four of which Protestants were in a clear majority.[61] The remaining two Northern Ireland counties, Fermanagh and Tyrone, had a majority Roman Catholic population (56.2 per cent and 55.4 per cent respectively). In the nine-county province of Ulster, the Protestants had a majority of approximately 56 per cent; in the six-county unit the figure was close to 66 per cent. The 1920 Act, therefore, incorporated the unionists' preference for including in Northern Ireland the largest possible area containing a Protestant majority without causing any instability which might have ensued from a closer numerical balance between the two communities. Although the 1920 Act thus divided Ireland, it did contain various significant (although ultimately non-operative)[62] all-Ireland provisions.[63] Section 2 made provision for a Council of Ireland and section 3 conferred on the two Irish Parliaments themselves the power to secure Irish union by their own constituent Acts if they desired so to legislate. The 1920 Act made no provision for the Westminster Parliament to be involved in the process, although under the terms of the 1920 Act the new all-Ireland Parliament would have been subject to Westminster's sovereign powers.

4. Pursuant to a resolution of the House of Commons of 4 June 1919,[64] a Speaker's Conference was established to consider, 'without prejudice to any proposals [the Government] may have to make with regard to Ireland',[65] and to report upon a 'measure of Federal Devolution'[66] for the regions of the United Kingdom. In light of the subsequent publication of the Government of Ireland bill, the conference 'felt [itself] absolved from the necessity of considering the special problems raised by Ireland'[67]

---

[61] See section 1(2) of the 1920 Act and note 56 above.

[62] Section 42 on the all-Ireland High Court of Appeal came into effect on 1 October 1921 and ceased to have effect on 8 December 1922. It heard a total of nine cases. See A. Quekett, *The Constitution of Northern Ireland* (HMSO, 1933), vol. 2, pp. 599–600.

[63] An official summary of the 1920 Act stated: 'Although at the beginning there are to be two Parliaments and two Governments in Ireland, the Act contemplates and affords every facility for Union between North and South, and empowers the two Parliaments by mutual agreement and joint action to terminate partition and to set up one Parliament and one Government for the whole of Ireland.' Quoted in Quekett, *Constitution of Northern Ireland*, p. 584. The details of sections 2, 3 and 7 of the 1920 Act merit close scrutiny.

[64] The following details are all contained in the Speaker's Conference report itself, namely Cmd 692 (1920). See also Fair, *British Interparty Conferences*, ch. 11. The speaker was James Lowther, later Viscount Ullswater.

[65] Cmd 692, p. 1.

[66] Ibid.

[67] Ibid., p. 2.

and concentrated upon formulating proposals for the implementation of devolution in Great Britain. It did not debate as such the arguments for and against the principle of devolution itself. The conference reached agreement on four key areas: the powers to be devolved, financial relations, the judiciary, and the areas in which the legislatures should be established (Scotland, Wales and, after discussion, England too as 'separate and undivided'[68] areas). The conference, however, divided upon the issue of the 'character and composition of the local legislative bodies themselves', namely whether they should be directly elected or not.[69] As Fair has pointed out, however, 'the extraction of the Irish issue from the conference agenda had sapped the vital component necessary to the ultimate success of [federal devolution] in Great Britain'.[70] That issue languished for another day.

5.   On the termination of the Anglo[71]-Irish War, the British prime minister, Lloyd George, entered into negotiations with (some of) the Irish leaders. On 6 December 1921 they formally concluded the Anglo-Irish Treaty[72] under the terms of which the twenty-six-county Irish Free State, as it was termed from 1922 until 1937, left the United Kingdom and became a self-governing dominion in the 'Community of Nations known as the British Empire'.[73] Article 3 of the treaty made provision for the representation of the Crown in Ireland and Article 4 for the oath of allegiance to the British monarch. Articles 11 and 12 addressed the question of Northern Ireland, whose Parliament since May 1921, having been elected, was operating under the provisions of the Government of Ireland Act 1920. These Articles empowered the Parliament of Northern Ireland to opt out of the terms of the agreement, if it so wished, leaving it subject to the continuing terms of the 1920 Act. If that Parliament were to exercise that choice—which it did rapidly—provision was made for institution of a boundary commission to 'determine in accordance with the wishes of the inhabitants, so far as may be compat-

[68] Cmd 692, p. 2.
[69] Ibid., p. 6 and Appendices I and II.
[70] *British Interparty Conferences*, p. 233.
[71] Much yet remains to be written about not solely *Anglo* (literally)—Irish relations, but also throughout this period Scottish–Irish relations.
[72] The correct British title for this is 'Articles of Agreement for a Treaty', reflecting the fact that under British law Ireland itself was not an independent state entitled to enter into 'The Treaty' per se. See Mansergh, *Unresolved Question*, ch. 8.
[73] Article 1.

ible with economic and geographic conditions, the boundaries between Northern Ireland and the rest of Ireland'.[74]

The legal force of the Anglo-Irish Treaty in British constitutional law, and also of the 1922 Irish Constitution, derives from the enactment by Westminster of the incorporating Act: the Irish Free State (Agreement) Act 1922 (as amended)—and thus Westminster, exercising its sovereign powers, redefined the United Kingdom by yielding twenty-six of its counties.[75] Assuming, and the argument is an important one, that this was a breach of Article 1 of the Anglo-Irish Acts of Union (establishing the Union forever), the procedure in accordance with which it was wrought is also significant: namely, an Act of the Westminster Parliament, preceded by negotiations with leaders of the Irish people culminating in a treaty.[76] The Union, as far as Northern Ireland was concerned, was not severed, a decision made effectively by the Parliament of Northern Ireland (albeit as operating for that jurisdiction under the terms of a Westminster Act of Parliament).

It is equally significant to note that, from the Irish perspective, the (1922) Irish Constitution and constitutional status did not derive from a British 'cession' of territory but from an assertion by the Irish people of their nationhood.[77] The 1921 treaty was ratified by the Dail, on 7 January 1922, by sixty-four votes to fifty-seven, and a provisional government was formed; an Irish general election was held in June 1922 at which sixty-eight seats were won by the pro-treaty party and nineteen by the anti-treaty party; a draft Irish Constitution was approved by the Dail and passed into law as the Irish Free State (Saorstat Eireann) Act 1922.[78]

The division within Ireland between the pro- and anti-Treaty faction manifested itself not solely in the Irish election of June 1922 (and, in many ways, in many subsequent elections) but also in the outbreak of the Irish civil war which lasted from June 1922 until May 1923, leaving over 900 people dead. The main point of disagreement at this stage

---

[74] Article 12.

[75] See also Westminster's Irish Free State Constitution Act 1922, which enacted (through section 1 and schedule 1) the Irish Constitution passed by the Irish constituent assembly. For British purposes, this is technically a reference to the Parliament of Southern Ireland established under the 1920 Act. For Irish purposes it was the Dail Eireann. See further text below.

[76] See Harry Calvert, *Constitutional Law in Northern Ireland* (Stevens, 1968), pp. 19–20. See also Brigid Hadfield, 'Learning from the Indians: The Constitutional Guarantee Revisited', *Public Law* (1983).

[77] See Calvert, *Constitutional Law*, and Mansergh, *Unresolved Question*, ch. 9.

[78] Mansergh, *Unresolved Question*, p. 212. See also the statute cited in note 75 above.

between the protagonists was essentially to be found in Articles 3 and 4 of the treaty: Ireland's 'subordination' to the British Crown. As the Irish constitution in later years became *de facto* and then *de jure* republican, the partition of Ireland, clearly significant in 1922, would achieve indisputable prominence. Further, during the Irish civil war the position— existence even—of Northern Ireland featured less significantly given the treaty provision relating to the establishment of the boundary commission. The commission eventually met from December 1924 until the end of 1925, technically with the remit of establishing the 'outer' borders of the United Kingdom, but in essence seeking to resolve the location and nature of the Irish border. Suffice it to state here,[79] that the extent of Northern Ireland as delineated by the Government of Ireland Act 1920 was in no wise altered, a decision ratified by a tripartite agreement (and Westminster legislation) on 3 December 1925.[80] By this stage, the nascent Northern Ireland state had itself already experienced a not inconsiderable amount of violence: in the two years from June 1920, there were over 2,000 casualties, including more than 400 deaths.[81]

By 1925, the all-Ireland dimensions and all the references to Southern Ireland had been deleted by Westminster from the 1920 Act.[82] The Irish Free State had left the United Kingdom and acquired dominion status. Northern Ireland, remaining in the United Kingdom, had devolved government—a system essentially not sought by Unionists, but the benefits of which for them were rapidly appreciated. The 'all round' aspects of devolution, for England, Scotland and Wales, had disappeared and Westminster embarked upon what it hoped would be minimal involvement in Northern Ireland. Arguments, as will be seen, had already commenced concerning Northern Ireland's *de facto* dominion status. This 'distancing' of Westminster's sovereign powers is considered in the next section.

---

[79] See Hadfield, *Constitution of Northern Ireland*, ch. 2; Mansergh, *Unresolved Question*, ch. 10; and *Report of the Irish Boundary Commission*, 1925 (not officially published until over forty years later), introduction by Geoffrey Hand (Irish University Press, 1969).

[80] Ireland (Confirmation of Agreement) Act 1925.

[81] See Buckland, *History of Northern Ireland*, p. 4.

[82] See, for example, especially Irish Free State (Consequential Provisions) Act 1922.

1925–65: Central insistence on homogeneity

During these forty years, there were within 'these islands'—no longer now the United Kingdom—three largely homogeneous blocs of power as perceived by the three respective governments, namely those of the Irish Free State, later the Republic of Ireland, of Northern Ireland and of Great Britain. Although the Irish Free State was no longer a part of the United Kingdom, brief reference will continue to be made to its constitution, for two very important reasons pertinent to the development of the United Kingdom, as a territorial state.

First, the interaction between the former and Northern Ireland, especially if not entirely, over the question of the reunification of Ireland (almost always addressed as required to take place outside the United Kingdom) provides evidence about the attitude of successive British governments as to what constitutes 'our' territory. Second, the evolution of the Irish Constitution and of British–Irish intergovernmental relations, both in the context of the border issue but also increasingly as European partners, has led to developments of significance, constitutionally, for the whole of the 'territorial' United Kingdom.[83]

To return specifically to events immediately subsequent to 1925, however, in terms of the relationship between Great Britain and the Irish Free State on the one hand and between the former and Northern Ireland on the other hand, there developed relationships of, respectively, mutual distance and unilateral indifference.

For the Irish Free State, dominion status was a created rather than evolutionary relationship, as it had been and would continue to be, between Westminster and the other dominions, such as Australia, Canada, New Zealand and South Africa. The sequencing of events over the twenty-five years from 1925 may be starkly stated. The oath of allegiance, provided for in Article 4 of the Anglo-Irish Treaty and included (not without considerable debate)[84] in Article 17 of the 1922

---

[83] The body with the most significance is the British–Irish Council, established under the Belfast Agreement 1998, and the intergovernmental treaty, signed in Dublin on 8 March 1999. This body, which includes representatives of the three devolved governments, as well as the British and Irish governments and those of the Channel Islands and Isle of Man, has in the context of devolution facilitated a wide range of bilateral and multilateral contacts throughout these islands—an element in many ways sadly missing throughout the twentieth century. See below.

[84] See also the Electoral Amendment Act 1927, and Mansergh, *Unresolved Question*, pp. 265–8. Mansergh, at p. 266, quotes de Valera as describing the oath 'as the cause of the strife and dissension in this country since the signing of the Treaty'.

Irish Constitution was repealed in 1933,[85] the same year as the abolition of appeals to the Judicial Committee of the Privy Council from the Irish Supreme Court.[86] The Crown was 'kept on the shelf, scarcely visible behind an apparatus of state symbolism and practice which was entirely republican',[87] while the powers of the governor-general, the representative of the Crown,[88] circumscribed at the outset,[89] were reduced and then almost totally eliminated by 1936. His sole remaining power stemming from the role of the king as 'symbol' of the Commonwealth was preserved by the Executive Authority (External Relations) Act 1936, and related to the accreditation of Irish diplomatic representatives. This Act itself was repealed in 1948 when the Irish Free State became the Republic of Ireland, and left the Commonwealth.[90] As the late Professor Kelly memorably wrote:

> Thus the royal and British theme descended between 1922 and 1948 in a chromatic scale until it ran off the constitutional keyboard; and the full republican chord, which might have been struck together in 1916 if the Easter Rising had succeeded, sounded (for twenty-six counties) in an arpeggio gradually formed over a quarter of a century.[91]

Meanwhile, the new Irish Constitution, Bunreacht na hEireann, of 1937 had by Articles 2 and 3 put the partition of Ireland constitutionally centre

---

[85] The legislation, introduced in 1932, was in essence de Valera's first act on becoming the first Fianna Fail (anti-treaty) prime minister.

[86] This was not peculiar to Ireland of the dominions. Canada, for example, had abolished appeals by 1949. The relationship between Ireland and the other dominions is completely outside the remit of this chapter, but the evolving nature of dominion status generally during this time should not be overlooked. See Mansergh, *Unresolved Question*, ch. 12, and D. Harkness, *The Restless Dominion: The Irish Free State in the British Commonwealth 1921–1931* (Butterworth, 1970). See also the later influence of de Valera's (1921) idea of 'external association'.

[87] J. M. Kelly, *The Irish Constitution*, 3rd edn (New York University Press, 1994), ed. G. Hogan and G. Whyte, p. xc. The preface continues: 'There were no royal visits. The Army was the Army of the Irish Free State and its officers held their commissions from the Government of the Irish Free State. The State's flag was the republican tricolour.'

[88] There were three governors-general in all: Timothy Healy (1922–8), for the significance of his method of appointment, see Mansergh, *Unresolved Question*, pp. 26ff; James MacNeill (1928–32); and Domhnal O'Buacalla/Donal Buckley 'who considerably reduced the visibility of the office'; *Oxford Companion to Irish History*, p. 227.

[89] Mansergh, *Unresolved Question*, pp. 264–5; Kelly, *Irish Constitution*, p. xc.

[90] Ireland had been the only dominion to be neutral during the Second World War. See Harkness, *The Restless Dominian*, n48, ch. 5. On the position of Northern Ireland, see Brian Barton, 'The Impact of Word War II on Northern Ireland and on Belfast–London Relations', ch. 4 in Catterall and McDougall (eds), *Northern Ireland Question*.

[91] Kelly, *Irish Constitution*, p. xc; see also the wording of the Constitution's Preamble.

stage. Article 2 read: 'The national territory consists of the whole island of Ireland, its islands and the territorial seas', while Article 3 addressed the issue of the application of the laws of the Irish Parliament 'pending the reintegration of the national territory'.

The 1937 Constitution, in Article 44.1.2° (removed after a referendum in 1972), stated:

> The state recognises the special position of the Holy Catholic Apostolic and Roman church as the guardian of the Faith professed by the great majority of the citizens.[92]

This provision, although itself of relatively limited legal effect, when bolstered by some judicial interpretation of the fundamental provisions of the Constitution[93] and more especially when coupled with the influence of the Roman Catholic Church within Irish society and upon the government (and indeed in the formulation of the 1937 Constitution itself) led to widespread perceptions (not least among the majority in Northern Ireland) of the Irish State as exclusively Roman Catholic.[94]

Meanwhile, in the Northern Ireland Parliament in 1934, the prime minister of Northern Ireland, James Craig, Viscount Craigavon uttered these often-quoted words:

> ... in the South they boasted of a Catholic state. They still boast of a Catholic state. All I boast of is that we are a Protestant Parliament and a Protestant state.[95]

Both the principles in accordance with which the borders of Northern Ireland had been delineated (including the balance of the populations between the two communities) and, from 1929, the first-past-the-post

---

[92] Article 44.1.3° (also removed by the Fifth Amendment of the Constitution Act 1972) provided that the state 'recognises the Church of Ireland, Presbyterian, Methodist, Quaker and Jewish congregations as well as the other religious denominations existing in Ireland at the date of the coming into operation of the Constitution'. The Protestant population in the Irish Free State was approximately 9 per cent at the time of partition. By 1926, it stood at 7.4 per cent and is around 4 per cent at the start of the twenty-first century.

[93] See Articles 40–3 and the case-law thereon in Kelly, *Irish Constitution*. Obviously, some of the cases arose after the period considered here.

[94] This is obviously a very brief summary. For a detailed consideration, see Dermot Keogh, 'The Role of the Catholic Church in the Republic of Ireland 1922–1995', and Terence Brown, 'Religious Minorities in the Irish Free State and the Republic of Ireland' (and the references in both chapters) in *Building Trust in Ireland*, studies commissioned by the (Irish) Forum for Peace and Reconciliation (Blackstaff Press, 1996).

[95] NI HC Deb., vol. 16, col. 1095, 24 April 1934.

system used for the Northern Ireland Parliament elections[96] meant that Craigavon's statement could be—and was—more than empty rhetoric.[97] It did not render it easy, to put it at its lowest level, for northern nationalists to identify with the Northern Ireland state.[98] A question which must, however, be addressed concerns the extent to which successive Westminster governments were prepared to intervene in matters which had been devolved to the Northern Ireland Parliament by the 1920 Act. Crucially, although the 1920 Act embodied a devolved system with Westminster's supreme powers carefully preserved in the Act, this was coupled with what may be termed a 'dominion attitude'. Although an Irish republican/ nationalist perspective on Northern Ireland (often) identifies British desire to 'hold on' to Northern Ireland as crucial to the continuance of partition, Westminster governments generally[99] throughout this period sought to put distance[100] between themselves and Northern Ireland. The *de facto* equation[101] of Northern Ireland to a dominion can be illustrated

---

[96] The consequences of the change, wrought by the Northern Ireland Parliament itself under section 14(5) of the Government of Ireland Act 1920, from proportional representation, did not directly impact upon the levels of unionist/nationalist representation in the devolved Parliament. Of more fundamental concern was the impact of the change on smaller parties (and against fragmentation) and the ways in which the legislation itself was perceived. See Sydney Elliott, 'Voting Systems and Political Parties in Northern Ireland', Brigid Hadfield (ed.), *Northern Ireland Politics and the Constitution* (Open University Press, 1992), and P. Buckland, *The Factory of Grievances: Devolved Government in Northern Ireland, 1921–1939* (Gill & Macmillan, 1979).

[97] See J. D. Brewer (with G. Higgins), *Anti-Catholicism in Northern Ireland 1600–1998: The Mote and the Beam* (Macmillan, 1998), ch. 3.

[98] The position of the minority within the Irish Free State/Republic of Ireland, proportionately small at its inception and continually dwindling, was of a different nature. See, for example, MacDowell, *Fate of Southern Unionists*, ch. 8.

[99] For discussion of the 'strategic' or defence value of Northern Ireland (and the change encapsulated in this regard in British government policy during the 1990s), see, for example, Barton, 'Impact of World War II', and B. Hadfield, 'From the Downing Street Declaration 1969 to the Downing Street Declaration 1993', *Contemporary Issues in Irish Law and Politics* (Sweet & Maxwell, 1998), vol. 1.

[100] This eventually culminated in a statutory declaration of a willingness to 'cede' Northern Ireland, subject to the consent criterion, in the cause of a United Ireland: now section 1 of the Northern Ireland Act 1998. The comments of Sir Alec Doughas-Home (as foreign secretary) on the undesirability of direct rule, made in 1972, are nonetheless typical of a prevalent attitude: '[Direct rule] means that we would end up being stuck with governing the province, permanently ... no sustainable framework for keeping Northern Ireland within the United Kingdom could ever be contrived'. His advice to the UK prime minister, Mr Edward Heath, was: 'start to push the people of Northern Ireland towards a United Ireland, rather than trying to tie them more closely in the United Kingdom'. Quoted by P. Hennessy, *The Prime Minister: The Office and Its Holders since 1945* (Penguin 2000), p. 347.

[101] This was an equation easier to make in the 1920s both with regard to Northern Ireland itself and with regard to the more influential nature of dominion status. References to

by a development early in the life of Northern Ireland. In 1922 the Northern Ireland government sought to introduce legislation to change the voting system employed in the local government elections from proportional representation to first past the post. This was a matter which fell squarely within that Parliament's powers as devolved under the 1920 Act. Under section 12(2) of the 1920 Act the governor of Northern Ireland had the power to reserve the royal assent to a bill passed by the Northern Ireland Parliament. This power[102] was used with regard to the Local Government bill (NI) and the royal assent was withheld from it from July 1922 until September 1922.[103] During this time conflicting arguments were presented by both the Irish (provisional) government and by the dominion analogy upon a British government, reluctant to intervene in devolved Northern Ireland affairs for fear of precipitating a Northern Ireland general election, the only outcome of which would be a re-elected Unionist government. Perhaps because the British government had no desire to reopen the question of its relationship with Northern Ireland (and certainly no desire to take a step which could have led to the 'reintegration' of Northern Ireland affairs at Westminster), the British government decided not to instruct the governor to withhold the royal assent from the 1922 bill. Winston Churchill had argued that for Westminster to intervene in clearly internal matters would set a precedent potentially limiting the future powers of the dominion Parliaments (of which the Irish Free State would shortly be one). The (counter-) arguments of the Irish (provisional) government, that the intentions

---

the quasi-dominion status of Northern Ireland, however, lasted into the 1950s: see 'The Constitution of Northern Ireland', in *Devolution of Government: The Experiment in Northern Ireland*, Foreword by D. S. Neill (Allen & Unwin, 1953), at p. 16. It should also be remembered that the Northern Ireland Parliament had, albeit within the context of a United Ireland, rejected dominion status. A variation on this theme recurred during 1974–5 when Prime Minister Harold Wilson toyed with the idea of dominion status for Northern Ireland in the context of a United Ireland: Hennessy, *Prime Minister*, p. 372. Of course, Northern Ireland as a part of the United Kingdom was unquestionably not in law the same as the dominions, as Professor Calvert cogently indicated. The fact that Northern Ireland possessed a governor with ceremonial functions helped to foster this analogy. All later devolution Acts have clearly placed conduct of relations from Westminster and Whitehall in the hands of a 'territorial' secretary of state with no 'devolution' of the Crown's ceremonial functions. See *Constitutional Law*, ch. 6 generally, specifically p. 90. The quasi-dominion analogy should not be confused with the quasi-federal analogy also used with regard to Northern Ireland.

[102] An equivalent power (vested in a secretary of state) is to be found in the later devolution Acts.

[103] This was before the boundary commission met.

behind the 1922 bill were both anti-nationalist and designed to pre-empt the work of the boundary commission, were not accepted by the British government. The power to reserve was never used again.[104] The distancing of Westminster's sovereign powers had begun. This was reinforced by the Speakers' Rulings, at Westminster and at the Northern Ireland Parliament, in 1923, precluding questions and debates on matters either respectively delegated by it or withheld from it.[105] Westminster's sovereign powers with regard to Northern Ireland were in effect to lie latent until the mid-1960s. Northern Ireland's centre-perceived homogeneity was not disturbed by Westminster. It should also be remembered that throughout this stage in Northern Ireland—as in the rest of the United Kingdom—for a variety of reasons what we would now term the public law role (and jurisprudence) of the courts was essentially a quiescent one. The courts had little or no role to play concerning the principles and procedures of public power.

Westminster's major 'territorial' contribution to the Irish/Ulster questions during the forty years considered here was the enactment of the Ireland Act 1949 in response to the Republic of Ireland's departure from His Majesty's dominions. Section 2 of the Act declared that, notwithstanding that fact, 'the Republic of Ireland is not a foreign country' for the purpose of United Kingdom law. Section 1(2) declared that Northern Ireland remained a part of the United Kingdom and the dominions and would not cease to be so[106] without the consent of the Parliament of

---

[104] See Buckland, *Factory of Grievances*, pp. 267–75.

[105] These issues are discussed by Calvert, *Constitutional Law*, pp. 94ff. Note also the Westminster home secretary's statement of 25 October 1967 (on pp. 93–4) and Calvert's pointed comment on it on p. 94: 'This, it is believed, is the first government utterance to evidence a proper understanding of the nature of constitutional relationships between Northern Ireland and the United Kingdom.' See also Bogdanor, *Devolution*, pp. 73–4 and 'Devolution: The Constitutional Aspects', in *Constitutional Reform in the United Kingdom: Practice and Principles* (Hart, 1998), p. 15.

[106] Section 1(2) which, of course, envisages separation albeit with consent and its 'replacement' section 1 of Northern Ireland Constitution Act 1973 did not actually spell out what the status of Northern Ireland would become were it to leave the United Kingdom, (although the questions asked in the border poll held in March 1973 under the Northern Ireland (Border Poll) Act 1972 clearly indicated that the sole alternative was a United Ireland outside the UK). The first statutory provision to indicate this was the Northern Ireland Act 1998—a position already indicated in the British Article 5 of the Sunningdale Agreement 1973, in Article 1 of the Anglo-Irish Agreement 1985 and in the Downing Street Declaration 1993. The difference between the opting out provision of the 1922 Treaty for the Northern Ireland Parliament and section 1(2) of the 1949 Act is that in 1922 Northern Ireland would have 'stayed' in dominion status (outside the United Kingdom); in 1949 (or later) it would have been opting out of the UK (and into a united non-dominion status Ireland).

Northern Ireland—a provision viewed with considerable hostility by the Dail[107]. Although there is recent evidence to suggest cross-border relations in Ireland during this period were not as sparse as is commonly believed,[108] the language of the 1925 tripartite agreement (signed after the boundary commission terminated) seemed remarkably dated twenty-five years later:

> ... whereas the progress of events and the improved relations now subsisting between the British Government, the Government of the Irish Free State, and the Government of Northern Ireland, and their respective peoples, make it desirable to amend and supplement the (1922) Articles of Agreement [the Treaty], so as to avoid any causes of friction which might mar or retard the further growth of friendly relations between the said governments and peoples:
>
> And whereas the British Government and the Government of the Irish Free State being united in amity in this undertaking with the Government of Northern Ireland, and being resolved to aid one another in a spirit of neighbourly comradeship ...[109]

During the forty years from 1925, viewing the constitutions through the centres of power (and not equating the two jurisdictions in all respects), it may be stated that on both sides of the Irish border there was what may be termed 'heightened homogeneity'. Meanwhile with regard to Great Britain, partly but not solely because of the distancing of the Irish and Ulster questions, homogeneity too ruled or so it seemed. Territorial questions, at least from the Westminster and Whitehall perspective, were no longer being asked and therefore (not logically, but practically) were not being addressed—a position in many ways justified not least, for several reasons, during the years of the Second World War.

This homogeneity was reinforced, if not mainly caused, by the virtual demise after the 1931 general election of the most constitutionally reform-minded party, the Liberals. From then on, throughout this forty-year period, party politics were dominated by two parties based on class rather than territory. In general terms, fundamental constitutional reform was not a part of the agenda of the Conservative (and Unionist) Party; the Labour Party regarded such reform as irrelevant to social and economic concerns, a commitment heightened by the Depression. The parties per-

---

[107] See Dail Eireann, Parliamentary Debates, vol. 115, col. 786, 10 May 1949.

[108] See M. Kennedy, *Division and Consensus: The Politics of Cross-border Relations in Ireland 1925–1969* (Institute of Public Administration, 2000).

[109] Schedule to the Ireland (Confirmation of Agreement) Act 1925.

ceived themselves and were perceived by the electorate as 'national' rather than territorial parties. The National Party of Wales/Plaid Cymru[110] was founded in 1925, with the aim of pursuing the idea of self-government for Wales in one form or another, initially through dominion status. The Scottish National Party (SNP) was founded in 1934, with the merger of the National Party of Scotland (1928) and the Scottish Party (founded in 1932),[111] to pursue a nationalist agenda. Yet as Vernon Bogdanor points out:

> As with the SNP, so also with Plaid Cymru—its birth was a sign not of the strength of peripheral nationalism but of its weakness. For both movements were founded on a recognition that neither national self-government nor even devolution were to be obtained from the other parties.[112]

Neither party gained any significant electoral[113] success until the Hamilton by-election of 1967 gave the (safe Labour) seat to Winnie Ewing of the SNP, and Gwynfor Evans, president of Plaid Cymru from 1945 to 1981, won Camarthen in a July 1966 by-election.[114] However, in the years from 1925 until the mid-1960s beneath the overall perception of national homogeneity and 'peripheral nationalism' (or the pursuit of laws and institutions to accommodate divergent national identity), certain significant changes did take place, not identical with regard to Scotland and Wales, which helped to pave the way for the nationalist parties' successes in the 1960s and for the establishment in 1969 of the Royal Commission on the Constitution.[115] The search for better government within a unitary state is not likely to assuage the desire for 'national' government but it can heighten the demand for it.

The Acts and Treaty of Union between England and Scotland had

---

[110] Now Plaid Cymru/Party of Wales.

[111] The SNP won its first seat at an April 1945 by-election. Parliamentary interest in Scottish home rule did not terminate totally at the end of the First World War. Bills to promote Scottish home rule had been debated by Parliament on several occasions both before (1908, 1911, 1912, 1913) and after the war (1924, 1927, 1928). For a consideration of Scottish politics throughout this era, see Finlay, *Partnership for Good?*; see also T. M. Devine, *The Scottish Nation 1700–2000* (Penguin 1999), ch. 14 (and for the earlier period ch. 13).

[112] Bogdanor, *Devolution*, pp. 152–3.

[113] The parliamentary seat (Motherwell and Wishaw) won by Dr Robert McIntyre in 1945 was lost in the general election three months later. He died in February 1998 before the first sitting of the Scottish Parliament had taken place.

[114] Plaid Cymru, however, won no seats in the 1970 general election. Equally significant in many ways in 1967, Plaid Cymru made vast inroads into the Labour majority in Rhondda West although it did not take the seat in the by-election.

[115] It reported in 1973; Cmnd 5460.

left many of Scotland's institutions of civic identity intact, not least the (Presbyterian) Church of Scotland, the legal and court systems, and education.[116] Consequently, the parliamentary and administrative reforms introduced during the middle years of the twentieth century not only created a series of steps important in terms of 'path dependency' but also by facilitating the identification of 'Scottish matters' at the heart of the processes of governing, thereby heightened the debate about the nature of the union between England and Scotland.

The office of secretary for Scotland was, as stated above, created in 1885 and from 1892 was, in peacetime, a Cabinet position. It has been persuasively argued that the creation of this post, generally regarded as of territorial significance, was in fact a centralising measure:

> Only after the passing of the Education Act of 1872, the extension of the franchise to the working class on a larger scale and the creation of the Scottish Office in 1885 was there a decisive movement towards a more centralised state. Until then the United Kingdom was probably more decentralised than any other country in Europe.[117]

This centralising office was, however, in turn to become a vehicle for both administrative and geographical devolution. The position became a full secretary of state in 1926 and an increasing number of powers concerning Scotland were located in the Scottish Office—Agriculture, Education, Fisheries, Health, Home, Prisons—which in 1936–7 became located in Edinburgh, St Andrew's House itself opening in 1939. That decision was made by the then Scottish secretary, Walter Elliot, who was, as Professor Devine has commented:

> motivated by the desire to bring a more efficient form of administrative devolution to Scotland while also firmly maintaining political control at the centre of power in London. But it was indeed ironic that it was a Unionist Minister who helped to boost the [Scottish] nation's sense of

---

[116] Devine, *Scottish Nation*, ch. 17, 'Educating the People'.

[117] Ibid., p. 288. He continued: 'In the second half of the twentieth century the enormous influence of the state, in education, health, welfare and economic management, is taken for granted. In the nineteenth century government intervention was, however, limited in the extreme and the system gave considerable autonomy to Scotland within the Union State.' He then quoted from Lindsay Paterson, *The Anatomy of Modern Scotland* (Edinburgh University Press, 1994) p. 49: 'There was a growing tendency for Scottish MPs to settle Scottish business outside Parliament, submitting the result for largely formal ratification to the full house. Thus the Scots functioned as an informal domestic Parliament within the imperial legislature.'

identity at a time when the cause of home rule was in the doldrums and the nationalists were marginalized by electoral humiliation.[118]

To this increasing administrative devolution must be added what was in effect the 'devolution' of Scottish affairs within the Westminster procedures. To provide a cumulative summary of what was introduced prior to and during this period:[119] a Scottish Grand Committee ('Grand' referring to its size, including all Scottish MPs, rather than to its functions) had deliberative powers with regard to, in effect, the second reading stage of Scottish bills, Scottish estimates and Scottish affairs; and two Scottish standing committees took the committee stage of Scottish bills, for government bills and private members' bills respectively. An *ad hoc* Select Committee on Scottish Affairs was put on a permanent footing in 1979 but had existed since 1969—the year in which the first oil field, the 'Montrose', was discovered off Aberdeen followed by the 'Forties' in 1970.

Meanwhile, as far as Wales was concerned during this period, Plaid Cymru itself was in many ways, in its early days, a language or cultural promotion organisation, language being the prime Welsh national concern (at least in some areas) post-disestablishment.[120] The Welsh Courts Act 1942 was the first legislative success[121] for the language. The Act removed any doubt as to the right of Welsh-speaking persons to testify in the Welsh language in the Welsh courts. Also, during the Second World War, the amount of administrative devolution or decentralisation to Wales (which had, to use the Kilbrandon Report's verb, 'halted' since 1919) increased to the point where by 1945 there were fifteen government department offices in Wales.[122] This was not, however, immediately

---

[118] Devine, *Scottish Nation*, p. 327.

[119] The *Report of the Committee on Scottish Administration* (the Gilmour Committee), Cmd 5563 (1937), the *Report of the Royal Commission on Scottish Affairs*, Cmd 9212 (1954) and a white paper on Scottish Affairs, Cmd 7308 (1948) all testify to the not inconsiderable concern during this period about the parliamentary and administrative attention given to Scottish affairs.

[120] David Foulkes in his *Current Statutes Annotated*, Wales Act 1978, wrote: 'In the 1920s and 1930s there were no significant changes in the law or administrative practice affecting Wales.'

[121] The Welsh Language Society, founded in 1885, had by this stage come to an end, but a national petition was launched at the 1938 National Eisteddfod calling for equal status for the English and Welsh languages in Wales. The petition received over a quarter of a million signatures and the support of all but six of the thirty-six Welsh MPs: see www.llgc.org.uk/ymgyrchu.

[122] Cmnd 5460, para. 131.

matched by the creation of a secretary of state for Wales.[123]. The Conservatives, however, in 1951 created the post of minister of Welsh affairs, a post held first by the home secretary, and from 1957 to 1964 by the minister of housing and local government. In 1957, the junior position of under-secretary of state for Wales became a minister of state for Wales.[124] In 1960 a Welsh Grand Committee was established at Westminster. Eventually in 1964, the incoming Labour government introduced a secretary of state for Wales. A major Act passed during the life of the 1966 Labour government was the Welsh Language Act 1967, which unusually for a twentieth-century statute has a preamble:

> Whereas it is proper that the Welsh language should be freely used by those who so desire in the hearing of legal proceedings in Wales and Monmouthshire; that further provision should be made for the use of that language with the like effect as English, in the conduct of other official or public business there; and that Wales should be distinguished from England in the interpretation of future Acts of Parliament . . .

Thus repealing, by section 4, section 3 of the Wales and Berwick Act 1746 which had provided that statutory references to England included Wales.[125]

In terms of non-governmental, non-parliamentary developments, if the discovery of North Sea oil—and later the 'Conservative' imposition of the poll tax/community charge on (Labour) Scotland before England—had a galvanising effect on Scottish national identity, two such matters with regard to Wales may be identified. One relates to the Welsh

---

[123] Nye Bevan feared that 'devolution of authority would divorce Welsh political activity from the main stream of British politics, as he felt was already happening in Scotland'. From James Griffiths, *Pages from Memory*, quoted by Foulkes, *Current Statutes Annotated*.

[124] For parliamentary interest in the administration of Wales during this time, see *Council for Wales and Monmouthshire: Third Memorandum*, Cmnd 53 (1957); *Government Administration in Wales*, Cmnd 334 (1957); and, on the Welsh language, the Elections (Welsh Forms) Act 1964 and the *Report of the Committee on the Legal Status of the Welsh Language*, Cmnd 2875 (1964). This led to the Welsh Language Act 1967, see below. For the funding of Welsh cultural/national events, see the Eisteddfod Act 1959, the Llangollen International Musical Eisteddfod Act 1967 and the Welsh National Opera Company Act 1971. For Scottish cultural activity, note especially the Edinburgh Festival established in 1947.

[125] For further provision on the Welsh language see the Welsh Language Act 1993, *inter alia* establishing Bwrdd yr Iaith Gymraeg/the Welsh Language Board and providing for full equality between the two languages. Before this, in 1974, the MPs' oath of allegiance was able to be taken in Welsh and in 1982 Sianel Pedwar Cymru (S4C), the all-Welsh television channel, was established. The Government of Wales Act 1998, section 47 requires equal treatment in Assembly proceedings for both languages.

language—the 1962 Reith Lecture, delivered by Saunders Lewis,[126] calling for the full restoration of the Welsh language by way of 'civil disobedience' if necessary.[127] The other was the enactment and then implementation of the Liverpool Corporation (Tryweryn) Act 1957, which allowed Liverpool Corporation to build a reservoir near Bala in (now) Gwynedd, drowning the village of Capel Celyn. In an article in the July/ August 1999 edition of the *Cambria Magazine*, Aled Sion wrote:

> The drowning of the Tryweryn valley in North Wales to create a supply of water for the city of Liverpool, was and remains a shameful example of English oppression on a Welsh Nation ... 1965, when the reservoir was officially opened and the village of Capel Celyn became a thing of the past ... [was] a year when it finally dawned on the Welsh nation the true meaning of British democracy.[128]

While not all would agree with (the wording of) these sentiments, few can argue the deep significance of the legislation for Wales: 'from this one event emerged a proud and determined nation'.[129]

In many ways nonetheless the biggest impact on the Labour government came from the rise in electoral support for both Plaid Cymru and the Scottish National Party. The Conservatives, indulging in the luxury of opposition, announced in May 1968 in the Declaration of Perth that a small constitutional committee should be established to explore the possibilities offered by devolution.[130] The Labour government, indulging

---

[126] One matter within the interest but neither the range nor the remit of the present author would be a comparative study of the influence of, for example, R. S. Thomas, Hugh MacDiarmuid (Christopher Murray Grieve) and Seamus Heaney on the creation of national identities during the twentieth century.

[127] As a result of this lecture, Cymdeithas yr Iaith Gymraeg/the Welsh Language Society was founded.

[128] On-line version available at www.lineone.net. The Tryweryn Memorial Fund was launched in 1999 for a memorial to mark the event.

[129] Ibid. One extra-parliamentary matter of significance with regard to Scottish national awareness was the taking from Westminster Abbey's coronation chair on Christmas morning 1950 by Scottish nationalists of the Stone of Scone/Stone of Destiny, which itself had been taken from Scotland by Edward I in 1296. It was recovered a few months later and restored to the Abbey, but on St Andrew's Day 1996 it was, on the decision of Prime Minister John Major, returned to Scotland to be placed with the Scottish crown jewels in Edinburgh Castle.

[130] The Scottish Conservative Party conference was held at Perth that year. The committee, chaired by Sir Alec Douglas-Home, reported in March 1970 in favour of a directly elected Scottish assembly or convention with limited powers. The committee's terms of reference were 'to keep the United Kingdom united; to make an effective effort to improve the machinery of government as it affects the people of Scotland; to allow the people of

in the responsibilities of government, announced the establishment of a Royal Commission.

The late 1960s to 2000: Decades of debate

The remit of what became the Kilbrandon Commission on the constitution[131] was not a model of precision or clarity: 'to examine the present functions of the central legislature and government in relation to the several countries, nations and regions of the United Kingdom; to consider ... whether any changes are desirable in those functions or otherwise in present constitutional and economic relationships'.[132] These terms of reference meant that for the Commission 'the mere identification of our task [was] a major preoccupation'.[133] Interpreting it by reference to the main intent behind its institution, the Commission considered a wide range of territorial options: independence, federalism, devolution in its various forms, regionalism and the 'parliamentary' or procedural devolution proposals recommended by the Conservative's Scottish constitutional committee.[134] With echoes of the Speaker's Conference on Devolution in 1920, the Commission's work on Northern Ireland was overtaken by events—increasingly euphemistically referred to as 'the Troubles'—and no recommendations were made with regard to Northern Ireland.[135]

Scotland to play their part in making decisions on Scottish legislation in Scotland, and to provide the Scots with an increased opportunity to propose and discuss United Kingdom policy as it affects Scotland'. See E. Heath, *The Course of my Life: My Autobiography* (Hodder & Stoughton, 1998), pp. 294–6; *Scotland's Government: The Report of the Scottish Constitutional Committee* (1970). The committee recommendations amounted to little more than moving the functions of the Scottish Grand and standing committees to a directly elected body sitting in Scotland. It was in effect the devolution of Westminster's procedures. For a similar but not identical process for Northern Ireland, see the Northern Ireland Act 1982, sections 3 and 4 and the work of the Northern Ireland Assembly 1982 to 1986. For a continuation of the Conservatives' approach, see *Scotland in the Union: A Partnership for Good*, Cm 2225 (March 1993).

[131] Lord Crowther, the first chair, was on his death replaced in March 1972 by Lord Kilbrandon: Cmnd 5460 (October 1973).

[132] Ibid., p. iii.

[133] Ibid., para. 12.

[134] Ibid., ch. 20.

[135] Ibid., paras 24, 25 and summary conclusion 212. Hennessy, *Prime Minister*, pp. 322–3 writes: 'Wilson did have early and explicit warnings about the danger of recrudescence of violence in Northern Ireland, especially as the fiftieth anniversary of the Easter Rising approached ... "events" rammed it into a high place on [the Cabinet's] agenda ... at the end of February 1969'.

The gap between the institution of the Commission in (eventually) April 1969 and the publication of its report in October 1973, during which period the United Kingdom had become a member of the European Economic Community[136], enabled the Conservative government, returned to power in June 1970, to defer implementation of its own proposals, formulated when in opposition, on parliamentary or procedural devolution. This decision was also, no doubt, facilitated by the fact that at the general election Plaid Cymru (0.6 per cent of the vote) and the Scottish National Party (1.1 per cent) had won only one seat between them. While Plaid Cymru's percentage share of the total votes cast remained at 0.6 per cent for the two 1974 general elections (winning the party two and then three seats), that for the Scottish National Party rose to 2 per cent (seven seats) and then 2.9 per cent (eleven seats) and 30 per cent of the Scottish vote—and this was combined with the return of a Labour government (until 1979) increasingly dependent upon Liberal support. Devolution—or at least talking about it—was back on the agenda. It is indeed interesting to note that during the thirty years from the time the Royal Commission was instituted until the close of the century, a considerable amount of parliamentary and government time was devoted to devolution. The actual existence or experience of devolution was, however, confined to little more than a handful of months: the Northern Ireland Parliament was prorogued in March 1972; the Northern Ireland Assembly sat during the first five months of 1974 and the Assembly[137] was in existence from December 1999 to February 2000, and again from May 2000; the Scottish Parliament and the Welsh Assembly were in existence from May 1999. Yet, as the following indicates, if—to return to the Speaker's Conference concerns of 1920—devolution has the merit of freeing Westminster's time to deliberate on other matters, it would appear that by the close of the century devolution had become imperative if only to stop Westminster debating it. The Acts which follow include three suspensory Acts (in 1972, 1974 and 2000) and two Acts (of 1978) rejected under the statutory terms by the people. The 1998 Acts,

[136] The EEC did not feature very prominently in the Kilbrandon Report, other than with regard to the Channel Islands and the Isle of Man: see Cmnd 5460, paras 404–14, 489–94.

[137] The Assembly sitting under the terms of the Northern Ireland Act 1982 from 1982 until 1986 did not have legislative power. For the terms of the Act and that Assembly's work, see Brigid Hadfield, 'The Northern Ireland Act 1982: Do-It-Yourself-Devolution?', *Northern Ireland Legal Quarterly* (1982), and 'The Northern Ireland Assembly: First Term Report', *Public Law* (1983). The most comprehensive treatment of the whole four-year period is in C. O'Leary, S. Elliott, R. A. Wilford, *The Northern Ireland Assembly 1982–1986: A Constitutional Experiment* (Hurst, 1988).

on devolution to Scotland, Wales and Northern Ireland, should not distort the picture of the United Kingdom as a territorial state throughout the twentieth century: actual experience of devolution has been the end-note, not the dominant theme. Even in the 'different' Northern Ireland, devolution—greatly, often hotly, debated—has been in existence for only just over a total of half the century.[138] The Northern Ireland legislation passed at Westminster during these thirty years is: the Temporary Provisions Act 1972, the Border Poll Act 1972, the Assembly Act 1973, the Constitution and the Constitution (Amendment) Acts 1973, the Northern Ireland Act 1974, the Assembly Disqualification Act 1975, the Northern Ireland Act 1982, the Northern Ireland (Entry to Negotiations etc) Act 1996,[139] the Elections Act 1998, the Northern Ireland Act 1998, and the Northern Ireland Act 2000. This list does not include the many government white papers or the reports of conventions, forums or independent inquiries into the preferred or possible forms of government for Northern Ireland.[140]

For Scotland and Wales, a flurry of white papers and legislative activity followed the February 1974 general election. Between 1974 and 1976 there were four white papers,[141] followed by the Scotland and Wales bill 1976 (lost effectively when the government's guillotine motion was lost), the Scotland Act 1978 and the Wales Act 1978. Section 85 and schedule 17 of the former Act and section 80 and schedule 12 of the latter Act made respective provision for a referendum before the Act came into force. The referendums—in many ways included as much to accommodate intra (Labour) Party divisions as to solicit popular

---

[138] The Northern Ireland Act 1974 in July 1974 introduced as a 'temporary' provision direct rule which was eventually terminated in December 1999, thus adding a whole new dimension to the meaning of temporary.

[139] Under section 4 of this Act, the referendum concerning the Belfast Agreement was put to the electorate in May 1998.

[140] These are discussed in Brigid Hadfield, *Constitution of Northern Ireland*, chs 4–8 up until 1989. For later reports, see Hadfield, 'From Downing Street Declaration', and 'Political Process: Peace Process?' *European Public Law* (1998); T. Hennessey, *A History of Northern Ireland 1920–1996* (Gill & Macmillan, 1997), ch. 5; B. O'Leary and J. McGarry, *The Politics of Antagonism: Understanding Northern Ireland* (Athlone Press, 1993), and *Explaining Northern Ireland* (Blackwell, 1995).

[141] *Devolution within the United Kingdom: Some Alternatives for Discussion* (June 1974); *Democracy and Devolution: Proposals for Scotland and Wales*, Cmnd 5732 (1974); *Our Changing Democracy, Devolution to Scotland and Wales*, Cmnd 6348 (1975); and *Devolution to Scotland and Wales, Supplementary Statement*, Cmnd 6585 (1976). In the event, our democracy did not change as rapidly as might have been expected. Note also the government's paper on England: *Devolution, the English Dimension* (1976).

consent—took place on 1 March 1979. The Welsh referendum comprehensively precluded the implementation of the Act: on a turnout of 58.8 per cent, 20.2 per cent voted yes, and 79.8 per cent voted no. In Scotland, the figures were respectively: 62.9 per cent, the yes vote being 51.5 per cent of those voting, the no vote 48.5 per cent. Crucially, however, in light of section 85(2), which required 40 per cent of the electorate to vote yes, the Act was not implemented, only 32.85 per cent of the electorate having voted in favour of the system of devolution it contained.[142] Eighteen years intervened between that referendum and the next— eighteen years of Conservative government essentially opposed to all forms of territorial devolution[143] (other than for Northern Ireland). During this time, in so many ways, the constitutional landscape changed. The European dimension became much stronger,[144] and the concept of an independent Scotland (and Wales) within a Europe of the regions tuned in more with prevalent values than the more introverted nationalism, in danger of being caught between dogmas of the left and of the right and also (in nations far less culturally uniform than so many assume them to be) in danger of being associated with only a part rather than a whole of the nation. Meanwhile the Conservative vote, and the number of seats it held, in Scotland and Wales declined (almost) progressively, a contributory factor in the former being the poll tax saga, until in the 1997 general election its percentage share of the votes yielded no seats.[145]

The New Labour government, elected in May 1997, rapidly moved to implement its constitutional reform agenda[146] by securing the enact-

---

[142] See Bogdanor, *Devolution*, pp. 188–91. The repeal of the Acts led to the institution of the select committees on Scottish and on Welsh Affairs.

[143] Bogdanor, *Devolution*, p. 137 quotes Margaret Thatcher: '[Edward Heath] had impaled the party on an extremely painful hook from which it would be my unenviable task to set it free. As an instinctive Unionist, I disliked the Devolution Commitment.'

[144] This is not discussed in this chapter, any more than the demise of the Empire has been, because of the chapters in this volume by Ian Loveland and Robert Holland.

[145] The Conservative Party in the five general elections from 1979 to 1997 inclusive received as a percentage of the votes (seats obtained) in Scotland the following: 31.4 per cent (22); 28.4 per cent (21); 24.9 per cent (10); 25.7 per cent (11)—the blip year; 17.5 per cent (0). For Wales the figures were 32.2 per cent (11); 31.1 per cent (14); 29.5 per cent (8); 28.6 per cent (6); 19.6 per cent (0). See A. McGonnell, 'Issues of Governance in Scotland, Wales and Northern Ireland', in R. Pyper and L. Robins (eds), *United Kingdom Governance* (Macmillan, 2000), p. 222.

[146] See generally Keith Sutherland (ed.), *The Rape of the Constitution?*, foreword by Michael Beloff (Imprint Academic, 2000); R. Blackburn and R. Plant (eds), *Constitutional Reform: The Labour Government's Constitutional Reform Agenda* (Longman, 1999); and specifically Noreen Burrows, *Devolution* (Sweet & Maxwell, 2000), ch. 1. For a rather different background on New Labour and devolution, see Andrew Rawnsley, *Servants of the People: The Inside Story of New Labour* (Hamish Hamilton, 2000), ch. 13.

ment of the Referendums (Scotland and Wales) Act 1997, which provided for a referendum in Scotland on 11 September 1997, on the establishment and tax-varying powers of a Scottish Parliament, and for a referendum in Wales on 18 September 1997, on the establishment of a Welsh Assembly. The sequencing of the dates was significant, the Welsh electorate were no doubt intended to be encouraged by the likely Scottish result—and needing to be encouraged. The referendum results in Scotland on a 60.4 per cent turnout were 74.3 per cent in support of a Scottish Parliament and 63.5 per cent in support of its tax-raising powers. In Wales, on a turnout of just over 50 per cent, 50.3 per cent were in favour (only one in four of the Welsh electors thus voting in favour of devolution).[147] The next two Acts at Westminster relevant to the territorial theme were, therefore, the Scotland Act 1998 and the Government of Wales Act 1998 translating the popular support for the principles of devolution (outlined in white papers preceding the referendums) into considerable detail.

The details of the three devolved systems lie beyond the bounds of this chapter, both in terms of extent and, more importantly, in terms of their projection towards the twenty-first century ('the radical century' as Tony Blair likes to term it) rather than as representing the essence of the twentieth.[148] Two matters of significance may, however, be briefly adverted to, namely the autochthonous and consensual nature of devolution and, second, the evolving nature of British–Irish relations.

The debate about whether a referendum can ever 'bind' the sovereign Westminster Parliament, a debate frequently aired with regard to the provisions of the (European) Referendum Act 1975 and the provisions in the Scotland and Wales Acts 1978, now seems rather passé.[149] There is an increasing, and possibly irreversible, acceptance on the part of British governments of seeking popular support for developments of constitutional significance. Northern Ireland has a long history of this; indeed the whole history of Northern Ireland illustrates it. Specifically, too, Northern Ireland constitutional history indicates a fascinating admixture of the situation where the consent of the Northern Ireland electorate has

---

[147] McConnell, 'Issues of Governance', n 145, p. 223 and p. 232.

[148] See Tom Nairn, *After Britain: New Labour and the Return of Scotland* (Granta, 2000); Andrew Marr, *The Day Britain Died* (Profile Books, 2000); and A. Taylor (ed.), *What a State! Is Devolution for Scotland the End of Britain*, (HarperCollins, 2000). From an English perspective see Simon Heffer, *Nor Shall My Sword: The Reinvention of England* (Weidenfeld & Nicolson, 1999).

[149] See Vernon Bogdanor, *Power and the People: A Guide to Constitutional Reform* (Gollancz, 1997), ch. 5.

been sought, namely the status of Northern Ireland, and those situations where it has not, namely issues which relate to the substance or the content of the union itself, including the symbols of the state. The debate about the existence and application of the 'unionist veto' is long and deep. Nationalists fear that it may operate to prevent, for example, cross-community or all-Ireland developments, or changes (under the parity of esteem principle) to policing and judicial appointments. Unionists fear that the status-consent provision will be rendered nugatory if the substance and symbols of the union are drained by developments over which they have no or limited control.

The increasing resort to the referendum becomes of greater significance when viewed in the context of the rise of other forms of 'popular sovereignty'. The non-parliamentary background to the Scotland Act 1998 illustrates this well. The work and influence of the Scottish Constitutional Convention, which held its inaugural meeting on 30 March 1989, not only assert the principle of popular sovereignty but show that, crucially, the issue of Scottish national identity has moved well beyond the custodianship of any political party or parties or class.[150] The Convention, although not contributed to by either the Conservative or the Scottish National parties as parties, represented a broad church:

> ... the Convention is beyond question the most broadly representative body in Scotland. It has enjoyed the support of the Scottish Labour Party, the Scottish Liberal Democrats, and a number of smaller parties. In all, the Convention has included 80 per cent of Scotland's MPs and MEPs; representatives of the great majority of local authorities; and many important elements in Scottish civic society including the Scottish Trades Union Congress, the Churches, ethnic minority groups, women's movements and sections of the business and industrial society.[151]

This membership thus gave massive force to the Convention's Claim of Right for Scotland:

> We, gathered as the Scottish Constitutional Convention, do hereby acknowledge the sovereign right of the Scottish people to determine the form of Government best suited to their needs . . .[152]

---

[150] Christopher Harvie, 'The Devolution of the Intellectuals', *New Statesman*, 28 November 1995, pp. 665–6, and 'Federal and Confederal Ideas in Scottish Political Culture', in English and Townshend (eds), *The State*.

[151] *Scotland's Parliament, Scotland's Right* (1995), p. 10.

[152] Declaration adopted at the Convention's inaugural meeting on 30 March 1989. For a historical perspective, see the Declaration of Arbroath 1320 and the Claim of Right 1689.

The Convention's[153] final report was published on St Andrew's Day 1995 and contained a detailed plan for devolution, much[154] of which formed the basis for the Scotland Act 1998. Significantly, just prior to the opening of the Scottish Parliament on 1 July 1999, the (Convention's) Claim of Right was ceremonially handed over to the Parliament's presiding officer for its future keeping.

The legal doctrine of Westminster's sovereignty meets its limits in the assertion of popular sovereignty. Crucially, the source of the Scottish constitution becomes rooted in the people[155] as well as in the Westminster Parliament.

The second notable feature of these thirty years relates to British–Irish intergovernmental relations. If 1949 rather than 1925 is the standard by which the evaluation is made, the relationship has become particularly harmonious (usually), although it has not been a linear development. Clearly 'the Troubles' provided a focal point for this, albeit one which, in light of the history of Northern Ireland, could have proved highly divisive, not least in terms of its impact on the majority community in Northern Ireland. The relationship nonetheless evolved: through the Sunningdale Agreement 1973, the Anglo-Irish Intergovernmental Council 1980, the Anglo-Irish Agreement and Conference 1985, the Downing Street Declaration 1993, the New (Joint) Framework for Agreement 1995

---

[153] For background to the Convention, especially the work of the Campaign for a Scottish Assembly (CSA), see Lindsay Paterson, *A Diverse Assembly: The Debate on a Scottish Parliament* (Edinburgh University Press, 1998), pp. 152ff. The aims of the Convention (a convention being 'a representative body convened to fill the democratic gap when the government of an existing state has partly or wholly failed, or when a government needs to be created for a new, or recreated for an old country') defined by the CSA in 1985 were to: '(1) articulate and represent the Scottish demand for an Assembly; (2) draft the provisions of an Assembly scheme . . .; (3) negotiate with the British Government the timetable and implementation of that scheme; (4) arrange any necessary test of Scottish support for the scheme'. *Diverse Assembly*, pp. 166–7.

[154] The Convention was 'adamant' that the powers of the Scottish Parliament 'should not be altered without the consent of the Scottish Parliament representing the people of Scotland'. It appreciated that the inclusion of any such amending formula in the Act was not feasible in light of the nature of the UK's constitution. 'The Convention however is firmly of the view that through widespread recognition of the Scottish Parliament's legitimate authority, both within Scotland and internationally, such a course of action is both practically and politically impossible.' The Convention's final report, *Scotland's Parliament, Scotland's Right*, p. 18. See *Scotland's Parliament*, Cm 3658 (1997), p. 12.

[155] For Northern Ireland equivalents to the Scottish Constitutional Convention—only this time granted by Westminster rather than asserted by the people—see the work of both the Northern Ireland Constitutional Convention 1975–6, elected under section 2 of the Northern Ireland Act 1974, and also the 1982–6 Northern Ireland Assembly's remit under sections 1 and 2 of the Northern Ireland Act 1982.

to the Belfast Agreement 1998 and the British–Irish Intergovernmental Conference. The multi-party agreement was successfully put to the Northern Ireland electorate in a referendum in May 1998 in Northern Ireland, and on the same day in the Republic of Ireland concerning approval for the consequential amendment to Articles 2 and 3 of the Irish Constitution.

The one part of the relationship which is of particular relevance to this chapter concerns two key provisions of the British–Irish agreement (a part of the Belfast Agreement)—provisions which indicate the subordination of territory as a principle of government to principles of identity, allegiance and non-territorially-based 'nationhood'. Article 1 first articulated the principle that the status of Northern Ireland as within the United Kingdom or a united Ireland was a matter for determination by the people of the island of Ireland alone, subject to the agreement and consent of a majority of the people of Northern Ireland. Nonetheless, however that choice was exercised:

> ... the power of the sovereign government with jurisdiction there shall be exercised with rigorous impartiality on behalf of all the people in the diversity of their identities and traditions and shall be founded on the principles of full respect for, and equality of, civil, political, social and cultural rights, of freedom from discrimination for all citizens, and of parity of esteem and of just and equal treatment for the identity, ethos and aspirations of both communities.

Furthermore, both governments 'recognised the birthright of all the people of Northern Ireland to recognise themselves and be accepted as Irish or British or both', a right which would not be affected by any future change in the status of Northern Ireland.[156]

This principle is reinforced by the establishment of the British–Irish Council (popularly known as the Council of the Isles),[157] a body composed of the representatives of all United Kingdom governments as well as those from the Republic of Ireland, the Isle of Man and of Jersey and of Guernsey. The inaugural meeting of the Council took place in December 1999 in London and is expected to meet yearly or twice yearly in summit format and regularly in ministerial or official sectoral format, with each member being given the lead role on a particular issue such as prevention of drug abuse, poverty and social exclusion or transport. Indeed, a wide variety of multilateral and bilateral contacts and arrange-

---

[156] Paragraphs (v) and (vi) of Article 1.
[157] Strand 3 of the multi-party Belfast Agreement.

ments is possible dealing with, for example, social, cultural, economic, educational, agricultural, environmental and transport issues. The British prime minister, Mr Tony Blair, at the inaugural meeting, described the council as:

> A framework with diverse functions but with the aim to build a new partnership for the new century. A partnership where we share what we have in common and respect what makes us different. A partnership which touches every corner of these islands, which deepens the ties between our diverse and vibrant regions and a partnership which brings together the devolved administrations and the islands themselves.[158]

The territorial events of the twentieth century, in many ways stemming from competing notions of the nation state, have thus culminated in a body which has the potential to take the 'territorial state' into the twenty-first century.

Conclusion

Looking back over the twentieth-century United Kingdom constitution, certain key evolutionary developments can be seen.

   1. The relationship between Britain and Ireland has moved through various, not always discrete, phases at the institutional level. The first period saw shared understanding (the Irish contribution to the First World War, the 1925 tripartite treaty) and bitter conflict; the middle period was the era of mutual antipathy; the final period witnessed developments which can carry the 'territorial' state into the twenty-first century— the linkages of the British–Irish Intergovernmental Conference[159] and the Council of the Isles.[160] The responsibilities of nation states towards their citizens of the diaspora coupled with their internal responsibilities in a multi-ethnic society point a flexible not rigid way forward concerning nationhood and identity. Interestingly, there yet remains to be addressed the English question as a question of national and not solely multi-regional identity.

   2. For Northern Ireland—Great Britain's 'outpost' physically, consti-

---

[158] BBC News, 17 December 1999.
[159] Belfast Agreement, strand 3: British–Irish Agreement signed in Dublin 8 March 1999. See also the Preamble to the British–Irish (Belfast) Agreement, April 1998.
[160] Vernon Bogdanor, 'The British–Irish Council and Devolution', *Government and Opposition* (1999), 287; Elizabeth Meehan, 'The Belfast Agreement: Its Distinctiveness and Points of Cross-fertilisation in the UK's Devolution Programme', *Parliamentary Affairs* (1999), 19.

tutionally and often emotionally—the relationship with Westminster has evolved through sovereignty and distance in the forty years from 1920 to what may be described in one of two ways: either sovereignty as coercion (the unionist perspective on the dismantling by Westminster of the British state in Northern Ireland) or sovereignty as indulgence (the nationalist and republican perspective on the undue regard paid by Westminster to the unionist veto). Yet, within Northern Ireland, evolving conceptions of citizenship, a heightened awareness of the responsibilities a nation owes to those of 'their' allegiance and identity, the possibilities offered by not solely the North–South Irish dimensions but also the British–Irish Council[161] indicate that a strong sense of territoriality may at least be conjoined with a more fluid concept of governance in and with regard to territory. Furthermore, from the time when the Westminster and Irish governments in December 1922 gave the Northern Ireland Parliament the opportunity to choose the form of its constitutional future, successive Westminster governments have, in both legislative and non-legislative form, accepted that in fact, if not also in legal theory, the constitutional status of at least one of the United Kingdom's 'component portions' cannot be altered without the consent of the people concerned.

3.   This principle may indeed be carried further with regard to Scotland, where a quasi-autochthonous constitution,[162] that is through the deliberations of the Scottish Constitutional Convention, has been legislated for by Westminster. In such a context, it is at the least an arguable proposition that Westminster, in exercising the constituent power in the Scotland Act 1998, has done so in a way that is self-embracing rather than continuing. Although it is possible to argue at this stage that devolution is central control at arm's length,[163] it is also possible to argue (at least tentatively) that devolution may lead to the emergence of not a federal United Kingdom but a (partially) confederal one, where the component nation states play a much more central role in the allocation of legislative responsibilities. This argument also has to be pursued in the context of a 'Europeanised' United Kingdom, and of 'Scotland in Europe'.

4.   With regard to both Scotland and Wales, and possibly Northern Ireland, devolution may be regarded as a response to questions of national identity. The new institutions, however, may—will—also

---

[161] G. Walker, 'Scotland and Northern Ireland: Constitutional Questions, Connections and Possibilities', *Government and Opposition* (1998), 21.

[162] The adjective may also, for different reasons, apply to Northern Ireland.

[163] In the work, for example, of the Joint Ministerial Committee and in the substance of the memorandums of understanding and the concordats; see Burrows, *Devolution, passim*.

heighten the sense of national identity, as well as provide new constitutional focal points even for those who originally opposed their introduction. That in turn will create a new political and national climate. It is hard even for someone who wishes to maintain central control to legislate for unanticipated consequences.

It is not easy to project forward in the twenty-first century, given that so many significant developments in the territorial United Kingdom took place in the last two or three years of the last century. Nonetheless, it should perhaps be stated that in some regards the nation state or even the multinational state seems rather outdated—the *arriviste parvenu* of globalisation has made its ubiquitous debut. As Anthony Giddens has written:

> Is the nation state becoming a 'fiction' . . . and government obsolete? They are not, but their shape is being altered. Globalisation 'pulls away' from the nation state in the sense that some powers nations used to possess . . . have been weakened. However, globalisation also 'pushes down'—it creates new demands and also new possibilities for regenerating local identities . . .
>
> Globalisation . . . is more than just the backdrop to contemporary policies; taken as a whole, globalisation is transforming the institutions of the societies in which we live.[164]

The debate, therefore, about the United Kingdom as a territorial state will now have to be conducted in the context of globalisation and Europeanisation,[165] whereas at the beginning of the twentieth century the concerns were of the nature and evolution of the British Empire. Also 'beneath' the nation state are the institutions of civil society. That, however, is primarily looking forward, not back, and it may well be that, for the future, pragmatism is all: in the words of Tony Blair, prime minister when the devolution Acts were passed: 'What matters is what works.'[166]

---

[164] Anthony Giddens, *The Third Way: The Renewal of Social Democracy* (Polity Press, 2000), pp. 31–3.

[165] See Martin Loughlin, *Sword and Scales: An Examination of the Relationship between Law and Politics* (Hart, 2000), ch. 10, 'Fractured Sovereignty'.

[166] Quoted by Andrew Rawnsley, *Servants of the People: The Inside Story of New Labour* (Hamish Hamilton, 2000), p. 7.

627

Bibliography

Official publications

Speaker's Conference on Devolution, Cmd 692 (1920).

Royal Commission on the Constitution (Kilbrandon), Cmnd 5460 (1973).

Scotland's Parliament, Cm 3658 (1997).

A Voice for Wales: The Government's Proposals for a Welsh Assembly, Cm 3718 (1997).

The Belfast Agreement: An Agreement Reached at the Multi-party Talks on Northern Ireland, Cm 3883 (1998).

Memorandum of Understanding between the United Kingdom Government, the Scottish Parliament, the Welsh National Assembly and the Northern Ireland Assembly, Cm 4444 (1999).

Department of the Environment, Transport and the Regions, *Regional Government in England: A Preliminary Review of Literature and Research Findings* (HMSO, 2000).

General

Bogdanor, Vernon, *Devolution in the United Kingdom* (Oxford University Press, 1999).

Coupland, Sir Reginald, *Welsh and Scottish Nationalism: A Study* (Collins, 1954).

Davies, Norman, *The Isles: A History* (Macmillan, 1999).

Evans, Neil (ed.), *National Identity in the British Isles* (Coleg Harlech, 1989).

Hodge, P. S. (ed.), *Scotland and the Union* (Edinburgh University Press, 1998).

Rawlings, Richard, 'Concordats of the Constitution', *Law Quarterly Review* (2000).

Rose, Richard, *Understanding the United Kingdom* (Longman, 1982).

Taylor, Bridget and Thomson, Katarina (eds), *Scotland and Wales: Nations Again?* (University of Wales Press, 1999).

Tomkins, Adam, *Devolution and the English Constitution* (Key Haven, 1998).

Northern Ireland

Bardon, Jonathan, *A History of Ulster* (Blackstaff Press, 1992).

Bogdanor, Vernon, 'The British–Irish Council and Devolution', *Government and Opposition* (1999).

Buckland, Patrick, *The Factory of Grievances: Devolved Government in Northern Ireland, 1921–39* (Gill & Macmillan, 1979).

Buckland, Patrick, *A History of Northern Ireland* (Gill & Macmillan, 1981).

Calvert, Harry, *Constitutional Law in Northern Ireland: A Study in Regional Government* (Stevens, 1968).

Hadfield, Brigid, *The Constitution of Northern Ireland* (SLS Legal Publications, 1989).

Hennessy, Thomas, *A History of Northern Ireland, 1920–1996* (Macmillan, 1997).

Kelly, J. M., *The Irish Constitution*, 3rd edn (Butterworths, 1999).

Lawrence, R. J., *The Government of Northern Ireland: Public Finance and the Public Services, 1921–1964* (Oxford University Press, 1965).

Mansergh, Nicholas, *The Government of Northern Ireland: A Study in Devolution* (Allen & Unwin, 1936).

Mansergh, Nicholas, *The Irish Question, 1840–1921* (Allen & Unwin, 1965).

Mansergh, Nicholas, *The Unresolved Question: The Anglo-Irish Settlement and its Undoing* (Yale University Press, 1991).

Quekett, A., *The Constitution of Northern Ireland*, 3 vols (HMSO, 1928–46).

Whyte, John, *Interpreting Northern Ireland* (Clarendon Press, 1990).

Wilson, T. (ed.), *Ulster under Home Rule: A Study of the Political and Economic Problems of Northern Ireland* (Oxford University Press, 1955).

Scotland

Bates, T. St John, *Devolution to Scotland: The Legal Aspects* (T. and T. Clark, 1997).

Brown, Alice, McCrone, David and Paterson, Lindsay, *Politics and Society in Scotland*, 2nd edn (Macmillan, 1996).

Devine, T. M. and Finlay, Richard (eds), *Scotland in the Twentieth Century* (Edinburgh University Press, 1996).

Dicey, A. V. and Rait, R. S., *Thoughts on the Union between England and Scotland* (Macmillan, 1920).

Finlay, Richard, *A Partnership for Good? Scottish Politics and the Union since 1880* (John Donald, 1997).

Hadfield, Brigid, 'Scotland's Parliament: A Northern Ireland Perspective on the White Paper', *Public Law* (1997).

Harvie, Christopher, *Scotland and Nationalism*, 2nd edn (Routledge, 1994).

Jones, Timothy, 'Scottish Devolution and Demarcation Disputes', *Public Law* (1997).

Keating, Michael and Bleiman, David, *Labour and Scottish Nationalism* (Macmillan, 1979).

MacCormick, Neil, 'The English Constitution, the British State and the Scottish Anomaly, *Scottish Affairs* (1998).

McCrone, David, *Understanding Scotland: The Sociology of a Stateless Nation*, 2nd edn (Routledge, 2001).

Mitchell, James, *Conservatives and the Union: A Study of Conservative Party Attitudes to Scotland* (Edinburgh University Press, 1990).

Mitchell, James, *Strategies for Self-government: The Campaigns for a Scottish Parliament* (Polygon, 1996).

Page, A., Reid, C. and Ross, A., *A Guide to the Scotland Act* (Butterworths, 1999).

Paterson, Lindsay, *The Anatomy of Modern Scotland* (Edinburgh University Press, 1994).

Paterson, Lindsay (ed.), *A Diverse Assembly: The Debate on a Scottish Parliament* (Edinburgh University Press, 1998).

Scottish Constitutional Convention, *Towards Scotland's Parliament* (1990).

Scottish Constitutional Convention, *Scotland's Parliament, Scotland's Right* (1995).

629

Wright, Kenyon, *The People Say Yes: The Making of Scotland's Parliament* (Argyll, 1997).

Wales

Butt, Philip Alan, *The Welsh Question: Nationalism in Welsh Politics, 1945–1970* (University of Wales Press, 1975).

Davies, John, *A History of Wales* (Penguin, 1993).

Foulkes, David, Jones, Barry and Wilford, R. A., *The Welsh Veto: The Wales Act 1978 and the Referendum* (University of Wales Press, 1983).

Morgan, Kenneth O., *Rebirth of a Nation: Wales, 1880–1980* (Oxford University Press and University of Wales Press, 1981).

Osmond, John, *Creative Conflict: The Politics of Welsh Devolution* (Routledge & Kegan Paul, 1977).

16.
Britain, Commonwealth and the End of Empire

ROBERT HOLLAND

Thirty years ago the constitutional historiography of the British Empire remained an important, prestigious and developing subject. This can no longer be said to be entirely the case today. In the recent five-volume *Oxford History of the British Empire* there is not a single chapter with the word 'constitution' (or 'constitutional') in its title, or one indeed which is substantially concerned with such themes, though of course there is a good deal on imperial 'governance'.[1] Preoccupation with the legal and constitutional aspects of imperial growth has been overwhelmed by a succession of competing perspectives, of which gender and 'culture' are just the most recent examples. For the same reason, it would be difficult, and perhaps impossible, to identify a single influential book appearing in this scholarly area during the past few years. For this reason alone it is worth attempting, as freshly as possible, to relate constitutional issues, very broadly conceived, to the outlines of imperial and Commonwealth history in the twentieth century.

The twentieth century ended in Britain as it began: with the constitutional structure of the United Kingdom a contested and vital subject of public discourse. The plasticity of notions surrounding how Britain should be governed, and in particular how an overseas imperium related to that governance, was reflected in Balfour's bitterly partisan comment in the immediate wake of the Liberal landslide in the 1906 general election that 'the great Unionist party should still control, whether in power or in opposition, the destinies of this great empire'. The contemporary Irish roots of this controversial contention we shall not be concerned with here, though Ireland will figure at points in our treat-

[1] Wm. Roger Louis (editor-in-chief), *The Oxford History of the British Empire*, 5 vols (Oxford University Press, 1998–9).

ment. With regard to the greatest dependency of all, however, there was a real concern among some critics in the early 1900s that the government of India's accountability to the Westminster Parliament was effectively being eroded. The conclusion of this chapter is that the transitions which characterised the Empire–Commonwealth over the next century, in this and in other cases, were ultimately constrained within the 'due process' of British constitutionalism, at least to the extent that formality and decent 'democratic' appearances required. We should recall, however, that this result was very far from inevitable when the challenges of the century began.

A preoccupation with the potentialities of building a British imperial 'superstate', capable of competing with the new types of continental politics of which the Wilhelmine Reich was the archetype, ran deep in Edwardian psychology. Its chief surface expression was the debate over tariff reform; and thereafter it was through a sporadic but occasionally intense controversy concerning the elaboration of a common tariff ('Empire free trade') that British politics came closest to being defined in imperial terms, most notably in the early 1920s and early 1930s. In the event, the limits of metropolitan protectionism were highlighted early on by the resignation of Joseph Chamberlain from the Unionist Cabinet in September 1903; they were never to be surmounted thereafter. Nevertheless, it is worth remarking that, had the movement for an imperial tariff system ever effectively broken through the lines of resistance opposed to it, the wider pattern of constitutional development in relation to empire would also have been different.

The first decade of the new century provided fresh evidence of an inherent flexibility in the modes and nomenclature of the Empire's constitutional structure. A critical example of this arises from the aftermath of the South African War of 1899–1902, in which both the Transvaal and Orange Free State reverted to Crown colony status. Following the 1906 general election, responsible government was restored in both territories, and in 1910 they became part and parcel of a unitary state through the South Africa Act. That union was locally made in its underlying politics, not least in its confirmation of a white-man's supremacy, but was imperially made in its constitutional legitimacy—legitimacy expressed most concretely through the preservation of the 'liberal' Cape coloured franchise and imperial oversight of the adjoining High Commission territories. In the context of this chapter, it was the continuing experimentation by the British with a model of colonial responsible government as a shot in its constitutional locker—that is, as a constitutional form which was not necessarily a solution in itself to any particular problem, but was of great utility in moving conveniently between statuses when required—which was to prove highly influential in the latter-day experience of decolonisation.

As for nomenclature, the 1907 imperial conference decided that the term 'dominion' (hardly a new one in the realm of Britain's overseas relationships) should have a special application to the self-governing colonies of the Empire.[2] This innovation met two deeply felt wishes within the 'empire of settlement'. The first was to exorcise the old bogey of 'Downing Street control' by recognising that self-governing colonies occupied a special constitutional and political zone within the Empire, cordoned off from the 'other' Empire of dependent colonies. Second, this experimentation was driven by a racial instinct (central not least to Australian and Canadian politics in these years) to erect a compartment between the white man's empire, and that of the lesser breeds. The tension between a deeply felt wish to distinguish between different qualities and rights pertaining to membership of the Empire–Commonwealth association, which was a feature of a good deal of British imperial thought after 1900, on the one hand, and the ineluctable forces conflating the range of experiences (at least constitutionally) into a broadly homogeneous whole, on the other, was to continue into the 1950s and 1960s.

Experimentation with nomenclature and categorisation ran alongside a heightened awareness of the realities and relativities of power. Status was one thing; function quite another. The function which really mattered in imperial terms was the preservation of the British Empire's integrity as a single body within the international system, and thus on its undifferentiated and efficient belligerency in war. The Committee for Imperial Defence, established in 1903, was the single most important innovation in the institutions of empire during the years leading up to 1914, and formed a model for the emergence thereafter of a modern Cabinet secretariat.[3] Yet one could not integrate planning for imperial defence without allowing for some modest enlargement of participation in decision-making concerning war and peace. At the 1911 imperial conference Sir Edward Grey, as foreign secretary, treated the dominion premiers to a confidential discourse on the current preoccupations within the foreign policy of the Empire. In retrospect this may be seen as the first

---

[2] John Kendle, *The Colonial and Imperial Conferences 1887–1911* (Longmans, 1967), pp. 45–57.
[3] See F. A. Johnson, *Defence by Committee: The British Committee of Imperial Defence, 1880–1959* (Oxford University Press, 1960).

sign of the dominions' emergence on to the stage of international power politics. But it also smacked of a metropolitan preference to allow imperial compatriots a tantalising glimpse into the inner sanctum of power, without actually allowing them inside.

The impact of the First World War on the imperial body politic, as in all other spheres of British life, was ambiguous and contradictory.[4] Although the British government was scrupulous after 3 August 1914 in ensuring that, when legislating for war machinery, the proper competences of dominion governments were not infringed, nonetheless the coming of belligerency revealed the fundamental unity of the Empire. In practice as well as in theory, the British Empire as a whole entered war with Germany as a result of the decision of the Westminster Parliament. Yet, there was a price to pay for that solidarity. How high that price might be would depend on the duration and cost—above all in lives— of the conflict. By late 1916 that price was high enough to overturn British domestic politics, and a coalition under Lloyd George was formed, with profound social consequences. It was also sufficiently high in imperial terms to affect the balance of wider imperial relationships. At the 1917 imperial war conference the self-governing parts of the Empire were promised that after the war the enhancement of their status would be definitively clarified. In retrospect it became a commonplace to observe that new dominion nationalities had been forged in the firestorm of 1914–18. Against that has to be set the fact that the war led to a marked recrudescence of pan-British feeling and loyalty. Sir Keith Hancock has captured the truth most neatly when remarking in his classic *Survey of British Commonwealth Affairs* that the self-governing dominions emerged from the First World War with a 'heightened self-consciousness'.[5] It was part of their predominantly English political culture, and reflective also of their own fragile internal balances, that this consciousness was above all constitutional in nature.

Embedded in the imperial politics of the war was the newly enshrined principle of 'no contribution without representation'—representation, that is, in what contemporaries termed 'the councils of the empire'. Robert Borden, the Canadian premier, was the first dominion leader to be invited to attend the British Cabinet, in July 1915, but it was Jan Smuts

---

[4] Robert Holland, 'The British Empire and the Great War', in Judith M. Brown and Wm. Roger Louis (eds), *The Oxford History of the British Empire*: vol. 4, *The Twentieth Century* (Oxford University Press, 1999), pp. 114–37.
[5] Sir Keith Hancock, *Survey of British Commonwealth Affairs*: vol. 1, *Problems of Nationality* (Oxford University Press, 1937), p. 1.

of South Africa who gained the distinction of being the only dominion statesman to become a full member of that body. In no other case did the nature and extent of the participation of a dominion in the conflict hinge so greatly on a single political personality as in that of Smuts. Alongside the 1917 imperial war conference there was also established an Imperial War Cabinet in which all dominion premiers were gathered alongside their British counterpart. This was the moment (though there was to be an echo of it again in 1940 in the plans to move the British government to Ottawa in the event of a successful German invasion) when the distinctness between the British and other Empire polities was most liable to blurring. Had this process gone further, separating out these elements of domestic and overseas sovereignties—that is, decolonisation in its most profound sense—might ultimately have proved harder to achieve. Yet, at the same time there was a superficiality about the imperialising tendencies induced by the war. Nobody was really under any illusion that the views of dominion prime ministers counted for much when it came to the big decisions in London, however much Hughes of Australia or Borden of Canada had to pretend otherwise to their own domestic constituencies. Meanwhile, it was in the war years that India, too, slipped at first imperceptibly, and obscured by repression in the Punjab, into a putative and modified dominionhood, initially signified to the world by the Montagu Declaration in August 1917, which established the goal of British policy in the subcontinent as responsible government.

The duality and flexibility of the dominions' constitutional situation by the end of the First World War was reflected in the fact that, while their representatives at the Paris Peace Conference in 1919 were part and parcel of the British Empire delegation, and gained leverage thereby in the acquisition of their own territorial desiderata, they also enjoyed a separate status signified by their independent signature of the Versailles Treaty.[6] This neatly illustrated the manner in which these burgeoning but still (in everything but geographical scale) small states had manoeuvred into a position where they were able to 'have it both ways': to enjoy the benefits of imperial partnership and yet increasingly to assert a measure of independence whenever it suited their interest. Perhaps this explains why the dominion status foreshadowed in 1917 was to prove a relatively comfortable constitutional halting-place until another great war upset

[6] R. M. Dawson, *The Development of Dominion Status, 1900–1936* (Oxford University Press, 1937), pp. 75–8.

the balance anew. In short, the very ambiguity behind the 'constitutional self-consciousness' in the overseas dominions reflected accurately their social and economic development; one may go even further and argue that under this ambivalent dispensation the societies concerned were rather more at ease with themselves than they were much later, once imperial ties had been cut. In line with the development heralded by Edwin Montagu, India also appended a separate signature in Versailles' Hall of Mirrors, and so to all intents and purposes acquired an international personality despite its dependent character. This was a paradox, however, not alleviated by the sort of cultural, political and racial uniformities which, by contrast, smoothed out the processes of Anglo-dominion relations.

The complex and subtle significance of the constitutional and political theory of dominionhood after the war of 1914–18 has been reassessed by John Darwin, who has stressed its 'distinctive blend of national status and Imperial identity',[7] as well as the appropriateness of that blend for the circumstances occupied by the metropole and outlying Britannic societies. Through its suppleness and adaptability the politics of dominionhood promised to underpin a genus of British imperial solidarity suited to twentieth-century conditions. The Indian expression of this tendency lay in the 'new' principle of dyarchy initially propagandised by Lionel Curtis which evolved from the Montagu–Chelmsford reforms of 1919, under which elected Indian ministers were to become constitutionally responsible for a prescribed range of portfolios at provincial level, without impinging on the authority of the central executive in Delhi in such key areas as defence and taxation. In truth, of course, there was nothing new about empires seeking to 'pay out rope', while keeping a tight grip on the essentials of power, but then Curtis was not so much an original thinker as a supplier of convenient ruses and slogans for men of power—a sort of constitutional spin doctor for his times, a role he played most importantly over Ireland in 1920–1.[8] Like all the best political theories, dominionhood could mutate over time, offering a menu of options—with regard to the balance to be struck between local and imperial citizenship, for example—which different partners could accept

[7] John Darwin, 'A Third British Empire? The Dominion Idea in Imperial Politics,' in Brown and Louis (eds), *The Oxford History of the British Empire*: vol. 4, *The Twentieth Century*, pp. 64–87.

[8] For a valuable biography of a seminal figure relating to the concerns of this chapter see Deborah Lavin, *From Empire to International Commonwealth: A Biography of Lionel Curtis* (Clarendon Press, 1995).

or reject as they found fit. Thus, the 1931 Statute of Westminster as the crowning charter of dominionhood could be 'eagerly endorsed in Dublin and Pretoria, carefully emasculated in Canada, and comprehensively ignored in Australia and New Zealand'.[9]

The 1931 statute was itself the legislative outcome of the 1926 Balfour Report on inter-imperial relations rather portentously unveiled at the imperial conference of that year. Immediately after the war all 'British' governments within the Commonwealth had been too preoccupied with economic problems to return to the issues of constitutional clarification flagged at the 1917 conference. Over the next few years, however, the balance of forces shifted in a way which pushed the unwritten imperial constitution further up the agenda. The defeat of the Conservative ministry of Arthur Meighen, and its replacement by Mackenzie King's Liberals, in Canada; the bigger shock for imperial enthusiasts at the 1924 South African election when Smuts was displaced as prime minister by Hertzog's Afrikaner Nationalist Party in coalition with Labour; and above all the establishment as a dominion of the Irish Free State in 1922; all combined to bring about a mood, and even necessity, for change.[10] Whether it was the Irish, the Canadians or the South Africans who played the decisive role thereafter in 'picking the lock' of post-war imperial reform is a question which used to be closely debated by historians,[11] though such issues have got lost with the more introspective concerns of component historiographies in recent decades.

The basic fact, however, is that by 1926 the British were not keeping a particularly jealous guard over the nature of their relationship with the self-governing empire, and were even prepared to take novel risks with other parts of their overseas patrimony (the recognition of Egyptian 'independence' in 1922 was a case in point). Most especially they exhibited no proclivity to stand in the way of redefining the complete autonomy of the overseas dominions, so that the Balfour Report recognised them, in the characteristically Balfourian word-play so often repeated in the textbooks, as

> autonomous communities within the British Empire, equal in status, in no
> way subordinate to one another in any aspect of their domestic or external

[9] Darwin, 'A Third British Empire?'.

[10] Robert Holland, *Britain and the Commonwealth Alliance, 1918–39* (Macmillan, 1981), pp. 53–67.

[11] See D. W. Harkness, *The Restless Dominion: The Irish Free State and the British Commonwealth of Nations, 1921–31* (Macmillan, 1969), pp. 198–205.

affairs, though united by a common allegiance to the Crown, and freely associated as members of the British Commonwealth of Nations.

Behind this pliability on the part of the imperial government, frequently pointed out but never perhaps entirely explained, there lay something quite profound: the disintegration of the ideal of the empire superstate which had been a presence in British public culture since the 1880s, and which the First World War had appeared to sublimate. Bonar Law signalled a new realism in his famous letter to *The Times* during the Chanak crisis of 1922 when he stated that the United Kingdom 'could no longer act alone as the Policeman of the World'. It was a statement, shaped by the fatigue and disillusion of the early post-war world, which had the immediate effect of helping to bring down the Lloyd George coalition, and which still more radically was to contribute to the intellectual and emotional genesis of appeasement. In the imperial context, the implication was that the dream of an integrated, pan-oceanic Britannic state capable of meeting all kinds of challenges single-handed—with allies if possible, but alone if necessary—was no longer feasible or desirable. Once this insight seeped into the official mind in Whitehall, the need to cling to the full panoply of constitutional and legal safeguards behind the automata of imperial unity was considerably devalued.

Yet we need to be clear what the process begun by the 1926 conference, climaxing in the Statute of 1931, did, and did not, actually do. Its main effect was to end the Empire-wide writ of the United Kingdom Parliament. The full implications of this change were exhaustively explored by very distinguished constitutional historians and commentators many years ago,[12] and we shall not seek here to go over the same ground—the change, for example, whereby governors-general in the dominions became representatives solely of the Crown, necessitating the appointment in those countries of United Kingdom high commissioners undertaking the business of Her Majesty's Government. What the new version of dominionhood did not do, or at least was not intended to do, was to subtract from the imperial sovereignty of the Crown. That Crown was to remain indivisible, so that, according to the constitutional analyst Sir Sidney Low, the 'one fatal heresy to guard against is the idea that there are many Crowns and that the King is King in different parts of the Empire in different senses'.[13]

---

[12] Most notably K. C. Wheare, *The Statute of Westminster and Dominion Status* (Clarendon Press, 1933).
[13] Holland, *Commonwealth Alliance*, p. 60.

In this spirit the one general area of legislation under the dispensation of the Statute of Westminster which all dominions, a category now including the United Kingdom, were not permitted to trench upon without consulting Commonwealth partners, was the succession to the throne. It was the Lord Chancellor in the Labour government after 1929, Lord Sankey, who remarked upon the irony that, despite the progressive diminution of the constitutional powers of the monarchy over many generations, the Crown had now become the last surviving link in the imperial chain and 'the most important factor in keeping things together'.[14] The last words of King George V on his deathbed in 1936 may or may not have been, as legend soon recorded, 'How is the Empire?', but over his last years he scanned all imperial legislation to ensure that the functions of the Crown were not impaired. Holding things together in Empire and Commonwealth, especially once the crisis of the abdication had been surmounted, gave the monarchy a meaningful role in British society over the following decades. It was to provide arguably the most distinctive motif in the reign of Queen Elizabeth II, at least until the very end of the century, when the crush of events and cultural change enforced a rather different gloss on the practice of monarchy in the United Kingdom.

This centrality of the Crown to the constitutional assumptions of the inter-war British Commonwealth of Nations arose most basically from the principle that 'when the King is at war, the Empire is at war'. The ideal of indivisibility had an obvious relevance in this regard. More than ever, what was important about the association for the metropole was not that it should have a great deal to do collectively in peacetime, but that it should act as one if and when another big war supervened. Metropolitan anticipations here were shaped overwhelmingly by memories of 1914. On that occasion the dependent Empire had been bound to a shared belligerency by the brutal realities of constitutional inferiority, whereas the self-governing territories had been carried along with a perhaps surprising ease and velocity ('to the last man and the last shilling', in the promise of the Australian premier of the day) by the emotional call of 'King and Country'. Throughout the 1930s the officials of the Dominions Office were prepared to turn a blind eye to imperfections in the orchestrated unity among 'the Commonwealth family'—as when one dominion took an initiative of its own at the League of Nations, for example—in the belief that during a major crisis everybody would

[14] Holland, *Commonwealth Alliance*, p. 61.

be pulled along in the roller-coaster fashion of 1914. Royal tours (most notably that to Canada in 1939, which repaired any damage done by the abdication in the most senior dominion, as witnessed by the large and enthusiastic crowds even in Quebec City) were significant to the locking-in of this expectation.

The concern in London, and above all the Foreign Office, to preserve the concept of 'Empire foreign policy' despite the developing international personalities of the dominions, blended these various psychological elements. There was a balance to be struck between the desire of the Foreign Office not to be lumbered with responsibility for managing the mass of local detail which the evolution of the dominions' burgeoning regional interests entailed, and a need to preserve the core elements in imperial diplomatic integrity. The first of these responses was evident in the welcome given in London to the precedent of the signing of the Halibut Treaty between Canada and the United States in March 1923, so offloading the hoary old chore of North American fishery problems.[15] Henceforth the dominions had a full capacity to conduct their purely local diplomacies as they thought fit.

The difficulty was that, although the United Kingdom also had regional (that is, European) preoccupations of its own, these were liable to involve all its Commonwealth partners willy-nilly in war. Significantly, the dominion governments did not sign the Locarno treaties of 1925 and thereby accept its obligations in the event of any infraction of either French or German borders by aggressors. This wedge driven into Empire-wide responsibilities was mitigated only by Article 9 of the treaties, which provided for dominion signatures at a later date. Yet, although this compromise was far from ideal, metropolitan decision-makers were in the end appreciative of the fact that common imperial action could never be guaranteed by the mere fact of contractual or constitutional commitment; perhaps the reverse. There was in this attitude a mixture of liberalism, self-interested calculation and *savoir faire* which was later to infuse decolonisation after 1945. Meanwhile, ministers and officials deflected occasional twitches of anxiety concerning empire togetherness with the prediction that the dominions would always 'turn up on the night'.

The nightmare of secession was the theoretical trapdoor beneath this lightweight and utilitarian Commonwealth structure constructed

---

[15] Philip G. Wigley, *Canada and the Transition to Commonwealth: British–Canadian Relations, 1917–1926* (Cambridge University Press 1977), pp. 175–85.

between 1919 and 1939. The 1926 report had stated the dominions to be 'freely associated', and it did not take unusual perspicacity to draw the deduction that members were therefore free to dissociate if they wished. For this reason Whitehall officials always jibbed at confronting this issue head-on. Whenever it was raised in private discussions, they reverted instinctively to the family metaphors embedded in Commonwealth thinking, stating that one might as well discuss the conditions of divorce even in the very act of marriage—an evasion with more validity, perhaps, for a society not yet acquainted with the notion of prenuptial contracts. Yet the striking thing is that none of the 'traditional' dominions took any actions which tended in this direction, and such actions became less, not more, likely as the inter-war years passed. Although some dominions appointed their own diplomatic representatives to certain foreign capitals during the 1920s (Canada sent 'its man' to Tokyo in 1928, for instance), no such appointment of this sort was made by any dominion between 1929 and the start of the Second World War.[16] The world became too dangerous a place for the dominions as small powers to relish a more extended exposure to its pitfalls. But the main roadblock across any approach to secession lay in the very nature of the dominion societies, with their anglophone—indeed, still, on balance, 'Britannic'—majorities, and where even francophone Quebec continued to look to the imperial connection as a constitutional guarantee of local rights. As Darwin puts it, the juridical and political settlement of 1926–31 is not to be regarded

> as a divorce nisi while the dominions waited for complete independence. The new Dominionhood was not the most that the dominions could extract from the grudging imperial centre: it was the most that the internal politics of the dominions themselves would permit.[17]

Secession, according to dominion norms therefore, lay well beyond the subtle limits defined by the interplay of the permissible and the unthinkable.

Still, in any empire norms are often honoured in the breach, and there are two cases which fit very uneasily with what has already been said about the inter-war Commonwealth. The lesser of this duo of exceptions is Newfoundland. This territory is interesting because it occupied a kind of no-man's-land between colonial and dominion status, defying precise

---

[16] Holland, *Commonwealth Alliance*, pp. 77–85.
[17] Darwin, 'A Third British Empire?', p. 71.

constitutional categorisation (as did both Southern Rhodesia and Malta, both of which had less claim to being a real dominion than Newfoundland, and yet were not mere colonies either—'colonies plus' we might call them today). There can be no doubt that in the 1920s Newfoundland was on the same conveyer-belt as all the other overseas dominions towards untrammelled autonomy. Yet, in 1933 Newfoundland was formally declared bankrupt—than which no more dismal fate could ever befall a British colony—and, in return for its debt being covered by the Treasury in London, its administration was put into the hands of a Commission of Government wholly appointed and supervised from Whitehall. Newfoundland was never to revert to the *status quo ante*, and in 1949 was incorporated—following a referendum the status of which has always been a matter of local notoriety—into the Canadian Confederation. During the inter-war years, then, the status of Commonwealth members was still clearly subject to regressions as well as advances, depending on certain standard metropolitan criteria such as solvency, in a way that would not have been true after 1945.

The greatest exception to the general rules of dominionhood, however, was provided by the experience of the Irish Free State. Perhaps it could never have been any other way. The south of Ireland was not a dominion like the others, for one fundamental reason: its status was bound by a treaty marred by imposition, and which carried with it an unenviable load of history. This gave the lie to the common argument of the time that, if only the British could treat the Irish Free State like a true dominion, the new state would act like one. In the Anglo-Irish agreement of 1921 it was laid down that the constitutional rights and duties of the Irish Free State would be the same as Canada (that is, the benchmark of the senior dominion within the Commonwealth). The debate which soon got under way as to whether the analogy referred to the situation of Canada as it was at the time, or as it might evolve thereafter, reflected the temptation on the part of some people to have second thoughts, encouraged by certain acts of the new government in Dublin. Notable among these was the registration of the treaty at the League of Nations as an internationally justiciable instrument, an act which conflicted with the rather fragile *inter se* doctrine of Commonwealth relations which held that these relations were *sui generis* and therefore outside international norms. In the event the Irish Free State did stick broadly within the accepted rules of the imperial game during the 1920s. More importantly, as Charles Townshend has written, that new and fragile polity 'took on the burdensome demands of constitutionalism'.[18] It was because they did so, Townshend goes on to state, that even the coming to power in Dublin of Eamon de Valera, the condemned rebel of 1916, at the 1932 general election did not mean a return to internal destabilisation. 'He [de Valera] took his place', Townshend concludes, 'in an orderly system of constitutional government whose unmistakably British assumptions survived . . .'.[19] Since some Irish people had played no mean part in operating and celebrating those assumptions over many decades, perhaps we should not be surprised.

Still, for many English contemporaries the triumph of de Valera at the head of his virulently republican Fianna Fail party is not to be underestimated. De Valera did not at first launch any frontal assault on the dominion settlement as it affected the Free State, testimony, arguably, to the durability and legitimacy of the reforms of 1926–31. But he did start to chip away at some of its most vulnerable spots, in particular refusing to take the oath to the sovereign, or to pay sums due to the Treasury in London arising from previous annuity arrangements. A military invasion of the south was considered by the British Cabinet, if only promptly to be abandoned as an option; but that such action against a fellow dominion was still at least thinkable is instructive. Ill feeling on these matters instead fed into the pettiness of a trade war—though in keeping with the unending irony of this particular relationship, even while conducting a trade war, at the ensuing imperial economic conference in Ottawa the British delegates got on better with the Irish than with any of the other participants.[20] This nonetheless remained an age when England's physical danger remained Ireland's constitutional opportunity and, although de Valera had to wait patiently, such an opportunity duly arrived with the Rhineland crisis of 1936, which (by diverting the attention of Stanley Baldwin's government) led de Valera to risk the inauguration of an External Relations bill in the Dail. This legislation erased any recognition of the Crown in the internal arrangements of the Free State constitution, and as such converted the dominion into a quasi-republic.

But, could a 'British' dominion become a republic without first leaving the Commonwealth altogether? It obviously could not do so without a

---

[18] Charles Townshend, 'The Meaning of Irish Freedom: Constitutionalism in the Irish Free State', *Transactions of the Royal Historical Society* (1998).
[19] Ibid., 70.
[20] Holland, *Commonwealth Alliance*, p. 159.

radical alteration in the very concept of dominionhood. What is most interesting about this interlude is how receptive metropolitan officialdom was to a fresh definition of dominion status which stripped it of complicating requirements, and held out the prospect that the association might be made so flexible as to permit India and Egypt—with both of which countries Britain's relations were currently at a stage of acute flux—to be fitted in at some later date.[21] As in 1926, so a decade later, shifts in Commonwealth constitutional assumptions were linked to strong undercurrents in Britain's world position and the responses they evoked in Whitehall. The Anglo-Irish defence agreement in 1938 simply worked out some of the practical consequences. It is true that the obverse of de Valera's caution in dealing with the external trappings of Irish statehood was the 'high Catholicism' of his internal policies, with bleak implications for any deal over partition. Yet, when Ireland remained neutral after 1939, it was a benevolent posture involving no danger to the British mainland—Churchill might have raged against the Irish, but it was in the same sulky, but knowingly pointless, way that he raged against Brahmins, Arabs, intellectuals and all those representative, as he had once put it to Lloyd George, of a new world order he affected to despise.[22]

Maybe in some profound way it was because the following war— with its blitzes, battles over Britain and occasional swagger sticks— served to make the English more consciously English than ever, which made it peculiarly difficult for Eire, as that country was now called, to remain any longer associated with the Empire through the dominion link. Certainly Eire, despite being led at the time by de Valera's domestic opponent, left the Commonwealth in a sudden huff in 1948, for reasons the immediacy of which were obscure then and since.[23] But the following year both India and Pakistan, and after them a number of other newly independent countries, were able to become republics within the Commonwealth, assisted by the Irish precedent. That it was Eamon de Valera who, through his actions after 1932, blazed a path which led towards a constitutionally and racially diverse, and therefore more sustainable, Commonwealth of Nations is a paradox worthy of Anglo-Irish history.

The war of 1939–45, in imperial and Commonwealth terms, proved

[21] Holland, *Commonwealth Alliance*, p. 161.

[22] See Robert Holland, *The Pursuit of Greatness: Britain and the World Role, 1900–1970* (Fontana, 1991), p. 92.

[23] For a treatmeant of this episode, see D. W. Dean, 'Final Exit? Eire, the Commonwealth and the Repeal of the External Relations Act, 1945–49', *Journal of Imperial and Commonwealth History* (1992).

to be a very different experience from that of 1914–18. For a start, there was not in September 1939 that rush to demonstrate imperial and loyalist credentials which had afforded August 1914 its pan-British trademark. Rather there was instead, in what one could still just about credibly describe as 'the self-governing Empire', a considered, rational and quali-fied decision to go to war alongside the United Kingdom. These entries into war, however, were now validated by separate Parliaments (though only after a change of government in South Africa) and, perhaps most significantly, became operational on different dates. In other words, the 'British' countries went to war against Germany in common, but according to their individual lights, not in a collective act of belligerency. We cannot, of course, say much here about the war which followed, but it is telling to note that no imperial war conference, let alone any Imperial War Cabinet, took place in these years, as they had done after 1916. Not only had the various dominions entered the war separately, they subsequently fought according to their own distinctive priorities. Wartime Australian governments, for example, strove to ensure that their troops should only be used in active service within their own region; while by the end of the war the very term 'dominion' had ceased to have real currency. Of all the more traditional elements in British life which, Brideshead-like, receded from view amidst the fog of conflict after 1939, one was the conception that the British Empire–Common-wealth existed as a distinct and integral constitutional entity.

For this reason, any attempt to write a coherent constitutional account of British imperial change in the decades after 1945 is plagued with difficulties. Constitutional themes and preoccupations were marginal to the far cruder struggle for power driving the process of decolonisation forward; it may be pertinent in this regard to recall Stanley de Smith's remark that after the Statute of Westminster the Commonwealth itself was 'already a singularly lawless association'.[24] Yet, clearly there is a constitutional dimension to events after the Second World War which historians of the end of empire have yet to get to grips with. For example, in what ways did the earlier politico-constitutional experience with regard to 'colonies of settlement' feed into the later management of change in the dependent empire? Is it the case, as some have contended, that, when it came to navigating the rapids of decolonisation, the British had an advantage over the French precisely in having a 'dominion model'

[24] S. A. de Smith, *The New Commonwealth and Its Constitutions* (Stevens, 1964), p. 1.

(that is, a framework for controlled devolution) imprinted on the official mind at many levels?

Suggestively, one analyst of what went wrong in the French possession of Madagascar after 1945, involving massive loss of life, argues that the problem for French colonial policy-makers was that, unlike their British counterparts, they had among their mental furniture no notion of half-way houses between rigid administration on the one hand, and rapid advances to self-government on the other.[25] As a result, when the reform process inevitably ran into problems, policy instantly ratcheted all the way back to violent repression, with disastrous consequences. Compare this with India, where, in the apparently extreme duress of July and August 1947, 'dominion status' was accepted by all the principal actors as a mechanism to at least see through the independence process in the subcontinent, without having to expose it to the destabilising complexities of a constituent assembly. Allowing Mountbatten his moment of glory in Delhi (we shall not speak of the situation in the Punjab, which was another matter entirely) constituted the last important contribution of the dominion idea — or, in this case, the dominion tactic — to British history.

Peter Burroughs has commented penetratingly on British experience in ending rather different sorts of empires at different times in its modern history. An extended quotation is required.

> The mid-Victorian disengagement from the settlement colonies was a major development in British colonial policy and an unprecedented transfer of power by an imperial state, comparable in its way with the decolonisation of Africa a century later. Despite certain obvious differences, principally the alien character of British political institutions in African societies and the international context of world war and the Cold War, the similarities between the two processes are striking. Stimulated into action by the Canadian rebellions of 1837–8 and the West Indian riots of 1937–8, the British government on both occasions fully recognised and positively promoted the movement towards colonial self-government. In neither case was it a question of the imperial authorities being caught napping and then fighting a rearguard action against nationalist demands. In the reshaping of imperial policy (the role of Durham and Grey late echoed by Lord Hailey and Malcolm MacDonald), much of the discussion centred on timing and pre-conditions, and on which colonists should be the recipients of the transferred power. While there was much concern with agitators and dema-

---

[25] Martin Shipway, 'Madagascar on the Eve of Insurrection, 1944–47: The Impasse of a Liberal Colonial Policy', *Journal of Imperial and Colonial Policy* (1996).

646

gogues, and whether or not they were susceptible to blandishments, the abandonment by Britain of the Canadian elites and attempts to work with assemblies were paralleled by British endeavours to convert elite nationalist movements in Africa into broadly-based, popular parties. In both instances Britain released a genie from the bottle, and after one test in each century— Canada and the Gold Coast—the pace of disengagement quickened and the timetables of apprenticeship and preparation were abandoned in an uncontrolled rush to autonomy. On both occasions the rapid process of decolonisation was accomplished with an air of British resignation, followed by a public mood of disillusion with newly self-governing territories. In neither case was decolonisation a result of British weakness, nor did a direct connection exist between the pace of political advance and the economic relationship of the colonies to Britain. It was a recognition of reality as much as a failure of will . . .[26]

We may, indeed, carry the comparison further by reminding ourselves that responsible government in the Canadas did not come about in one fell swoop in the wake of Durham's famous—if largely abortive—report in 1839. Rather it came into being incrementally and almost imperceptibly as the balance shifted in colonial assemblies between governors and elected members. What happened in the Colonial Empire a century later was broadly similar. In 1945 only nine out of fifty-two dependent territories had legislatures with elected majorities. The characteristic pattern of development in the remaining forty-one was for nominated members to be progressively introduced into the Executive Council at the governor's discretion; simultaneously the process of local consultation in the making of such appointments was extended; an elective element would shortly ensue, followed by an elective majority; somewhere along the line a ministerial system would be instituted, and sooner rather than later the position of chief minister; finally, the governor and ex-officio members would disappear completely from the council in the run-up to full independence. Thus Jamaica was accorded an elected element in the Executive Council in 1944, an elective majority supervened in 1953, 'internal self-government' arrived in 1959 and independence in 1962; though as de Smith, the most lucid commentator on these issues, commented with regard to the Jamaican example, 'a decorous progression of this order could seldom be maintained in the 1960s'.[27]

It is difficult to specify the decisive juncture in this politico-consti-

[26] Peter Burroughs, 'Colonial Self-government', in C. C. Eldridge (ed.), *British Imperialism in the Nineteenth Century* (Macmillan, 1984), pp. 62–3.
[27] De Smith, *The New Commonwealth*, p. 64.

tutional progression. Stanley de Smith describes the appointment of a chief (or prime) minister as 'the most significant step of all'.[28] This at least would nicely mimic British constitutional tradition. The argument also fits with the more strictly political side of the story. The Conservatives under Winston Churchill's leadership were returned to power in November 1951. The tories' general platform of reviving British 'greatness' after the shilly-shallyings of Attlee's socialist government was not expected to incline the new ministry to look favourably on any more concessions to nationalist politicians overseas. The first major decision relating to a colonial constitution waiting for Churchill and his colonial secretary, Oliver Lyttelton, however, was whether or not to confirm the title of prime minister on Kwame Nkrumah in Gold Coast Colony. They let it go through, and this indication of their willingness to stay with the existing 'grain' of policy was of real importance. For a few years thereafter there was considerable interest in Whitehall in developing some kind of 'mezzanine' statehood for the smaller, poorer or strategically more indispensable overseas territories such as Malta or Singapore.[29] Hesitation about the fundamental policy, and a related proclivity to make certain distinctions when it was convenient, was illustrated by the discussion within government as to the desirability of substituting the looser phrase 'self-government' for the more precise term 'independence' whenever possible.[30] There was potential here for constitutional permutations capable of making decolonisation an infinitely varied and prolonged experience. But to hold the positions implicit in such an approach would have required the metropole not to have pulled resources out of the Empire while it was being run down, but to have put more in; and certainly after about 1956–7 this was not the point of the exercise at all.

As in the constitutional advance of the old dominions, so in that of their latter-day colonial successors, the suppleness of constitutional vocabulary, and related notions of status and procedure, proved an advantage. Certain phases in the standard evolution could therefore be missed out altogether if it proved politically convenient to do so, so that in Tanganyika, once policy took an accelerated turn after 1958, the usual

---

[28] De Smith, *The New Commonwealth*, p. 66.

[29] W. David McIntyre, 'The Strange Death of Dominion Status', *Journal of Imperial and Commonwealth History* (1999).

[30] David Goldsworthy (ed.), *British Documents on the End of Empire: The Conservative Government and the End of Empire, 1951–57: Part 3, Politics and Administration* (HMSO, 1994), pp. 49–53.

transitional period in which nominated unofficial members held the balance between official and elected members in the legislature simply got omitted. Colonial constitutions in the age of decolonisation could be played like a concertina, the full range of possibilities being exploited, or compressed, into a more intense finale. It was natural that in this process the role of the local governor, assisted by his executive council, was gradually effaced as colonial constitutions moved through the successive gears of elected majorities, responsible government, full internal self-government and eventual independence. But this effacement was occasionally subject to reversals and qualifications; nor should the position of the governor necessarily be conflated with that of the secretary of state for colonies in London. One of the controls or 'stabilisers' built into the decolonisation process was the power of the governor to 'refer' key areas of legislation to the responsible minister in Her Majesty's Government, so taking the issue out of the increasingly contested realm of territorial politics. It was similarly orthodox procedure to keep control over the public services and law enforcement agencies out of the hands of locally elected politicians until the end of the process, though quite how late depended on how far the latter were felt to be trustworthy. In both Kenya and Uganda the governor (and beyond him the colonial secretary) remained constitutionally responsible for the police right up until independence.

In this connection de Smith remarks upon the paradoxical effect that during these various stages, when government and administration were increasingly intrusive within the societies concerned, the 'direct influence of the Secretary of State over the course of events may actually increase rather than diminish, if only because he may have occasion to exercise it over a wider range of political and constitutional questions than ever before'.[31] This increase in direct authority was acceptable to the main nationalist politicians because they looked forward to inheriting before long the enlargement of powers concerned. The description rings true also with regard to the essential *modus operandi* of metropolitan decolonisation, which was to devolve as many of the burdensome chores of government consonant with maintaining a firm grip on the essentials of power until the expiring moment of British responsibility. In the British case, at least, decolonisation was by no means always synonymous with weakness, let alone abject collapse, at the centre.

In discussing these aspects, de Smith is careful to state that, neverthe-

---

[31] De Smith, *The New Commonwealth*, p. 51.

less, it was not possible for a British minister to 'play the actor-manager' in the scene-change of decolonisation. 'The dynamics of colonial nationalism', he adds, 'will normally have created a situation in which he [the secretary of state] must be an umpire, a time-keeper, a conciliator and a candid friend'.[32] Yet the more we understand the way decolonis-ation happened, the more powerful and shaping these precise roles appear to be. The umpire, after all, determines who stays on the field of play, and who goes; while most people will have experienced at some point in their lives how shattering the 'candid friend' can indeed be. But it is in the capacity of time-keeper that the very distinctive power of the decoloniser—at once residual, intense and decisive—is most character-istically derived. Speed, in other words, is of the essence in the climaxes of many imperial departures, though rarely to such a marked degree as in India and Palestine, where the compressing of deadlines went to the heart of British tactics in extricating themselves from otherwise imposs-ible situations. Yet it is often the less well-known instances of the abandonment of colonial responsibility which carry with them important truths of a general kind. Thus, one historian has written with regard to the case of Newfoundland to which we have already referred:

> ... what the British eventually did was not to propose a particular consti-tutional solution ... but to establish a timetable and a procedure for political change there. To outward appearances this put them above the fray; but in truth, by asserting their right to establish how political change would occur in Newfoundland, they positioned themselves brilliantly to influence strongly what that change should be.[33]

Thus constitutionally, just as politically, it was not important that the British should always dictate in matters of detail, but that they should shape broad lines of movement and chronology. One area where they largely failed to achieve this was in the Mediterranean, if only because local nationalisms and state-building in that region had a dynamic entirely their own. This was obviously so in the special case of mandatory Palestine. Cyprus proved to be the only Crown colony where the British had no in-put into determining the basic structure of the independence constitution; it was Greece and Turkey which had that privilege, with a Swiss lawyer to chair the committee which filled in the less important

---

[32] De Smith, *The New Commonwealth*, p. 54.
[33] Peter Neary, *Newfoundland in the North Atlantic World, 1929–49* (Queens University Press, 1988), p. 246.

blanks.[34] But, despite such instances, for the most part the British remained sufficiently in control to supervise, in dialogue with local interlocutors, the drawing-up of independence constitutions—the real test of success for any departing imperial power. Whether what was put down on paper remained in place for very long was another matter, but this was not absolutely vital so long as by then the British had successfully divested themselves of responsibility with dignity and no great material damage to themselves.

One facet of the end of empire that requires special mention given the broad concerns of this volume is power-sharing, especially with regard to minorities. Although it was true that both the main British political parties could not easily be differentiated in terms of attitudes to colonial policy after 1945, generally Labour politicians showed a basic sympathy towards the involvement of indigenous representatives in constitution-making, while their Conservative counterparts were much more prone to exclude them. Yet, even in Labour circles, the scope of 'involvement' was often very circumscribed, as the actions of the Attlee ministry in the early phases of the move towards a Central African Federation showed. Afterwards, the interests of tribal or regional minorities tended to be shunted to one side in the deal-making between rulers and political legatees that was the essence of decolonisation. Where this did not happen it was because the diverse interests themselves were too powerful, as in Nigeria, or because the British had special reasons for according a preference, as with regard to the Turkish minority in Cyprus. The key point here is that in presiding over colonial constitutional change, the British usually, if not quite invariably, found it made things easier to marginalise those elements which did not easily fit the dominant configuration. It may be surmised that had decolonisation worked differently—and had the British learned more as a result about the theory and practice of power-sharing in plural societies—they might have been more inventive and tenacious when confronted by their own metropolitan dilemmas in Ulster from the later 1960s onwards.

Some of the above themes are especially well illustrated by the endgame of the Rhodesian imbroglio as it was played out at the Lancaster House conference of 10 September–21 December 1979. At that conference

---

[34] There was a certain pathos in the plea of the British colonial secretary to the Greek and Turkish foreign ministers in London on the eve of the Lancaster House conference in early February 1959 that 'the British Government . . . should take part in the process of [Cypriot] constitution-making'. Quoted in Robert Holland, *Britain and the Revolt in Cyprus, 1954–59* (Oxford University Press, 1998), p. 308.

the British delegation, led by the foreign secretary, Lord Carrington, performed the sort of tactical volte-face which often accompanied climaxes of decolonisation, whereby old enemies suddenly became friends, and old friends became dispensable. Thus it was that Carrington turned his patrician charm on Robert Mugabe, whilst other black African politicians, principally Joshuo Nkomo, discovered that they were not to be admitted to the inner circle. Nkomo later captured something of the essence in the working of such conferences when he described Lord Carrington as situated in the centre of a spider's web, drawing successive parties into his orbit, and proceeding to plenary conclusions only when matters had been so arranged as to conform to the basic requirements of his own government.[35]

The Rhodesian aftermath of the Lancaster House conference in 1981 evokes something even more fundamental about the experience of British decolonisation, implicit in the remark by one British observer in Salisbury (today's Harare) that he was struck at the time by how many of the participants, including Lord Soames as the last governor of the territory, 'were playing roles which had been well-scripted'. The same writer proceeded to expand on this theme by stating that there had always been something peculiar and anomalous about the rebel regime following the Unilateral Declaration of Independence in November 1965, and that after the Lancaster House settlement

> with the return of the Queen's authority, with the presence of a Governor, with the Union Jack flying over Government House, all, as it were, returned to normality. This restoration of normality, the restoration of well-tried and familiar roles—with the Governor and Mary Soames playing ... almost a vice-regal role—created the atmosphere of a well-scripted drama ... It was a drama returning to its proper course after being hijacked for a couple of intervening acts.[36]

This description captures very neatly the general truth behind the Rhodesian finale that in a curious and striking manner all those involved (and not just the departing British rulers) 'knew their place' in the ordering of the end of empire, and accepted it, if only because they were

---

[35] Michael Charlton, *The Last Colony in Africa: Diplomacy and the Independence of Rhodesia* (Blackwell, 1990), p. 57.

[36] Ibid., pp. 134–5. The role of a *grande dame* in decolonisation—like a bit-part in a film which, if well played, could steal a surprising amount of the limelight—had been brilliantly invented by Edwina, Lady Mountbatten in India during 1947. Lady Soames in Harare was a sort of understated version of this original.

afraid of being written out of their part. The proper 'constitutionalising' of Rhodesian independence reflected how deep this went, and revealed the advantages deriving from their own sovereign jurisdiction which the British had even in a territory where things had come so badly off the rails along the way.

Twenty years after the birth of Zimbabwe, that country, still governed by Mugabe and his Zanu PF Party, appeared to have come off the rails again, albeit in a post-colonial style defined by political 'kleptocracy' and plain incompetence. The undoubted failures common to 'new statehood' in Africa and elsewhere are not our concern here. Nevertheless, the scripted and crafted nature of British decolonisation helped to cultivate the easy impression that such later failure arose purely from errors by decolonised elites. Those 'nationalist' elites had certainly never been preoccupied in any serious way with issues of economic management. 'Seek Ye First the Political Kingdom' was the principle enshrined by Kwame Nkrumah in West Africa, which in its most cynical rendering simply meant, if you get hold of the power, the jobs and the perks will follow. For nationalist entrepreneurs, the 'Westminster model' fitted this outlook, since it represented their only idea as to how a political kingdom might be organised; as a slogan, it also helped to deflect any danger that they might be fobbed off with something less than untrammelled independence.

What is becoming clearer as the documentation is unearthed by researchers, however, is the degree to which the British commitment to Westminster-style democracy in putative 'new states' itself ebbed away in the final phases of decolonisation. Such widely quoted remarks as that by the last governor-general of Nigeria, Sir John Robertson, to the effect that it was now time for the British to leave the Africans to make their own mistakes, however bad the consequences might be for the locals, were not simply jocular. Behind such asides lay an important reconfiguration of constitutional and moral priorities in the ending of empire; and, just as the criteria for economic 'viability' were progressively watered down in the 1950s and 1960s, so were the criteria for the sustainability of democratic (and perhaps even 'good') governance.

Key elements in this change can be gleaned, for instance, from the interdepartmental debate within Whitehall during 1959 on 'Aspects of UK Strategic Policy—the next 15 years'. A draft of the resulting memorandum argued that 'the world being what it was ... democratic government on the Western pattern cannot suit the emerging backward countries',[37] and that as such it was important to develop a 'relativistic attitude' as to where democracy was likely to be appropriate, and where the opposite might prove to be the case. Most of Africa, undoubtedly, fitted into the latter category. 'The paper asks', one official summarised, 'whether we ought not to grant independence under some other kind of regime than the Westminster model'.[38] In fact, once 'the winds of change' began to blow so strongly later in that year, policy proceeded on the basis of the models ready to hand, and which reinforced the apparent liberality of the departing rulers, even if there was little faith that a real democracy would long survive. Part of the psychological complexity shaping the climax of the end of empire, in its metropolitan dimension, lies in this disjuncture behind the official rhetoric of generous optimism, and the more private flows of disillusionment, pessimism and even cynicism as to what the future held.

The 'jerry-building' feel to the constitutional and political structures consequent on decolonisation feeds, too, into the federalising impulse which sometimes made itself felt. As John Kendle has noted in his book, *Federal Britain*, 'if the federal idea had ever had much encouragement in British political life it had been in the imperial setting',[39] and certainly it got a fresh boost in the context of problems of colonial political advance after 1945, beginning with the Montego Bay conference on Caribbean federation in September 1947. The personnel involved in the specialised task of framing federal constitutions were often the same. For example, Sir Kenneth Wheare, adviser to the Newfoundland Convention after 1947, which looked closely at the details whereby that territory might be joined to the Canadian Confederation, was, partly on the basis of that experience, employed by the Colonial Office to sketch a Central African Federation just a few years later. After that it was downhill most of the way so far as the federal experience in decolonisation went. The West Indian and Central African federations, we can now see, were really doomed before they started, collapsing in 1962 and 1963 respectively. Then there was the South Arabian Federation, whose credibility can be summed up by recalling that it was the only constitutional entity ever invented which had a capital, Ittihad, without a permanent civil population. Kendle concludes his analysis with the acid, if not inapt, comment

[37] Minutes of the first meeting of the subcommittee on UK strategic policy, 8 May 1959, ZP15/13 FO371/143694, Public Record Office of the United Kingdom (PRO).
[38] Minute by P. C. Heppel, 26 June 1959, ibid.
[39] See John Kendle, *Federal Britain: A History* (Routledge, 1997), pp. 123–49.

that 'so long as the British were playing with other people's sovereignty, and not their own, the federal idea held little fear for them'.[40] Against this judgement, however, can be set the fact that the British are now conducting a quasi-federal experiment on themselves, though with what long-term consequences remain to be seen.

Definitions of British citizenship also changed with the ending of empire, though very much as a secondary effect—almost as an after-thought. The first trigger here was the Canadian Citizenship Act of 1946, which breached the 'common status' originally accorded by the British Nationality and Status of Aliens Act 1914. It did so not by rejecting outright British citizenship for Canadian nationals, but by asserting the primacy of Canadian nationality. The British Nationality Act 1948 followed suit but continued a common code system by creating 'a Citizenship of the UK and the Colonies'. Nobody then foresaw the pressure on entry into the United Kingdom resulting from the labour shortage after the mid-1950s and the influx of immigrants from the West Indies, followed after a short interval by flows from south Asia.

By the next decade economic needs (not least in the National Health Service) and an espousal of moral leadership clashed with the domestic politics surrounding immigration, a politics shaped by perceptions of material and national decline. The Commonwealth Immigration Act 1962 was the first of a long line of attempts to limit the rights of immigration without overt discrimination against people with a 'British' provenance; the 'patrial' system introduced in 1971 marked a new stage, including the so-called 'grandfather clause' exempting Canadians, Australians and New Zealanders from controls. In effect, what it meant to 'belong' to the United Kingdom was therefore only gradually improvised in the wake of the flux in these debates about immigration; and it was not until the British Nationality Act 1981 that the medley of improvisations was collated into a coherent legislative framework.[41] 'Over a period of twenty years', David McIntyre has written, '. . . migration rules changed from being part of a liberal imperial heritage to being a pragmatic response to social pressures and prejudices in Britain'.[42] So far as immigration went, by the end of the century those prejudices were more likely to be directed against people of Balkan extraction than, say, Jamaicans or

---

[40] Kendle, *Federal Britain*, p. 149.
[41] For a valuable discussion of this process, see Reiko Karatani, *Defining British Citizenship: Empire, Commonwealth and Modern Britain* (Frank Cass, 2003).
[42] W. David McIntyre, *The Significance of the Commonwealth, 1965–90* (Macmillan, 1991), pp. 89–92.

Barbadians. This might be said to mark the generally beneficent advance of multiculturalism in Britain, but it also reflected an endlessly revolving grudge against outsiders.

In terms of the actual decision-making process in the United Kingdom, there is one anecdote touching on British constitutional and governmental practice which should be mentioned. This is the confession by Iain Macleod that he could not recall 'having a single discussion . . . anyway in depth, on colonial matters' with either Prime Minister Harold Macmillan or his deputy, R. A. Butler, after he became colonial secretary in late 1959.[43] This is a remarkable comment on Cabinet government, though it is testimony also to Macmillan's determination at the time to load the responsibility on to Macleod in case affairs in the remaining colonies (especially East Africa) went badly wrong. Certainly colonial questions in the age of decolonisation did not significantly enter into the life of the Westminster Parliament. There is on Hansard's record no great parliamentary discourse on the termination of Britain's modern colonial empire to compare in any way with, say, Burke on the American colonies in the later eighteenth century.

In fact only two parliamentary occasions in the realm of colonial policy after 1945 are usually recalled as having had any real importance in themselves; and in both cases the reasons were essentially domestic. The first concerned Cyprus, on 28 July 1954, when a junior Conservative minister incautiously appeared to use the word 'never' when referring to the possibility of local self-determination. This intervention was rather unfairly depicted by the opposition as the cause of subsequent violence in the island, including the deaths of British servicemen. The other instance concerned the Hola Camp atrocity in Kenya during 1959, when the ensuing debate in Parliament—during which Enoch Powell emerged as the most powerful critic of its official handling—crystallised a shift in the moral foundations on which residual colonialism was based. 'Hola Camp was not about the British Empire, it was about ministerial responsibility', Powell remarked years later.[44] In general, British governments were bent on keeping issues of decolonisation outside the parliamentary arena as much as legislative decency allowed, and more often than not the opposition—for whom they also presented pitfalls—were only too happy to co-operate in doing so.

The parallels between British constitutional, and para-constitutional,

---

[43] Robert Shepherd, *Iain Macleod* (Hutchinson, 1992), p. 163.
[44] Robert Shepherd, *Enoch Powell: A Biography* (Hutchinson, 1996), p. 195.

experience in the respective spheres of Empire and Europe are important to an overall perspective on this theme. The clash between these rival orbits goes back further and deeper in recent British history than is usually recognised, even in strict terms of economic integration. An up-and-coming Foreign Office official, with a brilliant career ahead, commented critically in February 1931 on the negative British response to French proposals for agricultural preferences on a continental basis:

> Sooner or later I am convinced we have to choose between Europe and the Empire: we would like to have both . . . But if we want to keep Europe . . . it is a strange thing to dissociate ourselves from the most important practical discussion of Europe's needs there has been for some time.[45]

This choice was before long obscured by the war after 1939—or rather, the British had the dilemma resolved for them at Dunkirk in June 1940, when they left on their little boats. But, even after 1945 they continued to want to have both. The British were hardly alone in wishing to have their cake and eat it. The French came to want economic integration with western Europe, and political leadership of it; it was just that they got away with their contradiction far longer (in fact, until the logic of German reunification in 1990 really began to unfold). In the British case, the argument, first fleshed out by Anthony Eden in the early 1950s, of the three 'circles' overlapping with the United Kingdom's distinctive orbit (Empire, Europe, Nation) was essentially a rhetorical device to stave off unwanted choices. Undoubtedly, continuing imperial inclinations shaped British resistance to inclusion within a consolidating European phenomenon.

The fact that this resistance was to continue long after the Empire had itself faded away, however, suggests that these interactions were more subtle than is frequently supposed. Empire and Europe, far from giving rise to contrasting British responses, triggered a very similar ambivalence—perhaps the very same ambivalence. Just as the question of Europe cut across party-political lines from the 1950s onwards, so in fact had the question of Empire protection from around 1900 through to the 1930s (or even later, if one examines the debate about the terms of the American loan in 1946). Embedded in these tensions were, of course, matters of commercial interest. But so were even more profound concerns about the nature and mutability of national sovereignty. In other words,

---

[45] Minute by Rex Leeper, 13 February 1931, FO371/15694 W1649, Public Record Office, Kew.

the claims of Empire and Europe form a continuum in British experience in which the integrity of British constitutional conceptions were eroded from without. There was, throughout, a tendency to resist, but the facts of power and modernity ratcheted up the pressure over time. Ultimately, if insular Britain was able to keep its Empire at arm's length, while profiting from it, it was not able to do the same with Europe later on. Empire, for example, was never able to find a lodgement within British institutions as 'Europe' did after 1972 through the judicial process, as Ian Loveland's chapter in this volume so clearly shows. Nevertheless, it is what these two great phenomena both tell us about British instincts and their limits, rather than their stark difference, which is most striking in twentieth-century experience.

The latter-day Commonwealth fits into this pattern. Having shrugged off many of the obligations of empire, assuming some new version of them through the Commonwealth link was the last thing desired by the British foreign-policy elite from the early 1960s. This was why at the 1964 Commonwealth Conference, for example, the New Zealand delegation could not detect among their British hosts any 'real enthusiasm . . . behind the noble platitudes' they were wont to offer on the Commonwealth theme.[46] Indeed, had the British had their way, there never would have been a Commonwealth Secretariat, which came into existence only through the exertions of others.[47] Similarly, it was the Canadian delegation led by Pierre Trudeau which did most to calm the waters at the 1971 Commonwealth conference in Singapore when the Heath government's policy over arms to South Africa proved deeply divisive. British ministers and officials showed many signs of wishing to ditch the Commonwealth, but they were caught on the two petards of nomenclature (it was, after all, the 'Foreign *and* Commonwealth Office' after the Whitehall reorganisation of 1968), and their own frequent moralisings about the wider world and its needs.

---

[46] W. David McIntyre, 'Britain and the Creation of the Commonwealth Secretariat', *Journal of Imperial and Commonwealth History* (2000), 137. On a larger plane, there was little proclivity in Britain to take any practical initiatives in the constitutional field so that the 'new Commonwealth' might evolve into something more than what H. V. Hodson called at the time essentially 'a system of friendship'. For instance, the campaign in Britain, and elsewhere in the Commonwealth, to institute a peripatetic Court of Appeal in place of the waning credibility of appeals to the Privy Council proved shortlived. For the latter, see David B. Swinfen, *Imperial Appeal: The Debate on the Appeal to the Privy Council, 1833–1986* (Manchester University Press, 1987).

[47] The best account of the Commonwealth in the 1960s is Arnold Smith, *Stitches in Time: The Commonwealth in World Politics* (André Deutsch, 1981).

In the event, the Commonwealth survived the Euro-fashion of the 1970s, and the uninterest and even dislike of Mrs Thatcher in the 1980s, and emerged in the 1990s as a very different type of organisation—far more multi-polar in its centres of gravity, less hesitant about annoying even some of its own erring members, and with a more precise agenda pivoting on the human rights principles enunciated in the 1991 Harare Declaration. Far from being afflicted by anxiety about membership, like some shabby golf club, its expansion breached the historic criteria set by past membership of the British Empire proper. Both Cameroon and Mozambique joined in the next few years, and by the end of the century the Palestinian National Authority, itself a nascent state of sorts, was banging on the door to be let in. In short, just as the British acquired the Empire in a fit of absence of mind, so they remained part of a Commonwealth despite an absence of affection, not to say a good deal of parsimoniousness.

This chapter has roamed widely beyond the more strictly constitutional and juristic concerns at the heart of this book. The slippery and evasive quality of any imperial association in a nation's life makes this inevitable. In the same digressive spirit, therefore, we may end by drawing a putative connection between the loss of empire and British constitutional method by referring to Macmillan's love for the novels of Anthony Trollope, avidly read by Macmillan as they were throughout his years in 10 Downing Street.[48] In *Phineas Finn* we find the following description of a fictional prime minister's approach to the dominating issue of suffrage reform in the mid-nineteenth century:

> Let us be generous in our concession... Let us at any rate seem to be generous. Let us give with an open hand—but still with a hand which, though open, shall not bestow too much. The coach [of reform] must be allowed to run down the hill. Indeed, unless the coach goes on running, no journey will be made. But let us have the drag on both the hind wheels. And remember that coaches running downhill without drags are apt to come to serious misfortune.

This seems to anticipate almost exactly not only Macmillan's cast of mind on the demise of empire in the mid-twentieth century as what he liked to call in his Edwardian way an 'act of grace', but also an instinctive British policy towards politico-constitutional change over a much longer period. A seeming generosity was the key to success, as was the appear-

---

[48] The following section is based on remarks in Robert Holland, 'Newfoundland and the Pattern of British Decolonization', *Newfoundland Studies* (1998).

ance of uninterrupted movement in the desired direction. Less transparent, but perhaps equally important in ensuring a safe arrival, was the ability and preparedness to call a temporary halt if circumstances at any point required it. Certainly in presiding over the end of empire Macmillan kept the drag on the hind wheels until the very last moment, knowing as he did that any 'serious misfortune' would tarnish his own premiership. When, eventually, decolonisation is absorbed into the more ingrained wisdom and tradition of British history, it will surely seem entirely natural that the British survived that experience by practising the codes and principles (including the education of new masters, and the preparedness to take a leap in the dark) that had allowed them to navigate successfully through the shoals of suffrage reform a century or so before.

Bibliography

Documentary publications

Ashton, S. R. and Stockwell, S. E. (eds), *British Documents on the End of Empire Series:* vol. 1, *Imperial Policy and Colonial Practice, 1925–45: Part 1, Metropolitan Reorganization, Defence and International Relations, Political Change and Constitutional Reform* (HMSO, 1997).

Goldsworthy, David (ed.), *British Documents on the End of Empire:* vol. 3, *The Conservative Government and the End of Empire: Part 3, Politics and Administration* (HMSO, 1994).

Hyam, R. (ed.), *British Documents on the End of Empire:* vol. 2, *The Labour Government and the End of Empire, 1945–51: Part 3, Strategy, Politics and Constitutional Change* (HMSO, 1992).

Keith, Arthur Berriedale (ed.), *Speeches and Documents on the British Dominions, 1918–1931: From Self-government to National Sovereignty* (Oxford University Press, 1936).

Louis, Wm. Roger and Hyam, R. (eds), *British Documents on the End of Empire:* vol. 4, *The Conservative Government and the End of Empire, 1957–64: Part 1, High Policy, Political and Constitutional Change* (HMSO, 2000).

Madden, Frederick and Darwin, John (ed.), *The Dominions and India since 1900: Select Documents on the Constitutional History of the British Empire and Commonwealth* (Greenwood, 1993), vol. 6.

Mansergh, Nicholas (ed.), *Documents and Speeches on British Commonwealth Affairs 1931–52* (Oxford University Press, 1953).

Mansergh, Nicholas (ed.), *Documents and Speeches on British Commonwealth Affairs 1952–62* (Oxford University Press, 1963).

Books

Coupland, Reginald, *The Empire in These Days* (Macmillan, 1935).

Coupland, Reginald, *The Indian Problem* (Clarendon Press, 1942).

Curtis, Lionel, *The Problem of the Commonwealth* (Macmillan, 1915).

Dale, William, *The Modern Commonwealth* (Butterworths, 1983).

Dawson, R. M., *The Development of Dominion Status, 1900–1936* (Oxford University Press, 1937).

Garner, J., *The Commonwealth Office, 1925–68* (Heinemann, 1978).

Hall, H. D., *The British Commonwealth of Nations* (Methuen, 1920).

Hancock, W. K., *Survey of British Commonwealth Affairs:* vol. 1, *Problems of Nationality, 1918–36* (Oxford University Press, 1937).

Holland, R. F., *Britain and the Commonwealth Alliance, 1918–39* (Macmillan, 1981).

Jebb, Richard, *Studies in Colonial Nationalism* (Edward Arnold, 1905).

Jennings, Sir Ivor, *The British Commonwealth of Nations* (Hutchinson, 1968).

Keith, Arthur Berriedale, *Responsible Government in the Dominions* (Stevens, 1909).

Low, D. A., *Constitutional Heads and Political Crises: Commonwealth Episodes, 1945–85* (Macmillan, 1988).

Lyon, P., Manor, James and Morris-Jones, W. H., *Transfer and Transformation: Political Institutions in the New States of the Commonwealth* (Leicester University Press, 1983).

Mansergh, Nicholas, *The Commonwealth Experience* (Weidenfeld & Nicolson, 1969).

Miller, J. D. B., *The Commonwealth in the World* (Duckworth, 1958).

Smith, Arnold, *Stitches in Time: The Commonwealth in World Politics* (André Deutsch, 1981).

de Smith, S. A., *The New Commonwealth and its Constitutions* (Stevens, 1964).

Wheare, K. C., *The Statute of Westminster and Dominion Status* (Clarendon Press, 1933).

Wheare, K. C., *The Constitutional Structure of the Commonwealth* (Oxford University Press, 1960).

Wight, Martin, *British Colonial Constitutions* (Clarendon Press, 1947).

Zimmern, Alfred, *The Third British Empire* (Oxford University Press, 1926).

17.
Britain and Europe

IAN LOVELAND

The United Kingdom's membership of the European Community (EC) has markedly affected traditional constitutional understandings. This change has occurred not simply in terms of a transfer of law-making authority from the United Kingdom qua country to its fellow EC member states and the institutions of the Community. It has also been evident in a profound restructuring of the relationship between the courts, the executive and Parliament and the electorate within the United Kingdom. In addition, a point often overlooked by constitutional lawyers, it has substantially undermined orthodox presumptions as to party political loyalty within the Commons and led to pronounced departures from accepted constitutional conventions concerning ministerial responsibility. In combination, these effects make it quite plausible to argue that accession to the Community has proved by far the most significant constitutional innovation undertaken by any government in the twentieth century.

The 1950s and 1960s: Founding principles

The EC was created in 1957 by six countries who signed the Treaty of Rome (West Germany, Italy, France, Holland, Belgium, and Luxembourg). The states' primary concern was to prevent another war between France, Germany and Italy by integrating their economies so closely that war would become impossible. The treaty's explicit objective (outlined in Articles 2 and 3) was to create a 'common market' between the member states. This would require that member states cede law-making authority to the EC on a wide range of important economic policy issues, particularly competition law, the power to place taxes and quotas on imports and exports, the cross-national mobility of labour and services, and the entire field of agricultural production. The Community's initial competence may ostensibly have been limited to 'economic' issues, but the breadth of its jurisdiction in that field was sufficient to make it clear that its institutions would necessarily wield considerable political power. The treaty's framers perhaps envisaged that increased economic interdependence would slowly lead to some kind of political union, but the EC was not a 'federal' structure in the orthodox, *de jure* sense. It may, however, be defensible to suggest that 'federalism' can be a *de facto* construct, and that specific allocations of powers between different organs of government can be of sufficient significance for us to conclude that a federal system has indeed emerged.

The treaty itself is the original source of EC law. It is a constituent document: the EC, and all its institutions, are bodies of limited competence; they can do only those things the treaty permits. Article 236 provides for the treaty to be amended, but this entails cumbersome procedures, involving an inter-governmental conference between the signatory nations, and their unanimous support in accordance with their respective constitutional amendment mechanisms for any changes.

The treaty's terms are, however, quite flexible. It was designed as a *traité cadre* rather than a *traité loi*: its text contains broadly framed objectives and basic principles about institutional structures and law-making procedures, and about the EC's various economic policy powers. Consequently, most EC law is made without the need for treaty amendment, and takes the form of 'regulations', 'decisions', and 'directives'. The bulk of it is made by the Council of Ministers, where each member state has one representative.

The Council may legislate in three different ways. In some fields, the treaty requires unanimous member state approval. In others, the Council may proceed by a qualified majority, in which each member state's voting power is (crudely) adjusted according to its population size. Third, the treaty also permits some laws to be made by a simple majority system, giving all member states equal weight.

These different methods illustrate a theme pervading the EC's institutional structure; namely a tension between inter-nationalism and supra-nationalism. A purely international Community, in which every action requires the consent of all member states, would permit short-term national interests (or temporary political pressures with a particular country) to frustrate achievement of Community policy. In contrast, too strong an emphasis on supra-national objectives and law-making processes might have dissuaded some countries from joining the EC at all. In crude terms, the more important an issue was to the national interests of member states, the more likely it was that the treaty would require unanimous voting—the most international law-making process. Simple majority voting, the most supra-national process, was rarely provided for in the EC's initial development.

Unlike the Council, the Commission was intended to be an avowedly supra-national body. It had nine members, not more than two of whom could be nationals of the same member state. Per Article 157, commissioners were to be 'chosen for their general competence and of indisputable independence'. Article 155 charged the Commission with various powers of promoting, implementing and monitoring measures 'with a view to ensuring the functioning and development of the Common Market'. It was also the Commission's task to introduce much of the legislation on which the Council would vote: the Council had minimal powers of legislative innovation. Thus, the supra-/inter-national complexities of the Council's various voting systems would be applied to measures which had themselves passed through the supra-national filter of the Commission's collective decision-making process.

The Parliament (Assembly) was composed of delegates chosen by each member state from their own legislatures in (crude) proportion to their population size. It had few powers. Some parts of the treaty specified that the Council had to consult the Parliament before enacting legislation, but the treaty did not compel the Council to take any notice of the Assembly's opinions. The Parliament also had to be consulted by the Council over the Community's budgetary process but, again, its views did not bind the Council's eventual decisions.

The EC established a very complex separation of powers within its constitutional structure. But this separation does not comfortably correspond to orthodox British understandings of that concept. No part of the EC was directly elected by its citizens, which clearly raises questions as to the Community's democratic base. Such electoral control as citizens exercised on EC law-making would pass through the indirect filter of their respective governments' representative on the Council of Ministers, and their governments' nominees to the Commission and Assembly. In British terms, the Commission appears to serve as the executive branch of the Community's government, but one should qualify this in several ways. It has, for example, some legislative powers, which, in theory at least, it can exercise independently of the Council. But it is in no way comparable to a national legislature in the scope of its power. More significantly, the Commission was (and remains) a small organisation, and consequently could not realistically be involved in the detailed implementation of Community law. For that task, the EC was to rely primarily on member state governments.

The EC Parliament was obviously not comparable to Parliament in the British sense. That it was not an elected body would seem of little import, given that it had no significant powers. But this perhaps raised the longer term question of whether the EC should contain a powerful, directly elected legislative branch. Quite where the Parliament would stand on the supra-/inter-national axis was initially unclear. Its members' status as governmental appointees, rather than directly elected representatives, suggested it might simply reproduce international tensions on the Council. But it was also the case that its members sat from the outset in blocs organised essentially by party rather than national allegiance. This obviously raised the possibility that the Parliament would gradually function as a pan-European forum.

The treaty was a constituent document so it was necessary to devise some mechanism to ensure, first, that the substance of the laws made via Article 189 and the processes by which those laws were made respected the limits imposed by the treaty; and, second, that all the other activities of the EC's institutions had a defensible legal base, either in the treaty's text, or in secondary legislation passed under its authority.

In the early years of the EC's history, the most important of its institutions appears to have been the European Court of Justice (ECJ). Under Article 164, the ECJ was to ensure that 'in the interpretation and application of this Treaty the law is observed'. By the mid-1960s, this vague term had enabled the ECJ to produce two legal doctrines which would subsequently prove of enormous significance to British constitutional law and practice. The text of the treaty offered no explicit indication of the relative importance of EC law vis-à-vis inconsistent national law. Nor did it specify how—or by whom—that relationship was to be policed. Answers to both of these vital questions were quickly offered by the ECJ.

The supremacy of and direct effect of EC law

The doctrine of the 'supremacy' of EC law emerged in 1964 in a case called *Costa* v. *ENEL*, in which the ECJ held:

> The transfer by the States from their domestic legal systems to the Community legal system of rights and obligations arising under the Treaty carries with it a permanent limitation of their sovereign rights, against

which a subsequent unilateral act incompatible with the concept of the Community cannot prevail.[1]

At much the same time, the ECJ also concluded that the supremacy of EC law was something that—at least in respect of treaty Articles— could be enforced against National Government and legislatures by national courts. This principle of 'direct effect' first appeared in the 1962 case of *Van Gend en Loos*, in which the ECJ indicated that the EC was in legal terms a body of law unlike any other that had existed before. The treaty was not simply 'an agreement which merely creates mutual obligations between the contracting states': rather, it was 'a new legal order of international law for the benefit of which the states have limited their sovereign rights, and the subjects of which comprise not only the member states but also their nationals'.[2] This new legal order demanded new legal procedures to protect the new legal benefits it created. If EC law was to be effectively enforced, the national courts would have to serve as fora where the conformity of a member state's laws with the treaty could be gauged at the instigation of individuals; only domestic courts were sufficiently numerous and proximate and familiar to citizens. As well as acting in defence of their own EC entitlements, citizens invoking direct effect would police member states' compliance with EC law.

The treaty has no obvious textual basis to support either the direct effect or supremacy principles. The ECJ purportedly 'found' both concepts in the 'spirit, scheme, and general wording'. *Van Gend* and *Costa* typify what is known as the 'teleological' or 'schematic' approach to legislative or treaty interpretation. This means that the ECJ's primary concern is with the *effet utile* of EC law—namely how best to ensure that the treaty's objectives are realised. To achieve this, it will interpret EC law in imaginative ways, and not allow itself to be bound by the treaty text.

Both these developments of the EC's legal order appeared at the time to pass by the notice of the British media, and of British constitutional scholars. Legal journals of the period make no mention of either case, and neither merited so much as a mention in the leading broadsheet newspapers. The law of the EC was, it seemed, 'a far away jurisdiction of which we knew nothing'.

Yet the significance of the supremacy and direct effect doctrines can

---

[1] Case 6/64 [1964] ECR 585, at 593.
[2] Case 26/62 [1963] ECR 1, at 12.

hardly be overstated. By the end of the 1960s, the principles had been extended to encompass not just treaty Articles, but also much EC secondary legislation. For the six member states, this represented a major shift in orthodox understandings of sovereignty. Power had shifted in an obvious international sense, away from national governments and legislatures to the EC itself. But it had also shifted in a less obvious, intra-national sense, away from national governments and legislatures to national courts. By 1970, British politicians and constitutional analysts had, it seemed, grasped the first of these points, but the significance of the second had passed most of them by.

United Kingdom accession

The United Kingdom tried to join the EC twice during the 1960s—in 1961 under a Conservative government and in 1967 under a Labour administration. However, new states could be admitted only with the consent of all the existing members, and on both occasions the French government vetoed British entry. British opponents drew on two substantial political arguments against accession. The first related to the United Kingdom's world role. Opponents of EC entry felt that the UK should align itself with the Commonwealth countries and the USA, linking those nations to the EC, rather than risk merging into a 'European superstate'. The second argument focused on 'sovereignty'. The principle of supremacy alarmed a small number of British politicians. This faction feared that some of Parliament's powers would be irretrievably lost to Community institutions. Opponents of entry argued that such a transfer of political power was undesirable. But they also argued that it was constitutionally impossible for the UK to honour the obligations EC membership entailed, since it had always been assumed that Parliament was a sovereign law-maker, unable to bind either itself or its successors as *Costa* would require. But this concern was not widely understood. Most early attempts to analyse the potential impact of EC membership on the British constitution appear woefully inadequate.[3] By the late 1960s, such analyses were becoming more sophisticated. Professor de Smith produced a prescient article in 1971, identifying the EC as 'an incohate functional federation', which, while not initially a federal state, was likely

---

[3] For example, P. Keenan, 'Some Legal Consequences of Britain's Entry into the European Common Market', *Public Law* (1962).

to evolve in a direction demanding the 'pooling' of sovereignty.[4] He suggested that national sovereignty need not be abandoned if the UK acceded to the treaty, since it might always withdraw from the Community. Nevertheless, he also presumed that 'full recognition of the hierarchical superiority of Community law would entail a revolution in legal thought'.[5] Yet, even de Smith, among the most eminent constitutional lawyers of his time, overlooked the direct effect point. No one, it seemed, had appreciated that the interactive effect of the supremacy and direct effect principle might be that the UK's courts would, consequent upon accession, acquire the power to enforce legal limits on Parliament's law-making competence; a power they had hitherto not been thought to possess.

But it seems that even the supremacy issue had yet to be properly understood by mainstream politicians. Harold Wilson's 1966–70 Labour government had proposed that all EC measures would take effect in the UK as delegated legislation,[6] an analysis which betokens the subordinacy rather than supremacy of Community law. Edward Heath's 1970–4 administration, which eventually secured the UK's accession, seemed similarly confused. The government boldly stated that, while it would introduce a bill to incorporate the treaty into domestic law, 'there is no question of any erosion of essential national sovereignty'.[7] The distinction between 'essential' and (presumably) 'non-essential' sovereignty is a novel one, and was replaced when the aforesaid bill was before the Commons by an equally odd proposition. Members of Parliament were informed that nothing in the bill undermined the 'ultimate' sovereignty of Parliament. What might happen to Parliament's penultimate sovereignty (whatever this might be) was unexplained. Neither of the main parties seemed willing to accept that it was either desirable or possible to entrench the supremacy and direct effect principles. Consistency between national and domestic law would have to be maintained by Parliament itself ensuring that it did not legislate in breach of EC law.

Opinon among the judiciary seemed to be divided. Writing in an academic journal, Lord Diplock had argued:

> It is a consequence of the doctrine of [parliamentary sovereignty] that if a

---

[4] S. de Smith, 'The Constitution and the Common Market: A Tentative Appraisal', *Modern Law Review* (1971).
[5] Ibid., at 613.
[6] *Legal and Constitutional Implications of United Kingdom Membership of the European Communities*, Cmnd 3301 (HMSO, 1967), para. 22.
[7] *The United Kingdom and the European Communities*, Cmnd 4715 (HMSO, 1921), para. 29.

subsequent Act . . . were passed that was in conflict with any provision of the Treaty which is of direct application . . . the courts of the United Kingdom would be bound to give effect to the Act . . . notwithstanding any conflict.[8]

For Lord Diplock, it seemed, there could be nothing 'special' about the European Community Act 1972 (ECA 1972).

Lord Denning was initially rather more equivocal. The case of *Blackburn* v. *Attorney General*[9] involved an attempt by an anti-EC campaigner to establish that accession would entail (per *Costa*) an irrevocable loss of national sovereignty. Blackburn's legal case was a hopeless one, but it did prompt Lord Denning to offer the following observation:

> We have all been brought up to believe that, in legal theory, one Parliament cannot bind another and that no Act is irreversible. But legal theory does not always march alongside political reality.[10]

Lord Denning assumed that Parliament would never legislate contrary to its EC obligations. If it did so, what would the courts decide? Lord Denning was non-commital: 'We will consider that event when it happens.'[11]

Relocating sovereignty? Initial impressions

The political question as to the desirability of EC membership also shattered the presumption that party loyalties were invariably the dominant force within the House of Commons. Both the Labour left and Conservative right wings opposed accession. Accession would have two domestic phases: a Commons vote on whether to accept the entry terms, which, if successful, would be followed by a bill incorporating the treaty into domestic law. At the 1970 general election the Conservatives had won 330 seats, Labour 287, and the small parties thirteen. A rebellion by twenty-one anti-EC Conservatives would have deprived the Heath government of a majority; forty announced they would not approve the terms.

Labour was more deeply split. As prime minister in the late 1960s, Wilson had supported EC membership. In 1971, he and most of his shadow Cabinet opposed it. Wilson authorised a three-line whip

---

[8] 'The Common Market and the Common Law', *Law Teacher* (1972), 8.
[9] [1971] 2 All ER 1380.
[10] Ibid., at 1382.
[11] Ibid., at 1383.

instructing Labour MPs to vote against the terms. Sixty-nine Labour MPs, led by the shadow chancellor, Roy Jenkins, defied the whip and voted with the government. Had the whip been respected, the terms would have been rejected. But many of the dissident Labour MPs would not defy the whip on votes during the bill's passage, in part because Heath had announced that he would treat the second reading as a confidence issue.[12] Only a few elevated what they saw as the United Kingdom's national interest in joining the EC above questions of party loyalty. On the bill's third reading, the government's majority was just seventeen.

The Act itself appeared at least to pay lip-service to the *Costa* and *Van Gend* principles. The crucial provision was section 2, which provided that all directly effective EC law was to be accorded supreme status by domestic courts if it conflicted with either existing or future legislation. This was a startling provision. There is no constitutional difficulty in the ECA 1972 telling a court to give effect to EC obligations even if there is a contradictory domestic law, if that domestic law predated the ECA 1972. The ECA, as the later statute, would prevail. But what would happen if the inconsistent British statute was passed after 1972? Orthodox theory would maintain that the courts should apply the later Act, irrespective of what Parliament might have said in 1972. Indeed, it had long been accepted that Parliament need not even be explicit in its use of language to achieve this effect. Orthodox theory maintained that the courts were obliged to give effect to later legislation which was merely impliedly inconsistent with the terms of a previous Act.[13]

Quite what the courts would make of the 1972 Act remained to be seen. But, in the immediate term, the consitutional implications of accession arose again in a purely political sense. Having already introduced a new fault line into the realm of party political loyalties, the EC then triggered a shift in accepted understandings of the relationship between Parliament and the people.

Labour's two narrow election victories in 1974 brought into power a party deeply split over the desirability of EC membership. Labour's 1974 election manifestos had promised that the electorate would be given the opportunity to vote on continued membership, either by another general

[12] P. Norton, 'Government Defeats in the House of Commons: Myth and Reality', *Public Law* (1978), 360.
[13] See *Vauxhall Estates* v. *Liverpool Corporation* [1932] 1 KB 723; *Ellen Street Estates Ltd* v. *Minister of Health* [1934] 1 KB 590.

election or by a referendum. A third general election was not a plausible option, so a referendum seemed inevitable. The question which then arose was how the referendum was to be conducted. Having renegotiated the UK's terms of membership,[14] Prime Minister Wilson then jettisoned several traditional constitutional principles.

The first casualty was the convention of Cabinet unanimity. Wilson decided to 'suspend' the convention for the referendum campaign. His justification was that the question transcended party politics, although most commentators suggest his real motivation for both the referendum itself and the suspension was his assumption that there was no other way to keep his party together.[15]

The second casualty was the Burkean notion of the MP as a representative law-maker rather than a delegate. Parliament had in effect chosen to divest itself of its sovereignty on membership, by allowing the people the unusual opportunity of expressing an opinion on a single matter. This in itself was a remarkable innovation, insofar as it presented an obvious political challenge to the sovereignty of Parliament.

Neither the government nor Parliament was legally bound to respect the outcome of the referendum, although one imagines it would have been impossible, as a matter of practical politics, for them to do otherwise in the case of a clear-cut result. The campaign was not fought along traditional party lines, but might crudely be described as a contest in which right-wing Conservatives and the left of the Labour Party united in opposing membership, while the Labour centre-right and Conservative centre-left supported it. The question was very simple: 'Do you think that the United Kingdom should stay in the European Community (the Common Market)?' The result was a resounding victory for the pro-EC lobby: 67.2 per cent to 32.8 per cent on a 65 per cent turnout

A more orthodox approach to constitutional practice then reappeared. The anti-EC members of Wilson's cabinet re-embraced the unanimity convention, and traditional interparty rivalries rapidly reappeared. Nevertheless, the mere fact that a referendum was held, the peculiar political divisions which it exposed, and the overwhelming support it revealed for EC membership, suggested that the Treaty of Rome was

---

[14] A Commons motion approving the new terms was carried by a majority of 226; but only 137 of the 315 Labour MPs voted in favour. The success of government policy was entirely dependent on Conservative support.

[15] The convention had previously been 'suspended' over the issue of tariff reform in 1932 by Ramsay MacDonald's National Government, but that was of course a coalition administration.

undoubtedly a 'special' ingredient in Britain's constitutional recipe. By the early 1980s, the UK's courts had taken some steps to reinforce that impression.

In the 1979 case of *Macarthy's* v. *Smith*,[16] Lord Denning suggested that the 1972 Act had, in some unexplained way, altered the traditional understanding of parliamentary sovereignty. To this point in time, it had been accepted by constitutional analysts that a later Act which was inconsistent with an earlier Act had to be applied by the courts, even if the inconsistency was only implied rather than explicit.[17] In *Macarthy's*, Lord Denning indicated that this rule would no longer apply when EC matters were in issue. Domestic courts should assume that, if ever a British statute was impliedly inconsistent with an EC obligation, the inconsistency arose because Parliament had erred in the language chosen: legislators could not have intended to achieve such a result, so the courts would save them from the consequences of their mistake by according supremacy to EC law.[18]

A few years later, in *Garland* v. *British Rail*,[19] the House of Lords took care neither to confirm nor deny Denning's theory. It offered instead a radical innovation of its own. Lord Diplock suggested that the ECA 1972, section 2 had introduced a new rule of statutory interpretation to which the courts were now subjected. A UK court should construe all domestic legislation in a manner respecting EC obligations: 'however wide a departure from the prima facie meaning of the language of the provision might be needed in order to achieve consistency'.[20]

Macarthy's and *Garland* did not go far enough to satisfy *Van Gend* and *Costa*, but their dynamism is undeniable. Yet, while British courts struggled to accommodate long established principles of EC law, the issue of the Community's impact on British constitutional understandings moved back into the political arena: not within the UK on this occasion, but between the member states themselves. Some thirty years after its birth, the EC's own constituent basis was about to be reformed, through the mechanism of the Community's first major treaty amendment—the Single European Act (SEA).

---

[16] [1979] 3 All ER 325.

[17] See I. Loveland, *Constitutional Law* (Butterworths, 1996), ch. 2.

[18] See T. S. R. Allan, 'Parliamentary sovereignty: Lord Denning's Dextrous Revolution', *Oxford Journal of Legal Studies* (1983).

[19] [1983] 2 AC 751.

[20] [1983] 2 AC 751, at 771. See O. Hood-Phillips, 'A Garland for the Lords', *Law Quarterly Review* (1982).

The Single European Act

The SEA's roots lay in the Commission's perception that the Community's original objectives were being achieved at a painfully slow rate. The Treaty of Rome had envisaged that the four fundamental freedoms of movement for goods, capital, persons, and services upon which the Community was to be based would be achieved by 1970. But, even by 1984, this objective remained unfulfilled: national laws still contained many barriers to the creation of a truly 'common market'.

The proposed treaty amendments announced the intention to create an 'internal market' by 1 January 1993. The guiding principle was to ensure that goods and services lawfully marketed in one member state should be saleable throughout the Community. The SEA also extended the Community's substantive competence into the fields of environmental protection, regional development, research and technical innovation, and some aspects of social policy.[21] The SEA further enhanced the Community's supra-national profile by extending the use of qualified majority rather than unanimous voting within the law-making process. It also increased the political power of the Parliament, which, since 1979, had been an elected rather than appointed assembly, and was beginning to look as though it might eventually stake a plausible claim to supercede the Council as the EC's dominant law-making institution.[22]

In an international rather than supra-national vein, the SEA nonetheless acknowledged that many areas of government activity could not sensibly be brought within the EC's legal competence. Perhaps the best example of this is the declaration attached to the SEA to the effect that the reforms to the treaty should not be construed as derogating from the member states' powers to take such measures as they considered necessary regarding immigration control for regulating the movements of non-EC nationals, combating crime, and preventing terrorism.

Notwithstanding these reservations, the SEA substantially extended the Community's competence, and necessarily, by a concomitant degree, curtailed the autonomy of member state governments and legislatures. Furthermore—and again the point seemed to be overlooked in the UK—the broadening of the range of matters within the EC's competence

---

[21] N. Forwood and M. Clough, 'The Single European Act and Free Movement', *European Law Review* (1987). See C. Ehlermann, 'The Internal Market following the Single European Act', *Common Market Law Review* (1987).

[22] D. Edward, 'The Impact of the Single European Act on the Institutions', *Common Market Law Review* (1987).

also promised to further enhance the powers of the UK courts vis-à-vis Parliament and the executive. It is ostensibly rather surprising that the nominally Euro-sceptic government of Margaret Thatcher—then in its second term and enjoying huge majorities in both the Commons and Lords—ratified the SEA with such alacrity. Dissent within the Conservative Party on the issue was muted and insignificant. It is perhaps indicative of the way in which British politicians have traditionally seen the constitution as a political rather then legal phenomenon that Thatcher's Euro-scepticism rose to an acute pitch not over the law of the SEA, but over the personal beliefs of the then president of the Commission, the French 'socialist' Jacques Delors, who in 1988 told the TUC that the European Community offered great advantages for the trade unions and the European Left.

The Bruges speech

Delors was committed to the incrementalist ideal of furthering political union between the member states, and suggested in a speech in 1988 that the EC would evolve into a federal government akin to that of the USA. Thatcher promptly publicised her own view of the Community's future development in a speech delivered in Bruges in September 1988. She premised her view of Europe's development on what she regarded as the essential issue of preserving British 'sovereignty':

> Willing and active co-operation between independent sovereign states is the best way to build a successful European Community ... It would be folly to try to fit [the member states] into some sort of identikit European personality ...
>
> We have not successfully rolled back the frontiers of the state in Britain only to see them reimposed at a European level with a European superstate exercising a new dominance from Brussels ... The lesson of the economic history of Europe in the 1970s and 1980s is that central planning and detailed control don't work, and that personal endeavour and initiative do ...[23]

The speech suggested that the Thatcher government would adopt a sceptical, obstructionist approach to all integrationist EC initiatives. The Commission described the Bruges speech as 'unrelentingly naive'. Its contents had not been cleared with the then foreign secretary, Sir Geoffrey Howe, who apparently viewed its style and content with 'weary horror'.[24]

[23] The speech is thoroughly reported in *The Times*, 21 September 1988.
[24] Hugo Young, *One of Us* (Pan, 1991), p. 550.

The speech was enthusiastically received by the party's Euro-sceptic wing,[25] but was met with dismay by several senior Cabinet members and a substantial number of Euro-enthusiast backbenchers.[26]

In the shorter term, it had a significant effect. In 1989, eleven member states had adopted a *Community Charter of Fundamental Social Rights of Workers*. The so-called *Social Charter* advocated a significant extension of the Community competence in social policy matters, to encompass workers' rights to fair remuneration and adequate protection against unfair dismissal, redundancy, and unsafe working conditions. The British government opposed such measures, seeing them as a re-expansion of the 'frontiers of the state'. The charter was merely a declaration, not a binding part of EC law. Even in this form, however, it was unacceptable to the Thatcher government, which refused to sign the declaration.[27]

The end of parliamentary sovereignty?

Despite their radical practical implications, *Macarthy's* and *Garland* could be portrayed simply as a new innovation in judicial interpretation of statutes. They did not involve a blunt challenge to legislation which could be reconciled with EC law only by affording the concept of 'interpretation' a meaning that paid no heed at all to linguistic limitations and encompassed the presumably distinct concept of defiance. That challenge, however, was presented to the courts by the Merchant Shipping Act 1988.

The *Factortame* litigation arose from a dispute over fishing rights in British waters. The Merchant Shipping Act 1894 had allowed foreign-owned vessels to register as 'British', and thereby gain the right to fish in British waters. By the late 1980s, some ninety-five boats owned by Spanish companies had done so. The British government, alarmed by the impact this 'foreign' fleet was having on fishing stocks, asked Parliament to enact the Merchant Shipping Act 1988 (MSA 1988). The 1988 Act altered the registration rules to require a far higher level of 'Britishness' in a ship's owners or managers.[28] None of the ninety-five Spanish ships could meet this test. Factortame, one of the affected companies, sub-

---

[25] Alan Clark, *Diaries* (Weidenfeld & Nicolson, 1993), pp. 225–7.

[26] See Young, *One of Us*, ch. 23.

[27] See generally J. Shaw, *EC Law* (Macmillan, 1993), ch. 16.

[28] Including, *inter alia*, requirements that individual owners had to be British citizens or residents, and that corporate owners had to be incorporated in Britain, with 75 per cent of their shares owned by British citizens/residents.

sequently launched an action in the British courts claiming that the 1988 Act was substantively incompatible with EC law.

The *Factortame* litigation was still ongoing in the late 1990s. But, from a constitutional perspective, the most important of the many judgements it generated was that of the House of Lords in *R. v. Secretary of State for Transport, ex p. Factortame (No. 2).*[29] In June 1990, the House of Lords announced that it had held in Factortame's favour and would 'disapply' the relevant provisions of the MSA 1988. The announcement provoked apocalyptic denuciations from Prime Minister Thatcher about loss of national sovereignty to the Commission. When the judgement was eventually issued, Lord Bridge attacked as misconceived the Thatcheresque argument that the decision 'was a novel and dangerous invasion by a community institution of the sovereignty of the UK Parliament'.[30] He reasoned that Parliament had been quite aware of the supremacy doctrine in 1972, so any 'limitation' of sovereignty that EC membership entailed was 'voluntary'. The ECA 1972 had ordered domestic courts to respect that 'voluntary limitation', so there was nothing novel in this judgement.[31]

The *Factortame* doctrine was unarguably a radical innovation in UK law, but one that had long been required by EC law. Nonetheless, it might initially have been thought to be a principle of limited application. One question initially left unanswered was whether the power to disapply legislative provisions belonged only to the House of Lords; or did it extend to all national courts and tribunals? The House of Lords subsequently endorsed the latter position in *R. v. Secretary of State for Employment, ex p. Equal Opportunities Commission.*[32] Within months of this case being decided, it emerged that even industrial tribunals, which occupy a distinctly lowly position in the United Kingdom's constitutional hierarchy, were applying the *Factortame* doctrine.[33] In practical terms, the

[29] [1991] 1 All ER 70; [1991] 1 AC 603. For comment see Paul Craig, 'Sovereignty of the United Kingdom Parliament after *Factortame*', *Yearbook of European Law* (1991).

[30] [1991] 1 AC 603, at 658.

[31] Lord Bridge perhaps oversimplified the issue. As suggested earlier, British judges and British governments displayed confusion in the late 1960s and early 1970s as to the nature and implications of *Costa* and *Van Gend*. Moreover, many innovative aspects of the ECJ's own constitutional jurisprudence had appeared after the UK's accession, so they could hardly have been embraced by UK politicians in 1972.

[32] [1994] ICR 317.

[33] See D. Nicol, 'Disapplying with Relish? The Industrial Tribunals and Acts of Parliament', *Public Law* (1996).

Factortame rationale rapidly became—as far as all courts were concerned—an unremarkable feature of our constitutional landscape.

EC law as 'fundamental law'?

One thing which *Factortame (No. 2)* did not do, however, was explain just how it was that in 1972 the UK Parliament managed to do something that had always been thought to be beyond its predecessors' grasp—namely 'voluntarily' to limit its sovereignty? As Professor William Wade subsequently observed, Lord Bridge's reasoning makes very little sense, in terms either of legal theory or practical politics.[34] The obvious problem is that, if Parliament managed in 1972 to entrench the ECA, it can presumably entrench other statutes as well. One might suggest perhaps that the EC is 'unique' in this respect. But it is no less plausible to say that other important moral or political factors could acquire a similar constitutional status, with the result that, as Wade puts it, 'the new doctrine makes sovereignty a freely adjustable commodity whenever Parliament chooses to accept some limitation'.[35]

It may well prove to be the case, as Paul Craig has argued, that *Factortame* rests on no more than an adjustment to or development of the courts' role as interpreters of legislative intent.[36] That assertion can only be proven 'correct' as a matter of law if political developments afford the opportunity to put it to a legal test. This could occur in one of two scenarios.

It seems to be widely accepted that, if Parliament enacted a statute which said in express terms that it was intended to breach EC law, the domestic courts would apply it. Nor is there much support for the argument that the courts would refuse to apply a statute purporting to withdraw the UK from the Community. Yet, such an argument is a perfectly logical development of the foundations laid by the European Court over thirty years ago in *Van Gend* and *Costa* and of those set down by the House of Lords in *Factortame No. 2*.

As noted above, the ECJ told us in *Van Gend* that the EC was 'more than just an agreement between member states'. It was rather: 'a new legal order of international law for the benefit of which the states have limited their sovereign rights, and the subjects of which comprise not

---

[34] 'Sovereignty—Revolution or Evolution?', *Law Quarterly Review* (1996).
[35] Ibid., 573.
[36] 'Sovereignty of the UK Parliament after *Factortame*', *Yearbook of European Law* (1991), 221.

only the Member States but also their nationals'.[37] In other words, we as citizens of the United Kingdom each enjoy certain entitlements (and are subjected to certain obligations) which our domestic organs of government, acting unilaterally, are not legally competent to alter. Any radical alteration in the UK's relationship with the EC could lawfully be accomplished only through the mechanisms of EC law. That is essentially the position adopted by the House of Lords in *Factortame (No. 2)*. The question then becomes how that alteration can be lawfully effected.

The Treaty of Rome and the SEA contain no express provisions for member state withdrawal. The only way that result could lawfully be achieved (as a matter of EC law, and hence, given the supremacy of EC law over contradictory domestic statutes, as a matter of domestic law) is if the EC treaties were amended to reconstitute the Community with one member less. That process, as specified in Article 236, requires the convening of an intergovernmental conference, at which all existing member states must agree to alterations to the treaty's provisions. As a matter of EC law, any one of the other member states could veto the UK's departure from the Community.[38] To suggest that UK courts might simply refuse to apply the provisions of legislation seeking to withdraw the UK from the Community is a fanciful argument. But it is perhaps no more fanciful from today's vantage point than *Factortame* itself would have seemed to constitutional scholars in 1972.

But in our 'political constitution', *Factortame* itself might be regarded, at least in the short term, as rather small beer when measured against the political consequences of Margaret Thatcher's increasingly strident anti-European tones.

The fall of Margaret Thatcher

Several factors contributed to Conservative MPs' decision to remove Margaret Thatcher as their leader (and thence as prime minister) in November 1990. The unpopularity of the poll tax led many Conservative MPs to fear defeat in the next general election. Others remained continuingly unhappy with her evident preference for a presidential style of Cabinet government, which had triggered the resignations of Michael

---

[37] Case 26/92 [1963] ECR 1, at para. 12.
[38] Since the EC is (per *Van Gend*) a 'new legal order of international law', the rules in 'ordinary' international law permitting unilateral state withdrawal from treaty arrangements would not apply.

Heseltine in 1985 and Nigel Lawson in 1989. But, the catalytic event was Thatcher's attitude towards the UK's EC membership.

The Treaty of Rome had contained various non-binding provisions to co-ordinate states' macroeconomic policies. These modest policies were seen by some observers as a tentative first step towards 'monetary union', which would ultimately require a single EC currency and a central EC bank controlling the Community's money supply and interest rates. Monetary union also had profound political implications. A single EC currency and a central EC bank would present a distinct challenge to orthodox notions of national sovereignty, by extending the *de facto* federal nature of the Community and adding further force to arguments for a full political federation on the American model.

Roy Jenkins, having resigned from the Labour government to become president of the Commission in 1977, put monetary union at the top of the Commission's list of priorities, and by 1979 the European monetary system (EMS) was in place. Its central feature was the exchange rate mechanism (ERM), which placed fairly tight limits on fluctuations in currency exchange rates. Member states were not, however, obliged to join the ERM, and successive Labour and Conservative governments chose not to do so.

The SEA made scant reference to monetary union. However, in 1988 the European Council instructed Jacques Delors to produce a plan for achieving full union. The 1989 *Report on Economic and Monetary Union* envisaged, first, a gradual 'convergence' of the member states' economies in respect of such matters as inflation rates and economic growth; second, the locking of all member states' currencies into a far tighter ERM; and, third, the introduction of the single currency.

While many member state governments welcomed the plan, the Thatcher government did not. The Conservative manifesto for the 1989 EC elections warned that monetary union would 'involve a fundamental transfer of sovereignty . . . The report, if taken as a whole, implies nothing less than the creation of a federal Europe.'[39] By mid-1990, the prime minister and some of her Cabinet colleagues were making distinctly hostile comments about the Delors plan. But the Cabinet was clearly split on the monetary union question. The UK finally joined the ERM in October 1990, yet immediately afterwards the prime minister launched a tirade against the Delors plan, describing her fellow heads of govern-

---

[39] Quoted in W. Nicoll and T. Simon, *Understanding the New European Community* (Harvester Wheatsheaf, 1994), p. 158.

ment, who wished to accelerate plans for further monetary integration, as living in cloud-cuckoo-land. She then accused Jaques Delors and the Commission of trying to 'extinguish democracy', and announced she would greet every 'federalist' EC measure with a resounding 'No!'

Thatcher's outburst prompted Sir Geoffrey Howe, leader of the House of Commons and deputy prime minister, to resign from the Cabinet. His resignation speech to the Commons had a profound and immediate political effect. Howe attributed many of the country's economic difficulties to the government's refusal to join the ERM in 1985. More broadly, Howe asserted that it was a serious error to regard closer European integration, as the prime minister appeared to do, as involving a 'surrender of sovereignty'. Making an overt reference to the Bruges speech, Howe argued that such hyperbolic language served only to create:

> a bogus dilemma, between one alternative, starkly labelled 'co-operation between independent sovereign states', and a second, equally crudely labelled alternative, 'centralised federal super-state', as if there were no middle way in between.[40]

Howe's criticism of Thatcher also addressed the question of her basic attitude towards the UK's EC partners. Howe saw no merit in what he termed Thatcher's 'nightmare image' of an EC; 'positively teeming with ill-intentioned people, scheming in her words to "extinguish democracy", to "dissolve our national identities" and to lead us "through the backdoor into a federal Europe" '.[41] Against such Europhobic 'background noise', it was impossible for the chancellor of the Exchequer to be taken seriously by other member states in any discussion of EC economic policy.

Howe's speech is a graphic example of the Commons' capacity to serve as a forum for calling the executive to account, a capacity which had been somewhat lacking in the 1980s. Thereafter, domestic political events moved with great rapidity. Michael Heseltine, five years after leaving the Cabinet, challenged Thatcher for leadership of the Conservative Party. Her failure to win an adequate majority in the subsequent election held among Conservative MPs led to her resignation as party leader and prime minister, and to the eventual succession of John Major.

These events reinforce the presumption that EC membership has wrought significant changes in both orthodox constitutional theory and

---

[40] HC Deb., vol. 18, col. 463, 13 November 1990.
[41] Ibid., at col. 464.

orthodox constitutional practice. In practical terms, the constitutional history of twentieth-century Britain has been dominated (except during the two world wars) by a straightforward party political division, in which single-party governments with relatively distinct and coherent ideological beliefs have deployed a Commons majority to use Parliament's legal sovereignty to pursue their preferred policy programmes. The demise of Margaret Thatcher, seen in conjunction with the extraordinary party political alignments produced in the 1972 accession controversy and the 1975 referendum, indicates that the EC has introduced a profound ideological fault line into the very core of the traditional party political divide. In 1990, it seemed plausible to suggest that neither the Labour Party nor Conservative Party could any longer rely on its MPs to present a unified front on EC questions. This held out the prospect of a significant weakening of prime ministerial authority vis-à-vis the Cabinet, and of government authority vis-à-vis the House of Commons. The prospect was realised with dramatic effect during the Major government's attempt to ratify the Maastricht Treaty.

The Maastricht Treaty

The Maastricht Treaty (formally, the Treaty on European Union, TEU) was, in substantive terms, a less expansive innovation than the SEA. It introduced several minor extensions in the EC's competence.[42] The Community gained powers over consumer protection, industrial policy, and some educational and cultural matters. More significantly, a specific timetable was set for phases 2 (1 January 1994) and 3 (1 January 1997 or 1999) of Delors' plan for monetary union.

The Maastricht negotiations emphasised the plurality of meanings attached to the concept of federalism, both by different member states, and by different political parties within an individual country.[43] The constitutional device eventually adopted to paper over these ideological cracks was the concept of 'subsidiarity', a term bearing several meanings relating to the decentralisation of decision-making power.[44]

---

[42] See R. Lane, 'New Community Competences under the Maastricht Treaty', *Common Market Law Review* (1993).

[43] See T. Koopmans, 'Federalism: The Wrong Debate', *Common Market Law Review* (1992).

[44] J. Peterson, 'Subsidiarity: A definition to Suit Any Vision', *Parliamentary Affairs* (1994); N. Emiliou, 'Subsidiarity: Panacea or Fig Leaf', in D. O'Keeffe and P. Twomey (eds), *Legal Issues of the Maastricht Treaty* (Chancery Law, 1994).

The TEU also introduced significant reforms in respect of the *Social Charter*. Eleven of the twelve member states had wished to place the 1989 declaration on a legal basis within the Treaty of Rome, thus making it directly effective in all member states. The Major government rejected this reform. This resulted in the rather peculiar legal creature of a Protocol on Social Policy, attached to the TEU, in which the other eleven states agreed to incorporate the charter, and all twelve states agreed that the eleven could use Community institutions (including the ECJ) to administer it.

But for both proponents and opponents of a united states of Europe, other aspects of the TEU may have seemed of greater long-term importance. The TEU provided that the EC itself was now to be seen as merely one 'pillar' of the 'European Union' (EU). The other two pillars would be a Common Foreign and Security Policy (CFSP) and Justice and Home Affairs (JHA), which in combination substantially extend the range of the former system of 'European Political Co-operation' introduced by the Single European Act. In formal, legal terms, the CFSP and JHA were not part of the EC, and should perhaps be seen as an exercise in traditional intergovernmental co-operation rather than another 'new legal order' operating in parallel to the Community.

The inference that Maastricht may have gone too far too fast may also be drawn from consideration of the fate of the plans to achieve monetary union within the EC. The integrity of the ERM was substantially undermined late in 1993, before the TEU came into effect. The member states could not maintain exchange rate stability in the face of massive speculation on the international money markets against the weaker currencies. Consequently, several countries, including Britain, left the system. The Community's failure to resist these forces undermined its credibility in the eyes of supporters of further integration, and was construed as a sign of more pervasive weakness by its opponents. It is therefore unsurprising that the ratification and incorporation of the treaty proved so tortuous in several member states.

The ratification and incorporation of the Maastricht Treaty

The people of Denmark had initially rejected the terms of the Maastricht Treaty in a referendum. Some rapid renegotiation between the member states ensued, whereupon the TEU was approved by a tiny majority in a second Danish referendum. Opinion was also divided in France, where the requisite referendum produced a very small majority in favour. In

Germany, the political argument was clearly won by pro-Maastricht forces, although the German government subsequently faced an (unsuccessful) legal challenge which argued that the TEU was inconsistent with provisions of Germany's basic law.[45]

'Ratification' of the TEU presented considerable political difficulties in the UK. Given the small size (twenty-one) of the government's Commons majority, and the presence of a dozen anti-EC backbenchers within Conservative ranks, it was not clear that the government could win Commons approval for the treaty. In the course of tortuous parliamentary proceedings in the Commons, the government was defeated by eight votes on a motion concerning the social policy protocol. The prime minister thereupon announced that the government's motion on the protocol would be the subject of a vote of confidence the next day, and implied that a defeat would lead to a dissolution. For rebel Conservative MPs, the prospect of a general election in which they might lose their seats was sufficiently daunting to bring them back into line. The government's majority in the confidence vote was forty. But the extraordinary convolutions that had gripped the Commons and divided the Conservative Party continued in the following months.

At the EC's 1992 Edinburgh summit, the member states had agreed to a modest increase in the Community budget from 1995 onwards. When the Major government introduced legislation in November 1994 to incorporate that obligation into domestic law, it encountered a substantial rebellion from backbench Conservative MPs who had opposed the Maastricht reforms. For a government whose majority was then only fourteen, the prospect of a Commons defeat was very real. The prime minister then announced that the second reading vote would be a matter of confidence, evidently on the basis that a government which could not honour its international obligations could not continue in office. The threat of a general election at a time when the Labour Party enjoyed a substantial lead in the opinion polls was again sufficient to bring most potential rebels back into the government camp. Nevertheless, eight Conservative MPs abstained at second reading and were promptly stripped of the party whip.

---

[45] *Brunner* v. *The European Union Treaty* [1994] 1 CMLR 57.

Conclusion

The Labour Party's 1997 general election victory took much of the political heat out of the constitutional controversies attending the United Kingdom's membership of the Community. The Labour Cabinet was firmly pro-European in outlook and, while a small number of backbench Labour MPs fell into the Euro-sceptic camp, they were an insignificant grouping within the parliamentary party as a whole. The Conservative Party under its new leader William Hague continued its stridently Euro-sceptic tone but, given the size of the government's Commons majority, Conservative Euro-scepticism had become almost wholly insignificant.

The Blair government immediately demonstrated its pro-EC credentials by incorporating the *Social Charter* into UK law. It stood back, however, from participating in the launch of the single European currency in 1999. The government's official position on this issue was that it supported the single currency in principle, but would not join until economic conditions were appropriate. The government also promised that the United Kingdom would not join until the electorate had voted to do so in a referendum.

The new government found itself plunged immediately into a new round of treaty amendment negotiations. The proposals aired in the Amsterdam Treaty were relatively modest in effect.[46] The treaty's most significant innovation was to transfer much of the justice and home affairs pillar of the EU into the EC, thereby bringing its terms within the jurisdiction of the ECJ. While the Amsterdam amendments did not incorporate the European Convention on Human Rights into the EC's legal order, the new treaty did extend the EC's competence into a range of overtly 'political matters'. Under Article 13, the Community now has powers to address discrimination not just on the basis of nationality, but also gender, sexual orientation, disability, race and ethnicity, religious belief.

These extensions to the Community's competence are minor matters compared to the changes that the first twenty-five years of membership have wrought on our constitutionaal theory and practice. A substantial and continually increasing proportion of the laws applicable in the United Kingdom are found in the treaties and secondary legislation. It is similarly clear that the gradual extension of the Community's competence beyond the nominally 'economic' sphere into a range of 'political'

[46] See Paul Craig, 'The Treaty of Amsterdam: A Brief Guide', *Public Law* (1998).

issues has lent the EC a far more obviously 'federal' identity than it possessed twenty years ago. In that respect, the effective 'sovereignty' of the UK as a nation has been curtailed. Whether Parliament retains the capacity to reclaim that authority, should it ever wish to do so, remains to be seen. But, even if we accept that the courts do not have power to disapply a statute purportedly withdrawing the UK from the EC, the innovative stream of jurisprudence flowing from *Macarthy's* through *Garland* to *Factortame* and beyond has substantially restructured the internal balance of constitutional power between the courts, the government and Parliament. Lastly, the UK's membership of the Community was a political issue which transcended the usual rigidities of ideological loyalty within the Conservative and Labour parties. The EC has in effect shown us that even the most firmly held of orthodoxies may break, and not simply bend, in response to the winds of legal and political change now blowing from western Europe across the constitutional landscape of the United Kingdom.

Bibliography

Primary sources

Case-law of the European Court of Justice

Van Gend en Loos v. *Nederlandse Administratie der Belastingen* 26/62 [1963] ECR 1; [1963] CMLR 105.
Costa v. *ENEL* [1964] ECR 585; [1964] CMLR 425.
Grad v. *Finanzamnt Traunstein* 9/70 [1970] ECR 825; [1971] CMLR 1.
Internationale Handelsgesellchaft 11/70 [1970] ECR 1125; [1972] CMLR 255.
Politi SAS v. *Italian Ministry of Finance* 43/71 [1971] ECR 1039.
Van Duyn v. *The Home Office* 41/74 [1974] ECR 1337.
Defrenne v. *Sabena* 43/75 [1976] ECR 455; [1976] 2 CMLR 98.
Administrazine delle Finanze della Stato v. *Simmenthal SpA* 106/77 [1978] ECR 629; [1978] 3 CMLR 263.
Von Colson & Kamann v. *Land Nordrhein-Westfalen* 14/83 [1984] ECR 1891; [1986] CMLR 430.
Marshall v. *Southampton AHA* [1986] ECR 723.
Francovich & Bonifaci v. *Italy* C-6 and 9/90 [1991] ECR I-5337; [1993] 2 CMLR 66.
Brasserie de Pecheur SA v. *Germany* C-46/93 [1996] ECR I-1029; [1996] 1 CMLR 889.

United Kingdom government official publications

Membership of the European Communities, Cmnd 3269 (1967).
Legal and Constitutional Implications of United Kingdom Membership of the European Communities, Cmnd 3301 (1967).
The United Kingdom and the European Communities, Cmnd 4715 (1971).
Membership of the European Communities, Cmnd 5999 (1975).

Case-law of the United Kingdom courts

Blackburn v. *Attorney-General* [1971] 2 All ER 1380.
McCarthy's v. *Smith* [1979] 3 All ER 325.
Garland v. *British Rail* [1982] 2 All ER 402.
Lister v. *Forth Dry Dock* [1990] 1 AC 546.
R. v. *Secretary of State for Transport, ex p. Factortame (No. 2)* (Lord Goff) [1991] 1 AC 603.

Secondary sources

Academic critiques of the case-law of the European Court of Justice

Craig, Paul, 'Once Upon a Time in the West: Direct Effect and the Federalisation of EC Law', *Oxford Journal of Legal Studies* (1992).
Craig, Paul, '*Francovich*, Remedies and the Scope of Damages Liability', *Law Quarterly Review* (1993).
Curtin, D., 'The Province of Government: Delimiting the Direct Effect of Directives in the Common Law Context', *European Law Review* (1990).
Pescatore, P., 'The Doctrine of Direct Effect: An Infant Disease of Community Law', *European Law Review* (1983).
Steiner, J., 'Making the Action Suit the Case: Domestic Remedies for Breach of EC Rights', *European Law Review* (1987).
Weiler, J., 'The Community System: The Dual Character of Supra-nationalism', *Yearbook of European Law* (1981).
Winter, J., 'Direct Applicability and Direct Effect', *Common Market Law Review* (1972).

Academic critiques of the case-law of the United Kingdom court

Allan, T. S. R., 'Parliamentary Sovereignty: Lord Denning's Dexterous Revolution', *Oxford Journal of Legal Studies* (1983).
Allan, T. S. R., 'Parliamentary Sovereignty: Law, Politics and Revolution', *Law Quarterly Review* (1997).
Craig, Paul, 'Sovereignty of the UK Parliament after *Factortame*', *Yearbook of European Law* (1991).
Gravells, N., 'Effective Protection of Community Law Rights: Temporary Disapplication of an Act of Parliament', *Public Law* (1991).
de Smith, S. A., 'The Constitution and the Common Market: A Tentative Appraisal', *Modern Law Review* (1971).

Szsczak, E., 'Sovereignty: Crisis, Compliance, Confusion, Complacency', *European Law Review* (1990).

Wade, H. R. W., 'The Constitution and the Common Market', *Law Quarterly Review* (1971).

Wade, H. R. W., 'Sovereignty and the European Communities', *Law Quarterly Review* (1972).

Wade, H. R. W., 'Sovereignty—Revolution or Evolution?', *Law Quarterly Review* (1996).

18.
Conclusion
VERNON BOGDANOR

I

In 1953, the distinguished American sociologist, Edward Shils, attending a university dinner, was surprised to hear 'an eminent man of the left say, in utter seriousness . . . that the British Constitution was "as nearly perfect as any human institution could be" '. He was even more surprised to find that 'No one even thought it amusing.'[1] British institutions seemed to have been validated by victories in two world wars and, in the immediate post-war years, the British system of government was widely admired as an exemplar of what a liberal polity should be; and, in the 1950s and 1960s, the Westminster model came to be exported to the ex-colonies of Africa and Asia, for whom indeed it seemed the very touchstone of democracy. The collapse of democracy in much of central Europe between the wars had served to discredit many of the nostrums of constitutional reformers, in particular perhaps, proportional representation. Thus, the standard textbooks of the 1950s, works such as Herbert Morrison's *Government and Parliament*, K. C. Wheare's *Government by Committee*, and Robert McKenzie's *British Political Parties*, tended to be in the nature of somewhat uncritical celebrations of British institutions.[2]

By the end of the century, in contrast, it would have been hard to find an equivalent to Shils's 'eminent man of the left', prepared to offer a similar encomium of the British constitution. The constitution had ceased to be an exemplar of modern democratic practice. Not one of the new post-communist democracies of central and eastern Europe had so much as contemplated adopting the Westminster model, although they

---

[1] Edward Shils, 'British Intellectuals in the Mid-twentieth Century', *Encounter* (April 1955), reprinted in *The Intellectuals and the Powers* (University of Chicago Press, 1972), p. 135.
[2] Herbert Morrison, *Government and Parliament* (Oxford University Press, 1954); K. C. Wheare, *Government by Committee* (Oxford University Press, 1955); R. T. McKenzie, *British Political Parties* (Heinemann, 1955).

were still prepared to learn from British parliamentary procedures. Moreover, Britain herself was abandoning many of the central features of her constitution, as the Labour government, elected in 1997, implemented the most radical programme of constitutional reform that Britain had seen since the time of the Great Reform Act.

Thus, while, at the beginning of the twentieth century, there still seemed widespread confidence in the virtues of the constitution, by the century's end, that confidence seemed to have evaporated. This loss of confidence coincided with, and was perhaps in part caused by, a collapse of national self-confidence that had begun in the 1960s, when the British political and intellectual elite began to come to terms with the fact that Britain was falling economically behind her continental competitors. From that time, many commentators came to look with approval on continental models—state planning in France as undertaken by the Commissariat du Plan or co-determination (*Mitsbesttimung*) in Germany. Political scientists too came to look at foreign models and, in particular, Germany, whose system of proportional representation and federal government, so it became fashionable to argue in the 1970s, had played a large part in that country's post-war social and economic progress.[3] So it was that, during the 1970s, constitutional reform, which had hardly been an issue in British politics since the 1920s, came once again to the forefront of the political agenda.

II

During the first twenty-one years of the century, three measures—the Parliament Act 1911, the Representation of the People Act 1918, and the Anglo-Irish Treaty of 1921—had served to remove constitutional issues from British politics.

The Parliament Act had established an effectively unicameral system of government in Britain. In consequence, representative government came to be identified with the supremacy of the House of Commons. 'We all of us start', Prime Minister H. H. Asquith had claimed during

[3] See, for example, S. E. Finer (ed.), *Adversary Politics and Electoral Reform* (Anthony Wigram, 1975); and Nevil Johnson, *In Search of the Constitution: Reflections on State and Society in Britain* (Pergamon, 1977). Johnson, in particular, advocated a raft of reforms derived from the experience of the German Federal Republic, whose political system he had earlier studied in his book, *Government in the Federal Republic of Germany: The Executive at Work* (Pergamon, 1973).

the second reading debate on the Parliament bill, 'from one common point—the assumption which lies at the root of representative government that the House of Commons, itself a product of popular election, is, under normal conditions, a trustworthy organ and mouthpiece of the popular will'.[4] Unionist opponents of the bill, however, had argued that the House of Commons could by no means be relied upon as a 'trustworthy organ and mouthpiece of the popular will'. At the inter-party constitutional conference which had met between June and November 1910, therefore, they had argued that a special category of 'constitutional' legislation should be recognised, and that such legislation should require the approval of the people, as well as Parliament, in a referendum. This proposal had been rejected by Asquith, who had cited 'the difficulties— difficulty of defining "constitutional questions" where there was no written constitution, difficulty of selecting a tribunal to decide on disputed cases, danger of producing a deadlock over nearly the whole field of legislation by the width of our definition'.[5]

The provisions of the Parliament Act, which enabled the Commons to overcome disagreement by the Lords, had put paid to the possibility of referring legislation to the electorate. It had ensured also that no tribunal other than the government of the day could make a judgement on the constitutional propriety of legislation. Thus the Parliament Act was, for Dicey, 'the last and greatest triumph of party government', and it underlined the fact that party government was 'not the accident or corruption, but, so to speak, the very foundation of our constitutional system'.[6] Admittedly, it took some time for this reality to be legally recognised. But, in 1937, the office of leader of the opposition was recognised as a salaried post, while, in 1975, monies were made available to assist the opposition parties with their work in Parliament. It was not until the end of the century, however, in the Political Parties, Elections and Referendums Act 2000, that political parties were finally recognised in law as a part of the constitution rather than being treated, as they had

---

[4] HC Deb., vol. 1, col. 1748, 21 February 1911.

[5] Notes of Meetings of the Conference on the Constitutional Question, 11th sitting, 26 July 1910, Austen Chamberlain Papers, University of Birmingham Library, 10.2.45, cited in Vernon Bogdanor, *The People and the Party System: The Referendum and Electoral Reform in British Politics* (Cambridge University Press, 1981), p. 23. The Austen Chamberlain Papers contain all of the minutes of the constitutional conference.

[6] A. V. Dicey, Introduction to 8th edn of *Introduction to the Study of the Law of the Constitution* (Macmillan, 1915), p. ci.

hitherto been, as essential voluntary bodies on the lines of golf or tennis clubs.

The Representation of the People Act 1918 had preserved, almost by accident and after a series of strange political vicissitudes, the plurality system of voting for elections to the House of Commons, and it effectively put an end to a period of lively and vigorous debate on alternative electoral systems.[7] The extension of the franchise, together with the growth of class feeling, contributed to the restoration of a two-party system, albeit with Labour, rather than the Liberals, as the main party of the Left. The two parties found their main areas of disagreement to lie primarily in matters of social and economic policy rather than the constitution. The Labour Party, unlike the Liberals, sought to transform society, not to change the constitution. The party's prime aim was to capture the state, not to reform it.

The 1921 Anglo-Irish Treaty had provided for the removal of all Irish MPs, except those representing Northern Ireland constituencies, from the House of Commons. It thus contributed to the establishment of a two-party system in the House of Commons because it made single-party majority government more likely. For, before 1921, a government would need over eighty more seats than the main opposition party if it was to enjoy an overall majority free from reliance on the eighty-odd Irish nationalists regularly returned to the Commons in every general election between 1885 and 1914. Thus, while four of the eight general elections between 1885 and 1914 had resulted in hung Parliaments in which no single party enjoyed an overall majority, only three general elections after 1918 until the end of the century—those of 1923, 1929 and February 1974—were to result in hung Parliaments. Moreover, the Anglo-Irish Treaty also removed the constitutional issue of Irish home rule from British politics, taking with it—or so at least it seemed for nearly fifty years—both devolution and the Ulster question. 'The two supreme services which Ireland has rendered Britain', declared Winston Churchill after the First World War, 'are her accession to the Allied cause on the outbreak of the Great War and her withdrawal from the House of Commons at its close'.[8]

In the 1920s, the British party system began to take on the shape

---

[7] See, on the political background to the 1918 Act, Martin Pugh, *Electoral Reform in War and Peace, 1906–1918* (Routledge & Kegan Paul, 1978), and Bogdanor, *The People and the Party System*, pp. 126–43.

[8] Winston S. Churchill, *The World Crisis*: vol. 5, *The Aftermath* (Thornton Butterworth, 1929), p. 283.

which it was to assume for over fifty years—a two-party system within which both parties emphasised the priority of socioeconomic questions. The liberal agenda of constitutional reform seemed to have been completed, and it was perhaps symbolic that the Liberal Party began its long decline during this decade.

The expansion of the suffrage, occurring at the same time as the development of a politically conscious working class, created the preconditions for a highly organised two-party system. But it was the development of tightly organised mass parties which helped to fossilise the movement for constitutional change.[9] For many of the constitutional reforms proposed by an earlier generation, such as the referendum, proportional representation and devolution, would have threatened the interests of the political parties. Defenders of the party system could claim that, with universal suffrage now achieved, the parties were themselves perfectly adequate vehicles for popular participation, so that constitutional reforms designed to increase participation were no longer necessary. It was not until the party system came gradually to unfreeze, in the years following 1974, that the constitution once again entered the political agenda, and reformers rediscovered the liberal critique of the constitution, whose challenge had been evaded rather than resolved by the settlement of the years 1911 to 1922.

III

The constitution first re-entered British politics in the post-war years in Northern Ireland, which, from the time of the third Government of Ireland Act 1920, providing for devolution in the province, had seemed insulated from the politics of the rest of the United Kingdom. In 1968, however, the activities of the civil rights movement led to violence between the Unionist and Nationalist communities, and the problems of the province began once again to force themselves upon the attention of successive British governments. The basic problem seemed to be that, in a political system where conflict was between two rather rigid tribal communities, rather than between mobile social classes, the Westminster model could not work effectively. For that model was predicated upon alternating or at least potentially alternating majorities, rather than a

---

[9] Michael Steed, 'Participation through Western Democratic Institutions', in Geraint Parry (ed.), *Participation in Politics* (Manchester University Press, 1972).

permanent majority for one particular community. For this reason, successive British governments found themselves proposing constitutional innovations in Northern Ireland, such as power-sharing, devolution, proportional representation, the referendum and a Bill of Rights, whose application to the rest of the kingdom they strenuously resisted.

In 1973, three constitutional innovations were introduced in Northern Ireland, consequent upon the abolition of the Northern Ireland Parliament, Stormont, which had contained a permanent Unionist majority.

The first of these innovations was a border poll designed to test whether the population of Northern Ireland wished to remain members of the United Kingdom, or to join with the Irish Republic. This border poll was an innovation in two senses. First, it was a referendum, something hitherto deemed unconstitutional in Britain, except when used to decide local matters such as liquor licensing in Wales. Second, the border poll implied that one part of Britain could, if it so wished, exercise a right of self-determination to leave the United Kingdom. This was an implication whose significance would not be missed by Scottish nationalists.

The second innovation was a new Northern Ireland Assembly, provided for in the Northern Ireland Constitution Act 1973, which departed significantly from the Westminster model of single-party majority government, in that it would be based upon the principle of power-sharing between the Unionist majority and the Nationalist minority. Thus, whatever the outcome of the election to the new Assembly, the minority would be guaranteed places in the executive government of Northern Ireland.

Moreover, and this was the third innovation, the new Assembly would be elected by the single transferable vote method of proportional representation, the first experiment with proportional representation in Britain since the abolition of the university seats in 1950. In addition, the new district councils in Northern Ireland would also be elected by the single transferable vote. It is hardly surprising that the Electoral Reform Society, which had been campaigning for this reform for nearly ninety years, labelled 1973 a 'red letter year' and declared:

> The reform this Society seeks is no longer an academic matter, capable of being dismissed as the concern of a few enthusiasts; it is now something actually operating within the United Kingdom ... The whole subject is topical as it has not been for half a century.[10]

---

[10] *Representation* (Journal of the Electoral Reform Society) (October 1973), 54.

Reforms in Northern Ireland, however, had little immediate impact on the rest of the United Kingdom. But the 1960s and 1970s saw the introduction of an even more momentous issue into British politics: British entry into the European Community. This issue had major constitutional implications, and indeed it threatened the fundamental principle of parliamentary sovereignty, because decisions previously taken by Parliament would in future be taken by a body—the Council of Ministers of the European Community—which was not and could not be responsible to Parliament. European Community institutions would in future have the power to make law, and future Community provisions would automatically become part of British law. They would, indeed, prevail over British law and the courts would have to give Community provisions priority.

Admittedly, this transfer of power from Parliament was, for the time being, masked by the so-called Luxembourg compromise, a constitutional convention of the European Community, according to which, even where the Treaty of Rome provided for majority decision-making, unanimity would be required. However, two major amendments to the Treaty of Rome, the Single European Act of 1986 and the Maastricht Treaty of 1992, were greatly to extend the scope of majority voting in the Community, and thus almost totally undermine the Luxembourg compromise.

Entry into the European Community, moreover, raised, as Northern Ireland had done, the issue of proportional representation. For Article 138 (iii) of the Treaty of Rome, committed the British government together with the governments of the other member states to direct elections to the European Parliament 'by direct universal suffrage in accordance with a uniform procedure in all member states'. That uniform procedure would almost certainly prove to be a proportional one because, of the nine member states of the European Community after 1973, Britain and France alone did not use a proportional system to elect their national legislatures. Moreover, the traditional arguments in Britain for the plurality system, namely that it provided stable government as well as close links between MPs and constituents, seemed irrelevant in the European context. For it was not the function of the European Parliament, by contrast with the House of Commons, to sustain a government, and so the argument that proportional representation would lead to weak or unstable government was hardly relevant. Moreover, constituencies in the European Parliament elections would each contain around half a million electors, and it seemed, therefore, that close contact between legislators and constituents would probably be unattainable whatever the electoral system. Nevertheless, the plurality system was employed for elections to the European Parliament until 1999, when a proportional system was introduced.

Britain's entry into the European Community was thus a major constitutional innovation, and it led directly to a further constitutional innovation in 1975, the country's first nationwide referendum on the question of whether Britain should leave the Community, or remain on the terms renegotiated by the Labour government which had come to office in 1974. The referendum had originally been proposed by Labour in opposition so as to avoid a split between opposing factions in the party. It was, in James Callaghan's graphic words, 'a rubber life raft into which the party may one day have to climb'.[11] It thus came to be adopted in British politics as an *ad hoc* response to what was thought of as a unique issue. It was not intended to create a precedent. 'It is not just that it is more important', declared a Labour junior minister, Gerry Fowler, during the debates in the Commons on the European Community referendum, 'it is of a different order. There is, and there can be, no issue that is on all fours with it. That is why we say that this issue is the sole exception, and there can be no other exception, to the principle that we normally operate through parliamentary democracy.'[12] But, of course, once the precedent of the referendum had been conceded, it was difficult to prevent it being invoked again, as it was to be, within eighteen months of the European Community legislation, in December 1976, when the Labour government introduced legislation providing for devolution to Scotland and Wales. On this occasion, however, the government was forced, following a backbench revolt, to make the devolution legislation dependent upon approval in referendums, since otherwise it might well not have passed the Commons. Devolution was, in the event, defeated as a result of referendums held in 1979, although eighteen years later, in 1997, devolution in Scotland and Wales was to be endorsed in referendums held by another Labour government. Indeed, the Labour government elected in 1997 was to hold referendums, not only on devolution to Scotland, Wales and Northern Ireland, but also on whether there should be a directly elected mayor and strategic authority in London; while the Local Government Act 2000 provided for referendums on directly elected mayors in other local authorities. Moreover, this Act also provided that 5 per cent of registered electors in any local authority

[11] Quoted in David Butler and Uwe Kitzinger, *The 1975 Referendum* (Macmillan, 1976), p. 12.
[12] HC Deb., 5th series, col. 1743, 22 November 1974.

could require that authority to hold a referendum on the mayor option. This was the first provision for the use of the initiative in British politics. In addition, the Labour government indicated that Britain would not enter the European single currency, the euro, without a positive vote in a referendum; and it committed itself to a referendum on the electoral system for elections to the House of Commons.

For the first two-thirds of the twentieth century, the British constitution had known nothing of the people. In 1964, a widely used and valuable interpretation of the British system of government, *Representative and Responsible Government* by A. H. Birch, stated: 'It has occasionally been proposed that a referendum might be held on a particular issue, but the proposals do not ever appear to have been taken seriously.'[13] Until the 1970s, the referendum had been widely dismissed as unconstitutional. But, by the end of the century, it could be argued that it had become an accepted part of the British constitution.

It may be indeed that a persuasive precedent has been created to the effect that the powers of Parliament should not be transferred without popular endorsement. For the referendums that have been held so far in Britain have all been concerned with the legitimacy of transferring the powers of Parliament, either by excluding an area from Parliament's jurisdiction—the Northern Ireland border poll—or by transferring powers, whether to the European Community, or to directly elected bodies in Scotland, Wales, Northern Ireland or London. 'The Legislative', Locke had declared, 'cannot transfer the power of making laws to any other hands. For it being but a delegated power from the People, they who have it cannot pass it to others.'[14] The requirement, therefore, that validation from the people is needed for a transfer of the powers of Parliament has a clear rationale in liberal thought; and the referendum has become in part an instrument of entrenchment since it prevents the powers of Parliament from being transferred without the approval of the people.

Devolution was a third constitutional issue, in addition to Northern Ireland and the European Community, to haunt governments in the 1970s. The referendums in Scotland and Wales in 1979 were to show that there was insufficient support at that time for devolution; but, in 1998, following further referendums, legislation was passed providing for a

---

[13] A. H. Birch, *Representative and Responsible Government: An Essay on the British Constitution* (Allen & Unwin, 1964), p. 227.
[14] John Locke, *Second Treatise of Government*, para. 141.

Scottish Parliament and a National Assembly for Wales. The establishment of these devolved bodies raised, as Europe had done, fundamental questions concerning parliamentary sovereignty and federalism, questions which successive governments sought to avoid answering. Moreover, devolution, like Northern Ireland and Europe, brought the question of proportional representation back on to the political agenda. In October 1973, the report of the Royal Commission on the Constitution (the Kilbrandon Report) had unanimously recommended that any assemblies established in Scotland, Wales or the English regions should be elected by the single transferable vote method of proportional representation. This recommendation was rejected by successive governments until, in 1998, it was proposed that the Scottish Parliament and the National Assembly for Wales be elected by the German method of proportional representation, sometimes called the additional-member system. The Northern Ireland Assembly would continue to be elected by the single transferable vote method.

By the end of the century, therefore, Britain enjoyed a system of asymmetrical devolution. Scotland had a Parliament with legislative powers, Wales a National Assembly with powers only over secondary legislation, and Northern Ireland an Assembly with legislative powers, but with provisions requiring the executive to contain representatives of both of the two warring communities in the province. England, the largest component of the United Kingdom, containing 85 per cent of its population, had no devolved body to represent its interests, and calls for an English Parliament had little resonance. These variations between different parts of the United Kingdom were defended as a justified response to dissimilar conditions. Yet, as Douglas Hurd put it, the outcome was 'a system of amazing untidiness ... a Kingdom of four parts, of three Secretaries of State, each with different powers, of two Assemblies and one Parliament, each different in composition and powers from the others'.[15]

IV

These issues—the government of Northern Ireland, Britain's entry into the European Community, and devolution—however fundamental, were

---

[15] Douglas Hurd, 'On from the Elective Dictatorship', first Hailsham Lecture to Society of Conservative Lawyers (June 2001).

nevertheless probably peripheral to the perceptions of most people in England, and did not immediately impinge upon them. In February 1974, however, the outcome of the general election, perhaps the crucial general election of the whole post-war period, served to bring the constitution back on to the political agenda for the whole of the United Kingdom, and it made it difficult for any elector to ignore it.

The outcome of this election is shown in Table 18.1.

Table 18.1 Results of UK general election, February 1974

	Seats	Votes (per cent)
Conservatives	297	37.9
Labour	301	37.1
Liberals	14	19.3
Scottish Nationalist Party	7	2.0
Plaid Cymru	2	0.6
United Ulster Unionist Council	11	1.2
SDLP	1	0.5
Others	2	1.4
Total	635	100.0

The election failed, for the first time since 1929, to yield an overall majority for one party. Moreover, it yielded a House of Commons in which each of the two major parties—Labour and Conservative—needed the support of at least two minor parties in order to achieve an overall majority. The Liberal Party, moreover, won just fourteen out of 635 seats despite gaining over 19 per cent of the vote. In Northern Ireland, the United Ulster Unionist Council, formed to oppose the agreement providing for a power-sharing executive in Northern Ireland, won eleven of the twelve Northern Ireland seats on just 51 per cent of the vote in the province, effectively dooming the power-sharing experiment. In Scotland, the SNP, despite winning 22 per cent of the Scottish vote, gained just seven of the seventy-one Scottish seats. In the event, Labour, which had won four more seats than the Conservatives, formed a minority government, even though it had secured fewer votes than the Conservatives.

The defeat of Edward Heath's government in the February 1974 election proved momentous in heralding the end of the post-war economic and social settlement, so preparing the way for what came to be called 'Thatcherism'. The Heath government was to prove 'the last loyal signatory' of the 1944 pact by which governments had promised to secure full employment in return for wage restraint.[16] But the February 1974 general election was equally significant for what it indicated about the electoral system and the working of the British constitution.

The election cast doubt on a number of assumptions which had hitherto governed British politics: the assumption that the plurality system yielded 'strong government'; the assumption of a two-party system; and the assumption that Britain was a homogeneous country rather than a territorially diversified multinational one. The minority Labour government formed after the February 1974 general election enjoyed the support of just 37 per cent of the voters, while the majority Labour government formed after the October 1974 general election had the support of just 39 per cent. Of the remaining five general elections in the twentieth century, three—those of 1983, 1987 and 1997—were to yield landslide majorities in the House of Commons based on just 42 or 43 per cent of the vote. Thus, the general election of February 1974 made it plausible to suspect that, in the words of one political scientist in 1980, there had been 'a prodigious change in the public perception of the nature of the political parties and the way they have carried out their functions. That change is part of the more subtle and half-concealed changes detectable once the facade of the parliamentary duopoly has been penetrated.'[17]

It is hardly surprising that the issue of proportional representation came, for the first time since before the First World War, to the forefront of the political agenda. Until 1974, the electoral system had seemed of concern only to the Liberals, whose arguments were dismissed as special pleading. As recently as 1964, A. H. Birch, in *Representative and Responsible Government*, had stated that 'the electoral system is no longer a bone of contention'.[18] Political scientists had tended, rather uncritically perhaps, to defend the plurality system on the grounds that, whatever its theoretical deficiencies, it provided 'strong' government, and this was equated with governments which enjoyed overall majorities in the House of Commons.

The outcome of the February 1974 general election reopened the debate on electoral reform. But the basis of the argument for proportional representation underwent an important change. Hitherto, supporters of

---

[16] Keith Middlemas, *Power, Competition and the State*: vol. 2, *Threats to the Postwar Settlement* (Macmillan, 1990), p. 390.

[17] S. E. Finer, *The British Party System, 1945–1979* (American Enterprise Institute, 1980), p. xiv.

[18] Birch, *Representative and Responsible Government*, p. 227.

reform had argued that proportional representation was fairer than the plurality system. Opponents might have conceded this point, but they countered with the argument that the plurality system was more practical. Proportional representation, so they contended, led to coalition or minority government which was, inevitably, weak or unstable government. It now came to be argued, however, that proportional representation was not only fairer but also more practical than the plurality system.[19] For adversary politics, an inevitable consequence of the plurality system, yielded bad government, and hindered instead of assisting Britain's economic progress, by undermining policies for economic stabilisation, regional policy and pensions policy. It also prevented Britain from developing an effective incomes policy, because each government's attempt to fashion one became subject to overbidding by the opposition. By contrast, the 'deadlock', which proportional representation could be expected to produce, was positively to be welcomed, since it could help to yield a consensus in economic policy.[20]

The electoral system, moreover, served to protect the two-party duopoly against the threat of new competition. Each party adopted policy positions which owed more to the views of their activists than to the wishes of the voters. Since new parties could not easily erode the base of the two established parties, the voters were deprived of more consensual options. Reversals of policy when a government of one political colour was succeeded by a government of the opposite political colour created a climate of uncertainty damaging to business. Thus, the adversary politics argument purported, in theoretical terms, to prove that Anthony Downs's economic model of the working of two-party systems, which postulated that they would converge towards the centre, did not necessarily hold.[21]

Admittedly, research published since the 1970s has shown that the adversary thesis cannot be sustained. For, as Richard Rose has shown, the bulk of an incoming government's commitments are determined by its inheritance and these cannot easily be reversed. Moreover, comparative analysis shows that the economic consequences of proportional representation are highly uncertain. Some countries which use proportional representation have proved more successful economically than Britain, while others have been less successful. Research seems to show that a country's economic success owes rather less to constitutional or

---

[19] See, for example, Finer, *Adversary Politics and Electoral Reform*.
[20] See S. E. Finer, 'In Defence of Deadlock', *New Society*, 662 (September 1974).
[21] Anthony Downs, *An Economic Theory of Democracy* (Harper, 1957).

electoral factors than had previously been thought. Thus, by the end of the century, any argument for proportional representation had once again to be based on principles of fairness rather than upon its supposed consequences for the economy.[22]

The advocates of proportional representation did not succeed in persuading governments to alter the basis for elections to the House of Commons from the plurality system. But, by the end of the century, it had come to be accepted that bodies other than the Commons and local authorities ought not necessarily to be elected by that system. Devolved bodies in Scotland and Wales, and the Greater London Assembly, were elected, not by the single transferable vote method as in Northern Ireland, but by a variant of the German additional-member method, while elections to the European Parliament were, from 1999, held under the regional-list system of proportional representation. The mayor of London was to be elected by the supplementary vote, a variant of the alternative vote system. Thus, while at the beginning of the twentieth century the country enjoyed a uniform electoral system but a diversified franchise, by the end of the century the opposite was true, and the country had come to enjoy a uniform franchise but a variety of electoral systems. However, the plethora of elections and the development of alternative electoral systems was to do little for democratic participation. Low levels of turnout were recorded in local government elections in the 1990s, in the election for the mayor of London in 2000 (34 per cent), in the first elections for the National Assembly for Wales in 1999 (46 per cent), in the European Parliament elections of 1999 (24 per cent), and, above all, in the general election in 2001, where the turnout at 58 per cent was the lowest since 1918, and particularly marked among young voters. The franchise which in 1918 had been recognised as a right of citizenship did not, at the end of the century, seem to be accompanied by any sense of a corresponding civic duty to vote.

These changes at the electoral level were bound to cast doubt on the desirability of the Westminster model which seemed to legitimise a massive concentration of power at the centre of government. In 1976, Lord Hailsham, in a widely noticed Dimbleby Lecture entitled 'Elective Dictatorship', declared that 'our constitution is wearing out. Its central

---

[22] See, *inter alia*, Richard Rose, *Do Parties Make a Difference?* (Macmillan 1980); expanded 2nd edn (1984); Richard Rose and Philip Davies, *Inheritance and Public Policy: Change without Choice in Britain* (Yale University Press, 1994); and Richard Rose, *What are the Economic Consequences of PR?* (Electoral Reform Society, 1992).

defects are gradually coming to outweigh its merits, and its central defects consist in the absolute powers we confer on our sovereign body, and the concentration of these powers in an executive government formed out of one party which may not fairly represent the popular will.'

Bagehot had defended the British constitution as a constitution which worked. Now many were coming to believe that it was ceasing to work. This viewpoint seemed particularly prevalent on the Left, in opposition between 1979 and 1997. Confronted by eighteen years of Conservative government, the longest period of one-party government since the 1832 Reform Act, Labour abandoned its position of constitutional quietism and committed itself to a sweeping programme of constitutional reform which it proceeded to implement when returned to power in 1997.

V

By the end of the century, no political institution seemed to be exempt from questioning. Even the monarchy, which had been taboo for much of the century, had lost its aura of sanctity so that its virtues and deficiencies had now become legitimate topics for debate. The magical monarchy had become transformed into the sentimental monarchy, but also into the practical monarchy.[23] Moreover, during the 1990s, there were signs of a revival of republican feelings, which had lain dormant since the 1870s. Republicanism, however, was to remain distinctly a minority taste, and survey evidence indicated that support for the monarchy in the 1990s did not fall below 70 per cent.

The monarchy thus remained, despite vicissitudes, a focus of national identity, as the Golden Jubilee celebrations of 2002 were to show, a fixed point in a continually changing world. Its central function remained, as it had been in 1900, that of representing the country to itself, a function whose importance had perhaps increased with devolution which had transformed Britain into an explicitly multinational state, a state which could not take its continued existence for granted, but had to be held together by the conscious application of statecraft. A monarchy which was neither English, Scottish, Welsh or Northern Irish, seemed able to play an important part in such an evolving statecraft.

---

[23] See Frank Prochaska, *Royal Bounty: The Making of a Welfare Monarchy* (Yale University Press, 1995), *passim*, and Vernon Bogdanor, *The Monarchy and the Constitution* (Oxford University Press, 1995), pp. 307–9.

Although republicanism made little headway in the 1990s, there was some questioning of the sovereign's constitutional prerogatives. In the early 1980s, when the rise of the Liberal/SDP Alliance had seemed to make hung Parliaments more likely, the left-wing Labour MP Tony Benn, who was later to become an avowed republican, had urged that the power of the sovereign to appoint a prime minister and refuse a dissolution be delegated to the speaker of the House of Commons, as had been done in Sweden, in that country's new constitution, the 1974 Instrument of Government.[24] Under the provisions of the Scotland Act 1998 providing for a Scottish Parliament, Benn's proposal was adapted to the conditions of a devolved legislature. For in Scotland, by contrast with the 1921–72 Northern Ireland Parliament, it was to be the presiding officer of the Scottish Parliament, rather than, as in Northern Ireland, the governor acting as the queen's representative, who would carry out the sovereign's functions. It was to be the presiding officer who would recommend to the queen the appointment of a first minister in Scotland, after the Scottish Parliament had chosen one of its members to undertake that position; while the circumstances in which the Parliament could be dissolved were strictly circumscribed and the sovereign seemed unable to exercise any discretion to refuse a dissolution when the circumstances were met.[25] With regard to Westminster, on the other hand, there seemed little pressure to curtail the queen's prerogatives, largely because it was assumed that they would never be employed in a controversial way. Thus, at the end of the century, the paradox remained that the sovereign's constitutional powers could be retained so long as one could rely on their not being used.

In the Commonwealth monarchies, by contrast with Britain, there were signs that support for the monarchy was weakening even though, in 1999, a referendum in Australia had resulted in a defeat for the republicans. Despite this, however, the Royal Titles Act 1953, formally recognising the divisibility of the Crown, seemed to be unravelling. For it rested on the premise that Canada, Australia, New Zealand and the other Commonwealth monarchies would, despite having become independent and sovereign nations, remain essentially 'British' in feeling. Only thus would they be willing to continue to accept an absentee and non-resident head of state who would be able to visit their countries only

---

[24] Tony Benn, 'Power, Parliament and People', *New Socialist* (1982).
[25] See Vernon Bogdanor, *Devolution in the United Kingdom* (Oxford University Press, 1999), pp. 202–9 and 213–18.

very infrequently. For the Royal Titles Act to work, the Commonwealth monarchies had to continue to regard Britain as the mother country. That assumption, while perhaps plausible in the 1950s, had become somewhat archaic by the end of a century which saw the growth of nationhood in the queen's overseas realms, and of multiculturalism in Canada and Australia. The monarchy continued to exist in the queen's overseas realms for historical reasons and because it was considered to be of benefit. It was questionable how long the monarchy would continue to be seen in this light. Even if, however, the queen were to cease to be queen of Canada, Australia, etc, that would not mean the end of the sovereign's overseas role. For the queen's role as head of the Commonwealth remained unchallenged, and it continued to give the British monarchy an international perspective which continental monarchies lacked.

VI

By the year 2000, the position of the Cabinet seemed weaker than at any time in the century, except perhaps for the years of the Lloyd George coalition government between 1916 and 1922. Under the Blair Cabinet, so it appeared, few if any formal decisions were being taken in full Cabinet, nor indeed in Cabinet committees, and it seemed to some as if there was a reversion to the informal procedures of eighteenth-century times, when Cabinet meetings had been little more than bonding sessions, meetings of the 'prime minister's friends'. It was not clear, however, whether this indicated a permanent trend in the development of Cabinet government, or whether a new administration would revert to the more formal procedures which had characterised much of the twentieth century.

There was a good deal of talk concerning a strengthening of the centre of government, 10 Downing Street, and creating more powerful institutional backing for the prime minister, something anathematised by critics as creating 'presidential government'. Few noticed that machinery to strengthen Number 10 had first been developed by Lloyd George in 1916, and that, during the post-war years, every prime minister since Harold Wilson in 1964 had spoken of it as an objective. The consequences, however, had always been far more minimal than the rhetoric implied, and perhaps Cabinet government in Britain, whose flexibility had so often been lauded, found it difficult to absorb into itself bodies which lacked clear-cut executive machinery. Indeed, the history of the Cabinet in the twentieth century showed how resistant it was to frontal reform, whether in the form of Lloyd George's non-departmental war cabinet, his 'garden suburb' of personal advisers, the 'overlords' in Winston Churchill's peacetime government, or Edward Heath's Central Policy Review Staff, the so-called 'think-tank'. It would perhaps be safe to conjecture that the system would be equally resistant to the idea of a Prime Minister's Department, much bruited by the Blair administration as it had been, for example, by Edward Heath. One well-placed senior official working for the Blair government said in 2002 that he had been more impressed by the weakness of Number 10 than by its strength.[26] There were, at the end of the century, around 150 people working in Number 10, as compared with over 1,000 in the Prime Minister's Departments in Canada and Australia; and, of the 150, only around forty were working in an executive role, and many of these were involved purely in presentation. While the office of prime minister could, in the right political circumstances, prove a powerful one, its infrastructure remained weaker than that which serviced chief executives in most other democracies.

VII

The 'decline of Parliament' was a familiar theme at the end of the century as it had been at its beginning. Here, too, much of the analysis was ahistorical, looking back to a golden age that had never been. Important reforms in the last part of the century, especially the creation of permanent departmentally related select committees in 1979, had succeeded in creating a House of Commons which was more professional than it had been at the beginning of the century, and one which now enjoyed the forensic resources to enable it to scrutinise the activities of government in a way that had not been possible before. It was, of course, up to MPs whether they succeeded in making effective use of these new opportunities. But, with the demise of the knights of the shires and the old-style trade union members for whom a seat in the Commons was often a reward for years of activity in the labour movement, there were probably fewer passive members of the House of the Commons at the end of the century than at any time during the preceding hundred years.

---

[26] Private information.

House of Commons reform, however, had been concerned primarily with the scrutiny of administration. Little had been done to modernise the legislative process, nor to improve scrutiny of public expenditure or delegated legislation. The standing committees of the House of Commons, instead of subjecting legislation to critical scrutiny, tended to reproduce the adversarial procedures of the floor of the House, and were generally regarded as ineffective.[27] These standing committees were indeed unique in Europe in being unable to question witnesses on legislation; and, in 1992, the report of a commission of the Hansard Society on parliamentary government on the legislative process criticised the standing committees as feeble and amateurish.[28] The deficiencies of Westminster had become more noticeable since the 1970s, when MPs were exposed to the practices of the European Parliament, and they became even more noticeable at the end of the century, with the creation of the Scottish Parliament. The European and the Scottish Parliaments, both of which were elected by proportional representation, showed that legislative procedures could be organised in a different, and to many a more effective, way from that chosen by Westminster. The Scottish Parliament, indeed, was to prove a laboratory for the reforms which academics such as Bernard Crick had, unavailingly, pressed upon Westminster since the 1960s.[29] Moreover, the coming of the Scottish Parliament suggested to some reformers that major changes in the procedures of the House of Commons might be dependent upon a prior reform of the electoral system.

The failure of the House of Commons to modernise its traditional procedures led many to believe, especially during the long hegemony of Margaret Thatcher between 1979 and 1990, and that of Tony Blair at the end of the century, that members of Parliament had become docile sheep, willing, in W. S. Gilbert's words in *Ruddigore*, to:

[27] The classic study is by J. A. G. Griffith, *Parliamentary Scrutiny of Government Bills* (Allen & Unwin, 1974). There is no reason to suppose that standing committees have become more effective since 1974.

[28] *Making the Law: Report of the Hansard Society Commission on the Legislative Process* (Hansard Society, 1992). The author was a member of this commission. The secretary to the commission was Michael Ryle, a former clerk of the House of Commons and part-author, with J. A. G. Griffith, of the standard work, *Parliament: Functions, Practices and Procedures* (Sweet & Maxwell, 1989).

[29] See Bernard Crick, *The Reform of Parliament* (Weidenfeld & Nicolson, 1964), and Bernard Crick and David Millar, *Making Scotland's Parliament Work* (John Wheatley Centre, 1991). David Millar had been on the staff of the secretariat of the European Parliament after serving in the House of Commons, and had been much influenced by that experience.

... vote black or white as your leaders indict,
Which saves you the trouble of thinking.

Yet, academic research indicated that party cohesion had been strongest, not at the end of the century, but during the years 1945–70, after which it had been in decline. In 1965, a noted American commentator on British politics, Samuel Beer, summarising contemporary research, had reached the conclusion:

> ... party cohesion had steadily risen until in recent decades it was so close to 100 per cent that there was no longer any point in measuring it. In the House of Commons were two bodies of freedom-loving Britons, chosen in more than six hundred constituencies and subject to influences that ran back to an electorate that was numbered in the millions and divided by the complex interests and aspirations of an advanced modern society. Yet day after day with a Prussian discipline they trooped into the division lobbies at the signals of their Whips and in the service of the authoritative decisions of their parliamentary parties. We are so familiar with this fact that we are in danger of losing our sense of wonder over them.[30]

It was in fact after 1959, and then during the government of Edward Heath, between 1970 and 1974, that dissent began to increase and, by 1981, Beer was able to write of the 'rise of Parliament'.[31] For, in the three Parliaments of the 1970s, MPs voted 'against their own side on more occasions than before, in greater numbers, and with greater effect'.[32] Between July 1905 and March 1972, governments had suffered just thirty-four defeats in whipped divisions. The Labour governments of 1974–9, however, in a minority for much of the time, suffered no fewer than thirty-six defeats attributable to their minority status and twenty-three defeats caused by backbench revolts.[33]   Table 18.2 shows how dissent increased during the post-war period.

This rebelliousness continued until the end of the century. In the 1992–7 Parliament, John Major's government suffered four defeats in whipped divisions, while during the first Parliament of Tony Blair's premiership, no fewer than 50 per cent of Labour backbenchers voted

[30] Samuel H. Beer, *Modern British Politics* (Faber, 1965), pp. 350–1.
[31] Samuel H. Beer, *Britain Against Itself* (Faber, 1982), p. 181.
[32] Philip Cowley, *Revolts and Rebellions: Parliamentary Voting Under Blair* (Politico's, 2002), p. 4. The increase in dissent in the 1970s was first charted by Philip Norton. See his *Dissension in the House of Commons, 1945–1974* (Macmillan, 1975), and *Dissension in the House of Commons, 1974–1979* (Clarendon Press, 1980).
[33] Cowley, *Revolts and Rebellions*, p. 6.

Table 18.2 Percentage of divisions witnessing dissenting votes, 1945–79

Parliament	
1945–50	7.0
1950–1	2.5
1951–5	3.0
1955–9	2.0
1959–64	13.5
1964–6	0.5
1966–70	9.5
1970–4	20.0
1974	23.0
1974–9	28.0

Source: J. A. G. Griffith and M. Ryle, *Parliament: Functions, Practice and Procedures* (Sweet & Maxwell, 1989), p. 119.

against their own government at some time during the Parliament.[34] Neither John Major, faced with the revolt of the Euro-sceptics, nor Tony Blair, faced with the hostility of so many of his backbenchers to his foreign policy, would have agreed with the proposition that MPs were docile sheep whose support could be taken for granted.

The trouble was, however, that almost all of the parliamentary revolts in the last two decades of the century were ineffective because, in three of the last four Parliaments of the century—those of 1983, 1987 and 1997—the victorious party enjoyed a landslide in the House of Commons. Large majorities meant that revolts on such matters as the poll tax were bound to prove ineffective. The Parliament of 1992–7, however—when John Major's government, returned with a majority of twenty-one, saw it gradually reduced through by-election losses— showed that the House of Commons, if it wished, was fully able to impose its will on the executive. Ironically, however, many of the same commentators who had previously deplored 'the decline of Parliament', now began to castigate 'weak government', and demanded that Major bring his backbench rebels to heel.

The greater professionalism of the House of Commons and greater willingness of MPs to rebel made little impact upon the public, who regularly told opinion pollsters that they had little respect for MPs, although often making an exception for their own MP whom they tended to regard as effective and concerned. It is perhaps a paradox that Parliament, although more democratic and representative than it had been at the beginning of the twentieth century, was, by the end, less respected

[34] Cowley, *Revolts and Rebellions*, pp. 4, 231.

and less trusted to protect civil liberties, and this of course was one reason for the increased prominence given to the courts.

Part of the reason for public disenchantment was that the public expected the House of Commons to play a role for which it was not suited and had not been suited since the middle of the nineteenth century, that of being a governing institution. All too often, criticism of the House of Commons was misdirected, in that it was really a criticism of the quality of government. The House of Commons was not, however, and had hardly ever in its history been, a governing institution. Its role was quite different, to scrutinise legislation and to act as a forum for debate and criticism of government policy. It could enjoy influence but not power, and at the end of the century the opportunities for it to enjoy influence were perhaps greater than they had ever been.

The House of Lords, too, had become more professional during the post-war period. The failure of Harold Wilson's 1966–70 government to reform the Lords, when the Parliament (No. 2) bill was withdrawn in 1969, convinced the more thoughtful peers that it would be difficult to secure the passage of any meaningful reform through the House of Commons, and that they would therefore have to find a role for themselves within an unreconstructed house. It was entry into the European Community in 1973 which gave them the opportunity. The House of Lords established scrutiny procedures for European legislation which came rapidly to be seen as among the most effective in the Community, and certainly more effective than those in the Commons. In 1977, a committee established by the Hansard Society for Parliamentary Government found itself

> struck by the relevance and businesslike nature of the results of the Lords' work in this field, and think it significant that the Commons, who represent the people of this country, have taken in contrast to the Lords, a largely inward-looking and conservative attitude where the opposite was required.

In 1982, a report of a study group of the Commonwealth Parliamentary Association on 'The Role of the Second Chamber' concluded that the Lords

> offered the only really deep analysis of the issues that is available to the parliamentary representatives of the ten countries in the Community . . . The Lords' reports are far more informative and comprehensive than those produced by the Commons committee on European legislation.[35]

[35] These reports are cited in C. Grantham and C. M. Hodgson, 'The House of Lords— Structural Changes—the Use of Committees', in Philip Norton (ed.), *Parliament in the 1980s* (Blackwell, 1985), p. 27.

The House of Lords also established permanent select committees on science and technology and on delegated legislation, and various *ad hoc* select committees on such matters as a Bill of Rights, overseas trade and the public service ethos. By the end of the century, it had been transformed from a rather somnolent chamber whose constitutional function was unclear, to a house of experts. As early as 1975, Lord Windlesham, a former leader of the Lords, had noticed the change.

> In any well-tuned parliamentary system there is a need and a place for a third element besides efficient government and the operation of representative democracy. This third element is the bringing to bear of informed or expert public opinion . . . It is now one of the principal roles of the Lords to provide a forum in which informed public opinion can take shape and be made known.[36]

Most of the experts, however, were life rather than hereditary peers, created under the Life Peerages Act 1958, whose purpose was, in the words of Lord Home, then leader of the Lords, to 'enable the socialist point of view to be put more effectively from the other side of the House'.[37] By 1997, when the Blair government took office, the life peers comprised around one-third of the House. The hereditary peers came to seem more and more anachronistic as the century progressed and, in phase 1 of House of Lords reform, accomplished in 1999, all but ninety-two of them were removed from membership of the House. No definite decisions had, by the end of the century, been taken on phase 2 of the reform, but it seemed inevitable to many that further reform would bring an elected element into the chamber. The House of Lords ended the century in a curious limbo, straddled uneasily between a world that was dead, and one waiting uncertainly to be born.

Thus, by the end of the century, the House of Lords was no longer an aristocratic or a plutocratic body, but had become predominantly a chamber of experts, albeit with a sprinkling of professional politicians to add water to the experts' wine. The House of Lords had changed radically from being a prescriptive chamber to one in which every member had been specifically chosen to sit in it. Peers were either life peers, or belonged to the ninety-two hereditary peers, almost all of whom had been elected by the hereditary peers acting as an electoral college. Moreover, thanks to the removal of the bulk of the hereditary peers and to numerous Labour creations under the Blair government, the House of Lords, for the

---

[36] Lord Windlesham, *Politics in Practice* (Cape, 1975), p. 142.
[37] HL Deb., vol. 206, col. 615, 3 December 1957.

first time in the twentieth century, no longer contained an automatic Conservative majority. The Conservatives, to win a vote, needed the support either of the bulk of the crossbenchers or of the Liberal Democrats, who were coming to assume a pivotal role in the reformed chamber. It is perhaps not surprising that the reformed House of Lords felt itself to be more legitimate than the old one had been. In the words of Lady Jay, leader of the House of Lords, in 1999, 'a decision by the [interim] House not to support a proposal from the Government will carry more weight, because it will have to include supporters from a range of political and independent opinion'.[38] There were signs, as the century ended, that the House of Lords might well become what it had not been for much of the twentieth century, an effective revising chamber, and that a government might have more to fear from opposition to its legislation in the Lords than in the House of Commons.

VIII

If those who insisted that Parliament was in decline were oversimplifying a complex phenomenon, assertions that local government had declined had come to seem almost platitudinous as the century came to an end. The twentieth century, indeed, saw a decline in both local and territorial loyalties. With the Irish settlement of the years 1920–1, territorial issues came to be removed from Westminster for nearly fifty years. The decline of the Liberals and the rise of Labour had replaced, as representative of the Left, a party whose instincts favoured decentralisation and the dispersal of power, with one whose tendency, from the 1920s to the 1960s, was towards centralisation. In its early days, admittedly, the labour movement had given considerable emphasis to local self-government, and the idea of municipal socialism had been pioneered by the Fabians. But much of this came to be forgotten when Labour developed as a national party in the 1920s. Moreover, the division within the Left between Labour and the Liberals allowed the Conservatives to dominate British politics. The Conservatives, however, were predominantly the party of England, and tended to be less sympathetic to the claims of 'the Celtic fringe'. The centralisation of politics seemed to be accompanied by a decline in the quality of local leadership, as the local leaders of the political parties came to be seen as the emissaries of

---

[38] Interview with *Parliamentary Monitor*, November 1999.

national political forces, while Britain—unlike France, for example—lacked a territorial upper house in which the interests of local government could be defended. Thus, without any institutional link between the centre and the localities, local government remained a separate and increasingly subordinate part of the political system.

These political changes coincided with social developments helping to unify the country and eradicating differences; growing use of the motor car, for example, and the extension of geographical and social mobility, both of which tended to an undermining of the sense of locality. The strength of local government, after all, had rested on a sense of community lying between the individual and the state. Because that sense of community seemed to be gradually disintegrating, fewer and fewer people were prepared to defend local government. By the end of the century, 'parish pump' had become a term of abuse, not of approbation. There was, so it seemed, no longer a place in Britain for the idea of local self-government.

From 1934, when the establishment of the Unemployment Assistance Board transferred various public assistance functions from local authorities, to the Local Government Act 1972, which transferred local health services 2to central government, local government had become denuded of its responsibility for social welfare. During the period of the Attlee government, the public utilities—gas and electricity as well as road transport—also came to be transferred from local government to the centre, and the Local Government Act 1972 completed the process by centralising the water authorities. During the post-war years, it came to be accepted that these supposedly local services were in fact national services, and access to them, it was argued, ought not to depend upon the geographical vagaries of local provision, which could sometimes be patchy, but upon national policy. Local standards were coming to be replaced by national standards. For, in a modern welfare state, so it had come to be argued, benefits should depend upon need and not upon geography, upon what was later to be called a postcode lottery. At the end of the century, the idea of local self-government seemed under further threat from the notion of joined-up or holistic government, much promoted by the Blair administration, which implied a unified attack upon deep-seated social problems, and thus, so it seemed, even more control from the centre.

The post-war years were also the period in which Keynesian techniques of macroeconomic management came to be accepted, and these too were hostile to the claims of local government, because they required central government to control the global total of public expenditure,

713

including local government expenditure. This imposed strict limitations on the amount which local authorities could be allowed to raise from their own resources, and also restrictions on local government expenditure. It was not, however, until the Keynesian era was coming to an end in the 1980s that local government was made subject to two radical constitutional changes. The first occurred with the Local Government Finance Act 1982, establishing expenditure targets for local authorities in the form of standard spending assessments. Before 1982, central government had contented itself with determining merely the global total of local government expenditure, not how much individual local authorities should be spending. Now, central government was moving from influence and advice to new forms of direct control on the spending of individual local authorities. The second constitutional innovation occurred with the Rates Act 1984, empowering the secretary of state for the environment to 'cap' the rates, that is impose maximum rate levels upon local authorities. Previously, central government had controlled local authority expenditure by varying the rate support grant which consisted of monies derived from central taxation. Now, it was moving from restricting its own contribution to local authority expenditure, to restricting the power of a local authority to decide how much money it could itself raise through local taxation.

The introduction of standard spending assessments was a declaration by central government that it knew better than local authorities how much they should spend; the introduction of capping was a declaration by central government that it knew better than local authorities how much they should raise. The Local Government Act 2000 sought to revive local authorities by providing for new forms of internal management in place of the committee system, which had been predominant since the Municipal Corporations Act of 1835. As the century ended, however, few were confident enough to predict that the twenty-first century would see a revival of local government.

The demise of local government would inevitably mean that more tasks became the responsibility of central government and of the civil service which served it. Yet, as the century ended, the civil service found itself more on the defensive than it had ever been, with the exception perhaps of the years of the Lloyd George premiership. While the fundamental constitutional principles of the civil service remained intact, those characteristics which had buttressed it as a profession had come under threat from governments, both Conservative and Labour, which emphasised public policy outcomes rather than constitutional procedures. The 'revolution in Whitehall' during the years of the Thatcher and Major administrations, designed to bring outsiders, many from the private sector, into Whitehall seemed to some to threaten the principle of a career and permanent civil service. The establishment of executive agencies under the Next Steps reforms appeared to threaten the unity of the civil service, so laboriously constructed by Sir Warren Fisher, putting in its place a much looser conglomeration of organisations, held together primarily by the constitutional convention of ministerial responsibility.

This convention, moreover, had come to be regarded as outworn by many, even before the Second World War. Reformers, such as W. A. Robson in his influential work, *Justice and Administrative Law,* and Ivor Jennings, were already arguing, in the inter-war period, for the establishment of an administrative court to control bureaucracy.[39] By the end of the century, hardly anyone believed that ministerial responsibility was sufficient as a check upon administrative action. Indeed, in an age of managerialism, ministerial responsibility seemed irrelevant, and it was coming, increasingly, to be supplemented by other arrangements, such as the ombudsman, set up in 1965. There were also calls for the specific accountability of civil servants, which would undermine the *Carltona* principle, according to which civil servants were constitutionally merely the creatures of their ministers, and could not be accountable to any other bodies.[40]

In 1964, A. H. Birch, contrasting British practice with that on the Continent, was able to write that in Britain: 'Nobody has seriously suggested that there should be political appointments to the civil service . . .'.[41] From the time of Harold Wilson's first administration in 1964, however, it had come to be accepted that ministers were entitled to bring 'special advisers' with them to assist with the political side of their duties. These 'special advisers' were, perhaps, a pale imitation of the French *cabinet* system, and by the end of the century they had aroused fears that the political neutrality of the civil service was being subverted. The civil service, however, remained politically neutral, and Britain was very far from adopting a spoils system of the American type, or even the intermingling of political and administrative roles characteristic of the Continent.

---

[39] W. A. Robson, *Justice and Administrative Law* (Macmillan, 1928); W. Ivor Jennings, 'The Report on Ministers' Powers', *Public Administration* (1932), 348–51.
[40] *Carltona Ltd* v. *Commissioners of Works And Others,* [1943] 2 All ER 560.
[41] Birch, *Representative and Responsible Government,* p. 241.

IX

At the beginning of the twentieth century, it was generally believed that Parliament was well able to protect the liberties of the citizen. This belief was largely shared by the nascent Labour Party as well as by Conservatives and Liberals. The *Taff Vale* decision of 1901 and the cases preceding it which had yielded judgements adverse to the trade unions had predisposed the Left, and in particular the Labour Party, to a distrust of the judiciary. The trade unions believed that the opposition of the judges was based on class and party political grounds. They did not believe, therefore, that the judges could be trusted to protect their liberties. Labour's distrust of the judges was to last for much of the century. As late as 1977, Michael Foot, as leader of the House of Commons, was to declare to the Union of Post Office Workers: 'If the freedom of the people of this country and especially the rights of trade unionists—if these precious things of the past had been left to the good sense and fair mindedness of the judges we would have few freedoms in this country at all.'[42]

In Britain the protection of civil liberties, so it was held, did not require the juridical paraphernalia which disfigured the governmental systems of continental countries. By the end of the century, however, the judges seemed more liberal than Parliament, rather than less liberal as they had been at its beginning, when the courts, so far as civil liberties were concerned, seemed part of the dignified rather than the efficient machinery of the constitution. By the end of the century, dissatisfaction with traditional forms of redress and distrust of the effectiveness of Parliament had led to a renewed emphasis on the role of the courts in protecting civil liberties and in defending the citizen against the administration. The traditional approach towards the rule of law championed by Dicey had left little scope for a systematic approach to civil liberties which, at the beginning of the twentieth century, enjoyed no special protection. Indeed, there seemed little scope even for demarcating them from other kinds of liberties. But, by the end of the twentieth century, the judiciary, which had not even been mentioned in Bagehot's *English Constitution* or Low's *Governance of England*, was no longer a 'dignified' part of the constitution but was playing a crucial role both in the control of the administration and in the protection of civil liberties.

At the beginning of the century, there seemed no need for a system

---

[42] *Daily Telegraph*, 16 June 1977.

of administrative law. For, just as Parliament could be trusted to protect civil liberties, so also it could be relied upon to conduct an effective scrutiny of the activities of officials. 'In England', Dicey had supposedly told a French professor, 'we know nothing of administrative law and wish to know nothing about it';[43] while in *The Law of the Constitution*, first published in 1885, Dicey had declared that administrative law 'rests on ideas foreign to the fundamental assumption of our English common law, and especially to what we have termed the rule of law'.[44] It was not until 1925 that J. H. Morgan, professor of constitutional law at the London School of Economics, found himself forced to confess that a comparison between the powers of the citizen in a jurisdiction governed by a proper system of administrative law and the United Kingdom was 'chastening to our pride'.[45] But, as late as 1954, Sir Edward Bridges, permanent secretary to the Treasury and a former Cabinet secretary, could say: 'The traditional British doctrine (as taught in my extreme youth by Dicey) is that administrative law is the devil incarnate. We have continued to pay lip service to the view that it is a nasty continental practice which we would never allow to take root in this country.'[46]

The last quarter of the twentieth century, however, saw the growth of judicial review as the judges came to lose confidence in Parliament's ability to control the executive. Indeed, in 1985, the civil service published a pamphlet entitled *The Judge Over Your Shoulder*, warning officials to bear in mind the possibility of judicial review when preparing legislation. By the end of the century, there had been a revolution in administrative law as the judges repudiated their earlier passivity replacing it with an active concern for principles of good administration. With the political system polarised by Margaret Thatcher and the diminution of the civil service, the judiciary alone seemed to represent the values of non-partisanship and a position beyond politics. Thus, during the eighteen years of Conservative government between 1979 and 1997, the Labour Party's traditional hostility towards the judiciary weakened considerably as the party came to appreciate the full force of Lord Hailsham's description of Britain's system of government as being one of 'elective dictatorship'.

[43] W. A. Robson, 'Administrative Law', in Morris Ginsberg (ed.), *Law and Opinion in the Twentieth Century* (Stevens, 1959).
[44] A. V. Dicey, *The Law of the Constitution*, 10th edn (Macmillan, 1959), p. 329.
[45] J. H. Morgan, 'Remedies against the Crown', in Gleeson E. Robinson, *Public Authorities and Legal Liabilities* (University of London Press, 1925), pp. xlix–l.
[46] PRO T222/678, cited in W. H. Greenleaf, *The British Political Tradition*: vol. 3, *A Much Governed Nation* (Methuen, 1987), Part 1, p. 625.

Moreover, the development of a multicultural and multidenomin- ational society, and the revolution in sexual behaviour which had begun in the 1960s, had destroyed whatever consensus there had once been on civil liberties. In a society characterised by diversity, there needed to be, so it seemed, a clearer statement of fundamental human rights. In addition, of course, the influence of Europe, both through the European Convention and the European Union, increased the pressure for such a statement. By the end of the century, the House of Lords, acting in its judicial capacity, seemed to have taken on the character of a constitutional court vis-à-vis the European Union; while the Judicial Committee of the Privy Council was given, under the Scotland Act 1998, explicitly constitutional functions, as the ultimate court of appeal on the powers of the Scottish Parliament.

By the end of the century, therefore, the Left's distrust of the judiciary had largely disappeared. In 1998, the Labour government passed a Human Rights Act which strengthened the role of the judges by giving them the power to issue a declaration of incompatibility if, in their view, government legislation could not be reconciled with the European Convention of Human Rights. Judges, in consequence, were coming to be far more involved in the political arena and, as the twentieth century came to an end, there were signs of a renewed interest in such questions as the social background of judges and the methods by which they were appointed.

The greater role of the judges in the defence of civil liberties and in administrative law reflected the development of a liberal agenda, which emphasised the fundamental importance of individual human rights. But it was a reversion also to a theme which had been present in the writings of conservative thinkers such as Maine and Lecky at the end of the nineteenth century: a fear of majoritarianism and populism, and an awareness that democratic government might not necessarily prove a particularly good friend to civil liberties.

X

The last years of the century, from 1997, were marked by a flurry of constitutional reforms as the Blair government put its radical manifesto into effect. It is of course far too early even to speculate with any degree of detachment upon the likely consequences of the extensive pro- gramme of constitutional reform which began in 1997. What seems clear, however, is that the British constitution is coming to lose its central characteristic of being, in Dicey's terms, a 'historic' constitution.

By calling the British constitution 'historic', Dicey had meant not just that it was very old, but that it was original and spontaneous, the product not of deliberate design but of a long process of evolution.[47] As Sidney Low had declared in *The Governance of England*, 'Other constitutions have been built; that of England has been allowed to grow . . .'. The constitution was based not on codified rules but on tacit understandings although, as Low ruefully went on to remark, 'the understandings are not always understood'.[48] At the end of the twentieth century, however, such an interpretation of the constitution as 'historic' is bound to appear rather more far-fetched than it did at the beginning. For the constitution seems to have been refashioned in a self-conscious and deliberate way to meet new exigencies. If, at the beginning of the twentieth century, Britain enjoyed a historic constitution, by its end, the constitution seemed to have been something created in large part by human agency.

The constitution of tacit understandings, however, was not replaced by a codified constitution, and Britain remained almost the only democracy without one. But constitutional reforms such as the European Communities Act, the devolution legislation and the Human Rights Act seemed likely in practice to erode the power and supremacy of Parliament and perhaps to take on the character of fundamental law. If that happened, they would yield something very akin to a codified constitution, and a codified constitution moreover of a quasi-federal kind. Britain would thus have undergone a unique constitutional experiment, in having transformed an uncodified into a codified constitution by piecemeal means. There seemed, however, little political will to complete the process, and little consensus on what the final goal should be. For the moment, however, Britain remained, constitutionally speaking, in a half-way house. Perhaps it could remain in such a state indefinitely. For the British, according to a member of the Nolan Committee on Standards of Conduct in Public Life, seemed to 'like to live in a series of half-way houses'.[49]

Yet, by the end of the twentieth century, Dicey's constitution seemed

---

[47] Dicey's characterisation of the British constitution as a 'historic' constitution can be found in his unpublished Lectures on the Comparative Study of Constitutions in the Codrington Library, All Souls College, Oxford, MS 323 LR 6 b 13.

[48] *The Governance of England* (T. Fisher Unwin, 1904), p. 12.

[49] Cited in Peter Hennessy, *The Hidden Wiring: Unearthing the British Constitution* (Gollancz, 1995).

at last to be dead, along with the worldly pragmatism of Bagehot's; and there were signs that Britain was coming to develop, once again, a constitutional sense, a sense that there ought to be publicly proclaimed legal rules limiting the power of government. Only in this way, so it appeared, could there be a *pouvoir neutre* over and above the interests of the government of the day. The British constitution, so it seemed, was no longer whatever worked; indeed, it could work successfully, it was increasingly being argued, only if it were to become a genuine constitution, that is, a set of public principles for organising and controlling political power. It remained, however, to be seen whether in the twenty-first century the constitutional programme begun in such a flurry of activity during the final years of the twentieth century would be completed; or whether the British would remain content to live, on a permanent basis, in a half-way house, the foundations of which had still to be effectively tested by experience.

Appendix 1
Twentieth-century Governments

1895–1902	Lord Salisbury (Unionist)
1902–5	A. J. Balfour (Unionist)
1905–8	Sir Henry Campbell-Bannerman (Liberal)
1908–15	H. H. Asquith (Liberal)
1915–16	H. H. Asquith (Coalition)
1916–22	D. Lloyd George (Coalition)
1922–3	A. Bonar Law (Conservative)
1923–4	Stanley Baldwin (Conservative)
January–November 1924	Ramsay MacDonald (Labour, minority government)
November 1924–9	Stanley Baldwin (Conservative)
1929–31	Ramsay MacDonald (Labour, minority government)
August–November 1931	Ramsay MacDonald (National Government)
November 1931–5	Ramsay MacDonald (National Government)
1935–7	Stanley Baldwin (National Government)
1937–40	Neville Chamberlain (National Government)
1940–May 1945	Winston Churchill (coalition)
May–July 1945	Winston Churchill (caretaker Conservative)
1945–51	C. R. Attlee (Labour)
1951–5	Winston Churchill (Conservative)
1955–7	Sir Anthony Eden (Conservative)
1957–63	Harold Macmillan (Conservative)
1963–4	Sir Alec Douglas-Home (Conservative)
1964–70	Harold Wilson (Labour)
1970–4	Edward Heath (Conservative)
1974–6	Harold Wilson (Labour, minority government from February to October 1974)
1976–9	James Callaghan (Labour, minority government from March 1977)
1979–90	Margaret Thatcher (Conservative)
1990–7	John Major (Conservative, minority government from 1996)
1997–	Tony Blair (Labour)

Appendix 2
Leaders of the Major Parties in the Twentieth Century

Conservative Party

1900–2	Lord Salisbury
1902–11	A. J. Balfour
1911–21	A. Bonar Law*
1921–2	Austen Chamberlain*
1922–3	A. Bonar Law
1923–37	Stanley Baldwin
1937–40	Neville Chamberlain
1940–55	Winston Churchill
1955–7	Sir Anthony Eden
1957–63	Harold Macmillan
1963–5	Sir Alec Douglas-Home
1965–75	Edward Heath
1975–90	Margaret Thatcher
1990–7	John Major
1997–2001	William Hague

* Bonar Law and Austen Chamberlain were leaders of the party in the House of Commons. Until October 1922, when the party was in opposition, there were separate leaders in the Commons and the Lords, and there was no leader of the party as such.

Liberal Party

1900–8	Sir Henry Campbell-Bannerman
1908–26	H. H. Asquith
1926–31	D. Lloyd George
1931–5	Sir Herbert Samuel
1935–45	Sir Archibald Sinclair
1945–56	Clement Davies
1956–67	Jo Grimond
1967–76	Jeremy Thorpe
1976–88	David Steel

Liberal Democrat Party

1988–99	Paddy Ashdown
1999–	Charles Kennedy

(From 1900 to 1969, when a new party constitution came into force, all Liberal leaders were leaders in the House of Commons, except when the party was in office.)

Labour Party

Chairman of the Parliamentary Labour Party

1906–8	Keir Hardie
1908–10	Arthur Henderson
1910–11	George Barnes
1911–14	Ramsay MacDonald
1914–17	Arthur Henderson
1917–21	Willie Adamson
1921–2	J. R. Clynes

Chairman and leader of the Parliamentary Labour Party

1922–31	Ramsay MacDonald
1931–2	Arthur Henderson
1932–5	George Lansbury
1935–55	C. R. Attlee
1955–63	Hugh Gaitskell
1963–76	Harold Wilson
1976–80	James Callaghan
1980–3	Michael Foot
1983–92	Neil Kinnock
1992–4	John Smith
1994–	Tony Blair

Appendix 3
General Election Results in the Twentieth Century

		Seats
1900	Unionists	400
	Liberals	184
	Labour	2
	Irish Party	84
	Total	670
1906	Unionists	157
	Liberals	401
	Labour	29
	Irish Party	83
	Total	670
January 1910	Unionists	273
	Liberals	275
	Labour	40
	Irish Party	82
	Total	670
December 1910	Unionists	272
	Liberals	272
	Labour	42
	Irish Party	84
	Total	670
1918	Coalition Unionist	335
	Coalition Liberal	133
	Coalition Labour	10
	Total Coalition	478
	Conservatives	23
	Irish Unionist	25

	Liberals	28
	Labour	63
	Irish Nationalist	7
	Sinn Fein	73
	Others	10
	Total	707
1922	Conservatives	345
	National Liberals	62
	Liberals	54
	Labour	142
	Others	12
	Total	615
1923	Conservatives	258
	Labour	191
	Liberals	159
	Others	7
	Total	615
1924	Conservatives	419
	Labour	152
	Liberals	40
	Others	4
	Total	615
1929	Conservatives	260
	Labour	288
	Liberals	59
	Others	8
	Total	615
1931	Conservatives	473
	National Labour	13
	Liberal National	35
	Liberals	33
	National Government supporters	554
	Independent Liberals	4
	Labour	52
	Others	5
	Total	615

1935	Conservatives, Liberal National and National Labour	432
	Labour	154
	Liberals	20
	Independent Labour Party	4
	Communists	1
	Others	4
	Total	615
1945	Conservatives	213
	Labour	393
	Liberals	12
	Communists	2
	Independent Labour Party	3
	Others	17
	Total	640
1950	Conservatives	298
	Labour	315
	Liberals	9
	Others	3
	Total	625
1951	Conservatives	321
	Labour	295
	Liberals	6
	Others	3
	Total	625
1955	Conservatives	344
	Labour	277
	Liberals	6
	Others	3
	Total	630
1959	Conservatives	365
	Labour	258
	Liberals	6
	Others	1
	Total	630

1964	Conservatives	304
	Labour	317
	Liberals	9
	Total	630
1966	Conservatives	253
	Labour	363
	Liberals	12
	Others	2
	Total	630
1970	Conservatives	330
	Labour	287
	Liberals	6
	SNP	1
	Others	6
	Total	630
February 1974	Conservatives	297
	Labour	301
	Liberals	14
	SNP	7
	Plaid Cymru	2
	Others	14
	Total	635
October 1974	Conservatives	277
	Labour	319
	Liberals	13
	SNP	11
	Plaid Cymru	3
	Others	12
	Total	635
1979	Conservatives	339
	Labour	269
	Liberals	11
	SNP	2
	Plaid Cymru	2
	Others	12
	Total	635

1983	Conservatives	397
	Labour	209
	Liberal/SDP Alliance	23
	SNP	2
	Plaid Cymru	2
	Others	17
	Total	650
1987	Conservatives	376
	Labour	229
	Liberal/SDP Alliance	22
	SNP	3
	Plaid Cymru	3
	Others	17
	Total	650
1992	Conservatives	336
	Labour	271
	Liberal Democrats	20
	SNP	3
	Plaid Cymru	4
	Others	17
	Total	651
1997	Conservatives	165
	Labour	419
	Liberal Democrats	46
	SNP	6
	Plaid Cymru	4
	Others	19
	Total	659

Appendix 4
Chronology

Date	Events of constitutional significance	Statutes of major constitutional significance	Cases of major constitutional significance	Reports of major constitutional significance
1901	Death of Queen Victoria. Accession of Edward VII.		*Taff Vale Railway Co. v. Amalgamated Society of Railway Servants* [1901] AC 426. House of Lords rules that trade unions are not legally immune, but liable for damage caused by their members during strikes.	
1902		Education Act. School boards absorbed into elected county councils.		
1904	Committee of Imperial Defence, set up in 1902, established on permanent basis. Functions eventually taken over by War Cabinet in 1916.			
1906		Trade Disputes Act. Frees trade unions from liability caused by calling of a strike.		

Date	Events of constitutional significance	Statutes of major constitutional significance	Cases of major constitutional significance	Reports of major constitutional significance
1908–10				Royal Commission on Electoral Systems, Report, Cd 5163 (1910) advocates alternative vote.
1909	House of Lords rejects Lloyd George's 'People's Budget'. Edward VII refuses to promise to create peers to pass a Parliament Act without a second general election.		*Amalgamated Society of Railway Servants v. Osborne* [1910] AC 87 (1909). House of Lords rules trade union contributions to a political party are illegal.	
1910	Death of Edward VII. Accession of George V. July. George V sponsors constitutional conference to seek agreement on reform of the Lords. Breakdown of conference followed by the king's agreement to create sufficient peers to pass the Parliament Act if the House of Lords rejects it and if the Liberal government is returned in the December general election.			
1911	Payment of members of Parliament.	Parliament Act, removing entirely the powers of the House of Lords over money bills, and replacing the absolute veto of the House of Lords with a	*Board of Education v. Rice* [1911] AC 179. House of Lords rules that in exercising quasi-judicial or administrative powers, government departments must	

	National Insurance Act, providing for health and unemployment insurance. Official Secrets Act, providing for the prosecution of persons involved in offences prejudicial to the safety or interest of the state.			
1913	Trade Union Act. Legalises political contributions by trade unions under precisely defined conditions.			
1914	George V sponsors abortive Buckingham Palace conference on Irish home rule.	Government of Ireland Act enacted, after having been twice rejected by House of Lords, providing for home rule for Ireland. Suspended for duration of war, and never in fact implemented. Welsh Church Act enacted, disestablishing Church of Wales, after having been twice rejected by the House of Lords. Comes into force in 1920.		
1915	Buckingham Palace conference on conscription.			*Local Government Board v. Arlidge* [1915] AC 120. House of Lords rules that government departments are not bound to adopt the procedure of a court of law in dealing with objections to the use of statutory powers.

Date	Events of constitutional significance	Statutes of major constitutional significance	Cases of major constitutional significance	Reports of major constitutional significance
1916	Easter Rising in Dublin. Buckingham Palace conference to choose prime minister following resignation of Asquith. The new prime minister, Lloyd George, establishes a Cabinet Secretariat and appoints Maurice Hankey the first Cabinet secretary.			
1917				Report of first Speaker's Conference, Cd 8463, unanimously supports female suffrage and proportional representation in rural constituencies, and, by a majority, the alternative vote in borough constituencies.
1918		Representation of the People Act (4th Reform Act). Provides for universal suffrage for men over 21 and for women over 30. Conscientious objectors disenfranchised for five years. Proportional representation rejected except for university seats.		Report on the Machinery of Government Committee (Chair, Lord Haldane), Cd 9230. Report of the Conference on the Reform of the Second Chamber (Chair, Lord Bryce), Cd 9038.
1919	Sir Warren Fisher appointed permanent secretary to the Treasury and designated head of the civil service			

1920	Report of Speaker's Conference on Devolution, Cmd 692, proposes either legislative devolution or devolution to grand committees of the House of Commons.
	Government of Ireland Act, providing for two home rule parliaments in Ireland. The Act implemented only in Northern Ireland whose Parliament opens in 1921.
1921	Anglo-Irish Treaty, providing for the twenty-six counties of the Irish Free State to become self-governing dominion within the British Empire, given legislative effect in 1922 by the Irish Free State (Agreement) Act.
	Tribunals and Enquiries Act.
1922	Local Government Act (NI), an Act of the Northern Ireland Parliament, providing for the abolition of proportional representation for local elections in the province.
1923	George V appoints Baldwin rather than Curzon as prime minister.
1924	First Labour minority government, January–November, following resignation of Baldwin after defeat on the address. In October, George V agrees to dissolution after government is defeated in vote on the Campbell case.

Date	Events of constitutional significance	Statutes of major constitutional significance	Cases of major constitutional significance	Reports of major constitutional significance
1925	Boundary Commission proposes only minor changes in border between Northern Ireland and the Irish Free State.		*Roberts v. Hopwood* [1925] AC 578. House of Lords rules Poplar council's minimum wage of £4 per week to be unlawful.	
1926	General Strike.			Balfour Report on Inter-Imperial Relations. Formula agreed by which the king becomes the constitutional link between the dominions.
1928		Equal Franchise Act (5th Reform Act). Vote extended to women over 21 on the same basis as men.		
1929		Local Government Act. Administration of poor law absorbed into local authorities.		
1929–32				Committee on Ministers Powers (Donoughmore Committee), Report, Cmd 4060 (1932) distinguishes between the 'judicial' and the 'quasi-judicial', and argues that no system of administrative law should be established in Britain.
1931	National Government formed in August and goes to the country in October.	Statute of Westminster, providing that United Kingdom legislation should not extend to a dominion without its request and consent.		

1932	National Government suspends convention of collective Cabinet unanimity on issue of Imperial preference.	
1936	Death of George V. Accession of Edward VIII (January). Abdication of Edward VIII (December). Accession of George VI.	Public Order Act. Prohibits use of threatening, abusive or insulting words or behaviour in public place with intent to provoke a breach of the peace, or whereby a breach of the peace is likely to be occasioned. His Majesty's Declaration of Abdication Act 1936, providing for the abdication of Edward VIII.
1942		*Liversidge v. Anderson* [1942] AC 206 (1941). House of Lords rules that whether a minister has reasonable grounds for exercising an emergency detention power is a matter to be judged in Parliament rather than in the courts. *Duncan v. Cammell Laird* [1942] AC 624. House of Lords rules that Crown may withhold documents or refuse questioning if minister certifies that the answer may be injurious to the public interest.

Date	Events of constitutional significance	Statutes of major constitutional significance	Cases of major constitutional significance	Reports of major constitutional significance
1943			*Carltona Ltd v. Commissioner of Works* [1943] 2 All ER 560. Rules the acts of civil servants are constitutionally acts of ministers, and that civil servants have no constitutional personality of their own.	
1945	First Labour majority government.			
1947		Crown Proceedings Act, enabling government departments to be sued in contract or tort while leaving unimpaired the sovereign's personal immunity.	*Franklin v. Minister of Town and Country Planning* [1948] AC 87 (1947). Court of Appeal rules that courts have no responsibility for procedural due process under New Towns Act.	
1948		Representation of the People Act. University seats abolished. Plural voting abolished. Representative democracy extended to local government. British Nationality Act, defining the status of a British subject as a citizen of the United Kingdom or colonies, the terms 'British subject' and 'Commonwealth citizen' being interchangeable.	*Associated Provincial Picture Houses Ltd v. Wednesbury Corporation* [1948] 1KB 22. Court of Appeal decides that the courts can intervene in a discretionary decision only if the body making the decision was acting so unreasonably that no reasonable body could so act.	

1949	Commonwealth prime ministers agree, in the London Declaration, that India can remain in the Commonwealth as a republic, provided that she recognises the king as Head of the Commonwealth.	Ireland Act, passed in response to Ireland declaring herself a republic, provides that Northern Ireland would not cease to remain a part of the United Kingdom without the consent of the Parliament of Northern Ireland. Parliament Act, further restricting suspensory veto of House of Lords over non-money bills to two sessions and one year.	
1952	Death of George VI. Accession of Elizabeth II.		*R v. Tronoh Mines Ltd* [1952] 1 All ER 697. Election expenditure to be declared only if specifically directed to secure the election of a particular candidate; i.e. only constituency expenditure, but not national expenditure, is regulated by law, a condition remedied by the Political Parties, Referendums and Elections Act 2000.
1953	The United Kingdom becomes a signatory to the European Convention of Human Rights.	Royal Titles Act 1953, providing for the style and title of Elizabeth II.	*MacCormick v. Lord Advocate* [1953] SC 396. Court of Session raises the possibility that the unlimited sovereignty of Parliament is only an English and not a Scottish doctrine.

Date	Events of constitutional significance	Statutes of major constitutional significance	Cases of major constitutional significance	Reports of major constitutional significance
1954	Crichel Down affair leads to resignation of minister for agriculture, Sir Thomas Dugdale, and the Maxwell Fyfe guidelines on ministerial responsibility.			
1956			*Smith v. East Elloe RDC* [1956] AC 736. House of Lords upholds statutory clause declaring that decision of an administrative body is not to be challenged by the courts after six weeks.	
1957	Disputed succession to the premiership. The queen appoints Harold Macmillan, rather than R. A. Butler, to succeed Sir Anthony Eden. Treaty of Rome signed by France, Germany, Italy and the Benelux countries, establishing European Economic Community.			Franks Committee on Administrative Tribunals, Report, Cmnd 218.
1958		Life Peerages Act, providing for the creation of both life peers and peeresses, women thus being enabled for the first time to become members of the House of Lords.		

1962	Commonwealth Immigrants Act, providing for the first time for the control of immigration into the United Kingdom from other parts of the Commonwealth.	*Van Gend en Loos* [1963] ECR 1. Establishes doctrine of 'direct effect', that EC Treaty Articles can be enforced against the governments and legislatures of member states by the courts of member states.	Final Report of Royal Commission on the Police, (Willink Commission), Cmd 1728.
1963	Disputed succession to the premiership. The queen appoints Lord Home, rather than Lord Hailsham, R. A. Butler or Reginald Maudling, to succeed Harold Macmillan. Peerage Act, providing for the disclaimer of hereditary peerages, and providing that hereditary peeresses might sit and vote in the House of Lords. London Government Act, establishing Greater London Council, in place of the LCC, and a lower tier structure of thirty-two boroughs in Greater London.		Lord Denning's Report on the Profumo Affair, Cmd 2152.
1964		*Ridge v. Baldwin* [1964] AC 40 (1963). House of Lords rules that, where an important interest is at stake, fairness requires that an affected person be granted a hearing. *Rookes v. Barnard* [1964] AC 1129. House of Lords rules that union members and officials are not immune from liability for conspiracy. The effect of this decision is reversed by the Trades Disputes Act 1965.	

Date	Events of constitutional significance	Statutes of major constitutional significance	Cases of major constitutional significance	Reports of major constitutional significance
			Costa v. Enel [1964] ECR 585. Establishes 'supremacy' of directly effective European Community Treaty Articles over incompatible domestic legislation.	
1965	Conservative Party adopts one MP one vote procedure for the election of its leader. British citizens granted the right of petition to the European Commission of Human Rights.	Race Relations Act, for the first time, outlaws racial discrimination in housing, provision of goods and services to the public, education and training, and sets up the Race Relations Board to assist in its implementation.		
1966	The United Kingdom government accepts the jurisdiction of the European Court of Human Rights.			
1967		Parliamentary Commissioner Act creates office of the Parliamentary Commissioner for Administration, generally known as the Ombudsman.		

1968		*Conway v. Rimmer* [1968] AC 910 (1967). House of Lords rules that courts have residuary power to determine whether public interest in suppressing them outweighs interests of parties and of public in securing justice. *Padfield v. Minister of Agriculture* [1968] AC 997. House of Lords rules that minister is required to exercise his statutory discretion so as to fulfil the policy of Parliament, as determined by the courts.	Report of the Royal Commission on the Civil Service (Chair, Lord Fulton), Cmnd 3638.
1969		Representation of the People Act. Voting age lowered to 18. *Anisminic v. Foreign Compensation Commission* [1969] 2 AC 147 (1968). The courts can exercise judicial review for errors of law by a body whose decisions have been protected by Parliament from appeal.	Report of the Royal Commission on Local Government in England (Chair, Lord Redcliffe-Maud), Cmnd 4040.
1970	Edward Heath's government establishes Central Policy Review Staff, the so-called 'Think Tank', whose first head is Lord Rothschild.		

Date	Events of constitutional significance	Statutes of major constitutional significance	Cases of major constitutional significance	Reports of major constitutional significance
1972		European Communities Act, providing for Britain's entry into the European Communities.		
		Local Government Act. First full-scale reorganisation of local government in England and Wales since the nineteenth century. Local government outside Greater London and metropolitan areas reorganised into two-tier system.		
		Northern Ireland (Temporary Provisions) Act. Northern Ireland Parliament suspended and direct rule instituted.		
		Border Poll Act, providing for border poll in Northern Ireland, which is held in March 1973.		
1973	UK enters the European Communities.	Northern Ireland Constitution Act, providing for the establishment of a power-sharing executive and assembly.		Report of Royal Commission on the Constitution (Chair, Lord Kilbrandon), Cmnd 5460, advocates directly elected assemblies for Scotland and Wales.

1974	Power-sharing executive provided for under the terms of the Northern Ireland Constitution Act is established, but resigns after five months, following strike by Ulster Workers Council. Direct rule reinstated and continued in the Northern Ireland Act 1974.	
1975	Referendum Act provides for first nationwide referendum, on whether Britain should remain in the European Communities. Cabinet unanimity suspended for the duration of the referendum campaign. Sex Discrimination Act (Great Britain), outlawing discrimination in employment, education and the provision of professional services. Establishes Equal Opportunities Commission.	
1977	Scotland and Wales bill withdrawn following failure of government to secure majority in guillotine motion. Reintroduced later in the year as two separate bills and passed in 1978.	

Date	Events of constitutional significance	Statutes of major constitutional significance	Cases of major constitutional significance	Reports of major constitutional significance
1978		Scotland and Wales Acts, providing for directly elected assemblies in Scotland and Wales, and incorporating a requirement that 40 per cent of the registered electorate, in addition to a majority, vote 'Yes' in referendums.		
1979	Referendums on devolution in Scotland and Wales. Devolution heavily defeated in Wales, but endorsed by a small majority in Scotland, falling well short of 40 per cent. Parliament repeals Scotland and Wales Acts. First direct elections to European Parliament. Departmentally related select committee system established in the House of Commons.			
1981		British Nationality Act, providing for three ways of acquiring United Kingdom citizenship: by birth, by naturalisation and by registration with the home secretary.		

1982		Northern Ireland Act, establishing new directly elected Assembly without legislative or executive powers in Northern Ireland Parliament, which sits until 1986.		
1983	Central Policy Review Staff abolished.		*Bromley London Borough Council v. GLC* [1983] AC 768 [HL]. GLC acted *ultra vires* and in breach of its fiduciary duty towards ratepayers by cutting fares by 25 per cent.	
1984		Rates Act, authorising the government to cap the amount of finance which local authorities can raise through the rates		
1985		Anglo-Irish Agreement 1985. Local Government Act, abolishing GLC and metropolitan county councils.	*Council of Civil Service Unions v. Minister for the Civil Service* [1985] AC 374. Some prerogative powers are reviewable and susceptible to judicial review.	
1987		Single European Act comes into force amending the Treaty of Rome and providing for more qualified majority voting in the Council of Ministers.		
1988	Efficiency Unit (Chair, Sir Robin Ibbs), *Improving Management in Government: The Next Steps* (report to the prime minister).	Local Government Finance Act, establishing in England and Wales the community charge, the so-called 'poll tax'.		

Date	Events of constitutional significance	Statutes of major constitutional significance	Cases of major constitutional significance	Reports of major constitutional significance
1989	Inauguration of Scottish Convention to draw up proposals for Scottish devolution.			
1991	*The Citizen's Charter*, Cm 1599.	War Crimes Act enacted under the Parliament Acts for the first time since 1949, after having been rejected by the House of Lords.	*R v. Secretary of State for Transport, ex p. Factortame Ltd (No. 2)* [1991] 1 AC 603. House of Lords rules that United Kingdom Acts of Parliament must be disapplied in British courts to the extent that they conflict with relevant provisions of Community law. *R v. Secretary of State for the Home Department, ex p. Brind* [1991] AC 696 (HL). House of Lords rules that it was not unreasonable to ban the broadcasts of the direct words of certain proscribed and nonproscribed paramilitary organisations.	
1992	Maastricht Treaty further amending the Treaty of Rome and providing for economic and monetary union.	Local Government Finance Act. Poll tax abolished and replaced by council tax.		

1993	*Pepper v. Hart* [1993] AC 593. House of Lords decides that legislative debates are, in certain specified circumstances, admissible as evidence in interpreting statutes.
1994	Committee on Standards in Public Life established, chaired first by Lord Nolan and then by Lord Neill. First report, laying down seven principles of public life, Cm 2850, published in 1995.
1995	*R v. Secretary of State for Employment, ex p. Equal Opportunities Commission* [1995] 1 AC 1. House of Lords rules that British legislation relating to protection of part-time workers violates European Community directives and should be disapplied. Parliamentary Commissioner for Standards established.
1996	*Report into the Inquiry into the Export of Defence Equipment and Dual-use Goods to Iraq and Related Prosecutions* (Scott Report), HC 115.
1997	Referendums (Scotland and Wales) Act, providing for referendums in Scotland and Wales on devolution.

Date	Events of constitutional significance	Statutes of major constitutional significance	Cases of major constitutional significance	Reports of major constitutional significance
1998	Referendum in Greater London approves proposals for a directly elected mayor and strategic authority.	Scotland Act and Government of Wales Act, providing for a Parliament in Scotland and a National Assembly in Wales. Northern Ireland Act, implementing Belfast or Good Friday Agreement, Cm 3883 (1998), and providing for a new directly elected assembly in Northern Ireland, a partnership form of government, together with a North–South Ministerial Council, a British/Irish Intergovernmental Conference, and a British–Irish Council. Human Rights Act, requiring public bodies to comply with the provisions of the European Convention of Human Rights, permitting judges to declare legislation incompatible with convention rights and providing for Parliament to alter such legislation by means of delegated legislation. Registration of Political Parties Act, requiring all parties wishing to put forward candidates for election to formally register.		*Report of the Independent Commission on the Voting System*, Cm 4090, chaired by Lord Jenkins of Hillhead, advocates alternative vote with 'topping-up' to produce proportional representation.

1999	First elections to Scottish Parliament and Welsh National Assembly result in coalition government in Scotland and minority government in Wales— replaced by a coalition government in 2000, the first in the democratic world to contain a majority of women.	House of Lords Act. Removal of all but ninety-two of the hereditary peers from the House of Lords.
	Greater London Authority Act 1999, creating a Greater London Authority and a directly elected mayor of London.	Royal assent given under the Parliament Acts to European Parliamentary Elections bill, following rejection by the House of Lords.

Date	Events of constitutional significance	Statutes of major constitutional significance	Cases of major constitutional significance	Reports of major constitutional significance
2000	Ken Livingstone, an independent candidate, elected first mayor of London.	Local Government Act. Requires local authorities to establish either executive mayors, cabinet or city manager regimes. Political Parties, Referendums and Elections Act, providing for the establishment of an Electoral Commission and for the control of donations and campaign expenditure in elections and referendums. Representation of the People Act, reforming the system of electoral registration and facilitating postal voting. Royal assent given under the Parliament Acts to the Sexual Offences (Amendment) bill, following rejection by the House of Lords.		Report of Royal Commission on Reform of the House of Lords, chaired by Lord Wakeham, *A House for the Future*, Cm 4534, recommends a mixed upper house based on appointed and elected members.

Table of Cases

Table of Statutes

Table of Reports

Index

suffragette movement, 408, 417, 420–1
Sunningdale Agreement (1973), 175
Supply, Committee of, 150, 165–7
supremacy, principle of EC law, 60–1, 62,
  666–9, 677
surveillance, 405, 436, 463, 563
Sweden, Instrument of Government
  (1974), 704
Syndicalist, The, 415

Tanganyika, 295, 648–9
tariff reform, Cabinet crisis (1903), 11, 19
tax,
  monarchs' immunity from liability, 84, 88
  and the wealthy, 344
tax law, 346–7
  and civil liberties, 344
Taylor, A.J.P., 175
Taylor, Lord, 358, 360, 362, 363
Teaching and Higher Education bill
  (1998), 219
television, political, 132, 186
Temperance (Scotland) bill (1913), 211
territorial state, United Kingdom as a,
  585–630
territoriality,
  and identity, 624–5
  and the rule of recognition, 588–91
terrorism,
  bombings (1974), 459–60
  Fenian, 410
  growth of state power in response to,
    433, 434–5, 442, 453–7, 580
  prevention legislation, 355, 437–8, 674
Thatcher government,
  and the Commonwealth, 659
  Euroscepticism, 675
  and the judiciary, 354, 356–63
  and marketplace ideology, 430
  and MPs, 707
  strengthening of state power, 388–9,
    437, 576
Thatcher, Margaret, 10, 75, 195, 218, 231,
  464
  Bruges speech on the EC (1988), 675–6
  culture shift in civil service, 258–65
  on EC, 677
  the fall of, 679–82
  influence on Cabinet, 121, 123–4, 130, 132
Thatcherism, 699–700
theatre, 448–9
theorising, constitutional, 32–3, 55–6
think-tanks *see* Policy Review Staff
Thomas, Hugh, 254
Thomas, J. H., 299

Thomas, Sir Robert, 180
Thomson, Basil, 410
Times, The, 357
Tocqueville, Alexis de, 29, 590
Top Salaries Review Body, 143
Torture, European Committee for the
  Prevention of, 462
totalitarianism, 398
Toulmin Smith, Joshua, 522
towns, incorporated, 525, 527–8
Townshend, Charles, 642–3
Trade and Industry Committee, 287
Trade Union bill (1984), 218–19
Trade Union and Labour Relations bill
  (1976), 211
trade union legislation (1906) and (1913),
  52, 339
traditionalism, 56
transport, 22
Transport bill, 213–14, 219
Transport, Ministry of, 109, 120
Transvaal, 632
Treasury, 103, 104
  and Cabinet, 110, 113–14, 122, 124, 126–7,
    131–2, 133
  control of the civil service, 240, 241–2,
    245–9
  first lord of the, 9
  permanent secretary as head of the civil
    service, 247–8
  and the police, 557, 560–1
  powers of inter-war, 248–9
Treasury and Civil Service Committee, 260,
  263–4, 271, 313
treaties,
  effect on municipal law, 439–40
  international, 439–40
  power to make, 75, 433, 440
Treaties Committee, recommended, 226
Treaty on European Union *see* Maastricht
  Treaty
Trenchard, Viscount, 570
Trend, Sir Burke, 130
trial,
  by jury right, 414
  right to fair, 461–2
tribunals,
  administrative, 53, 59, 345, 383
  use of military, 412, 413
Trollope, Anthony, 659–60
Troup, Sir Edward, 566
'truce of God', 5–6
Trudeau, Pierre, 658
Tryweryn valley affair, 180, 616
Tumim, Stephen, 438, 462
Turkey, 115, 650–1
Turks, in Constantinople, 109, 110